CONSUMER PROTECTION IN ASIA

This book looks at the consumer protection offered in a range of Asian countries, for example China, Japan and South Korea in key areas such as consumer sales law, unfair terms, product liability and unfair commercial practices. However, it is interesting to note that consumer protection is on the rise everywhere and to compare how this differs depending upon the legal cultures. It is also fascinating to reflect on the influence of models for law reform such as the EU laws. ASEAN has also affected the development of consumer policy for its member states.

The book takes the form of national reports which explain the development of the law and also shed light on how the law works in practice. The book also contains thematic reports which look at each area of the law from a comparative perspective. Commentators from around the globe reflect on their impression of Asian consumer law based on their own differing legal systems and benchmarks.

A must-read for anyone with an interest in consumer law in Asia and beyond, this book will form the basis of further research and discussion internationally.

Consumer Protection in Asia

Edited by
Geraint Howells
Hans-W Micklitz
Mateja Durovic
and
André Janssen

• HART •
OXFORD • LONDON • NEW YORK • NEW DELHI • SYDNEY

HART PUBLISHING

Bloomsbury Publishing Plc

Kemp House, Chawley Park, Cumnor Hill, Oxford, OX2 9PH, UK

1385 Broadway, New York, NY 10018, USA

29 Earlsfort Terrace, Dublin 2, Ireland

HART PUBLISHING, the Hart/Stag logo, BLOOMSBURY and the Diana logo are trademarks of Bloomsbury Publishing Plc

First published in Great Britain 2022

A catalogue record for this book is available from the British Library.

A catalogue record for this book is available from the Library of Congress.

Library of Congress Control Number: 2022934813

ISBN: HB: 978-1-50995-753-8
ePDF: 978-1-50995-755-2
ePub: 978-1-50995-754-5

Typeset by Compuscript Ltd, Shannon

FOREWORD

Mateja Durovic, Geraint Howells and André Janssen were all working in Asia at the City University of Hong Kong when this book was first proposed in connection with a conference held from 13–14 January 2017 at the School of Law, City University of Hong Kong (supported by City University of Hong Kong research grant: 9380074 Consumer and Product Liability in Europe and Asia) and the Faculty of Law, University of Helsinki (supported by the Finland Distinguished Professor Programme, led by Hans-W. Micklitz), Hans-W. Micklitz joined with the Hong Kong based team in his research on the global reach of EU Consumer Law. Asia was a good case study as several jurisdictions in the region have historical links back to European legal traditions. It is also a region that has been influential in producing consumer goods for global markets in recent times. Many Asian jurisdictions have seen a rise in consumerism that has accompanied increased affluence.

It was therefore appropriate to make an assessment of how consumer protection law has developed in the region. The following pages demonstrate a rich tapestry of legal systems at different stages of evolution and in particular many are only just starting to assess the impact of technology of consumer protection needs – a topic that has become even more important since this project took form. There is surely far more work to be done going forward, but our hope is that this book will provide the impetus for more intense research in this area.

The chapters in this book have been through several drafts. We thank the authors for their patience and for responding diligently to our various requests. We also would like to thank Raphaelle Teenie Chan (City University of Hong Kong) for her help with research, Hilma Mäkitalo (University of Helsinki) who tirelessly helped ensure the revised chapters were submitted on time and our colleague, Jonathon Watson, who managed the project across the finish line. Thanks to, respectively, the Finland Distinguished Professor Programme of the University of Helsinki and NUI Galway for supporting their work.

We are only too well aware that our coverage is not complete either in terms of Asian jurisdictions or subject area (credit and financial services are major omissions). However, the book is already a large tome and we sincerely hope it is useful both within Asia and for global scholars of consumer protection law. There are many useful insights from Asian consumer law and it will surely be a place of increasing legal innovation.

Mateja Durovic, Geraint Howells, André Janssen and Hans-W. Micklitz

CONTENTS

LIST OF CONTRIBUTORS

Meika Atkins is a Research Fellow at Curtin Law School, Curtin University, Australia.

Michel Cannarsa is Dean of Law, Lyon Catholic University, France. Member of the Sciences and Humanities Confluence Research Center – UCLy.

Marta Cantero Gamito is Associate professor in IT law at the University of Tartu, Estonia.

Alberto De Franceschi is Full Professor of Private Law, Intellectual Property Rights and Environmental Law at the University of Ferrara, Italy.

Mateja Durovic is a Reader in Law at King's College London, United Kingdom.

Jerry G Fong is Jointly Appointed Professor of Law, College of Law & College of Business, National ChengChi University, Taiwan.

Johannes Gunawan is Professor of the Law of Obligations and Consumer Protection Law, Parahyangan Catholic University, Indonesia.

Hisakazu Hirose is Professor emeritus of law at the University of Tokyo, Japan.

Geraint Howells is Executive Dean of the College of Business, Public Policy and Law at NUI Galway, Ireland, and Visiting Professor of Law at the University of Manchester, United Kingdom.

André Janssen is a Chair Professor of European Private Law at Radboud University, The Netherlands.

Jin Jing is Associate Professor at the Civil, Commercial and Economic Law School of the China University of Political Science and Law (CUPL), People's Republic of China.

Shindong Jung is Professor of Law at the Gangneung-Wonju National University, South Korea.

Karl-Friedrich Lenz is Professor of German Law and EU Law, Aoyama Gakuin University, Japan.

Gary Low is Vice-President (Legal and Regulatory Engagement) for Lazada Singapore and RedMart (Alibaba Group), and Central Committee member for the Consumers Association of Singapore.

Hans-W Micklitz is Professor of Economic Law at the Robert Schuman Centre for Advanced Studies, European University Institute, Italy, and Finland Distinguished Professor, University of Helsinki, Finland.

Tjakie Naude is Professor of Private Law, University of Cape Town, South Africa.

James P Nehf is Professor of Law and Cleon H. Foust Fellow, Robert H. McKinney School of Law, Indiana University, United States.

Rémi Nguyen is Associate Researcher at IRASEC (Research Institute on Contemporary Southeast Asia) (CNRS-MAEE), Thailand.

Luke Nottage is Professor of Comparative and Transnational Business Law at the University of Sydney Law School, Australia.

Ashok R Patil is Chair Professor of the National Law School of India University, Chair on Consumer Law & Practice, India; Director, Online Consumer Mediation Centre; Member, Central Consumer Protection Council; Legal Education Innovation Awardee.

Ângelo Patrício Rafael is a Ph.D. candidate at the Faculty of Law of the University of Macau.

Gail Pearson is Professor of Business Law at the University of Sydney, Australia.

Jeremy Pui is a Research Assistant at King's College London, United Kingdom.

Tadashi Shiraishi is Professor of Law, University of Tokyo, Japan.

Aimpaga Techaapikun is Assistant Professor in Private Law at Thammasat University, Thailand.

Sakda Thanitcul is Professor and former Dean at the Faculty of Law, Chulalongkorn University, Thailand.

Nguyen Van Cuong is General Director of Institute of Legal Studies, Ministry of Justice of Vietnam.

Bernadette M Waluyo is Professor of Civil Procedure Law, Law of Obligations and Consumer Law, Parahyangan Catholic University, Indonesia.

Eileen Webb is Professor of Law, Discipline of Justice and Society, The University of South Australia, Australia.

Dan Wei is Full Professor at the University of Macau.

Zalina Zakaria, is a Senior Lecturer, Department of Syariah and Law, University of Malaya, Malaysia, and Director, University Malaya Halal Research Center, University Malaya.

PART 1

Introduction

1

Introduction to Asian Consumer Law

GERAINT HOWELLS AND HANS-W MICKLITZ

I. Background

This project originated with a conference on 'Consumer Protection in Asia' held from 13–14 January 2017 at the School of Law, City University of Hong Kong. The conference was co-organised by the School of Law, City University of Hong Kong (and supported by research grant: 9380074 Consumer and Product Liability in Europe and Asia) and the Faculty of Law, University of Helsinki (supported by the Finland Distinguished Professor Programme). At that event, national reports were presented on the state of consumer law in Mainland China, Hong Kong, India, Japan, Macau, Malaysia, Singapore, Thailand and Vietnam. Subsequently, expert reports from Indonesia, Myanmar and Taiwan were added. We asked the rapporteurs to cover various topics: information and the right of withdrawal, sale of goods, unfair terms, product liability, product safety, adaptation to the digital age, unfair commercial practices and access to justice. The reports also typically explain the general structures for promoting consumer protection and its public enforcement. We considered adding consumer credit and financial services, but finally concluded the list was comprehensive enough and those topics deserved separate treatment in a future project. These national reports were revised on various occasions up to 2021.

We wanted to explore the state of consumer protection in Asia through two additional dimensions. By inviting internationally renowned scholars to make comparative surveys of the substantive themes, an impression of the different approaches adopted within Asia, influences on the law's development and relative level of consumer protection existing within Asia could be established. We also wanted to reflect on how the development of consumer protection in Asia compared from regional (Africa, Australia, Europe, North and South America) and global (UN) perspectives, and so asked the invited commentators to compare their country or region to Asia as well as looking at international influences. Overall, we hope that the book provides for a comprehensive overview and analysis of where consumer law in Asia is standing, what kind of influences have been exerted and from whom. Last but not least we hope to demonstrate how and where Asian consumer law has to be located in the development of consumer law internationally.

II. Implications and Incentives

A. The Five Parts of Asia

First and foremost, the title *Consumer Law in Asia* seems to suggests that the book covers all parts of Asia geographically speaking: *North Asia* (Russia), *Central Asia* (former Russian-ruled, later Soviet republics of Kazakhstan, Kyrgyzstan, Tajikistan, Turkmenistan and Uzbekistan), *Western Asia* (21 countries out of which 13 are part of the Arab world). The most populous countries in *Western Asia* are Iran, Turkey (the Asian side), Iraq, Saudi Arabia and Yemen; in *South Asia* Afghanistan, Pakistan, India, Nepal, Bhutan, Bangladesh, the Maldives and Sri Lanka; in *East Asia* China, North and South Korea, Japan; in *South East Asia* Cambodia, Laos, Myanmar, Peninsular Malaysia, Thailand, Vietnam, Brunei, East Malaysia, East Timor, Indonesia, the Philippines and Singapore. In light of a geographical categorisation, the present book on consumer law covers *South Asia* (India), *East Asia* (China, including the SARs of Hong Kong and Macau, Japan, South Korea and Taiwan) and *South East Asia* (Myanmar, Malaysia, Thailand, Vietnam, Indonesia and Singapore) and even the countries that come under these umbrella categories are not covered in full. This is partly due to the difficulty of finding rapporteurs for the country reports.

The three parts of Asia under review are not tied together through a particular economic and/or political agreement. The South East ASEAN countries – Brunei, Cambodia, Indonesia, Laos, Malaysia, Myanmar, Philippines, Singapore and Taiwan – are not only tied together to some form of regional market building, they are also gradually moving towards a cautious form of harmonisation of consumer law.[1] The deeper reason might very well be that the countries are exporting their products to Europe and the United States inter alia, and have to abide by the production standards of the importing countries. Consumers within ASEAN are then indirectly benefitting from the economic interaction of ASEAN with the western world. This is a kind of Brussels effect.[2]

B. The Consumer Society

Looking beyond the ASEAN countries, the array of countries here under review that belong to South, East and South East Asia are extremely heterogeneous in size, in their economic power, their per capita income and not least their history. Despite all these differences they all share the development of the consumer society which has been compressed into a shorter time span than in the West.[3] However, the

[1] L Nottage et al, *ASEAN Consumer Law, Harmonisation and Co-operation* (Cambridge: Cambridge University Press, 2019) 11.

[2] A Bradford, *The Brussels Effect: How the European Union Rules the World* (Oxford: Oxford University Press, 2020).

[3] F Trentmann, *Empire of Things* (London: Penguin, 2016) 355 et seq.

consumer society is now pervasive throughout many parts of Asia. In the country with the largest population, China, there were already 300,930.8 billon RMB (1 USD = approximately 6.5 RMB) sales in 2015. Some states, such as Hong Kong, Japan, South Korea and Singapore, are seen as shopping tourist destinations as they have reputations for high consumer standards. Admittedly, in some other states the markets are less developed, but everywhere there is a sense that the development of consumption will be an important part of the economy going forward. Middle class affluence brings increased demand for quality products and services, whereas safety scandals have brought understanding that consumer protection is needed to protect all, but especially the most vulnerable. This is recognised particularly in ASEAN taking action in the field of consumer protection and the raft of measures introduced in many states as documented in the national reports. Online sales are also beginning to take off. They are largest in China with 35 per cent of all sales being online and estimated to account for RMB 144.44 trillion sales in 2020. Online trading also promotes cross-border sales particularly as there are some major companies in China, for instance Alibaba, JD.com and Pinduoduo, that reach beyond national borders.

It cannot be overlooked though, that in many of the lesser developed economies there is a deep divide between those consumers who can afford Westernised, often imported products, and those with scarce resources who have to buy the local products which might be counterfeited and substandard. The potential impact of a divided economy and divided society on the elaboration of an appropriate consumer law belongs to one of the key topics that are under-discussed, under-researched and under-theorised. The potential risk of a one-size-fits-all consumer law approach might very well be that the most vulnerable consumers in the respective countries are those who benefit the least from high consumer protection standards. The only effort undertaken to research this issue, to our knowledge, is an impact assessment of the Draft Consumer Law in Georgia.[4] Georgia has concluded an association agreement with the EU and is supposed to integrate the EU consumer law into its own legal system. The Regulatory Impact Assessment demonstrates by way of an empirical investigation how a one-size-fits-all-consumer law, based on EU standards, risks deepening the divide in the Georgian economy and society. The counterargument by Porter is that high standards are needed to compete for production and sales of high value-added value goods.[5] This would mean that the only way for Georgia out of the misery of a divided economy would be to take over the higher consumer standards provided so as to be competitive. Whilst this might be true in theory, the vulnerable consumer appears as a kind of collateral damage.

[4] Regulatory Impact Assessment of the Draft Law of Georgia on Consumer Rights Protection 2019, The Regulatory Impact Assessment was conducted and the report was prepared at the initiative of the Committee on European Integration of the Parliament of Georgia, with the financial and technical assistance of the Deutsche Gesellschaft für Internationale Zusammenarbeit (GIZ).

[5] M Porter, 'The Competitive Advantage of Nations', Harvard Business Review, March–April 1990, available under https://hbr.org/1990/03/the-competitive-advantage-of-nations.

C. The Legacy of the Western Legal Systems

With the exception of (most of) China, Japan and Thailand, the countries under review have been colonised chiefly by the British Empire, France, the Netherlands or Spain. The colonial times have left deep legacies in the South Asian, East Asian and South East Asian countries. Somewhat oversimplified, one might argue that the national systems can be divided into those with a common law and those with a civil law background. The Western influence can even be traced in countries with no or limited colonial legacy. The rise of consumer law had therefore to be merged with the already existing common law and/or civil law systems. Throughout the various fields of consumer law, but in particular in consumer sales law and unfair commercial practices law, the common law and civil law traditions are omnipresent, in particular when it comes to judicial consumer redress.[6]

The contributions united in the book also demonstrate a correlation between economic and political independence and the preparedness to overcome the historical legacy, to disconnect from the former colonial power and to engage into a much more open exchange of the possible pros and cons of common law and civil law systems when it comes to the elaboration of consumer laws. Here the path dependency is much looser anyway as the consumer society leads to a relatively homogeneous set of consumer problems which do not require identical but rather similar answers. Depending on perspective and on the degree of scrutiny one might be surprised by the relatively homogeneous answers to consumer problems throughout Asia. Vice versa the path dependency is stronger and stubborner when consumer law interferes in the core of the common law or the civil law system, such as consumer sales law or the control of standard terms. China, Japan and Singapore may serve as outstanding examples, where the historical legacies are weakening. These countries can no longer be easily classified as common or civil countries, as the legal orders combine all sorts of elements depending on the relevant subject matter.

D. The Impact of European Law

One of the key questions already in the seminar in Hong Kong and later during the many exchanges and zoom meetings in order to finalise the book was whether, and to what extent, EU consumer law has a direct or an indirect impact on the development of the national consumer laws in South, East and South East Asia. A sophisticated answer would have required empirical research in tracing back the legislative history and the involvement of the EU or EU experts or national experts coming from the EU. Whilst such an undertaking was beyond our ambition, there is clearly evidence from the country reports that some Asian countries take the law of the former colonial power into consideration. If the colonial power is a member of the EU, the Asian country might

[6] M Cantero Gamito, 'Access to Justice', in this volume.

adjust its law to the consumer law of the colonial power, which in fact is EU law. Brexit might very well have an impact, in particular when it comes to the emerging 'consumer law 2.0.' – the consumer law of the digital economy, which is about to take shape within the EU in the next couple of years.[7] It is likely that many states around the world are closely following if and how the EU regulates the digital economy and society and what kind of rules will be introduced in the name of consumer protection.

III. The Actors: Governments, Courts and Consumer Organisations

A. The Legal Design of Consumer Law

Setting aside the divide between common law and civil law as well as doctrinal battles of key concepts, the consumer law in South, East and South East Asia looks amazingly similar. There is a common core, which dates back to the Kennedy declaration in 1962. The consumer law is built around these rights – not only in the Western World but also in the countries under scrutiny. One can only speculate what happens when policymakers in South, East and South East Asia are called to draft or to revise a consumer law. Harking back to the now dominating paradigm of evidence based policymaking,[8] a perfect starter would in theory be a kind of serious stock-taking of the socio-economic situation in the respective country. What kind of problems do consumers suffer from in the respective countries? What are the most urgent problems? And who is in need of protection? Such a stock-taking does not necessarily require a genuine political dimension of consumer law, whether it serves to stabilise the market and the government like in China[9] or whether consumer law is part of a programme to democratise a country – such as in Greece, Portugal, Spain and in Brazil. It might very well be that the open texture of consumer law – its multifunctional usability – from correcting deficits in the market to questioning inequality in society, forms an integral part of its success and explains the relative homogeneity worldwide. This can be seen as a strength as it affords political acceptability across the board for consumer protection measures. It can also be seen as a weakness as the foundational principles can remain obscured.

With regard to the countries investigated it seems fair to assume that none of them undertook this kind of stock-taking. Otherwise, the data would have become known in one way or the other. It equally means that governments and parliaments are operating from the idea that the consumer society produces similar problems whatever the country might be. This is both correct and wrong. It is correct, as mass production leads to nearly identical problems provided the products are available throughout the countries. Dieselgate is a wonderful example. The social and economic problem – consumers

[7] A De Franceschi, 'Adaptation of Asian Consumer Law to the Digital Age', in this volume.
[8] P Cairney, *The Politics of Evidence-Based Policy Making* (Basingstoke: Palgrave MacMillan, 2017).
[9] F Trentmann, *Empire of Things*, 355 et seq.

being cheated through misleading information, to put it politely – concerns all consumers, in Europe and Asia. Only the legal and political solution differs considerably. However, the assumption is wrong in that there are differences depending on whether the countries are exporters or importers of consumer mass production and what their position is in the global value chains, whether the national companies are the chain leaders or are rather at the lower tail.[10] These differences are not visible in the existing body of consumer laws, although they would and should affect the rights and remedies available.

B. The Actors

Setting aside Japan, there is a remarkable conspicuousness that two actors who play a key role in the development of consumer law in the Western world are by and large missing: the courts and consumer organisations. Courts were at the forefront in the development of consumer law in the United States, in Western European and more recently Middle and Eastern European countries, and last but not least also in the EU itself through the European Court of Justice. One of the major battlefields of consumer law, where the courts played a key role, was product liability. Many key cases decided in courts concerned the liability of car manufacturers,[11] in the aftermath of the thalidomide catastrophe pharmaceuticals,[12] and tobacco.[13] Even at the EU level, it needed the European Court of Justice to tackle the social problem of consumers who were evicted from their houses at times of the financial crisis in 2008/2009, because they could no longer pay their mortgages or were unable to repay loans concluded in foreign currency (Swiss Francs in particular).[14] Litigation in courts quite often served as a last resort for the victims of consumer harm to seek compensation and justice. The national reports on the South, East and South East Asian countries amply demonstrate that national courts did not play a similar role. Consumer law very much remains in the hands of the government not only with regard to the law-making but also when it comes to law enforcement. One branch of government – the judiciary – is by and large excluded.

A similar observation can be made on the role and function of the consumer organisations. In a perfect world, consumer organisations would grow out of the middle of the society, would be sponsored by the members of the civil society and monitored through the civil society. In the Western world, the role and function of consumers

[10] For an overview see J Salminen and M Rajavuori, 'Transnational Sustainability Laws and the Regulation of Global Value Chains: Comparison and a Framework for Analysis' (2019) 26 *Maastricht Journal of European and Comparative Law* 602; A Beckers and H-W Micklitz, 'Une perspective holistique sur la réglementation des chaînes d'approvisionnement mondiales' (2020) 3 *Revue Internationale De Droit Economique* 343–59.

[11] R Nader, *Unsafe at Any Speed* (New York: Grossman, 1965).

[12] https://en.wikipedia.org/wiki/Thalidomide_scandal.

[13] G Howells, *The Tobacco Challenge: Legal Policy and Consumer Protection* (Farnham: Ashgate, 2011).

[14] F Gómez and M Artigot, 'Ex-Post Fairness Controls and Contract Design: The Spanish Experience' in K Mathis and A Tor (eds), *Consumer Law and Economics. Economic Analysis of Law in European Legal Scholarship* (Cham: Springer, 2021) 133; M Jazon, 'Judicial Governance by Unfair Contract Terms Law in the EU: Proposal for a New Research Agenda for Policy and Doctrine' (2020) 4 *European Review of Private Law* 909.

vary considerably, in particular with regard to their political and economic power.[15] Many Western democratic states subsidise consumer organisations to such a degree that they look much more like outsourced branches of government than organisations of the civil society. In some states such as Hong Kong, Macau and Singapore there are state-backed Consumer Councils that might provide a similar function. These are different from grassroots consumer organisations. In the South, East and South East Asian countries, setting aside Japan and maybe to some extent India, Malaysia and Taiwan, consumer organisations are by and large out of the picture when it comes to consumer politics, to the making of consumer law and to the enforcement of consumer law through collective action. Even if they exist and even if the respective law provides for rights granted to consumer organisations, their practical importance is very limited. The consequence for the place of consumer law and policy is rather far reaching: consumer law is not really anchored in the civil society, perhaps maybe in the form of individual expectations, but not institutionally anchored through organisations that claim to speak for the consumer society in the respective countries.[16] It needs to be explored whether in some states, such as China, consumer groups have the power and independence to take on this role.

IV. Substance of Consumer Law

A. Private Law Controls

There are plenty of private law rules regulating consumer sales. These transactions are subject to the general rules of contractual and non-contractual liability. Most systems have, for instance, a system of liability for contractual non-conformity derived from civil law code traditions or the English Sale of Goods Act. In some Asian countries, aspects of consumer sales might be found in special consumer protection statutes, but there is surprisingly little development of a sales regime explicitly aimed at consumers modelled on EU reforms, at least in comparison with the widespread impact of the Product Liability Directive.[17],[18] There are some examples of EU sales law impacting on consumer sales law in Asia – this is clearly evidenced in Macau and in Singapore, for whilst it might not have been expressly stated to be based on the EU law, their sales law reforms are clearly influenced by the European model.[19] Typical sales law remedies involve rejection of the goods and/or damages, but some other Asian countries, alongside those mentioned above that have been influenced by EU law, such as China, Japan,

[15] S Nessel, 'Consumer Policy in 28 EU Member States: An Empirical Assessment in Four Dimensions' (2019) 42 *Journal of Consumer Policy* 455.

[16] H-W Micklitz and G Saumier, 'Enforcement and Effectiveness of Consumer Law – General Report' in H-W Micklitz and G Saumier (eds), *Enforcement and Effectiveness of Consumer Law* (Cham: Springer, 2018) 3–45.

[17] Council Directive 85/374/EEC of 25 July 1985 on the approximation of the laws, regulations and administrative provisions of the Member States concerning liability for defective products, OJ 1985 No L210, p 29.

[18] G Pearson, 'Sale of Goods: A Comparative Perspective', in this volume.

[19] A Loke, 'The Lemon Law and the Integrated Enhancement of Consumer Rights in Singapore' (2014) *Singapore Journal of Legal Studies* 285.

Macau and Thailand, have also developed cure remedies in relation to consumer sales. In South Korea, cure remedies are available in practice due to guidance that is normally complied with.

Product liability has been described as one of the most successful legal exports at least on paper.[20] This is certainly true for Asia with Cannarsa illustrating how many countries have adopted strict liability.[21] To varying degrees this has been inspired and developed in line with the EU Product Liability Directive, but in any event that Directive has been an impetus for reform alongside knowledge of US developments in this field. However, like in so many jurisdictions outside North America, having strong substantive laws has not ensured that victims have access to justice as the number of reported cases remains low, perhaps with the exception of Australia.

Unfair terms regulation probably lies somewhere between product liability and conformity as regards the extent to which the laws have been adapted to the needs of consumers. Nehf notes reliance has been placed on broad concepts such as unconscionability and good faith.[22] There are tensions between procedural and substantive fairness. Normally a concern for procedural fairness dominates, but Malaysia provides a distinctive approach. Based on a non-implemented recommendation of the Indian Law Reform Commission, it clearly distinguishes procedural from substantive fairness. Promoting substantive fairness can also be underpinned by prohibitions on specific unfair terms. Often these relate to controls on exclusion clauses, but also cover matters such as unilateral variations by the trader or forcing consumers to arbitrate. Some of the controls in Asian common law jurisdictions, such as Hong Kong and Singapore, reflect in part the UK's Unfair Contract Terms Act 1977. The EU law in this area has not been a force for approximation of Asian laws to the same extent as the Product Liability Directive, though the Korean law has some similarities. Vietnam used the EU law as a reference, but stopped short of introducing a general unfairness clause. Indeed, the EU approach of pre-emptively regulating contracts through undertakings and injunctions is not a common feature of the Asian regulatory landscape. Such a power does exist for the Council of Consumers in Macau, but is not exercised in practice. By contrast, Taiwan provides an example of a system imposing official mandatory contract term requirements or prohibitions of terms in specific contracts.

Information is central to most regimes of consumer protection. In comparison to Europe the position in Asia looks underdeveloped or at least patchwork. This is because the combination of the Unfair Commercial Practices Directive[23] (with its obligation not to omit material information) and the Consumer Rights Directive[24] with its positive information obligations potentially covering all sales provide both a comprehensive regime and one linked to remedies as the information can become part of the terms of the contract. Atkins and Webb neatly explain the patchwork of rules operating in Asia.

[20] M Reimann, 'Product Liability in a Global Context: the Hollow Victory of the European Model' (2003) 2 *European Review of Private Law* 128.

[21] M Cannarsa, 'Product Liability', in this volume.

[22] J Nehf, 'A Comparative Analysis of the Regulation of Unfair Terms in Asia', in this volume.

[23] Directive 2005/29/EC of the European Parliament and of the Council of 11 May 2005 concerning unfair business-to-consumer commercial practices in the internal market, OJ 2005 No L149, p 22.

[24] Directive 2011/83/EU of the European Parliament and of the Council of 25 October 2011 on consumer rights, OJ 2011 No L304, p 64.

Some information duties are derived from a duty not to mislead and in a few jurisdictions this also extends to obligations in relation to omissions. There are also examples of positive pre-contractual duties, especially in financial services contracts. Some legal systems include a principle on the consumer's right to information, but it is unclear how effectively these are operationalised in practice. China, Macau, Taiwan and Vietnam provide examples of jurisdictions that have extensive mandated pre-contractual information duties. South Korea has adopted extensive obligations for e-commerce.

Rights of withdrawal are another area where Asia seems to lag behind Europe. Such rights are also less well-developed in other areas of the world that have a track record for adopting consumer laws, such as North America and Australasia. Where rights of withdrawal exist, they tend to be in the context of doorstep and other forms of direct selling. There are only isolated instances of the right applying to distance selling.[25] China, Korea, Taiwan and Thailand provide examples of a developed right of withdrawal which applies to Internet sales. Such rights are being proposed in Macau. By contrast, in Hong Kong there have even been arguments put forward as to why the right of withdrawal should not apply to Internet sales.[26] Japan seeks to develop a nuanced approach by allowing the trader not to offer a right of withdrawal in Internet sales, but only if this is made clear to the consumer. This is, however, an area ripe for further consideration by Asian legislators, though it has already been noted that the concept is not as enthusiastically embraced outside Europe. There are also theoretical arguments mustered to at least question whether the right should be maintained or qualified. These come from both those who want to use Big Data to give personalised withdrawal rights depending on individual preferences[27] and the environmental lobby concerned by the waste and transportation implications of goods being returned when they are in good order.[28]

B. Public Law Controls

Unfair commercial practices lie on the cusp of private and public law. Many private law rules can apply to counter unfair commercial practices, but specialised laws either focusing on specific problematic practices or increasingly based on broad standards such as misleading, unfair and aggressive practices are being adopted. Asia has several examples of jurisdictions adopting these broad standards (Hong Kong, India, Japan, Singapore) whose adoption was influenced in the earlier days by North American, particular Canadian, and Australian laws and more recently by the EU Directive. Micklitz describes a trend for systems that have more sophisticated enforcement structures to move beyond criminal sanctions to allow for civil law remedies such as injunctions.[29]

[25] M Atkins and E Webb, 'Information Duties and the Right of Withdrawal, in this volume.

[26] M Durovic, G Howells and A Janssen, 'Hong Kong,' in this volume.

[27] O Ben-Shahar, 'Personalizing Mandatory Rules in Contract Law' (2019) 86 *The University of Chicago Law Review* 255.

[28] B Keirsbilck et al, 'Sustainable Consumption and Consumer Protection Legislation How can sustainable consumption and longer lifetime of products be promoted through consumer protection legislation?' IP/A/IMCO/2020-13 (May 2020); B Keirsbilck and E Terryn (eds), *Circular Economy and Consumer Protection* (Cambridge: Intersentia, 2019).

[29] H-W Micklitz, 'Commercial Practices: A Comparative Perspective,' in this volume.

There are rare examples, for example Hong Kong, where breach of the regulatory controls gives a private right of redress, but no evidence that this is widely invoked; though that is true also in many European jurisdictions where private redress is available. It often needs a collective redress mechanism to make such recovery practical and effective.

Malaysia was an early adopter of a general safety obligation. Such laws are also now found in Hong Kong and Macau, where the introduction is linked to copying of reforms in the United Kingdom and Portugal. Some countries have quite sophisticated regimes linked to pre-market controls of goods such as in Japan and Singapore. The Singapore model links control to the standardisation process. However, the scope of such laws is limited to particular categories of goods. Thailand allows for testing to verify if products are safe. Indeed, in many Asian countries national standardisation bodies have a strong influence over the product safety culture: this is a feature often seen in countries having significant state control of the economy. India allows for unsafe goods to be withdrawn from the market or recalled if in the hands of consumers. However, in many Asian jurisdictions the most common regulatory powers are those that allow for post-market control. Whilst it is good that most states have such controls, there seems to be a clear need to develop a more holistic approach to product safety and this is indeed being fostered by ASEAN as a priority.[30]

C. Consumer Law in the Digital Age

The comparative state of consumer law may be patchy at the national level and often lacking an overall underpinning policy framework and philosophy. The position as regards e-commerce trading is even more embryonic. Whilst many jurisdictions have data protection laws and rules on e-contracting, there has not been a widespread adoption of rules adapting consumer law to the digital environment.[31] Even cooling-off periods for online purchases are not universally available in Asia[32] and are even explicitly rejected in Hong Kong by their Consumer Council.[33] That said, laws are starting to address the consumer concerns involved in online trading.[34] This is certainly an area to monitor developments and will doubtless come to the fore in the future as an area of regulatory activity.

V. Enforcement of Consumer Law

The gap between the law in the books and its impact in practice is well-documented and particularly significant in relation to consumer protection law.[35] Individual consumers

[30] L Nottage, 'Consumer Product Safety Law', in this volume.

[31] A De Franceschi, 'Adaptation of Asian Consumer Law to the Digital Age', in this volume.

[32] See M Atkins and E Webb, 'Information Duties and the Right of Withdrawal', in this volume.

[33] M Durovic, G Howells and A Janssen, 'Hong Kong', in this volume.

[34] A De Franceschi, 'Adaptation of Asian Consumer Law to the Digital Age', in this volume.

[35] H-W Micklitz and G Saumier, 'Enforcement and Effectiveness of Consumer Law – General Report' in H-W Micklitz and G Saumier (eds), *Enforcement and Effectiveness of Consumer Law* (Cham: Springer, 2018) 3–45.

face several disadvantages when seeking to resolve consumer problems. They often lack the technical and legal skills needed to identify the source of the problem and seek redress. This is even more problematic for poorer consumers who have less resources. Vulnerable consumers may also be less good advocates, perhaps even lacking basic literacy skills.[36] Whereas retaining the custom of high net worth customers may persuade traders to deal with them favourably on the basis of commercial judgement, this is rarely the case with the more marginal disadvantaged consumer. For all consumers, though, the amounts at stake in many cases are small compared to the effort needed to pursue a claim. As Leff noted, to bring a consumer claim the consumer needs 'super-spite'.[37] All these generic problems affect consumers on a global scale and are also present in Asia, indeed many parts of Asia have relatively poor income levels and so consumer purchases can be significant for them. This was made very evident by the example of the Vietnamese tourist who bought a phone for his girlfriend and was surprised to find he had signed up for an expensive guarantee contract.[38] There are of course even more basic concerns facing poor consumers in many parts of Asia.

It is often argued that the problems for consumer redress are accentuated in Asia by cultural habits that do not favour inter-personal conflict and litigation.[39] Politeness and respect for authority and hierarchies are certainly features that one recognises from even a casual acquaintance with Asia. However, there needs to be some caution before embracing a theory that Asian consumers *en masse* shun litigation. This may be true for certain sectors of society and it may even be the case that there may be a preference for less confrontational means of dispute resolution, such as mediation. But, as we shall see, the popularity of various forms of dispute resolution geared to the needs of consumers suggests that many Asian consumers are more than happy to raise their complaints and seek redress. Not litigating for Asian consumers may be a natural response to the difficulties they face when bringing claims and the outcome of a cost-benefit analysis of the decision to seek redress. In this regard they are no different from consumers around the globe.

Likewise, in accordance with legal regimes around the globe, there have been experimentations with new procedures and institutions to assist consumers having access to justice. Mediation has been adopted as a mechanism to enhance dispute resolution in many countries (such as the important roles played by the Hong Kong Consumer Council, the Korean Consumer Dispute Settlement Commission, Macau's Consumer Council's Centre for Arbitration of Consumer Conflicts, the Consumer Disputes Mediation Service run by local authorities in Taiwan and the mediation role of the Vietnam Consumer Protection Association). In Indonesia, the Consumer Dispute Settlement Agency allows consumers to choose between mediation and arbitration.

[36] C Riefa and S Santier (eds), *Vulnerable Consumers and the Law: Consumer Protection and Access to Justice* (London: Routledge, 2020).

[37] A Leff, 'Ignorance, Injury and Spite' (1970) 80 *Yale Law Journal* 1.

[38] See 'Singapore jails 4 salesmen in phone shop that cheated Vietnamese tourist', *The Thanhnien Times*, thanhiennews.com, 14 October 2015.

[39] AHY Chen, 'Mediation, Litigation, and Justice: Confucius Reflections in a Modern Liberal Society' in DA Bell and H Chaibong (eds), *Confucianism for the Modern World* (Cambridge: Cambridge University Press, 2003) 259.

Whether these ADR innovations are linked to the supposed Asian preference to avoid confrontation or are part of a wider trend in dispute resolution is hard to discern. Certainly, arbitration is also adopted in Asia, especially in relation to financial services (see, for example, Hong Kong's Financial Dispute Resolution Scheme, Singapore's Financial Industry Dispute Resolution Centre and Taiwan's Financial Ombudsman Institute). But, whilst arbitration may be less daunting and more relaxed in style than court proceedings, bringing a claim to arbitration involves being prepared to confront the other side just as much as in formal litigation.

There are also some instances of court procedures being modified to enable consumers to bring small claims more effectively, but these seem to have had mixed success. Thailand seems to have positively adopted its system to assist consumers, although some issues remain in need of further reform. In Hong Kong, the small claims procedure does not seem to be widely used, perhaps because the alternatives to litigation offered by, for example, the Consumer Council are more attractive. Singapore builds mediation into the small claims procedure. It has also adopted a novel procedure for the accelerated hearing of claims involving tourists. By contrast, there are also examples in Asia of special consumer tribunals being established with an ethos that makes them more user-friendly. India has a system of District, State and National Consumer Dispute Redress Agencies. Malaysia has a very extensive and effective network of Consumer Tribunals.

Leaving aside the above attempts to ameliorate the position of the consumer in the litigation process, the overwhelming impression is that in many Asian jurisdictions the courts are overwhelmed and under-resourced so that consumer litigation is deterred by the length of the process. There is a notable lack of substantive consumer case law on topics in many jurisdictions despite the prompting of the editors to encourage discussion of reported cases and the endeavours of the national contributors to discover such material. There are some signs that this might change as public interest litigation (in China, where consumer organisations are given the role as plaintiff) or class action procedures are made available (Japan, Thailand) or promoted as reform options (Hong Kong). In China there is the intriguing *Wang Hai* phenomenon, where it has become a business model to seek out infringing goods and sue to make a profit from generous damages laws.

Regulatory agencies in many Asian jurisdictions do not routinely bring test cases. There are some exceptions of course and the enforcement activities of state agencies in Taiwan are noted.[40] In many Asian jurisdictions consumer organisations remain weakly organised. There are exceptions like in Hong Kong and Singapore, where consumer organisations have state funding. Malaysia is one state where grassroots organisations have been particularly active, especially the consumer group based in Penang. Consumer organisations can seek injunctions in Japan and also through a two-stage class action process can first establish breaches of law and then recover damages in a secondary procedure. Vietnam has the right for consumer organisations to bring litigation, but the

[40] JG Fong, 'Taiwan (Republic of China)', in this volume.

right is also circumscribed with conditions. However, routinely litigating in the courts is not a primary objective of consumer organisations in many Asian jurisdictions.

It is not an easy task to evaluate the effectiveness of consumer redress mechanisms. This is equally the case with regulatory enforcement. There are certainly jurisdictions with structures to promote compliance. Sometimes these are independent consumer agencies, at other times they are linked to other functions such as competition. There are also examples of regulatory overlap with different agencies having competing competencies. It is clear though that many agencies in the region have only limited resources and the scale of the resource problem is often related to the wealth of the economy. There seem to be some limited moves in a few jurisdictions to more modern forms of enforcement, for example seeking undertakings rather than simply relying on the criminal law or administrative fines. But we seem a long way off a fully embracing sophisticated enforcement regime as expounded in works such as that of Ayres and Braithwaite that advocates a pyramid of levels of regulatory enforcement.[41]

VI. Conclusions

This project has been a complex one for several reasons. The wide variety of jurisdictions, yet still only representing partial coverage of the region, is one factor. Another is the *ad hoc* adoption of consumer policy that has not been derived from a clear policy blueprint for the consumer economy. It seems at least in part to have been driven by the need to conform to international standards in a region that has become the workshop for the world. Though increased affluence seems also to be bringing domestic pressures for consumer reform.

There are clear differences in the sophistication of the legal regimes within Asia and their practical effectiveness. Often this is linked to the wealth of the nations. Consumer protection is becoming more important, but in legal policy debate it still needs to be elevated further to reach the level of importance accorded to the subject in Europe. However, it should be noted that consumer law only really came to the fore in general legal doctrine when its scope broadened and connections were found with reform of the general civil and commercial law and it became central to broader private law debates related to the potential development of a European Civil Code. That is unlikely to be the spur in Asia, although there are some projects seeking to replicate the European civil code debates.[42] However, the so-called Consumer 2.0 project linked to the digital economy may promote interest in consumer law as a subset of issues related to e-commerce. This area is currently under-developed, but could provide the catalyst for fresh Asian thinking on consumer law. To date, Asian consumer law largely reflects patterns from

[41] I Ayres and J Braithwaite, *Responsive Regulation* (Oxford: Oxford University Press, 1992); F Cafaggi and H-W Micklitz (eds), *New Frontiers of Consumer Protection – the Interplay between Private and Public Enforcement* (Mortsel: Intersentia, 2009).

[42] See M Durovic, 'Harmonisation of Contract Law in the Eastern and South-Eastern Asia: What Can Be Learnt from the CISG and the ECL Experience?' (2018) 7 *Global Journal of Comparative Law* 207.

the Western world. Potentially in the digital sphere it can become a leading participant in the debates. However, consolidation of the values of consumer protection and their effective enforcement should also remain key goals in the region. In seeking such development, key roles can be played by ASEAN, the UN and leading legal systems in the region that can provide policy development and models of legal regulation for jurisdictions in the region.

PART 2

National Reports

2

China

JIN JING

I. Introduction

China is one of the largest countries of consumption around the world. In 2020, China's total retail sales of social consumer goods reached RMB 39,198 billion (approximately USD 6125 billion).[1] Along with these tremendous numbers there are a large number of consumer complaints. In 2020, the National Consumers Association accepted a total of 982,249 consumer complaints and resolved 749,317 complaints.[2] Since the establishment of The Law on the Protection of Consumer Rights and Interests (hereinafter: Consumer Rights Law)[3] in 1993, the development of China's consumer protection laws over the past two decades has reflected the development of the market economy and private legal autonomy in China: it has fluctuated back and forth between the ideal and reality. However, the sufficient implementation of legislation related to consumer protection is still lacking, and the current legislation has lagged behind the development of new forms of consumption in the digital world. Although consumer protection has become an important legal area in China, theoretically, controversies remain in the Consumer Rights Law, such as the scope of application, the controls on unfair contract terms, contractual remedies and other issues. Additionally, the judicial applications remain inconsistent. A large number of legislative gaps between financial and digital consumers still exist. This contribution will try to find out the most important issues in Chinese consumer protection law, especially the key issues of the 2013 revision of the Consumer Rights Law and the core problems to be solved by legislation in the future.

[1] Summarised under www.stats.gov.cn/english/PressRelease/202101/t20210119_1812515.html.

[2] Statistics from the China Consumers Association. Available (in Chinese) under www.cca.org.cn/tsdh/detail/29923.html.

[3] The first Consumer Rights Law came into force in 1993, and was amended in 2009 and 2013. The current law is the 2013 amendment version. Of the total number of articles of the Consumer Rights Law, both the 1993 and 2009 versions have 55 articles in total, but the number of provisions in the 2013 amendment increased to 63 articles. In terms of the legal structure, neither of the two amendments changed the original legislative structure of the 1993 version, all include eight chapters, which are general principles, consumer rights, the obligations of business operators, State protection of legal rights and interests of consumers, consumer organisations, dispute resolution, legal liability and supplementary provisions.

II. Sources of Consumer Law

A. Legislation

Since the establishment of the Consumer Rights Law in 1993, China has already formed a complex legislative system of consumer protection, which can be divided into three levels: (1) special legislation on consumer protection issues, (2) general private law and (3) industry-specific regulations or administrative measures. First of all, concerning special legislation on consumer protection issues, the current legislation mainly includes two parallel acts: the Consumer Rights Law and Product Quality Law.[4] The Consumer Rights Law focuses on the systematic regulation of consumer protection issues, while the Product Quality Law focuses on tort law issues in relation to product liabilities. The two pieces of legislation are the most important laws in the field of consumer protection. Secondly, the Chinese Civil Code constitutes the general legal framework involving consumer protection issues such as remedies for breach of contract and tort liability. They function as the general private law and follow the basic *lex specialis* doctrine. Finally, in addition to special consumer protection law and general laws, China also initiated a large number of industry-oriented, consumer protection-related as well as specific content-oriented special legislation or administrative regulations, including the E-Commerce Law, Advertising Law,[5] Food Safety Law, Pharmaceutical Administration Law, Tourism Law and Telecommunication Regulation etc.

B. Guiding Cases and Judicial Interpretations

The Guiding Cases issued by the Supreme People's Court are particularly noteworthy. From 20 December 2011 to 16 March 2017, the Court has issued 16 Guiding cases[6] (from a total number of 87). From the 16 cases, four involve consumer disputes: No 64[7] on information duty in the telecommunications service contract, No 51[8] on flight delay damage compensation in transport contract, No 23[9] on punitive damages in case of breach of food safety provisions and No 17[10] on contract fraud in automobile

[4] Similar to the Consumer Rights Law, the first Product Quality Law came into force in 1993 and was amended in 2000 and 2009. The current law is the 2009 amendment version, including 74 articles and six chapters which are general principles, supervision and control of product quality, product quality responsibilities and obligations of producers and sellers, damages, penalty provisions and supplementary provisions.

[5] Meanwhile, the State Administration for Industry and Commerce (SAIC) issued the Interim Measures for Administration of Internet Advertising and specifies the regulation in the area of internet advertising.

[6] Statistics from the Supreme People's Court of the PRC. Available under www.court.gov.cn/shenpan-gengduo-77.html.

[7] No 64 Guiding Case (2016), *Liu Chaojie v China Mobile*, regarding a telecommunication contract, available (in Chinese) under www.court.gov.cn/shenpan-xiangqing-27571.html.

[8] No 51 Guiding Case, (2015), *Abdul Waheed v China Eastern Airline*, regarding an air passenger transport contract, available (in Chinese) under www.court.gov.cn/shenpan-xiangqing-14249.html.

[9] No 23 Guiding Case (2014), *Sun Yinshan v Auchan supermarket Nanjing*, regarding a sales contract dispute, available (in Chinese) under www.court.gov.cn/shenpan-xiangqing-13326.html.

[10] No 17 Guiding Case (2013), *Zhang Li v He Li Hua Tong Automobile Ltd.*, regarding contract fraud, available (in Chinese) under www.court.gov.cn/shenpan-xiangqing-6003.html.

sales. Although the status of the Guiding cases as a legal resource is not clear, due to the Court's institutional function as a legal interpretation body, Guiding Cases have become deciding grounds with weak normative binding force on the basis of subordinate institutional authority and can be deemed as 'quasi-legal sources'.[11] Additionally, the weight of a Guiding Case is less than a statute or a judicial interpretation, and the Guiding Cases, in fact, have been affected by various realistic and institutional factors.[12] Although the above four guiding cases are limited in their explanation of the whole picture of consumer protection, they have been involved in most core areas of consumer protection (pre-contractual information, damages) and the judicial influence should still not be underestimated.

It should also be noted that although there is no specific judicial interpretation of the Consumer Rights Law, the Supreme People's Court has adopted two judicial interpretations of the Contract Law (hereinafter: 'Contract Law Interpretation I'[13] and 'Contract Law Interpretation II'[14]) and one judicial interpretation on the trial of cases of disputes over sales contracts (hereinafter: the 'Sales Contract Interpretation'[15]). Although the Court is entitled to make statutory judicial interpretations, the legal effects of such interpretations remain unclear. Such interpretations are outside the formal hierarchy of legal norms, but the Court insists that statutory judicial interpretations have legal effects.[16] Therefore, in a sense, the judicial interpretations also constitute a part of the contract law, and a number of provisions of the interpretation are directly related to consumer protection, such as Articles 6, 9 and 10 of the Contract Law Interpretation II on content and validity of standard contract terms and Articles 21–23 of the Sales Contract Interpretation on the buyer's remedies in case of non-conformity. As the number of provisions of the Consumer Rights Law is not so large, and numerous more detailed contract rules are contained in the judicial interpretations, it can be understood that the judicial interpretations related to the Civil Code have constituted the legal source of consumer protection law, and play a very important role in the formation, effectiveness and remedy of consumers' contracts.

C. Remarks

In terms of the legal structure of consumers' protection law in China, it is necessary to pay special attention to the interaction between multilayered legislation as well as the cross-application paradox between different levels of legal sources, and to the special role of judicial interpretations and Guiding Cases. First of all, the legislation generally

[11] L Lei, 'Rethinking of the Status of Legal Source of Guiding Cases' (2015) 1 *China Legal Science* 272 (in Chinese).

[12] ibid.

[13] 'The Interpretation I of the Supreme People's Court of Several Issues concerning the Application of the Contract Law of the People's Republic of China', promulgated and entered into force on 29 December 1999.

[14] 'The Interpretation II of the Supreme People's Court of Several Issues concerning the Application of the Contract Law of the People's Republic of China', promulgated and entered into force on 13 May 2009.

[15] 'The Interpretation of the Supreme People's Court on Issues Concerning the Application of Law for the Trial of Cases of Disputes over Sales Contracts', promulgated and entered into force on 1 July 2012.

[16] C Wang, 'The Study on the Legal Effect of Judicial Interpretation' (2016) 28(1) *Peking University Law Journal* 263 (in Chinese).

shows the interactive relationship between the special laws and the general laws, among them the Consumer Rights Law is the core special legislation and Book Three of the Civil Code is the main general legal resource. In addition, many by-laws exist as a sort of 'satellite system'. Although there are plenty of laws and regulations on consumer protection, because of the lack of a unified and general law, for example a legal code, there is inevitably a phenomenon of fragmentation in consumer protection law. The legal application of the same situation varies greatly, such as the contradictory provisions on content control of standardised contract terms between Articles 9 and 10 of the Contract Law Interpretation II and Article 496 of the Civil Code. Meanwhile, the new models of transactions and disputes, such as those dealing with financial consumers for example, still lack special legislation. There are still a large number of cross-cutting areas in the existing laws. Secondly, the significance of the guiding cases should not be underestimated. Despite the limited number of guiding cases, the Chinese 'case law' clearly shows the basic opinions of the Supreme People's Court on typical cases and has a certain guiding function for judicial practice. However, the guiding cases as a normal legal resource is still controversial, in theory. Finally, special attention should be paid to the codification of Chinese civil law on the one hand, and to the legislation of the E-Commerce Law and other (digital) related laws on the other. The current general status is that the Consumer Rights Law is excluded from the Civil Code and remains as a single law. The E-Commerce Law has been in effect since 2019. These new laws will take a hybrid legal reception approach, and will seemingly rely heavily on the existing legislative experiences of the EU and the United States. Concerning the Consumer Rights Law itself, it has obviously been improved during the two amendments in 2009 and 2013. The latest amendment of the Consumer Rights Law in 2013 introduced specific rules on personal information protection,[17] withdrawal rights,[18] specific performance,[19] triple punitive damages in case of contract fraud,[20] defective product recall obligations of the seller,[21] online shopping rule[22] and other new consumption patterns such as obligations of the seller in case of financial product sales.[23] During the revision, the 2013 amendment also learned from the legislative experiences in the EU, Japan and South Korea.[24]

III. Concept of Consumer

The concept of consumer is a fundamental issue of consumer protection law and is also a controversial issue of Consumer Rights Law itself. Article 2 of the Consumer Rights Law defines a consumer as the legal subject involved in purchasing and using goods or receiving services for daily consumption. The meaning of this provision is not only to clearly define

[17] Consumer Rights Law, Art 14.
[18] ibid, Arts 24–25.
[19] ibid, Art 19.
[20] ibid, Art 55.
[21] ibid, Art 19.
[22] ibid, Art 25.
[23] ibid, Art 28.
[24] Law Commission of the NPC Standing Committee, *Legislation Background and Point on Protection of Consumer Rights and Interests* (Beijing: Law Press, 2013) 317–76 (in Chinese).

the concept of consumers but also to delineate the scope of application of the Consumer Rights Law. It is worth noting that during the amendment to this Law, its scope of application was one of the most controversial issues and generated considerable debates.

A. Controversies

Firstly, there was a suggestion that the expression of the 'daily consumption needs' should be modified to 'the purpose is not to make production or business activities' since there are different understandings of the meaning of 'daily consumption needs' in legal practice, therefore it causes much confusion. Ultimately, no change was made and the new amendment maintains the original expression, although a flexible interpretation of the term was suggested.

Secondly, there were also suggestions that the Consumer Rights Law should learn from the EU and United States during the legislative process on financial consumers and incorporate 'financial consumer' into the concept of consumers and allow medical education services to fall under the Consumer Rights Law.[25] The new amendment recognises that financial services in general fall into its scope of application and Article 27 of the Consumer Rights Law stipulates an information duty of the financial service providers. However, from observations of current judicial practice, this has not been effectively implemented. In judicial practice, the financial consumer disputes cases will be judged according to Book 3 of the Civil Code rather than the Consumer Rights Law. In the process of revision, it was also determined that, due to the fact that emergency medical treatment and compulsory medical care belong to the statutory obligation of the hospital and compulsory education, it is thus a kind of public welfare. Further, because a consensus was not achieved concerning the current application of the law to medical education services, and because these services are very complex and special, the Consumer Rights Law does not specify whether it applies to these services as a whole, but rather specific judgments will rest on the basis of the 'daily consumption needs' of the transaction.[26]

Two further issues concerned the questions whether the Consumer Rights Law should protect the consumer who knowingly purchases fake goods, and whether the consumer concept should be limited to natural persons. Although during the revision process there were considerations to extend the legal subject of Article 2 from natural persons to legal persons and NGOs and to exclude the 'professional counterfeit hunter', the final amendment ultimately limits its concept of consumer to natural persons and does not exclude the professional anti-fake product buyer from its scope of application. It is, however, worth paying attention to the No 23 Guiding Case of the Supreme People's Court, in which the Court affirmed that the prerequisite elements of punitive damages do not consider the buyer's subjective state of mind.[27]

[25] H Su, 'Study on Some Important Issues of the Revision of CRL' (2013) 2 *Western Law Review* 2 (in Chinese).

[26] S Li (ed), *Interpretations and Explanations on CRL* (Beijing: Law Press, 2013) 5–17 (in Chinese).

[27] No 23 Guiding Case (2014), *Sun Yinshan v Auchan supermarket Nanjing*, available (in Chinese) under www.court.gov.cn/shenpan-xiangqing-13326.html.

B. 'Financial Consumer' Disputes

Article 28 of the Consumer Rights Law stipulates that sellers providing securities, insurance, banking and other financial services shall provide this information for the consumers, including the business address, their contact details and the content of the services. This means that financial consumers are not excluded from the Consumer Rights Law's scope of application in its 2013 revision. However, from the perspective of judicial practice, a large number of insurance contract disputes or trust contract disputes rely mostly on Book Three of the Civil Code rather than the Consumer Rights Law, which inevitably has unfavourable results for the protection of financial consumers. Regarding this, the main problem lies in the so-called over-protection of financial consumers. Besides, banks and other financial institutions insisted that if the Consumer Rights Law were to be directly applied, the result would be an over-protection of consumers and so they advocated that judgments should be made on the basis of the financial consumer contract itself according to Book Three of the Civil Code. At present, most courts only apply Book Three of the Civil Code and do not regard the Consumer Rights Law as the main legal basis, although many disputes have been caused because insurance sellers have not fulfilled their information obligations.

Another tricky question is whether punitive damages could be applied in financial consumer contracts. According to Article 28 of the Consumer Rights Law (2009 version), it is clear that the information disclosure obligations of the sellers cover specific areas such as online shopping, video shopping, mail order and financial services. Therefore, it is clear that financial consumers also belong to the group of consumers in the Consumer Rights Law. This produces a difficult problem, namely whether punitive damages can apply in relation to a fraudulent act in financial consumer contracts. In fact, China's current bank, securities and insurance industries recognise the concept of 'financial consumers' and do not distinguish between the average investors, financial consumers and normal consumers. As a result, fraudulent activities in the financial consumption area can also apply the triple punitive damages of the Consumer Rights Law. However, it should be noted that, although the current laws and judicial interpretations are not clear about the questions mentioned above, the practice is very cautious. As financial consumer contracts often involve a relatively high amount of the contract price, it will cause such a result: once the punitive damages rule is applied, the punishment will be very severe and the punitive damages will be very high. At present, although the punitive damages in the area of financial consumer contracts have not yet appeared in litigation, such a rule design in the Consumer Rights Law is undoubtedly dangerous, and equating financial consumers to normal consumers with regard to punitive damages is undoubtedly misplaced. The financial consumers have their own characteristics: the essence of financial consumption is the consumption of risks. The financial consumer contracts with the risk as the consumption purpose should be clearly distinguishable from the general consumer contracts in the Consumer Rights Law in the future, with respect to the determination of fraudulent acts and the application of punitive damages. If punitive damages were to apply in the financial consumption area, special rules on punitive damages should be introduced. More specific rules need to be introduced on the constituent elements, such as the specific rules between appropriateness principles, fraudulent acts and the information duty, which can adapt to the behavioural characteristics of financial consumers, and can achieve a truly deterrent effect in this special area. The construction of special rules on punitive damages in financial consumer contracts can also prevent the dangerous possibility of excessive expansion of punitive damages in the current Consumer Rights Law. It remains to be seen whether the future financial consumer protection needs to be complemented by existing legal provisions in the Consumer Rights Law or by separate special legislation. It is clear, however, the protections concerning financial consumers should be strengthened in the future.

IV. Pre-contractual Information Obligations

A. Civil Code

The pre-contractual information obligation is one of the pre-contractual obligations found in the general provisions of Book Three of the Civil Code and the special provisions of the Consumer Rights Law, respectively. Book Three of the Civil Code distinguishes between pre-contractual and post-contractual obligations. Articles 500 and 501 of the Civil Code mainly prescribe the pre-contractual obligations, which refer to various types of contractual obligations arising from the course of contract negotiation, preparation or similar transactions based on the principle of good faith. The obligations of non-disclosure and confidentiality are typical pre-contractual obligations in the Civil Code. Breach of such obligations constitutes *culpa in contrahendo* and necessitates payment for damages as a result. These provisions on pre-contractual obligations of the Civil Code are general provisions and apply not only in consumer contracts but also in other types of contracts. According to Article 500 of the Civil Code, the party shall be liable for damages if its behaviour causes losses to the other party. As a result, the losses are the necessary prerequisite for damages in case of *culpa in contrahendo* under Article 42 of the Civil Code.

In comparison with the Civil Code, the Consumer Rights Law contains more detailed provisions on contractual information duties, which saw heated issues in the 2013 amendment. From the legislative approach, the contractual information duties can be divided into direct and indirect provisions in the Consumer Rights Law.[28] For the indirect provisions on pre-contractual obligations, the consumer's right to information and the right to enjoy education are defined separately in Chapter II of the Consumer Rights Law ('Consumer Rights'), which indirectly provides that consumers are entitled to be provided with relevant information.[29] For the direct provisions on pre-contractual obligations, Chapter III of the Consumer Rights Law (Obligations of Sellers) contains three provisions. Articles 18(1) and 19 of the Consumer Rights Law expressly specify the obligations of the operator on explanations and warnings with regard to products,

[28] Q Lu, 'The Information Duties of Consumer Protection Law' (2014) 8 *Tsinghua University Law Journal* 156 (in Chinese).

[29] ibid.

which may endanger the safety of persons and property. In particular, Article 20 of the Consumer Rights Law stipulates that the sellers shall provide consumers with true and complete information on the quality, performance, use and validity period of goods or services.

B. Consumer Rights Law

Articles 20 and 21 of the Consumer Rights Law are the main provisions on pre-contractual information duties. The pre-contractual information obligation and its corresponding legal consequences constitute an important part of the 2013 amendment. Although the pre-contractual information obligations have featured since the first version of Consumer Rights Law in 1993 and were not modified in the 1999 amendment,[30] three important amendments were introduced into Article 20 during the 2013 revision. Firstly, Article 20 of the Consumer Rights Law explicitly lists the important types of pre-contractual information in practice, including but not limited to information about the quality, performance, use and validity period of goods or services. Secondly, the information provided by sellers to consumers shall be real and true. In practice, there are situations where the seller may deliberately conceal some important information that may affect the consumer's choice, therefore in addition to the real information obligation the sellers must provide comprehensive information to consumers. Accordingly, the current version of the Consumer Rights Law requires that sellers provide not only true but also comprehensive information for consumers. Thirdly, the restriction on false and misleading advertising was changed to restriction on false *or* misleading advertising.[31] The new amendment distinguishes between false advertisement and misleading advertisement, which is in line with the restriction of false or misleading content in advertisement in Article 4 of the Advertising Law. Finally, it should be pointed out that Article 20 of the Consumer Rights Law is one of the most widely applied articles in consumer contract disputes, according to the PKU Law Database. The number of legal cases involving the Consumer Rights Law is approximately 4000, from which approximately 800 concern Article 20 of the Consumer Rights Law, which shows that pre-contractual information liability is an important factor of consumer disputes in judicial practice.

C. Punitive Damages

i. Scope

Punitive damages in consumer contracts is an important legal institution in the Consumer Rights Law and is an essential component of the 2013 amendment. It is also one of the most controversial issues in legal theory and practice. As a typical legal institution of the common law system, the introduction of punitive damages in

[30] Consumer Rights Law (1993 and 1999), Arts 19–20.
[31] Consumer Rights Law (1999), Art 19; Consumer Rights Law (2013), Art 20.

China is based on comparative law and relies especially on the legislative experiences of common law.[32] Article 47 of the Tort Law used the 'punitive damages' expression for the first time in 2010 and since then the legal institution of punitive damages has been established. Still, there was no clear calculation method in the Tort Law. Article 49 of the Consumer Rights Law (1999 version) stipulated that sellers who engage in fraudulent activities in the supply of goods or services shall, on the demand of the consumers, increase the compensations for victims' losses. The increased amount of the compensation shall be double the costs that the consumers paid for the goods or services. This is referred to as double punitive damages. The 2013 amendment of the Consumer Rights Law changes the double punitive damage to triple punitive damage in cases of consumer contract fraud with the minimal compensation threshold of RMB 500 (approximately USD 80) in Article 55 of the Consumer Rights Law. Sellers, who fraudulently provide goods or services shall, as required by consumers, increase the compensation for consumers' losses, and the increase in compensation shall be three times the payment made by a consumer for the goods or the service *or* be RMB 500 if the increase calculated before is less than RMB 500. In tort cases, Article 55(2) of the Consumer Rights Law stipulates that when sellers knowingly provide consumers with defective goods or services, causing death or serious damage to the health of consumers or other victims, the victims have the right to claim punitive compensation no more than two times the amount of losses incurred. In addition, in Article 55(1) there is an exception. This exceptional regulation is in line with other provisions such as Article 148(2) of the Food Safety Law, which states that a consumer may require a producer of food who fails to meet the food safety standards or a trader knowingly dealing in such food to pay an indemnity of 10 times the price paid or three times the loss. If the amount of the additional compensation is less than RMB 1,000 (approximately USD 155), it shall be RMB 1,000, except for a defect in the labels or instructions of the food which neither impairs food safety nor misleads consumers. Although the Consumer Rights Law and the Food Safety Law both stipulate compensation for punitive damages, they have different prerequisites: fraud is the necessary precondition for punitive damages in the Consumer Rights Law, but not under the Food Safety Law.

ii. Professional Counterfeit Hunters

In judicial practices of punitive damages in China, the most extreme, controversial and unique situation is the so-called 'buying fake while knowing it' lawsuits. In 1995, a consumer found that he could not only profit from punitive damages but also deter the sale of counterfeit goods. The consumer deliberately purchased the counterfeit goods, then sued to obtain punitive damages. Such intentional purchase of counterfeit goods and making huge profits through litigation, according to punitive damages rules, are known as the 'buying fake while knowing it' behaviour, and such consumers are called 'professional counterfeit hunters'. For example, in *Beijing Ninetowns Tianshi Ecological Agriculture Co, Ltd. v Tian Junwei*, a consumer purchased 24 bottles of mineral water

[32] L Yang, 'New Development of the Punitive Damages in Consumer Protection Law' (2014) 4 *The Jurist* 90 (in Chinese); L Wang, 'On the Compensation of Punitive Damages in the United States of America' (2003) 5 *Journal of Comparative Law* 1 (in Chinese); Li, 'Interpretations and Explanations', 266–73.

labelled 'healthy function' at the price of RMB 3537 (approximately USD 550). The next day, the consumer bought 264 bottles of the same mineral water at a total price of RMB 34,257 (approximately USD 5350). The consumer then claimed that the health functions on the label constituted misleading information and were in violation of Article 55 of the Consumer Rights Law. The consumer claimed for triple compensation as punitive damages because of false advertisement. The Beijing Third Intermediate People's Court supported the consumer's claim and held that the company's publicity content had constituted consumer fraud. Meanwhile, the Court held that the purpose or motive of the purchase of the consumer did not affect the composition of fraud. The consumer was to return the goods and the operator to return the purchase price and pay three times the purchase price as punitive damages compensation. This is a typical case of a 'professional counterfeit hunter' and the Court also supported the punitive damages claims. Although the courts in China still have different opinions on the 'professional counterfeit hunter' cases, most of them maintain that punitive damages can be applied to 'professional counterfeit hunter' cases.

In Chinese judicial litigation, 'professional counterfeit hunter' cases have some unique characteristics and are easy to identify. First of all, such cases are characterised by the high claim value. The amount of compensation for contract fraud is often very high. While the current triple compensation or 10 times compensation in the Consumer Rights Law and the Food Safety Law take the purchase price as the basis for calculation, the professional hunter purchases many items or even hundreds or thousands of pieces of goods, and then triggers the litigation, such as purchasing a large number of television sets or computers, and then claiming for triple compensation because of false advertisement. As a result, this high claim value is based on the intentional 'use' of punitive damages rules on the basis of calculation method, and the plaintiff often increases the number of purchases to achieve the intention of increasing the fine. Secondly, the same plaintiff may trigger a number of cases with repetitive features. As the current Consumer Rights Law stipulates in its Article 55, the minimum compensation threshold of RMB 500, the professional counterfeit hunter deliberately purchases goods at a very low price, and then can rely on the minimum compensation of RMB 500. The same hunter may sue for similar reasons several times in order to make profit. Thirdly, the reasons for litigation are similar. Although the purpose of punitive damages is mainly to deter fraudulent sellers, there have been a large number of 'professional counterfeit hunter' lawsuits and the fraudulent activities mostly are related to the false information on labels, for example, the clothing label is listed as a fur coat and the actual fur content is only 60 per cent. In this case, the label constitutes a false piece of information. In fact, the wrong or inaccurate information on the label should be recognised as behaviour that differs from traditional fraud activities. Since the current legislation does not clearly distinguish these two types of behaviour, incorrect label information becomes the main cause to trigger the punitive damages in litigation. Last but not least, in Chongqing, Jiangsu, Shanghai and Beijing, it easily falls into the punitive damages litigation. Although there are no clear statistics, this may be related to regional 'professional counterfeit hunter' groups. According to some investigations, such professional hunters in Shenzhen, Guangdong and other southern regions even have formed professional and corporate bodies or teams.

From the unique characteristics mentioned above, there are some significant differences between 'professional counterfeit hunter' litigation and real consumer litigation. 'Professional counterfeit hunter' lawsuits bring the majority of punitive damages litigations in judicial proceedings, and are easy to identify. This kind of litigation may constitute a malicious action actually. However, according to the relevant provisions of the Chinese Civil Procedure Law on malicious litigation, malicious litigation is still limited to the malicious collusion of the parties attempting to (1) infringe the lawful rights and interest of the other parties by litigation or (2) to evade the performance of obligations determined in a legal instrument by litigation.[33] As a result, it is not possible for the court to classify 'professional counterfeit hunter' litigation as malicious actions, which is a major flaw in the procedural law.

V. Right of Withdrawal

The right of withdrawal is a special provision of the Consumer Rights Law, and its legal nature is a contractual termination right. It is a statutory termination right stipulated in the special law. The withdrawal rights in the Consumer Rights Law can be divided into two types: Article 24 concerns the right of withdrawal in cases of non-conformity, whereas Article 25 concerns the right of withdrawal in specific situations in which no reason is required in order to exercise the right (referred to below as 'no reason withdrawal rights').

A. Withdrawal for Non-conformity

Article 24 of the Consumer Rights Law stipulates the conditional withdrawal right: in cases where the goods or services provided by sellers fail to meet the quality requirements, consumers may return them in accordance with the provisions of the statute or as agreed upon by the parties, or require sellers to fulfil their obligations of replacement or repair. In the absence of such provisions of the statute or agreements between the parties, consumers may, within seven days of receiving the goods, return them; and consumers may, if the statutory conditions for rescission of a contract are met after the seven-day period, return them in a timely manner, or, if not met, require sellers to fulfil their obligations of replacement or repair. For the return, replacement or repair, sellers shall reimburse consumers for return costs and other necessary expenses.

B. 'No Reason Withdrawal Rights'

The introduction of a right for a consumer to withdraw from particular contracts without a particular reason is a new important element in the 2013 amendment. During the revision, the legislative experiences of the EU, Japan, South Korea and Taiwan in

[33] Chinese Civil Procedure Law, Art 112.

off-premises and distance contracts were summarised and analysed and such information played a role in the formation of provisions on withdrawal rights.[34] As far as the right of withdrawal with no reason is concerned, the core contents in the Consumer Rights Law include the scope of application, exclusion situations and the rules of expenses. These provisions are contained in Article 25 of the Consumer Rights Law and the withdrawal right is also described as 'return without a reason'.

First, the right of withdrawal without a reason applies only to situations where sellers sell goods via the Internet, television, over telephone or by mail order, or other sales methods. The applicable situations for the exercise of withdrawal right should be broadly understood, not only including the use of networks, television, telephone, mail and other long-distance sales, but also including doorstep sales, direct sales and other off-premises sales.[35] Secondly, the expression of 'other sales method' in Article 25 of the Consumer Rights Law means that the sales through the Internet, television or telephone are only examples. It is therefore possible to grant the consumer a withdrawal right as long as the sales are different from the traditional sales model and where the information asymmetry seriously affected the consumer's freedom in the process of contract formation. Therefore, this provision has left space for new transaction models in the future. Thirdly, Article 25(1) and (2) of the Consumer Rights Law contains the statutory situations in which the right of withdrawal does not apply. Article 25(1) lists four kinds of goods which shall not be subject to the withdrawal right, namely custom-made goods; fresh, live or perishable goods; audio-visual recordings, computer software and other digital goods downloaded online or unpacked by consumers; and newspapers or periodicals delivered. In addition to these goods, the return without a reason shall not apply to goods unsuitable for return by nature as confirmed by consumers at the time of purchase.

In exercising the withdrawal right, consumers must comply with provisions on the withdrawal period and costs. That is to say, consumers shall return the goods within seven days after receipt of the goods. Furthermore, the goods returned by consumers shall remain intact. Sellers shall, within seven days of receipt of the returned goods, refund the payments made by consumers for the goods. The consumer shall pay the costs for the return of goods, except as otherwise agreed upon by sellers and consumers.

C. Implementing Regulations

Although the 2013 amendment of the Consumer Rights Law introduced the withdrawal right, there are still different interpretations and understandings of the provisions. Therefore, the administrative regulations are worth noting as they introduce more detailed provisions on the withdrawal right. The State Administration for Industry and Commerce had in August and September 2016 promulgated Draft Measures for Implementation of the Consumer Rights Law and the Draft Measures for Implementation of the Withdrawal Right in case of Network Sales and the Measures for Implementation of the Withdrawal Right in case of Network Sales, which came into effect on 15 March 2017. In order to

[34] Shishi, 'Interpretations and Explanations', 99–105 (in Chinese); Law Commission of the NPC Standing Committee, 'Legislation Background', 247–51.

[35] Shishi, 'Interpretations and Explanations', 100.

clarify the scope of the no-reason withdrawal right, Article 12 of the Draft Measures for Implementation of the Consumer Rights Law stipulates that the applicable situations shall not be allowed to expand and the following goods may not be eligible for withdrawal right when confirmed by the consumers at the time of purchase: goods that once opened are liable to cause changes in the nature or affecting personal safety, life and health; goods whose value will decrease greatly once activated or tried; goods with a short use-by date, indicated on purchase. Additionally, in order to clarify the meaning of Article 25 of the Consumer Rights Law that the goods returned by consumers should be '*intact*', Article 13 of the Draft Measures for Implementation of the Consumer Rights Law further clarified that if the commodity can maintain its original quality, function, including the commodity itself, accessories, trademark logo, user's guidebook completely, the goods can be seen as 'intact'. If consumers need to open the packaging of goods, or do reasonable debugging in order to confirm the quality or function of goods, such behaviour does not have an effect on whether or not the goods are intact. Therefore, it is foreseeable that after these two draft implementation measures enter into force in 2017, the exercise of the withdrawal right will be clearer. Especially, the withdrawal right with no reason in cases of network transactions will have a more detailed legal basis. It is noteworthy that, since the introduction of a no-reason withdrawal right, the actual application in practice is still difficult to evaluate and more data needs to be assessed. There are presently only eight judgments concerning no-reason withdrawal rights. On the other hand, the withdrawal right in case of non-conformity has been more widely exercised with approximately 148 cases listed in the database.

VI. Sale of Goods: Remedies for Non-conformity

The remedies for non-conforming goods in consumer sales contracts can be divided into three types: (1) special provisions on certain goods ensuring the 'three guarantees' [三包], (2) the special regulations on remedies in the Consumer Rights Law and (3) the general provisions in Book Three of the Civil Code. However, it is necessary to pay special attention to repair, replacement and return. At present, they are understood as the methods of remedies in breach of contract, but from the historical development of the three guarantees liability system, repair replacement and return is the local and unique administrative control in an era of planned economy. Therefore, from the perspective of original and historical background, repair, replacement and return are completely different from western contract law.

A. From 'Three Guarantees' to 'Repair, Replacement and Return'

The 'three guarantees' can be regarded as a local legal institution in China.[36] From the point of view of historical interpretation, the remedies for breach of consumer contract

[36] R Zhong, 'General Review of Chinese "Three Guarantees" Institution' (2005) 2 *Tsinghua University Law Journal* 67 (in Chinese).

in the Consumer Rights Law can be traced back to the provisions on the so-called 'three guarantees', namely repair, replacement and return of goods. The earliest provisions of the 'three guarantees' appear in the Industrial Product Quality Liability Regulation and the Three Guarantees Provisions on Some Domestic Appliances in 1986, since abolished ('Old Three Guarantees'). The former is an administrative regulation, while the latter is its implementation. According to Articles 1 and 5 of the Three Guarantees Provisions on Some Domestic Appliances the 'Old Three Guarantees' can only apply to six domestic appliances (colour televisions, black and white televisions, refrigerators, washing machines, electric fans, tape recorders), and if the products sold by the producer and distributor fail to meet the requirements of the relevant laws and regulations, quality standards and the contractual agreements during the warranty period, the producer and distributor shall be responsible for the consumers in the form of 'three guarantees'. Therefore, China's earliest 'three guarantees' provisions arise from the planned economy era and was a kind of administrative measure.

The corresponding effective legal act for 'three guarantees' ('New Three Guarantees'), are the Provisions on the Liability for the Repair, Replacement and Return of Some Commodities promulgated by the State Economic and Trade Commission in 1995. Regarding the terminology, the 'New Three Guarantees' used repair, replacement and return instead of the original expression in 'Old Three Guarantees', which is in line with the Consumer Rights Law and the General Principles of Civil Law. The 'New Three Guarantees' are the demarcation point of the three liabilities system. Starting from the 'New Three Guarantees', the three guarantees began to incorporate with the remedy system of the traditional civil law. These provisions on '*three guarantees*' are mandatory rules and only applicable for the goods as the products listed in the Catalogue of Some Commodities for 'Three Guarantees' in the Provisions such as cars, televisions, refrigerators, microwave ovens, air conditioners, etc. In general, although the 'New Three Guarantees' adopted modern contract law terms, the current provision is still mandatory in relation to limited product types listed in the Catalogue of Some Commodities for 'Three Guarantees'. Therefore, it is more specific than the Consumer Rights Law.

B. Consumer Rights Law

Repair, replacement and return are also remedies in the Consumer Rights Law. The remedies for breach of contract are mainly stipulated in Articles 24, 41, 45, 48 and 55 of the Consumer Rights Law, including repairs, replacements, returns, damages (punitive damages), and most are combined with the stipulation of damage compensation in tort law. According to Article 24, if the goods or services provided by sellers fail to meet the quality requirements, consumers may return them in accordance with the provisions of the statute or as agreed upon by the parties, or require sellers to fulfil their obligations of replacement or repair. If there are no special statutory provisions or agreements between the parties, consumers may, within seven days of receiving the goods, return them; and consumers may, if the statutory conditions for rescission of a contract are met after the seven-day period, return them in a timely manner, or, if not met, require sellers to fulfil their obligations of replacement or repair.

C. Civil Code

According to Article 48 of the Consumer Rights Law, if the Consumer Rights Law does not expressly stipulate, then the liability for breach of contract should be governed by the general provision of Article 812 of the Civil Code: where the quality fails to satisfy the agreement, the breach of contract damages shall be borne in the manner as agreed upon by the parties. Where there is no agreement in the contract on the liability for breach of contract, where such agreement is unclear, or where it cannot be determined in accordance with the provisions of Article 510 of the Civil Code, the damaged party may, in light of the nature of the subject matter and the degree of loss, reasonably choose to request the other party to bear the liabilities for the breach of contract such as repairing, substituting, reworking, returning the goods, or reducing the price or remuneration. Therefore, repair, replacements, returns (termination) and price reduction constitute the system of remedies for breach of contract. Additionally, where there is no clear sequence between different remedies, the parties need to make a reasonable choice.

VII. Unfair Contract Terms

The control on contract terms is an important institution in Chinese contract law and can be divided into three dimensions: (1) general control on the contract terms under the Civil Code, applicable to all kinds of contracts and to all contractual clauses; (2) general control on the standardised contract terms under the Civil Code, applicable to all standardised contract terms in all kinds of contracts and (3) special control on standardised contract terms in consumer contracts under the Consumer Rights Law, only applicable to consumer contracts.

The control of the standard contract terms is complicated and controversial. It can be considered that the control of the standard contract terms is one of the most controversial elements of the Civil Code. First of all, the Civil Code does not clearly distinguish between the control of the conclusion of a contract and the control of the validity. Theoretically, Article 496 of the Civil Code is usually regarded as the control of the conclusion of a contract, while Article 497 is regarded as the control of the validity. According to Article 497, when standard terms are under the circumstances stipulated in Article 506 of the Civil Code or the party which supplies the standard terms exempts itself from its liabilities, increases the liabilities of the other party and deprives the material rights of the other party, the terms shall be invalid. According to Article 10 of the Contract Law Interpretation II, where the party providing the standard clauses violates the Article 39(1) of the Contract Law and falls under any of the circumstances as described in Article 40 of the Contract Law, the people's court shall determine the standard clauses as invalid. Therefore, the invalidity of a standard term should violate both Article 496(1) and Article 497 of the Civil Code.[37]

[37] H Xie, *New Development of Study Contract Law* (Beijing: China Social Science Press, 2014) 153 (in Chinese).

Although the provisions of the Civil Code concerning unfair standard contract terms appear to be complex and controversial in their theory, because Article 26(2) and (3) of the Consumer Rights Law clearly stipulate the control on unfair standard terms in consumer contracts, it is not so difficult to determine whether standard consumer contract terms are unfair. According to these provisions, sellers shall not, by standard terms and conditions, notices, declarations, on-site posters and other means, impose unfair or unreasonable rules on consumers to exclude or restrict consumer rights, reduce or waive the responsibilities of sellers or aggravate the responsibilities of consumers, and shall not force consumers into any transactions by standard terms and conditions and technical means. If the standard terms and conditions, notices, declarations and on-site posters, among others, contain any rules as mentioned in the preceding paragraph, such rules shall be void. In practice, the relevant disputes occurred often in the sales of house contract, insurance contracts, contracts of sale, contract of carriage and other types of contracts. According to the PKU Law Database, almost half of the cases involving Article 26 of the Consumer Rights Law concern real estate, showing that control of unfair contract terms is an important institution when the contract price is very high, for example, when buying a house.

VIII. Product Liability

The liability for defective products is classified as tort liability and is recognised as a specific type of tort liability under the Tort Law. From the perspective of a normative system, the laws concerned can be divided into three types. First, the Product Quality Law promulgated in 1993 and revised in 1999 is a special law on product quality and liability, in which the liabilities of producers and sellers are clearly defined and damage rules are stipulated. Secondly, in Book 7 of the Civil Code (Tort Liability), the product liability is also defined as an independent type of tort liability in Chapter 4, in which six articles stipulate the responsible legal subjects of the liability for defective products, the imputation principles and punitive damages. Thirdly, in case of consumer products, in addition to the general provisions of Book 7 of the Civil Code and the special provisions of the Product Quality Law, several provisions under the Consumer Rights Law on product liabilities are also applicable, namely the sellers' guarantee duty of product safety and warning duty of dangers products,[38] recall duty of defective products,[39] damages for defective products[40] and punitive damages for defective products in cases causing death and disability.[41] In addition, there are a number of special laws and administrative regulations on food safety, industrial standards of products and defective product recall systems, such as the Regulation on the Administration of Recall of Defective Auto Products, Administrative Measures for Food Recalls and the Food Safety Law.

[38] Consumer Rights Law, Art 18(1).
[39] ibid, Art 18(2).
[40] ibid, Art 14.
[41] ibid, Arts 41, 55, 59.

A. The Notion of Defective Products

The criteria on defective products under the Product Quality Law are slightly different from the other national laws. While other national laws often have one standard for defective products, namely *irrational dangers* criteria, Article 46 of the Product Quality Law sets two standards for defective products, namely irrational dangers and the national or industry standards.[42] Book 7 of the Civil Code does not provide a definition of product defects. In practice, the definition of defects in Article 46 of the Product Quality Law can function as a standard of defective products. The provisions of the Product Quality Law introduce a general standard of defects, but in practice, it still should be judged on a case-by-case basis. In general, the product is defective if the product is 'irrationally dangerous'. According to Article 6 of the Standardisation Law, national standards shall be formulated for the technical requirements that need to be unified nationwide. Where, in the absence of national standards, technical requirements for a certain trade need to be unified, industry standards may be formulated. Therefore, if the product meets the national standards or industry standards, then the product defects refer to 'does not meet the standards', which is to facilitate the identification of defective products. However, compliance with the national mandatory standards does not mean that the product is completely flawless. If a product complies with a national mandatory standard, but one performance indicator of the product is not regulated in the industry standards, it is possible that this does not meet the protection of personal and property safety requirements and may cause damage. In this case, the product can still be identified as a defective product.

B. Imputation Principle

The imputation principle of product liability was a controversial issue during the legislative process of the Tort Law. The main points of contention are strict liability, negligence liability, presumption of liability and binary liability, that is strict liability in principle, but the application of negligence liability in special circumstances.[43] Article 1202 of the Civil Code stipulates that producers should bear strict liability; Article 1203 provides that the sellers are liable for fault. Accordingly, the current general opinion of the imputation principle is that Article 1202 of the Civil Code is a provision on strict liability while Article 1203 of the Civil Code is on negligence liability. The Civil Code acknowledges binary liabilities on product liability.[44]

[42] Law Committee of the Standing Committee of the National People's Congress (ed), *Explanations, Legislative Reasons and Relative Provisions of the Tort Law* (Beijing: Peking University Press, 2010) 173 (in Chinese).

[43] ibid, 172.

[44] H Liang, 'The Tort Law of China', in *Studies on Civil Law in China and Japan*, Vol 17 (Beijing: Law Press China, 2011) 48 (in Chinese).

C. Burden of Proof and Exemptions from Liability

Product liability is a special kind of infringement. Considering the information asymmetry between users, consumers and producers, the cause of damage is not easy to prove (especially for high-tech products), as such the producers are required to prove that there is no causal relationship between damages and defects. Where no such proof can be furnished, the product is defective and there is a causal relationship between the defect and the damage. According to Article 4 of the Provisions of the Supreme People's Court on Evidence in Civil Cases, in cases of defective products, the producers are required to prove the exemption cases regulated in the law.

Although product liability is in principle a strict liability, it is not absolute liability. The producers can still in some cases reduce or exempt their liabilities. Although in the drafting process of the Tort Law there was a separate provision on exemption from liability of the producers in the draft, during the legislative process there were opinions that the provision was the same as the related provision in the Product Liability Law and there was no need to introduce the same regulation in the Tort Law. Therefore, the Tort Law does not provide for liability exemption of the producers. At present, the exemption from liability of producers is mainly regulated in Article 41(2) of the Product Quality Law, which lists the following three types of exemptions: the products have not been put into circulation; the defects are non-existent when the products are put into circulation; the defects cannot be found at the time of circulation due to scientific and technological reasons. Producers shall not be held responsible if they can prove one of these cases.

D. Punitive Damages as Tort Liabilities under the Food Safety Law

Given the scandals on milk products such as in *Sanlu*,[45] China introduced punitive damages in the Food Safety Law. In particular, Article 148 of the Food Safety Law provides that a consumer claiming damages may require the producer or the seller to pay 10 times the purchase price. The reason for 10 times compensation is that food price is usually not so high and the introduction of 10 times price as punitive damages will deter and prevent the malicious tort in the field of product liability.[46] However in fact, it is very doubtful whether 10 times compensation is enough to achieve the deterrent effect. Notably, Article 148(2) of the Food Safety Law provides that

> in addition to claiming damages, a consumer may require a producer of food failing to meet the food safety standards or a trader knowingly dealing in such food to pay an indemnity of ten times the price paid or three times the loss.

[45] See 'China dairy products found tainted with melamine', bbc.com, 9 July 2010, available under www.bbc.com/news/10565838.

[46] Y Zhu Yan and W Pan, 'A Study on Punitive Damages in China' (2014) 9 *Frontiers of Law in China* 359, 372 (in Chinese).

It is clear that the subjective requirements of the producer and the trader are different: whether the food producer knows the fact that the food is not in conformity with the standards or not, the consumer is always entitled to claim punitive damages. However, the consumer can claim punitive damages against the trader in cases of 'knowingly dealing'. This rule adopts a different subjective standard of responsibility for food producers and traders, although the appropriateness of this subjective rule is still worthy of further discussion.[47] In addition, Article 15 of the Food and Drug Disputes Interpretation also clarifies that the consumer is entitled to both compensatory and punitive damages. Accordingly, Article 148 of the Food Safety Law and Article 15 of the Food and Drug Disputes Interpretation form the current norms system for food safety punitive damages. Therefore, punitive damages is regarded as a special tort liability[48] in food and drug dispute cases, whose application no longer requires fraud as a prerequisite, and the only condition for punitive damages is that the food or medicine does not meet safety standards.

The standard of punitive damages stipulated in Article 148 of the Food Safety Law is 10 times the purchase price. In the process of legislative discussion, most opinions do not support this provision. The reason is that for most consumers the prices are normally quite low, so 10 times the purchase price would be little in the amount of compensation. The costs for food producers or traders are not high enough to deter violations, as a result the protection of consumers is not sufficient. However, this majority opinion was not adopted in legislation. This is why the current food safety punitive damages mechanism does not function as well as consumer contract fraud activities. It is notable that the number of litigation on punitive damages related to the Food Safety Law is clearly lower than the number of cases in the Consumer Rights Law.

On the other hand, it is a remarkable fact that Article 55(2) of the Consumer Rights Law following its 2013 amendment provides a new provision on punitive damages in the field of tort liability, which is completely free from the reliance on commodity prices or service charges as the calculation base. According to Article 55, if sellers knowingly provide consumers with defective commodities or services, causing death or serious damage to the health of consumers or other victims, the victims shall have the right to require business operators to compensate them for losses in accordance with Articles 49 and 51 of the Consumer Rights Law, and have the right to claim punitive compensation of not more than two times the amount of losses incurred. In the provision, the calculation of punitive damages provides for the first time the 'loss suffered' by the consumer as the basis for the determination of punitive damages. The scope of the relative loss is stipulated in Articles 49 and 51 of the Consumer Rights Law, namely medical expenses, care expenses, travel expenses and other reasonable expenses incurred for treatment and rehabilitation; lost wages; expenses on assisting devices for disability and pay disability compensation; funeral expenses and death compensation; mental damage compensation. As the current Food Safety Law and the Interpretation stipulate that the calculation of punitive damages should be 10 times the prices of food or drugs, if the food does not meet the food safety standard causes death or serious health damages, Article 55 of the

[47] S Gao, 'The Purpose and Institution of the Punitive Damage in Food Safety' (2013) 6 *The Jurists* 58 (in Chinese).

[48] B Shui, 'The Normative Construction of Punitive Damages' (2015) 4 *Law Science* 99 (in Chinese).

Consumer Rights Law and Article 148 of the Food Safety Law are therefore both applicable. As a result, the consumer is entitled to choose the Consumer Rights Law or the Food Safety Law as a legal base in litigation.

IX. Product Safety

There is no separate 'product safety' law in China's current laws. However, through the promulgation of the Standardisation Law, China has established a series of unified technical requirements for agriculture, industry and other fields, and established mandatory standards and recommended standards at the national level. The mandatory standards must be implemented. Many national compulsory standards contain specific requirements for product safety. For example, the National Safety Standard for Milk Quality sets specific standards for the quality and safety of dairy products, and the National Standardisation Management Committee coordinates the standard work.

At the legislative level, the relevant legislation related to product safety is mainly the Product Quality Law, the Agricultural Product Quality Safety Law (revised in 2018), the Food Safety Law (revised in 2018) and the Special Equipment Safety Law effective since 2014.

At the level of administrative regulations, the State Council has also issued separate quality and safety supervision and management regulations, including the Regulation on the Supervision and Administration of Quality and Safety of Dairy Products implemented in 2008, and the Regulations on Safety Supervision of Special Equipment (revised in 2009), the Regulations on the Safety Supervision and Administration of Agricultural Machinery (revised in 2019) and the Regulation on the Implementation of the Food Safety Law (revised in 2019). In addition, the State Council issued the Special Rules of the State Council on Strengthening the Supervision and Administration of the Safety of Food and Other Products in 2007. The administrative regulations have regulated the safety of food, edible agricultural products, medicines and other products related to human health and life safety. Items such as the raw materials, auxiliary materials and additives used in the products must comply with mandatory standards.

X. Adaptation to the Digital Age

Under the current legal system in China, there is no clear normative basis for digital content or digital services. China has neither introduced special rules on digital content within the current system of the Civil Code nor has it adopted separate legislation. Furthermore, legislative proposals for separate legislation have not even been found at any legislative level. To some extent, digital content or digital services seem to have become a 'blind spot' in the rules of private law in China. Under existing law, protection can only be based on copyright or trade secrets law, depending on the specific type of data. However, litigation disputes related to digital content can only be resolved by returning to the existing general rules, that is, applying the general norms of the Civil Code.

A. Digital Content under the Civil Code and the E-Commerce Law

In terms of providing digital content, the relevant rules in the field of civil law are mainly embodied in the General Principles of Civil Law and the E-Commerce Law. Article 127 of the General Principles of Civil Law, which came into effect in 2017, establishes general norms for data protection. 'The provisions on the protection of data or network virtual properties shall be abided by': this is a principle provision of the General Principles of Civil Law on data and network virtual property, which does not specify the legal attributes of data or network virtual property. This rule is just an inducible norm, which is too concise and lacks operability. This clause is incorporated into Article 127 of the current Civil Code.

The E-Commerce Law, which came into effect in 2019, clarifies the rules on time of delivery and place of performance of the contract. Article 51(2) of the E-Commerce Law stipulates that where the subject matter of contract is delivered via online transmission, the date of entry of the subject matter of contract into the designated specific system of the transaction counterparty, which can be searched and identified, shall be the date of delivery. Article 51 of the E-Commerce Law has been retained in the Article 512 of the current Civil Code.

Regarding the date of delivery of the subject of the contract, the E-Commerce Law distinguishes between the two types of delivery of goods and provision of services. If the subject matter of contract is provision of services, the date stated in the generated electronic receipt or hard copy receipt shall be the date of delivery; if the aforesaid receipt does not state the date or the date stated does not match the date of actual provision of services, the date of actual provision of services shall be the date of delivery. Where the subject matter of contract is delivered via online transmission, the date of entry of the subject matter of contract into the designated specific system of the transaction counterparty, which can be searched and identified, shall be the date of delivery. In terms of the date of delivery, whether the services provided are tangible or digital, the date of delivery shall be the date specified in the receipt or the date of actual provision of services. If there is a conflict between the two, the date of actual provision of services shall prevail. Therefore, the main application of the so-called 'delivering the subject matter of contract via online transmission' as referred to in Article 51(2) of the E-Commerce Law lies in provision of digital content. At this time, the date of delivery shall be the date of entry into the designated system which can be identified. This rule constitutes the rule for date of delivery established by the E-Commerce Law for the provision of the subject matter of digital content. Given that the delivery of the subject matter is closely related to the transfer of risks, unifying the date of delivery naturally determines the date of risk transfer. Correspondingly, Article 512 of the current Civil Code established the same rule for date of delivery. Article 512 stipulates that where the subject matter of contract is delivered via online transmission, the date of entry of the subject matter of contract into the designated specific system of the transaction counterparty, which can be searched and identified, shall be the date of delivery.

The E-Commerce Law also addresses the special problems of electronic payment services by establishing a series of special rules, which mainly involve notification obligation, security guarantee obligation, obligation of inquiry assistance[49] and compensation liability for damages of electronic payment providers.[50] In terms of the notification obligation, security guarantee obligation and obligation of inquiry assistance of electronic payment providers, electronic payment service providers shall notify users of the functions of electronic payment services, use method, points to note, the relevant risks and fee rates etc, and shall not impose unreasonable transaction conditions. Electronic payment service providers shall ensure the integrity, consistency, traceability and non-tamperability of electronic payment instructions.[51] Electronic payment service providers shall provide an account reconciliation service and transaction records from the past three years to users free of charge.[52] Regarding the compensation liability for damages of electronic payment providers, it mainly focuses on three situations where the electronic payment service fails to meet the requirements of: security management, the payment instruction is incorrect and the payment is not authorised. Where the electronic payment services provided by an electronic payment service provider do not comply with the administrative requirements of the State on payment security, causing users to suffer losses, the electronic payment service provider shall bear compensation liability.[53] Where there is an error in a payment instruction, the electronic payment service provider shall promptly investigate and identify the reason, and adopt the relevant measures to make correction. Where the error causes the user to suffer losses, the electronic payment service provider shall bear compensation liability, except where it can be proven that the error in the payment instruction is not caused by the electronic payment service provider.[54] Losses arising from an unauthorised payment shall be borne by the electronic payment service provider; where the electronic payment service provider is able to prove that the unauthorised payment is due to the user's fault, it shall not be held accountable. When an electronic payment service provider discovers an unauthorised payment or is notified by a user of an unauthorised payment, it shall forthwith adopt measures to stop the losses from escalating. Where the electronic payment service provider does not promptly adopt measures to stop the losses from escalating, it shall bear liability for the portion of losses which has escalated.[55]

B. Copyright Law and Law Against Unfair Competition

Article 14 of the Copyright Law defines a compilation work. If data with originality constitutes a compilation work, it is protected by the Copyright Law. Article 9(4) of the

[49] E-Commerce Law, Art 53.
[50] ibid, Arts 54, 55 and 57.
[51] ibid, Art 53(2).
[52] ibid, Art 53(3).
[53] ibid, Art 54.
[54] ibid, Art 55(2).
[55] ibid, Art 57(2) and (3).

Law Against Unfair Competition defines trade secrets, that is, commercial information such as technical information and business information, which is not known to the public and has commercial value and for which the rights holder has adopted the corresponding confidentiality measures. Data such as technical information and business information that meet the above conditions can be protected as trade secrets.

XI. Unfair Commercial Practices

The Anti-Monopoly Law and the Anti-Unfair Competition Law constitute the two main pieces of legislation against unfair practice and protecting the interests of consumers, and the functions of the two laws are quite different.

A. Consumer Protection under the Anti-Monopoly Law

Monopoly has the potential to cause great harm to the rights and interests of consumers. The main manifestation is that monopoly severely infringes on the status of consumers, the right to choose, the right to fair transactions, and monopoly hinders technological progress, which can damage consumer welfare. From the perspective of the history of the development of the Anti-Monopoly Law, the protection of consumer rights and interests promoted its birth and development. Therefore, the protection of consumer rights is an important driving force behind the Anti-Monopoly Law. At the same time, the protection of consumer rights is the basic purpose of the Anti-Monopoly Law: the protection of consumer rights is one of the legislative goals and forms a part thereof. One of the main values is an important aspect of the public interest in the Anti-Monopoly Law. In the case of monopoly, the rights to choose and to fair transactions will be severely restricted. Consumers merely defending their rights in accordance with the Consumer Rights Law cannot fundamentally change their weak position in terms of economic strength, transaction information acquisition and redress seeking. The Anti-Monopoly Law, through the regulation of monopoly, makes competition tend to be healthy and orderly, and guarantees that consumers obtain fairer results in transactions. For example, the prohibition of cartels is conducive to lowering the price of products and expanding the range of consumer choices. According to Article 1 of the Anti-Monopoly Law, its function is mainly to prevent and curb monopolistic conducts, protect fair market competition, enhance economic efficiency and maintain the consumer interests and the public interests. The Anti-Monopoly Law defines three types of behaviour as 'monopolistic conducts', that is, monopoly agreements reached between business operators, abuse of dominant market position by business operators and concentration of business operators that may have the effect of eliminating or restricting competition.

After more than 10 years of protecting consumers' interests since the implementation of the Anti-Monopoly Law, China's antitrust agencies have rich experience in the areas of prohibiting monopolistic agreements, prohibiting abuses of market dominance and prohibiting the elimination or restriction of competition by abuses of administrative power. As a result, three supporting regulations to the Anti-Monopoly Law were promulgated on 26 June 2019, coming into effect on 1 September 2019: the Interim Provisions for Prohibiting Monopolistic Agreements, the Interim Provisions for Prohibiting Abuse of Market Dominance and the Interim Provisions for Prohibiting Eliminating and Restricting Competition by Abuse of Administrative Power.

B. Consumer Protection under the Anti-Unfair Competition Law

The Anti-Unfair Competition Law aims to encourage and protect fair competition, stop unfair competition and protect the legitimate rights and interests of operators and consumers. The law defines unfair competition as behaviour that illegally disrupts the order of market competition and damages the legitimate rights and interests of other operators or consumers in production and business activities, thereby protecting the rights and interests of consumers. The Anti-Unfair Competition Law focuses on the competitive relationship between operators and protects consumers. Its fundamental goal is to maintain the orderly conduct of competition and the fairness of the results of competition. However, for the intervention and maintenance of the competition order, the relevant State agencies (the administrative department for industry and commerce) bear the main responsibilities; and the realisation and protection of consumer rights are more realised through the supervision of consumer associations and other mass organisations and judicial relief.

XII. Access to Justice

A. Civil Public Interest Lawsuits

i. Consumer Associations and Public Prosecutors

In general, the 2012 Amendment of the Civil Procedure Law (hereinafter: Civil Procedure Law 2012 Amendment) had already introduced rules on the public interest litigation in areas of environmental and consumer issues. The Civil Procedure Law states that the authority or relevant organisation may bring a public interest lawsuit to the court.[56] But in fact, until the Consumer Rights Law was amended in 2013, a clear rule on consumer related civil public interest litigation rule was introduced for the first time into the Consumer Rights Law itself. According to the Article 47 of the Consumer Rights Law, the China Consumers' Association and consumer associations formed in provinces, autonomous regions and municipalities directly under the Central Government may file lawsuits in the people's courts against the infringement upon the lawful rights and interests of vast consumers. The China Consumers' Association and consumer associations established above the provincial level will be responsible for the public interest litigation. According to the Opinions of Consumer Public Interest

[56] Civil Procedure Law, Art 55.

Litigation provided by the Civil Law Department of the National People's Congress Law Commission, the organisations that are entitled to bring the public interest litigation are limited to a certain range that is 'appropriate'.[57] The main reasons are as follows: firstly, it is conducive to prevent abuse of public interest litigation; secondly, it is in line with the actual situation of Chinese consumers' organisations; thirdly, it is conducive to the implementation of consumer public interest litigation; and fourthly, it can be reconciled with the existing judicial and administrative redress systems.[58] In addition, until the 2013 revision of the Consumer Rights Law, local courts had not yet heard any consumers' public interest litigation cases.[59] Since the Consumer Rights Law introduced a rule of public interest litigation, because its scope of application and the specific application rules were not clear, it therefore needed to be further clarified. Although the relevant rules still need to be further clarified, on 1 July 2015, China's first consumer related public interest litigation started in Shanghai.[60]

In terms of procedural rules of public interest litigation, the Interpretation of the Supreme People's Court on the Application of the Civil Procedure Law clarifies the procedural acceptance conditions of public interest litigation. According to its Article 284, where an organ or relevant organisation initiates a public interest action, if the action meets the following conditions, the people's court shall accept such action if: (1) there is a clear defendant; (2) there are specific claims; (3) there is preliminary evidence that public interests have been damaged; (4) the case is within the scope of civil actions accepted by the people's courts and under the jurisdiction of the people's court with which the action is initiated.

Though the Civil Procedure Law and the Consumer Rights Law establish the rules on civil public interest litigation for consumers, it is particularly noteworthy that, in the revision of the Civil Procedure Law of 2017, Article 55(2) was introduced to authorise the public prosecutors to bring public interest litigation in specific areas. In the case of consumer protection, the public interest litigation of the public prosecutors is limited to food safety cases. Therefore, according to the current Chinese law, the main body that can bring the consumer civil public interest litigation mainly includes two categories: firstly, the China Consumers' Association and the consumer associations, and they are the main institutions of public interest litigation. Secondly, the public procurators, and they can initiate the litigation only in food safety areas.

ii. Judicial Interpretation on Consumer Civil Public Interest Litigation

Most importantly, the Interpretation of the Supreme People's Court concerning Several Issues on the Application of Law in Hearing Consumer Civil Public Interest Litigation (hereinafter: 'Interpretation on Consumer Civil Public Interest Litigation') took effect

[57] Law Commission of the NPC Standing Committee, 'Legislation Background', 284.

[58] ibid, 284–85.

[59] ibid, 281.

[60] *Shanghai Consumer Council v Tianjin Samsung Communication Technology Co, Guangdong Oupo Mobile Communications Co, Ltd*, see the website of the China Consumers' Association under www.cca.cn/en/viewpoints/26545.html.

on 1 May 2016, aiming to provide clarity to and reflects the efforts by the Supreme People's Court to establish a judicial framework for consumer public interest lawsuits.

The Interpretation on Consumer Civil Public Interest Litigation clarified many problems on the consumer civil public interest litigation, such as plaintiff qualification, scope of application, the types of social public interest, the jurisdiction of the court, the restrictions on the plaintiff's disposition rights, the relationship between public interest litigations and private litigations, etc. Article 2 of the Interpretation on Consumer Civil Public Interest Litigation is the central provision. It provides five categories of specific situations in which the consumers' association can initiate consumer civil public interest litigation.

B. Small Claims Procedure

According to Article 274 of the Interpretation of the Supreme People's Court on the Application of the Civil Procedure Law, China clearly recognises the small claims procedure. However, its scope of application is limited to pecuniary payment cases. When a court tries a small claim lawsuit, its judgment shall be final. According to Article 274, small claims proceedings may concern the following (consumer) situations: sales contracts, loan or lease contracts; utilities contracts; bank cards; and property, telecommunications or any other service contracts.

XIII. Concluding Remarks: The Way Further Forward?

The relationship between the Consumer Rights Law and the Civil Code is complex. There are several overlapping norms between the Civil Code and the Consumer Rights Law. Additionally, in the application of the law, the questions such as whether the financial consumer disputes should directly apply the Consumer Rights Law or rather apply the Civil Code, need to be clearer in future judicial practice and require some improvements. As the new E-Commerce Law has been effective since 2019, consumer protection moves from traditional consumer protection to consumer protection in the digital age. A number of new issues, such as protection of digital product sales and financial consumer protection, have become a legislative focus. Due to the rapid development of e-commerce and digital consumption in China, the special legislation on consumer protection has to some degree lagged behind the development of the reality, which puts more demands on judicial judgment. Besides, considering that the Consumer Rights Law is not integrated into the Civil Code and remains as a separate law, dealing with the relationship between the Civil Code and the Consumer Rights Law will become a central task in the codification in the future.

3

Hong Kong

MATEJA DUROVIC, GERAINT HOWELLS AND ANDRÉ JANSSEN*

I. Overview

Hong Kong is a Special Administrative Region (SAR) of the People's Republic of China with a population of approximately 7.5 million people.[1] In 2020, its GDP per capita was HKD 359,343 (approximately USD 46,300).[2] Most of the consumer goods in Hong Kong are imported. Goods from Mainland China account for 45.2 per cent of the total value of imports.[3] Of the total imports, consumer goods account for 19.3 per cent and food stuffs 4.2 percent. Ninety per cent of Hong Kong's food is imported, with China again being the main source; many locals will shop for food at wet markets that were subject to enhanced regulation in the 1970s in a response to the introduction of supermarkets in order to ensure they remained competitive.[4] Shops serving the local community have struggled to survive in the face of rising rent prices and the development of malls aimed at the tourist market. Although not a significant producer of consumer goods, Hong Kong has an important retail sector that caters primarily to tourists from Mainland China. Hong Kong has low prices in comparison to the Mainland as it imposes no VAT and is a free port that does not levy custom tariffs on imports or exports.

Chinese consumers are also attracted by the comparably strong protection of intellectual property in Hong Kong. The Hong Kong Customs and Excise Department conducts raids to combat counterfeit goods and the infringement of intellectual

* The work described in this book chapter was fully supported by two grants from City University of Hong Kong (Project Nos 7004797 and 9380074). Financial support from City University of Hong Kong is acknowledged. This Paper represents a revised version of our paper M. Durovic, G. Howells and A. Janssen 'Reforming Consumer Protection in Hong Kong: How to Adequately Protect Consumers?' (2019) 49 *HKLJ* 571

[1] See Census and Statistics Department of the Hong Kong Special Administrative Region, www.censtatd.gov.hk/en.

[2] Census and Statistics Department of the Hong Kong Special Administrative Region, www.censtatd.gov.hk/en/web_table.html?id=31.

[3] Census and Statistics Department of the Hong Kong Special Administrative Region, 'Analysis of Hong Kong's Imports of Goods' (September 2019) 5.

[4] Consumer Council, 'Grocery Market Study: Market Power of Supermarket Chains Under Scrutiny' (December 2013).

property. Since 1998 many retailers have joined the 'No Fakes Pledge' scheme[5] and have posted 'No Fakes' stickers in their shops. These cover consumer sectors as diverse as electrical appliances, pharmaceuticals, jewellery and ceramics. It has also been suggested that at times Chinese manufacturers might produce two standards of products and save the higher standard for export to markets like Hong Kong, though the evidence of this is anecdotal and from some media reports, there appear to be efforts to ensure domestic and export products are made to uniform standards to prevent the need for Chinese shoppers to shop abroad to be guaranteed quality products. Hong Kong's legal system is another reason why consumers feel safe shopping there. Tourists purchasing from shops under schemes run by the Tourist Board have additional rights beyond their legal rights.[6]

Despite being part of the People's Republic of China, Hong Kong has, due to its history as a former British colony from 1841–1997, a substantially different legal system from the Mainland Chinese legal system and it is one of the Special Administrative Regions of China (adopting the principle of 'one country, two systems'). Its law is based on the common law legal tradition inherited from when it was under British rule. Accordingly, many of the familiar rules and principles of the common law are found in Hong Kong. There is less of a move to assert an independent jurisprudence than might be detected in, say, Singapore. Many of the signature English statutes such as the Sale of Goods Act 1893 of the United Kingdom (UK) have been more or less replicated in Hong Kong Ordinances. These have been updated from time to time, though not to the same extent as in the UK. Until Brexit, English law, including consumer law, was substantially influenced by the impact of European Union (EU) law.[7] Some of these reforms have found their way into Hong Kong law, normally following their adoption by the UK. Several other reforms have been proposed notably by the Hong Kong Law Reform Commission and the Consumer Council. However, law reform is notoriously slow in Hong Kong with the Legislative Council often in political stalemate, which can affect the progress of even relatively uncontroversial matters such as consumer protection reform. As it stands now, responsibility for consumer policy lies with the Commerce, Industry and Tourism Branch of the Commerce and Economic Development Bureau.

There has been a shift in the consumer policy as concerns have changed over the years. In the 1970s, there was a need to establish the Consumer Council owing to the high inflation on essential daily commodities caused by the global oil crisis. In the following decade, the focus was more on the quality of goods (especially food) and services as the rapid economic development transformed Hong Kong from an industrial society to a financial centre with more affluent consumers. In the 1990s, there was increasing public demand for the regulation of sale practices. In the 2000s, when the Hong Kong economy was affected by the severe acute respiratory syndrome (SARS) outbreak and the financial crisis, followed by the Lehman Brothers mini-bond default,

[5] Intellectual Property Department of the Government of the Hong Kong Special Administrative Region, '"No Fakes Pledge" Scheme', www.pid.gov.hk/eng/promotion_edu/no_fakes.htm.

[6] Travel Industry Council of Hong Kong, 'Refund Protection Scheme (Registered Shops) for Inbound Tour Group Shoppers (revised) Resolution No. 225' (Inbound Directive).

[7] G Howells, C Twigg-Flesner and T Wilhelmsson, *Rethinking EU Consumer Law* (London: Routledge, 2018).

policy revolved around these major issues as the Hong Kong economy recovered. There was a shift to emphasise consumer protection in the financial services sector. In 2020, the global pandemic of Covid-19 also had a serious impact on Hong Kong's economy and its real impact is still to be assessed.

The main goals of the currently valid Hong Kong consumer policy are to regulate consumer contracts in general, consumer safety, consumer credit, consumer health and unfair trade practices. As a result of this policy, some of the recent developments in the area of consumer law in Hong Kong include the Trade Descriptions (Unfair Trade Practices) (Amendment) Ordinance (Cap 362), Competition Ordinance (Cap 619), and the Residential Properties (First-hand Sales) Ordinance (Cap 621). Besides the mentioned ordinances, the legal framework for consumer protection in Hong Kong has been established by a number of additional separate and independent pieces of legislation relating to consumer contracts. Important rules on consumer contracts can be found under the Sale of Goods Ordinance (Cap 26), Control of Exemption Clauses Ordinance (Cap 71), Supply of Services (Implied Terms) Ordinance (Cap 457) and Unconscionable Contracts Ordinance (Cap 458). There is also legislation covering specific types of consumer credit, but these are not dealt with by us in detail: Money Lenders Ordinance (Cap 162) and Pawnbrokers Ordinance (Cap 166). Unfair commercial practices, heavily inspired by UK and EU law, are covered in the Trade Description Ordinance and consumer safety in the Consumer Goods Safety Ordinance (Cap 456). A recent focal point of Hong Kong's consumer policy (that is, in the 2010s) has been on sustainable consumption and personal privacy. Especially the latter aspect is attributed to the rapid technology development and proliferation of internet shopping.[8]

The contribution starts with issues relating to consumer contract law such as information duties and the right of withdrawal, consumer sales law and unfair contract terms. It then moves to topics such as product liability and product safety, to the question of the adaption of consumer law to the digital age and to the problem of unfair commercial practices in Hong Kong. The contribution then discusses the status quo of access to justice in Hong Kong before coming to some final conclusions and suggesting possible ways forward.

II. Information Duties and Right of Withdrawal

There is no particular mandatory set of general information for all consumer contracts that has to be given by a business to a consumer. The Money Lenders Ordinance does provide for some information rules in relation to money lending, but in general the information to be given in this context is mainly determined (only) by the Trade Descriptions Ordinance (Cap 362) and the rules on misrepresentation, which include the common law and the Misrepresentation Ordinance (Cap 284). Most of these rules concern controlling misleading information and the unfair trade practices that consumers encounter are forbidden by the Trade Descriptions Ordinance.[9] However, since the

[8] Consumer Council, 'Landmark Events of the Council in 40 Years'.

[9] Consumer Council, 'Online Retail: A Study on Hong Kong Consumer Attitudes, Business Practices and Legal Protection' (November 2016) 62.

2012 amendment, the Trade Descriptions Ordinance contains obligations, according to section 13E, relating to omitting or concealing material information, providing material information in an unclear, unintelligible or untimely manner and failing to identify material information. 'Material information' includes a variety of factual information (for example the trader's identity). A failure to identify commercial intent also amounts to a misleading omission. This amendment was inspired by rules from the EU Unfair Commercial Practices Directive[10] that had been implemented in the UK. Consumers who suffer damage as a result of the deceptive or misleading practice may seek redress under relevant consumer protection legislation, such as the Misrepresentation Ordinance or Trade Descriptions Ordinance and common law for rescission and/or damages.[11]

To improve transparency, a requirement for a mandatory set of information to be given by the business to the consumer is being discussed in Hong Kong – in particular for the quickly growing online trade sector. According to the recommendations of the Consumer Council both online and offline retailers should be required to provide information to ensure full disclosure of essential information.[12] This information should include the total price of the goods or services (inclusive of delivery charges, taxes and any other costs); the full identity and contact details of the trader; the duration of the contract; details about the right to withdraw (if applicable); and the complaints handling policy. The legislator has not yet taken any action to implement this proposal.

Unlike in the EU or Mainland China, a statutory right of withdrawal to provide consumers with cooling-off periods for different kinds of business to consumer contracts does not exist in Hong Kong. However, there are some voluntary schemes (for instance in relation to insurance, telecommunications, some financial products and where there is direct selling) and some traders (online and offline) have developed their own 'goodwill' returns policies offering exchange, replacement, credit notes or refund. Nonetheless, return policies still vary greatly between stores and trades. Most of the time only defective goods can be returned.

The 2010–11 government consultation on the reform of the unfair trading practices law had proposed introducing cooling-off periods for goods and services contracts of more than six months' duration and for contracts concluded during unsolicited visits to the consumer's home.[13] This was not introduced due to business lobbying. In recent years, the Consumer Council issued a major report, 'A Report to Advocate Mandatory Cooling-Off Period in Hong Kong',[14] that recommends a seven-day cooling off period for off-premises contracts, distance contracts (other than online contracts) and for fitness centres, beauty treatments and timeshares. The exclusion of online transactions under the latest proposal is surprising given that in the recent past the Consumer Council had supported such a right for online trade to enhance consumer confidence.[15] This change

[10] Directive 2005/29/EC of the European Parliament and of the Council of 11 May 2005 concerning unfair business-to-consumer commercial practices in the internal market, OJ 2005 No L149, p 22.

[11] Consumer Council, 'Online Retail: A Study on Hong Kong Consumer Attitudes, Business Practices and Legal Protection' (November 2016), 62.

[12] ibid, xii.

[13] Consumer Council, 'Report on Public Consultation Paper on Legislation to Enhance Protection for Consumers Against Unfair Trade Practice' (2011).

[14] Consumer Council, 'A Report to Advocate Mandatory Cooling-off Period in Hong Kong' (April 2018).

[15] ibid, viii.

of heart seems to be based on consumer satisfaction with online shopping, the competitive market and small margins that may be threatened by the granting of a cooling-off period and problems of defining online shopping and legal difficulties arising from the cross-border nature of the transaction. These reasons do not seem very compelling as European online businesses manage with these rules, which are also often part of voluntary codes. The lack of knowledge of quality of online goods would seem to be a reason why consumers should be granted protection. If there is a feeling that consumers should be allowed to take a risk on low value goods, then perhaps an exemption could be made for such low value goods. However, general consumer law would continue to apply even to low value goods. The Hong Kong government has recently signalled plans to introduce the right of withdrawal for fitness and beauty services where pre-paid plans are entered into for more than HKD 3,000 (approximately USD 385) following scandals in these two very popular industry sectors.

III. Consumer Sales Law

A comprehensive consumer sales law as a part of a separate consumer law act (as for example in Italy) or as a part of the general sales law (as for example in Germany) is missing in Hong Kong. Hence, a 'real' consumer sales law as known in some countries does not exist. The Hong Kong sales law follows the traditional common law approach and is regulated by the Sale of Goods Ordinance (Cap 26), which is modelled after the old UK Sale of Goods Act 1893.[16] The Ordinance itself has only a few consumer law elements and seems therefore to be outdated in comparison to other (European) legal systems.[17] In this respect it now diverges from the UK which has fashioned a separate consumer sales regime in the Consumer Rights Act 2015. Section 2A(1) of the Sale of Goods Ordinance defines 'dealing as consumer' in line with a mainstream definition as where:

(a) the party neither makes the contract in the course of a business nor hold itself out as doing so;
(b) the other party does make the contract in the course of a business; and
(c) the goods passing under or in pursuance of the contract are of a type ordinarily supplied for private use or consumption.[18]

A. Goods

The Sale of Goods Ordinance only codifies the law relating to the sale of *goods*. The Law Reform Commission's proposal to enact a statute governing other supply contracts

[16] See in general for the Hong Kong Consumer Sales Law L Chen, 'Consumer Sales Law in Hong Kong' in L Chen, C Twigg-Flesner, G Howells and HW Micklitz (eds), *Comparative Consumer Sales* (London: Routledge, 2018) 69.

[17] M Durovic, 'Consumer Sales in the European Union', in L Chen, C Twigg-Flesner, G Howells and Micklitz(eds.), *Comparative Consumer Sales*, (London: Routledge, 2018), 39.

[18] This introduction of the notion of consumer in the Sale of Goods Ordinance was done as the Ordinance is sometimes deviating from the general sales law in case of a business-to-consumer sales (see eg s 37(3) for the acceptance of goods).

has not been acted upon.[19] Other supply contracts are left to the common law, which may imply similar terms, but may have different remedies as they rely on common law principles rather than the statutory scheme. Following the recommendation of the Law Reform Commission,[20] the Supply of Services (Implied Terms) Ordinance (Cap 457) was adopted implying terms into service contracts.

'Goods' under section 2(1) of the Sale of Goods Ordinance are defined to include all chattels personal other than things in action and money. From this definition, it seems that digital content supplied in tangible form (for example as a CD or DVD) is subject to the rights and remedies in the sale of goods legislation, but digital content supplied in intangible form (through downloads, streaming or other means) is not subject to similar statutory regulation. As yet, there is no other specific statutory regime for digital content in Hong Kong. The Consumer Council recommends taking action and regulating this area of law,[21] but no action has been taken yet by the Hong Kong legislator.

B. Implied Terms

The Sale of Goods Ordinance is embedded in the traditional common law with its distinction between express and implied terms, and warranties and conditions. It has the following implied terms (but not limited to business-to-consumer transactions):

- implied condition that the seller has the right to sell;[22]
- implied warranty that the buyer shall have and enjoy quiet possession of the goods and that the goods shall be free from any charge or encumbrance;[23]
- implied condition that the goods shall correspond with the description (in the case of sale by description) and sample (in the case of sale by description and sample);[24]
- implied condition that the goods must be of merchantable quality where the seller sells goods in the course of a business.[25] Merchantable quality is defined as being when the goods are
  - (a) as fit for the purpose or purposes for which goods of that kind are commonly bought;

[19] The Law Reform Commission of Hong Kong, 'Contracts for the Supply of Goods' (2002).
[20] ibid.
[21] Consumer Council, 'Online Retail: A Study on Hong Kong Consumer Attitudes, Business Practices and Legal Protection' (November 2016), 84 et seq: 'The Council recommends that proper consideration be given to exploring the legislative options of specifying the legal rights and remedies for purchasing digital content. Such options may for example include (i) amending the definitions of goods to include digital products or extending the application of the Sale of Goods Ordinance to digital products regardless of their status as goods or otherwise. It also requires suitable amendments to ensure the practical application of the rights and remedies of the goods framework to digital content, for instance, transfer of property and delivery provisions cannot be easily applied to intangibles; (ii) enacting a new subject specific 'digital content' legislation; and (iii) a more long-term and holistic approach, following UK experience where a wider reform is undertaken of consumer protection law, with an aim to consolidate consumer protection provisions covering contracts for goods, services and digital content etc. in one single statute'.
[22] Sale of Goods Ordinance, s 14(1)(a).
[23] ibid, s 14(1)(b).
[24] ibid, s 15(1).
[25] ibid, s 16(2).

(b) of such standard of appearance and finish;
(c) as free from defects (including minor defects);
(d) as safe; and
(e) as durable,

as it is reasonable to expect having regard to any description applied to them, the price (if relevant) and all the other relevant circumstances;[26]

- implied condition that, where the seller sells goods in the course of a business and the buyer, expressly or by implication, makes known to the seller any particular purpose for which the goods are being bought, the goods supplied under the contract are reasonably fit for that purpose.[27]
- implied condition in sales by sample that:

(a) the bulk shall correspond with the sample in quality;
(b) the goods shall be free from any defect rendering them unmerchantable which would not be apparent on reasonable examination of the sample; and
(c) the buyer shall have a reasonable opportunity of comparing the bulk with the sample.[28]

Other additional implied terms which can be found in other jurisdictions in a business-to-consumer context, such as the liability of the final seller for non-conformity based on public statements (his own or those of the producer) or for incorrect installation or installation instructions are unknown in the Sale of Goods Ordinance.[29]

The Hong Kong Law Reform Commission in its 'Sale and Supply of Goods Report' had rejected replacing merchantable quality with a label such as 'adequate' or 'acceptable', noting merchantable has a '(spurious) connotation of precision',[30] but its recommendation to include a list of relevant factors was acted upon. In the 'Contracts for the Supply of Goods Report' it favoured the adoption of satisfactory quality as had been enacted in the UK.[31] This recommendation has not yet been enacted.

C. Remedies

The Hong Kong legislation makes it clear whether the implied terms are conditions or warranties. Where there is a breach of an implied condition, which is the case for the terms relating to quality, under the Hong Kong legal system the buyer can repudiate the contract, reject the goods and sue for any damages. The right to repudiate the contract is lost if the goods are accepted. Acceptance occurs when the buyer intimates to the

[26] ibid, s 1(5).
[27] ibid, s 16(3).
[28] ibid, s 17(2).
[29] See Articles 2(2)(d) and 2(5) of Directive 1999/44/EC of the European Parliament and of the Council of 25 May 1999 on certain aspects of the sale of consumer goods and associated guarantees, OJ 1999 No L171, p 12 ('Consumer Sales Directive').
[30] The Law Reform Commission of Hong Kong, 'Report on Sale of Goods and Supply of Services' (February 1990) 8.
[31] The Law Reform Commission of Hong Kong, 'Report on Contracts for the Supply of Goods' (February 2002).

seller that he has accepted them;[32] or when the goods have been delivered to him and he does any act in relation to them which is inconsistent with the ownership of the seller;[33] or by retaining the goods after the lapse of a reasonable time he retains the goods without intimating to the seller that he has rejected them.[34] However, following reforms based on recommendations of the Law Reform Commission, acceptance will not occur where goods had not been previously examined by the buyer until he has had a reasonable opportunity of examining them or (though this is more likely to be relevant in a commercial context) merely because of sub-sale or other disposition. The move in the UK to create a distinct remedies regime for consumers that differentiates between a short-term and long-term right to reject and includes the remedies or repair and replacement has not yet been followed in Hong Kong.[35] Where the term breached by the seller is an implied warranty, the buyer is only entitled to a claim for damages.[36] The Sale of Goods Ordinance also foresees the possibility to reduce the price in case of a breach of warranty.[37] The limitation period for a sale of goods contract is, according to section 4(1)(a) Limitation Ordinance (Cap 347), six years beginning from the date on which the cause of action accrued.[38] A presumption in favour of the consumer that any lack of conformity which becomes apparent within a particular period of time after delivery shall be presumed to have existed at the time of delivery (see for example the six months presumption of Article 4(3) of the Consumer Sales Directive) is unknown in Hong Kong. Hence, the burden of proof regarding the non-conformity is fully on the buyer under the Sale of Goods Ordinance.

IV. Unfair Contract Terms

A. Exemption Clauses

Exemption clauses were controlled indirectly by rules of common law such as those requiring the term to be incorporated[39] or construed *contra proferentum*.[40] The need for the sometimes strained judicial application of the common law rules has been reduced due to statutory intervention. The Control of Exemption Clauses Ordinance (Cap 71) followed the recommendations of the Hong Kong Law Reform Commission's 'Report of Control of Exemption Clauses'[41] and is modelled on, from a modern consumer law perspective, a rather old-fashioned UK Unfair Contract Terms Act 1977 and aims to

[32] Sale of Goods Ordinance, s 37(1)(a).
[33] ibid, s 37(1)(b).
[34] ibid, s 37(4).
[35] Consumer Rights Act 2015 (UK), ss 19 et seq.
[36] Sale of Goods Ordinance, s 13(2).
[37] ibid, s 55(1)(a).
[38] That is considerably longer than the two-year limitation period of Art 5(1) of the Consumer Sales Directive.
[39] Incorporated by signature: *L'estrange v Graucob Ltd* [1934] 2 KB 394; incorporation by notice: *Olley v Marlborough Court Ltd* [1949] 1 KB 532, *Thornton v Shoe Lane Co Ltd* [1970] EWCA Civ 2, *Parker v South Eastern Railway Co Ltd* [1877] 2 CPD 416; incorporation by course of dealing: *J Spurling v Bradshaw* [1956] 1 WLR 461, *Kendall (Henry) & Sons v William Lillico &Sons Ltd* [1969] 2 AC 31.
[40] *Andrews Bros ltd v Singer Cars* [1934] 1 KB 17, *Ailsa Craig Fishing v Malvern Fishing* [1983] 1 WLR 964.
[41] The Law Reform Commission of Hong Kong, 'Report on the Control and Exemption Clauses' (1986).

limit the extent to which civil liability for breach of contract, or for negligence or other breach of duty, can be avoided by means of contract terms and otherwise; and to restrict the enforceability of arbitration agreements.

Exemption clauses that exclude liability for death and personal injury are not effective.[42] For those that exclude liability for financial loss or damage to property, their validity is subject to a 'reasonableness' test.[43]

In consumer contracts, terms cannot allow the seller to perform contractual performance substantially different from that which was reasonably expected of him; or to render no performance at all unless the contract term satisfies the requirement of reasonableness.[44] Nor can the consumer's rights to implied terms relating to title and to conformity under the Sale of Goods Ordinance be excluded.[45] Consumer guarantees cannot exclude liability for defects caused by negligence in the manufacture or distribution of goods.[46] Agreements to arbitrate prior to a dispute arising do not bind consumers.[47]

B. Reasonableness

In assessing the reasonableness of a contract term, a court or arbitral tribunal should assess whether the term was a fair and reasonable one to be included having regard to the circumstances which were, or ought reasonably to have been, known to or in the contemplation of the parties when the contract was made. Schedule 2 of the Control of Exemption Clauses Ordinance sets out some guidelines on what may be considered 'reasonable', including the strength of the relative bargaining positions of the parties; any inducement to agree to the term; the opportunity of entering into a similar contract with other persons without having to accept a similar term; whether the customer knew or ought reasonably to have known of the existence and extent of the term; the practicability of complying with any condition whose non-compliance triggers the exclusion or restriction; and whether the goods were manufactured, processed or adapted to the special order of the customer.

C. Services

The Supply of Services (Implied Terms) Ordinance (Cap 457) consolidates and amends the law with respect to the terms to be implied in contracts for the supply of services. It is implied in service contracts that:

- services should be carried out with reasonable care and skill (which generally means the services must meet the standard that a reasonable person would regard as satisfactory);[48]

[42] Control of Exemption Clauses Ordinance, s 7(1).
[43] ibid, s 7(2), (3).
[44] ibid, s 8.
[45] ibid, s 11(2).
[46] ibid, s 10.
[47] ibid, s 15.
[48] Supply of Services (Implied Terms) Ordinance, s 5.

- services should be performed within a reasonable time if the time of performance has not been fixed by the contract;[49] and
- a reasonable charge should be paid if the charge has not been fixed by the contract.[50]

If service suppliers fail to meet any of the above conditions, they would be in breach of the service contract and liable for compensation to consumers. These implied terms cannot be excluded or restricted by reference to any contract term in the contract.[51]

D. Unconscionable Contracts

The Unconscionable Contracts Ordinance (Cap 458) empowers courts to give relief in certain contracts found to be unconscionable. However, 'unconscionable' is not defined and, therefore, the court refers to a non-exhaustive list in section 6(1) of the Ordinance and common law definitions[52] that tend to focus on the totality of the circumstances and conduct that give rise to unfairness in the bargaining process. There have only been six reported cases invoking the Unconscionable Contracts Ordinance. In *Shum Kit Ching v Caesar Beauty Centre Ltd*[53] the test was said to be a harder one to satisfy than the unjust test in the law of New South Wales. In fact the law was modelled after Australia's Federal Trade Practices Act 1974,[54] whose unconscionable conduct provisions had been interpreted to require objective rather than subjective unconscionability.[55] The Consumer Council in a 2012 Report noted 'the court would tend to focus on the totality of the circumstances and conduct that give rise to unfairness in the bargaining process rather than the meaning and effect of the term alone'.[56] Under the UK's Unfair Terms in Consumer Contracts Regulations 1999, as confirmed in the subsequent Consumer Rights Act 2015 that replaced the Regulations, the relationship between the requirement that for any term to be unfair it must cause a significant imbalance and also be contrary to good faith is unclear. It seems that some terms will be so unfair that their mere use is contrary to good faith. However, in Hong Kong substantive unfairness alone may not be enough. It was held in *Shum Kit Ching v Caesar Beauty Centre Ltd* that to be considered unconscionable, the other party has to have knowledge of the weaknesses of the consumer. However, the case of *Chang Pui Yin and Others v Bank of Singapore Ltd*[57]

[49] ibid, s 6.
[50] ibid, s 7.
[51] ibid, s 8(1).
[52] *Chitty on Contracts* 28th ed (London: Sweet & Maxwell, 1999) Vol 1, 452, mn 7-078 applied by *Shum Kit Ching v Caesar Beauty Centre Ltd.* [2003] 3 HKLRD 422.
[53] ibid.
[54] Federal Trade Practices Act 1974 (Australia).
[55] Under the Australian Consumer Law that replaced it see *Australian Competition and Consumer Commission v Lux Distributors Pty Ltd* [2013] FCAFC 90 Allsop JA linked the normative standard of unconscionability to community norms and values: 'the task of the Court is the evaluation of the facts by reference to a normative standard of conscience. That normative standard is permeated with accepted and acceptable community values'. See J Paterson, A Robertson and A Duke, *Principles of Contract Law* 5th edn (Sydney: Thomson Reuters, 2015).
[56] Consumer Council, 'Report on Unfair Terms in Standard Form Consumer Contract' (2012) 5.
[57] [2016] HKEC 1721.

may mark a change in direction. It concerned investment decisions which had been made based on a higher risk exposure than the bank knew its clients wanted to accept. Clauses excluding the bank's liability for advice were held to breach both the Unconscionable Contracts Ordinance and the Control of Exemption Clauses Ordinance. Taking note of recent Australian case law imposing normative standards of conscience that were not limited by the general equitable concept of unconscionability, the Court of Appeal judges were clearly concerned that the banks should not get away with breaching Codes of Conduct. However, the Court did not need to hold all breaches of codes as coterminous with unconscionability as in the circumstances of the case the bank's misleading the clients as to the nature of the investments and services offered was considered to be 'so aberrant from the commercial norms' that their reliance on a clause excluding liability could be characterised as unconscionable. The Court also held that these consumer rules were available to all consumers regardless of how wealthy they were.

The burden of proof is on the party seeking to rely on the unfairness. The court may (1) refuse to enforce the contract; (2) enforce the remainder of the contract without the unconscionable part; (3) limit the application of, or revise or alter, any unconscionable part so as to avoid any unconscionable result.[58] Since the enactment of the Unconscionable Contracts Ordinance, there have only been five successful challenges to unfair terms thereunder.[59]

Note that there is no specific legislation controlling consumer unfair terms beyond exclusion clauses. An unfair term on its own is not sufficient to make out a case for unconscionable contract.[60] In practice the Unconscionable Contracts Ordinance is ineffective in protecting consumers from unfair terms in standard form contracts, due to ineffectual legislation, lack of a specific enforcement body and restrictions on accessing legal aid.[61] The Consumer Council has recommended the introduction of a legislation modelled on the UK's Unfair Terms in Consumer Contracts Regulations 1999, with appropriate modifications in view of the differences in culture and marketplace.[62] It is unclear what is intended by the mention of local culture and marketplace.

V. Product Liability

Product liability law in Hong Kong remains based on traditional common law principles. There are no reported cases in recent times that would be identified as traditional

[58] Unconscionable Contracts Ordinance, s 5(1). See eg *Cheung Kam Sing & Another v International Resort Developments Ltd* [2003] 2 HKLRD 113 where the court refused to enforce an unconscionable contract.

[59] ibid; *Lau Ying Wai v Emperor Regency International Ltd*, DCCJ 1600/2013; *Hang Seng Credit Card Ltd v Tsang Nga Lee* [2000] 3 HKLRD 33; *James Manuel Ho and Another v Grand Pacific Vacation (Hong Kong) Ltd* [2005] HKCU 1016. See also L Mason, 'Hong Kong Consumers Deserve Fairer Deal in Goods and Services Contracts', scmp.com, 14 July 2014.

[60] See eg *Hang Seng Credit Card Ltd v Tsang Nga Lee* [2000] 3 HKC 269; *Shum Kit Ching v Caesar Beauty Centre Ltd* [2003] 3 HKC 235.

[61] L Mason, 'Inadequacy and Ineffectuality: Hong Kong's Consumer Protection Regime Against Unfair Terms in Standard Form Contracts' (2014) 83 *HKLJ* 93.

[62] Consumer Council, 'Fairness in the Marketplace for Consumers and Business' (February 2008); Consumer Council, 'Report on Unfair Terms in Standard Form Consumer Contract' (April 2012).

consumer product liability claims. If the defective goods were bought under a contract and injured the buyer, then the provisions of the Sale of Goods Ordinance will normally provide a remedy as consequential damages for personal injury and damage to other property will be covered under general contractual damages. However, contractual remedies do not allow redress against the non-retail manufacturer or third parties such as by-standers or even probably those given the goods as a gift.

Normally a claim will be brought against the manufacturer in negligence. Other agents handling the goods will also be potentially liable if their conduct in relation to the goods causes foreseeable harm. Wholesalers might incorrectly store goods or assemblers put goods together in a dangerous manner. However, in all these instances there is a need to show a duty of care (normally easy to establish in relation to personal injury, death and property damage) and a breach of that duty of care. In theory it might be possible for a manufacturer to be found to have satisfied the duty of care by providing a good system of work and adequate supervision.[63] But for manufacturing defects, where products deviate from the model, the English courts came to recognise that either the system was not adequate or that someone for whom the manufacturer was vicariously liable must have erred. There was no need to show exactly what went wrong.[64] Recovery for manufacturing defects would normally be possible even under a negligence regime. However, when it came to challenging the design or the appropriateness of warnings or instructions the negligence standard is more favourable to defendants. So long as they followed a reasonable practice, they would be likely to escape liability. Their actions could only be judged in the light of the knowledge that it was reasonable to expect them to have at the time of their conduct. Thus, in the Thalidomide Scandal, the effect of the drug on the foetus *in utero* was probably not attributable to negligence on the part of the manufacturer as no one at the time of manufacture had contemplated drugs ingested by the mother would affect the growing baby.[65] This case was the impetus for a reform debate in the UK[66] and continental Europe[67] that eventually led to the Product Liability Directive in Europe.[68]

In 1998 the Hong Kong Law Reform Commission issued a 'Report on Civil Liability for Unsafe Products' that recommended adopting strict liability along the lines of the Product Liability Directive. Its proposals were quite progressive. In relation to the three options available under the original directive it would have included unprocessed agricultural food;[69] have placed no cap on personal injury damages;[70]

[63] See *Daniels v R White & Sons Ltd and Tabard* [1938] 4 All ER 258.

[64] See *Grant v Australian Knitting Mills Ltd* [1936] AC 85; *Hill v James Crowe (Cases) Ltd* [1978] 1 All ER 812.

[65] J Stapleton, *Product Liability* (Cambridge: Cambridge University Press, 1994) 42–44; K Horsey and E Rackley, *Tort Law* (Oxford: Oxford University Press, 2017) 353.

[66] The Law Commission and The Scottish Law Commission, 'Report on Liability for Defective Products' (Law Com No 82, Scot Law Com No 45, Cmnd 6831) (1977) and 'Royal Commission on Civil liability and Compensation for Personal Injury', Cmnd 7054 (1978).

[67] In 1976, the Council of Europe issued the Strasbourg Convention on Products Liability in regard to Personal Injury and Death.

[68] Council Directive 85/374/EEC on the approximation of the laws, regulations and administrative provisions of the Member States concerning liability for defective products: OJ 1985 No L210, p 29. The first proposal had been issued in 1976.

[69] The Hong Kong Law Reform Commission, 'Report on Civil Liability for Unsafe Products', para 7.45. This option was subsequently removed from the European Directive.

[70] ibid, para 7.75.

and whilst it would have included the development risks defence it would not have allowed it to apply where there was a failure to comply with a statutory recall order.[71] The recovery of damages would also have been more generous than under the Product Liability Directive as it was proposed not to have a minimum threshold on recovery of property damages[72] and damage to the product itself would be included as it was argued sometime the only expensive damage was to the product itself.[73] The Report was also ahead of its time in addressing the issue of software as a product and would have included within the definition standardised software integrated into a computer without which the computer cannot function.[74] In addition it accepted a 10 year cut-off limitation period, but with some hesitation and felt it should be kept under review.[75] One restriction on liability would be that Hong Kong law should not apply to goods that in the entrepôt trade had simply passed through Hong Kong for re-export.[76] The Law Commission Report was a well thought out response to international trends in product liability and the failure to implement its recommendations leaves Hong Kong lagging behind many states in the level of protection afforded to consumers. Given the small manufacturing base in Hong Kong and large retail market it would have a lot to gain in terms of consumer confidence and little to lose by adopting such a more protective regime.

VI. Product Safety

Hong Kong has a number of product safety regulations that seek to prevent unsafe products reaching the market and to remove those that make it into the marketplace. For example, it has a Toys and Children's Products Safety Ordinance (Cap 424). Most significantly it has since 1994 had the Consumer Goods Safety Ordinance (Cap 456). This seems to be modelled on the early UK Consumer Protection Act 1987 before English law was revised based on the European General Product Safety Directive.[77] The enforcer is the Commissioner for Customs and Excise. However, several products have their own regulations and regulators. For example, electrical products are governed by the Electrical and Mechanical Services Department.

The Consumer Goods Safety Ordinance contains a general safety requirement breach of which is a criminal offence. There is no civil liability for a breach of the product safety regulations in Hong Kong. The factors to be taken into account in assessing safety broadly accord with the UK Consumer Protection Act 1987 and are less fine

[71] ibid, para 7.63.
[72] ibid, para 7.72.
[73] ibid, para 7.78.
[74] ibid, para 7.39.
[75] ibid, para 7.95.
[76] ibid, para 7.97.
[77] Directive 2001/95/EC of the European Parliament and of the Council of 3 December 2001 on general product safety, OJ 2002 No 11, p 4.

grained than subsequent EU inspired rules. Under section 4 of the Ordinance, such factors are:

(a) the manner in which, and the purpose for which, the consumer goods are presented, promoted or marketed;
(b) the use of any mark in relation to the consumer goods and instructions or warnings given for the keeping, use or consumption of the consumer goods;
(c) reasonable safety standards published by a standards institute or similar body for consumer goods of the description which applies to the consumer goods or for matters relating to consumer goods of that description; and
(d) the existence of any reasonable means (taking into account the cost, likelihood and extent of any improvement) to make the consumer goods safer.

The measures that can be taken if consumer goods are considered unsafe include notices to warn,[78] prohibition notices[79] and recall notices.[80] Notices to warn allow the enforcer to require a person to publish a notice specifying the steps needed to make a product safe, if he reasonably believes consumer goods are unsafe in certain circumstances. Prohibition notices can be served for six months prohibiting a person from supplying consumer goods that the Commissioner reasonably believes do not comply with approved safety standards or safety standards or specification established by regulation or, if there are no safety standards, are otherwise unsafe. This six-month period equates with the suspension notice in the UK Consumer Protection Act 1987. In Hong Kong the prohibition notice can only be extended if the Commission has taken proceedings against the person concerned in relation to the notice or the goods or sought to have the goods seized or destroyed. The recall notice requires the immediate withdrawal of consumer goods from the market and to the extent reasonably possible to deal with those already supplied. There is nothing called a forfeiture order in Hong Kong – as there was in UK Consumer Protection Act 1987 – but the equivalent is the provision for the destruction of the goods or their return subject to the condition they be rendered safe.[81] Hong Kong therefore has the basic framework to protect the consumers against unsafe goods, but it has failed to follow up on EU-inspired later changes, such as imposing obligations on traders to inform the authorities of problems with their goods.

VII. Adaption to the Digital Age

The Digital Age represents particular and numerous different challenges for consumer law.[82] Online retailing in Hong Kong is increasing, especially as a consequence of a global

[78] Consumer Goods Safety Ordinance, s 7.
[79] ibid, s 8.
[80] ibid, s 9.
[81] ibid, s 31.
[82] See the insightful book, A de Franceschi (ed), *European Contract Law and the Digital Single Market: The Implications of the Digital Revolution* (Cambridge: Intersentia, 2016).

Covid-19 pandemic. Hong Kong has adopted modern data protection legislation.[83] It also has an Electronic Transactions Ordinance (Cap 553). However, it does not have rules mandating consumer information in online sales or a mandatory cooling-off period for online consumers. Hong Kong has not adopted any specific rules related to digital consumer contracts, such as for digital downloads (for example, apps) or streaming which are not covered by the existing consumer legislation.[84] In that context, the recent development in English consumer law (in particular the Consumer Rights Act 2015) but also the EU Digital Content Directive,[85] EU Modernisation Directive[86] and the proposed EU Digital Services Act[87] might represent good inspirations for related progress of Hong Kong law. When it comes to digital means to be used for the resolution of consumer disputes, there is also little development of Online Dispute Resolution (ODR).[88] Here the EU law on Online Dispute Resolution might serve as a useful model to look at.[89] However, in order to respond to an anticipated increase in disputes related to the Covid-19 pandemic, Hong Kong has introduced a (Covid-19) Online Dispute Resolution Scheme in order to offer fast and effective means to resolve disputes and avoiding face-to-face contact between parties.[90] Although the scheme is limited to Covid-19-related disputes, its approaches may later impact on a future consumer ODR scheme.

VIII. Unfair Commercial Practices

The field of unfair commercial practices represents one of the broadest and most important areas of consumer law which aims at securing fairness in business-to-consumer relations. In Hong Kong, particular problems in this area of consumer law seem to exist in the fitness industry[91] and beauty industry.[92] The principal source of the rules

[83] Personal Data (Privacy) Ordinance (Cap 486); see S Wong and G Zhu, *Personal Data (Privacy) Law in Hong Kong: A Practical Guide on Compliance* (Hong Kong: City University of Hong Kong Press, 2016).

[84] L Chen, 'Consumer Sales Law in Hong Kong', in L. Chen, C. Twigg-Flesner, G. Howells and H.W. Micklitz (eds.), Comparative Consumer Sales, (London: Routledge, 2018) 74.

[85] Directive (EU) 2019/770 of the European Parliament and of the Council of 20 May 2019 on certain aspects concerning contracts for the supply of digital content and digital services, OJ 2019 No L136, p 1.

[86] Directive (EU) 2019/2161 of the European Parliament and of the Council of 27 November 2019 amending Council Directive 93/13/EEC and Directives 98/6/EC, 2005/29/EC and 2011/83/EU of the European Parliament and of the Council as regards the better enforcement and modernisation of Union consumer protection rules, OJ 2019 No L328, p 7.

[87] European Commission, 'Proposal for a Regulation of the European Parliament and of the Council on a Single Market for Digital Services (Digital Services Act) COM(2020) 825 final; European Commission, Proposal for a Regulation of the European Parliament and of the Council on contestable and fair markets in the digital sector (Digital Markets Act) COM(2020) 842 final.

[88] Consumer Council, 'Online Retail: A Study on Hong Kong Consumer Attitudes, Business Practices and Legal Protection' (November 2016), 72 et seq.

[89] See Regulation (EU) No 524/2013 of the European Parliament and of the Council of 21 May 2013 on online dispute resolution for consumer disputes and amending Regulation (EC) No 2006/2004 and Directive 2009/22/EC (Regulation on consumer ODR), OJ 2013 No L165, p 1.

[90] See the statement by the Secretary for Justice (T Chang), 'Online Dispute Resolution Effective' (13 April 2020), available under www.news.gov.hk.

[91] C Lau, 'Hong Kong Chief Executive Looks to Improve Consumer Protection In Wake of California Fitness Collapse', scmp.com, 14 July 2016.

[92] 'Too much chaos in the beauty industry', orientaldaily.on.cc (in Chinese).

on unfair commercial practices in Hong Kong is the Trade Descriptions Ordinance (Cap 362). The Ordinance prohibits false trade descriptions for goods[93] and services.[94]

A. Background

Until a few years ago, Hong Kong rules on unfair commercial practices were insufficiently developed to secure properly a high level of fairness in business-to-consumer relations.[95] They mirrored the English Trade Descriptions Act 1968,[96] but only applied to goods and were formulated in a very clumsy manner. The only sanctions were criminal in nature.[97] This is why eventually in 2012, the Trade Descriptions Ordinance was enacted in response to the use of dubious or exaggerated claims in advertisements and high-pressure tactics to induce consumers to enter into a transaction for goods and services. The coverage was extended from goods to services and the regulation of specified unfair trade practices, came into effect. Under the amended legislation, six types of unscrupulous trade practices will be prohibited: applying false trade descriptions of goods and services; misleading omissions; aggressive commercial practices; bait advertising; baiting and switching; and wrongly accepting payment.[98] The structure is a little awkward as the goods provisions still use the language of the UK's Trade Descriptions Act 1968 (which was repealed in the UK when the UK adopted the EU Unfair Commercial Practices Directive), but the other general clauses on omissions and aggressive practices mirror the new UK law based on the Directive. The rationale for retaining the trade description law for goods was apparently that it also applied to business-to-business transactions, but this does not seem sufficient reason to make the consumer provisions less coherent.

B. Commercial Practice

The notion of commercial practice has been taken from EU law.[99] Accordingly, the commercial practice is defined in a very broad manner to include any act, omission, course of conduct, representation or commercial communication (including advertising and marketing) by a trader which is directly connected with the promotion of a product to consumers or the sale or supply of a product to or from consumers, whether occurring before, during or after a commercial transaction (if any) in relation to a product. The benchmark for assessment of fairness of commercial practice is the same as in

[93] Trade Descriptions Ordinance, s 7.
[94] ibid, s 7A.
[95] SHC Lo, 'Consumer Remedies for Misleading or Deceptive Marketing Practices: Reform of the Law in Hong Kong' (2008) 37 *Common Law World Review* 117.
[96] Trade Descriptions Act 1968 (UK).
[97] See: SHC Lo, 'Limitations in the Regulation of Unfair Marketing Practices in Hong Kong' (2008) 7(1) *Journal of International Business and Law* 77.
[98] Amended by the Trade Descriptions (Unfair Trade Practices) (Amendment) Ordinance 2012, ss 13E–13I.
[99] See M Durovic, *European Law on Unfair Commercial Practices and Contract Law* (Oxford: Hart Publishing, 2016) 34.

the EU – the average consumer which is understood as a reasonably well informed and circumspect and observant consumer.[100] However, the Hong Kong law has not adopted the concept of vulnerable consumer as a subsidiary benchmark to be used for assessment of fairness of commercial practices in cases when particular practice is targeted towards consumers who are vulnerable due to their their mental or physical infirmity, age or credulity.[101]

C. Enforcement

The trade descriptions work of the Customs and Excise Department is divided between its Intellectual Property Investigation Bureau (IPIB) that deals with trade descriptions matters relating to services and specified types of goods (ginseng, dried seafood and mobile phones which may involve syndicate crimes) and the Trade Descriptions Investigations Bureau (TDIB).[102] In 2017, the Customs & Excise Department received 6,922 Trade Descriptions-related complaints.[103] The IPIB completed 1,997 investigations and instigated 22 prosecutions.[104] Seventy-four persons were arrested.[105] The TDIB completed 1,491 investigations and instigated 50 prosecutions.[106] Amongst those 1,491 completed investigations, 163 cases resulted in enforcement actions and 1,328 cases did not. Between July 2013 and December 2017 there was a 27 per cent prosecution rate for goods (314 cases) and a much lower prosecution rate for services 6 per cent (26 cases); with respective conviction rates of 95 per cent and 78 per cent.[107] The prosecution rate seems to have increased to 57 per cent due to a decrease in detailed investigations allowing more proactive enforcement in the period from May 2016–December 2017.[108] The low rate for services is explained by the difficulty of obtaining evidence as there is often no physical evidence as in the case of goods.[109]

D. Case Examples

There have, however, already been a number of notable cases in Hong Kong in the area of unfair commercial practices. These are not normally reported as they are often heard in the Magistrates' Court, but some are documented in a booklet produced by the

[100] Unfair Commercial Practices Directive (EU), recital 18 and Art 5(2)(b).
[101] Unfair Commercial Practices Directive (EU), Art 5(3).
[102] Audit Commission, at vii. Telecommunications matters are dealt with by the Office of the Communications Authority (OFCA).
[103] Audit Commission of the Government of the Hong Kong Special Administrative Region, 'Consumer Protection Against Unfair Trade Practices, Unsafe Goods, and Short Weights and Measures' (Report No 70, Chapter No 2) (April 2018), at para 1.7.
[104] ibid, Executive Summary, para 5.
[105] ibid, para 2.22(d).
[106] ibid, Executive Summary, para 5.
[107] ibid, para 2.6. In Table 5, this figure combines Customs and Excise Department and OFCA.
[108] ibid, para 2.7(b).
[109] ibid, para 2.6.

Customs and Excise Department.[110] In that sense, the *Private Eye Case* of 2014[111] was the first case after amending the Trade Descriptions Ordinance. The case concerned a private detective who was misleading his customers as to the services his company provided. He had falsely stated on his website that his firm had 30 years of investigative experience and that investigations would be planned and led by former police officers. In fact, the company was founded in 2008 and none of the staff were former police officers. Although the company did occasionally carry out investigations with unofficial advice from a police officer, the police officer was merely a friend of the private detective and was never employed by the company. The defendant was convicted for offering services where there was a false trade description and was fined HKD 30,000 (approximately USD 3,800). It must however be noted that, as the magistrate emphasised, the monetary nature of the sentence could not be used as a precedent for future penalties. Rather, the sentence was imposed on the grounds that it was the first case involving false trade description of services, but not the worse of its kind.

The *Dried Fish Maw Case* of 2015 was a case about a defendant being convicted of a charge of 'misleading omission' in relation to the sale of fish maw. It involved a common deceptive trade practice of fooling people over the measuring unit used when the price quoted differs from the actual measuring unit being charged. This happened at a dried seafood store where a Mainland Chinese tourist enquired about a price sign of a tray of fish maw. When being asked whether this is the price per catty, the defendant repeated the price without making any reference to the unit. It was only after the tourist agreed to buy that the defendant revealed that the price referred to the price per gram. By that time, the product had already been cut up and the tourist was put under pressure to pay and settle the bill. In this case, the defendant was found to have purposefully misled the victim with respect to the measurement units and was sentenced to 10 weeks' imprisonment – the heaviest penalty to date for the offence of 'misleading omission' – in addition to a compensation of HKD 10,000 (approximately USD 1300) that he was ordered to pay to the victim.

The third case is the *Body Treatment Case* of 2015[112] which involved the use of aggressive commercial practices in a beauty store. The victim was undergoing a beauty treatment when a store consultant visited and persuaded her to allow the manager to enter and examine her breasts, after which she was told that lumps were found and that they might become cancerous in the future. The victim was then urged to purchase a therapy package worth HKD 140,000 (approximately USD 18,000) to cure the problem. Despite the victim's repeated refusal, the defendants continued persuading for more than an hour. Eventually, she agreed and paid a deposit of HKD 70,000 (approximately USD 9,000) for the therapy. Later it was discovered during a medical check-up that she was in fact healthy. Both the manager and consultant of the beauty store were convicted

[110] Customs & Excise Department, *Booklet on Cases under the Trade Descriptions Ordinance: Successful Prosecution and Accepted Undertaking Cases*, 2nd edn (March 2018).
[111] KTCC6664/2013.
[112] KCCC 3903/2014.

for the use of aggressive commercial practices, and were each sentenced to three months' imprisonment. This is the first case in which an immediate custodial sentence was imposed on traders who performed aggressive commercial practices.

The fourth case was the *School Fees Case* of 2015 where the defendant wrongly accepted private tuition school fees. The defendant ran an education business after he retired. Knowing that he could not deliver some of the requested courses on their designated dates, he still accepted tuition fees from two students. The court decided that the defendant had no reasonable grounds to believe that he would be able provide the courses because of the financially difficult situation the company was in. The defendant was sentenced to 14 days' imprisonment and ordered to compensate the victims for the tuition fees paid.[113]

E. Enforcement Authorities

Enforcement is by the Customs and Excise Department. There is a broader debate about whether this is the right body to be bringing such actions or if a consumer agency should be established.[114] Traditionally criminal sanctions were used. The recent reforms allowed for civil sanctions such as undertakings and injunctions. This allowed Hong Kong to come into line with modern regulatory practice, however criminal enforcement seemed to remain the default position, as between July 2013–April 2016 of the 1,363 cases handled only 10 led to written undertakings under the civil compliance-based mechanism. Practical enforcement remains a problem with many consumers not wanting to engage once their own problem is resolved. We have already noted the low prosecution rate for services. It is also reported that the Customs and Excise Department found that 70 per cent of complaints relating to the service sector were withdrawn and the complainants refused to assist the investigation.[115] The Audit Commission also noted problems of delays in completing investigations, lack of effectiveness of spot checks and improper classification of cases.

The Consumer Council has also been influential in addressing unfair practices through a process of naming and shaming.[116] In 2011 two audio-visual shops were named for persistent use of bait and switch tactics and making misrepresentations to tourists; in 2012 a beauty salon was named after it refused to provide redress following high pressure sales involving misrepresentations; and in 2016 a fitness centre chain was named for using high pressure and intimidatory sales practices to pressure consumers into membership and buying highly priced private lessons. The bad publicity eventually led to the collapse of the chain.

[113] KCCC 843/2015.

[114] Consumer Council, 'Report on Unfair Terms in Standard Form Consumer Contract'.

[115] Consumer Council'Online Retail: A Study on Hong Kong Consumer Attitudes, Business Practices and Legal Protection' (November 2016).

[116] V Tang, 'Enforcement of Consumer Law in Hong Kong' in H Micklitz and G Saumier (eds), *Enforcement and Effectiveness of Consumer Law* (Cham: Springer, 2018) 331 et seq.

IX. Access to Justice

A. Consumer Council

Almost 50 years have passed since the establishment of the Consumer Council in 1974.[117] One of its earlier important functions was to monitor the price of essential goods in the wake of the global oil crisis in the early 1970s. It was also originally tasked to deal with issues of consumer rights related to the sale of goods. In 1975, its functions were extended to cover also services. The Consumer Council is an Executive and Council Member of Consumers International. The Council participated in the revision of the UN Guidelines for Consumer Protection by completing a matrix related to the application of the Guidelines in Hong Kong, and suggesting areas of concern that should be incorporated into the Guidelines in the future.[118]

The Council provides comments to consultations of the OECD, including the G20 High-level Principles on Financial Consumer Protection.[119] It also has produced the Good Corporate Citizen's Guide to further its objectives which are influenced by the international standards (for example, electronic commerce complying with OECD Guidelines for Consumer Protection in the Context of Electronic Commerce).[120]

In addition to this policy work, the Consumer Council, although not an enforcement authority in Hong Kong, helps to resolve consumer complaints through conciliation. In the years 2019–20, it resolved 9,713 cases, with the resolution rate being 62 per cent.[121] From 2017 to 2020, it received a total of 77,729 cases with an average resolution rate of 67 per cent.[122] In 2020, the main cause of consumer complaints were travel matters followed by medical services and telecommunication services.[123] The most important problems with travel matters related to air tickets, with the key complaint areas concerning contract variation/termination and shop closure.[124]

The Alternative Dispute Resolution (ADR) mechanism is established by the Consumer Council. It is initiated by complaints from consumers. When the Consumer Council finds that the complaint is a consumer dispute, it will contact the trader and request prompt follow-up on the case. The progress of the case is dependent on the voluntary cooperation of the trader. The consumer will then receive the outcome when the trader gives a substantive reply. Although the Consumer Council is willing to assist in the conciliation of consumer complaints, it acknowledges that 'aggrieved consumers … are faced with the daunting task of taking civil action on their own as the only redress option'.[125] Furthermore, since consumer disputes are settled out of court

[117] For an overview of the history of the Consumer Council see www.consumer.org.hk/ws_en/history.

[118] ibid.

[119] Consumer Council, 'Hong Kong Consumer Council's Comments on the OECD's Draft G20 High-level Principles on Financial Consumer Protection Public Consultation' (26 August 2011).

[120] Consumer Council, 'Consumer Council Good Corporate Citizen's Guide' (15 March 2005).

[121] Consumer Council, 'Consumer Council Annual Report 2019–2020', 22.

[122] ibid.

[123] Consumer Council, 'Complaints Statistics 2019–2021'.

[124] Consumer Council, Annual Report 2019–2020', 19.

[125] Consumer Council, 'Fairness in the Marketplace for Consumers and Business' (February 2008) 3, para 7, cited in Mason, 'Inadequacy and Ineffectuality', 90.

privately, while the result may satisfy that individual aggrieved consumer, there is no judicial precedent set for the benefit of all other consumers who are subjected to the same mistreatment (for example unfair standard form contract terms).[126]

B. Consumer Dispute Resolution Centre

Like in other countries, in Hong Kong costly and time-consuming litigation is often the only option for consumers in dispute with traders who fail to reach an out of court-settlement and want to further pursue their potential claims. Currently, arbitration and adjudication are predominately used to resolve commercial but not consumer disputes. The application of arbitration and adjudication to consumer dispute resolution in Hong Kong are basically confined to the finance and insurance industries with the schemes respectively operated by the Financial Dispute Resolution Centre and the Insurance Claims Complaints Bureau. Therefore, the Consumer Council has proposed to establish a general Consumer Dispute Resolution Centre.[127] This Centre envisaged by the Consumer Council would be government-funded and be capable of both providing preliminary legal advice to consumers as well as a dispute resolution mechanism on a 'mediation first, arbitration next' model. However, at the moment it is unclear how the Consumer Dispute Resolution Centre might operate. Nonetheless, a number of the recommendations will outline the idea of the Consumer Council, including:

- no charge for consumers to use the initial services offered by the Consumer Dispute Resolution Centre;
- amounts handled by the Consumer Dispute Resolution Centre to be capped at HKD 200,000 (approximately USD 25,750);
- prohibition of legal representation during the process of mediation initiated by the Consumer Dispute Resolution Centre; and
- introduction of mechanisms to allow the Consumer Council and the Judiciary to refer consumer disputes to the Consumer Dispute Resolution Centre.

C. Courts

The courts, however, remain the main formal means of enforcing consumer rights. There is no specific enforcement agency in charge of enforcement of consumer law. In general, the basis for the authority of the Hong Kong judiciary is laid down in Articles 80–96 of the Hong Kong Basic Law (the 'constitution' of Hong Kong). Article 80 of the Hong Kong Basic Law provides that '[t]he courts of the Hong Kong Special Administrative Region at all levels shall be the judiciary of the Region, exercising the judicial power of the Region'.

[126] ibid.

[127] Consumer Council, 'Advocating for Establishing a "Consumer Dispute Resolution Centre" to achieve triple wins in consumer dispute resolution for Hong Kong' (31 August 2016).

As for the manner in which courts may enforce consumer rights, brief information can be accessed from the offices and websites of the Consumer Council[128] and various relevant bodies (for example the Customs and Excise Department), as well as legal public education websites (for example the Community Legal Information Centre). However, accessibility does not mean there is always awareness.

The major law courts in Hong Kong include the Magistrate's Courts, the District Court, the High Court (comprises the Court of Appeal and the Court of First Instance) and the Court of Final Appeal. The Court of Final Appeal is the highest appellate court in Hong Kong. It hears appeals on civil and criminal matters from the High Court. There are also special courts and tribunals, particularly the Small Claims Tribunal. The Small Claims Tribunal provides an informal, quick and inexpensive means to deal with claims up to HKD 50,000 (approximately USD 6,400). The main types of claims handled by the Tribunal include debts, services charges, damage to property, goods sold and consumer claims.

There are no specialised court tariffs/taxes (or their exemption) for consumer disputes.[129] If the consumer is not submitting the claim to the Small Claims Tribunal, and wishes to have it tried in the District Court or the High Court, he may apply for legal aid if certain conditions set out by the Legal Aid Department are satisfied. For civil cases, consumers must pass the merits test and the means test.[130] For the merits test, one needs to show reasonable grounds for taking or defending proceedings. For the means test, one's financial resources must not exceed the financial eligibility limit, currently HKD 420,400 (approximately USD 54,000). Consumers with financial resources lower than HKD 52,550 (approximately USD 6750) will receive free legal aid. Those with financial resources higher than the said amount are required to pay contributions according to a scale.[131] The Director may waive the financial eligibility limit in meritorious cases in which a breach of the Hong Kong Bill of Rights Ordinance (Cap 383) or an inconsistency with the UN International Covenant on Civil and Political Rights is an issue.

Consumers can also access the Consumer Legal Action Fund (CLAF). This provides legal assistance to consumers in cases where there is a public interest. In successful cases the money is recovered together with 10 per cent of the benefit to the consumer deriving from the judgment (the 'Benefit Value'), subject to a cap of 25 per cent for matters before the Small Claims Tribunal and 50 per cent in other matters. The Consumer Legal Action Fund is not always appealing to consumers due to a non-refundable application fee, the risk of liability for costs and expenses if true and accurate information is not provided (even unwittingly), and because funding can be terminated at any time. It also requires the use of mediation, which may settle individual dispute, but not improve law or general market conditions. This seems at odds with supporting cases because of their public interest dimension.

Compared with complaining to the Consumer Council, the Court has the power of adjudication. Also, it has power to make various orders which the Council is not

[128] See for example: Consumer Council, 'Guide to Consumer Rights and Responsibilities' (2006).

[129] The Consumer Council has proposed a Consumer Tribunal. See 'Fairness in the Marketplace for Consumers and Business' (February 2008) 42–43.

[130] Legal Aid Department, 'Ordinary Legal Aid Scheme'.

[131] Legal Aid Department, 'Ordinary Legal Aid Scheme Civil Cases'.

empowered to make. Generally, compared with complaining to the Consumer Council or the Customs and Excise Department, judicial enforcement of consumer rights takes a longer time and is costlier.

D. No Class Action

There is no class action in Hong Kong. In May 2012, the Law Reform Commission proposed that a mechanism for class actions should be adopted in Hong Kong and recommended phasing its implementation by starting with consumer cases.[132] No action has been taken to implement the recommendation. Under the existing law, the sole machinery for dealing with multi-party proceedings is a rule on representative proceedings under Order 15 Rule 12 of the Rules of the High Court (Cap 4A) which was criticised as restrictive and inadequate by the Chief Justice's Working Party on Civil Justice Reform in its Final Report in 2004.[133]

i. Who May Initiate Representative Actions?

A representative action is begun in the name of one person, but every person represented is a party to the action within the meaning of section 2 of the High Court Ordinance (Cap 4), even if not named on the record. The court has the power to add individuals as a necessary party under Order 15 Rule 6 of the Rules of the High Court or to amend the proceedings by substituting an unnamed person for a named plaintiff so as to bring him in as at the date of the issue of the original writ. It is not necessary to name every plaintiff or defendant in the group. It is essential, however, to define the group represented with sufficient clarity so that the court can determine whether they have the requisite common interest and whether the relief claimed is for the benefit of all members of the group. The writ of summons must state that the person is suing or being sued in a representative capacity,[134] and this should also be specifically pleaded in the body of the statement of claim and in the prayers.

ii. Opt-in

Order 15 Rule 12(3) of the Rules of the High Court provides that a judgment or order given in representative proceedings shall be binding on all persons represented as being those represented by the plaintiffs or defendants, but shall not be enforced against any person not a party to the proceeding except with the leave of the court. If a representative action is properly constituted, any person represented in, but not a party to, the action is bound by any judgment given in the action. No leave is required to enforce the judgment in representative proceedings as against the parties actually before the court. However, the judgment can only be enforced with the leave of the court against a person represented in, but not a party to, the proceedings.

[132] The Law Reform Commission of Hong Kong, 'Report on Class Actions' (May 2012).
[133] Chief Justice's Working Party, 'Final Report on Civil Justice Reform' (March 2004).
[134] Rules of the High Court, Order 6 Rule 3.

iii. Criteria for the Representative Proceedings

The representative proceedings procedure governed by Order 15 Rule 12 of the Rules of the High Court applies to all causes and matters. However, the action must satisfy the necessary criteria imposed by the rules. For example, the mere existence of a common wrong will not necessarily suffice if there is no common right or common purpose. A representative action may be begun by a person or persons claiming to represent numerous other persons having the same interest. No leave or representation order is necessary either before or after the action is begun. There would appear to be no limitation on who may bring an action in representative proceedings, provided that the representative plaintiff seeks to represent others having the same interest.

X. Conclusion

The consumer law situation in Hong Kong seems to be unsatisfactory. The Hong Kong SAR Government often adopts the 'wait and see' approach and only reacts to problems as they emerge.[135] Since the early 1990s, laws were introduced or existing laws amended to address obvious concerns over unconscionable conduct, deception in the supply of services and the widespread use of exemption clauses. Furthermore, ineffective enforcement led to more and more problems such as unfair sales tactics in the fitness industry and beauty industry. However, the consumer law as a whole has not really been identified as a legal issue yet and the legal framework looks more like a patchwork than one reflecting a holistic approach of the government. The consumer law in Hong Kong lags behind important developments and it seems to be the law of the twentieth rather than the twenty-first century: an adaption to the legal state of the art in consumer law worldwide has not taken place and important consumer law features of other legal systems as for example, the EU, Mainland China or Singapore are just missing (for example, the right of withdrawal). Likewise, it is fair to say that the Hong Kong consumer law is an 'analogue law' as it hardly deals with legal issues of the digital age. It needs to be seen whether the Hong Kong government is willing and able to bring its consumer law into the twenty-first century, something that will certainly be needed in a post-Covid-19 world. There is great room for a substantial improvement and we would welcome Hong Kong having a fundamental review of its consumer policy that should inform the modernisation of its consumer law and its adaptation to the particularities of the increasing digitalisation of the market and society.

[135] Editorial, 'Consumers in Hong Kong Deserve Stronger Laws to Protect Their Interests', scmp.com, 19 August 2015.

4

India

ASHOK R PATIL

I. Introduction

Worldwide, India is the seventh-largest country by area and the second-most populous country with over 1.2 billion people. The Indian consumer durables market is broadly divided into urban and rural markets, and is attracting marketers from across the world. The sector comprises a huge middle class, relatively large affluent class and a small economically disadvantaged class. Global corporations view India as one of the key markets from where future growth is likely to emerge. The growth in India's consumer market would be primarily driven by a favourable population composition and increasing disposable incomes. The Indian GDP per capita is expected to reach USD 3,273.85 in 2023, increasing from USD 1,983 in 2012. The maximum consumer spending is likely to occur in food, housing, consumer durables and the transport and communication sectors.[1]

With its ever-increasing population and status as third-largest consumer market behind only the United States and China, the need for consumer protection in India is paramount given the demand for many goods and services of which is there is no matching supply. Beginning with a brief overview, this chapter highlights that some aspects of consumer protection are not unfamiliar to the law of India, but that India has also moved to address other issues relating to consumers, such as information and the right of withdrawal, sales law and unfair contract terms. The chapter also covers matters such as product liability, product safety, e-commerce, unfair trade practices as well as access to justice, before drawing some conclusions and making suggestions for possible ways forward.

II. Overview

A. History

Broadly speaking, consumer protection in India began during King Chandragupta's reign from 321 BC, during which time minister *Kautilya* wrote the Arthashastra,

[1] www.ibef.org/industry/indian-consumer-market.aspx.

which contains references to the concept of consumer protection with punishment against exploitation by means of trade and industry, short weights and measures and adulteration.[2]

Moving forward to modern times, British crown rule had revolutionised the Indian legal system by bringing about a unified nationwide modern legal system. Key legislation relevant to consumer interests, such as the Indian Contract Act, 1872, Sale of Goods Act, 1930, Indian Penal Code, 1860, Drugs and Cosmetics Act, 1940 and Agriculture Procedure (Grading and Marketing) Act, 1937, were passed during the British regime and were based on most of the principles and doctrines of English common law and English legislation.

India gained independence from British rule in 1947. The Constitution of India – the supreme legal document – took effect on 26 January 1950. Through its Articles 21, 38 and 47, the Constitution guarantees that it is the primary duty of the State to guarantee the right to live with human dignity, free from exploitation, secure a social order for the promotion of the people's welfare, and it shall effectively work to achieve a social order and to raise the level of nutrition and the standard of living to improve public health, and to prohibit the consumption of intoxicating drinks or drugs which are injurious to the health of everyone living in it. In order to transform the constitutional mandate, several pieces of consumer welfare legislation were enacted post-independence such as the Competition Act, 2002,[3] the Food Safety and Standards Act, 2006,[4] the Legal Metrology Act, 2009[5] and the Bureau of Indian Standards Act, 2016.[6] The Government of India also established regulatory authorities and ombudsmen under special legislations related to sectors such as insurance, banking, electricity and telecommunications, to protect consumers.[7]

In 1986, the Government of India enacted an exclusive law for consumers – the Consumer Protection Act, 1986 – which covers broadly the United Nations Guidelines on Consumer Protection, 1985.[8] The Consumer Protection Act 1986 has since been amended three times to achieve better protection for consumers by plugging the gaps. However, it did not address various issues such as contracts between the consumer and product manufacturer or with a service provider, disputes relating to e-commerce, product liability, etc. It was also evident that the three-tier redressal system at national, state and district levels was overburdened due to the time-consuming procedure adopted by the consumer commissions.

In order to address these challenges, the Law Commission of India recommended new and separate legislation. The Consumer Protection Bill, 2015 was presented before the Parliament and was examined by the Standing Committee on Consumer Affairs which submitted its report in April 2016. The Committee made several recommendations with

[2] *Kautilya's Arthasastra*, 8th edn, translation by R Shamashastry (Mysore: Mysore Printing and Publishing House, 1967) 115.

[3] Repealing the Monopoly Restrictive and Trade Practice Act, 1969.

[4] Repealing the Prevention of Food Adulteration Act, 1954.

[5] Repealing the Standard Weights and Measures Act, 1976 and the Standards of Weights and Measures (Enforcement) Act, 1985.

[6] Repealing the Bureau of Indian Standards Act, 1986.

[7] See below under s X.D.

[8] General Assembly Resolution 39/248 of 9 April 1985.

regard to: (i) product liability; (ii) powers and functions of the regulatory body (Central Consumer Protection Authority) being established; (iii) penalties for misleading advertisements and endorsers of such advertisements; and (iv) pecuniary jurisdiction of the adjudicatory body at the district level. The Consumer Protection Act, 2019 was introduced in Lok Sabha by the Minister of Consumer Affairs, Food and Public Distribution on 8 July 2019. It received presidential assent on 9 August 2019 and came into force partly on 20 July 2020 and partly on 24 July 2020, repealing the Consumer Protection Act 1986.

A further notable and recent development concerns the establishment of the Central Consumer Protection Authority (CCPA). The CCPA has since been established with effect from 24 July 2020 with the objective to regulate matters relating to violation of consumers rights, unfair trade practices and false or misleading advertisements which are detrimental to the interests of public and consumers and to promote, protect and enforce the rights of consumers as a class. The Central Consumer Protection Authority structure as well as its powers and functions are set out extensively in the Consumer Protection Act, 2019.[9] For example, the CCPA is empowered not only to inquire or cause an inquiry or investigation to be made into violations of consumer rights or unfair trade practices, either *suo motu* or on a complaint received or on the directions from the Central Government, but it may also file complaints or intervene in any proceedings before the District Commission, the State Commission or the National Commission. Moreover, the CCPA may recommend the adoption of international covenants and best international practices on consumer rights to ensure effective enforcement of consumer rights, but also undertake and promote research in the field of consumer rights as well as spread and promote awareness on consumer rights.[10]

B. Defining the Consumer

The Consumer Protection Act, 2019 has broadened the scope of the definition of the consumer: a person who buys any goods or hires or avails of any services including offline or online transactions through electronic means or by teleshopping or direct selling or multi-level marketing for consideration.[11] The user of such goods, with the approval of the buyer, and any beneficiary of such services with the approval of the hirer, has also been included within the ambit of the concept of consumer, enlarging its scope to a great extent. The consideration for such goods or services may be paid or promised or partly paid or partly promised or covered under any system of deferred payment. However, a person who, in the case of goods, obtains the goods for resale or for any commercial purpose or who, in case of services, avails of such services for any commercial purpose is excluded from the definition of consumer. The explanation further states that the expression 'commercial purpose' does not include use by a buyer of such goods or hirer of services, exclusively for the purpose of earning his livelihood by means of self-employment.[12]

[9] Consumer Protection Act 2019, ss 10–27.
[10] ibid, s 18(2).
[11] ibid, s 2(7).
[12] ibid, s 2(7).

III. Information and Right of Withdrawal

In India, if the seller refuses, after selling goods or rendering services, to take back or withdraw defective goods or to withdraw or discontinue deficient services and to refund the consideration thereof, if paid, within the period stipulated in the bill or cash memo or receipt or in the absence of such stipulation, within a period of 30 days, it would be considered as an Unfair Trade Practice.[13] Similarly, under the Consumer Protection (E-Commerce) Rules 2020 and Consumer Protection (Direct Selling) Rules 2021, it is the mandatory duty of the e-commerce or direct selling entity that it may not impose any cancellation charges on consumers cancelling after confirming purchase unless similar charges are also borne by the e-commerce or direct selling entity, if they cancel the purchase order unilaterally for any reason and further the e-commerce or direct selling entity shall not refuse to take back goods, or withdraw or discontinue services purchased or agreed to be purchased, or refuse to refund consideration, if paid, if such goods or services are defective, deficient or spurious, or if the goods or services are not of the characteristics or features as advertised or as agreed to, or if such goods or services are delivered late from the stated delivery schedule, provided that in the case of late delivery, this sub-rule shall not be applied if such late delivery was due to *force majeure*. In order to protect the consumers from unfair trade practices in India, they are guaranteed the right to be informed about the quality, quantity, potency, purity, standard and price of goods, product or services. Further consumer rules and regulation of consumer welfare legislation such as the declaration to be made under the Legal Metrology Act 2009; the information as to compliance with standards as prescribed under the Bureau of Indian Standards Act, 2016, Food Safety and Standards Act, 2006, and the Drugs and Cosmetics Act, 1940 etc, and also information relating to the name of the manufacturer, seller, grievance redressal officer and other information mandatorily required to be declared by the e-commerce or direct selling entity to all consumers under Consumer Protection (E-Commerce) Rules 2020 and the Consumer Protection (Direct Selling) Rules 2021 respectively.

IV. Consumer Sales Law

A. Sale of Goods Act, 1930

The Sale of Goods Act, 1930 (SGA 1930) provides certain safeguards to the buyer of goods. A buyer aggrieved by a good acquired under contract of sale may – subject to certain exceptions – rely on express undertakings of the seller under section 12 as well as 'implied conditions and warranties' under sections 14–17 SGA 1930. Section 16 SGA 1930 deals with implied conditions relating to 'fitness for purpose' and 'merchantable quality', that is, goods must satisfy that they are genuine according to name, kind and

[13] ibid, s 2(47)(iii).

description, saleable in the market, fit for ordinary use and purpose of such good and free from defects.[14]

It is the duty of the seller to make proper disclosure of all information about the usage of goods and to make the buyer aware of any defects in goods. In case of failure the seller will be liable if the goods do not adhere to standards as required by the law even though he has taken all possible care. As regards product liability under contract law, these standards are implied by the Sale of Goods Act. In case of breach of contract, consumers have a right to sue for the price of goods, damages for non-acceptance, damages for non-delivery and subject to the provisions of Specific Relief Act, 1877 may file a suit for breach of contract to deliver specific or ascertained goods under sections 55–61 of this Act.

B. Consumer Protection Act, 2019

The concept of defect in goods under the Consumer Protection Act, 1986 is incorporated in the Consumer Protection Act, 2019.[15] According to this provision, defect means any fault, imperfection or shortcoming in the quality, quantity, potency, purity or standard which is required to be maintained by or under any law for the time being in force or under any contract, express or implied, or as is claimed by the trader in any manner whatsoever in relation to any goods. The phrase 'required to be maintained by or under any law for time being in force' means the quality, quantity, potency, purity or standard which is specifically required to be maintained under consumer welfare legislation of specific goods.

V. Unfair Contract Terms

A. Indian Contract Act, 1872

The Indian Contract Act, 1872 was enacted during the British regime and is one of the oldest pieces of legislation in India. Although general in application, the Act contains provisions relevant to consumer protection – the contract must consist of a lawful object and a lawful consideration, and in the event of breach the consumer can also claim the protection of their interests and seek compensation;[16] the consumer may also seek recourse to the Specific Relief Act, 1963. However, the scope of the Indian Contract Act, 1872 is limited due to the principle of privity of contract, which prevents third parties from seeking relief and thereby excludes a large number of consumers from its ambit.

[14] M Krishnan Nair, 'Quality Control: Conditions and Warranties in Sale of Goods' in P Leelakrishnan (ed), *Consumer Protection and Legal Control* (Lucknow: Eastern Book Company, 1981) 143.

[15] Consumer Protection Act 2019, s 2(10).

[16] ibid, ss 10, 73.

In 2006, the Law Commission submitted a Bill on Unfair (Procedural and Substantive) Terms in Contract which proposed to divide unfair terms into 'procedural' and 'substantive' to meet an urgent need of persons who are parties to contracts in the markets today as well as to other contractual transactions on the basis of the observation made in 1984 in its 103rd Report.[17] But even after the Law Commission reports, courts could declare contracts void or voidable only if they fall under one or another of the corresponding provisions of the Indian Contract Act, 1872. At present, neither the Indian Contract Act, 1872 nor the Sale of Goods Act, 1930 contain a general provision whereby courts can give relief to the consumer – or the weaker party – by holding such terms in contracts as void on the ground of their being unreasonable, or unconscionable or unfair.

The inequality of bargaining power between parties and of the unfair advantage of one party over the other features in the Indian Contract Act, 1872 under 'undue influence' – one of the parties to the contract is in a position to dominate the will of the other and uses that position so as to obtain an unfair advantage over the other.[18] Pursuant to section 16(2), 'dominate the will of another' means when one party holds a real or apparent authority over the other or stands in a fiduciary relation to the other; or makes a contract with a person whose mental capacity is temporarily or permanently affected by reason of age, illness or mental or bodily distress. The burden of proof under such unconscionable transactions lies with the person who was in a position to dominate the will of the other.

Section 23 of the Indian Contract Act is a further relevant provision which requires discussion as it deals with 'substantive' matters which invalidate a contract, namely the legality of the consideration and objects, although it does not refer to 'unconscionability' specifically. The consideration or object of an agreement is lawful, unless it is forbidden by law, is of such a nature that, if permitted, it would defeat the provisions of any law, is fraudulent, involves or implies injury to the person or property of another, or if the court regards it as immoral, or opposed to public policy. In each of these cases, the consideration or object of an agreement is said to be unlawful. Every agreement of which the object or consideration is unlawful is void. The same was upheld by the Supreme Court in *Central Inland v Brojo Naths*[19] while discussing the position that the English law regarding unreasonable and unfair contract terms is mostly judge-made, whereas the law of contracts in India is enacted in a statute, namely the Indian Contract Act, 1872.

B. Consumer Protection Act, 2019

'Unfair contract' was not defined in the Consumer Protection Act, 1986, but it is defined in the Consumer Protection Act, 2019 as a contract between a manufacturer or trader or service provider on one hand, and a consumer on the other, having terms which cause

[17] Law Commission of India, 199th Report on Unfair (Procedural and Substantive) Terms in Contracts (August 2006).

[18] Indian Contract Act, s 16.

[19] AIR 1986 SC 1571.

significant change in the rights of such consumer.[20] The provision identifies six types of unfair terms: (i) manifestly excessive security deposits; (ii) disproportionate penalties on the consumer for the breach of contract; (iii) refusal to accept early repayment of debts on payment of applicable penalty; (iv) right to unilaterally terminate the contract without reasonable cause; (v) permitting or having the effect of permitting one party to assign the contract to the detriment of the other party who is a consumer, without his consent; (vi) imposing on the consumer any unreasonable charge, obligation or condition which puts such consumer at a disadvantage. Further the State Commission and National Commission may also declare any terms of contract, which are unfair to any consumer, to be null and void.[21]

VI. Product Liability

Indian law previously did not contain any specific product liability chapter or legislation, but manufacturers or product sellers or service providers were held liable to pay compensation to the aggrieved consumer who proves that the good is defective or the service is deficient under the Consumer Protection Act, 1986, relying on the standards mentioned under the specific legislation such as the Food Safety and Standards Act, 2006; the Drugs and Magic Remedies Act, 1940; the Legal Metrology Act, 2009; the Bureau of Indian Standards Act, 2016; and the Indian Contract Act, 1872.

However, the new Consumer Protection Act, 2019 contains a new chapter with specific provisions on product liability.[22] Under the provisions, the consumer may bring an action and file complaint against the manufacturer, service provider or product seller for any harm caused by a defective product manufactured by a product manufacturer or serviced by a product service provider or sold by a product seller or for any harm caused to him on account of a such defective product.[23] Pursuant to section 84 CPA 2019, strict liability applies to product manufacturers and covers aspects such as manufacturing defects, non-conformity with a warranty or the failure to provide warnings regarding improper use (where the exceptions in section 87 do not apply). According to section 85 CPA 2019, a product service provider shall be liable for, inter alia, faulty or inadequate performance as required by statute, contract or otherwise, or an act of omission or commission or negligence or conscious withholding any information which caused harm. The scope of liability of a product seller who is not a product manufacturer is set out in section 86 CPA 2019. According to this provision, liability applies to a product seller insofar as, for example, he has exercised substantial control over the designing, testing, manufacturing, packaging or labelling of a product that caused harm.

In *CN Anantharam v Fiat India Ltd and Ors*[24] the complaint concerned noise from the engine and the gear box. There was no other major defect which made the vehicle incapable of operation, particularly when the engine was replaced. The issue was

[20] Consumer Protection Act 2019, s 2(46).
[21] ibid, ss 49(2) and 59(2).
[22] ibid, ss 82–87.
[23] ibid, s 83.
[24] AIR 2011 SC 523.

whether there was a manufacturing defect in the engine of the vehicle. The Supreme Court directed that the independent technical expert was of the opinion that there were inherent manufacturing defects in the vehicle, the petitioner would be entitled to refund of the price of the vehicle and the lifetime tax and monthly instalments along with interest at 12 per cent per annum and costs, as directed by the State Commission. The decision of the court is strongly appreciated for upholding higher standards of product liability in India. With the industrial growth and numerous manufacturers producing varied products, higher standards are an imperative.

VII. Product Safety

India may be the world's second-fastest growing economy with manufacturers regularly launching improved variants of consumer products, but it is behind in protecting consumer interests, specifically via legislation.

Although India lacks a general consumer safety law, the CCPA in pursuit of the objective to protect, promote and enforce the rights of consumers as a class may issue safety notices to alert consumer against dangerous or hazardous or unsafe goods or services.[25] Moreover, if on the basis of an investigation there is sufficient evidence, the CCPA is empowered to recall goods or order the withdrawal of services which are dangerous, hazardous or unsafe.[26]

Specific legislation such as the Agricultural Produce (Marking and Grading) Act, 1937, the Drugs and Cosmetics Act, 1940, the Food Safety and Standards Act, 2006 and the Bureau of Indian Standards Act, 2016, have prescribed mandatory safety standards. If these standards are not followed, manufacturers and service providers are held liable for both damages and penal sanctions under these pieces of legislation as well as under the Consumer Protection Act, 2019.

A. The Agricultural Produce (Marking and Grading) Act, 1937

The regulatory measures for standardisation and quality control of agricultural commodities are contained in the Agricultural Produce (Marking and Grading) Act, 1937 – the pioneering legislation in the field of quality control and standardisation in India. Section 3 of this Act empowers the Central Government to make rules to carry out the functions of prescribing grade designations.

The Directorate of Marking and Inspection has set conditions which govern the use of standards and lays down the procedure for grading, marking and packing of a broad range of agricultural produce, such as fruits, vegetables, dairy produce and poultry products, spices condiments, tobacco, tea, etc. The quality marks provided under the Act – AGMARK[27] – are based on physical as well as internal attributes of commodity

[25] Consumer Protection Act 2019, ss 18(1)(a), (2)(j).
[26] ibid, s 20.
[27] Agricultural Marketing.

such as weight, colour and contents; the marks are also subject to periodical revisions. These standards signify an agricultural seal ensuring purity and quality which benefit the consumer insofar as the product can be easily assessed.

B. The Drugs and Cosmetics Act, 1940

The Drugs and Cosmetics Act, 1940 was enacted with an intent to regulate import, manufacture, distribution and sale of drugs and cosmetics so as to provide better protection to consumers and public at large. It provides special measures for standardisation and quality control. 'Drugs' include a wide variety of substances, diagnostic and medical devices; 'cosmetics' are products that are meant to be applied to the human body for the purpose of beautifying or cleansing.

The salient features of the Act concerning product safety are the standard of quality for drugs defined under section 16, the suspension of a manufacturer of misbranded drug defined under section 18 read with section 17 and fake and adulterated drugs under section 27. The Act also contains requirements for information to be disclosed on labels as well as penalties for failing to comply with standards such as manufacturing, sale or distribution of sub-standard, adulterated and spurious drugs and cosmetics, and the manufacture, sale or distribution without a licence.

C. The Food Safety and Standards Act, 2006

To strengthen food safety and standards, the Parliament passed new legislation in 2006 – the Food Safety and Standards Act, 2006 (FSSA) – calling upon the Central Government to establish the Food Safety and Standards Authority of India (FSSAI), an autonomous regulatory body responsible for protecting and promoting public health through the regulation and supervision of food safety.

To protect consumers, the FSSA imposes responsibilities on 'food business operators' to ensure the articles of food satisfy the requirements of the Act and the rules and regulations made thereunder. Food business operators shall not, for example, manufacture, store, sell or distribute any article of food which is unsafe or misbranded or sub-standard or contains extraneous matter or required as per the conditions of licence, or prohibited by any law or food authority or Central or State Government.[28]

If a food business operator considers or believes that the food processed or manufactured or distributed is not in compliance with the Act or rule or regulation or is unsafe to consumers, he shall withdraw the food from the market and consumers by indicating reasons to competent authorities and action taken to prevent risk to consumers.[29] The Food Safety and Standards (Food Recall Procedure) Regulations, 2017 prescribe procedures to recall the good in order to ensure removal of food under recall from

[28] FSSA, s 26.
[29] ibid, s 28.

all stages of the food chain in accordance with section 28 FSSA and ensure dissemination of information to concerned consumers and customers; and ensure retrieval, destruction or reprocessing of food under recall. A food business operator shall follow the conditions and guidelines Food Safety and Standards (Food Recall Procedure) Regulations, 2017 notified by FSSAI. In case of violation of the same, the operator shall be punished pursuant to sections 48–67 of the Act. As part of its efforts, the FSSAI directed the top 200 food companies to submit their food recall plans. The letter was also sent to other key domestic players to submit their food recall plans within two months, to implement food recall guidelines which shall include details of the procedures and mechanisms to retrieve their food or food products from the food chain in case a product is found to be unsafe for consumption and details of their recall management teams.[30]

D. The Bureau of Indian Standards Act, 2016

The Bureau of Indian Standards Act, 2016 entered into force on 12 October 2017 with an objective to provide for the establishment of a national standards body – the Bureau of Indian Standards (BIS).[31] This national body certifies goods, services, articles, processes and systems and helps to provide the harmonious development of the activities of standardisation, conformity assessment and quality assurance, and for matters connected therewith or incidental thereto. The BIS certifies the 'ISI' mark for industrial products, 'BIS hallmark' for purity of gold jewellery and 'Ecomark' is an ecolabel for various products. The Act has also empowered the Central Government to notify certain goods, articles etc, which must carry a standard mark. In exercising this power, the Central Government has notified some products under the mandatory certification list, for instance milk powder, condensed milk and infant milk food, food colours and additives, cement, LPG cylinders, dry cell batteries, electric appliances and accessories, etc.

These Standards were formulated in view of the national programmes prioritising industrial development, technical needs, export promotion, consumer welfare, health, safety, national security etc. The BIS was also empowered to work in co-operation with all the regulatory authorities in case of powers enumerated to it such as recall of goods or articles from traders which are already out for sale or supply when such goods or articles do not satisfy the required standard. The BIS has also empowered to impose the penalties for offences relating to (i) the improper use of the standard mark by testing and marking centres, and (ii) manufacturing or selling goods and articles which do not carry a standard mark and have been mandated to do so.

[30] M Ambwani, 'FSSAI asks top 200 companies for details of their food recall plans', thehindubusinessline.com, 26 March 2018.

[31] For details see https://bis.gov.in/.

VIII. E-Commerce in the Digital Age

In India, as across the globe, the electronic commerce market has experienced consistent growth in recent years. The Indian B2C e-commerce market was valued at USD 38.5 billion in 2017 and is estimated to rise to USD 200 billion in 2026, while B2B e-commerce was estimated to be approximately USD 300 billion. Despite the high rate of growth of e-commerce in India, the sector is still at a nascent stage and according to some estimates, it is about 3 per cent of the retail market worth USD 860 billion, excluding travel and tourism.[32]

The Consumer Protection Act, 2019 represents the first time that statute refers to the online sale of goods or services: section 2(7)(ii)(b) includes online transactions through electronic means with respect to the purchase of goods or acquisition of services. Moreover, section 2(16) defines 'e-commerce' as the buying or selling of goods or services including digital products over digital or electronic networks, with section 2(17) defining the 'electronic service provider' as a person who provides technologies or processes to enable a product seller to engage in advertising or selling goods or services to a consumer and includes any online marketplace or online auction sites. According to section 94 CPA 2019, the Central Government is authorised to take measures to prevent unfair trade practices in e-commerce so as to protect the interest and rights of the consumer.

To undertake the aforesaid measures, the Ministry of Consumer Affairs, Food and Public Distribution in exercise of the power under section 101(1)(zg) CPA 2019, recently passed the Consumer Protection (E-Commerce) Rules, 2020 (CPR 2020) which entered into force on 23 July 2020. The rules apply to all goods and services bought or sold over digital or electronic networking including digital products; *all* models of e-commerce, including marketplace and inventory models of e-commerce;[33] all e-commerce retails, including multi-channel single brand retailers and single brand retailers in single or multiple formats; and all forms of unfair trade practices across all models of e-commerce.[34]

The legislation is novel insofar as it makes express reference to marketplace models of e-commerce, including references to platforms and in this context drawing a distinction to sellers offering goods or services for sale on a marketplace e-commerce entity.[35] In this respect, the CPR 2020 subjects e-commerce entities to a range of duties and liabilities.[36] For example, whereas the e-commerce entity is to disclose particular information and may not adopt any unfair practice, it shall also require sellers through an undertaking to ensure that, inter alia, descriptions pertaining to goods or services on their platform are accurate and correspond to the good as advertised on the platform.

[32] https://dipp.gov.in/sites/default/files/DraftNational_e-commerce_Policy_23February2019.pdf.
[33] See CPR 2020, s 3(f) and (g).
[34] CPR 2020, s 2(1).
[35] ibid, s 3(b).
[36] ibid, ss 4–5.

IX. Unfair Trade Practices

'Unfair trade practice' means a trade practice which, for the purpose of promoting the sale, use or supply of any goods or for the provision of any service, adopts any unfair method or unfair or deceptive practice.[37] Such practices include but are not limited to misleading advertisements, not issuing bill/memos for the goods and services, failing to take back defective goods or deactivate defective services, not refunding the amount within stipulation and manufacturing spurious goods or offering such goods for sale, etc. To regulate matters surrounding unfair trade practices, false or misleading advertisements the Central Government established the Central Consumer Protection Authority (CCPA) to promote, protect and enforce the rights of the consumers as a class.

The unfair trade practices listed in section 2(47) CPA 2019 are not exhaustive. In *Rupasi Multiplex v Mautusi Chaudhuri*[38] the issue was whether restrictions on carrying a drinking water bottle inside the cinema hall/Multiplex, amounts to an unfair trade practice under section 2(1)(r) CPA, 1986. The National Consumer Dispute Redressal Commission (NCDRC) held that it is obligatory for the cinema hall to make water – being a basic necessity for human beings – available to the movie-goers in case they decide not to allow the drinking water to be carried inside the cinema hall. NCDRC noted 'Not everyone may be in a position to afford drinking water at such huge price, which normally is many times more than the price at which such water is available in the market outside the cinema halls'. It was held that free portable and pure drinking water must be provided inside the cinema halls, NCDRC directed a Multiplex owner to pay compensation of Rs. 11,000/- to the respondents for refusing to allow them to carry a water bottle inside the hall.

In *Fortune Infrastructure and another v Trevor D'lima and others*[39] the issue was whether there was deficiency of service on the part of the builders'/appellants' delay in granting possession to a flat. The Supreme Court observed that a time period of three years would have been reasonable for completion of the contract. As the respondents were made to wait indefinitely for the possession of the flats and there were no valid reasons for the transfer of the property to a third party, the Supreme Court was drawn to an irresistible conclusion that there was a deficiency of service and an unfair trade practice on the part of the appellants. Accordingly, the appellants were directed by the Supreme Court to refund the amount of Rs. 1,87,00,000 which they had received from the complainants, to pay a sum of Rs. 2,27,20,000 as compensation, a sum of Rs. 20,00,000 as compensation for one unit of parking lot and Rs. 10,000 as the cost of litigation to the complainants.

X. Access to Justice

'Access to Justice' is a fundamental right guaranteed under Article 21 of the Constitution of India. At its core, the State must provide an *effective adjudicatory mechanism*; the

[37] CPA 2019, s 2(47).
[38] 2015 SCC OnLine NCDRC 2331.
[39] (2018) 5 SCC 442.

mechanism so provided must be *reasonably accessible in terms of distance*; the process of adjudication *must be speedy*; and the litigant's access to the adjudicatory process must be *affordable*.[40]

A. The Consumer Protection Act, 2019

The Consumer Protection Act, 2019 is a marked improvement over the pre-existing consumer protection as it provides compensation and its remedies are in addition to and not in derogation of the provisions of any other laws for the time. The remedies available to a consumer under section 100 CPA 2019 constitute an additional dispensation. This improves the previous system whereby remedies thereunder are basically punitive or preventive in nature and are designed to provide relief only in specific situations. Since the Consumer Protection Act, 2019 does not derogate from existing laws and is supplementary in nature, its provisions do not debar a consumer from approaching a civil court to seek compensation for loss or damage caused by a defect in the goods or deficiency in services. Therefore, a consumer may initiate proceedings in a civil court under the law of contract, sale of goods, law of torts, or any other existing law depending on the circumstances.

i. Consumer Dispute Redressal Agencies

A consumer aggrieved by a defective product or deficiency in service may file a complaint before the Consumer Dispute Redressal Agencies, that is, the National Consumer Dispute Redressal Commission (NCDRC), State Consumer Dispute Redressal Commission (SCDRC) and District Consumer Dispute Redressal Commission (DCDRC). Under the Consumer Protection Act, 2019, the pecuniary and territorial jurisdiction of these agencies has increased. These agencies are given authority to provide relief to consumers who suffer losses due to defective products or deficiency in services. The complaint can be made in relation to those goods which, for example, suffer from one or more defects or are hazardous to life and safety of public at large in contravention of any standards relating to safety of such goods

The access to the consumer court has been enhanced by an increase in the pecuniary jurisdiction of the commissions. For example, under the Consumer Protection Act, 1986 jurisdiction of the National Commission was calculated on the basis of compensation claimed (not the consideration paid), which was very difficult to the consumer to calculate and may be one reason where consumers assign an authorised agent to appear in their case. The Consumer Protection Act, 2019 also allows consumers to file their complaint at the jurisdiction where the complainant resides or personally works. The court fee to file a consumer complaint is also very negligible and is prescribed under the Consumer Protection (Consumer Disputes Redressal Commission) Rules, 2020 as displayed in Table 1.

[40] *Anita Kushwaha v Pushap Suda*, (2016) 8 SCC 509.

Sl. No.	Value of goods or services paid as consideration	Amount of fee payable
(1)	(2)	(3)
District Commission		
(1)	Up to rupees five lakh	Nil
(2)	Above rupees five lakh and up to rupees ten lakhs	Rs.200
(3)	Above rupees ten lakh and up to rupees twenty lakhs	Rs 400
(4)	Above rupees twenty lakh and up to rupees fifty lakh rupees	Rs.1000
State Commission		
(5)	Above rupees fifty lakh and up to rupees one crore	Rs.2000
(6)	Above rupees one crore and up to rupees two crore	Rs.2500
National Commission		
(7)	Above rupees two crore and up to rupees four crore	Rs.3000
(8)	Above rupees four crore and up to rupees six crore	Rs.4000
(9)	Above rupees six crore and up to rupees eight crore	Rs.5000
(10)	Above rupees eight crore and up to rupees ten crore	Rs.6000
(11)	Above rupees ten crore	Rs.7500

Case statistics[41] as on 31 August 2021 of the total number of consumer complaints filed/ disposed since inception under the Consumer Protection Act, 1986 specifically for unfair trade practices, defective goods and services, etc are as displayed in Table 2.

Sl. No.	Name of Agency	Cases filed since inception	Cases disposed of since inception	Cases Pending	% of total Disposal
1	**National Commission**	**138676**	**116508**	**22168**	**84.01%**
2	State Commissions	874562	755863	118699	86.43%
3	District Commissions	4472029	4057971	414058	90.74%
	TOTAL	**5485267**	**4930342**	**554925**	**89.88%**

ii. Mediation

Mediation is recognised in Indian statute law.[42] Furthermore, the Supreme Court held in 2010 in *Afcons Infrastructure Ltd v Cherian Varkey Construction Company Pvt Ltd*[43]

[41] http://ncdrc.nic.in/stats.html.
[42] Civil Procedure Code, s 89.
[43] (2010) 8 SCC 24.

that cases relating inter alia to consumer disputes can be referred to alternative dispute resolution. In view thereof, the Government of India introduced a chapter on mediation in the Consumer Protection Act, 2019.[44] The State Government shall establish a consumer mediation cell to be attached to each of the District Commissions and the State Commissions of that State.[45] The Central Government shall establish a consumer mediation cell to be attached to the National Commission and each of the regional Benches. The National Commission or a State Commission or a District Commission, as the circumstances may be, will appoint a mediator who shall attempt to resolve the dispute between the parties by facilitating discussion between parties directly by guiding the parties in identifying issues, reducing misunderstandings, exploring different ways to find a compromise by generating options in an attempt to solve the dispute.

B. E-Commerce

In 2019, the Department for Promotion of Industry and Internal Trade (DPIIT) released a draft National E-commerce Policy (draft policy). The main objective is to enable India to benefit from digitalisation by creating a governance framework for various stakeholders and strategies for data localisation, consumer protection and promoting micro, small and medium enterprises (MSMEs) and start-ups. Consumer Protection is discussed as a strategy under clause (F) as the atypical nature of an e-commerce transaction necessitates a consumer protection framework specific to this sector. India will move towards a system for electronic redressal of grievances including making available compensation to the aggrieved consumer electronically. It is only rational that a transaction completed online should have an online system of grievances redressal which will, in turn, boost consumer confidence. In this regard, mechanisms will be developed to establish e-consumer courts as part of the mission mode e-government project in order to address grievances online. Unsolicited commercial messages (on various platforms including but not limited to SMS, email, etc) and calls will be regulated. A legal framework for this will be developed.[46]

In addition, in 2016 the Ministry of Consumer Affairs established the 'Online Consumer Mediation Centre' (OCMC) as a pilot project at the National Law School of India University (NLSIU) under the directorship of the author. Its mission is to provide innovative technology for e-consumers and e-commerce companies to manage and resolve conflicts and to propel online mediation as a first choice to resolving consumer disputes. The OCMC runs with a vision to provide for an innovative online mediation tool that affords consumers better access to justice through quick and easy redressal mechanism and at the same time provide opportunity for businesses to maintain good customer relations. Its core values include easy accessibility, security, confidentiality, cost-effectiveness, neutrality and integrity.[47] The online platform is compatible for mobile phones also.

[44] CPA 2019, ss 74–81.
[45] ibid, s 74.
[46] https://dipp.gov.in/sites/default/files/DraftNational_e-commerce_Policy_23February2019.pdf.
[47] http://onlinemediationcenter.ac.in.

C. Writ Petitions Enhancing Consumers' Access to Justice

i. Karnataka State

The Consumer Chair established by the Ministry of Consumer Affairs in 2008 at the National Law School of India University (NLSIU), Bengaluru, has undertaken many activities to reach needy people in society. Under the guidance of the Consumer Chair, NLSIU students conducted empirical research on 'Implementation of the CPA, 1986 in Karnataka State'. On the basis of this research report, the students filed a Public Interest Litigation (PIL) before the High Court of Karnataka contending that more than half of the 30 district consumer disputes redressal forums across the Karnataka State – including the State Commission – had not appointed a president and the stipulated number of members to be present in Forum. In the districts of Ramanagar, Yadgir and Chikkaballapur, the consumer forum had not yet been established and there was lack of administrative staff, proper infrastructure, meagre salary for members; district councils and state councils were also not established in Karnataka. On 2 April 2013, the High Court of Karnataka in view of the above research directed the State Government to fill vacancies and solve other issues in the District Forum and State Commission within six months.[48]

ii. Supreme Court Report

In *State of U P and Ors v All U P Consumer Protection Bar Association*[49] the Supreme Court constituted a committee on 14 January 2016 under the chairmanship of the former Supreme Court judge, Justice Arjit Pasayat. The committee submitted its interim report on 17 October 2016. On the basis of this report, the Supreme Court directed the Central Government to constitute a committee to frame rules for the procedure to appointment of members and their terms and conditions to achieve the object of the Consumer Protection Act, 1986. Accordingly, the Central Government constituted an expert committee under the chairmanship of the Secretary, Ministry of Consumer Affairs on 7 December 2016. The author was also one of the experts of the committee who framed the rules. These rules helped in drafting the rules and regulations enacted under the Consumer Protection Act, 2019 such as the Consumer Protection (Qualification for appointment, method of recruitment, procedure of appointment, term of office, resignation and removal of the President and members of the State Commission and District Commission) Rules, 2020 (15 July 2020) & Consumer Protection (Salary, allowances and conditions of service of President and Members of the State Commission and District Commission) Model Rules, 2020 (15 July 2020).

The Honourable Supreme Court in *In RE: Inaction of the Governments in appointing President and Members/Staff of Districts and State Consumer Disputes Redressal Commission and inadequate infrastructure across India*,[50] has sou moto directed the

[48] *Basavana Gouda and other v Government of Karnatka*, WP No 50856/2012.

[49] AIR 2016 SC 5368; 2016 6 AWC6412SC; 2017(1) CDR41(SC); IV(2016)CPJ 15(SC); 2016(12)SCALE182.

[50] *In RE: Inaction of the Governments in appointing President and Members/Staff of Districts and State Consumer Disputes Redressal Commission and inadequate infrastructure across India*, W P No 2/2021; 2021 SCC OnLine SC 604.

State and Central Government to appoint the president, member and admin staff of District and State Consumer Commissions; to frame rules and notify with regards to salaries and allowance under section 44; and to constitute selection committee. It is also acting as a watchdog and on every hearing it is taking note of compliance of the implementation of the Consumer Protection Act 2019 in true spirit.

D. Regulatory Authorities

The aggrieved consumers may approach the Regulatory Authority established in specific sectors to seek justice. Examples of very important regulatory authorities are the 'Telecom Regulatory Authority of India', the 'Reserve Bank of India', the 'Food Safety and Standard Authority of India', the 'Insurance Regulatory Authority of India', the 'Security and Exchange Board of India' and the 'Central Electricity Regulatory Commission'.

E. Ombudsman

Aggrieved consumers may also obtain a remedy from sector ombudsmen:

- *Banking*. The Reserve Bank of India introduced the Banking Ombudsman Scheme in 1995 to provide an expeditious and inexpensive forum to bank customers for resolution of their complaints relating to banking services.[51]
- *Insurance*. The Insurance Ombudsman is appointed under the Insurance Ombudsman Rules, 2017. These rules seek to resolve all complaints of all personal lines of insurance, group insurance policies, policies issued to sole proprietorship and micro enterprises on the part of insurance companies and their agents and intermediaries in a cost effective and impartial manner.
- *Income tax*. The Income Tax Ombudsman Guidelines, 2010 seek to enable the resolution of complaints relating to public grievances against the Income Tax Department.
- *Electricity*: Any consumer may make a representation for the redressal of his grievance to an authority to be known as Ombudsman. The Ombudsman is to be appointed or designated by the State Electricity Regulatory Commission and shall settle the grievance of the consumer within a time and manner as specified by the Commission.[52]

XI. Conclusion

The State has a duty to frame proper guidelines and effective policies to protect consumers from traders and service providers who exploit consumers' rights. The product safety standards, service standards and fair business play an important role in our daily

[51] Banking Regulation Act, 1949, s 35A.
[52] Electricity Act, 2003, s 42(6).

lives. As standards are developed in response to our needs, it is difficult to imagine modern life without them. In one way or another, standards make life easier, safer and more comfortable. It is also a duty of every citizen of India under Article 51A of the Constitution to abide and strive towards excellence in all spheres of individual and collective activity so that the nation constantly rises to higher levels of endeavour and achievement.

It is well-known that without the active participation by the people, the Government alone cannot protect consumers from defective products, deficiency of services, unfair and restrictive trade practices. There are plenty of laws, regulatory authorities and ombudsmen to take care of consumers and their numbers are constantly increasing. However, their effectiveness has to rely upon the alertness of consumers and the sincerity of the authorities in their implementation by the state governments.

The new strong Consumer Protection Act, 2019, not only has more teeth but also a stronger bite to better protect consumers in the digital era. As legislation enacted by Central Government, the success of the Consumer Protection Act, 2019 depends on effective implementation by all the State Governments. Then the market will shift in principle from *caveat emptor* to *caveat venditor*.

5

Indonesia

JOHANNES GUNAWAN AND BERNADETTE M WALUYO

I. Overview

Indonesia is a diverse archipelagic nation consisting of more than 300 ethnic groups within its population of approximately 260 million – the world's fourth most populous nation. It is the largest economy in Southeast Asia. An emerging middle-income country, Indonesia is currently a member of the G-20, having made an enormous poverty rate reduction of more than half since 1999, namely to 9.78 per cent in 2020.[1]

In light of the projected increases in Gross Domestic Product, Gross National Income and population,[2] it can be estimated that consumers of Indonesian goods and services will be increasingly vulnerable, both in terms of quality standards, prices/tariffs and availability of goods and services, as well as their bargaining position towards business actors and service providers.

The 1945 Constitution of the Republic of Indonesia does not specifically regulate consumer protection; however, Article 33(2) – as amended by the Fourth Amendment – regarding the economy and people's welfare is indirectly related: 'Production sectors that are vital to the state and that affect the livelihood of a considerable part of the population are to be controlled by the state'. Thus, it can be inferred that there are production sectors (goods and services) that are vital and affect the lives of many people, and production sectors (goods and services) that are not vital and do not affect many people.

Vital goods and services that affect the lives of many people are to be controlled by the state, in the sense of being regulated, managed and supervised by the state.[3] It follows that goods and services that are not vital and do not affect many people can be left to the society in a competitive market. The task of the state in the latter case is to ensure and guarantee that the market for goods and services formed is a well-functioning one, that is to say, the markets for such goods and services are protected from monopolistic behaviour. These goods and services in the market form the objects

[1] www.worldbank.org/en/country/indonesia/overview.
[2] https://data.worldbank.org/country/indonesia.
[3] Decision of the Constitutional Court of the Republic of Indonesia No 001-021-022/PUU-i/2003.

of Law No 8/1999 concerning Consumer Protection (hereinafter: Consumer Protection Law). Likewise, a Consumer Protection Bill is in the process of being drafted.[4]

II. Position of Consumer Protection Law

Long before the projected growth interactions of the three factors mentioned above were expected to affect consumers of goods and services in Indonesia in increasingly vulnerable conditions, awareness of the need for consumer protection had been growing since the 1970s.

This awareness was marked with the establishment of the first country-wide consumer organisation, the Foundation of *Yayasan Lembaga Konsumen Indonesia*, in the early 1970s. While the Consumer Protection Law as a so-called umbrella act was enacted in 1999, other laws which had a bearing on consumer protection include the Hygiene Act of 1966, the Health Act 1992, the Food Act 1996 and the Banking Act 1998. These sectoral provisions were applied based on the principle *lex specialis derogat legi generali* governing the Consumer Protection Law. With respect to financial services in particular, advancement has been made by the enactment of Law No 21/2011 concerning the Financial Services Authority, where one of the chapters regulates the protection of consumers of financial services businesses.

Finally, as an unprecedented regulation, Presidential Decree No 50/2017 concerning the National Strategy of Consumer Protection in Indonesia was adopted in order to synergise, harmonise and integrate the implementation of consumer protection in Indonesia.

A. History of Law No 8/1999 Concerning Consumer Protection

i. Asian Financial Crisis of 1997

The Asian financial crisis of the late 1990s hit the Indonesian economy hard. The Rupiah (IDR) crisis began in July and August 1997 and intensified in November 1997 when the effects of the Indonesian Rupiah devaluation policy showed up in corporate balance sheets. Before the Rupiah crisis, the exchange rate between the Rupiah and the US Dollar was roughly 2,600:1. The rate fell to over 11,000:1 on 9 January 1998, and over 14,000:1 during 23–26 January 1998. In June 2021, the rate was approximately 14,420:1.

Coming to the rescue in this crisis, the International Monetary Fund (IMF) stepped in on 29 July 1998 to initiate a USD 43 billion programme to stabilise the Indonesian economy.

ii. Law Concerning Consumer Protection as an IMF Requirement

In the 1970s, the Foundation of *Yayasan Lembaga Konsumen Indonesia* had actually drafted a Consumer Protection Bill, but this initiative did not receive a positive response

[4] Johannes Gunawan is the Chairman of the Drafting Team of the Indonesian Consumer Protection Bill.

from the Government, so the Bill was never actually submitted to Parliament. Suddenly, in October 1998, the Government submitted a Consumer Protection Bill to Parliament because it was one of four laws that had to be enacted by Indonesia as a condition for receiving aid from the IMF.

Considering that the monetary crisis in Indonesia was already acute, the process of passing the four laws, including the Consumer Protection Bill, was conducted in Parliament in a rapidly executed marathon. The Consumer Protection Bill was passed within six months, on 20 April 1999. Article 65 of the Consumer Protection Law stipulated that this law shall be enforced after one year, counting from the date of promulgation.

iii. Mistakes in Law No 8/1999

Due to the rapid legislative process behind the Consumer Protection Bill, it is not surprising that the Consumer Protection Law contained many kinds of mistakes, including mistakes in grammar and systematic mistakes in legal construction, as well as mistakes concerning consumer dispute settlement and consumer protection institutions.

One fundamental mistake is that the Consumer Protection Bill had been drawn up as a bill on consumer protection of goods, but when it was to be approved by Parliament, questions arose about consumer protection of services. Since the effort to overcome the urgent monetary crisis had to be implemented, a simple solution was adopted where each time the word 'goods' appeared, the phrase 'and/or services' was added. Having said this, the character of goods and services is very different, including differences in the forms of legal liability for goods and service providers.

In 2012, an initiative arose from the National Consumer Protection Agency to amend the Consumer Protection Law. According to the National Consumer Protection Agency, the above-mentioned mistakes should be amended, otherwise they would create difficulties in applying this particular Law.

B. Present Version

i. Structure

Judging from its title, one would think that the Consumer Protection Law is concerned with consumers, indeed some provisions expressly concern consumer rights.[5] But the reality is that it is dominated by provisions relating to business actors as the framework used in drafting the Consumer Protection Law is that this law protects consumers by regulating the behaviour of business actors.[6] The articles are grouped into 15 chapters: I: General Provision; II: Principle and Objectives; III: Rights and Obligations; IV: Prohibition Imposed on the Business Actors; V: Provisions on the Inclusion of Standard Clauses;

[5] Consumer Protection Law, Art 4 on the rights and obligations of the consumers.

[6] As mentioned above, the Consumer Protection Bill of this Consumer Protection Law is designed as a Consumer Protection Bill concerning goods. This is why this Law uses only the term 'business actor' and not 'service providers'.

VI: Obligation of Business Actors; VII: Coaching and Supervision; VIII: National Consumer Protection Agency; IX: Non-Governmental Consumer Protection Organisations; X: Dispute Settlement; XI: Consumer Dispute Settlement Agency; XII: Investigation; XIII: Sanctions; XIV: Transition Provision; XV: Concluding Provision.

ii. Scope

The scope of the Consumer Protection Law consists of goods and/or services. Goods are all objects, that is to say, both tangible and intangible, both movable and immovable, those that are consumable or inconsumable, and those that can be traded, used or utilised by consumers.[7] Services comprise every service in the form of work or achievement provided for the society to be utilised by consumers.[8]

a. Consumer

In addition, it should be stated that the term 'consumer' in the Consumer Protection Law represents every user of goods and/or services available in society, both for oneself, one's family, others and other living creatures, and not intended for trade.[9] The 'Person' in the definition consists of natural persons and legal entities who become a user of goods and/or services on the basis of a purchase agreement, an exchange, a lease, a grant, etc. The goods and/or services must be already available in society, meaning that the goods and/or services have been delivered to the market. The goods and/or services are used for personal, family, other people's interests or that of other living creatures, whereby 'not for trading' means that the consumers referred to in this law are end-users, excluding intermediate consumers.

b. Business Actor

Furthermore, the term 'business actor' in the Consumer Protection Law is any individual or business entity, whether in the form of a legal entity or not, established and domiciled or carrying out activities within the jurisdiction of the Republic of Indonesia, both individually and jointly through agreements organising business activities in various economic fields.[10]

'Business actor' is used for both goods and service providers because originally this law was merely designed to protect the consumer of goods. As a result, some professional service providers who do not aim to make a profit, but make a living (livelihood), for example medical doctors, are not willing to be subject to this law.

The phrase 'established and domiciled in the jurisdiction of the Republic of Indonesia' means that if a business actor establishes a business entity, said business entity must be established based on Indonesian law and domiciled in Indonesia.

[7] Consumer Protection Law, Art 1(4).
[8] ibid, Art 1(5).
[9] ibid, Art 1(2).
[10] ibid, Art 1(3).

'Or carrying out activities within the jurisdiction of the Republic of Indonesia' means that the intended business actor is not established and is not domiciled in Indonesia, but is conducting activities in Indonesia through export-import activities with Indonesian business actors using a distributorship contract or agency contract.

'Business activities in various economic fields' through the grammatical interpretation method means business activities for profit-making or for making a livelihood.

III. Unfair Contract Terms

Provisions on standard clauses (not standard contracts) are provided in Article 18 of the Consumer Protection Law:

Article 18

(1) Business actors in offering goods and/or services intended for trading are prohibited from making or including standard clauses on each document and/or agreement if:
  (a) it purports to transfer the liability of business actors;
  (b) it states that the business actor has the right to refuse to return the goods purchased by consumers;
  (c) it states that the business actor has the right to refuse to return the money paid for goods and/or services purchased by consumers;
  (d) it declares authorisation from consumers to business actors both directly and indirectly to carry out all unilateral actions relating to goods purchased by consumers in instalments;
  (e) it regulates proof of loss of use of goods or use of services purchased by consumers;
  (f) it grants business actors the right to reduce the benefits of services or reduce the assets of consumers who are the object of buying and selling services;
  (g) it declares that consumers are subject to regulations in the form of new, additional, advanced and/or continued changes made unilaterally by the business actor in the time the consumer utilises the services s/he bought;
  (h) it states that the consumer authorises the business actor for the imposition of mortgage rights, liens, or guarantee rights on goods purchased by consumers in instalments.

(2) Business actors are prohibited from including standard clauses whose location or form is difficult to see or cannot be read clearly, or whose disclosures are difficult to understand.
(3) Every standard clause that has been determined by a business actor on documents or agreements that meet the provisions referred to in paragraphs (1) and (2) is declared null and void.
(4) Business actors are obliged to adjust standard clauses that conflict with this law.

Each of the standard clauses mentioned above is an exoneration/exemption clause. The inclusion in standard contracts is prohibited because they have the potential to harm consumers. The sanctions for violating the prohibition of inclusion of the standard clauses are making the offending standard clause null and void. Further, Article 62 of the Consumer Protection Law regulates criminal sanctions for violating prohibitions concerning the inclusion of these kinds of standard clauses.

IV. Product Liability

The Consumer Protection Law features a product liability regime, as regulated in its Articles 19 and 28:

Article 19

(1) Business actors are responsible for providing compensation for damage, pollution and/or loss of consumers due to consuming goods and/or services produced or traded.
(2) Compensation as referred to in paragraph (1) can be in the form of refunds or replacement of goods and/or services of a similar or equivalent value, or health care and/or compensation in accordance with the provisions of the applicable laws and regulations.
(3) The compensation is given within seven days after the transaction date.
(4) Giving compensation as referred to in paragraph (1) and paragraph (2) does not eliminate the possibility of criminal prosecution based on further evidence regarding the existence of an element of fault or wrongdoing.
(5) The provisions referred to in paragraph (1) and paragraph (2) do not apply if the business actor can prove that the fault is the fault of the consumer.

Article 28

Proof of whether there is an element of fault in the claim for compensation as referred to in Articles 19, 22, and 23 is the burden of the business actors.

From Articles 19 and 28 above, it can be stated that the product liability regime in the Consumer Protection Law is based in tort law as regulated in Article 1365 of the Indonesian Civil Code (ICC), but the burden of proof of the element of fault is transferred to business actors as defendants to prove that they are innocent. Shifting the burden of proof for fault elements from plaintiffs (consumers) to defendants (business actors) is a derivation of tort law, often referred to as strict liability. This derivation is depicted below in Table 1.

Table 1 Product liability system

	Tortious Liability		**Product Liability**	
	Burden of proof		**Burden of proof**	
Element that must be proven	**Consumers (plaintiff)**	**Business actors (defendant)**	**Consumers (plaintiff)**	**Business actors (defendant)**
Unlawful act	+		+	
Fault	+			+
Loss	+		+	
Causal relationship between unlawful act and loss	+		+	

V. Access to Justice

A. Institutions

Based on the Consumer Protection Law, there are four institutions involved in the implementation of consumer protection in Indonesia.

i. National Consumer Protection Agency

The National Consumer Protection Agency, which is accountable to the President, has the function of providing advice and consideration to the government in efforts to develop consumer protection in Indonesia. Its members consist of the government, industry actors, non-governmental consumer protection organisations, scholars and various experts. To carry out its function, the Agency provides, inter alia, advice and recommendations to the government in the context of formulating policies in the field of consumer protection; conducts research and studies of the applicable laws and regulations in the field of consumer protection; encourages the development of non-governmental consumer protection organisations; and receives complaints concerning consumer protection from the general public, non-governmental consumer protection organisations or business actors.

ii. Consumer Dispute Settlement Agency

Consumer dispute settlement can be reached in in-court or out-of-court settlements based on the voluntary choice of the parties to the dispute.

Out-of-court consumer dispute settlements are carried out through mediation, conciliation or arbitration to reach an agreement regarding the form and amount of compensation and/or regarding certain actions to guarantee that the loss suffered by the consumer will not recur in the future.

iii. Courts

In court, consumer dispute settlements are carried out in accordance with provisions governing the general courts, based on Indonesian Civil Procedure Law.

iv. Non-Governmental Consumer Protection Organisations (NGOs in Consumer Protection)

The government recognises NGOs in Consumer Protection that meet certain requirements so that they have the opportunity to play an active role in realising consumer protection. NGOs in Consumer Protection have the legal standing to sue business actors before the general court. The tasks of NGOs in Consumer Protection include, inter alia, the dissemination of information to increase awareness of the rights and obligations and caution of consumers in consuming goods and/or services, advising and assisting consumers, including receiving consumer complaints; and conducting joint supervision by the government and the public on the implementation of consumer protection.

B. Sanctions

The Consumer Protection Law regulates three types of sanctions. Civil sanctions are in the form of annulling and voiding standard clauses; compensation in the form of refunds or replacement of goods and/or services of a similar or equivalent value; or health care and/or compensation in accordance with the provisions of the applicable laws and regulations.

The Consumer Dispute Settlement Agency has the authority to impose administrative sanctions on business actors violating certain articles in the form of determining compensation at a maximum of IDR 200 million (approximately USD 14,000).

Business actors who violate the provisions of certain articles are sentenced to imprisonment of between two to five years or a fine of between IDR 500 million approximately USD 35,000) up to a maximum of IDR 2 billion (approximately USD 140,000). For violations that result in serious injury, serious illness, permanent disability or death, applicable general criminal provisions apply, that is, additional punishment may be imposed in the form of, for example, confiscation of certain goods, injunctions, compensation, withdrawal of goods from circulation or revocation of business licences.

C. In-Court and Out-Of-Court Consumer Dispute Settlement

Article 45 of the Consumer Protection Law regulates the settlement of civil disputes between consumers and business actors, namely through institutions tasked with resolving these civil disputes, or through courts within the General Court.

Based on Article 49 of the Consumer Protection Law, the institution tasked with resolving disputes between consumers and business actors referred to in Article 45 of the Consumer Protection Law is the Consumer Dispute Settlement Agency. Consumers who feel disadvantaged by business actors can therefore sue through the General Court or the Consumer Dispute Settlement Agency based on the agreement between the disputing parties.

i. In-Court Consumer Dispute Settlement

a. Structure

The powers of the Judiciary in Indonesia are exercised by the Supreme Court and the judicial bodies below it, that is, the general courts, religious courts, state administrative courts, the military court and the Constitutional Court. See Table 2. General courts and religious courts have jurisdiction to resolve consumer disputes.

Table 2 Structure of the judiciary

Supreme Court				**Constitutional Court**
General Court	**Religious Court**	**State Administrative Court**	**Military Court**	
High Court	Religious High Court	State Administrative High Court	Military High Court	
District Court	Religious District Court	State Administrative District Court	Military Court	

In principle, all disputes in civil and/or criminal contexts can be resolved through the courts of general jurisdiction, unless the law specifically regulates otherwise. Thus, consumer disputes, which can be related to civil and/or criminal aspects, can be resolved through general courts, namely district courts, high courts and the Supreme Court.

The General Court will examine, decide and settle disputes in the civil and/or criminal fields in general except for the settlement of cases specifically regulated by other laws. Specific laws in question include resolving disputes in the field of Sharia Economics, for example Law No 3/2006 concerning the Amendment to Law No 7/1989 concerning Religious Courts governing the authority of the Religious Courts. See Table 3.

Table 3 Authority of District Court versus Authority of the Religious Court

Authority of the District Court	Authority of the Religious Court
Examine, decide and resolve civil and criminal cases in general. Cases concerning consumer protection can be related to civil and/or criminal aspects. As a consequence, the district court has the authority to settle consumer disputes.	Examine, decide, and resolve cases at the first level among Muslims in the areas of: a) Marriage b) Inheritance c) Testament d) Grant e) *Zakat* (alms-giving as a religious obligation) f) *Infaq* (disbursement to please God) g) *Shadaqah* (voluntary charity/donation) h) Sharia Economics

b. Requirements

In the process of resolving consumer disputes through the courts, there are a number of important matters that need to be discussed before a lawsuit is heard in court, namely:

Basis

In principle, the basis for filing a lawsuit is dependent on the legal relationship that underlies the relationship of the parties to the dispute, unless the legislation has been set up specifically in a different manner.

If the basis of the relationship between the parties is the agreement and achievement that must be measured, then the basis of the lawsuit is in default of the agreement. If the basis of the relationship between the parties is the law, then the basis of the lawsuit is an unlawful act. Over time, the Consumer Protection Law has begun to adhere to strict liability, causing a shift in the burden of proof.

Parties

In a consumer dispute, there are at least two parties, that is, the plaintiff who filed the lawsuit, and the defendant(s) who feel that their rights have been violated. The plaintiff is principally an interested legal subject (individual or entity).

The person of interest as plaintiff has the right to act as a party in court, either material or formal (*legitima persona standi in judicio*). As a material party, it means that the plaintiff has a direct interest in the dispute concerned, and at the same time is a formal party, which means the plaintiff attends court proceedings.

People can also act as plaintiffs in court based on agreements, for example a lawsuit filed by a power of attorney based on a power of attorney agreement, or the person acting in that court because of the law, for example a guardian or person who acts as a party before a court of law in his own name but for the benefit of the person he represents.

Legal entities that are parties to a dispute in court are represented by their management. The legal entity is regarded as a material party, but because it is not possible to conduct their own case, the management will act on behalf of the legal entity.

Judge's Authority

In civil procedures, authority can be distinguished between absolute and relative authority.

Absolute Authority

To find out the type of judicial body, it can be discerned in the provisions of Article 18 of Law No 48/2009 concerning judicial authority, which divides up the four judicial bodies. For example, a case regarding a lawsuit on Sharia banking falls under the authority of the Religious Court.

As for the settlement of disputes, where the parties have previously chosen the resolution of the dispute through arbitration, the District Court has absolutely no authority. The District Court's authority over so-called absolute authority, namely the authority of the judiciary views of their kind in the courts, examines certain types of cases that cannot be examined by another court.

Relative Authority

Relative authority concerns the distribution of judicial authority, that is, the distribution of powers to adjudicate between similar courts, which are dependent on the jurisdiction of a court. Relative authority is regulated in Article 118 of the Revised Indonesian Regulations,[11] which contains the principle that the court authorised to adjudicate a dispute is the District Court in the jurisdiction where the defendant lives. This is called the principle of *actor sequitur forum rei*. There is an exception, namely the principle of *sequi rei forum sequitur actor* if the lawsuit is filed in the District Court in the Plaintiff's jurisdiction, for instance, the plaintiffs are minors, underprivileged persons, civil servants or workers who live in the employer's house.

ii. Out-of-court Consumer Dispute Settlement

Based on Article 49(1) of the Consumer Protection Law, the government should form a Consumer Dispute Settlement Agency in the cities and districts for the resolution of consumer disputes outside the court system. In Indonesia, there are 514 cities and

[11] *Het Herziene Indonesische Reglement*; HIR.

districts, but there are only 171 Agency branches that have been established, and only 120 of these are currently functional.

As noted above, Consumer Dispute Settlement Agency members consist of government members, consumers and business actors, who are appointed and dismissed by the Minister in charge. In carrying out its duties, the Agency is assisted by a Secretariat, whose appointments and dismissals are carried out by the Minister.

As the implementing regulations of the Consumer Protection Law, on 10 December 2001, Decree of the Minister of Industry and Trade No 350/MPP/Kep/12/2001 concerning Implementation of Duties and Powers of the Agency was issued.

One of the tasks of the Agency is to settle consumer disputes by means of mediation, arbitration or conciliation based on the agreement of the parties.

According to the provisions of Article 46(1) in conjunction with Article 46(2) of the Consumer Protection Law, a consumer dispute that can be resolved through the Consumer Dispute Settlement Agency is a consumer dispute in the form of a claim for violation of business actors, by disadvantaged consumers or where the consumer's heirs are concerned.

Settlement by the Consumer Dispute Settlement Agency tended to reach an agreement on the form and amount of compensation, and/or regarding certain actions to guarantee that the loss would not recur. In practice, it is possible that business actors do not agree that disputes that arise should be resolved through the Agency. In such cases, the consumer as the injured party will inevitably have to submit their case through the District Court. It will hamper non-litigation consumer dispute resolution through the Agency, even though the intention of establishing the Agency is precisely to resolve consumer disputes simply and quickly at a low cost.

Article 45(2) of the Consumer Protection Law states that settlement of consumer disputes can be reached through the court or outside the court based on the voluntary choice of the parties to the dispute.

If the disputing parties have agreed to settle a dispute arising out of court through the Consumer Dispute Settlement Agency, the parties still have to choose the way to resolve the dispute, whether by conciliation, mediation or arbitration.

Settlement of consumer disputes is carried out by means of conciliation and mediation, in the form of an agreement as outlined in a written agreement signed by the parties to the dispute and strengthened in a decision by the Agency. Meanwhile, the settlement of consumer disputes by arbitration will be examined and decided by the arbitrators who also contribute to the Agency's decision. Settlement of these disputes must be resolved no later than 21 working days from the time the request is received by the Secretariat to the Consumer Dispute Settlement Agency.

Article 7 of the Decree of the Minister of Industry and Trade No 350/MPP/Kep/12/2001 states, with regard to consumer dispute decisions through either conciliation, mediation or arbitration, that the parties to the dispute can submit an objection to the District Court no later than 14 working days, counted from the notice of the decision of the Agency received by the disputing party.

In order for the Agency's decision to have the power of execution, its execution must be requested at the District Court in the residence of the injured consumer according to Article 57 of Consumer Protection Law in conjunction with Article 42(2) of the Decree of the Minister of Industry and Trade No 350/MPP/Kep/12/2001. The cost of requesting fiat executions that must be borne by consumers is often not proportional to the actual losses incurred.

VI. Consumer Protection Bill

A. Need For Amendment

Since the draft of the Consumer Protection Law was prepared in a great hurry, namely within six months, it is not surprising that various mistakes were made.[12] The first fundamental mistake was that the draft of this Consumer Protection Law was prepared for consumer protection of goods, but in the final stages of discussion, the phrase 'and/or services' was added each time the word 'goods' appeared. As a result, the liability of business actors which can be based on tort liability (in case of there being no direct relationship between business actors and consumers) or the contractual liability (in case of there being a direct relationship between business actors and consumers), also applies to the liability of service providers, almost all of which should be based on contractual liability, except that there are no measured rights and duties provided in the contract. In the latter case, liability of service providers should be based on tort liability even though there is a contract.

B. Fundamental Changes

To overcome the above-mentioned mistakes, the amendment[13] of the Consumer Protection Law includes some fundamental changes, including regulations concerning the use of electronic agreements (e-contracts or digital contracts) that have not been regulated in the Consumer Protection Law as well as changes to the consumer dispute settlement structure. Due to the vast scope of the changes, it is only possible here to refer to a select few.

i. Consumer

The definitions of 'consumers' and 'end consumers' are clarified, so that they do not lead to various interpretations in their enforcement. The consumer is the end consumer who is an individual or entity, whether in the form of a legal entity or not, who uses goods and/or utilises services with the aim of not being traded again or not being an element in producing goods and/or producing other services.

[12] See above at s II.A.iii.
[13] One of the authors of this chapter (Johannes Gunawan) is the Chairperson of the Amendment Team in charge of the Consumer Protection Law. The team has been working since 2017, and a new Consumer Protection Bill will be discussed in the House of Representatives in 2021.

ii. Business Actors

A clear distinction is drawn between 'business actors' and 'service providers', so there is no reluctance of professional service providers including doctors, lecturers and notaries to be bound by the new laws.

Goods Business Actors are individuals or business entities, both in the form of legal entities or non-legal entities that are established and domiciled or conducting activities offline or online within the territory of the Republic of Indonesia both alone and together through agreements, organising business activities aimed at producing, importing and/or trade in goods.

Service Providers are individuals or business entities, both in the form of a legal entity or not, established and domiciled or conducting activities offline or online within the territory of the Republic of Indonesia, both alone and together through agreements, organising service activities aimed at producing and/or providing services.

iii. Classification of Goods and Services

The classification and the nature of 'goods' and 'services' is to be clarified so as to provide legal certainty in the regulation of liability (see Table 4). Goods are tangible or intangible objects, moveable immoveable, consumable or inconsumable, and that have been put into circulation; services are commercial or professional services in the form of work or achievements that have been put into circulation.

Table 4 Definition of goods

<table>
<tr><td rowspan="4">Goods</td><td rowspan="3">Tangible</td><td rowspan="2">Moveable</td><td>Consumable</td></tr>
<tr><td>Inconsumable</td></tr>
<tr><td>Immoveable</td><td></td></tr>
<tr><td>Intangible</td><td></td><td></td></tr>
</table>

iv. Scope of Liability

Contractual liability is used for goods business actors that have a direct relationship with consumers, whereas those that do not have a direct relationship use product liability based on strict liability.

Contractual liability is used for service providers who generally have a direct relationship with consumers if their performance is measured, whereas strict liability is used for service providers whose performance is not measurable, among others medical doctors and lawyers.

v. Standard Contracts and Terms

As the Consumer Protection Law only regulates standard clauses, it is necessary to clarify the notions of 'standard contracts' and 'standard clauses' and regulate the legal consequences of using standard contracts and standard clauses.

Goods business actors and/or service providers are prohibited from making and using standard contracts that contain standard clauses concerning:

(1) transfer of obligations of goods business actors and/or service providers to consumers;
(2) the right of the goods business actors to refuse the return of the goods purchased by the consumers;
(3) the right of the goods business actors and/or the service providers to refuse the return of money paid for the goods used and/or the services utilised by the consumer;
(4) granting authority from consumers to goods business actors and/or service providers, both directly and indirectly, to carry out all unilateral actions of goods purchased and/or services utilised by consumers in instalments;
(5) proof of the loss of usefulness of the goods or benefits of the services purchased by the consumer;
(6) the right of the goods business actors and/or the service providers to reduce the usefulness of the goods and the benefits of the services or reduce the consumer assets that are the object of the transaction;
(7) subject consumers to new, additional, advanced and/or amended rules made unilaterally by the goods business actors and/or service providers during the period the consumer uses the goods or utilises the services s/he obtained;
(8) granting consumer authority to the goods business actors for the imposition of mortgage rights, liens, or fiduciary rights over the goods purchased by the consumer at the cost of a third party;
(9) regulations that goods business actors and/or service providers are only bound to the standard clauses stated in the standard contracts;
(10) regulations that goods business actors are not liable for consumer losses caused by the actions of legal subjects under their responsibility; and/or
(11) establishment of a dispute settlement forum other than the forum residing in the consumer's domicile.

In addition, goods business actors and/or service providers are prohibited from making and using standard contracts that contain standard clauses which:

(1) are placed in a position that is difficult to be seen;
(2) contain the standard clauses whose size and shape of letters cannot be read clearly; and
(3) contain the standard clauses in Indonesian (*Bahasa Indonesia*) with terms and phrases that are difficult to understand.

The standard contract which contains the standard clause as referred to above is null and void. Cancellation of the standard contract is submitted by the consumer to the court or the Consumer Dispute Settlement Agency. Cancellation of the standard contract can be accompanied by civil sanctions, namely:

(1) return of money equivalent to the value of the goods and/or services or replacement of goods of similar or equivalent value accompanied by costs, losses and/or interest; and/or
(2) health care and/or compensation of permanent disability/death in accordance with the statutory provisions.

The standard contract model for each line of business is determined by the Central Government after coordinating with:

(1) The Association of Goods Business Actors and/or Service Providers in a related line of business; and
(2) The Association of Consumer of Goods and/or Services in a related line of business.

The standard contract model established by the Central Government must be used in the standard contract drawn up by the goods business actors and/or the service providers in accordance with the statutory provisions.

Goods business actors and/or service providers who use the standard contract must provide an explanation and opportunity for the consumer to understand the contents of the standard contract before the consumer closes the standard contract (it is usually called the 'free look'). Goods business actors and/or service providers who violate this provision are subject to administrative sanctions in the form of administrative fines, temporary suspension of business activities and/or revocation of licences.

C. Liabilities Of Goods Business Actors and Liabilities of Service Providers

In the amendment to the Consumer Protection Law, there is a separation between the liabilities of goods business actors and the liabilities of service providers, because between the two there are fundamental legal liability differences.

i. Tort Liability

The liability of goods business actors that do not have a direct relationship between consumers and goods business actors (producers, distributors, sub-distributors and wholesalers) is to be regulated. This liability is called product liability, which uses strict liability.

The legal construction of strict liability in product liability is as follows. Firstly, when an event is detrimental to a consumer of goods, the goods business actor is directly presumed guilty. Secondly, according to Article 1865 of the Indonesian (Dutch) Civil Code, consumers in the dispute settlement process (in-court or out-of-court) bear the burden of proof, for which (in tort liability), there are four elements that must be proven, namely that the goods business actor has carried out an unlawful act, mistakes have been made by the goods business actor, and causation giving rise to the loss suffered by the consumer. It should be noted that out of the four elements that must be proven by consumers, the heaviest burden of proof is to prove the mistakes of goods business actors.

As a derivation of tort liability, the strict liability that is used in product liability adheres to the presumption of fault, that is to say, the business actor of goods is considered guilty when events that harm the consumer occur. In the process of dispute settlement, the goods business actor must postulate and prove innocence. Thus, there is a shifting of the burden of proof of the fault element from the consumer to the goods business actor.

With the legal construction above, there is a concern shown for the interests of consumers of goods, that is, proof of the element of fault of the goods business actor is not a burden on consumers of goods.

The responsibility of professional service providers who have a direct relationship with service consumers, along with unmeasured rights and obligations (for example between doctors and patients as consumers where doctors cannot promise healing), cannot be based on contractual liability. The reason is that there is a contract between the doctor and the patient, but the rights and obligations in the contract, especially the doctor's obligation cannot be measured, so the requirements to sue based on the breach of contract are not fulfilled. In these cases, doctors must be sued based on the derivation of tort liability, that is, strict liability in professional liability. The legal construction of professional liability is mutatis mutandis identical to product liability as stated above.

ii. Contractual Liability

First, it must be stated that in the civil law system, at least in Indonesia, there are two conditions that must be met by consumers of harmed goods and/or services who will sue based on the breach of contract through the process of resolving consumer disputes (in-court or out-of-court), that is, there are contracts, both written and unwritten; and the achievements (rights and obligations) of the parties to the contract can be measured.

Second, the liabilities of goods business actors who have a direct relationship with consumers of goods, along with measurable rights and obligations to each party (for example between retailers of goods and consumers of goods, or between producers of goods that sell them directly to consumers of goods), are based on contractual liability. This means that when consumers of goods are harmed, then goods business actors will be sued through a consumer dispute settlement process (in-court or out-of-court) based on the breach of contract.

Third, the liabilities of commercial service providers who have a direct relationship with service consumers, along with measurable rights and obligations (for example between a bank and a customer as a consumer where the bank can promise the amount of deposit interest), can be based on contractual liability. The reason is that there is a contract between the bank and the consumer and the rights and obligations in the contract (especially the bank's obligations) can be measured, so the requirements to sue based on the breach of contract are fulfilled. In cases like this, banks must be sued through the process of resolving consumer disputes (in-court or out-of-court) based on breach of contract.

It should be noted that there are professional service providers whose performance (rights and obligations) can be measured, for example services from architects, accountants or civil engineers, so that in the event that consumers are harmed, professional service providers are responsible based on contractual liability. Therefore, the settlement of consumer disputes will be carried out through the process of resolving consumer disputes (in-court or out-of-court) based on breach of contract, because it has fulfilled both conditions as stated above.

The overall legal structure of Liabilities of Goods Business Actors and Liabilities of Service Providers is as follows in Table 5.

Table 5 Liability of goods business actors/service providers

	Goods Business Actors			**Service Providers**	
	Contract with consumer			**Contract with consumer**	
Liability based on	**Measured rights and duties**	**Unmeasured rights and duties**	**No contract with consumer**	**Measured rights and duties**	**Unmeasured rights and duties**
Tort liability derived as strict liability		+	+		+
Contractual liability	+			+	

VII. Consumer Protection in the Digital Era

The regulation of consumer protection in the digital era in Indonesia has not yet extensively developed, so amendments to the Consumer Protection Law need adequate attention.

Changes in the mode of business transactions involve changing patterns of attitude from Indonesian Customary Law to laws that are able to enter into international relations. As we know, Indonesian Customary Law has the characteristics of cash and *religio magis*. The characteristic of cash as hard currency means that changes in attitude require relatively long periods of time, caution and tenacity. This attitude will form a new business ethic in the business world in Indonesia, which in turn requires a mode of consumer protection that is consistent with these changes. Due to the fact that digital transactions are increasingly widespread nationally, it becomes more important to create a legal basis in the Amendment instead of merely adhering to Central Bank Regulations to protect consumers' rights as well as those of business enterprises.

In the field of financial services, the UNCTAD Report[14] 'Voluntary Peer Review of Consumer Protection Law and Policy in Indonesia' states that efforts from the business community have been noted in the financial services sector. As many as 43 business members of the Indonesian FinTech Association (AFTECH) signed the Code of Conduct of Responsible Lending (LPMUBTI) in August 2018. The Code of Conduct is drafted by FinTech Association's working group on financial inclusion and was agreed upon voluntarily by its members providing online loans to consumers in Indonesia.

[14] UNCTAD, 'Voluntary Peer Review of Consumer Protection Law and Policy in Indonesia' (2019), 20.

VIII. Misleading Advertising and Unfair Commercial Practices

Article 10 of the Consumer Protection Law states that in offering the goods and/or services for trading, business actors are prohibited from offering, promoting, advertising or providing incorrect or misleading statements regarding the price or rate of a certain goods and/or services, the use of the goods and/or services, the condition, warranty, guarantee, rights or compensation on certain goods and/or services, the discount or attractive prizes offered, and the danger of using the goods and/or services.

In addition, Article 7 of the Consumer Protection Law stipulates that business actors are obliged to, among other things, act in good faith in conducting the business; provide correct, clear end honest information with regard to the condition and warranty of the goods and/or services and provide explanation on the use, repair and maintenance; treats or serves consumers properly and honestly and is not discriminatory; guarantee the goods and/or services produced and/or traded based on the prevailing quality standard provisions of the goods and/or services.

6

Japan

HISAKAZU HIROSE, KARL-FRIEDRICH LENZ AND TADASHI SHIRAISHI*

I. Structure of Japanese Consumer Law

Statutes or legal institutions with a title that specifically refers to the 'consumer'[1] appeared in Japan during the 1960s. Since then, a fairly unified, cross-sectional system of 'consumer law', covering both private law and public law, seems to have been constructed.[2] Firstly, the underlying governmental policy is provided by the Basic Act on Consumer Policies (2004).[3] The two main issues, consumer contracts and products

* Hisakazu Hirose (Sections I to VI, IX) – I would like to express my thanks to Simon Vande Walle and Yoshihisa Nomi for their constructive comments on my earlier draft. Karl-Friedrich Lenz largely wrote Section VII, and Tadashi Shiraishi Section VIII.

[1] The legal concept of 'consumer' has been converging on 'an individual (natural person) not engaging in business'. A corporations, an association or an individual engaging in business, etc., are 'enterprises' (Consumer Safety Act 2009, Art 2(1). The Consumer Contract Act 2000 contains a similar definition in its Art 2(1)). The term 'business' includes non-profit activities. However, this has not been carried through in case of consumer law in the substantial meaning. The fundamentals of consumer law are discussed in A Omura, *Shouhishahou* [*Consumer Law*] 4th edn (Tokyo: Yuhikaku, 2011). One element of his thesis (distinction between an 'individual interest' of a specific consumer ('micro' consumer law) and a 'general interest' of the public ('macro' consumer law) has received support from H Sono, 'Private Enforcement of Consumer Law' (2012) 16 *Hokkaido Journal of New Global Law and Policy* 63–80. Further discussions on 'consumers' from the enlarged viewpoints including market, government and society would also be fruitful. Ss V.B.ii, iii and V.C below are connected to this problem.

[2] Based on the infrastructural change after the World War II with the Constitution of 1946 and the State Redress Act of 1947 (below, at s V.B.iii) toward the popular sovereignty with the emphasis on individual dignity, freedom and equality, the development has unfolded as follows. From the 1960s to the early 1980s, pollutions and products accidents accompanied industrial recovery. Ministries started to enforce regulative measures based on the notion of consumers as an object of governmental support (eg Consumer Protection Fundamental Act 1968 or Consumer Product Safety Act 1973). From the mid-1980s to the turn of the century, trade conflict with the United States, market globalisation and end of Japan's economic bubble caused a policy shift towards emphasising deregulation and privatisation, and in the area of consumer law to view the consumer as an independent market-player (eg Consumer Contract Act 2000 and Basic Act on Consumer Policies 2004). From 2009, the new re-regulative movement towards a more comprehensive system of consumer protection has started with the establishment of the tripartite governmental organs. Their efforts to face actual problems directly and to extend consideration for vulnerable consumers, in terms of their age, has become fruitful (see ss II.A.ii.a–d, IX.B.ii). A Osawa, 'La mise en oeuvre et l'effectivité du droit de la consommation au Japon' in H-W Micklitz and G Saumier (eds), *Enforcement and Effectiveness of Consumer Law* (Cham: Springer, 2018) 371–89 is an informative survey.

[3] Act No 78 of 1968 (reformed from Consumer Protection Fundamental Act 1968). Article 2(1) provides that 'the consideration of the *disparity in the quality and quantity of information and negotiating power* between

(and services) safety, are dealt with respectively by the Consumer Contract Act (2000)[4] and the Consumer Safety Act (2009) as well as various product-related Acts and regulations (for example the Consumer Product Safety Act (1973)).[5] From the procedural perspective, not only the special litigation systems conducted by specified and qualified consumer organisations (so-called 'Japanese class action') but ADR or consultation activities have been gradually institutionalised.[6] With regard to administrative organs, since 2009, the tripartite cooperation[7] of Consumer Affairs Agency,[8] Consumer Commission[9] and National Consumer Affairs Center[10] has taken an initiative to collaborate with other concerned Ministries, Agencies and local consumer institutions.

However, these are only part of the larger group of Japanese laws which substantially concern consumers: ever since the introduction of western, modernised legal systems by the Meiji government in the late nineteenth century,[11] consumers have been protected, for example in the private law field, by the Civil Code,[12] the Commercial Code[13] or other statutes,[14] and by case law developments. However, these protections have applied to such individuals in their capacity as 'a person', 'a lessee', 'a customer', etc.[15] A similar phenomenon is observable in the public law area. This implies that consumer laws in the substantial meaning had not only existed long before the emergence of the formal 'consumer law' noted above, but that they continue to be applicable to cases not covered by the formal 'consumer law'. In this respect, among many others, the recent enactment of the largely reformed Civil Code of 2017 (hereinafter: Civil Code), which took effect in 2020, deserves special attention.[16] This chapter strives to cover both formal and substantial consumer laws.

consumers and enterprises' is the basis of the legislation (emphasis added). The same consideration had been already featured in the Consumer Contract Act 2000, Art 1. English translations of these Acts are provided by the Japanese Law Translation Database System: www.japaneselawtranslation.go.jp.

[4] Act No 61 of 2000. See below at ss II–IV, IX.

[5] See below at s VI.

[6] See below at s IX.

[7] For details see www.cao.go.jp/consumer/en/e-index.html.

[8] An external bureau of the Cabinet Office founded by the Act for Establishment of the Consumer Affairs Agency and Consumer Commission (Act No 48 of 2009). See the Agency's survey report on its first 10 years: www.caa.go.jp/en/publication/annual_report/2019/white_paper_summary_09.html.

[9] An independent, third-party organisation in the Cabinet Office, monitoring the consumer administration generally and offering recommendations and opinions to the Prime Minister and the relevant government Ministries.

[10] Originally established in 1970, newly founded in 2003 by the Act on National Consumer Affairs Center of Japan (Act No 123 of 2002). See www.kokusen.go.jp/ncac_index_e.html and below, at s IX.

[11] The Meiji government (1868–1912) made much effort to absorb western legal systems with the intention of revising the unequal treaties the previous shogunate government had been forced to conclude. For the historical background, see H Oda, *Japanese Law* 4th edn (Oxford: Oxford University Press, 2021) 4–5, 11–18.

[12] With the exception of the parts on family law and inheritance law, the original Civil Code (Act No 89 of 1896), had mostly survived until 2020, when the largely amended Civil Code promulgated in 2017 came into effect.

[13] Act No 48 of 1899. Its Arts 596–98 provide a responsibility of inn keepers, etc for the loss of the customer's belongings.

[14] eg Interest Rate Restriction Act (Dajyôkan-Fukoku No 66187 of 1877) providing the maximum limit of interest rates per annum. See below at s IV.C and n 89.

[15] For a recent overview in French, P Bloch et al (eds), *Droit japonais des affaires* (Brussels: Lacier, 2019).

[16] See below, at ss II–IV.

II. Information Duties and Right of Withdrawal

A. Information Duties Regulated under Private Law

The Civil Code adopts the basic principle of private autonomy with the idea of self-responsibility,[17] and thus does not provide a general contractual 'duty to inform'.[18] However, in the field of consumer law, both the Basic Act on Consumer Policies of 2004 and the Consumer Contract Act of 2001 prescribe a duty for enterprises to provide consumers with necessary information.[19] Nonetheless, the nature of the Basic Act is to declare governmental policy guidelines (so-called 'program provisions') and Article 3(1) of the Consumer Contract Act obliges an enterprise only to 'make an effort' to provide plain and clear information regarding the contents of the consumer contracts.[20] These provisions therefore usually do not have direct, specific legal effect, though the provision of the Consumer Contract Act seems to have assisted judges in deciding cases (for example on damages liability) or consumer consultants solving problems.[21]

At the same time, we should not overlook that courts and the legislature have developed at least two types of measures for a 'customer' (including a consumer) to face these information problems: entitling a customer to claim damages and allowing the customer to rescind the contract or withdraw therefrom.

i. Damages

Courts have often used the principle of good faith under the Civil Code[22] to affirm the damages liability of an enterprise for infringements of pre-contractual information duties against the customer. As the Supreme Court has recognised the nature of this liability as tortious,[23] the claimant (that is, the customer) must prove, inter alia, negligence[24] by the defendant (that is, the enterprise), causation and the amount of loss.[25] The main areas affirmed by the courts have been real estate transactions,

[17] Civil Code, Art 521.

[18] For a comparison to French law, though partly outdated, M Maeda, 'Les contrats du consommateur au Japon', in Association Henri Capitant (ed), *Le consommateur* (Paris: Bruylant 2007) 151–58. For a more recent survey, K Nakata, 'Die Modernisierung des Rechts der Willenserklärungen in Japan' (2019) 47 *Zeitschrift für japanisches Recht* 247; M Nozawa, 'L'information et la désinformation des consommateurs: Papport Japonais' in G Straetmans (ed), *Information Obligations and Disinformation of Consumers* (Cham: Springer, 2019) 447–56.

[19] Basic Act on Consumer Policies of 2004, Art 5(1)(ii); Consumer Contract Act of 2001, Art 3(1).

[20] The Consumer Contract Act recommends enterprises to 'make an effort' to provide pre-contractual, plain and clear information regarding the contents of consumer contracts, considering the knowledge and experience of each consumers (Art 3(1)).

[21] In contrast to these private law measures, public law (regulative) measures intervene more directly into the consumer transactions on which we will see in ss II.B and VI.A.

[22] See Civil Code, Art 1(2).

[23] Supreme Court judgment of 22 April 2011, Minshu 65, 3, 1405. Theoretical overview by K Yamamoto, 'Basic Question of Tort Law from a Japanese Perspective' in H Koziol (ed), *Basic Questions of Tort Law from a Comparative Perspective* (Vienna: Jan Sramek Verlag, 2015) 559–62.

[24] In this report, the word 'negligence' is mainly used for tortious liability and 'fault' for contractual liability.

[25] Civil Code, Art 709. The prescription period is three years (five years for personal injury) from the time the victim comes to know of the damage and of the identity of the perpetrator (or 20 years from the time of the tortious act). Civil Code, Arts 724 and 724-2.

financial transactions, insurance contracts, franchise agreements and medical malpractices cases, where the enterprise possesses structural superiority regarding information, knowledge, experience and information processing ability over the customer. In cases where the defendant is a trusted specialist (for example a lawyer, a doctor or a specialist in the securities market), courts not only affirm the duty to inform but may further accept that the specialist should positively give advice and/or warning to the customer. Moreover, in case of a risky speculative market, the Supreme Court acknowledged the possibility of adopting a 'suitability rule' so that a stockbroker was obliged to carefully propose a product which is suitable to the individual customer, or to refuse to solicit in an unsuitable situation.[26]

In 2000, this case law development gave birth to the 'Act on Sales, etc. of Financial Instruments',[27] which contains a pre-contractual information duty with special damages sanctions, protecting in particular non-professional customers. The targeted products broadly cover securities, insurance, and derivatives, as well as bank deposits and savings. The Act provides for a special tort liability with the distinguishing features of: non-negligent characteristics, presumption of the causal relationship and presumption of the amount of loss, all of which, compared to the aforementioned general tort law, supports the claimant by making it easier to claim damages and facilitates the rapid resolution of the financial market conflict. This Act, originally of private law character, plays a role as one of the important counterparts of administrative regulations.[28]

ii. Rescission and Withdrawal

The second measure focuses on the manifestation of contractual intention by the customer to whom the imprecise or false information was provided and allows for rescission or withdrawal from the contract. There are three levels of provisions, which range from the general to the specific: Civil Code, Consumer Contract Act and more specific statutes. In this section, we shall treat the right to withdraw – as a 'cooling off' right – separately.

a. Civil Code

The Civil Code has rules on mistake,[29] fraud and duress[30] which entitle a customer to make the contract voidable. However, because of the difficulties the customer

[26] Supreme Court judgment of 14 July 2005, Minshu 59, 6, 1323. The question arises as to the relationship between this severe liability to the 'warning defect' of product liability, see below at s V.

[27] Act No 101 of 2000.

[28] See s II.B.

[29] Civil Code, Art 95. The Civil Code largely amended the law on mistake, reflecting the case law development. For example, its effect has become 'voidable' (from 'void') and its conditions are more explicit. In case of 'motivation mistake' ie when the mistake derives from the untrue perception on the basic circumstances of the contract, the fact that such circumstances were the basis of the contract must have been *indicated* at the transaction (Art 95(2)). The mistake must be *material* (Art 95(1)), and the mistake must *not* be made by the declarant's *gross negligence*, unless the other party knew (or did not know with gross negligence) or was under the same mistake (Art 95(3)). See more in detail, Nakata, 'Die Modernisierung', 251–57.

[30] Civil Code, Art 96. Fraud and duress, as traditional causes of rescission, have mostly remained unchanged in the Civil Code. Both may also be subject to criminal sanctions (Penal Code, Arts 246, 246-2, 248–50).

usually faces,[31] these provisions are not so helpful, except for their longer prescription periods.[32]

b. Consumer Contract Act

As to the second level, the Consumer Contract Act,[33] which applies to almost all types of contracts between an enterprise and a consumer, has introduced a refined version of rescission rules in seeking to respond to actual consumer complaints.[34]

In the area of fraud, the Act picked up three 'misleading' types of conduct: 'misrepresentation' as to the material information,[35] 'affirmation of conclusive evaluation' of uncertain items subject to future change[36] and representation of only advantageous facts while intentionally or with gross negligence omitting disadvantageous facts.[37]

Second, adding to the Act's original two types of 'overwhelming' duress by the enterprises (that is, detainment and confinement),[38] six new types of their coercive and fraudulent solicitations were included in 2018, among which are information-related cases[39] such as prompting fears of the consumer and conveying that the goods, rights or services are necessary to fulfil their aspirations, although there is no reasonable grounds or rational basis;[40] causing anxiety about their breaking of falsely enchanted romantic relationships with the salesman/woman;[41] exploiting uneasiness of the aged or disadvantaged consumers about maintaining their current life;[42] or unreasonable indication of the future suffering of a serious incident which, according to the enterprises, could be avoided by their services.[43]

In 2016, the Act introduced a special case of 'excessive provision' where the enterprise knowingly supplies the object of the contract in a quantity that grossly exceeds what would normally be required by that consumer.[44]

[31] Especially in case of fraud or duress, a client is obliged to prove the other party's (enterprise) intention to deceive or coerce the client, which is difficult to establish. Mistake has been more frequently invoked by clients, however, with various hurdles, as outlined above in n 29.

[32] Five years from the time that ratification became possible or 20 years from the time of the conclusion of the contract (Civil Code, Art 126).

[33] A. Ohsawa, 'La réforme de la loi sur les contrats de consommation au Japon' (2020) 2 *RIDC* 523–43.

[34] Consumer Contract Act, Art 4. This right of rescission is subject to prescription of one year from the time that ratification became possible or five years from the time of the conclusion of the contract. Consumer Contract Act, Art 7(1). The periods are shorter than tortious liability or mistake and fraud under the Civil Code.

[35] The 'material information' is further categorised in detail (Consumer Contract Act, Art 4(5)), which makes it easier to decide whether legal steps should be taken.

[36] See also Consumer Contract Act, Art 4(1).

[37] ibid, Art 4(2).

[38] ibid, Art 4(3)(i) and (ii).

[39] As duress does not always concern information problems, we refer here only to examples which concern the exploitation of the information asymmetry.

[40] eg such essential desires as 'admission to schools, finding employment, marriage, etc', or as 'improvement of style, figure, or any other important physical state'. These are typically the cases of such young adult consumers who are 'lacking in the sufficient experience of life in society' (Consumer Contract Act, Art 4(3)(iii)).

[41] Consumer Contract Act, Art 4(3)(iv). This is an interesting feature which requires further detail: in essence, the saleswoman creates the impression for the consumer that she is in love with him and the consumer purchases goods as a reciprocation of his love.

[42] Consumer Contract Act, Art 4(3)(v).

[43] ibid, Art 4(3)(vi).

[44] ibid, Art 4(4), amended in 2016. Elderly consumers living alone with a weakened judgement ability have been victimised by these crooked traders. To compare to the similar rule in the Act on Specified Commercial Transactions, see text below.

Compared to the rescission rules under the Civil Code, the conditions noted here are in a way broadened in favour of consumers (especially regarding vulnerable consumers), but are in another way restricted to the narrowly formulated, concrete categories, which enhances foreseeability but limits their spheres of protection.

c. Specific Statutes

Among the third level of specific statutes, the Act on Specified Commercial Transactions[45] provides a similar rescission system but only in five types of such potentially aggressive or tempting selling practices. Further, an additional cancellation system in case of 'excessive sales' is stipulated for just Door-to-Door Sales and Telemarketing Sales. The difference from the excessive sales noted above is that here the victim can rescind by proving objectively only the gross 'excessiveness', without proving the knowledge of the enterprise. This is again a measure to protect vulnerable consumers.

d. 'Cooling Off'

A consumer may be permitted to withdraw from the contract without requiring any reason (the right to withdraw or 'cooling off'), although within a short period (for example, eight to 20 days usually after the receipt of the formal documents from the enterprise) and only in certain limited transactions. The Act on Specified Commercial Transactions is the most prominent statute which contains this right.

First, only Mail Order Sales lack a cooling-off measure because they involve neither surprise visits nor complex or intriguing contracts. However, in order to protect the mail-order customer from the information deficit of a 'sight unseen purchase', the Act provides an alternative (but a weaker, non-mandatory) measure of cancellation by returning the goods within eight days after their delivery.[46]

Second, an additional 'termination' measure after the expiration of each cooling-off period applies in multilevel marketing transactions and for the provision of specified continuous services. It often takes longer for a customer to realise the real problems accompanying such transactions and thus the protective measures are more extensive.

Third, since around 2010, the elderly living alone have become targets for Door-to-Door Purchases, in which they have been persuaded by enterprises to sell products (for example their personal jewellery) in their homes fraudulently or/and forcefully. Together with 'excessive sales', these incidents picked up by this Act are symbolic examples of victimisation not only of the vulnerable but also of well-off elderly persons often living alone.

e. Act on Specified Commercial Transactions: Overview

Table 1 provides an overview of the different rights under the Act on Specified Commercial Transactions, as referred to above.

[45] Act No 57 of 1976 see Table 1.

[46] This does not apply when the enterprise had indicated a special provision concerning the cancellation in its advertisement following the regulations (Art 15-3). This measure is a result of a compromise.

Table 1 Act on Specified Commercial Transactions

	Private Law					Public Law		
						Regulation of		
	Cooling-Off	**Rescission**	**Termination**	**Excessive sales cancellation**	**Injunction***	**disclosure****	**solicitation**	**advertising**
'Surprising visit'								
Doorstep sales	8 days	Yes	No	Yes	Yes	Yes	Yes	No
Doorstep purchase***	8 days	No	No	No	Yes	Yes	Yes	No
Telemarketing	8 days	Yes	No	Yes	Yes	Yes	Yes	No
'Intriguing group								
Multi-level marketing	20 days	Yes	Yes	No	Yes	Yes	Yes	Yes
Business opportunity	20 days	Yes	No	No	Yes	Yes	Yes	Yes
Continuous services	8 days	Yes	Yes	No	Yes	Yes	Yes	Yes
'Sight unseen'								
Mail order	Yes/No****	No	No	No	Yes	No*****	Yes/No	Yes

* By a Qualified Consumer Organisation. See s IX.A.ii.
** Documentation is mandatory. See s II.B.
*** Referring to situations in which the consumer sells to the business. See s II.A.ii.d.
**** Art 15-3 allows the enterprise to exclude the right to withdraw under the mandatory advertisement requirement. See s II.A.ii.d and n 46.
***** Written notification of acceptance is, however, necessary in cases of pre-payment. Art 13 (1).

B. Information Duties Regulated under Public Law

Governmental efforts in the form of administrative regulations have also played a significant role in tackling consumer information problems. Many government bodies have played a part, though the Consumer Affairs Agency and the Financial Services Agency are the most notable.

The Consumer Affairs Agency started in 2009, taking initiative in its three areas of competence: consumer transactions, consumer safety and labelling and representation. Each is related to information issues, but consumer safety is still supplemental to the traditional administrative authorities discussed below. Here the focus is on consumer transactions. The 'public law' sections in Table 1 above cover (i) the 'regulation of disclosure' (for example mandatory disclosure of the sales purpose and of the main elements of the contract before solicitation, mandatory delivery of contract documents right after its conclusion, etc), (ii) the 'regulation of (unfair) solicitation' (for example prohibition of fraudulent, aggressive, or unsuitable solicitations), and (iii) the 'regulation of advertisements' (for example, prohibition of misleading advertisement and mandatory indication of certain material facts in the advertisement) under the Act on Specified Commercial Transactions (now under the jurisdiction of the Consumer Affairs Agency). The sanctions against the enterprise that violates these regulations include, for example, an administrative action, an order to improve or to suspend the business, etc, and sometimes a criminal penalty.

A particularly conspicuous development is seen also in the field of finance law supervised by Financial Services Agency (in charge of, for example, the Financial Instruments and Exchange Act, Insurance Business Act, etc). Here the three features (i) to (iii) above are also present. The striking example of (ii) (regulation of solicitation or suitability) is that business money lenders must investigate the customer's solvency and are prohibited from lending more than one-third of the annual income (Money Lending Business Act, Article 13-2). Behind these tendencies of governmental intervention were two inter-related background factors. One is the aging of the Japanese society producing a large older generation with savings prepared against the poor annuity system, who so often became the target of shrewd businesses. Another is the fact that particularly since the 'Japanese financial big bang' at the end of twentieth century, a traditional prohibition on banks, insurance companies, etc, to do business in the speculative financial market was removed and a growing number of ordinary consumers, including the elderly with assets, have begun to enter into such markets. The government who backed up this market vitalising policy became obliged to enact regulations to stop it going too far.

C. Comments

Although the private law versus public law divide introduced in the nineteenth century has been firmly institutionalised in the Japanese legal system, we could also observe a tendency that private law measures such as damages, rescission, cancellation and withdrawal and the aforementioned public law measures have started to complement each other. The injunction by the qualified consumer organisations is usually classified as a private law measure, but has quasi-public law characteristics, too.

Dealing with consumer problems, there seem to exist at least two different approaches: one towards looking into the concrete facts of each case and characteristic of individual customers (their ability, needs or even psychological inclination), the other towards more formal or objective categorisation of the client's or enterprise's conduct. In the face of the increasing problems caused by sophisticated business practices trying to evade the clutches of the regulations, the former approach seems inevitable, especially in court. On the other hand, the latter approach would be in conformity with the demand of consumers for easier claims, with enterprises' need for predictability, and with the requirement of administration for equal and efficient treatment.

III. Sale of Goods: Consumer Sales Contract

A. Overview and Status Quo

Although the Consumer Contract Act applies to almost all types of contracts, including the sale of goods, the Act deals only with (1) contract formation,[47] (2) unfair terms[48] and (3) a special litigation procedure for qualified consumer organisations.[49] Substantive rules such as contractual obligations on consumer sales are therefore found in the Civil Code, especially in its section on sales as well as in the sections commonly applicable to contracts or obligations in general (Part III: Law of Obligations), which we explain, focusing on the particularly important topic of conformity of goods.[50]

B. Civil Code

Articles 562–66 of the Civil Code afford a buyer (a consumer or an enterprise) with four rights in the event the delivered goods do not conform to the sales contract: cure, price reduction, damages and cancellation of the contract. The non-conformity liability of seller may not be disclaimed in a consumer contract.

i. Right to Cure

The right to cure permits a buyer to demand from the seller either repair, delivery of substitute goods or delivery of the missing part.[51] These measures have long

[47] Above at s II.

[48] Below at s IV.

[49] Below at s IX.

[50] In case of non-conformity of transferred right to terms of contract, Art 565 provides the *mutatis mutandis* application.

[51] Civil Code, Art 562(1).

existed in Japanese business practices. Partly inspired by international legislative movements including the UN Convention on Contracts for the International Sale of Goods (CISG)[52] and the UNIDROIT Principles of International Commercial Contracts (PICC),[53] they are newly introduced in the Civil Code as special provisions for sales and other onerous contracts.[54] As to the choice between these three types of cure, although a buyer can first choose any one of the three (for example repair), the seller can cure the performance by a different means than chosen by the buyer (for example substitute delivery), provided that the seller's choice would not put a disproportionate burden on the buyer.[55]

ii. Price Reduction

The remedy of price reduction comes into play if cure is unsuccessful (that is, the additional reasonable period for cure, having been set by the buyer, has expired without the seller's performance). However, the buyer may demand cure immediately if, inter alia, the cure itself was impossible or unrealistic.[56] As this price reduction is considered to be a partial cancellation of the contract, the repair and delivery of a substitute correspond to those of the general cancellation system considered below.

With regard to the remaining two rights – damages and cancellation – the Civil Code states that they are not precluded by the claim either for cure or for price reduction,[57] so that they therefore fall under the more general rules of the Civil Code.

iii. Damages

Article 415 of the Civil Code concerns the buyer's claim for 'damages' against the seller for non-performance. According to this provision, the buyer (obligee) cannot claim damages from the seller (obligor) where the latter's non-performance is due to grounds not attributable to him. Whether this implies the continuation of the traditional 'fault' (or 'negligence') principle or not has been the subject of discussion. However, a substantial difference in consequence between these seemingly different opinions is not so significant especially when the former conceives 'fault' objectively as a breach of duty legally (and sometimes extensively) required under the circumstances, which has been the position taken by the Japanese courts. We must watch the future developments.

With regard to the effect side of the non-performance, the question arises as to how far the damage or harm should be compensated by the obligor (seller). Under the

[52] CISG, Art 48, substantially Art 46. Japan ratified the CISG in 2008 (entry into force in 2009).
[53] PICC, Arts 7.1.4 and 7.2.3. T Uchida, 'Contract Law Reform in Japan and the Unidroit Principles' (2011) *Uniform Law Review* 705, 710.
[54] Civil Code, Art 559.
[55] ibid, Art 562(1).
[56] ibid, Art 563(2) states concrete cases as follows: impossibility of cure; apparent rejection of cure by the seller; delayed performance where time is of the essence; and other cases where there is apparently no prospect for curing performance.
[57] ibid, Art 564.

Civil Code, the obligor's foreseeability over the circumstances causing the harm is a prerequisite for confirming the compensatory liability.[58] International sets of rules, and almost all the contractual damages rules in the world, hold the view of judging this foreseeability at the time of conclusion of the contract, considering that the contractual parties would take measures (for example setting the appropriate price or buying insurance) to meet the future risks foreseeable at the time of its conclusion.[59] However, according to established Japanese case law, the obligor's foreseeability should be judged at the time of non-performance. This reveals the weakness of the 'contract' idea in the Japanese contractual damages rule.[60] Japanese judges seem to be inclined to make sure that, even in case of circumstances that were unforeseeable at the time of conclusion but had become foreseeable at the time of (non-)performance, the obligor should perform reasonably so as not to cause (or increase) damage which might spring out of such special circumstances. This is an idea closer to 'negligence' liability in tort.

iv. Cancellation

The contract cancellation[61] (termination) system in the Civil Code abandoned the traditional 'fault' ('negligence') principle much more clearly than in the new damages system. Instead it focuses on the degree or seriousness of the breach (or non-performance).[62]

IV. Unfair Terms

The restriction of the use of unfair terms under Japanese private law is spread across three levels: the Consumer Contract Act, the Civil Code, which contains general provisions and special provisions on unfair terms in standard form contracts[63] and other specific statutes.

A. Consumer Contract Act

Unfair terms in a consumer contract are regulated by the Consumer Contract Act. These provisions are general and specific in their application. Unfair terms are

[58] ibid, Art 416(2).

[59] CISG, Art 74; PICC, Art 7.4.4.

[60] This remark was first made by Y Nomi, 'Proportionality in Tort and Contract Law' in E Hondius (ed), *Modern Trends in Tort Law* (Alphen aan den Rijn: Kluwer, 1999) 216–17.

[61] I follow here a Japanese semi-official translation ('*cancellation*') for the legal term '*Kaijo*'.

[62] Under the Civil Code, cancellation is divided into cancellation after demand (eg delayed performance), where cancellation is possible if the degree of breach is not trivial (Art 541), and cancellation without demand (eg impossibility of performance): cancellation is possible if it is impossible to accomplish the purpose (Art 542). The degree of the breach is the principal question in both.

[63] Civil Code, Arts 548-2 to 548-4.

not only void but are also subject to a special injunction by Qualified Consumer Organisations.[64]

i. General Provision: Nullity of Terms that Impair the Interests of Consumers Unilaterally

According to Article 10 of the Consumer Contract Act, any consumer contract term is void that restricts the rights or expands the duties of the consumer more than the application of provisions unrelated to public order in any other laws and regulations (1),[65] and which unilaterally impairs the interests of the consumer, in violation of the fundamental principle of good faith (2).

A case about the renewal fee for an apartment lease illustrates how this provision functions in practice.[66] The lease contract provision in Article 601 of the Civil Code mentions the payment of *rent* as a duty of the lessee, but not the *renewal fee*. Therefore, the Supreme Court affirmed the first pre-requisite (1), saying that the renewal fee term expands the duty of the lessee more than as prescribed in the Civil Code. However, it denied the second pre-requisite (2) stating that the gap between the contract parties as to the information and the negotiation power was not so significant, the renewal fee term was clearly and concretely stated in the contractual document, and the amount of the renewal fee (two month rental payment) also was not too excessive. Hence the term was deemed valid.

The comprehensive consideration of both objective and subjective factors resembles the consideration in case of profiteering decisions under Article 90 of the Civil Code ('Public Policy and Good Morals').[67] However, the rigidly ordered, two-stage assessment procedure provided in Article 10 merits attention. In particular, the first stage of screening unfair terms focusing on their objective contents with a measure of non-mandatory rules of law may function to screen unfair terms by way of a 'grey' list (with room for discretion) as provided in the European Unfair Terms Directive.[68] The comparatively limited number of unfair terms in the ('black') list given below seem thus supplemented by these non-mandatory legal norms referred to in the first pre-requisite, although the room for discretion is much wider here (due to the second pre-requisite) and the final judgment is less predictable for both consumers and enterprises.

[64] Consumer Contract Act, Arts 12 et seq. See also s IX.A.ii.

[65] The Supreme Court judgment of 15 July 2011, Minshu 65, 5, 2269 interpreted the first pre-requisite extensively that compared 'provisions unrelated to public order' should include not only statutory provisions but general legal principles. In this provision, a term where 'the Consumer is deemed to have manifested his/her intention to offer or accept the Consumer Contract based on his/her inaction' is referred as an example of this first pre-requisite (eg a rental contract term under which the fee is free for the period of three months but becomes fee-charging if the customer continues using it after that expiration date without retuning the item). Such a term may restrict the right of consumer more than what the general principle of contract formation requires. Therefore, it may fulfil the first pre-requisite. However, it will become void only if the second pre-requisite is also fulfilled.

[66] ibid. See M Okino, 'Recent Developments in Consumer Law in Japan' (2002) 4 *UT Soft Law Review* 10 at 14.

[67] Below at s IV.B.ii.

[68] Council Directive 93/13/EEC of 5 April 1993 on unfair terms in consumer contracts, OJ 1993, No L95, p 29.

ii. List of Unfair Terms

Articles 8–9 of the Consumer Contract Act contain a list of specific unfair terms. For exemption clauses, Articles 8 and 8-2 provide that the following terms are void:[69]

- Terms which fully exempt an enterprise from liability arising from either non-performance or a tort,[70] or which authorise an enterprise to decide whether the enterprise is liable or not.[71]
- Terms which partially exempt an enterprise from liability, or terms authorising an enterprise to decide the limit of its liability, arising from either non-performance or a tort in case of an intentional act or gross negligence on the part of the enterprise.[72]
- Terms which fully exempt a seller[73] from liability to compensate a consumer, or terms authorising a seller to decide whether not at all or to what extent the seller is to compensate the consumer, for damages caused by the non-conformity of the goods delivered, provided that the enterprise seller is to be liable for cure or for price reduction in case the delivered goods do not conform to the sales contract.[74]
- Terms which force consumers to waive their right to cancel, or terms authorising the enterprise to decide whether the consumers have the right to cancel in case of non-performance by the enterprise.[75]

With regard to terms stipulating the amount of damages to be paid by consumers, the following are void to the extent provided in each respective item:

- Terms that stipulate an amount of liquidated damages (and/or a fixed penalty) in the event of consumer's cancellation, wherein the total amount exceed the normal amount of damages: The term is void by the amount the total exceeds the normal amount.[76]

[69] Consumer Contract Act, Art 8-3 is a notable provision responding to a practice whereby a lease (housing) contract could be terminated if the leaseholder becomes an adult ward (eg in the event of illness such as dementia). Such terms are now void. The rule is quite symbolic of the focus towards protecting vulnerable members of society.

[70] Only in case the tort is committed during the enterprise's performance of a consumer contract.

[71] Consumer Contract Act, Art 8(1)(i) and (iii).

[72] ibid, Art 8(1)(ii) and (iv).

[73] Art 8(2) of the Consumer Contract Act stipulates more generally on onerous contracts and on non-conformity of the delivered object, however the text here focusses on sales contracts.

[74] ibid, Art 8(2).

[75] ibid, Art 8-2.

[76] ibid, Art 9(1)(i). For example, applicants for university entrance examinations had to pay each university not only the examination fee, but once passed, entrance fee as well as part of the tuition fees, often before the date of passing announcement of some other universities. Therefore, most of those successful candidates would pay such fees to several universities even though they would enter into only one. The Supreme Court in its judgment of 27 November 2006, Minshu 60, 9, 3597 interpreted these fees to be the liquidated damages in case of cancellation by the successful candidate and applied Article 9(1)(i) of the Consumer Contract Act. Although the entrance fee is valid (entitling the successful candidate to acquire the possibility of entering into that university), the judgment says, the tuition fee should be regulated by the Act as liquidated damages and the amount by which the total exceeds the normal amount is to be invalid. As in most of these cases the cancellation took place before the beginning of a school year on 1 April, 'normal amount' is zero as the school does not start yet. This judgment not only ended the conflict between the claimants and the defendant universities but entirely changed the traditional custom of excessive tuition payment in Japan. This kind of policy direction is one important function that consumer litigation can fulfil. S Kozuka takes up this judgement in his, 'Judicial Activism of the Japanese Supreme Court in Consumer Law: Juridification of Society through Case Law?' (2009) 27 *Zeitschrift für japanisches Recht* 84–86.

- Terms that stipulate an amount of liquidated damages (and/or a fixed penalty) in the event of a total or partial default by the customer, wherein the total amount exceeds the amount calculated by deducting the amount actually paid from the amount which should have been paid on the due date and multiplying the result by 14.6 per cent per annum in accordance with the number of days from the due date to the day on which the money is actually paid: The term is void by the amount by which the total amount exceeds the calculated amount.[77]

B. Civil Code

i. *Unfair Terms in Standard Form Contracts*

Legislation of the law on standard form contracts had been the subject of a long, heated controversy between business groups and academics during the promulgation process. The Civil Code has finally succeeded in introducing a group of special provisions on standardised transactions.[78] First, it permits an enterprise to authorise the inclusion of its standard terms[79] not only by an 'agreement' with the customer, but by the enterprise's easier 'manifestation of intention' to the customer.[80] Second, for controlling unfair terms, it stipulates a general provision similar to Article 10 of the Consumer Contract Act.[81] Finally, no list of unfair terms is provided, but one special provision on amendment of the standard terms has been inserted.[82] These were the results of a compromise and some worry has been expressed as to the possibility of regression of customers' protection (especially that of consumers and small businesses).

[77] ibid, Art 9(1)(ii).

[78] A standard transaction is a transaction conducted by a specified person (enterprise) with an *unspecified and large number of persons as the counterparties*, in which the *uniformity of the whole or part of the transaction is reasonable to both parties* (Civil Code, Art 548-2(1)). The italicised parts reveal the typically targeted enterprises to be such big entities facing the general public as transportation companies or electricity (or gas) supplying companies. In this regard, these provisions are not directly facing the global issue of an abuse of bargaining power by commercial enterprises enforcing their one-sided general conditions. Although the German law development on general conditions has been quite influential among Japanese academics since Ludwig Raiser's *Das Recht der Allgemeinen Geschäftsbedingungen* (Hamburg: Hanseatischer Verlag, 1935), the exceptional measure regarding the general conditions for public services in the German Civil Code (BGB) § 305a seems to have become the central issue in the Japanese Civil Code. This focus, linked to the privatisation of these services as well, was a result of the compromise due to the confrontation during the promulgation process.

[79] According to Article 548-2(1) of the Civil Code, standard terms are a collection of provisions prepared by that specific person (enterprise) with the purpose of applying them as the terms of a contract for a standard transaction.

[80] ibid, Art 548-2(1).

[81] ibid, Art 548-2 (2).

[82] ibid, Art 548-4. An enterprise may be deemed to have been agreed by customers to amended terms, without making any individual agreement with them, if the necessary announcement beforehand by Internet etc is made, and also (1) if the amendment to the standard terms conforms to the general interest of the customers, or (2) if the amendment is not contrary to the purpose of the contract and is reasonable in light of the need to change, the appropriateness of the contents after the change, whether there is the provision of possibility of amendment to the standard terms, the contents of such provisions and the other circumstances relating to the amendment.

ii. Other Provisions

The Civil Code sets the limits to the basic principle of contractual freedom by providing some specific mandatory rules[83] (for example Article 572)[84] and such general principles of a juristic act as respecting 'Public Policy and Good Morals',[85] and 'Good Faith'.[86] Unfair terms in any type of contract have fallen under these restrictions. However, since the enforcement of the Consumer Contract Act with its general and specific mandatory provisions, the significance of these prohibitive rules in the Civil Code has considerably decreased.[87]

C. Other Specific Statutes

It is rather the mandatory provisions outside the Civil Code which continue to take a lively role for substantive control over unfair contract terms. Several tenant protection measures in the Act on Land and Building Leases[88] and mandatory, maximum (for example 20 per cent) ceiling of annual interest rate in the Interest Rate Restriction Act[89] are well known examples of direct governmental intervention for protecting the lives of weaker contractual parties.

D. Comments

There have been at least three different approaches toward 'unfair terms': (1) focussing on consumer contracts, (2) on standard terms and (3) on the type of unfairness of the term itself (usually with the specific characteristics of the typical contractual situations: for example maximum interest-rate ceiling for a money lending contract, or a maximum duration of an immovable lease). The styles of legal intervention are at least twofold: 'standard' ('general clause') and 'rule'-oriented. The former is fit for the

[83] ibid, Art 91.

[84] ibid, Art 572 invalidates an exemption agreement of seller's non-conformity liability in case the seller knew but did not disclose the existence of the non-conformity of the sold object.

[85] ibid, Art 90. Supreme Court decision of 1 May 1934, Minshu 13, 875.

[86] ibid, Art 1(2).

[87] For example, contrary to Art 572 of the Civil Code, even an innocent seller cannot exempt himself from the non-conformity liability under Consumer Contract Act (Art 8(2)). As regards a general provision of Public Policy and Good Morals under Article 90 of the Civil Code, its important role of settling unfair term disputes against the profiteers (considering both a subjective, exploitative element and an objective excessive profit-making element), has been largely replaced by Consumer Contract Act (Art 10 and other specific mandatory rules) in consumer-related cases.

[88] For example, the Act on Land and Building Leases states that the Land Lease Right shall be 30 years (Art 3) and that any contractual provisions that run counter to these provisions and which are disadvantageous to the Land Lease Right Holder shall be invalid (Art 9). Therefore, a contract term providing a land-lease for 10 years for example is invalid and the lease continues for 30 years.

[89] The Interest Rate Restriction Act stipulates mandatory, maximum ceiling of annual interest rate between 15 per cent and 20 per cent depending upon the amount of the principal. There are also criminal sanctions against the business contract with the interest rate exceeding 20 per cent (Act Regulating the Receipt of Contributions, the Receipt of Deposits, and Interest Rates, Act No 195 of 1954, amended in 2007).

traditional, judicial system of courts solving the conflict ex post between the specific parties, considering the individual facts and situations in detail, whereas the latter is in conformity with the forward-looking direction of everyday practices considering the foreseeability, efficiency and policymaking for the concerned mass market transactions. The developments we have seen here show both the polarisation and the combination (for example Article 10 of the Consumer Contract Act) of these two styles.[90]

V. Product Liability

Damage caused by a defective product can be recovered in both contract and tort[91] under the Civil Code. However, since the Product Liability Act 1994[92] introduced the 'defect' liability against manufacturers and importers, this Act has become the main source of recovery.

A. Characteristics of the Japanese Product Liability Act

At first glance, the Japanese Product Liability Act appears to resemble the European Product Liability Directive.[93] However, there are at least three distinguishable points.[94] First, with regard to the recoverable damage, Article 3 of the Product Liability Act mentions only 'damages arising from the infringement of life, body or property of others', without stating any further restrictions of its coverage as are stated

[90] Cf above, at s II.C.

[91] Long before the promulgation of the Product Liability Act, the courts have taken the meaning of 'negligence' of tortious liability (Civil Code, Art 709) objectively and flexibly. Especially in case of damages from medicines or food as well as those from pollution in the 1970s and 80s, the courts interpreted the word 'negligence' very extensively and affirmed the damages claims of injured victims. Some commentators on the famous, medicine-induced suffering case of SMON (Tokyo District Court judgment of 3 August,1978, Hanrei Jiho 899, 48) observed the court's interpretation of negligence getting infinitely close to a non-fault, strict liability. These judgments can be interpreted as extending a helping hand to the victims of the dark side of the post-war rapid – but sometimes rough – industrial development.

[92] Act No 85 of 1994. Regarding the original text with explanations as well as its promulgation process, see A Omura, 'The Product Liability Law of Japan' (1997) 5(5) *Consumer Law Journal* 153 and L Nottage, *Product Safety and Liability Law in Japan: From Minamata to Mad Cows* (Abingdon: Routledge, 2004). For a more recent overview, Y Shiomi, 'Product Liability in Japan' in K Oliphant et al (eds), *Product Liability: Fundamental Questions in a Comparative Perspective* (Berlin: de Gruyter, 2017) 62–79. A brief survey of Japanese consumer safety law in French, see H Hirano, 'La sécurité du consommateur au Japon' in Association Henri Capitant (ed), *Le consommateur* (Paris: Bruylant 2010) 407–14.

[93] Council Directive 85/374/EEC of 25 July 1985 on the approximation of the laws, regulations and administrative provisions of the Member States concerning liability for defective products, OJ 1985 No L210, p 29. For example, similar to this Directive, Articles 3–4 of the Japanese Product Liability Act provide a non-fault 'defect' liability as a rule with some 'defences' as exceptions. The substantive content of the 'defect' standard with the three important – but not the exclusive – list of circumstances is quite similar. The Japanese Product Liability legislation (1994) was considerably inspired by the European Product Liability Directive of 1985 and also by many other foreign product liability legislation.

[94] The concept of 'product' ('movable which is manufactured or processed', Art 2(1)) excluding primary agricultural products is more limited than the Directive. However, the definition was partly inspired by the European Product Liability Directive of 1985 (Art 2). Regarding 'processed' fish for food, see the case at n 102.

in Article 9(1)(b) Product Liability Directive (limiting property damage to *consumer* property). Therefore, the extent of liability is subject to the general tort law rule under the Civil Code,[95] which means it is fairly extensive, without the lower threshold of the European Directive (500 ECU), nor clearly excluding pure economic loss. The orientation of the Japanese Product Liability Act towards consumer protection is less significant.[96] Second, the targeted responsible enterprises extend to a 'substantial manufacturer' who did not actually manufacture the product, nor had such appearance (name, brand etc,) as manufacturer of the product, but who substantially committed to the process of making or/and distributing such a product.[97] Third, the starting point for calculating the limitation period (prescription) becomes flexible in case where the human damage (for example disease) was caused by the product with a long incubation period.[98]

B. Cases under the Product Liability Act

The cases after the enactment of the Product Liability Act have already been the subject of some detailed work in English.[99] We only pick up on those topics not yet fully discussed but which may become important.

i. 'Negligence' versus 'Defect'

At the time of the promulgation process concerning the Product Liability Act, the then government stressed the substantial continuity of the case law on 'negligence' to the newly introduced 'defect' liability, which was persuasive to the business side. The actual phenomena after the enactment has not been so clear. The 'defences', especially the development risk defence, has not yet been affirmed by the courts and the decision as to the 'defect' has become vital for both parties. The results of court decisions as to 'defect' might not be so different from their 'negligence' decisions if the 'negligence' is extensively and objectively interpreted as before.[100] However, instead of one whole

[95] Product Liability Act, Art 6.

[96] Compare Article 1 of the Product Liability Act ('Purpose': to protect the victim of the injury to life, body, or property …) to the idea of *consumer* protection expressed in the preamble of the Product Liability Directive. One of the reasons for our extended application beyond consumers was the necessity to assist Japan's numerous small and medium enterprises.

[97] ibid, Art 2(3)(iii). The 'substantial producer' is included by the experience of a medicine's side-effect case of SMON (n 91), where not only the actual producer of the medicine but also the well-known medicine producing and selling company (with a label '*Hanbai-moto*' (a selling agency)), who had the substantial monopolistic power over the whole distribution process and who had let another smaller company produce this medicine, was claimed damages by the victims. The lower courts admitted the claim and the case was settled. The Product Liability Act did not extend the liability to a seller even when manufacturers are not found (as the Product Liability Directive did). Instead, it introduced this type of substantial extension as to the responsible entity.

[98] ibid, Art 5(3). This derives also from such medicine-induced suffering cases as SMON (n 91).

[99] For example, Nottage, *Product Safety and Liability Law in Japan*, an additional survey by the same author and M Kato, including the Product Liability Act with cases on until approx. 2006; Nottage, *Business Law in Japan*, 175–312.

[100] See n 91. A similar argument appeared (above at s III.B.iii) on the contractual liability between non-fault v. fault interpretation.

concept of 'defect', the three categories of 'defect', namely, manufacturing defect, design defect and warning or instruction defect, have become popularly used in recent litigation and it seems that a tendency towards more fragmented decision-making focusing on each of these sub-categories has become observable. There might exist a danger of leaving some important facts, which might have been more comprehensively argued over the proof of 'negligence', out of the subject of discussion.[101] The fragmented decision-making of 'defect' liability might sometimes become less protective to victims than 'negligence' liability.

ii. 'Defect' Liability and Insurance

The problem related to the function of insurance has become one of the controversial issues for deciding the defect. Sometimes it is related to the development risk defence provided in Article 4(1). An interesting decision involved a small restaurant owner in Chiba Prefecture, who cooked and served a fish (raw and grilled) rarely found in that district (named a striped beak perch), which turned out to be infected with ciguatera (food-poisoning bacteria which is nearly impossible for a chef to discover and which has strong resistance to high heat cooking as well). Some customers suffered from food-poisoning and sued the restaurant owner based on the Product Liability Act. The defendant owner alleged the development risk defence. The Tokyo District Court rejected the defence saying that the level of knowledge necessary for the development risk defence must be measured objectively by the best scientific or technical knowledge of the whole society at that time (and not subjectively by that of the specific defendant).[102] The court in this case mentioned also that the availability of liability insurance and the fact that the defendant restaurant had actually taken out such insurance should justify this non-fault liability.[103]

This argument gives us a possibility of looking at the product liability problem from a perspective of the risk distribution through insurance. Some countries already adopted product liability law with a compulsory insurance system.[104] Japan also has the SG mark system using an insurance mechanism.[105] However, not only problems such as moral hazard (the insured enterprise might become less cautious about taking

[101] In the Supreme Court judgment of 12 April 2013, Minshu 67, 4, 899, concerning a side-effect of a new drug ('Iressa'), the issue of discussion was narrowed down to whether there existed a warning defect on the side of the import (and selling) company and the argument became focussed on (1) the foreseeability of the fatal side-effect risk at the time of the delivery and (2) the appropriateness of the warning expression on the attached document for doctors. Other surrounding circumstances such as the actual conduct by the defendant before and after the delivery (including the side-effect information gathering and its prompt giving to the customers (ie doctors)), which might have been discussed in a litigation of 'negligence' liability, were paid much less attention.

[102] Tokyo District Court judgment of 13 December 2002 Hanrei Jiho No 1805, 14. The Appellate Court dismissed as well: Tokyo High Court judgment of 26 January 2005, LEX/DB 28101913.

[103] Although this insurance argument has not always been discussed by the commentators, according to the writer's opinion, it was certainly one of the decisive factors for this decision.

[104] For example, the Austrian Product Liability Law (*Produkthaftungsgesetz*), Art 16, see R Welser and C Rabel, *Produkthaftungsgesetz Kommentar* 2nd edn (Vienna: LexisNexis, 2004) 189–91; Scandinavian Product Liability Act, see G Howells, *Comparative Product Liability* (London: Dartmouth, 1993) 147 et seq.

[105] See below at s VI.C.

safety measures) but the question of how to realise a fair mechanism for the distribution of risk by the (private) insurance market should be further considered.[106]

iii. Product Liability and State Liability

One characteristic feature of Japanese law related to the question of product liability is that the State (or the government) can be liable under the State Redress Act.[107] For example, in cases of medicine-induced sufferings, not only the manufacturer of the medicine, but also the State (Japanese government) may be liable if the public officer in charge of supervising the safety of the medicine negligently overlooked the dangerous side-effect of the medical products. Regarding medicines whose distribution into the market is only allowed under the strict, prior governmental approval,[108] damage caused by side effects that went negligently unnoticed in prior governmental examinations, may be compensated by the government.[109] On the other hand, regarding automobiles whose safety is supposed to be checked and maintained by the initiative of each car driver,[110] who is licensed by the national examination, the government is not easily considered to be liable even when the defects of an automobile which went negligently unnoticed at the official car inspection caused damage.[111] According to an administrative law specialist, the difference is based on the degree of the people's expectancy toward the governmental intervention.[112] This opinion is supportable as here the actual and final burden of compensation (in case of an affirmative decision of damages) is put on the populace generally through tax.

C. Comment

Japanese law features diverse paradigms to distribute the product-related risk. If we focus on who will be put under the final burden, possibilities thus far are (1) victim (refusal to attribute liability or by exemption clause), (2) enterprise (by non-fault liability),

[106] Interesting discussions took place between F Nagano and H Koziol in H Koziol (ed), *Comparative Stimulations for Developing Tort Law* (Wien: Jan Sramek, 2015) 38–43, 50–51.

[107] Act No 125 of 1947, Art 1(1). See above, at s I.

[108] Pharmaceuticals and Medical Devices Act (originally, 'Pharmaceuticals Affairs Act' Act No 145 of 10 August 1960).

[109] In the SMON case, the claim against State as well as against the medicine manufacturing company were affirmed (see n 91). However, the Supreme Court judgment of 23 June 1995, Minshu 49, 6, 1600 (chloroquine case) dismissed the claim with a remark that the State's liability would be affirmed only when the non-use of the competent power by the public officer deviated from the permissible limits and became grossly unreasonable. In the recent Iressa case, the Supreme Court (n 101) rejected not only the importer's liability but also the State's liability (the government's rapid approval – the first purchaser in the world, permitting the phase III trials exceptionally *after* the approval – with the permission of the insufficient documental warning, which became later officially amended, were questioned). Some commentators expressed criticism that this kind of unpredictable risk should not be put solely on the victims but be shared by the whole society. Concurring opinions (by Judges Takehiko Otani and Masaharu Ohashi) in that Supreme Court judgment suggested also that idea of social distribution.

[110] Road Transport Vehicle Act (Act No 185 of 1951).

[111] For example, Kanazawa District Court judgment of 16 July 1976, Hanrei Jiho 824, 40.

[112] K Uga, *Kokka Hosho Ho* [*State Compensation Law*] (Tokyo: Yuhikaku, 1997) 164–66.

(3) participants of the insurance market (by insurance system) and (4) tax payers (by State liability), and the discussion should be continued. However, we must also take a forward-looking perspective from the viewpoint of risk prevention, which we consider next.

VI. Product Safety

A. Overview

The present consumer safety system can be divided into three stages: the pre-market, design and production stage, the in-market stage and the post-accident stage. Having discussed the post-accident stage above, this section focuses on the preceding stages, for which the governmental control systems consist of both item (product)-specific, vertical regulations by each responsible Ministry and a supplemental, horizontal regulation by the Consumer Affairs Agency (CAA).[113] Table 2 provides an overview.[114]

Table 2 Main Product Safety Legislation

Item	Main Legislation	Competent Authorities
Food	Food Sanitation Act (No 23 of 24 December 1947)	Ministry of Health, Labor and Welfare & Consumer Affairs Agency
	Food Safety Basic Act (No 48 of 2003)	Food Safety Commission (Cabinet Office)
	Food Labeling Act (No 70 of 2013)	Consumer Affairs Agency
Medicine	Act on Securing Quality, Efficacy and Safety of Products Including Pharmaceuticals and Medical Devices (No 145 of 1960)	Ministry of Health, Labor and Welfare
Automobiles	Road Transport Vehicle Act (No 185 of 1951)	Ministry of Land, Infrastructure, Transport and Tourism
Electrical Appliances	Electrical Appliance and Material Safety Act (No 234 of 1961)	Ministry of Economy, Trade and Industry
Other Goods	Consumer Product Safety Act (No 31 of 1973)	Ministry of Economy, Trade and Industry & Consumer Affairs Agency
Buildings	Building Standards Act (No 201 of 1950)	Ministry of Land, Infrastructure, Transport and Tourism
Generally	Consumer Safety Act (No 50 of 2009)	Consumer Affairs Agency

[113] See above at s I.

[114] Movable items are mostly selected from the list of regulative laws provided by the Appended Table (related to Art 2) of the Consumer Product Safety Act.

B. Consumer Product Safety Act

The Consumer Product Safety Act is theoretically a core statute[115] for the pre- and in-market regulations, and classifies consumer products into three kinds, with differing levels of pre-market control:

- 'Specified products' (10 items)[116] must be inspected and verified by the manufacturer to ensure that the products conform to the technical requirements[117] (self-inspection). The inspection record must be prepared and preserved. After the verification, the 'PSC Mark' (signifying Product Safety Consumer Goods) is to be placed on the products.
- 'Special specified products' (four items)[118] are among 'specified products', but are specially required to be inspected by a third party (a registered conformity inspection body) in addition to self-inspection. The 'PSC Mark' on the products is to be placed after the verification.
- The un-designated, 'un-specified products' (all other consumer product items not included in the 'specified products' above) can be manufactured and distributed in the market without the aforementioned inspection.

Regarding the in-market control, manufacturers of the 'specified products' (including 'special specified products') are subject to the following administrative orders: Order for improvement of manufacturing (or inspection, etc); Order for prohibition of labelling; Hazard Prevention Order;[119] and Collection of Reports and On-Site Inspection. Manufacturers of 'un-specified products' can also be subject to the following orders: Hazard Prevention Order[120] and Collection of Reports and On-Site Inspection. Most of these orders are accompanied by penal sanctions against their infringements.[121]

[115] However, note that this Act does not cover such important movables as food, medicines, automobiles, etc., nor immovables as Table 2 (other goods versus other items) shows.

[116] 'Specified Products' are autoclaves and pressure cookers for household use; helmets (limited to those for riding a two-wheeled motor vehicle or motorised bicycle); baby beds; climbing ropes; portable laser application devices; hot water circulators for baths; oil water heaters; oil bath boilers; oil heaters; lighters.

[117] These requirements are under the control of the government.

[118] 'Special specified products' include baby beds; portable laser application devices; hot water circulators for baths; lighters.

[119] 'When the competent minister believes that there exists a risk of danger to the lives or bodies of general consumers regarding specified products, and when the minister finds it particularly necessary to prevent the occurrence and increase of such danger, the minister may order the business enterprise to recall the products and otherwise to take all necessary measures' (Art 32).

[120] 'When "serious product accidents" have occurred due to defects in the consumer products other than specified products or when serious danger has occurred to the lives or bodies of general consumers or the occurrence of such danger is considered to be imminent, and when the competent minister finds it particularly necessary to prevent the occurrence and increase of such danger, the minister may order, to the extent necessary, to recall the consumer products and to otherwise take measures necessary to prevent the occurrence and increase of serious danger to the lives or bodies of general consumers' (Art 39).

[121] Consumer Product Safety Act, Arts 58–62 provides imprisonment with work for not more than one year or a fine of not more than JPY one million (approximately USD 9100).

C. 'SG Mark' System

A weakness of the above-mentioned system of consumer product safety is that the number of targeted items is very small.[122] A great many items classified as 'un-specified products' fall outside the scope of the pre-market safety controls and even at the in-market stage are only subject to a few exceptional orders. Their safety controls rely upon the post-accident, damages liability systems of the Product Liability Act or tort law. However, we should remember that, when the Consumer Product Safety Act was enacted in 1973, it introduced another subsidiary system: the Safe Goods Mark (SG Mark). It is run by the organisation 'Consumer Product Safety Association' (hereinafter: CPS Association).[123] Over one hundred items of various consumer products have been (and continue to be) registered under the mark and the victim of the product accident is protected by a kind of insurance system.[124] After the de-regulation movement, the Association changed its nature to a general foundation in 2012. However, the SG Mark continues to be functioning as a unique subsidiary system to support the Consumer Product Safety Act.

D. Product Recall

For the safety measures at the in-market stage, product recall has become a major scheme. The Consumer Product Safety Act prepares administrative, compulsory orders to require the manufacturers recall the products (including un-specified products) in case the products pose a risk of danger to the lives or bodies of general consumers.[125] There have been cases of actual implementation of these orders,[126] but most of the recalls in this area are voluntarily exercised by enterprises without a specific legal basis.

If we extend our observation to such special areas as medicine, food and automobiles, their recalls as well as their pre- and in-market safety activities in general are far more strictly controlled by regulatory laws than by the Consumer Product Safety Act and, although their recalls are mostly started at the initiative of each enterprise as well, those enterprises are usually obliged to report to the competent authority when they start a recall,[127] which the authority will monitor. For an enterprise not falling under any responsible authorities, the direct recall system by the Consumer Affairs Agency (the Prime Minister) has been introduced.[128]

[122] 'Specified products' (including 'Special specified products') cover only 10 items.

[123] www.sg-mark.org.

[124] M Ramseyer, 'Product Liability Through Private Ordering: Notes on a Japanese Experiment' (1996) 144 *University of Pennsylvania Law Review* 1823, 1828–40; H Sarmida, 'Comparative Institutional Analysis of Product Safety Systems in the United States and Japan: Alternative Approaches to Create Incentives for Product Safety' (1996) 29 *Cornell International Law Journal* 79.

[125] See nn 119 and 120.

[126] For example, hot air heaters with a danger of carbon monoxide poisoning were recalled compulsorily in 2005 by the Hazard Prevention Order.

[127] Pharmaceuticals and Medical Devices Act, Art 68-11, Food Sanitation Act, Art 58, Road Transport Vehicle Act, Arts 63-2, 63-3, 63-4.

[128] Consumer Safety Act, Arts 40–42.

E. Accidents Reporting (and Publication) Systems

In 2006, after some serious accidents,[129] the Consumer Product Safety Act was revised and introduced the following reporting and publication system: an enterprise, who becomes aware that 'serious product accidents' (including the accidents where the actual or potential danger is serious) have originated with its manufactured or imported consumer products, shall report to the competent minister the details of the accidents within 10 days after knowing of the accident.[130] The competent minister, having received the report, shall make public the name and type of the consumer products pertaining to said serious product accidents, the details of the accidents and any other matters that contribute to avoiding the dangers.[131]

The Consumer Safety Act of 2009 provided that the head of the administrative organ (etc[132]) becomes obliged to notify the Prime Minister (CAA) of such information as a 'serious accident'[133] immediately and a 'consumer accident'[134] promptly, both of which cause actual or potential harm to the consumer's life and person.[135]

VII. Adaption to Digital Age

The Consumer Policy Development Plan adopted by the Cabinet in March 2015 notes[136] that the development to a highly developed information society has resulted in a massive increase in Internet consumer transactions. Between 2008 and 2013, these grew by a factor of 1.8, from JPY 6.1 trillion to 11.2 trillion (approximately USD 55.7 billion to 102.3 billion).

This in turn has increased the number of consumer enquiries to consumer protection centres that concern information services to more than 20 per cent of all enquiries. The topics concern contracts for telecommunication services, Internet distance contracts and their payment methods, problems related to adult and game Internet sites, spam mail and leaking of personal information.

[129] For example, a fatality caused by carbon monoxide poisoning through a defective water heater, and injuries caused to a baby whose fingers became entangled in a paper shredder.

[130] Consumer Product Safety Act, Art 35(1), Cabinet Office Order, Art 3.

[131] ibid, Art 36(1).

[132] Besides the head of an administrative organ, prefectural governor, municipal mayor and president of the National Consumer Affairs Center of Japan are listed (Consumer Safety Act, Art 12(1)).

[133] The 'serious accident' (ibid, Art 2(7)) which concerns harm to the consumer's life or person (not just that to property damage), is similar to the 'serious product accident' in the Consumer Product Safety Act mentioned above, but the 'serious accident' here is not limited to the accident caused by 'consumer products' but extends to consumer services.

[134] ibid, Art 2(5). The 'consumer accident' is that which does not amount to a 'serious accident' but the notification becomes necessary in cases where the harm will increase in scope or that a similar type of the accident will occur.

[135] As regards a 'consumer accident', the notification is necessary only in case it is likely that the harm will increase in scope or that a similar type of the accident will occur (ibid, Art 12(2)).

[136] *Shōhisha kihon keikaku*, Cabinet decision of 24 March 2015, p 6.

A. E-commerce Regulation

As regards issues of the E-commerce regulation, there are four relevant topics: minimum information requirements, input error protection, cooling-off periods and credit card abuse.

i. Minimum Information Requirements

Internet commerce is not tied to a physical address. Therefore, if the consumer needs to contact or even sue the seller, they need a physical address displayed on the relevant home pages.

The largest damage to consumers in Japan in recent years (measured in hundreds of millions of dollars) resulted from the collapse of the Bitcoin Internet exchange MtGox in 2014. While this exchange was active, it did not display its physical location on its home page. It did display such a location in its terms of use, but that address did not actually exist.[137] Obviously, such a state of affairs is unacceptable from a point of view of consumer protection.

The consumer protection law dealing with this problem is Article 11 of the Act on Specified Commercial Transactions.[138] That Article requires the selling price, time and method of payment, time of delivery, matters regarding return and exchange and any matters specified by an Ordinance of the Ministry of Economy, Trade and Industry to be disclosed in all commercial communications about distance contracts. The relevant Ordinance[139] requires in its Article 8 No 1 that the seller includes information about his name and address. Article 8 No 2 requires information about the legal representative if the seller is a legal person.

ii. Input Error Protection

When ordering goods over the Internet, a consumer may sometimes be confused by the webpage layout and order a different number of items than intended or click on some item without actually wanting it. The Japanese system to tackle such problems is covered in the Act on Special Provisions to the Civil Code Concerning Electronic Consumer Contracts of 2001.[140] This works by providing an exception to Article 95 of the Civil Code.[141] According to this provision, a manifestation of intention is voidable if it is based on a mistake wherein the person lacks the intention that corresponds to the manifestation of intention and if the mistake is material in light of the purpose of the juridical act and the common sense in the transaction.[142] However, if a mistake is due to gross negligence on the part of the person making the manifestation of intention, that person may not rescind a manifestation of intention.[143]

[137] See K-F Lenz, 'Where is MtGox?', 21 October 2013, available under bit.ly/3hmp3dw.
[138] Act No 57 of 1976 (above n 45). See above at II.B and Table1.
[139] Ordinance No 89/1976 of the Ministry of Economy, Trade and Industry.
[140] Act No 95 of June 2001, amended in 2017.
[141] Act No 89 of April 1896, amended in 2017. See above at II.A.ii. a and n 29.
[142] Civil Code, Art 95(1).
[143] ibid, Art 95(3).

The Act on Electronic Consumer Contracts works by first exempting consumers from the requirement of not being grossly negligent in Article 95 of the Civil Code and grants an exception for cases where the merchant in question has taken measures to confirm the consumer's intention to make an offer or accept the offer by electromagnetic means on the visual browser, or where the consumer manifests expressly the intention to the business entity that there is no need for such confirmation measures.[144]

Since most merchants will be interested in being granted this exception, they will usually provide a step in the ordering process for finally confirming orders. That gives the consumer a chance to correct all potential mistakes. If merchants do so, all mistakes by consumers in gross negligence leave the contract intact. Keeping up an error even after looking at a confirmation screen is gross negligence, so the merchant will be protected in most such cases.

iii. Cooling Off

In contrast to EU law,[145] Japan has no consumer protection regulation in place that guarantees consumers a cooling-off period in all distance contracts. In principle, consumers have a cooling-off period of eight days, however merchants (in mail order sales) can indicate special provisions on withdrawal in its advertisement, such as excluding the right or subjecting it to particular conditions.[146]

Considering that consumers are able to compare prices and quality of goods more easily when shopping over the Internet than when actually walking around through physical stores, this approach seems to be not without merit. The fact alone that consumers use the Internet as opposed to a contract in a physical shop does not mean that their ability to acquire information on the goods in question is fully impaired. While it is true that consumers may not be able to see the goods before concluding a contract with distance sales, the consumer in a physical shop is not able to see prices at competing shops easily. On the other hand, if the seller does not wish to grant the consumer a right of withdrawal, it seems to be fair to ask him to say so clearly before receiving an order. The Japanese system achieves this. The right of withdrawal is not granted unconditionally. If the consumer knows that there is no such right and still orders anyway, the seller is not forced to accept a withdrawal.

iv. Credit Card Abuse

Since Internet commerce contracts are distance contracts, until recent years the only way for the consumer to pay was using a credit (or debit) card. Compared to using a cryptocurrency like Bitcoin, this is inherently unsafe. The consumer needs to hand over all information needed for payment to the merchant. If the merchant's database is hacked or some employee of the merchant sells the consumer's card data, any third

[144] Act on Electronic Consumer Contracts, Art 3.
[145] Directive 2011/83/EU of the European Parliament and of the Council of 25 October 2011 on consumer rights, OJ 2011 No L304, p 64.
[146] Act on Specified Commercial Transactions, Art 15-3(1). See above, at II.A.ii.d, especially n 49.

party can use that data for fraudulent payments. As a consequence, annual global credit card fraud has reached USD 28.65 billion in 2019; by 2025 gross card fraud is projected to reach over USD 35 billion.[147]

Japanese law does not protect consumers from losses related to credit card fraud. However, that does not mean that consumers actually pay for these losses.

Most credit cards come with a special insurance called 'theft insurance' (*tōnan hoken*). That insurance covers losses from credit card fraud as a general rule. There is no protection if someone living with the cardholder abuses the credit card or in cases of gross negligence (for example choosing a birthday date for a PIN number).

In the absence of regulation requiring the credit card issuer to cover these losses, such an insurance model is what is expected to happen. If the credit card issuers did not provide for insurance, consumers would be reluctant to use credit cards. Therefore, providing this form of consumer protection is also in the interest of the credit card companies.

v. Anti-spam

The Japanese anti-spam law[148] is based on an opt-in model. The outdated translation available at the Japanese government translation site still shows the original opt-out concept of 2002. That was changed in 2009. Now this Act requires prior consent for sending of commercial email messages. Article 3 of the Act restricts sending of spam mail to the cases of prior consent, the receiver giving their mail address to the sender, or an existing business relationship. Article 4 of the Act requires the sender to include their name in the spam mail. Articles 5 and 6 prohibit sending spam mail from false or fictitious mail addresses.

B. Bitcoin Consumer Protection

Japan has enacted legislation in 2016[149] to regulate cryptocurrency exchanges. This law introduced a new chapter in the Payment Services Act (*Shikin kessai ni kan suru hōritsu*).[150] This was in response to the MtGox bankruptcy. In 2014, MtGox was the world's largest bitcoin exchange. Mainly because it lost several hundred thousand bitcoins due to 'theft' (worth several hundred million dollars even at the time), it collapsed. This resulted in a bankruptcy procedure with over 20,000 creditors, most of them based outside of Japan, and claims of over JPY 40 billion (approximately USD 365 million). At the time, anybody could start a bitcoin exchange. There was no special regulation in place. To avoid such spectacular failures damaging great numbers of investors, the new legislation requires registering any cryptocurrency exchange with the Financial Services Authority (*Kinyūchō*), for which minimum requirements apply.[151]

[147] 'Card Fraud Losses Reach $28.65 Billion', nilsonreport.com, 1 December 2020.
[148] Act on Regulation of Transmission of Specified Electronic Mail, Act No 26 of 2002.
[149] Act No 62 of 2016 changing the Payment Services Act.
[150] Act No 59 of 2009, Arts 63-2 to 63-22.
[151] Payment Services Act, Art 63-5.

The applicant needs to be a stock company. A foreign operator of an exchange needs to have a representative resident in Japan. The applicant needs to show a financial base sufficient for operating the exchange, set by Cabinet Ordinance[152] to a capital of JPY 10 million (approximately USD 91,000). The applicant must be able to safely and appropriately execute the exchange business. It must show an organisation that makes sure the relevant rules are followed. The executives of the exchange may not be bankrupt or convicted of crimes.

Article 63-11 of the Payment Services Act orders exchanges to keep their own funds (fiat currency and virtual currency) separate from their customers' funds. These funds need to be audited regularly. Article 63-14 requires regular reports on these funds. These measures give some minimum assurance against large scale failures like the MtGox case. The new regulation also gives the regulator oversight powers.

As a result, Japan was able to capture a large percentage of worldwide bitcoin trading volume[153] with the newly regulated exchanges being more trustworthy. This in turn helps Japan to develop its financial industry and position the Japanese financial market for the twenty-first century, which is already seeing a strong increase in the use of trustless blockchain assets.

VIII. Unfair Commercial Practices

A. Overview

'Unfair Commercial Practices' is a vast concept that may concern almost all the parts of this chapter. Especially the fraudulent and coercive commercial practices have been the subjects of our survey as a part of the information-related topics. Although we examined the problems from the viewpoints of both private law (for example the Civil Code and Consumer Contract Act) and administrative regulations (for example some provisions in the Act on Specified Commercial Transactions), we have not yet covered the consumer protection aspects of competition law in Japan.[154]

B. The Antimonopoly Act

The Antimonopoly Act[155] – the Japanese competition law – covers cartels, resale price maintenance (RPM), refusals to deal and predatory pricing, among others. If the customers of the relevant market are end consumers, competition law enforcement of those categories of conduct logically protects end consumers.

[152] Cabinet Office Ordinance on Virtual Currency Exchanges, Cabinet Office Ordinance No 7 of 2017.
[153] W Suberg, 'Japan Tops Bitcoin Trading Volume Again', Cointelegraph.com, 7 August 2017.
[154] In general see S Vande Walle and T Shiraishi, 'Competition Law in Japan' in J Duns, A Duke and B Sweeney (eds), *Comparative Competition Law* (Cheltenham: Edward Elgar, 2015) 415–42.
[155] Act No 54 of 1947.

The Antimonopoly Act also covers abuse of a superior bargaining position (ASBP). It is logically an equivalent of the exploitative abuse prohibition in EU competition law.[156] The ASBP prohibition by Article 2(9)(v) of the Antimonopoly Act could be applied to abusive conduct against end consumers because there is no statutory restriction in the provision. Even offensive behaviour regarding personal data, such as the alleged conduct by Facebook under probe by the *Bundeskartellamt* (German Federal Cartel Office), could be prohibited under the Article 2(9)(v). However, there is no precedent in which the Japan Fair Trade Commission (JFTC) applied the ASBP prohibition to abusive conduct against end consumers. It is arguably because the JFTC has enforced the ASBP prohibition following political pressures in favour of small and medium enterprises. Moreover, after the 2009 Amendment of the Antimonopoly Act, the ASBP prohibition has been equipped with a nondiscretionary fine, which the JFTC is obliged to impose when it issues cease-and-desist orders. This introduction of a tight obligation has arguably reduced the incentive of the JFTC to apply the statute to end consumer abuse cases. The JFTC created guidelines in 2019 to incorporate the idea above concerning application of the ASBP prohibition to personal data abuse, apparently inspired by the German case above. Still, actual enforcement is to be seen as of December 2021.

C. The Misrepresentation and Premium Act

The Japan Fair Trade Commission used to also prohibit misrepresentations and excessive premiums under the Misrepresentation and Premium Act.[157] In 2009, when the Japanese Government established the Consumer Affairs Agency (CAA), the JFTC transferred the relevant division to this newly created Agency. Article 1 of the Misrepresentation and Premium Act used to identify its purpose as the maintenance of fair competition. However, it was just an expedient to justify the JFTC's jurisdiction in the Act. In 2009, Article 1 was amended to identify its purpose as consumer protection, which had been the hidden purpose of the Act even before 2009. The Misrepresentation and Premium Act does not regulate unfair trade practices other than misrepresentations and excessive premiums. However, the Act has now become one of the core statutes for administrative regulation of consumer protection. It covers misleading representations which involve: (i) quality or content; (ii) price or other conditions; or (iii) other matters (for example, country of origin) designated by the Prime Minister. The Consumer Affairs Agency can issue cease and desist orders (Article 7). A Qualified Consumer Organisation can seek an injunction at courts to stop illegal conduct by the defendant (Article 30). The November 2016 Amendment has enabled the CAA to impose administrative fines, the amount of which is equivalent to three per cent of the relevant turnover (Article 8).

[156] T Shiraishi, 'The Exploitative Abuse Prohibition: Activated by Modern Issues' (2017) 62 *Antitrust Bulletin* 737, at 743–48.

[157] Act No 134 of 1962.

In addition to this prohibitive, negative control, the CAA can now exercise more positive and disclosure-enhancing control pursuant to other statutes such as the Food Labeling Act which provides a pre-contractual mandatory disclosure of the essential facts listed by the administrative 'standard' (Articles 4 and 5) and the Household Goods Quality Labeling Act which sets also the mandatory labelling standards (for example, components, performance, usage, and storage conditions) for the specified products of daily use (for example, textile goods, plastic goods, electrical appliances and apparatuses, and other goods specified by Cabinet Order). Such obligations have enabled consumers to obtain adequate information that could be hard to get without the regulations.

D. Private Enforcement

The Antimonopoly Act and the Misrepresentation and Premium Act could also be enforced by private plaintiffs. Private plaintiffs can rely on Article 709 of the Civil Code by arguing that the conduct by the defendant violated the Antimonopoly Act or the Misrepresentation and Premium Act and constituted an infringement in the meaning of Article 709. Private plaintiffs could also seek injunctions under the Article 24 of the Antimonopoly Act. Those cases could include private lawsuits by end consumers against abusive conduct, which the Japan Fair Trade Commission tends to avoid.[158] Under the Misrepresentation and Premium Act, a Qualified Consumer Organisation could seek injunctions against illegal misrepresentation, while the victim end consumers themselves could seek injunctions under the Article 24 of the Antimonopoly Act. There has been only limited private enforcement in Japan, so far, arguably because of the scarcity of plaintiff lawyers. Private enforcement of the Antimonopoly Act and the Misrepresentation and Premium Act could potentially flourish.

IX. Access to Justice

A. Overview

Based on the Constitutional right of access to the courts,[159] consumers may complain to the district court in case the amount sued for is more than JPY 1.4 million (for example product liability cases) and to the summary court not more than JPY 1.4 million (approximately USD 12,700). The following three special court systems are also open to consumers.

i. Small Claim Action

In 1996 'Small Claim Action', a special procedure before a summary court, was added in case the value of the subject matter of the action is not more than JPY 600,000

[158] Above at s VIII.B.
[159] Constitution of Japan, Art 32.

(approximately USD 5,400).[160] The trial shall be completed on the first date for oral argument and the court shall render a judgment immediately after the conclusion of the argument.[161] The examination of evidence shall be limited to what can be examined immediately, and the court may examine a witness even by a telephone.[162] After a judgment is made, only an objection to the same court is allowed, not an appeal to the court of second instance.[163]

As it was foreseeable that this action would be widely used by business money lenders or sellers against their clients (that is, obligors=debtors unable to repay), a limit on the frequent use of this action was provided (maximum 10 times per year).[164] In order to help poor defendants having difficulty in paying immediately the sum required by the judgment, the court may stipulate a provision concerning the period for payment or a provision authorising payment through instalments, both within three years of the judgment.[165] The defendant who pays following such judgment shall have the benefit of exemption from the obligation to pay any delay damages accrued after the filing of the action. About 10,000 cases appear before the small claim courts each year.

Under this system – as well as in other cases handled by the summary courts – parties often proceed themselves, without attorneys.[166] Generally speaking, the burden of attorney's fee makes consumers hesitant to litigate. In Japan a system of payment of the attorney's fee of both sides by the losing party does not exist.[167] There exists a government legal aid, 'Japan Legal Support Center',[168] offering a legal consultation free of charge. In case of litigation, it will advance the attorney's fee on the consumer's behalf. However, the consumer must pay back the cost later.[169] However, systems are in place which may overcome at least partly these financial difficulties of consumers by letting Qualified Consumer Organisations handle their claims.

ii. Injunction Demand by a Qualified Consumer Organisation

In case an enterprise conducts certain improper acts to many unspecified consumers in soliciting a consumer contract, a Qualified Consumer Organisation[170] may demand the said enterprise to stop or to prevent such acts. This injunction system was first created by the reform in 2006 of the Consumer Contract Act.[171] The targeted acts of the enterprise are classified into two groups: (1) the enterprise's act of entering into

[160] Code of Civil Procedure, Part VI: Arts 368–81.
[161] ibid, Art 374(1). 'Principle of Trial on Single Date' (Art 371).
[162] ibid, Art 372(3).
[163] ibid, Arts 377, 378(1). When a lawful objection is made, the action shall be restored to the stage before the conclusion of oral argument. In this case, ordinary proceedings shall be applied to the trial (Art 379(1)).
[164] In case of the same plaintiff obligee at the same summary court (Code of Civil Procedure, Art 368(1)).
[165] ibid, Art 375 ('Grace of Payment by Judgment').
[166] Not only in summary court proceedings, but in Japanese law suits in general, parties are allowed to take part in the litigation proceedings without being represented by an attorney.
[167] In case of tort law suits exceptionally, the plaintiff (consumer side) can in essence recover the attorney's fee by way of including the cost into the amount of damage.
[168] Comprehensive Legal Support Act, Act No 74 of 2004.
[169] Only exceptionally such poor people as welfare recipients can be excused from paying the attorney's fee.
[170] At present 22 Qualified Consumer Organisations have been certified by the Prime Minister.
[171] Consumer Contract Act, Arts 12 et seq. See above at s II.A.ii.b.

a contract which contains an unfair clause:[172] the clause is not only void but is also a subject of this injunction;[173] (2) the enterprise's act inducing mistake[174] or duress[175] of a consumer:[176] the act is not only a cause of rescission by the consumer but is also a subject of this injunction.[177]

In 2009, as part of the reforms of the Act on Specified Commercial Transactions[178] and the Misrepresentation and Premium Act,[179] and in 2013 with the promulgation of the Food Labeling Act,[180] similar systems of injunction by a Qualified Consumer Organisation were also institutionalised. Thus, Qualified Consumer Organisations have come to play a semi-governmental role of ensuring public security under the indirect control by the government (for example, through certification, supervision or revocation by the Consumer Affairs Agency), but they are having a difficult time to manage without financial support from the government. These developments are achievements under the new regime of the Consumer Affairs Agency but the strengthening and support of the activities of these Consumer Organisations would be a new problem to overcome.

iii. Special Collective Court Proceedings for Consumers (Japanese Class Action)[181]

The injunction system above does not help recover damages already caused to the consumers. Special measures for the collective recovery of damages for harm that commonly affected a considerable number of consumers became necessary. In 2013, a two-stage litigation procedure similar to the French system was introduced. In the first-stage proceedings, a Specified Qualified Consumer Organisation[182] files an action seeking to obtain a declaratory judgment on whether a 'common obligation' of the defendant enterprise exists concerning consumer contracts.[183] In case the Specified Qualified Consumer Organisation wins the first-stage, the common obligation of the enterprise having been affirmed, the second-stage proceedings for determining the

[172] ibid, Arts 8–10 et seq. See above, at s IV.A.

[173] Only those Qualified Consumer Organisations certified by the Prime Minister can process this injunction.

[174] Art 4(1)–(4) of the Consumer Contract Act. See above at s II.A.ii.b.

[175] ibid, Art 4(3). See above at s II.A.ii.b.

[176] ibid, Art 4.

[177] This might be fairly unique. However, for a victimised consumer, no longer the injunction but rather the recovery of the damage seems more important.

[178] Above at s II.

[179] Above at s VIII.C.

[180] Act No 70 of 2013.

[181] Act on Special Measures Concerning Civil Court Proceedings for the Collective Redress for Property Damage Incurred by Consumers' (Act No 96 of 2013) entering into force in 2016.

[182] Specified Qualified Consumer Organisations are Qualified Consumer Organisations specially certified by the Prime Minister as those capable of proper performance of the court proceedings for consumer damage recovery (Act on Special Measures, Arts 65 et seq). There exist four at present.

[183] This action is possible with regard to monetary payment obligations borne by an enterprise against a consumer which pertain to the following claims concerning consumer contracts: (1) a claim for performance of a contractual obligation; (2) a claim pertaining to unjust enrichment; (3) a claim for damages for non-performance of a contractual obligation; (4) a claim for damages based on a warranty against defects; and (5) a claim for damages based on the tort provisions of the Civil Code.

target (damages) claim commences. Each consumer now subscribes to the proceedings and delegates their power to the Specified Qualified Consumer Organisation, authorising it to bring an action for the consumer's claim. The Organisation then files these claims and if the defendant enterprise neither approves the claims, nor arrives at a mutual settlement, the court issues a simple determination order. This system tries to adjust to a common feature of the present-day consumer transactions that take place repeatedly with uniform products and services. For example, when a defect in a manufactured product causes damage, it often takes place in other products of the same type as well and tends to cause similar damages to many consumers, as far as their property damages are concerned – in contrast, damages as to personal injury resulting from the same product defect would vary significantly according to each case so that these human injury cases are exempted from application of this collective procedure. This is the reason why this procedure limits the target obligations narrowly and why the Act makes it necessary to check the existence of a 'common obligation' at the first stage. However, consumers would be reluctant to use the action whose successful result would only compensate the common damage among litigants but not the actual individual damage. The Government, faced with the fact that the mechanism is rarely used, has started to consider its reform.

B. Alternative Dispute Resolution[184]

Japan has three types of alternative dispute resolution (ADR) which are available to consumers: judicial, executive and private. Here we focus on the successful executive type ADR, comprising national ADR and local ADR.

i. National ADR: Consumer ADR Committee of the National Consumer Affairs Center of Japan

The National Consumer Affairs Center of Japan (NCAC)[185] handles consumer issues in collaboration with the government and local consumer centres located throughout Japan. The NCAC not only provides advice to consumer counsellors working in local consumer centres and cooperates to resolve their cases, but since 2009, it has conducted ADR of its own, establishing the ADR Committee which has an independent authority to carry out mediation and arbitration to resolve important consumer conflict cases that are necessary to be solved on a nationwide scale. The summary of the outcomes of the mediation and arbitration procedures is released as necessary in order to prevent the occurrence of similar problems and to hold back the expansion of the existing problems.[186] The NCAC also inaugurated in 2015 the Cross-border Consumer Center

[184] S Kakiuchi, 'Die Förderung der außergesetzlichen Konfliktlösung in Japan' (2014) 37 *Zeitschrift für japanisches Recht* 3.

[185] See n 10.

[186] For a map showing the flow of the procedure up to the decision by the Consumer ADR Committee in National Consumer Affairs Center (NCAC), see www.kokusen.go.jp/e-hello/about_ncac/data/ncac_adr.html; www.kokusen.go.jp/adr/pdf/adr_l.pdf.

Japan (CCJ) for the purpose of handling increasing troubles between consumers in Japan and businesses outside Japan (Cross-border Consumer Troubles).[187]

ii. Local ADR

The Basic Consumer Act provides that local governments shall endeavour to engage in such activities as the mediation of complaint processing between consumers and enterprises so that the complaints are appropriately and promptly dealt with based on expert knowledge.[188] Based on such provisions, Consumer Affairs Centers have been set up by prefectural and municipal governments. In the present, rapidly aging Japanese society and also at a time when the age of majority has been lowered from 20 to 18, the danger of victimisation of the elderly and young adults will be increasing, and the importance of these local consumer centres will grow as well.[189] The actual problems faced by these centres and the voices from consumer consulting practices all over the country will, by way of a National Consumer Affairs Center, become one of the important sources of inspiration for future legislative reforms.

C. Final Comment

Japan seems to have developed a fairly balanced consumer law system, as seen at the beginning of this chapter. In various consumer-related laws, the result of the difficult compromise between business and consumer interest can be observed. The triparty governmental organs (including the Consumer Affairs Agency) have conspicuously taken on a leadership role since 2009, and the courts have played an important role as well. Nonetheless, significant procedural and practical hurdles remain for consumers and consumer organisations to obtain effective redress. Hence, it could be said that Japan still has a long way to go.

At the same time, one must also acknowledge the limits of what can be achieved through the actions by government organs. Although they can play an enabling role, ultimately, it is the alert, everyday consumer, who will lead the way towards true progress in our global consumer society.

[187] See www.kokusen.go.jp/pdf/n-20150305_2_2.pdf. The NCAC has started in 2018 a hotline, 'Consumer Hotline for Tourists' for foreign visitors to Japan, for dealing with complaints from foreigners about consumer products and services they purchased in Japan.

[188] Basic Consumer Act, Art 19(1). On consumer safety matters, Consumer Safety Act, Art 8(1)(ii)(a), (b) and (2)(i), (ii).

[189] Since 2015, a public telephone service, 'Consumer Hotline' (dial 188), has started which connects a call of any consumer to a local consumer centre nearby.

7

Macau

DAN WEI AND ÂNGELO PATRÍCIO RAFAEL

I. Introduction

The Special Administrative Region of Macau of the People's Republic of China (Macau)[1] is a territory of 32.9 km^2 that was under Portuguese administration from the sixteenth century, until China resumed sovereignty over the territory from 1999. Today, Macau enjoys a high degree of autonomy and maintains executive and legislative powers as well as independent judicial authority until the last instance of appeal (Article 2 Basic Law of Macau). After the handover, most of the previous laws reflecting the Portuguese legal system were kept in place and are still in force today. Among those laws are most of the Consumer Law legislation. Legislative processes after the handover also normally take into consideration the legislative developments in Portugal and, by extension, in the European Union, although most Consumer Law legislation currently in force has not been reviewed since its enactment.

In 2020, Macau had a population of 683,100, and a GDP per capita of MOP 285,314 (approximately USD 35,600).[2] Its economy largely revolves around the gaming and tourism industries. Since 2001, Macau imports more goods than it exports. For example, in 2020, the Region exported goods valued in around MOP 10.8 billion (approximately USD 1.35 billion), against imports valued in around MOP 92.5 billion (approximately USD 11.5 billion), meaning a trade deficit of almost MOP 82 billion (approximately USD 10.2 billion).[3] Around 73 per cent of goods imported in 2020 were consumer goods, most of them from mainland China, the European Union, Hong Kong and Switzerland.[4]

[1] On the Status of Macau, see Article 31 of the Constitution of the People's Republic of China www.npc.gov.cn/zgrdw/englishnpc/Constitution/node_2825.htm, and the Macau Basic Law 1993 available as an unofficial translation under www.um.edu.mo/basiclaw/english/main.html, and the Joint Declaration on the Issue of Macau 1987.

[2] Statistics and Census Service of the Government of Macau Special Administrative Region, *2021 Macau in Figures* (2021), 1, available from the website www.dsec.gov.mo.

[3] ibid, 13.

[4] ibid.

In 2019, Macau received approximately 39 million tourists, over 70 per cent of which came from mainland China, followed by those from Hong Kong and Taiwan.[5] On average, each tourist spent approximately 1600 MOP (approximately USD 200) during an average stay of one day.[6]

The economic structure and the consumption patterns in Macau has evolved greatly since the first legislative efforts aimed specifically at protecting consumers in the 1980s, due to structural changes and significant development of the gaming industry in the 2000s. Yet, most of the consumer legislation has not changed. The Consumer Protection Law 1988 only establishes general principles and does not address specific problems. There is a wide range of separate legislation dealing, inter alia, with consumer health and safety, protection against unfair commercial practices, right to information, and standard form contracts. For all other matters not specifically regulated by special legislation, the Civil Code 1999 (hereinafter: Civil Code) and the Commercial Code 1999 (hereinafter: Commercial Code), apply.

II. Information Duties and Right of Withdrawal

A. The Right to Information

i. Overview

The right to information of the consumer is protected by the Consumer Protection Law 1988. While Article 3(b) announces the right, Article 9 contains the details on its content, its objective and those subject to the obligations. The right serves to enable the consumer to make a conscious and rational choice between competing goods and services and to use, under the best conditions, these goods and services. It consists of the obligation to provide true and clear information on the essential characteristics of the goods or services to be supplied, and cannot be limited under pretence of a manufacturing secret not protected by law. The obligation is placed on the producer, the manufacturer, the importer, the distributor, the packer, the warehouseman and the retailer or the service provider.

Interestingly, in the *18k Gold Watch* case decided by the Consumer Mediation and Arbitration Centre (hereinafter: Arbitration Centre),[7] the arbitrator decided in favour of the seller, considering that as the seller stated the good was an '18k pink gold watch' the buyer should not have believed that 'the whole watch was made of 18k gold', because 'it is common sense that an 18k gold watch is not made only with [gold]', and therefore it could not be said that the seller induced the buyer's error.[8] In this case, the consumer

[5] ibid, 15. Note that due to travel restrictions because of the global pandemic, the figures for 2020 are not an accurate representation of the number of tourists visiting Macau and therefore the statistics for 2019 are used.

[6] ibid, 15–16.

[7] For information consult 'CMACC' on the homepage of the Macau SAR Government Consumer council at www.consumer.gov.mo.

[8] A summary of the case is available (in Portuguese and in Chinese) from the Macau SAR Government Consumer Council (2016) 278 (26) *O Consumidor*. The full proceedings of the cases handled by the Council of Consumers are not published and the names of the parties are not disclosed.

believed that the watch was not in conformity due to later discolouration on the crown. The arbitrator found 'common sense' or the 'norms of experience' as limits to the duty of information. The decision seems to ignore the aforementioned provision on the right to information which provides information on the essential characteristics of the goods must be true and clear.

Taking a somewhat different approach, the arbitrator of the *Damaged Carpet* case – in which the dispute was triggered by the damage to a carpet following laundry services – considered that the business operator violated the duty of information, notwithstanding the latter argument that 'shrinking and deformation' were not an abnormal occurrence due to the material that the carpet was made of. The arbitrator considered that, having professional knowledge on the matter, it was the responsibility of the business operator to provide such specific information to the consumer before the services were provided to allow a rational and informed decision on whether to conclude the contract.[9]

The Standard Form Contract Clauses Law 1992 also provides for the right to information of the receiving party (often a consumer), imposing on the offeror not only the duty of adequate communication in advance, where the other party only accepts the terms,[10] but also imposes the duty to inform of the content and provide clarifications when asked.[11] Other examples of consumer legislation which provide for the right to information or the corresponding duty include the Administrative Regulation No 17/2008 of 7 July 2008[12] – the General Product Safety Regime – and Decree-Law No 50/92/M of 17 August 1992 on labelling of foodstuffs; both were inspired by Portuguese law and, by extension, European Union law.[13] The provisions of these special laws are in line with the general principle of good faith in the formation of contracts, which is normally understood as also comprising the duty to inform.[14]

ii. *Consequences of Violation*

The Consumer Protection Law 1988 is silent on the legal consequences of a violation of the right of information. Accordingly, unless another special law applies, the general regime of the Civil Code applies and, therefore, there will only be liability if the obligor acted with fault and caused damage to the other party.[15] However, in particular cases, it may be difficult for the consumer to prove that the provider of goods or services has violated the duty to provide information with fault, as is required by the general law.[16]

[9] A summary of the case is available (in Portuguese and in Chinese) from the Macau SAR Government Consumer Council (2017) 287 (25) *O Consumidor*.

[10] Standard Form Contract Clauses Law 1992, Art 5(1) and (2).

[11] ibid, Art 6.

[12] Specifically, Art 5(1) No 1.

[13] See Decree-Law 383/89 of 6 November (amended by Decree-Law 131/2001 of 24 April 2001) which in turn followed the Council Directive 85/374/EEC of 25 July 1985 on the approximation of the laws, regulations and administrative provisions of the Member States concerning liability for defective products, OJ 1985 No L210, p 29 (amended by the Directive 1999/34/EC of the European Parliament and of the Council of 10 May 1999, OJ 1999 No L141, p 20).

[14] Civil Code, Art 219.

[15] ibid, Art 219 and Arts 477 et seq.

[16] ibid, Art 480.

The question of compensation was discussed in the *Damaged Carpet* case where the arbitrator ordered the business operator to pay compensation to the consumer for the damaged carpet. However, there was no need for the consumer to prove the fault of the business provider as the arbitrator applied the rules on non-performance of contractual obligations, which impose the burden to prove the absence of fault on the defaulting party,[17] making it a special rule in relation to the general rules on compensation.[18]

The Draft Consumer Protection Law 2019 proposes the introduction of administrative penalties ranging from MOP 2,000 to 60,000 (approximately USD 2,500 to 7,500), depending on the severity, to those who violate the right to information. As to the relevance of fault and the allocation of the burden of proof, the Draft Consumer Protection Law 2019 lacks a general rule on such issues. However, it appears from the proposed rule for civil liability for provision of defective goods that the consumer is also exempted from the requirement to prove the fault of the business operator for lack of information on the defective nature of the product before the conclusion of the contract, in addition to the exemption from the need to prove the fault of the business operator for the provision of a defective product – which is the main focus of the provision.[19] A similar provision is lacking in the corresponding provision for civil liability for the provision of defective services.[20] This reinforces the need for an autonomous general provision on the relevance and burden of proof of the fault for violations of the right to information, which would eliminate the recourse to a provision from the Consumer Protection Law in relation to defective goods and a provision from the Civil Code in relation to the provision of defective services.[21]

For pre-contractual information in distance and off-premises contracts, and in prepayment contracts, the burden of proof of compliance with the duty of information on the business operator.[22] However, the provisions fall short of addressing the allocation of burden of proof of the fault for non-compliance, which is one of the conditions for civil liability claims. The wording leaves room for situations where even if the business operator cannot prove compliance with the duty of information, the consumer is still left with the most difficult task to prove that the business operator acted with fault in failing to comply with such duty. In the absence of a special rule, unless the matter could be dealt with according to Article 34 of the Draft (if approved) or Article 788 of the Civil Code, the general rule of Article 480 of the Civil Code would apply, with the burden of proof falling on the consumer, which represents an unreasonable burden for the exercise of consumer rights. A general rule exempting the consumer from proving the fault of the business operator for the violation of the right to information would be a more appropriate solution.

[17] ibid, Art 788.
[18] ibid, Art 480.
[19] Draft Consumer Protection Law 2019, Art 34(1) and (2).
[20] ibid, Art 40(1) and (2).
[21] Civil Code, Art 788.
[22] Draft Consumer Protection Law 2019, Arts 45(3) and 48(3).

Where the obligation to provide information relates to standard form contract clauses, the legal consequence of the breach of such obligation is the exclusion (juridical non-existence) of the clauses which had not been communicated, including incorrect communication.[23] Under the general terms provided in the Civil Code, the adhering party may be entitled to compensation for loss resulting from this exclusion.

Administrative Regulation No 17/2008, of 7 July 2008 (on product safety) and Decree-Law No 50/92/M of 17 August 1992[24] (on the labelling of foodstuffs) impose fines for the breach of the obligation to provide information to the consumer. Unfortunately, both lack special rules on compensation. Moreover, under the current legislation, the mechanism of control of compliance by business operators is weak, as the specialised body that deals with consumer issues – the Council of Consumers – does not have the power to demand business operators to provide information relating to their activities. This latter situation will hopefully change soon, as the Draft proposes the extension the Council of Consumers' authority to encompass supervisory powers, including the right to demand that business operators provide information.[25] The Draft also proposes to grant the Council of Consumers powers to apply the necessary administrative penalties.[26] This is clearly a leap forward in strengthening the enforcement system. However, only time would tell how effective the new rules would be, if they are approved.

B. Right of Withdrawal

Current legislation does not provide the consumer with the right to withdraw from a contract. However, the Draft proposes the introduction of a seven day cooling-off period during which the consumer may withdraw from the contract without the need to provide any justification.[27] In distance and off-premises contracts, this cooling-off period would be extended to an additional 30 day period in case of violation of the duty of information.[28] These provisions on the right of withdrawal were among the most debated during the preparation of the Draft, so it remains to be seen if they will be approved as proposed, subject to modifications or eliminated from the final version. If approved, these rules would be highly beneficial for consumers, especially the extended period for distance and off-premises sales in the current context where electronic transactions are on the rise. However, despite (or maybe even because of) the inclusion of detailed provisions on how this right of withdrawal is to be exercised, exceptions to the right, and on the responsibilities of the parties, it can be expected that this issue may be a hotspot for disputes if the provisions are approved.

[23] Standard Form Contract Clauses Law 1992, Art 9.

[24] Amended by Administrative Regulation No 7/2004 of 1 March 2004.

[25] Draft Consumer Protection Law 2019, Art 58.

[26] ibid, Art 64.

[27] ibid, Art 51. A list of exceptions to this right is presented in Art 57, and includes, for example, cases where the contract involves a good produced according to the consumer's specifications, a good which cannot be returned without deteriorating, and hospitality and transportation services, where the contract includes a performance date or period.

[28] ibid, Art 51(3).

III. Consumer Protection in the Sale of Goods and the Provision of Services: The Standards of Non-Conformity

Without prejudice to the special rules that may be applicable to the sale of certain goods or to the provision of certain services or in relation to certain types of sale or provision of services, the Civil Code establishes the general regime for sales contracts and for contracts for the provision of services.[29] Macau does not have a special law on the sale of consumer goods, which is unfortunate considering that most of the trade in the Region involves consumer goods. This means that solutions such as those recommended in the EU Consumer Sales Directive[30] on the sale of consumer goods (and more recently in the Sale of Goods Directive)[31] have not found their way into Macau's current consumer law. However, the Draft under discussion adopts many of those recommendations.

A. Sales

For sales not subject to a period of guarantee, the buyer has the right to demand the repair of the thing.[32] However, the alternative right to demand replacement is subject to two conditions: replacement being 'necessary' and the thing in question being 'fungible'.[33] While the second condition can be easily assessed, determining the first condition can surely give rise to disputes. A case-by-case analysis will have to be undertaken to make such determination.

For both repair and replacement, the buyer does not have such rights if the seller acted without fault. However, as mentioned when discussing fault in relation to the violation of the right to information, the burden of proof of the seller's fault for selling defective goods lies with the seller.[34] When related to seeking compensation, this is a special rule in relation to the general rule of Article 480 of the Civil Code, which places the burden of proof on the party seeking compensation. The consumer only bears the burden of proving the defective nature of the goods, as there is currently a presumption of conformity at all times. The Draft proposes the introduction of a special provision whereby consumers are exempted from proving that the seller acted with fault when selling defective goods.[35]

[29] Civil Code, Arts 865 et seq and Arts 1080 et seq.

[30] Directive 1999/44/EC of the European Parliament and of the Council of 25 May 1999 on certain aspects of the sale of consumer goods and associated guarantees, OJ 1999 No L171, p 12.

[31] Directive 2019/771 of the European Parliament and of the Council of 20 May 2019 on certain aspects concerning contracts for the sale of goods, OJ 2019 No L136, p 28. This Directive repeals the EU Directive 1999/44/EC, with effect on 1 January 2022; see also, Directive 2019/770 of the European Parliament and of the Council of 20 May 2019 on certain aspects concerning contracts for the supply of digital content and digital services, OJ 2019 No L136, p 1.

[32] Civil Code, Art 906.

[33] ibid, Art 907.

[34] ibid, Art 788.

[35] Draft Consumer Protection Law 2019, Art 34(2).

The buyer must notify the defect to the seller within 30 days of knowing of the defect or one year after the thing is delivered.[36] If the seller acted with intent, the buyer can file directly for the annulment of the contract and compensation for the damages that would not have been suffered if the contract was not concluded.[37] Such right to annulment and compensation can be exercised within one year after discovering the defect where the seller acted with intent.[38] In cases of error,[39] the right to annulment and compensation may only be exercised if the buyer reported the defect to the seller within the aforementioned time periods and sought annulment within six months after reporting the defect.[40]

In the *Scratched Bed Frame* case, a consumer requested the annulment of a contract of sale and the reimbursement of the price paid, alleging that the bed delivered was not in conformity with the contract due to scratches on the frame.[41] The arbitrator dismissed the consumer's request considering that the defect only affected the aesthetic appearance and did not affect the functionality, thus ordering the seller undertake the necessary repair, based on Article 914 of the Civil Code.

The Draft Consumer Protection Law 2019 proposes the introduction of a rebuttable presumption that a defect detected within six months after the good is delivered already existed at the time of delivery.[42] After six months, a presumption of conformity would exist and the consumer would need to prove any alleged non-conformity. This represents a partial reversal from the current regime as, according to the general rules of the Civil Code, there is an implicit general presumption of conformity at all times, as the burden of proof of non-conformity with the contract falls entirely on the consumer. It is apparent that the Draft was inspired by the EU Consumer Sales Directive with regard to the presumption of non-conformity in the first six months after the delivery of the good.[43] Nevertheless, the Draft maintains the period of one year already present in the Civil Code 1999, within which the seller is responsible for any non-conformity of the goods with the contract,[44] which differs from the two years under the Consumer Sales Directive.[45] Additionally, the Draft maintains the time limit of 30 days for the consumer to inform the seller of the non-conformity, which also represents a lower standard than the (minimum) two month period under the Consumer Sales Directive.[46]

Where a period of guarantee applies, the fault of the seller is irrelevant for the exercise of the right to repair or replacement.[47] The defect must be reported within the

[36] Civil Code, Art 909(2).
[37] ibid, Arts 896 and 900, by force of Art 905.
[38] ibid, Art 280.
[39] There is 'error' where the decision to buy was tainted by a wrong or inexact understanding of reality, and such 'mistake' was both 'essential' (determinant) to the decision of the buyer to conclude the contract and 'cognoscible' by the seller (see Civil Code, Art 240).
[40] Civil Code, Art 910.
[41] A summary of the case is available (in Portuguese and in Chinese) from the Macau SAR Government Consumer Council (2017) 284 (20) *O Consumidor*.
[42] Draft Consumer Protection Law 2019, Art 33(2).
[43] Consumer Sales Directive (EU), Art 5(3).
[44] Draft Consumer Protection Law 2019, Art 33(1).
[45] Consumer Sales Directive (EU), Art 5(1).
[46] ibid, Art 5(2).
[47] Civil Code, Art 914.

guarantee period and 30 days after the defect is known, except where otherwise agreed by the parties.[48] The right to file for annulment and compensation can also only be exercised within six months after the defect has been reported to the seller and is subject to the condition of such reporting within the legally or contractually agreed period. In this case, there is no difference in the time limitations between the cases where there is intent and the cases where an error by the buyer.

B. Services

For typified service contracts (mandate, deposit and construction contracts) only the construction contract contains rules on defective services. As for sales contracts, the defects must be reported within 30 days from the date of their knowledge;[49] the right to initiate arbitration or litigation expires within one year of the rejection of the defective construction or of its acceptance with reservation.[50] The owner has the right to demand the elimination of defects if possible, or to require a new construction if defects cannot be eliminated.[51] However, the right to repair and re-construction ceases if expenditure is disproportionate to the price – such rule does not exist for sales contracts.[52] The alternative for the owner is to demand reduction of the price or the termination of the contract, and compensation in the general terms.[53]

The case *Non-uniform Kitchen Tiles* decided by the Arbitration Centre concerned an alleged non-conformity of a construction service as the construction company had affixed on one of the kitchen walls, tiles with different designs from the tiles affixed onto the remaining three walls.[54] In dismissing the consumer's complaint, the arbitrator focused on the time limitation to report the defects and to initiate arbitration or litigation proceedings. As the complainant had reported the defects after more than a year, the arbitrator dismissed the complaint on the grounds that the relevant time limitation had expired.

The Draft proposes the regulation of consumer services, establishing rules for services to conform with the contract. It establishes a rule exempting the consumer from the need to prove the fault of the services provider when seeking compensation.[55] It also establishes a rule establishing that where the services are to be provided again to replace a previous defective provision of services, they shall be provided within 30 days.[56]

[48] ibid, Art 914(3).

[49] ibid, Art 1146.

[50] ibid, Art 1150.

[51] ibid, Art 1147(1).

[52] ibid, Art 1147(2). However, the Draft proposes a similar solution in relation to consumer contracts involving the provision of goods and services, Art 34(3) and (4) and Art 40(3).

[53] ibid, Arts 1148 and 1149.

[54] A summary of the case is available (in Portuguese and in Chinese) from the Macau SAR Government Consumer Council (2018) 303 (23) *O Consumidor*.

[55] Draft Consumer Protection Law 2019, Art 40(2).

[56] ibid, Art 40(4).

IV. Unfair Contractual Clauses and Standard Form Contracts

The inclusion of unfair contractual clauses constitutes a violation of the consumer's right to equality and loyalty.[57] It also constitutes a breach of the general principle of good faith.[58] The Standard Form Contract Clauses Law 1992 contains lists of absolutely prohibited and another of relatively prohibited clauses;[59] Macau does not adopt a general unfairness test. The nullity of clauses, both absolutely prohibited and relatively prohibited clauses that are found to be unfair can be relied on at all times, in accordance with Article 14(2) of the Standard Form Contract Clauses Law 1992 and Article 279 of the Civil Code.

In addition to the prohibition of the use of certain clauses, the Standard Form Contract Clauses Law 1992 has another mechanism of control against unfair contractual clauses: the judicial or procedural control activated through an injunction.[60] Besides the (main) lawsuit intended at obtaining a definitive prohibition, the law allows entities with standing to apply for an interim measure for a provisional prohibition where there is a well-founded fear that the contractual clauses being challenged will be included in individual contracts. This would happen if, for example, when conducting arbitration of a consumer dispute or after receiving a complaint from a consumer, the Council of Consumers finds that a service provider has incorporated prohibited clauses in their standard contract and despite advising it to make corrections, the service provider expressly refuses to do so or remains inert. Under the current framework, however, this provision is of little practical relevance and we are not aware of its use to assert consumer rights. In part, this may be due to the limited powers of the Council to obtain information from business operators. With the possible expansion of those powers if in the Draft are approved, it is possible that this mechanism of control gains more practical importance.

The Standard Form Contract Clauses Law 1992 only grants standing to file for an injunction against the use or recommendation of standard form contract clauses to the following entities: the Council of Consumers, professional associations or associations of economic interests legally constituted acting within the scope of their attributions, and the Public Prosecutor's Office either on its own initiative or at the request of any interested party.[61] However, individuals also appear to have such standing based on the Civil Procedural Code general rule on the protection of diffuse interests.[62]

If the use of abusive contractual clauses is demonstrated, the court declares them null and void, and may issue such declaration on its own initiative, both in relation to absolutely prohibited clauses and in relation to clauses that are relatively prohibited.[63]

[57] Consumer Protection Law 1988, Art 7.
[58] Civil Code, Art 219.
[59] Standard Form Contract Clauses Law 1992, Arts 12 and 13.
[60] ibid, Arts 17 et seq.
[61] ibid, Art 18(1).
[62] Civil Procedural Code, Art 59.
[63] Standard Form Contract Clauses Law 1992, Art 14 and Civil Code, Art 279, second part.

Those who have suffered damages from the use of prohibited standard form contract clauses may seek compensation under the general terms of civil law, subject to the practical difficulties brought by the legal requirement of proving the fault of the infringer when seeking compensation.[64]

Despite the law establishing severe consequences for the use of unfair contractual clauses, we have found only few challenges to these clauses either in court or in arbitration. Of course, this may be because business operators abide by the law and consumers are satisfied or this may be because of other factors. A significant part of consumers in Macau are typically day tourists for whom it may not be convenient to initiate and proceed with judicial or even arbitration proceedings in Macau.

Nonetheless, the *Express Transport Services* case involved a Macau consumer who bought watercolour paints online from a store in mainland China.[65] The watercolour paints were damaged at the time of delivery, whereby the consumer filed a complaint with the Council of Consumers against the transport services company, demanding compensation. The transport services provider was only willing to pay MOP 50 (approximately USD 6), invoking a clause in the transport services standard form contract which limited its liability up to such amount, notwithstanding that the value of the damaged goods was MOP 500 (approximately USD 600). The arbitrator excluded the standard form contract clause and awarded compensation to the consumer equivalent to the value of the damaged goods.

Macau law does not expressly distinguish between substantive unfairness and procedural unfairness. However, it is possible to identify rules in which the legislator strives to protect the consumer (and other subjects) from substantive unfairness and other rules in which the legislator appears to seek to tackle procedural unfairness. An example of the former is the prohibition of some standard form contract clauses.[66] An example of the latter is apparent in the protection of consumers against 'aggressive methods of sales promotion that undermine conscious evaluation of the contractual clauses and the free formation of the contracting decision'.[67]

V. Product Liability

Articles 85–95 of the Commercial Code contain a product liability regime. Article 85(1) establishes a system of strict liability of the producer (manufacturer, importer or distributor).[68] This legal solution, as the whole section on product liability, was based on the Portuguese Product Liability Act,[69] which in turn followed the EU Product Liability Directive 85/374/EEC.[70]

[64] Civil Code, Arts 477 et seq, Art 480.

[65] A summary of the case is available (in Portuguese and in Chinese) from the Macau SAR Government Consumer Council (2018) 290 (22) *O Consumidor*.

[66] Standard Form Contract Clauses Law 1992, Art 12.

[67] Consumer Protection Law 1988, Art 7(a), second part.

[68] Commercial Code, Art 85(2) and (3).

[69] Decree-Law 383/89 of 6 November 1989, amended by Decree-Law 131/2001 of 24 April 2001.

[70] J Fan and AD Pereira, *Commercial and Economic Law in Macau* (Alphen aan den Rijn: Kluwer Law International, 2011) 128–29; JC da Silva, *Responsabilidade Civil do Produtor* (Coimbra: Almedina, 1990) 451 et seq.

Both personal injury and property damages are compensable.[71] However, property damages to goods other than the defective product, are only compensable if they are usually intended for private use or consumption and the injured party mainly used the good in such manner.[72]

The right to compensation is subject to a three-year prescription period from the date on which the injured person had or should have been aware of the damage, defect and identity of the business operator;[73] it expires in any event within 10 years from the date on which the business operator put the product causing the damage into circulation, except where an action brought by the injured party is pending.[74]

VI. Product Safety

The general product safety regime is provided for by the Administrative Regulation No 17/2008 of 7 July 2008 (hereinafter: Regulation), which, in general, adopts the standards of the EU General Product Safety Directive.[75] The Regulation establishes a general safety obligation, determining in succinct and peremptory terms that 'only safe products can be placed on the market'.[76] It excludes from its scope of application, inter alia, all foodstuffs.[77] Safe products are defined as those 'which, under normal or reasonably foreseeable conditions of use, present no risk or present a low risk, compatible with its use and considered acceptable according to a high level of protection of the health and safety of consumers'.[78] Compliance with product safety regime is monitored by the Directorate of Economic Services (DSE).[79]

In addition to the general safety requirement, the Regulation also contains several specific obligations of the producer and the distributor.[80] The legislator attaches particular importance to the duty to provide information, which is patent in several respects in the various obligations imposed on the producer and distributor. For example, the producer is required to take appropriate measures, depending on the characteristics of the product supplied, and to keep the consumer informed about the risks that the product may present.[81]

The recall of dangerous products may take place at the initiative of the producer and/or the distributor, or by order of the Chief Executive.[82] The costs for the recall and eventual destruction of dangerous products are borne by the respective producers and

[71] Commercial Code, Art 91.
[72] ibid, Art 91, final part.
[73] ibid, Art 93.
[74] ibid, Art 94.
[75] Directive 2001/95/EC of the European Parliament and of the Council of 3 December 2001 on general product safety, OJ 2002 No L11, p 4.
[76] Regulation No 17/2008, Art 4.
[77] ibid, Art 1(2) No 1.
[78] ibid, Art 3(1).
[79] ibid, Art 7(1).
[80] ibid, Arts 5 and 6.
[81] ibid, Art 5(1) No 3.
[82] ibid, Arts 5(1), (3), 6(3) and 8(2).

distributors.[83] The process of recall of dangerous products, that is, the specific steps to be followed and the responsibilities for carrying out those steps, is not regulated in detail, although the general obligations established in Article 6 puts the responsibility on the distributor to ensure that the recall process is conducted in a safe manner.

VII. Adaptation to the Digital Age

Law No 5/2005 of 8 August 2005 regulates electronic documents and signatures – recognising electronic documents, for example, as having the same legal value as written (paper) documents if their content can be represented as a written declaration and their integrity can be demonstrated.[84] There is no other legislation dealing specifically with substantive aspects of electronic transactions and there is no special adjective legislation dealing with the matter. E-commerce consumer transactions and related disputes are therefore regulated by the existing special consumer legislation and subsidiarily by the general provisions of the Civil Code and of the Civil Procedural Code 1999 (hereinafter: Civil Procedural Code), respectively.

The number of online transactions in Macau has constantly increased in recent years. Indeed, in 2020, the number of online shoppers increased to 145,000 Internet users (an increase of 17 per cent percent from 2019), while the average spending remained stable at MOP 1,000 (approximately USD 125).[85] In 2020, 82.9 per cent of Macau's population used internet services. This means that despite the increase and the large coverage of internet services, the percentage of online shoppers in relation to the number of people with Internet access and in relation to Macau's total population remains low. Nonetheless, the trend shows that the number of online shoppers will continue to increase in the near future, and in any event e-commerce consumer relations already deserve better regulation.

In that light, the matter has been considered in the Draft Consumer Protection Law 2019 which includes provisions on distance contracts. It imposes strict information requirements on business operators.[86] Regarding the proposed cooling-off period, the business operator is subject the special obligation of informing the consumer on this right, its time limitation and the method of exercise.[87] The violation of this special duty of information would trigger the automatic extension of the cooling-off period by an additional 30 days during which the consumer could exercise the right of withdrawal.[88]

The proposals contained in the Draft would be a major leap forward in the protection of online shoppers. Notwithstanding, even if approved the provisions would in practice be of limited reach, especially in a context of cross-border transactions.

[83] ibid, Art 14.
[84] Law No 5/2005, Art 3.
[85] Statistics and Census Bureau, 'Survey on Information Technology Usage in the Household Sector for 2020' (March 2021).
[86] Draft Consumer Protection Law 2019, Arts 45 et seq.
[87] ibid, Art 45(1) No 10.
[88] ibid, Art 51(3).

The effectiveness of the proposed rules largely depends on upgrading of other regional consumer protection laws and on increased cooperation especially concerning the use of alternative dispute resolution mechanisms, such as through online dispute resolution systems. Thus far, legislation containing provisions similar to the ones in the Draft described above are lacking in Hong Kong[89] and in mainland China the protection standards differ (for example, there is no rule on the extension of the seven day cooling-off period, which apply to all transactions, including online transactions),[90] although some online retailers and platform operators have voluntarily adopted better standards.[91]

VIII. Unfair Practices in Relation to Consumers

A. Unfair Commercial Practices

The Consumer Protection Law 1988 declares the right of the consumer to protection of health and safety against unfair or irregular advertising or supply of goods or services.[92] It also establishes protection against abuse resulting from the adoption of standard form contracts and aggressive methods of sales promotion, which undermine the conscious evaluation of contractual clauses and on the unenforceability of the payment of goods or services the provision of which was not expressly requested.[93]

The Standard Form Contract Clauses Law 1992 also imposes some barriers on the adoption of clauses that may give rise to unfair commercial practices, imposing absolute prohibitions and relative prohibitions, as well as mechanisms of control, as described above.[94]

The Draft proposes the introduction of detailed provisions on unfair commercial practices, which would include 'misleading commercial practices' and 'aggressive commercial practice'.[95] It includes provisions containing long lists of practices that are considered misleading or aggressive. In cases considered as serious violations, in addition to fines ranging from MOP 20,000 (approximately USD 2,500) to 60,000 (approximately USD 7,500), the Draft proposes the application of the sanctions of closure of the business establishment and/or an injunction on practising the relevant business activity.[96]

Notwithstanding the fact that unfair commercial practices appear to be one of the major focuses in the Draft, no major cases involving the issue have been reported in Macau. This does not mean that the problem does not exist, but the absence of legislation listing practices considered unfair, such as the ones in the Draft, may be a practical obstacle for consumers to identify them.

[89] See the national report on 'Hong Kong' in this book.

[90] See the Law of the People's Republic of China on the Protection of Consumer Rights and Interests 2013, Art 25.

[91] China Daily, 'Revised law will apply to online shopping', chinadaily.com, 15 March 2014.

[92] Consumer Protection Law 1988, Art 3(a).

[93] ibid, Art 7(a), (c).

[94] See above at s IV.

[95] Draft Consumer Protection Law 2019, Arts 23 et seq.

[96] ibid, Art 63.

B. Unfair Advertising Practices

Law No 7/89/M of 4 September 1989 represents the Law on Advertising Activities. In its Preamble, it is indicated that this Law was inspired by two Portuguese laws on advertisement activities, namely Decree-Law No 303/83 of 28 June 1983 and Law No 96/88 of 17 August 1988.[97] Thus, it becomes clear that, like most of its contemporary Macau legislation, the Law on Advertising Activities was directly inspired by solutions adopted in Portuguese law and, by extension, by EU law.

As general principles, the Law establishes that advertising messages must be lawful, identifiable (as advertisement) and truthful, and must respect the principles of free and fair competition and consumer protection.[98] The same Law lists a series of prohibited forms of advertising and forms of advertising subject to conditions.[99]

Unlike the Consumer Protection Law 1988 and the Standard Form Contract Clauses Law 1992, which are silent as to the liability of the infringer for the violation of the consumer's rights, the Law on Advertising Activities contains a rule on liability, declaring joint and several liability of the owners of advertising apparatus and the advertising agent with the advertiser for damages caused to third parties as a result of dissemination of illegal advertising messages.[100] The Law also contains a provisions on criminal liability and on administrative liability.[101]

IX. Access to Justice

The Consumer Mediation and Arbitration Centre of the Council of Consumers aims to solve consumer disputes of no more than MOP 50,000 (approximately USD 6,200) in the territory of Macau through mediation, conciliation and arbitration.[102] Business operators may adhere in advance, in writing, to the Centre's regulation regime for arbitration of consumer disputes.[103]

The process begins with a complaint by the party that feels that their rights have been violated and such complaint shall be made according to Article 8 of the Regulation No. 11/1998. Complaints can be submitted face-to-face, or through an out-of-hours call

[97] Decree-Law No 303/83 was later repealed by Decree-Law 330/90, which, inter alia, harmonised Portuguese legislation with EU legislation (Council Directive 84/450/EEC of 10 September 1984 relating to the approximation of the laws, regulations and administrative provisions of the Member States concerning misleading advertising, OJ 1984 No L250, p 17 (no longer in force) and Council Directive 89/552/EEC of 3 October 1989 on the coordination of certain provisions laid down by Law, Regulation or Administrative Action in Member States concerning the pursuit of television broadcasting activities, OJ 1989 No L298, p 23 (no longer in force), and the European Convention on Television Without Borders [1989] ETS No 132).

[98] Law No 7/89/M, Art 3.

[99] ibid, Arts 7–9.

[100] ibid, Art 25.

[101] ibid, Arts 26 and 27.

[102] Regulation No 11/1998 of 18 March 1998, Art 1, as amended by the Order of the Secretary for Economy and Finance of 3 May 2001.

[103] ibid, Art 7.

recording service.[104] The parties are then notified for an attempt to conciliate or, if this results in failure, a trial. If the parties reach an agreement in the conciliation procedure, such agreement shall be officially approved and shall have the same value as a decision rendered in arbitration, which, in turn, has the same enforcement force as a court judgment.

The existence of an arbitration agreement is an impediment for the parties to submit the case to the courts, but if the case is submitted to a court in violation of such agreement, the lack of jurisdiction must be raised before the first statement of defence.[105] The parties are bound by the arbitral decision of the Centre, although they may challenge its validity with the courts under the same terms as other arbitral decisions.[106]

The Council of Consumers established in March 2018 an online dispute resolution system which is especially aimed at dealing with cross-border consumer disputes.[107] To materialise its operation, the Council of Consumers concluded cooperation agreements with its counterparts of the Greater Bay Area, which includes cities from the Guangdong province in mainland China, and Hong Kong. In November 2018, the system was used to conduct a successful conciliation between a consumer from Macau and a real estate agent from the Hengqin district in the neighbouring city of Zhuhai (mainland China).[108] The plan is to gradually extend the use of this online dispute resolution system to cross-border disputes involving parties not only from mainland China but from other parts of the world.

The parties may, if the value of the case does not exceed MOP 100,000[109] (approximately USD 12,500) and provided that there is no arbitration agreement, submit their dispute to the Judicial Base Court. It will be heard under a special process – 'the process for small claims'.[110] If the value exceeds MOP 100,000, the case shall nevertheless be submitted to the Judicial Base Court, but it will be heard under the common procedure.[111] Where the value does not exceed MOP 250,000 (approximately USD 31,000) it will be handled under the expedited procedure; claims exceeding that threshold will be handled under the ordinary procedure.[112]

Besides individual lawsuits, class actions, in an opt-out system, are also admitted in Macau for the protection of consumer and other diffuse interests.[113] Individuals, consumer associations and foundations, municipalities, and the Public Prosecutor's Office all have standing to bring and intervene in such lawsuits. Moreover, other types of plurilateral actions can be used, namely joint actions (*litisconsórcio*) and

[104] For more details, including the forms for complaint, for information and for suggestion, visit: Macau SAR Government Consumer Council, 'Consumers Complaint and Enquiry' (constantly updated) under www.consumer.gov.mo.

[105] Civil Procedural Code 1999, Art 31.

[106] Decree-Law No 29/96/M of 11 June 1996, Arts 37–39.

[107] https://app.consumer.gov.mo/wapp.

[108] Macau SAR Government Consumer Council (2018) 304 (18) *O Consumidor*.

[109] This is the value up to which courts of first instance can decide without the possibility of appeal, Law 9/1999 of 20 December 1999, Art 18(1).

[110] Law 9/1999 of 20 December 1999, Arts 10(2), 27(1) and 29-A; Civil Procedural Code, Art 1285(1)(b).

[111] Civil Procedural Code, Art 369(2), final part.

[112] ibid, Art 371.

[113] ibid, Art 59.

colligation (*coligação*).[114] Joint actions are used for cases based on the same material legal relationship.[115] Differently, colligation is used where, despite the diversity of material legal relationships, the cause of action is the same with different requests; there is a relationship of dependency between the requests; the decision depends on the appreciation of the same facts, or on the interpretation and application of the same legal rules or of perfectly analogous contractual clauses.[116] Except the cases where a joint action is 'necessary' by force of law, of contract or by the nature of the basic material legal relationship, voluntary joint actions and colligations rely on an opt-in system, and there is simply an accumulation of lawsuits and the different parties to the action maintain their independency.

However, from the 97 judgments issued by the Judicial Base Court at the time of writing, published on the page of the Macau SAR courts, not one deals with consumer disputes. Obviously, this does not mean that there are no consumer disputes that may have been submitted to courts, since most decisions of the Judicial Base Court are not published.

Macau courts have, in general, jurisdiction over cross-regional consumer disputes involving an element from mainland China, Hong Kong or Taiwan, or even transnational disputes that involve a personal or patrimonial element in Macau and an element of other foreign jurisdictions. As a principle, Macau has jurisdiction over all (consumer) cases in the territory.[117] The Civil Procedural Code contains more detailed rules on jurisdiction of Macau courts. If the facts that gave rise to the dispute occurred in Macau, or if there is a personal or patrimonial connection of the dispute with Macau, Macau courts have jurisdiction.[118]

Cross-regional disputes, especially those involving parties from Macau and mainland China are increasingly common, especially disputes involving tourists who visit Macau and, to some degree, Macau residents who buy products from the mainland online. As mentioned above, for now, Macau does not have any legislation dealing specifically with e-commerce disputes or even substantive norms on electronic transactions. Thus, e-commerce disputes are dealt with according to the general provisions of the Civil Procedural Code and relevant provisions from special consumer legislation.

X. Conclusion

The sources of consumer law in Macau are dispersed across several pieces of legislation. The Consumer Protection Law 1988, which is the general law on consumer protection, is outdated, as it has not followed the socio-economic developments of the last decades, especially since the development of the gaming industry in the 2000s. This

[114] See ibid, Arts 60–66.
[115] ibid, Arts 60 and 61.
[116] ibid, Art 64.
[117] Macau Basic Law, Art 19; Law 9/1999 of 20 December 1999, Art 1.
[118] Civil Procedural Code, Art 15.

status is attenuated by the various specific regimes and the general rules of the Civil Code and of the Commercial Code, but the inherent risk of fragmentation and lack of harmony materialises in relation to several aspects. For example, there are situations of 'passive conflict' between the different pieces of legislation, especially in relation to the remedies for violation of consumer rights and interests. For example, for the violation of the right to information, which is a cornerstone of consumer law, none of the analysed laws seem to offer adequate protection, especially for matters of compensation, as the Consumer Protection Law 1988 is silent on the issue, the Standard Form Contract Clauses Law 1992 only provides for the exclusion of the relevant clause and the Regulation No 17/2008 on product safety only prescribes administrative penalties against the offender. This scenario means that the applicable regime for matters of compensation is the regime of the Civil Code, the standards of which are very detrimental to a proper protection of consumers, as the consumer is required, as a general rule, inter alia, to prove that the provider of goods or services acted with fault when violating consumer rights. The consumer is only exempted from proving the fault of the business operator when the violation is linked to a non-performance of the contract.

We submit that, in the realm of consumer law, the ideal solution would be a general rule excluding the need for the consumer to prove the fault of the business operator for violations of consumer rights, and whenever deemed appropriate, special exceptions to that general rule would be put in place. The current solution is the opposite, and the Draft Consumer Protection Law 2019 basically maintains the status quo, notwithstanding exempting the consumer from proving the fault of the business operator for violations of its rights in most instances. However, the approach of regulating each issue specifically, without a general (consumer law) rule, has left a loophole in relation to the rules on the provision of services, which would continue to rely on the rules of the Civil Code 1999 if the Draft Consumer Protection Law 2019 is approved as it is.

In general, however, the Draft proposes to bring consumer protection in Macau closer to the best standards of consumer protection in the world. It addresses many of the weaknesses of the current regime. Indeed, it goes beyond just establishing general principles of consumer protection, as the current Consumer Protection Law 1988 does, to establish detailed rules on several issues, including on the right to information, on unfair commercial practices, on the conformity of the goods or services with the contract, on distance contracts and off-premises contracts, on pre-payment contracts, on the sanctions for the violation of consumer rights and mandatory legal rules, and on the (expanded) powers of the Council of Consumers.

Only time will tell how effective the new Law will be, considering the special economic reality consumer structure of Macau, which largely depends on the tourism industry (linked with the gambling industry) with consumers that stay in the Region for less than a day and half on average. Another relevant factor which is and will continue to impact consumer relations and will test the effectiveness of the law and its supporting enforcement structure is the increase in cross-border transactions (both online and offline) also involving the local population. The increased economic integration which is ongoing in the Greater Bay Area – which includes Macau, Hong Kong and several cities in the Guangdong province in mainland China – will likely increase cross-border consumer transactions and disputes and will test the different legal systems, enforcement structures and dispute resolution mechanisms in place. The work developed by the Council of Consumers in cooperation with its counterparts in the neighbouring cities, namely the signing of cooperation agreements for enhancing information exchange and mutual reception and transfer of consumer complaints between consumer protection agencies, and the introduction of an online dispute resolution system is a step in the right direction.[119] Notwithstanding, a debate on the possible approximation of consumer laws to accompany the increased economic integration and the possible rise in consumer disputes, seems timely. In such debate, the experiences of the European Union can be particularly valuable.

[119] Macau SAR Government Consumer Council, 'Estabelecer a plataforma de cooperação na área de defesa do consumidor da Grande Baía Guandong-Hong Kong-Macau' (2018) 297 (17) *O Consumidor*.

8

Malaysia

ZALINA ZAKARIA

I. Overview

Consumer rights and consumer protection law provide a way for individuals to fight back against abusive business practices. Such laws are designed to prevent businesses that engage in fraudulent or specified unfair practices from gaining an advantage over competitors. It is a form of government regulation whose aim is to protect the rights of consumers. In Malaysia, proper recognition of consumer protection began in 1999 through the introduction of the Consumer Protection Act which was based on the model established by Consumers International based on UN Guidelines. The main consumer associations fought for more than 20 years for the Act to be enacted.[1] It was said by the then Minister of Domestic Trade and Consumer Affairs that there were more than 30 laws that had consumer protection characteristics, yet none contained a comprehensive single law specific to consumers. This Minister explained that it took so long for the Act to materialise due to the fact that some agencies thought that the focus should be on consumer education rather than law. It was also reported in the *News Straits Times* on 25 July 1999 that the Ministry, together with consumer movements and other social organisations had, since 1992, sought to put in place the Consumer Protection Bill. The consumer protection regime was therefore introduced after many years of effort and much work convincing all stakeholders. The uproar over the strength of this Act had reduced and it was then introduced and finally gazetted on 9 September 1999.

There are several improvements that have been brought by the Consumer Protection Act, as the specific act on consumer protection. This report will explain the improvements particularly from the perspective of consumer protection, namely information duties and the right of withdrawal, sales law, unfair contract terms, product liability, product safety, adaptation to digital age and consumer access to justice.

II. Consumer Protection Timeline

In Malaysia, the history of consumer protection can be divided into two main phases: the colonial era and post-colonial era.

[1] For detail, see M Hamdan Adnan, *Perjuangan Perundangan Pengguna* (Petaling Jaya: IBS Buku, 2005).

A. Colonial Era

Malaysia was colonised by four nations. Firstly, Malaysia was colonised by the Portuguese from 1511 until 1641. It was then taken over by the Netherlands. By virtue of an Anglo-Dutch treaty, the British took over Malaysia from the Dutch in 1824. From 1941 until 1945, Malaysia was subjected to Japanese conquest and occupation. Finally, in 1945 the British reoccupied Malaysia and this set it on its path to being an independent country in 1957. Although it was occupied by four separate powers, the law for the country's administration comes from the British, as the British occupation lasted for more than 150 years. This was especially true in relation to mercantile law. Sections 3 and 5 of the Civil Law Act 1956 provide for the reception of English common law and statutes in areas of mercantile law where there is no Malaysian statute. However, the law to be imported is the law 'as would be administered in England in the like case on 7 April 1956 [the date the Act first came into force] if such issue had arisen in England'. Unless the Malaysian Parliament enacts new laws or amends those inherited at the time of independence, the English law as at 7 April 1956 will apply.

During the British colonial era, two laws were implemented: the Contracts Act 1950 (Amendment 1974) and the Sale of Goods Act 1957. These two statutes are of great significance in consumer purchases. Both can be traced back to the English nineteenth-century ideal of equal bargaining power between contracting parties and the maxim of freedom of contract.[2] The Contracts Act 1950 codified the English common law pertaining to contracts and applies to all contracts including those between producers and consumers. The Malaysian Sale of Goods Act 1957 is based on the English Sale of Goods Act 1893. In the UK, the Sale of Goods Act 1979 has superseded the Sale of Goods Act 1893. The latter Act has itself been amended on several occasions, thus giving added protection to consumers.[3] However, the enhanced rights conferred by the UK Sale of Goods Act 1979 and subsequent amendments to it have not yet been included in the Malaysian Sale of Goods Act 1957. Hence, for instance, in the Malaysian context, the implied terms that the goods match the description, be of merchantable quality, and be fit for their purpose could be excluded by an express term of the contract.[4] This situation remained until the adoption of the Consumer Protection Act in 1999.

B. Post-Colonial Era

Before 1999, there were approximately 30 Acts related to consumer protection that have been enforced under different ministries,[5] whereby some of these Acts existed before Malaysian independence in 1957, such as the Dangerous Drugs Act 1952, Poisons

[2] N Amin, 'Product Liability Under the Consumer Protection Act 1999' (1999) 7(2) *IIUM Law Journal* 175.

[3] NB the Consumer Rights Act 2015 (UK) now contains an – in part – separate system for consumer contracts.

[4] Sale of Goods Act 1957, s 62.

[5] S Shaik Ahmad Yusoff and R Ismail, 'Perlindungan Pengguna Di Bawah Undang-Undang: Pembekalan Barang & Perkhidmatan' (2008) 12 *Jurnal Undang-Undang dan Masyarakat* 48.

Act 1952 and Contracts Act 1950. Other Acts that also uphold consumer rights include: Sale of Goods Act 1957, Food Act 1983, Medicines (Advertisement and Sales Act 1956), Sale of Drugs Act 1952, Control of Drugs and Cosmetics Regulations 1984, Registration of Pharmacies Act 1951, Electricity Supply Act 1990, Gas Supply Act 1993, Road Transport Act 1987, Railways Act 1991, Control of Supply Act 1961, Price Control Act 1977, Sale of Goods Act 1957, Weights and Measures Act 1972 and Trade Descriptions Act 1972.[6]

Although approximately 30 Acts were introduced, there was no specific general regulation on consumer protection in Malaysia. This only occurred with the Consumer Protection Act, which entered into force on 15 November 1999 following a lengthy process. There are two reasons for this. First, the government did not want to burden foreign investors with comprehensive and rigid consumer protection legislation. Second, the Act indeed required a long period to be drafted; traders opposed it as they feared it would stifle their business affairs. There were a number of reactions during the debate on the consumer protection bill in the Malaysian Parliament. In addition, this Act was opposed by several ministries, namely the Ministry of Health and Ministry of Housing and Local Government, because it would reduce these ministries' jurisdictions and would create an overlap of enforcement powers. The Act was placed under the ambit of the Ministry of Domestic Trade, Co-operatives and Consumer Affairs.[7] This is the main ministry that has been mandated with governing most consumer affairs in Malaysia. Currently, there are a number of Acts that are enforced by this ministry, for example the Price Control Act 1946, Supply Control Act 1961, Trade Descriptions Act 2011, Hire Purchase Act 1967, Weights and Measures Act 1972, Copyright Act 1987, Direct Sales and Anti-Pyramid Scheme Act 1993, Franchise Act 1998, Consumer Protection Act 1999 and Optical Discs Act 2000, Goods and Services Act 2014.

Apart from the Ministry of Domestic Trade, Co-operatives and Consumerism, there are other ministries that regulate consumer goods. The Ministry of Health, for example, governs several other Acts such as the Food Act 1983, Dangerous Drugs Act 1952, Poisons Act 1952, Medicines (Advertisement and Sale) 1956, Sales of Drugs Act 1952 and Control of Drugs and Cosmetics Regulations 1984. These Acts were enacted and enforced to protect consumers from the adverse effects of consumer products that are dangerous and of poor quality especially in relation to important consumer goods such as foods, pharmaceuticals and cosmetics.

The Ministry of Science, Technology and Innovation has also played its role in consumer protection in Malaysia. This ministry promoted the Research Institute of Standards Malaysia (Corporation) Act 1975 through which the Department of Standards Malaysia was established. The department was tasked with drafting various standards relating to the protection and safety of consumers.[8] Malaysia also has an effective national body, the Standards and Industrial Research Institute of Malaysia, to certify products and develop product standards. Its role is geared more to assisting

[6] Hamdan Adnan, 'Perjuangan Perundangan Pengguna'.

[7] ibid.

[8] For example, Standard of Information Security Management System MS ISO / IEC 27001: 2007 and Food Safety Management Standard EN ISO 220000: 2012.

the manufacturing sector to produce products that meet Malaysian and international standards. Although its role is to develop standards, it has no enforcement powers. It tests products voluntarily submitted by manufacturers for a fee and sells them its standard marks if they meet the required standards under its Certification Marketing Scheme. It is considered that with these labels, the manufacturers may have an edge over other competitors in Malaysia. However, the Standards and Industrial Research Institute does not collect accident statistics related to consumer products or develop mandatory standards for all manufacturers and importers to comply with. The Consumer Protection Act now permits the Minister of Domestic Trade and Consumer Affairs to specify mandatory standards.

Another important ministry is the Ministry of Urban Wellbeing, Housing and Local Government. This ministry implements Housing Developers (Control and Licensing of 1966 Act (Revised 1973), Rent Control Act 1966, and Pawn Act 1972 in order to uphold consumer rights related to housing.

The Ministry of Transport is responsible for the Road Transport Act 1987, Malaysian Institute of Road Safety Research Act 2012 and Road Transport Rules, and the Railways Act 1991. These were enacted to regulate the policies and regulations related to road safety, vehicle technical specifications, enforcement, railways assets and the railways sector developments.

The Ministry of Information, Communication and Culture has under its jurisdiction the Communications and Multimedia Act 1998, Communications and Multimedia Commission Act 1998 and Personal Data Protection Act 2010. These were enacted to provide a regulatory framework to cater for the convergence of the telecommunications, broadcasting and computing industries. Apart from that, it is tasked with regulating communications and multimedia activities in Malaysia and enforcing the communications and multimedia laws of Malaysia and other related matters.

III. Information Duties and Right of Withdrawal

A. Information

Information regulation is an important instrument that is significant under a consumer protection regime in any jurisdiction. Information regulation is regarded as a 'smart' option as it preserves consumer choice, improves competition among firms and does not include technical rigidity which may be caused by product standards. In short, consumer protection mechanisms help to create an atmosphere where producers take responsibility themselves for not only producing their products but also for monitoring and reacting to dangers. The law indeed plays a role by imposing requirements on producers to create procedures to detect and react to concerns about their products.

There is no particular mandatory set of provisions on general information rules under Malaysian law. The Consumer Protection (Electronic Trade Transactions) Regulations 2012 provide that any person who operates a business for the purpose of supply of goods or services through a website or in an online marketplace (goods or services marketed by a third party) shall disclose certain key information on the website where the business is conducted.[9] Such information includes, for example, the name of the business, a description of the main characteristics, the full price (including delivery costs), the terms and conditions and the method of payment.[10]

However, what can be found in the Consumer Protection Act 1999 could be linked to information duties, which is mentioned in relation to misleading and deceptive conduct, false representation and unfair practices.

Some literature in Malaysia linked information duties with advertisement and false description.[11] In 2011, there was a significant amendment to the Trade Description Act of 1972. Through the preamble, it states the aim of promoting good trade practices by prohibiting false trade descriptions and false or misleading statements, conduct and practices in relation to the supply of goods and services and to provide for matters connected therewith or incidental thereto. The main purpose of this Act is to punish offenders who commit acts of misleading and falsehood descriptions in their businesses or trading. The goods sold or services rendered must tally to the information provided, either by descriptions displayed on the label of the goods or the brochures or other documents related to the services advertised. In short, the labels or advertisements shall not give misleading or false descriptions that induce the customers to purchase the goods or hire the services.

The representations made by the seller are usually by way of advertisement. Advertisement is capable of informing the consumers of the benefits of a product, but at the same time it may also mislead the consumers. Advertisement is a powerful medium in today's businesses. Without regulation by the law, consumers would be subject to the mercy of the sellers. In the Trade Description Act 2011, 'advertisement' means every form of advertising (whether or not accompanied by or in association with spoken or written words or other writing or sounds and whether or not contained or issued in a publication) by the display of notices or by means of catalogues, price lists, circulars, labels, cards or other documents or materials or by the exhibition of films or of pictures or photographs, or by means of radio or television, or in any other way including through electronic means.[12]

The Trade Descriptions Act 2011 is a statute of criminal application. It is stated that a false trade description is a trade description which is false to a material degree.[13] The terms of 'false' or 'misleading' have been defined to mean any conduct, representation, statement or practice which is capable of leading any person into error.[14] It could be linked to information regulation in a way information attached to any product or services must be accurate and not mislead anyone.

[9] Consumer Protection (Electronic Trade Transactions) Regulations 2012, s 3(1).

[10] ibid, schedule 3.

[11] KH Hassan, 'E-commerce and Consumer Protection in Malaysia: Advertisement and False Description' (2012) 32 *IPEDR* 45.

[12] Trade Description Act 2011, s 2.

[13] ibid, s 7(1).

[14] ibid, s 13.

B. Right of Withdrawal

i. Cooling-off Period

At present, the only law that contains a cooling-off period provision is the Direct Sales and Anti Pyramid Scheme Act 1993. This Act is under the purview of the Ministry of Domestic Trade and Consumer Affairs. This Act provides for the licensing of persons carrying on direct sales business, for the regulation of direct selling, for prohibiting pyramid scheme or arrangement, chain distribution scheme or arrangement or any similar scheme or arrangement, and for other matters connected therewith. 'Direct sale' means a door-to-door sale, a mail order sale or a sale through electronic transaction within the meaning of this Act.[15] 'Electronic' means the technology of utilising electrical, optical, magnetic, electromagnetic, biometric, photonic or other similar technology.

It is specifically required that in any direct sales contracts, in respect of a door-to-door sale for the supply of goods or services and a contract in respect of a mail order sale, the contract must be in writing where the goods or services have a value of MYR 300 or more (approximately USD 70); and must contain immediately above the place provided for the signature of the purchaser the statement 'this contract is subject to a cooling-off period of 10 working days' which is specified to be printed in upper case in type not smaller than 18 point and shall be signed both by vendor and the purchaser. During the cooling-off period, no goods or services will be performed until the cooling-off period has expired.[16] However, the consumer in a direct sales contract may require the seller to perform during the cooling-off period. The request has to be made in writing and, if performance is requested, the consumer waives the right of withdrawal.[17]

Although this cooling-off period is a good provision that permits the consumer to withdraw from the order within a specified period of time, it is also subject to criticism. It was said that the 10-day cooling-off period is not reasonable in giving the consumer adequate time to withdraw. In particular, it was suggested that that the 10-day cooling off period should start from the date the customer receives the goods ordered and not from the time of ordering. Another point that has been raised is that the cost of returning the goods is borne by the buyer.

ii. Warming-up Period

The 2019 amendment to the Consumer Protection Act 1999, by adding Part IIIB, extends it to credit sale transactions. The provisions, however, do not apply to a credit sale transaction entered into between a purchaser and a corporative society that is registered under Co-operative Societies Act 1993 or any sale transaction involving a credit card.

[15] Direct Sales and Anti-Pyramid Scheme Act 1993, s 2.
[16] ibid, s 25(1).
[17] ibid, s 25(2).

The reason for the insertion of the new provisions of credit sale transactions is due to the Minister's decision based on the higher percentage of household indebtedness every year. It was also due to the fact that many credit facility providers have charged consumers at a very high interest rate that could result in their exploitation in easy-payment schemes. Credit facility has been defined in this new provision as 'a facility provided by a credit facility provider under a credit sale transaction which allows the payment of goods to be made in instalments' which has been spelt out in section 24L Consumer Protection Act 1999. Preconditions for a credit sale agreement have to be met before any credit sale agreement is entered into in respect of any goods or class of goods between a seller or any credit sale provider, or anyone on behalf of the seller or credit sale provider. A written statement relating to the summary obligation of the prospective purchaser must be served on the prospective purchaser and must be signed by the seller. The prospective purchaser is under no obligation to enter into any credit sale agreement,[18] however, if there is the wish to proceed with the purchase, then this may be done after three days of the service of the written statement by the credit sale provider.

This will give the prospective purchaser a reasonable time to either proceed with the sale or not, and such time would allow them to read and understand the statement more thoroughly or at least give them time to ask around, if there is uncertainty about any of the conditions in the facility provided, either in terms of the total payment, time of payment, the annual percentage rate etc. If the purchaser decides to proceed with the purchase, then a credit sale agreement must be prepared by the credit facility provider, which shall be made in writing and in the national language (that is, Bahasa Malaysia) or the English language at the choice of the purchaser before the agreement is signed.[19] The credit sale agreement also spells out the rights and obligations of the purchaser as well as the credit facility provider. Another important provision in this credit sale agreement is regarding the limitation on charges, whereby they shall not exceed the prescribed rate in respect of the goods/class of goods.

IV. Sale of Goods

In Malaysia, the common law principles during the eighteenth and nineteenth centuries, which were based on the practice of freedom of contract as well as the *laissez faire* concept, were the basis of the law of sale of goods in Malaysia. The Sale of Goods Act came into the picture in 1957, the same year as Malaysia's independence. It was previously known as the Sale of Goods (Malay States) Ordinance and is the main piece of legislation governing the supply of goods in Malaysia affecting the content of a contract for the sale of goods, in general. Parallel to the Sale of Goods Act 1957, the Consumer Protection Act 1999 contains a system of guarantee rights and remedies available to consumers in contract for the *supply* of goods, that is, the scope is not limited to

[18] Consumer Protection Act 1999, s 24N(7).
[19] ibid, ss 24O and 24R(1)(a).

contracts of sale. Pursuant to section 30 of the Consumer Protection Act, the guarantees apply whether or not the goods are supplied in connection with services.

A. Implied Guarantees

Sections 31–37 of the Consumer Protection Act 1999 contain a list of implied guarantees where goods are supplied to a consumer. Whereas some of these guarantees have counterparts under the Sale of Goods Act 1957 – such as the implied guarantee of title,[20] compliance with sample[21] and description[22] – there are a number of notable distinctions. For example, in contrast to the Sale of Goods Act 1957, the provisions on implied guarantee of title also feature and detail an information obligation whereby the supplier is to first orally advise the consumer as to the way in which the right to quiet possession of the goods may be varied.[23] The quality guarantee under section 32 of the Consumer Protection Act 1999 also differs from section 16 of the Sale of Goods Act 1957, not only in relation to its general application but also the quality standard. For consumer goods, there is an implied guarantee that the goods are of 'acceptable quality' (contrast 'merchantable quality'), bearing resemblance to section 14(2B) of the English Sale of Goods Act 1979, with the list of quality criteria, for example durability, fitness for purpose, safety, etc.

Sections 36 and 37 of the Consumer Protection Act 1999 are two novel guarantee rights. Section 36 concerns an implied guarantee as to the price. Pursuant to this provision, there is an implied guarantee that the consumer shall not be liable to pay more than the reasonable price where the price is not otherwise determined. If the supplied breaches this guarantee, the consumer only has a right to refuse more than the reasonable price. Section 37 concerns an implied guarantee as to repairs and spare parts. This provision places the manufacturer and the supplier under the obligation to take reasonable action to ensure that facilities for the repair of goods and the supply of spare parts are reasonably available for a reasonable period after supply. This obligation does not apply where reasonable action has been taken to inform the consumer that the manufacturer or supplier does not undertake that repair facilities and spare parts will be available.

B. Right of Redress

Under the Consumer Protection Act 1999, the consumer has a right to seek redress against a supplier of goods and, in some circumstances, against a manufacturer of goods for breach of the implied guarantees.

[20] Sale of Goods Act 1957, s 14; Consumer Protection Act 1999, s 31.
[21] ibid, s 17; ibid, s 35.
[22] ibid, s 15; ibid, s 34.
[23] Consumer Protection Act 1999, s 31(2)–(4).

i. Supplier

Sections 39–49 of the Consumer Protection Act 1999 set out the redress mechanisms available to consumers against suppliers in the event of a breach of the implied guarantees in sections 31–37 of the Act. According to section 41(1) Consumer Protection Act 1999, the remedies available to the consumer may depend on whether or not the defect can be remedied. If the defect can be remedied, the consumer may require the supplier to remedy the failure within a reasonable time.[24] The supplier may satisfy this requirement through repairing or replacing the goods, curing any defect in title or refunding the consumer where the supplier cannot be reasonably expected to satisfy the requirement by these means.[25] If the supplier refuses or neglects to remedy in a reasonable time, the consumer may seek cure elsewhere (and obtain from the supplier all reasonable costs incurred) or reject the goods.[26]

If the defect cannot be remedied or is of a 'substantial character',[27] the consumer may reject the goods or obtain damages in compensation for any reduction in value.[28] Whereas section 45 of the Consumer Protection Act 1999 details the manner of rejecting goods, section 43 states the circumstances in which the right is lost.

ii. Manufacturer

Sections 50–52 state the consumer's rights against manufacturers in respect of guarantees in the supply of goods. The implied guarantees concerned, however, only include acceptable quality, correspondence with description and the failure to comply with the guarantee as to repairs and spare parts.[29] The liability for breach of the implied guarantees of quality and description can be excluded where the manufacturer is not responsible for the breach (for example, act by another).[30]

The redress available to the consumer vis-à-vis the manufacturer for breach of an implied guarantee is limited to damages (a) for loss in value calculated against the purchase price; and (b) for consequential loss or damage to the consumer.[31] The consumer may, under an express guarantee by the manufacturer, require the manufacturer to repair or replace the goods. However, where the consumer requires repair or replacement, the claim for damages relating to loss in value is not available unless the manufacturer refuses or fails to remedy, or does not do so in a reasonable time.[32]

[24] ibid, s 40(1)(a).
[25] ibid, s 42(1)(a)–(d).
[26] ibid, s 41(3).
[27] As defined in s 44 of the Consumer Protection Act 1999. According to this provision, substantial character includes significant deviation from description/same/model, substantially unfit for purpose, unsafe goods.
[28] ibid, s 41(1)(b).
[29] ibid, s 50(a)–(c).
[30] ibid, s 51.
[31] ibid, s 52(1).
[32] ibid, s 52(2).

V. Unfair Terms

A significant improvement to the protection of consumer rights has been made by the Consumer Protection (Amendment) Act 2010, which was brought into effect in 2011. This amendment has to a certain extent resolved the issue of the inadequacy of the Contracts Act 1950, which had no provisions regarding unfair contract terms. It also served as an amendment to the Consumer Protection Act 1999, which did not specifically deal with unfair contract terms to provide redress in the situation.[33] Previously, this was the major loophole in the Malaysian consumer protection law. The amendment is particularly significant as Malaysia usually follows the UK, Australia and New Zealand, but on this occasion it has adopted the Indian Law Commission's Report on Unfair (Procedural and Substantive) Terms in Contract, which divides unfairness into 'procedural' and 'substantive' unfairness.[34] It was stated that such a division has not been done in any other country so far.[35]

A. Definition

Unfair contract terms provision has been dealt with by the Consumer Protection Act 1999. Section 24A(c) defines an unfair term as 'a term in a consumer contract which, with regard to all the circumstances, causes a significant imbalance in the rights and obligations of the parties arising under the contract to the detriment of the consumer'.[36] This general test of unfairness inevitably raises difficult issues of interpretation, which are subjective. From the definition, a fair contract term requires a perfect balance between the rights and obligations of the parties to the contract.

B. Scope

In order to deal with unfair contract terms, a new Part has been included in the Consumer Protection Act 1999, namely Part IIIA. Section 24B states that 'the provisions of this Part shall apply to all contracts', but this is misleading as it is clearly restricted to business-to-consumer contracts, given that the stated purpose of the Act is only the protection of consumers. A further unclear aspect is whether Part IIIA applies to all types of consumer contracts or whether just to matters within the scope of the Act. This Part aims in particular to protect consumers against unfair terms in a standard form contract, a type that is commonly adopted by traders and is the basis for the majority of contracts in consumer transactions.[37]

[33] N Amin, 'Protecting Consumers Against Unfair Contract Terms In Malaysia: The Consumer Protection (Amendment) Act 2010' (2013) 1 *Malayan Law Journal* 89.

[34] Law Commission of India, '119th Report on Unfair (Procedural & Substantive) Terms in Contract' (August 2006).

[35] Amin, 'Protecting Consumers', 89.

[36] Consumer Protection Act 1999, s 24A(c).

[37] Amin, 'Protecting Consumers', 91–92.

C. Assessment

In order to assess the fairness of a contract/a term, the 'procedural' and 'substantive' division has been made in the 2019 amendment to the Consumer Protection Act. Procedural unfairness is based on the manner/process of making a contract, whereas substantive unfairness looks at the content. The concept of such a division has been recognised under the common law and can be found in the statute on contract law. It must be remembered that sometimes even a correct procedure would not be able to produce fairness since a consumer's ability to make rational decisions when entering into contracts may be limited by various factors.[38] Therefore, adopting both a procedural and substantive approach on unfairness would make it clearer that a contract or term in a contract can be declared to be unfair by itself despite its compliance with requirements of transparency and clarity.

i. Procedural Unfairness

According to section 24C(1) Consumer Protection Act 1999, a contract or a term of a contract is procedurally unfair if it has resulted in an unjust advantage to the supplier or unjust disadvantage to the consumer on account of the conduct of the supplier or the manner in which or circumstances under which the contract or the term of the contract has been entered into or has been arrived at by the consumer and supplier.

In determining procedural unfairness, a court or consumer tribunal may take into account the following list of considerations, that are: (a) the knowledge and understanding of the consumer in relation to the meaning of the terms of the contract or their effect; (b) the bargaining strength of the parties to the contract relative to each other; (c) reasonable standards of fair dealing; (d) whether or not, prior to or at the time of entering into the contract, the terms of the contract were subject to negotiation or were part of a standard form contract; (e) whether or not it was reasonably practicable for the consumer to negotiate for the alteration of the contract or a term of the contract or to reject the contract or a term of the contract; (f) whether expressions contained in the contract are in fine print or are difficult to read or understand; (g) whether or not, even if the consumer had the competency to enter into the contract based on their capacity and soundness of mind, the consumer was not reasonably able to protect their own interests or of those whom they represented at the time the contract was entered; or suffered serious disadvantages in relation to other parties because the consumer was unable to appreciate adequately the contract or a term of the contract or its implications by reason of age, sickness, or physical, mental, educational or linguistic disability, or emotional distress or ignorance of business affairs; (h) whether or not independent legal or other expert advice was obtained by the consumer who entered into the contract; (i) the extent, if any, to which the provisions of the contract or a term of the contract or its legal or practical effect was accurately explained by any person to the consumer who entered into the contract; (j) the conduct of the parties who entered into the contract in

[38] ibid, 95.

relation to similar contracts or courses of dealing between them; and (k) whether the consumer relied on the skill, care or advice of the supplier or a person connected with the supplier in entering into the contract.

In the above consideration, transparency is the most significant requirement in procedural fairness. It denotes that any difficult term or any ambiguous jargon should be clarified to the consumer who wants to enter into a contract to allow for an informed decision.

ii. General Substantive Unfairness

For general substantive fairness, section 24D(1) of the Consumer Protection Act 1999 states that a contract or a term of a contract is substantively unfair if the contract or the term of the contract (a) is in itself harsh; (b) is oppressive; (c) is unconscionable; (d) excludes or restricts liability for negligence; or (e) excludes or restricts liability for breach of express or implied terms of the contract without adequate justification. However, all the five terms do not have clear definitions, or at least some illustrations. This could lead to different interpretations. It could be argued that the terms are vague and could carry ambiguity. Accordingly, the terms such as 'harsh', 'oppressive' and 'unconscionable'[39] need further clarification.

In determining substantive unfairness, a court or consumer tribunal may take into account a list of considerations (a) whether or not the contract or a term of the contract imposes conditions: (i) which are unreasonably difficult to comply with; or (ii) which are not reasonably necessary for the protection of the legitimate interests of the supplier who is a party to the contract; (b) whether the contract is oral or wholly or partly in writing; (c) whether the contract is in standard form; (d) whether the contract or a term of the contract is contrary to reasonable standards of fair dealing; (e) whether the contract or a term of the contract has resulted in a substantially unequal exchange of monetary values or in a substantive imbalance between the parties; (f) whether the benefits to be received by the consumer who entered into the contract are manifestly disproportionate or inappropriate to their circumstances; (g) whether the consumer who entered into the contract was in a fiduciary relationship with the supplier; and (h) whether the contract or a term of the contract: (i) requires manifestly excessive security for the performance of contractual obligations; (ii) imposes penalties which are disproportionate to the consequences of a breach of contract; (iii) denies or penalises the early repayment of debts; (iv) entitles the supplier to terminate the contract unilaterally without good reason or without paying reasonable compensation; or (v) entitles the supplier to modify the terms of the contract unilaterally.

Looking at the long list of considerations in determining substantive unfairness, it should be noted that it is difficult to fathom how 'whether the contract is oral or wholly or partly in writing', and 'whether the contract is in standard form' could relate to substantive fairness assessment having understood that substantive fairness assessment should not focus on the 'procedural aspects' of contract making.

[39] ibid, 100.

D. Effects

Section 24G(1) of the Consumer Protection Act 1999 states that a court or consumer tribunal may declare an unfair contract term under subsections 24C and 24D to be unenforceable or void. Alternatively, a court or tribunal may consider the unfair term to be severable and give effect to the remaining terms. In a case where the contract is able to stand without the unfair term, a court or tribunal has the discretion to determine the extent and the manner to enforce and give effect to the remaining contract term. In addition to civil liability, Part IIIA imposes criminal liability. Section 24I makes the contravention by any person of any provision of Part IIIA an offence. In other words, not only can unfair terms be set aside, a criminal action can also be taken against traders who insert such terms. Although such provision could be seen as a rationale to creating a deterrent effect on traders, it is highly doubtful if this criminal sanction could be invoked as the nature of the contravention has not been spelt out clearly in the provisions especially on what are considered as unfair and mandatory procedural compliance. It is pertinent to note that other jurisdictions have so far not seen the need to make any inclusion of an unfair contract term an offence.

E. Case Example: *Fairview International School*

In so far as case law is concerned, the issue of unfair terms has been discussed in a case brought to judicial review in 2017.[40] The principal ground of this case involves the review of the decision-making process such as 'excess of jurisdiction' or 'error of law' by the Tribunal for Consumer Claims Malaysia. In this case, the applicant operated the Fairview International School (Subang Jaya Campus) ('the School'). The first respondent was the Consumer Claims Tribunal ('Tribunal'), while the second respondent was the parent of Sabheena binti Mohd Adam ('Sabheena') who enrolled as a student in the School. Sabheena enrolled in the School in Year 8 on 25 April 2011. At that time, the School operated on three terms of four months duration per academic year. Sabheena's enrolment was subjected to the School's Regulations ('terms and conditions') which were, inter alia, as follows: (i) in the event of withdrawal of the student from the School, one full academic term notice in writing must be given in advance failing which the security deposit shall be forfeited in full; and (ii) the School reserved the right to amend the terms and conditions from time to time. The second respondent was unhappy with the School's decision not to allow Sabheena to take Chemistry as a subject in Year 10 on the grounds that Sabheena's performance in Chemistry did not qualify her to take the subject further. Hence, on 21 January 2013 the second respondent served the withdrawal notice on the School to withdraw Sabheena from the first semester, academic year 2012/2013 as from 23 January 2013 and requested the School to refund the security deposit amounting to MYR 12,500 (approximately USD 3000). The School refused to

[40] *Fairview International School Subang Snd Bhd v Tribunal Tuntutan Pengguna Malaysia & Anor* [2015] 1 CLJ 224, Judicial Review No 25-69-11-2013.

refund the security deposit contending that the notice of withdrawal was insufficient notice. The second respondent then filed a claim with the Tribunal and the Tribunal held in favour of the second respondent. The applicant brought this application for judicial review against the award of the Tribunal. The applicant primarily contended that the Tribunal had acted *ultra vires* and without jurisdiction as the applicant was not covered by the Act. And even if the Tribunal had jurisdiction, it erred in construing the enrolment contract between the applicant and the second respondent. On the other hand, the second respondent contended that the first respondent was clothed with jurisdiction and correctly awarded the second respondent the refund of the deposit as claimed. The first respondent found and held that the applicant's amended semester duration of six months was void because of section 24A of the Consumer Protection Act in that it was made unilaterally by the applicant without informing the second respondent. However the first respondent overlooked that the contract empowered the applicant to make such amendments. She did not construe this empowerment provision *vis-a-vis* sections 24A to 24D and even if this provision was void, whether the original provision that required one full academic term of four months' notice was similarly void. In light of the competitive environment that private schools operate including this school, the Court did not consider the original provision that require the full academic term of four months' withdrawal notice to be neither imbalanced to the detriment of the parent or pupil nor substantively unfair in contravention of section 24A or section 24D of the statute. The Court thought that it was a reasonable provision to enable the school to properly plan its intake of student population. As a matter of public policy, such provision according to the court also instilled commitment and discouraged students from switching schools at their whims and fancies thereby depriving other students of a place. As per the provision empowering the school to unilaterally amend the terms and conditions, the Court thinks that such a provision per se is neither objectionable nor unreasonable. It is situational depending on how the provision is utilised and the resultant contents and effect of the amended term or condition. For example, an amendment to tighten school discipline to curb rising student delinquency should be acceptable. Conversely, an unjustified sudden major hike in school fees would be unacceptable. The problem here concerned the unilateral alteration by the applicant of an academic year comprising three terms of four months' duration to two semesters of six months' duration. Consequently, it affected the period of service of withdrawal notice. The purpose of the change could be the betterment of the system of student learning which the Court did not find objectionable. This is considered neither procedurally nor substantively unfair by the Court. It is also not heavily imbalanced to the detriment of the parent or student. The position would however be different if the dominant purpose of the applicant was just specifically to increase the period of service of the notice but there was no evidence adduced by the second respondent to that effect. It was therefore held that the first respondent fell into error when it construed this amended provision as void for contravening section 24A of the Consumer Protection Act. That notwithstanding, the problem here is not that the second respondent gave four instead of six months' withdrawal notice that was inadequate. In fact the applicant was only given two days' notice by the second respondent. Even if the amended provision is void, the second respondent was still bound by the original notice provision and the first respondent had obviously again overlooked or disregarded that provision. The first respondent appeared to be more influenced by the factual version of the events advanced by the second respondent over the conflicting factual version of the applicant. It is not the Court's function to review the relative merits of the evidence adduced and the resultant findings of fact by the first respondent. In any event, there was plainly no evidence of waiver of the notice provision on the part of the applicant. It was also not the second respondent's case that the applicant repudiated the contract. In other words, the second respondent did not terminate the contract, but had merely withdrawn his daughter from the school after giving two days' notice. In such a scenario, the terms of the contract were in the court's view fully operative and must be observed. In the circumstances, the Court therefore found that the first respondent fell into the more serious error for holding that there were extenuating circumstances that justified the second respondent withdrawing his daughter from the school without giving the required notice. There was plainly short notice and this error of law warranted judicial intervention. It was held that *certiorari* order was granted quashing the first respondent's award dated 7 October 2013 and order costs of RM7,500 made to be paid by the second respondent to the applicant.

VI. Product Liability

Product liability law is set out in the law of contract, tort of negligence common law principles, strict liability and in a number of statutes. Both the common law and legislation offer different rights to compensation for loss or damage of goods to different classes of people. The Consumer Protection Act 1999 was enacted to provide improved legal protection to consumers so a product liability clause has also been included in this Act (Part X).[41]

The Consumer Protection Act 1999 introduces a system of liability in respect of death, personal injury and damage to property caused by defective products. Such a system is believed to overcome the problems inherent in contractual and negligence remedies and accordingly gives better protection to the consumer. The Act provides that with respect to any defect in a product that causes any damage at all, the liability for causing the damage shall be borne by the producer of the product, or the person putting their name/mark on the product, or the importer.[42] The provision indicates that even in the absence of any contractual relationship or proof of fault liability can still be imposed. Thus, to succeed in a product liability claim, the plaintiff only has to prove damage, a defect in the product and a causal link between the two.

This approach has advantages for the consumer as liability may be proved from a defect alone. However, the plaintiff still has the onus of proving such a defect in the product, which might create substantial obstacles for consumers, especially in relation to proving design defects. Proof of causation will also pose a problem as in many cases the evidence used to establish causation will be extremely similar to the efforts required of previous consumers to establish fault.[43]

[41] Amin, 'Product Liability', 175.
[42] Consumer Protection Act 1999, s 68(1).
[43] Amin, 'Product Liability', 177.

The Act also helps consumers in terms of procedure as it relieves them of the need to prove fault. Although they do still need to prove that their injury was caused by the defect, they do not, it appears, need to prove that the producer was responsible for the defect. In contrast to contractual liability, some commentators have noted that liability under the Act cannot be limited or excluded, either by a contract term, a notice or other provisions.[44]

A. Product

Despite the wide definition of 'product' provided by the Act, it certainly does not cover every product. In certain cases, the definition of product appears to raise some difficulties. Section 66 defines 'product' as: 'any goods and, subject to sub-section (2), includes a product which is comprised in another product, whether by virtue of being a component part or raw material or otherwise'. In this definition, three types of products are clearly covered by the Act, namely, goods, component parts and raw materials. Section 3 provides that 'Goods' means goods which are primarily purchased, used or consumed for personal, domestic or household purposes, and includes, for example, goods attached to, or incorporated in, any real or personal property, animals (including fish), vessels and vehicles. It does not include choses in action, including negotiable instruments, shares, debentures and money.

B. Persons Liable

The Act does not make every person connected with the product liable. The persons liable under the Act can be divided into two categories, namely the primary defendant and secondary defendant. The primary responsibility for damage caused by a defective product is placed on the primary defendant, in particular the 'producer'. The secondary defendant will only be liable in certain circumstances and that liability may be channelled back to the primary defendant. Section 68(1) lists three principal persons who may be strictly liable under the Act: the producer of the product, the own-brander and the importer.

i. Producer

Section 66(1) of the Consumer Protection Act 1999 states that 'producer', in relation to a product, means:

(a) the person who manufactured it;
(b) in the case of a substance which has not been manufactured, won or abstracted, the person who won or abstracted it;
(c) in the case of a product which has not been manufactured, won or abstracted but essential characteristics of which are attributable to an industrial or other process having been carried out, the person who carried out that process.

[44] ibid.

The definition of 'producer' appears to be broad enough to extend to every person in the manufacturing chain. Every 'manufacturer' of a component part is jointly or severally liable under the Act.

ii. Own-brander

Strict liability also applies to any person who, by putting their name on the product or using a trade mark or other distinguishing mark in relation to the product, has held himself out to be the producer of the product.[45] Such 'own brand' products are often found in supermarkets and department stores, whereby products are manufactured in accordance with the seller's own specifications. The extension of strict liability to such 'own-branders' is a significant approach under the Consumer Protection Act,[46] yet in consideration of the 'own-brander's' typically strong economic position and choice of manufacturer, the decision to impose strict liability is justifiable from the perspective of their control over the product.[47] Nonetheless, it has been questioned whether the own-brander is liable where it has clearly indicated (even in small print) that it is not the manufacturer.[48]

iii. Importer

The Act apportions further significant liability to importers. Section 68(1)(c) attaches liability to anyone who has imported a product in the course of business to supply it to a third party. The purpose of this provision appears to be to overcome the practical problem of having to sue a foreign producer in its own country. By contrast, the supplier's liability is secondary in that it only surfaces when it fails to tell the injured person the identity of the producer, own-brander, importer or supplier of the product in a reasonable time.[49]

C. Defences

The various defences to product liability are stated in section 72(1) Consumer Protection Act 1999. According to this provision, it can be a defence if the defect is attributable to compliance with any requirement imposed under any written law; if the defective product was not supplied at any time to another person; if defect did not exist in the product at the relevant time;[50] if the state of scientific and technical knowledge at the relevant time was not such that a producer of products of the same description as the product in question may reasonably be expected to discover the defect if it had

[45] Consumer Protection Act 1999, s 68(1)(b).
[46] ibid.
[47] ibid.
[48] ibid.
[49] N Amin, 'Product Liability Under The Consumer Protection Act 1999' [1999] *IIUM Law Journal*.
[50] Defined in Consumer Protection Act 1999, s 72(2).

existed in his product while it was under his control; or if the defect (i) is a defect in a product in which the product in question is comprised therein (the 'subsequent product'); and (ii) is wholly attributable to the design of the subsequent product; or compliance by the producer of the product in question with instructions given by the producer of the subsequent product.

VII. Product Safety

Before 1999, there were seven parent pieces of legislation which regulated product safety in various goods, and these are still in force.[51] These were added to by the Consumer Protection Act 1999 which has brought significant changes to product safety. The law on product safety in Malaysia can be found in two forms of legislative instruments: general legislation related to general safety standards for all products, and sectoral legislation that deals piecemeal with specific products.[52] An outline of product safety legislation in Malaysia is given in Table 1 below.

Table 1 Product Safety Legislation

Type of Product	Legislation	Objectives	Government Agency
Pesticides	Pesticides Act 1974	To control the importation, production, sale and storage of pesticides through registration of import and export permits.	Ministry of Agriculture and Agro-Based Industry Malaysia
Pharmaceuticals (Prescribed medicines, over-the-counter medicines, traditional and complementary product)	Dangerous Drugs Act 1952	To control and make regulations on the importation, exportation, production, sale and use of opium and other dangerous drugs.	Ministry of Health Malaysia
	Poisons Act 1952	To control the importation, possession, manufacturing, storage, transportation and use of poisons.	
	Sale of Drugs Act 1952		
	Medicine (Advertisement and Sales) Act 1956	To prohibit certain advertisement relating to medical matters and to regulate the sale of substances recommended as a medicine.	

(continued)

[51] S Sothi Rachagan, *Consumer Law Reform: A-Report* (United Nations Development Programme 1992).
[52] Rahmah Ismail et al, 'Consumer Right To Safe Product: The Application Of Strict Criminal Liability In Product Safety Legislations In Malaysia' [2012] *Pertanika Journal of Society, Science & Humanity* 20.

Table 1 *(Continued)*

Type of Product	Legislation	Objectives	Government Agency
Electrical Installations and Appliances	Standards of Malaysia Act 1996	To establish the Department of Standards Malaysia to formulate policies, programs, scheme, projects and activities on standardisation related to electric installations and appliances such as Household and Similar Electrical Appliances.	Department of Standards Malaysia under Ministry of Sciences, Technology and Innovation
Vehicles	Road Transport Act 1987	To regulate motor vehicles and road traffic and other matters linked with roads and vehicles.	Ministry of Transportation Malaysia
	Malaysian Institute of Road Safety Research Act 2012	To protect third parties against risks arising from the use of motor vehicles in addition to assigning a method/way for construction and the use of motor vehicles.	
	Road Transport Rules	To reinforce the existence of the MIROS as a corporate body (body corporate) and give legal protection to the relevant Institutions in implementing the function properly.	

The safety of consumer products that do not have specific safety standards is governed by the Consumer Protection Act 1999. This provides general safety standards that must be complied with by the manufacturer and supplier. The specific provision dealing with product safety is in Part III, section 19(1) which authorises the Minister to set regulations that prescribe the safety standards in respect of any goods or class of goods and any services or class of services, and may prescribe different safety standards for different goods or services, or classes of goods or services. Part III of the Act deals with the safety of goods and services. It provides for the declaration of safety standards and compliance with them. Also provided for is a general safety requirement for goods. A special defences section is included, that is, covering compliance with a requirement imposed by law or a standard determined in accordance with the Act. For suppliers, the special defences are the absence of knowledge and the absence of a reasonable ground to believe that the goods failed to comply with the standard specified.

Part III also confers on the Minister the power to declare any goods or class of goods to be prohibited where such goods are likely to cause injury to any person or property or are otherwise unsafe. Such a prohibition order may additionally require the supplier to undertake remedial measures including the recall of unsafe goods at the supplier's own cost. This part of the Act is based on the Australian Trade Practices Act 1974, the New Zealand Fair Trading Act 1986 and the UK Consumer Protection Act 1987. Unfortunately, this part of the Act does not apply to health-care goods and food.[53] In Malaysia, there are rarely any cases brought before the court on product liability and product safety matters. However, the recent case in 2017 on breach of contractual promise has shown that the issue of liability and safety has not been totally left out. The case of *Prestige Dynamic Industries Snd Bhd v Clariant Masterbatches (M) Snd Bhd*[54] was an appeal case against the decision of the learned Judicial Commission who previously dismissed the plaintiff's claim against the defendant for a breach of contract in respect of a plastic component sold and supplied to the plaintiff by the defendant. The component was subsequently incorporated into the plaintiff's product which was sold and supplied by the plaintiff to Bosch. Bosch incorporated the plaintiff's product into its tools, which were marketed in the EU countries. Bosch later informed the plaintiff that the products were not in compliance with the EU Directive 2002/95/EC on the Restriction of Hazardous Substances[55] as they contained cadmium of 1800 ppm whereas the permissible limit under the EU Directive was 100 ppm. Bosch claimed compensation from the plaintiff for the cost of corrective action taken on the product supplied to him. The plaintiff then claimed the substantial amount of MYR 3,196,841.71 (approximately USD 778,000) from the defendant for loss and damage suffered as a consequence of the defendant's alleged breach of contract. It was clear from the contract that the defendant must attach the Certificate of Analysis and Test Report for Hazardous Substance in every delivery and that no hazardous substance is allowed in all products and packaging supplied to the plaintiff. The appellate court accepted the appellant's claim that the material supplied by the respondent contained hazardous substances. The contention made by the Judicial Commission that was reversed in the appellate court is that, even though there was a breach of contract by the defendant, the plaintiff s acceptance of the said products was construed as a waiver of the breach and that it was in the plaintiff's knowledge that the product contained hazardous substances. The appeal was allowed unanimously and the learned Judicial Commission's decision was set aside. It was the defendant's obligation to prove that it had supplied safe products and the onus was not on the plaintiff to prove that the products were safe. This is due to the fact that the plaintiff could not have known of the defect by 'a mere visual inspection' of the said products.

Ideally, a comprehensive product safety policy should provide for surveillance of consumer products on the market in order to identify product-related injuries and analysis of unreasonable risks through data collection and other sources.[56] Clearly, information derived from data collection systems such as for home accident and

[53] Z Zakaria, 'Cosmetic Safety Regulation: A Comparative Study of Europe, The USA and Malaysia', PhD Thesis, University of Manchester (2012).

[54] [2017] 1 LNS 67.

[55] OJ 2003 No L37, p 19.

[56] L Krishnan, 'An Insight Into The Law Of Product Safety' (2006) 5 *Malayan Law Journal* 30.

injury-reporting relating to consumer products are vital to develop standards on all consumer goods available in the market, be it manufactured locally or imported. Thus, data collection systems of injury and death statistics related to consumer products are an important source of such information. The Act does not make provision for such 'preparatory action'.[57]

It is an essential element of any safety law that the scope of such law must extend to a wide range of consumer goods not covered by specific legislation. However, the Act does not apply to healthcare goods and food. The Act needs to be amended to provide for primary agricultural produce to come within the meaning of a 'product'.[58] Another improvement that could help consumers is the development of voluntary recall. Although product recall is a very important part under product safety, it has not been frequently used by the manufacturer. For example, it was shown that for five years from 2015–20, only 15 products were recalled in Malaysia.[59] Examples of products that have been recalled are a beach chair, baby seat for a bicycle, quite a number of IKEA products and a screwgate carabiner.[60]

VIII. Adaptation to the Digital Age

Despite its advantages, e-commerce has also brought with it problems and challenges in terms of the legal protection of consumers. The main e-consumer concerns in Malaysia are payment security, data protection, validity and enforceability of an e-contract, satisfactory information disclosure, product quality and enforcement of rights. The way online shopping is conducted has become more sophisticated compared to a traditional transaction, which has increased consumer vulnerability to unfair trade practices. A consumer faces a number of problems, for example, difficulty in placing an order; no delivery or wrong delivery of goods even though there has been payment with a credit or debit card. In addition, the supplier may refuse to give a refund if the consumer changes his mind once the goods have been received.

In Malaysia, various pieces of legislation have a direct or indirect impact on e-commerce.[61] The Contract Act 1950 and the Sale of Goods Act 1957 also apply, but have not been updated in light of modern practices. As noted above,[62] the Consumer Protection (Electronic Trade Transactions) Regulations 2012 sets out information obligations for websites, but also contains provisions allowing for rectification of input errors and acknowledgement of receipt.[63]

However, the Electronic Commerce Act 2006 takes account of features of e-commerce. The Act provides for legal recognition of electronic messages in

[57] ibid.

[58] R Ismail et al, 'Consumer Right To Safe Product: The Application Of Strict Criminal Liability In Product Safety Legislations In Malaysia' (2012) 20 *Pertanika Journal of Society, Science & Humanity* 57.

[59] On recalled products see https://mysafe.kpdnhep.gov.my.

[60] ibid.

[61] For detail see N Amin and R Nor, 'Online Shopping In Malaysia: Legal Protection For E-Consumers' (2013) 5 *European Journal of Business and Management* 79, 80–81.

[62] Above at s III.A.

[63] Consumer Protection (Electronic Trade Transactions) Regulations 2012, s 4.

commercial transactions, the use of the electronic messages to fulfil legal requirements and to enable and facilitate commercial transactions through the use of electronic means. However, the Act does not regulate how electronic transactions could be done in a safe way and in a secure environment, which is crucial for e-consumer protection.

The Consumer Protection Act was initially inapplicable to any trade transactions by electronic means until its amendment in 2007. The protection for e-consumers has been further strengthened by the enactment of the Consumer Protection (Electronic Trade Transactions) Regulations 2012. Similarly, the 2010 amendment to the Direct Sales and Anti-pyramid Scheme Act 1993 includes e-commerce within the definition of mail order sales.

Malaysia has also developed legislation concerning other online activities, for instance the Computer Crime Act 1997 and Digital Signature Act 1997. Although the Computer Crime Act 1997 primarily concerns criminal offences such as unauthorised access to computers, it is of importance as, to some degree, it protects e-consumers' interests with regard to security of online payments.[64] The Digital Signature Act 1997 also protects e-consumers insofar as it establishes the legal validity, enforceability and admissibility of digital signatures.

Other important pieces of legislation include the Communications and Multimedia Act 1998, the Communications and Multimedia Commission Act 1998 and the Personal Data Protection Act 2010. In particular, the Communications and Multimedia Commission Act 1998 provides for a Malaysian Communications and Multimedia Commission with powers to supervise and regulate the communications and multimedia activities in Malaysia and to enforce the communications and multimedia laws of Malaysia and other related matters. One of the Commission's functions is to provide protection to consumers in the information, technology communications and multimedia industries generally. Consumer disputes on issues related to communication and multimedia can be addressed to the Communications and Multimedia Consumer Forum of Malaysia, which has been designated with this task by the Commission.[65]

The National Consumer Complaints Centre, a centre that was established under the purview of Selangor and Wilayah Persekutuan Consumer Association has published the Malaysia Complaints Series annually. Through the summary of complaints for 2015 and 2016 by NCCC, it was found that e-commerce has topped the overall complaints for both years. The number of complaints are 7,692 in 2015 with potential loss amounted to MYR 4,915,752 (approximately USD 1.1. million). Although the number of complaints has declined to 7,371 in 2016, however the potential loss has increased to MYR 5,011,383.00 (approximately USD 1.2 million). The complaints on e-commerce revolve around the delivery, scams, product quality, return and refund, misleading advertisements, unauthorised cancellation, missing items, etc.[66]

It is undeniable that e-commerce offers many benefits to consumers. They do not need to queue to wait for opening store hours; they can shop even from overseas and can enjoy more online sales with just a click of a mouse. Having said that, there is also

[64] ibid, 81.
[65] ibid.
[66] NCCC, 'Annual Consumer Complaints Report 2016', 9.

another vital question, that is, how safe is buying/shopping online and does Malaysia have adequate regulations to minimise the risk due to increasing issues in e-commerce? Malaysia's current e-consumer protection law is almost equivalent to the protection afforded in developed jurisdictions such as the USA and European Union. However, it was mentioned that some areas remain unregulated, such as unsolicited commercial e-mails (anti-spam law). A local law would not be enough to protect e-consumers in online cross-border transactions. Further improvement to current regulations is also clearly needed to provide a strong basis for national consumer protection in e-commerce. This would increase consumer confidence and bolster their protection.

IX. Access to Justice

A. Tribunal for Consumer Claims

The right to receive redress is a consumer right that has been recognised universally. Malaysia has one of the most effective consumer tribunal claims. The Ministry of Domestic Trade, Corporative and Consumerism has been given the power to establish this tribunal. The function of this tribunal is very significant as it provides the means to secure redress with respect to numerous consumer rights, including in cases of defective and unsatisfactory goods and services under contract law, tort law as well as the Consumer Protection Act 1999, which established the Tribunal for Consumer Claims.[67] The rationale behind the Tribunal's establishment was that consumers are often burdened with lengthy and expensive procedures when bringing a case involving defective products/services to the court. This could normally intimidate consumers, especially those consumers making a complaint against a large, powerful corporation that has unlimited resources. In other words, the central aim of establishing the Tribunal is to provide consumers, who are the vulnerable party, with an alternative medium to file claims in a simple and easy procedure. The fees are extremely cheap (RM 5 = approximately USD 1.2) compared to a more expensive court fees. Also, most cases are heard and settled within 40 days.

The Tribunal hears and determines claims filed by consumers under the Consumer Protection Act 1999. Such claims may concern the supply of goods or services, as well as unfair trade practices such as misleading advertisements or price indications, provided that the total amount in respect of which an award is sought does not exceed MYR 25,000 (approximately USD 6,000).[68] The Tribunal may also hear complaints rooted in other statutes, such as hire purchase or direct sale, which fall within the ambit of the Ministry of Domestic Trade and Consumer Affairs.[69] The chairman and deputy chairman are appointed from members of the judicial and legal service, with no less than five Tribunal members being persons who are members of the judicial and legal

[67] See Consumer Protection Act 1999, Part XII.

[68] Consumer Protection Act 1999, s 98(1).

[69] Section 99 of the Consumer Protection Act 1999 lists the matters that do not fall within the Tribunal's jurisdiction, including claims for the recovery of land, claims under a will, etc.

service (or are qualified under the Legal Profession Act 1976, etc) and therefore could help both parties to settle their disputes in a fair manner.[70]

The consumer has the right to sue the manufacturer that supplied the defective product or service. Since most consumer claims are small and of low value, a redress system that is simple, cheap and fast is highly desirable. In this respect, the ordinary court system is obviously unable to handle consumer claims effectively due to its high costs, as well as the lengthy and formal procedures.[71] As such, the establishment of the Tribunal for Consumer Claims in 1999 may be considered a major development in the development of consumer protection law in Malaysia.

The Tribunal has two methods of resolving disputes, namely, by assisting the parties to negotiate an agreed settlement or by conducting a proper trial. Based on section 107 of the Consumer Protection Act 1999, before a proper hearing is conducted the Tribunal should assess whether it is appropriate to assist the parties to negotiate an agreed settlement in relation to the claim. The Tribunal provides room for disputes to be settled through negotiations between the claimant and respondent, a development that 'exemplifies the true spirit of the [Alternative Dispute Resolution] concept'.[72] However, there are still ambiguities in respect of the negotiation process as there are no clear guidelines on how it is to be carried out, with section 118 of the Consumer Protection Act 1999 stating that the Tribunal may adopt any procedure it thinks fit and proper. Therefore, the provision leaves the matter to the discretion and skill of the presiding officer in the negotiation process.

Where the parties reach an agreed settlement, the Tribunal shall approve and record the settlement, which shall take effect as if it is an award of the Tribunal.[73] However, if the negotiation session fails, a proper hearing will be conducted in a 'court set-up' room but the parties are not allowed to be represented by an advocate and solicitor.[74] During the hearing, the parties may 'adduce evidence, call any witness or produce any document and other relevant information related to their case'.[75] The decisions of the tribunals are final and shall be deemed an order of a Magistrate's court.[76] The party must comply with the award made by the tribunal within the stipulated time. Failure to comply with such an order amounts to an offence and may be subject to a criminal penalty.[77]

B. ADR Schemes

Apart from having the Consumer Tribunal, the system of settling consumer disputes in Malaysia has also been helped by the ADR schemes. This is the important role played by consumer councils/associations. For example, the National Consumer Council

[70] See Consumer Protection Act 1999, s 86(1).

[71] N Amin, 'Consumer Redress Mechanisms in Malaysia: Prospects and Challenges' (2007) 15 *IIUM Law Journal* 231.

[72] ibid, 237.

[73] Consumer Protection Act 1999, s 107(3).

[74] ibid, s 108(2).

[75] Amin, 'Consumer Redress Mechanisms', 237.

[76] Consumer Protection Act 1999, s 116.

[77] ibid, s 117.

and Penang Consumer Association have become a place for mediation between the consumers and the traders. In some cases, the Council/Associations have succeeded in helping consumers to settle disputes with traders. For consumers, after all, what they wanted from the traders in the first place is to get their refund or claims back. Even some traders are quite comfortable in this kind of settlement as they do not want their good name tarnished if the dispute goes to the consumer tribunal or court system. These associations are also active in helping the Domestic Trade and Consumer Affairs Ministry in providing data and statistics on consumer issues and complaints. The National Consumer Complaints Centre, for example, publishes its Annual Consumer Complaints reports. These are complaints on goods and services by consumers that have sought assistance from this Council. The increase in complaints has shown that more and more consumers are braver to exert their rights. The Consumer Association of Penang is the oldest and one of the most active consumer associations in this country. It reaches out to consumers even in rural areas as well as providing education not only through programmes but also through its publications. Recently, both the National Consumer Council and Penang Consumer Association have issued a memorandum asking for a review of Malaysia's current Consumer Protection Act by taking the example of several other countries' systems to strengthen the current consumer protection in Malaysia.

C. Enforcement of Regulations on Unfair Commercial Practices

Consumer enforcement has always fallen under the purview of the Ministry of Domestic Trade and Consumer Affairs. As its name suggests, this Ministry exercises two significant functions: developing domestic trade and addressing consumer affairs. The Ministry of Domestic Trade, Cooperatives and Consumer Affairs is responsible for ensuring that consumers are protected while at the same time ensuring that enterprises can operate efficiently, innovatively and competitively. The scope of work of this Ministry in terms of domestic trade is to improve the socio-economic standing of the Malaysian citizen by developing business opportunities through wholesalers and retailers, franchise opportunities, direct selling, hawkers and petty traders and sectors downstream from the petroleum industry; to determine and monitor prices of essential goods; to control and monitor the sales and distributions of essential goods, petroleum and petrochemical products and direct-sales goods; and to implement regulations on metric weights and measures. The Ministry also regulates companies and businesses based on relevant legislation while encouraging good corporate governance practices. Lastly, this Ministry also develops and administers the intellectual property protection system. The scope of work for consumer affairs is to carry out consumer education programmes, to enhance programmes on consumer awareness and consumer protection, and to encourage and assist consumer movements.

It may appear that the Ministry focusses more on domestic trade than consumer affairs – but regulating domestic trade can help protect consumers, too. When the matters pertaining to domestic trade are well-regulated, especially when industry best practices are encouraged, consumers will benefit. The Enforcement Division was established on 17 April 1972, but at that time it was part of the Ministry of Trade and Industry and had the objective of helping the government to curb the inflation occurring at that time. On 27 October 1990, the Ministry of Trade and Industry was restructured into two ministries: the Ministry of International Trade and Industry and the Ministry of Domestic Trade and Consumer Affairs. The Enforcement Division was placed under the latter, with its core duties identified as the enforcement of trade laws and the protection of consumer rights; this includes eradication of malpractice in the sale of subsidised controlled goods and other unfair commercial practices. For the latter, the responsibilities of the Enforcement Division lie in the investigation of consumer complaints and eradicate unethical business activity in order to protect consumers from being exploited. Consumer protections are codified in the Hire Purchase Act 1967, Weights and Measures Act 1972, Direct Sales and Anti-Pyramid Scheme Act 1993, Consumer Protection Act 1999 and Trade Description Act 2011; as a group, they regulate sale activities, door-to-door sales, hire purchase agreements, verification of weighing and measuring equipment and the use of halal terms. In addition, the Enforcement Division also promotes good trade practices under the Trade Descriptions Act 2011 by prohibiting false trade descriptions and false or misleading statements in relation to the supply of goods and services.

D. Regulatory Action against Profiteering Activities

i. Price Control and Anti-Profiteering Act 2011

One of the Ministry of Domestic Trade and Consumer Affairs' main enforcement activities is curbing price hikes and other price manipulation. For this purpose, the Ministry has introduced the Price Control and Anti-Profiteering Act 2011. This is an Act intended to control prices of goods and charges for services, to prohibit profiteering and to provide for matters connected therewith. The Act was enacted with a view to ensuring that there is no exploitation or manipulation by businesses during implementation of the Goods and Services Tax (GST).

Sections 14 and 21 of the Price Control and Anti-Profiteering Act deal with offences. Under section 14(1), any person who, in the course of trade or business, profiteers in selling or offering to sell or supplying or offering to supply any goods or services commits an offence. For the purpose of this Act, to 'profiteer' means to make unreasonably high profit. Section 21 relates to the power of the Assistant Controller to require provision of information.

ii. Festive Season Price Control Scheme

The Ministry of Domestic Trade and Consumer Affairs is also tasked with enforcing the Festive Season Price Control Scheme, implemented under the Price Control and Anti-Profiteering Act 2011 to protect consumers from traders who increase the prices of key commodities during the festive seasons.[78] Under this Scheme, a number

[78] Hari Raya Puasa, Chinese New Year, Deepavali, Christmas, Pesta Kaamatan and Hari Gawai.

of essential festive season goods are identified as price-controlled goods, meaning that their maximum selling price is fixed for specified periods (though the price ceiling varies among areas and districts). The objectives of this Scheme are to protect consumers against profiteering, to determine the maximum price of essential festive goods, and to ensure that these goods are readily available and sold at the price determined. This Scheme is enforced throughout Malaysia at the producer, wholesaler and retailer level.

Under this Scheme, it is an offence if price-controlled goods are sold above the maximum price, or if vendors fail to label price-controlled goods with both price tags and certain coloured labels that indicate their status as price-controlled goods. A fine of up to MYR 100,000 (approximately USD 25,000) and/or three years' imprisonment can be imposed for individuals who fail to comply, while for corporations, a fine of up to MYR 500,000 (approximately USD 121,100) can be imposed.

In 2019, the scheme was prolonged from 51 days to 102 days; this has had a positive impact on consumers. The scheme is more effective because it now covers the time directly before and after the festive season. This initiative indirectly helps consumer spending during the festive season. In 2019 alone, there were 143,503 enforcement activities conducted and 738 actions taken against traders who sold price-controlled goods at prices that exceeded the relevant ceiling and/or failed to use a price tag.

iii. Enforcement

The Ministry of Domestic Trade, Cooperatives and Consumerism has enforced regulations relating to profiteering in trade and industry. For example, during 2019, a total of 460 notices under section 21 of the Price Control and Anti-Profiteering Act 2011 were issued. Of that total, 33 per cent were issued to manufacturers and producers. A total of 142 cases were produced during 2019; 86 per cent of the cases were offences recorded under section 14(1) of the Price Control and Anti-Profiteering Act 2011.

In June 2019, cement prices rose dramatically: by 40 or even 50 per cent. This had a significant impact on society, not only raising concerns for developers but also creating nervousness among consumers, as house prices could be expected to rise as a result. Within a week, the Ministry had issued a notice to the offending companies under section 21 of the Price Control and Anti-Profiteering Act 2011.

E. Collaboration between Agencies in Fighting Smuggling of Controlled Goods

Enforcement activities related to controlled goods also encompass efforts to ensure that the money directed through subsidies of controlled goods is not mishandled. This is an issue that affects consumers. Inspection and auditing of companies associated with liquefied petroleum gas (LPG) were carried out in several states. Inspection is one of the actions developed to address the issue of subsidised cooking oil leakages. A total of 13 companies or business premises in Tawau including LPG filling depots, wholesalers, retailers and others (including prisons and car wash centres) were inspected. As a result of the inspection and auditing, two wholesaler companies were cited for suspicion of involvement with subsidised LPG controlled goods. Inspections of cooking oil were also conducted in several selected states. A total of 82 businesses, comprising packaging, wholesalers and retailers were audited; 43 cases were produced.

Many of the enforcement actions by the Ministry of Domestic Trade, Cooperatives and Consumer Affairs are as a result of collaborations with other enforcement agencies, such as the Malaysian Maritime Enforcement Agency; the Royal Malaysia Police, including the General Operations Force; The Royal Malaysian Customs Department; Malaysia Border Control Agency; Marine Police Force; Malaysian Anti-Corruption Commission; and the Malaysian Armed Forces. Without these collaborations, it may have been difficult to break the chain of companies, organisations and individuals smuggling controlled goods such as diesel, petrol, cooking oil and LPG. In 2019, for example, a total of 146 cases were submitted to the Ministry from these agencies to be prosecuted under the Supply Control Act 1961. It was reported that the most cases were submitted by the Marine Police Force: 69 cases, or 47 per cent of the total. The state of Sabah received the most submissions (56 cases). The commitment and cooperation from various enforcement agencies has had a positive impact on the Ministry's efforts to ensure that subsidised goods are accepted by eligible target groups.

F. The Role of the Ministry under Competition Law

The Ministry of Domestic Trade, Cooperatives and Consumerism is responsible for ensuring that consumers are protected while at the same time ensuring that enterprises can operate efficiently, innovatively and competitively. This process will be complete with the implementation of competition law, which will ensure a competitive business environment. Enforcement of the Competition Act 2010 began on 1 January 2012 with the establishment of the Malaysia Competition Commission (MyCC). Today, MyCC is one of the key Ministry agencies working to regulate the country's competitive ecosystem to ensure that the people benefit from the growth and prosperity of the nation's economy.

The Competition Act 2010 is part of the transformations and economic reforms undertaken by the government to strengthen competitive economies and achieve developed-nation status. In line with that aim, the Competition Commission Act 2010 established a commission capable of monitoring competition issues in Malaysia. Competition can facilitate efficiency and innovation: it encourages enterprises to take initiative, increase efficiency and innovate to produce a wide range of high-quality products and services at low cost. This competition law is one of the measures taken by the government to ensure that the country's economy remains competitive and free of anti-competitive practices that can undermine economic development. Awareness of this law is still lacking in society, especially among industry players and users. The implementation of the competition law is a complex process and requires careful judgement to ensure its effectiveness. However, the Malaysia Competition Commission has implemented a series of high-impact advocacy programmes to educate the public, especially business enterprises, in how to comply with this law.

MyCC has come a long way since it was established on 1 April 2011. In 2018, MyCC organised more than 20 advocacy and engagement programmes in both the public and private sectors to increase awareness, especially among enterprises, of the importance of fair competition in the market and the role of the Commission under the Competition Act 2010 in maintaining a fair market. The Commission has played a vital role in implementing the Strategic Plan 2017, working to achieve some of the high-impact Key Performance Indicators (KPIs), including those involving international programmes and co-operation, market review, advocacy programmes, and the E-Learning System Competition Compliance Program for Small and Medium Enterprises.

9

Myanmar

RÉMI NGUYEN*

I. Introduction

Unlike other Asian countries, the Republic of the Union of Myanmar recently implemented the 'Consumer Protection Law'.[1] In 2011, after five decades of economic isolation under military rule and sanctions imposed by the international community,[2] the Myanmar government undertook significant economic and legislative reforms to stimulate the economy.[3] The second Myanmar Foreign Investment Law was issued in 2012[4] in order to promote and regulate foreign investments.[5] The basic principles of this legislation include the promotion of exports, import substitution, large investment projects, development of modern industry, development of banking services as well as promoting modern service provision.[6]

Before focusing on Consumer Protection Law in Myanmar, it is important to emphasise that at a certain time, trading was complicated in Myanmar.[7] The goods traded in the economy were restricted, but trade restrictions have been dismantled gradually. Firstly, in 2013, the Ministry of Commerce allowed local traders to trade freely

* Due to the unrest in Myanmar during the editing process, this contribution has not been updated in the interest of the author's safety.

[1] *Handbook on ASEAN Consumer Protection Laws and Regulation* (Jakarta: ASEAN Secretariat, June 2018).

[2] For more information about the legal situation during the socialist period, see H Aung, 'State and Law in Contemporary Socialist Legal Thought' (1967) 50 *JBRS* 261.

[3] S Turnell, 'Legislative Foundations of Myanmar: Economic Reforms' in M Crouch and T Lindsey (eds), *Law, Society and Transition in Myanmar* (Oxford: Hart, 2014) 183.

[4] The first Myanmar Foreign Investment Law was in 1988 (The state Law and Order Restoration Council Law No 10/88). The ambit of this legislation has been limited.

[5] Myanmar Constitution 2008, s 35: 'The economic system of the Union is market economy system; Myanmar Constitution 2008, s 36: The Union shall: (a) permit all economic forces such as the State, regional organizations, co-operatives, joint-ventures, private individual, so forth, to take part in economic activities for the development of National economy; (b) protect and prevent acts that injure public interests through monopolization or manipulation of prices by an individual or group with intent to endanger fair competition in economic activities; (c) strive to improve the living standards of the people and development of investments'.

[6] Foreign Investment Law No 21/2012.

[7] See Government of the Union of Burma, *Pyidawtha the New Burma* (Aylesbury and London: Hazell Watson and Viney Ltd, 1954); M Maung, *Burma's Constitution* (The Hague: Martinus Nijhoff, 1959).

(without a licence to import or export) 318 types of goods (including 152 export items and 166 import items).[8] Secondly, in 2014, the Ministry issued a notification to waive the import licence requirement on 152 types of goods for all local and foreign importers.[9] Thirdly, in 2015, the Management Committee of the Thilawa Special Economic Zone issued an instruction[10] to the companies established therein.[11] Thereafter, the Ministry of Commerce issued a notification to allow foreign joint ventures to engage in the trading of agricultural products and healthcare equipment.[12] Fourth, in 2016, the Ministry of Commerce issued a notification to allow foreign joint venture to trade construction materials subject to certain conditions[13] and another notification to specify the items allowed to be traded under the previous two notifications.[14]

In 2018, the Ministry of Commerce relaxed trade restrictions[15] and has detailed key terms and conditions with exceptions for retail and wholesale business for both local and foreign companies such as 100 per cent foreign-owned companies, joint-venture companies between Myanmar citizens and foreigners and 100 per cent Myanmar-owned companies in Myanmar and the prioritised sectors allowed for wholesale and retail operations.[16]

[8] Notification No 16/2013 from Department of Trade, Ministry of Commerce (Liberalisation on Import and Export).

[9] Notification No 11/2014 from Department of Trade, Ministry of Commerce.

[10] Instruction No 02/2015 from the Management Committee of Thilawa Special Economic Zone (Instruction on the Scope of 'Trading Activities Permitted for Investors in the Thilawa Special Economic Zone').

[11] www.thilawasez.gov.mm/page/about-us: 'The Thilawa Special Economic Zone – located on the outskirts of Yangon – is the first Special Economic Zone (SEZ) to be built in Myanmar, and will be fully (commercially) operational within 2015. Inside Thilawa SEZ, (where) both (the) hard and soft infrastructure – from roads and utilities to supporting services such as maintenance – will be developed up to the international standard. It is located at 14 miles (23 km) South-East of Yangon, which is the biggest commercial city of Myanmar. The construction of all the hard infrastructures inside the zone has commenced since November 2013. The required soft infrastructures are being build up to be in line with the international standards'.

[12] Notification No 93/2015 Department of Trade, Ministry of Commerce.

[13] Notification No 56/2016 Department of Trade, Ministry of Commerce (Permitting the JV to Trade the Construction Materials).

[14] Notification No 85/2015 Department of Trade, Ministry of Commerce (HS lines for Medical Device and Construction Materials for JV).

[15] Notification No 25/2018 from Union Minister's Office, Ministry of Commerce in the Terms and Conditions for Retail/Wholesale, s 1: 'in the economic reforms of the Union of Myanmar, relaxation [of rules] is being provided in commercial sectors in order to increase employment opportunities and to improve technology through foreign investment. In doing so, it has become necessary to allow foreigners to carry out sales and distribution services in the domestic market, not only to provide better prices and more choice in quality to consumers, but also to be in accord with regional treaties. Hence, to bring about conditions favourable to the interest of the consumer and also not detrimental to the domestic Small-and-Medium Enterprises, retail/wholesale among commercial activities related to distribution and sales will be allowed for foreigners'; See Eurocham Myanmar, *Consumer Goods Guide 2019* (2018) 23.

[16] Notification No 25/2018 from Union Minister's Office, Ministry of Commerce in the Terms and Conditions for Retail/Wholesale, ss 5, 8, 9, 15, 16: 'Joint-Ventures between Myanmar citizens and foreign investors, in which the Myanmar shareholder(s) hold at least 20% of the shares are subject to the following minimum capital requirements: The Joint-Venture wholesale company must have a minimum capital of USD 2 million (excluding land rental fees); The Joint-Venture retail company must have a minimum capital of USD 0.7 million (excluding land rental fees). For 100% foreign-owned companies and Joint-Venture companies with less than 20% Myanmar-owned shareholding, are subject to the following minimum capital requirements: The 100% foreign-owned of Joint-Venture company carrying out wholesale activities must have a minimum capital of five million United States Dollar (excluding land rental fees); The 100% foreign-owned or Joint-Venture company carrying out retail activities must have a minimum capital of USD 3 million (excluding land rental fees). The 100% foreign-owned company or joint-venture company shall not engage

In this regard, the spread of the retail and wholesale activities in Myanmar had to be followed by the protection of the consumer.[17] The consumer should be protected against defective goods and services coming from around the world.[18] In any international legal treatise or law manual, such protection should preserve safety and public health.[19] Thus the Parliament decided to legislate in this field.[20] The first definition of consumer appeared in 2014 as a 'person who takes or uses goods or services not for trading'.[21] The purpose of the Consumer Protection Law is important for individuals, who deserve the right to purchase goods of the requisite safety and quality and to obtain accurate, unbiased information about goods and services purchased.[22]

However, the Consumer Protection Law can be a burden for companies that lack the manpower or capacity to comply with the legislative requirements.[23] Companies are already facing many difficulties when doing business in Myanmar because of, for example, administrative, infrastructure, logistics and banking issues. For the company, legislative compliance can contribute to improving reputation, increasing profitability and competitiveness, if it can survive.[24] In Myanmar, it is difficult for companies complying with all the relevant legislation, especially the Consumer Protection Law, to remain competitive against companies established on the grey and black markets.[25]

in retail distribution, including mini-markets and convenience stores in premises less than 100% Myanmar citizen owned companies whose capital is less than USD 700,000 that are operating a retail/wholesale business prior to the enactment of the Directive are required to register with the Ministry of Commerce within 150 days from 9 May 2018'.

[17] Underground Market and some of the cases including but not limited to condominiums, soft drinks or butter cakes demonstrate the relevance and the need for a Consumer Protection Law in Myanmar for the purposes of protecting the health and safety of consumers.

[18] On the need for an International Consumer Law, see M Durovic, 'International Consumer Law: What Is It All About?' (2020) 43 *Journal of Consumer Policy* 25–143.

[19] N Reich et al, *European Consumer Law* 2nd edn (Cambridge: Intersentia, 2014); G Howells, I Ramsay and T Wilhelmsson (eds), *Handbook of Research on International Consumer Law* 2nd edn (Cheltenham: Edward Elgar, 2018); G Howells, H-W Micklitz and T Wilhelmsson, *European Fair Trading Law: The Unfair Commercial Practices Directive* (Farnham: Ashgate, 2006); P Cortés, *The Law of Consumer Redress in an Evolving Digital Market: Upgrading from Alternative to Online Dispute Resolution* (Cambridge: Cambridge University Press, 2018); M Durovic and H-W Micklitz, *Internationalization of Consumer Law: A Game Changer* (Vienna: Springer, 2017); J Calais-Auloy, M Depincé and H Temple, *Droit de la consummation* 10th edn (Paris: Dalloz, 2020); Y Picod, *Droit de la consummation* 4th edn (Paris: Sirey, 2018); S Piedelièvre, *Droit de la consummation* (Paris: Economica, 2008); G Raymond, *Droit de la consummation* 5th edn (Paris: LexisNexis, 2019); C Noblot, *Droit de la consummation* (Paris: LGDJ, 2012).

[20] The enactment of Consumer Protection Law in Myanmar does not mean that consumer law is a separate branch of law. However, it may be a possibility that the State is in the best position to defend the general interest, as in France. See J Stuyck, 'European Consumer Law after the Treaty of Amsterdam: Consumer Policy in or beyond the Internal Market?' (2000) 37 *Common Market Law Review* 370.

[21] Consumer Protection Law 2014, s 2(a). The concept of consumer is defined in a broad manner. It will be interesting in the future to be enlightened on the issue that all the consumers are concerned with this law or the weaker consuming party against a powerful professional supplier and if a businessman can be considered as a consumer in some circumstances.

[22] S Bakhytovna Zharkenova and L Shalbaevna Kulmakhanova, 'Consumer Rights Protection in International and Municipal Law: Problems and Perspectives' (2015) *European Research Studies* 149: 'Consumer rights are among basic civil human rights together with the right to life, right to a healthy environment, right to liberty, etc.'; see also https://aseanconsumer.org/cterms-consumer-protection/why-is-consumer-protection-important.

[23] In practice, most of the local companies were not prepared to comply with the Consumer Protection Law.

[24] The doctrine of *caveat emptor* became the new philosophy of the law of sales in Myanmar but the gap is still important between the theory and the practice in the country.

[25] For instance, www.frontiermyanmar.net/en/in-myanmar-chang-faces-its-own-black-market/.

In wholesale and retail business, local companies compete with foreign companies[26] and with companies which do not use the legal channels.

II. Background

In light of the above, it is relevant to study the different legal tools to protect the consumer. After an overview of consumer protection prior to 2018, this section will analyse the new Consumer Protection Law 2018 and its implementation.

A. The Protection of the Consumer before 2014

Before 2014, the protection of the consumer was not taken into consideration. Nevertheless, Colonial Law[27] could be used to protect the consumer and different laws concerning various sectors were protecting indirectly the consumer. With the liberalisation of the economy in 2012, it was necessary to protect the consumer via specific legislation. Hence, in 2014, the first Consumer Protection Law was adopted in order to provide the consumer with more direct protection.

i. British Colonial Law

During the colonial period, the British administration transplanted a wide range of laws from the codification of Indian Common law.[28] At that time, these legal tools were mainly used to regulate the economy within the colonies and to impose British laws on the country.[29] However, most of the economic legal tools from the colonial period are still enforced. Accordingly, the general laws in colonial period are still very useful to

[26] www.mmtimes.com/news/locals-call-more-regulation-retail-sector.html: During the Private Sector Development Committee meeting with President U Myint Swe on 27 April 2019, Daw Su Hlaing, Secretary of Myanmar Retailers Association, voiced concern for the survival of local retailers in the face of foreign competition, stating that the government should have a plan to protect local retailers before allowing foreign companies to compete in the market, adding that local companies face challenges such as a lack of funds, high interest rates and expensive rental, making it difficult for them stay profitable.

[27] On Colonial law in Myanmar, see E Forchhammer, *The Jardine Prize: an Essay on the Sources and Development of Burmese Law from the Era of the First Introduction of the Indian Law to the Time of the British Occupation of Pegu* (Sagwan Press, 2015); M Collis, *Trials in Burma* (Bangkok: AVA Publishing House, 1996); J Dautremer, *Burma under British Rule* (New York: Charles Schribner's Sons, 1913); MB Hooker, *Legal Pluralism. An Introduction to Colonial and Neo Colonial Laws* (Oxford: Clarendon Press, 1975).

[28] For the concept of transplantation, see A Watson, *Legal Transplants: an Approach to Comparative Law* 2nd edn (Athens, GA: The University of Georgia Press, 1993); D Berkovitz, K Pistor and J-F Richard, 'The Transplant Effect' (2003) 51 *American Journal of Comparative Law* 171; F Barrière, 'Le Code civil français aujourd'hui : influences' in J-P Dunand and B Winiger (eds), *Le Code civil français dans le droit européen* (Brussels: Bruylant, 2005) 95; P Legrand, 'The Impossiblity of Legal Transplants' (1997) 4 *Maastricht Journal of European and Comparative Law* 111.

[29] U Tun Wai, *Economic Development of Burma from 1800 to 1940* (Rangoon: University of Rangoon, 1961) 95; JS Furnivall, *An Introduction to the Political Economy of Burma* 3rd edn. (Rangoon: People's Literature Committee and House, 1957).

protect the consumer even if laws were enacted by the Parliament in order to protect the consumer in different sectors.

a. Myanmar Contract Act 1872

The Myanmar Contract Act 1872 may be used in order to protect the consumer.[30] Before signing any purchase contract, the free consent of parties is an essential element to turn an agreement into a valid contract. Without free consent, the contract cannot legally be enforced before the courts. Consent can be defined as an act of reason, accompanied with deliberation, the mind weighing the good or evil on each side. Free consent means that a person has to conclude a contract out of their own will or volition. Under section 14 Myanmar Contract Act, consent is said to be free when it is not caused by coercion,[31] undue influence,[32] fraud,[33] misrepresentation[34] or mistake, subject to some provisions.[35] A person to whom money is paid or anything delivered by mistake or under coercion must repay or return what was received.[36] Consent is invalid when it would not have been given but for the existence of such coercion, undue influence, fraud, misrepresentation or mistake. If the contract is entered into by coercion, undue

[30] A Briggs and A Burrows, *The Law of Contract in Myanmar* (Gosport: Ashford Colour Press, 2017) 258.

[31] Myanmar Contract Act 1872, s 15: '"Coercion" is the committing, or threatening to commit, any act forbidden by the Penal Code or the unlawful detaining or threatening to detain, any property, to the prejudice of any person whatever, with the intention of causing any person to enter into an agreement'.

[32] Myanmar Contract Act 1872, s 16: (1) 'A contract is said the be induced by "undue influence" where the relations subsisting between the parties are such that one of the parties is in a position to dominate the will of the other and uses that position to obtain an unfair advantage over the other. (2) In particular and without prejudice to the generality of the foregoing principle, a person is deemed to be in a position to dominate the will of another – (a) where he holds a real or apparent authority over the other or where he stands in a fiduciary relation to the other; or (b) where he makes a contract with a person whose mental capacity is temporarily or permanently affected by reason of age, illness, or mental or bodily distress. (3) Where a person who is in a position to dominate the will of another, enters into a contract with him, and the transaction appears, on the face of it or on the evidence adduced, to be unconscionable, the burden of proving that such contract was not induced by undue influence shall lie upon the person in a position to dominate the will of the other. Nothing in the sub-section shall affect the provisions of s 111 of the Evidence Act, 1872'.

[33] Myanmar Contract Act 1872, s 17: '"Fraud" means and includes any of the following acts committed by a party to a contract, or with his connivance, or by his agent, with intent to deceive another party thereto or his agent, or to induce him to enter into the contract: (1) the suggestion, as a fact, of that which is not true, by one who does not believe it to be true; (2) the active concealment of a fact by one having knowledge or belief of the fact; (3) a promise made without any intention of performing it; (4) any other act fitted to deceive; (5) any such act or omission as the law specially declares to be fraudulent'.

[34] Myanmar Contract Act 1872, s 18: '"Misrepresentation" means and includes (1) the positive assertion, in a manner not warranted by the information of the person making it, of that which is not true, though he believes it to be true; (2) any breach of duty which, without an intent to deceive, gains an advantage to the person committing it, or any one claiming under him, by misleading another to his prejudice of any one claiming under him; (3) causing, however innocently, a party to an agreement to make a mistake as to the substance of the thing which is the subject of the agreement'.

[35] Myanmar Contract Act 1872, s 20: 'Where both the parties to an agreement are under a mistake as to a matter of fact essential to the agreement, the agreement is void'; Myanmar Contract Act 1872, s 21: 'A contract is not voidable because it was caused by a mistake as to any law in force in the Republic of the Union of Myanmar; but a mistake as to a law not in force in the Republic of the Union of Myanmar has the same effect as a mistake of fact'; Myanmar Contract Act 1872, s 22: 'A contract is not voidable merely because it was caused by one of the parties to it being under a mistake as to a matter of fact'.

[36] Myanmar Contract Act 1872, s 72.

influence, fraud, misrepresentation or mistake, one party can claim compensation for any loss and damage resulting from the non-performance[37] or the breach of the contract.[38]

b. Myanmar Sale of Goods Act 1930

Under the Myanmar Sale of Goods Act 1930, some legal mechanisms could be used in order to protect a consumer. Normally, the seller does not provide any implied condition or warranty for the quality or fitness of goods but there are exceptions,[39] which are presumed by law and impose implicit conditions on a seller for any default in the goods that are being sold by him. This is an exception to the rule of *caveat emptor*. Damages for non-delivery may be claimed where the seller wrongfully neglects or refuses to deliver the goods to the buyer, the buyer may sue the seller for damages for non-delivery.[40] Where a condition is breached, the buyer may reject the goods and treat the contract as repudiated.[41] Moreover, damages can also be claimed for breach of warranty.[42]

c. Others

Furthermore, the Specific Relief Act 1877 states that any person suing for the specific performance of a contract may also ask for compensation for its breach, either in addition to, or in substitution for such performance.[43]

[37] Myanmar Contract Act 1872, s 53: 'When a contract contains reciprocal promises, and one party to the contract prevents the other from performing his promise, the contract becomes voidable at the option of the party so prevented; and he is entitled to compensation from the other party for any loss which he may sustain in consequence of the non-performance of the contract'.

[38] Myanmar Contract Act 1872, s 73: 'When a contract has been broken, the party who suffers by such breach is entitled to receive, from the party who has broken the contract, compensation for any loss or damage caused to him thereby, which naturally arose in the usual course of things from such breach, or which the parties knew, when they made the contract, to be likely to result from the breach of it. Such compensation is not to be given for any remote and indirect loss or damage sustained by reason of the breach; When an obligation resembling those created by contract has been incurred and has not been discharged, any person injured by the failure to discharge it is entitled to receive the same compensation from the party in default, as if such person has contracted to discharge it and had broken his contract'.

[39] Myanmar Sale of Goods Act 1930, s 16.

[40] ibid, s 57.

[41] ibid, s 12(3).

[42] ibid, s 59: (1) 'Where there is a breach of warranty by the seller, or where the buyer elects or is compelled to treat any breach of a condition on the part of the seller as a breach of warranty, the buyer is not by reason only of such breach of warranty entitled to reject the goods; but he may (a) set up against the seller the breach of warranty in diminution or extinction of the price; or (b) sue the seller for damages for breach of warranty. (2) The fact that a buyer has set up a breach of warranty in diminution or extinction of the price does not prevent him from suing for the same breach of warranty if he has suffered further damage'.

[43] Myanmar Specific Relief Act 1877, s 19: 'Any person suing for the specific performance of a contract may also ask for compensation for its breach, either in addition to, or in substitution for such performance. If in any such suit the Court decides that specific performance ought not to be granted, but there is a contract between the parties, which has been broken by the defendant and that the plaintiff is entitled to compensation for that breach, it shall award him compensation accordingly. If in any such suit the Court decides that specific performance ought to be granted, but that it is not sufficient to satisfy the justice of the case, and that some compensation for breach of the contract should also be made to the plaintiff, it shall award him such compensation accordingly. Compensation awarded under this section may be assessed in such manner as the Court may direct'.

Thereafter, the Civil Procedure Code 1908 provides a right to recovery to persons entitled to the possession of specific immovable property or specific movable property.[44]

Lastly, section 415 of the Penal Code (1860) may apply in relation to practices which 'cheat' the consumer: whoever, by deceiving any person, fraudulently or dishonestly induces the person, or to consent that any person shall retain any property, or intentionally induces the person so deceived to do or omit to do anything which he would not do or omit if he were not so deceived, and whose act or omission causes or is likely to cause damage or harm to that person in body, mind, reputation or property, is said to 'cheat'.[45] If the conditions are fulfilled, this provision is the most efficient protection before the court. The criminal procedure is faster than the civil procedure. Also, the sanctions are dissuasive if a party cheats a consumer.[46] Moreover, the Penal Code punishes fraudulent use of false instruments for weighing, fraudulent use of false weights and measures and anyone in possession of a false weight.[47] In addition, the Penal Code contains sanctions concerning the spread of infections[48] and on adulteration of food or drink, adulteration of drugs, sale of adulterated drugs and sale of drugs as a different drug or preparation, which may be punishable with imprisonment.[49]

ii. Sectoral Legislation

First and foremost, Myanmar has different laws for unsafe and low-quality goods or expired goods.

a. Foodstuffs

The National Food Law 1997[50] aims to enable the public to consume food of genuine quality, free from danger and that is hygienic.[51] The law strives to prevent the public

[44] Myanmar Civil Procedure Code 1908, s 16: 'subject to the pecuniary or other limitations prescribed by any law, suits (a) for the recovery of immoveable property with or without rent or profits, (b) for the partition of immoveable property, (c) for foreclosure, sale or redemption in the case of a mortgage of or charge upon immoveable property, (d) for the determination of any other right to or interest in immoveable property, (e) for compensation for wrong to immoveable property, (f) for the recovery of moveable property actually under distraint or attachment, shall be instituted in the Court with the local limits of whose jurisdiction the property is situate: provided that a suit to obtain relief respecting, or compensation for wrong to, immoveable property held by or on behalf of the defendant may, where the relief sought can be entirely obtained through his personal obedience, be instituted either in the Court within the local limits of whose jurisdiction the property is situate, or in the Court within the local limits of whose jurisdiction the defendant actually and voluntarily resides, or carries on business, or personally works for gain'.

[45] For instance, A, by putting a counterfeit mark on a good, intentionally deceives Z into believing that the good was made by a certain manufacturer, and thus dishonestly induces Z to buy and pay for the good. A cheats. Or, A, by exhibiting to Z a false sample of a good, intentionally deceives Z into believing that the good corresponds with the sample, and thereby dishonestly induces Z to buy and pay for the good. A cheats. The conclusion is that an untrained consumer is a good prey for trained professionals.

[46] By awarding compensation, the law of tort is primarily concerned with redressing wrongful civil actions. See H Htet Zaw, 'Nuisance Under Law of Tort' (2018) 8 *Dagon University Research* 133: Tort is not an enacted law; it can therefore be said that it is a customary law which is the outcome of the English common law.

[47] Myanmar Penal Code (1860), ss 264–67.

[48] ibid, ss 269–71.

[49] ibid, ss 272–76.

[50] National Food Law 1997 was amended in 2013 by Law Amending the National Food Law on 13 August 2013.

[51] ibid, s 3.

from consuming food that may cause danger or is injurious to health, and provides for the systematic supervision of controlled food as well as for the systematic control and regulation of the production, import, export, storage, distribution and sale of food.[52]

A Board of Authority was established[53] for laying down the policy relating to the production, storage, distribution and sale of food and for determining good production practices with respect to quality assurance of food. Its mission is to also set out the policy relating to the inspection, control and laboratory analysis of food labelling and advertising of food, determining the kinds of controlled food and food additives and determining detailed criteria and standards for food, differing from other standards. The Board of Authority coordinates with the relevant Ministries on matters concerning the import and export of food for the safety of consumers.[54]

For the protection of the consumer, a person desirous to produce controlled food shall apply for a licence to the Government department or organisation, which is authorised to issue the licence, only after obtaining recommendation from the Department of Health.[55] Without a licence, a person can be punished with imprisonment for a term, which may extend to five years and/or with a fine, which may extend from a minimum of MMK 5,000 (approximately USD 3) to a maximum of MMK 50,000 (approximately USD 30).[56]

b. Drugs

Under the National Drug Law 1992 (amended in 2014), the Myanmar Food and Drug Board of Authority was formed to enable the public to use genuine quality, safe and effective drugs, to register drugs systematically, to enable the public to consume genuine quality and safe food, to systematically control and regulate manufacture, import, export, storage, distribution and sale of food and drugs.[57] This model is similar to the food model and requires licences,[58] quality assurance[59] and labelling and advertising[60] are necessary for a person who desires to manufacture, import, export, store, distribute

[52] Government of The Republic of the Union of Myanmar, Ministry of Agriculture, Livestock and Irrigation, Formulation and Operationalization of National Action Plan for Poverty Alleviation and Rural Development through Agriculture (NAPA), 'Food Safety and Quality Standard', Working Paper 14 (2016).

[53] National Food Law 1997, s 4.

[54] ibid, s 6.

[55] ibid, s 9; See also www.fda.gov.mm. The Food and Drug Administration (FDA) was established in 1995 as one of the divisions under the Department of Health. The FDA division was upgraded to a separate department in April, 2013. The aim of the department is to ensure the safety and quality of Food, Drugs, Medical Devices and Cosmetics in the country. Its headquarters are located in Nay Pyi Taw, the capital city of Myanmar, with five major divisions: Administrative division, Drug Control division, Food Control division, Cosmetic and Medical Device Control division and Laboratory division while pre-existing Yangon and Mandalay branches acting are still as major branches, control activities have greatly expanded with the establishment of new FDA branches in other Regions and State. In addition, FDA has also established branches in important border trade zones such as Muse, Kalthaung, Myawaddy and Tamu.

[56] ibid, s 29.

[57] National Drug Law 1992, s 3.

[58] ibid, s 8: 'A person desirous of manufacturing storing, distributing and selling pharmaceutical raw material or registered drug shall apply for a licence in the prescribed manner'.

[59] ibid, s 9: 'A person who has been granted the right to manufacture, import, export, store, distribute or sell pharmaceutical raw material or registered drug shall abide strictly by the order, directive and conditions issued by the Board of Authority in respect of quality assurance of the drug'.

[60] ibid, s 10: 'A person who has been granted registration of the drug or who has obtained a licence shall abide strictly by the order, directive and conditions issued by the Board of Authority in respect of labelling and advertising'.

or sell drugs. In case of any violation, a person can be punished with a fine, which may extend from a minimum of MMK 5,000 (approximately USD 3) to a maximum of MMK 50,000 (approximately USD 30) or with imprisonment for a term, which may extend to seven years, or with both.[61]

The Traditional Drug Law 1996 (amended in 2014) aims to promote and develop traditional medicine and traditional drugs and to enable the public to consume genuine quality, safe and efficient traditional drugs. This law provides a systematic registration of traditional drugs and a control and regulation of the manufacture of traditional drugs. A traditional drug must be registered by the Board of Authority[62] and a licence is required to manufacture a registered traditional drug.[63] Punishment can be a fine, which may extend to MMK 30,000 (approximately USD 18) and/or with imprisonment for a term which may extend to three years.[64]

c. Others

Consumer protection legislation also exists in the information and communication technology (telephone, Internet services and e-commerce):[65] the Telecommunications Law 2013[66] and the Electronic Transaction Law 2004[67] (amended in 2014).

In the banking sector, some indications with regard to consumer credit may be found in the Financial Institutions Law 2016[68] and the Central Bank of Myanmar Law 2013.[69] In the healthcare sector, legislation includes, but is not limited to, the Lunacy Act 1912, the Myanmar Medical Degree Act 1916, the Poison Act 1919 and the Geneva Convention Implementing Act 1936.[70]

[61] ibid, s 18.

[62] Traditional Drug Law 1992, s 10. Actually, the Myanmar Food and Drug Board of Authority is chaired by the Minister of Health and Sports and Central Food and Drug Supervisory Committee is chaired by the Director General, Department of Food and Drug Administration (FDA). The FDA is the regulatory/implementing agency for food and drug safety, guided by above-mentioned steering bodies: See Myanmar Consumer Union, 'Myanmar Consumer Report August 23, 2016 to September 29, 2017' (2017).

[63] ibid, s 17.

[64] ibid, s 31.

[65] Deloitte, 'The Myanmar Consumer Survey Poised for take-off' (2020) 8. Although Myanmar's digital economy remains nascent, its penetration rates for Internet, mobile, and social media have been steadily increasing, and moving closer towards the overall average for Southeast Asian economies.

[66] Telecommunications Law 2013, s 4(d).

[67] Electronic Transactions Law 2004, s 3(b).

[68] Financial Institutions Law 2016, s 71: '(a) It shall be the responsibility and duty of the Central Bank to promote consumer protection and financial capability of the bank consumers and financial consumers generally. (b) For the purposes of carrying out the responsibility and duty under sub-section (a), the Central Bank shall be empowered to (1) plan, formulate an implement a strategy for financial consumer protection in Myanmar; (2) co-ordinate consumer protection measures carried out by other financial sector regulators; (3) receive all necessary information from other financial sector regulators and financial institutions; (4) issue directions to the general financial sector in areas that are not supervised by the other financial sector regulators and where there are gaps; (5) promote an out of court dispute resolution system to deal with disputes between financial institution and its customers; (6) promote and consolidate consumer research and data collection; (7) create an effective financial literacy network of stakeholders; (8) keep the Government and public informed of the activities and issues in the area of financial consumer protection. The Central Bank may issue regulations necessary to give effect to sub-section (a) and (b)'.

[69] Central Bank of Myanmar Law 2013, s 40.

[70] See also Public Health Law 1972, Law relating to the Nurse and Midwife 1990, Prevention and Control of Communicable Diseases Law 1995, Prevention and Control of Communicable Diseases Law 1995, Eye Donation Law 1996 amended in 2013, Blood and Blood Product Law 2003, The Control of Smoking and Consumption of Tobacco Product Law 2006, the Law relating to Private Health Care Services 2007,

B. Consumer Protection Law 2014

If the legislation from colonial period and special legislation in different sectors were applicable in order to afford the consumer with indirect protection, the adoption of a Consumer Protection Law was justified by the increase of goods and services in Myanmar after 2012.[71] For the first time, Myanmar decided to protect the interests of consumers with a separate law and to advocate theoretically for a paternalistic approach[72] in contrast to a market-oriented approach.

The first Consumer Protection Law was enacted on 14 March 2014. It is divided into 12 chapters and 31 sections. The objectives of the Consumer Protection Law are to help consumers understand their rights and to prevent fraud and to create a system which protects the rights of the consumer. This law can be combined with the Competition Law 2015 with a general view to protect the consumer.[73] In addition, this law makes it possible to establish a consumer protection scheme in order to provide the consumer with correct and transparent information and to encourage the entrepreneur to take responsibility towards consumer protection. Ultimately, the Consumer Protection Law serves to provide for the fulfilment of goods or services that ensures a high quality for safety, health and satisfaction of the consumer.[74] For the first time in Myanmar legal history, the Consumer Protection Law reflects legislation that is focused on rights and duties for the consumer and entrepreneur.[75]

i. Fraud

The Consumer Protection Law 2014 altered the definition of fraud contained in the Myanmar Contract Act 1872[76] in order to protect the consumer. Under the amended

Body Organs Donation Law 2015, Myanmar Red Cross Law 2015, Myanmar Medical Council Law 2016, Maternal and Child Welfare Association Law 2018, Myanmar Dental and Oral Medical Law 2018, Traditional Medicine Council Law 2019.

[71] In Myanmar, law enforcement is difficult due to weaknesses within the judicial system. See M Zan, 'The "New" Supreme Court and Constitutional Tribunal Marginal Improvement or More of the Same?' in N Cheesman, M Skidmore and T Wilson (eds), *Myanmar's Transition Openings, Obstacles and Opportunities* (Singapore: Institute of Southeast Asian Studies Singapore, 2012) 262.

[72] On paternalism, see M Trebilcock, *The Limits of Freedom of Contract* (Cambridge, MA: Harvard University Press, 1993) 147 et seq.

[73] For instance, Competition Law 2015, s 2(f): 'Competition Policy means policies laid down by the State to cause direct effect on production, services, trade, investment and businesses in order to emerge fair competition in the market and protect the interests of the consumers from monopolization'. Competition Law 2015, s 2(h): 'Unfair Competition means competitive practices by businesses during the business process which cause or may cause damage to the interests of the State or the legitimate rights and interests of other businesses or of consumers'. Competition Law 2015, s 17(a): 'The acts for the purposes of unfair competition under this law include as follows (a) misleading of consumers'; Competition Law 2015, s 20: 'No businessman shall coerce consumers or partners of other business by threatening or compelling them not to transact or to cease the transaction with such business'. Competition Law 2015, s 27(b): 'No businessman shall, by abusing influence in the market, carry out any of the following acts, causing to the detriment of consumers by sale or purchase the goods or services at unreasonable price to market price or by fixing sale price for retailers'.

[74] Consumer Protection Law 2014, s 3.

[75] ibid, s 2(g): '"Entrepreneur" means an individual person or organization conducting production, distribution, storage, transportation, sale, reproduction, exportation, importation, resale of goods, providing services or advertisement'.

[76] Myanmar Contract Act 1872, s 17.

definition, fraud is an act which is not done in good faith or a wrong statement or an incorrect advertisement with the intention to mislead the consumer with respect to goods or services and the act done dishonestly to deceive the public concerning the natural quality, manufacturing process, activity process, characteristic, specified standard, intention or quantity relating to goods or services.[77] According to section 10 of the Consumer Protection Law 2014, entrepreneurs shall, in selling and buying, not deceive or mislead consumers, listing several different misleading or deceptive practices such as stating incorrectly that the goods or services meet the prescribed standard and quality or concealing the quality of the goods or services. The entrepreneur may not substitute the proposed goods with other goods or increase the price of the goods or services before sale promotion of the goods or services. The entrepreneur shall not sell by redecorating or mixing the goods that are already expired. Lastly, fraud can be attested when an entrepreneur sells by mixing goods that are similar and lower in quality.[78]

ii. Consumers

Section 6 of the Consumer Protection Law lists the rights and obligations for the consumer. Under section 6(a), the consumer has numerous rights, such as obtaining the promised value for the chosen goods or services and the complete and correct information relating to the terms, conditions and warranty of the goods or services. The consumer can also hear and settle disputes related to the used goods or services and obtain correct settlement in order to receive a fair and non-discriminatory treatment and service.

However, according to section 6(b) the consumer shall comply with the information and guidelines related to goods or services for safety. The consumer must comply with the decisions of the Consumer Dispute Settlement. In Myanmar, many consumers complain in bad faith on social media for different goods or services. For this reason, the consumer shall avoid false accusation intended to harm entrepreneurs and avoid saying, writing and acting in order to harm relevant entrepreneurs in the media or by other means while these persons are settling the consumer dispute.

iii. Entrepreneurs

Section 7 of the Consumer Protection Law sets out the rights and obligations for entrepreneurs. According to section 7(b), entrepreneurs have the duty to provide clear and relevant information to the consumer. They have to act with business ethics, to treat consumers with non-discrimination. Entrepreneurs shall guarantee that the goods or services are traded or produced based on stipulated standards and quality. Entrepreneurs must also conduct any necessary quality tests prior to purchase. In terms of responsibility regarding the contract, they have to guarantee the goods or services regarding the damage during the warranty period. They shall be responsible if the good received or used by the consumer is inconsistent with the agreement. Lastly, they also have to avoid

[77] Consumer Protection Law 2014, s 2(h).
[78] ibid, s 10.

saying, writing and acting in order to harm the consumer by any media or by other means while the relevant person is settling the consumer dispute.

Furthermore, entrepreneurs shall produce or trade goods if they are providing information regarding the label, net weight, net volume, total amount, quality, grade, position, mode, batch number, expiry date, side effect, poisonous materials, name and address of manufactured company, name of distribution, trademark, information and preparation or style of the goods. In addition, entrepreneurs shall label in Myanmar language or jointly in Myanmar and other language for the information or instruction from the date stipulated by the Central Committee. The place of production shall be identified. For the goods, the nutritional information and a guarantee for the health are important with reference to scientific research on the relevant organisation and they must comply with the standards and norms. Services are to be performed in compliance with the advertisement and sale promotion.[79] The entrepreneur shall not sell, promote or advertise at a special price within a designated period.[80] Finally, the entrepreneur shall not sell or advertise goods or services, which can result in physical or mental health of the consumer.[81]

According to section 7(a) of the Consumer Protection Law, entrepreneurs have the right to defend themselves in a consumer dispute. They are able to prove their goodwill if the injury and loss of the consumer is not due to their goods or services. Entrepreneurs can prove their goodwill if it is provable regarding the law that the injury and loss of the consumer is not due to the goods or services purchased.

iv. Consumer Protection Central Committee

The Consumer Protection Central Committee was formed pursuant to section 4 of the Consumer Protection Law in order to ensure the protection of consumer.[82] As stated in section 5, its functions and duties are to successfully implement the provisions of the Law, to carry out the policies of consumer protection and to protect the safety of the consumer regarding goods and advisory services. This Committee provides recommendations and assistance to the Union Government in order to protect the safety of consumer regarding goods and services. This protection is achieved through the publication of information by the media to the consumer, international organisations, regional organisations, relevant departments or organisations, and the settlement of complaints related to consumer protection from the consumer, consumer protection organisations and other organisations. The Consumer Protection Central Committee can conduct (and review) surveys by collecting statistics related to consumer protection business. This Committee can implement studies by expert groups and laboratories. This institution has also the pedagogical assignment to educate entrepreneurs. Lastly, the Consumer Protection Central Committee can appeal cases when an administrative

[79] ibid, s 8.
[80] ibid, s 11.
[81] ibid, s 13.
[82] The Consumer Protection Central Committee has been established in accordance with the Union Cabinet's Executive Order No 38/2014, No 112/2016 and No 15/2017.

penalty is requested by the Consumer Dispute Settlement Body and co-operate with non-governmental consumer protection associations. The Department of Consumer Affairs is under the jurisdiction of the Ministry of Commerce and serves as a form of secretariat to the Central Committee.

v. Dispute Resolution

The Consumer Protection Law provides a special jurisdiction with the establishment of Consumer Dispute Settlement Bodies at state, regional and district levels by the order of the Central Committee.[83] In settling a consumer dispute, the Consumer Dispute Settlement Body shall, pursuant to section 18 of the Consumer Protection Law, examine the entrepreneur who is accused of violation, the person who knows the consumer dispute, eye-witnesses and expert. This Settlement Body examines and decides if the consumer has suffered a loss. In the meantime, it issues notifications to entrepreneurs that they are in violation of provisions prescribed in the Consumer Protection Law. In the event that the Consumer Dispute Settlement Body finds that the entrepreneur has failed to comply with any duties prescribed in the Consumer Protection Law, it can take actions such as warning, finding remedy, prohibiting the sale of goods for a limited period, destroying the goods which are dangerous for the consumer or revoking the licence temporarily or permanently with the relevant Ministries' coordination.[84] Regarding the Consumer Protection Law, any entrepreneurs in violation[85] can be punished with imprisonment for a term not exceeding three years and/or with a fine not exceeding MMK 5 million (approximately USD 3000).[86] Finally, the consumer may sue for their injury under civil litigation, if possible.[87]

C. The Protection of Consumers after 2018

The Consumer Protection Law 2014 was a milestone in the protection of the consumer, yet its impact was more theoretical due to its poor results in practice.[88] As a consequence, a reform was needed in order to provide consumers with clear and effective protection.[89]

i. Labelling

Before enacting the Consumer Protection Law 2019, the Central Committee of Consumer Protection was active in order to protect the consumer. On 26 October 2018,

[83] Consumer Protection Law 2014, s 16.
[84] ibid, s 19.
[85] ibid, ss 9–14.
[86] ibid, s 23.
[87] ibid, s 24.
[88] Businesses and administration were not prepared to implement the provisions prescribed in the Consumer Protection Law 2014 due to the lack of information and knowledge about this law.
[89] T Ko Ko, 'Well-Received New Consumer Rights Law Brings Clarity', mmtimes.com, 5 April 2019.

the Central Committee issued a notification[90] regarding the rights prescribed in the Consumer Protection Law.[91] In this notification, the Central Committee insisted on the obligation of information from the sellers. It expressed the need for companies to use a label in Burmese language or a bilingual label (Burmese and another language) on products.[92] This label shall include a list of indications, which is compulsory depending on the type of products. Indeed, companies may have to include indications about direction for use, storage condition/instruction, hypersensitivity reaction, warning/precaution and adverse effect.[93] In order to give time to label as prescribed, this notification has been effective six months after the issue date.[94] Although companies shall comply with this order announcement from the Central Committee regarding the Consumer Protection Law 2014, no labelling in Burmese was undertaken.[95]

On 17 January 2019, the Consumer Protection Central Committee issued another notification[96] for entrepreneurs to comply with the regulation of labelling products regarding the notification in 2018. This notification concerns, inter alia, foodstuffs,[97] household goods,[98] children's goods,[99] communication goods,[100] drugs and supplements,[101] chemical products,[102] cosmetic products,[103] consumer goods[104] and business goods.[105] Regarding the goods, usage instructions, storage instructions, allergic reactions, warnings and sides effects shall be mentioned on the label. Consequently, information for consumers is essential for the Consumer Protection Central Committee.

The new law further refines product labelling issued by the Central Committee for Consumer Protection. Although the notification has been enforced in April 2019, the issuance of the Consumer Protection Law made this notification effective on 15 March 2020.

[90] Order announcement No 1/2018 from the Central Committee of Consumer Protection.
[91] Consumer Protection 2018, s 31(b).
[92] Notification No 1/2018 (Central Committee of Consumer Protection), s 1.
[93] ibid, s 2.
[94] ibid, s 3.
[95] ibid, s 4.
[96] Notification No 1/2019 (Central Committee of Consumer Protection).
[97] ibid, Annex: the food concerns juices and jams, milk and dairy products, meat and meat products, egg and egg products, canned goods, edible oils, coffee and tea mixes, instant noodles, instant foods, frozen foods, drinking water, food flavourings, chilli sauce and sauces, ready-made snacks, children's nutrition supplements, betel flavouring, cigarettes, alcoholic beverages and other pre-packaged food.
[98] ibid, Annex: it concerns household electric goods.
[99] ibid, Annex: Children's goods concern strollers, walkers, toys, cribs and personal hygiene products.
[100] ibid, Annex: Communication goods concern corded phones, cordless phones, cell phones and telephone accessories.
[101] ibid, Annex: for drugs and supplements, the labelling into Burmese language applies to non-prescription Over-the-counter oral drugs, non-prescription Over-the-counter balms, nutritional supplements and traditional medicine.
[102] ibid, Annex: for chemical, it concerns fertilizers, pesticides, chemicals used in food products, chemicals used in consumer goods, chemicals used in cosmetics.
[103] ibid, Annex: for cosmetics, it concerns cosmetics (above 10 g), cosmetics (below 10 g) and hair care products.
[104] ibid, Annex: for consumer goods, it concerns toothpaste, liquid soap, bar soap and powdered soap.
[105] ibid, Annex: for business goods, it concerns agriculture tools and healthcare supplementary goods.

ii. Consumer Protection Law 2019

a. Overview

The new Consumer Protection Law was enacted on 15 March 2019.[106] This text repeals the former Consumer Protection Law[107] and this law is part of the regional economic integration in the Association of Southeast Asian Nations.[108] The adoption of a new Consumer Protection Law in 2019 was quite unpredictable[109] and the provisions it contained triggered an intense discussion between foreign entities, interested departments of Ministries and the Parliament. Its implementation is still raising concerns among businesses and relevant ministerial departments.

The new legislation aims to combine all the consumer rights and to promote awareness relating to consumer protection in a broad manner. It is divided into 25 chapters[110] and 84 sections; it provides precise and clear legal definitions[111] As a matter of fact, a 'consumer' is a person who purchases, uses, leases goods and services for their personal use or for other members of their households but not for trading.[112] The Consumer Protection Law 2019 tries to strike a balance between the rights of consumers and the duties of entrepreneurs. Indeed, no one shall behave with dishonest conduct such as inducing the customer to make a complaint, to give a false statement, to distribute false news or to infringe on existing laws.[113]

The obligation of information is very important through the distribution of correct and transparent information to consumers. The high quality of goods and services

[106] Pyidaungsu Hluttaw Law No 09/2019.

[107] Consumer Protection Law 2019, s 84.

[108] https://asean.org/asean-economic-community: Myanmar is a member of the Association of Southeast Asian Nations (ASEAN). The establishment of the ASEAN Economic Community (AEC) in 2015 is a major milestone in the regional economic integration agenda in ASEAN. Consumer protection is an essential tool in building a people-oriented ASEAN Economic Community (AEC). The AEC prioritises the interests and welfare of consumers in the implementation of strategies for achieving an integrated economic region. Consumer protection is also an important component of a modern, efficient and competitive marketplace. Confident and informed consumers who make well-reasoned decisions, represent powerful drivers for innovation and productivity, thereby contributing towards the development of the AEC; see also L Nottage et al, *Integration with Competition Policies, Laws and Institutions: Opportunities for ASEAN Consumer Protection. ASEAN Consumer Law Harmonisation and Cooperation: Achievements and Challenges* (Cambridge: Cambridge University Press, 2019).

[109] The date of the adoption and implementation of this law was unclear and created legal uncertainty.

[110] Chapter 1: Title, Enforcement and Definitions; Chapter 2: Objectives; Chapter 3: Formation of the Commission; Chapter 4: Authority and Duties of the Commission; Chapter 5: Authority and Duties of the Department; Chapter 6: Duties of the Investigating Officer; Chapter 7: Formation of the Consumer Affair Committee; Chapter 8: Authority and Duties of the Committee; Chapter 9: Rights and Duties of the Consumer; Chapter 10: Duties of Entrepreneur; Chapter 11: Giving Guarantee relating to Goods; Chapter 12: Rights claimed by the Consumer on the Giving Guarantee relating to Goods; Chapter 13: Giving Guarantee relating to Service; Chapter 14: Rights claimed by the Consumer relating to the Guarantee of the Service Businesses; Chapter 15: Safety of Goods or Service; Chapter 16: Re-storing of dangerous goods from the market or Prohibition of sale and Dangerous Service; Chapter 17: Responsibility on Goods or Service; Chapter 18: Labelling Guidelines of Goods; Chapter 19: Complaint and Authentication, negotiation and settlement: Chapter 20: Administrative Action; Chapter 21: Appeal; Chapter 22: Associations relating to Consumer Protection and facts to be performed; Chapter 23: Prohibitions; Chapter 24: Offences and Penalties; Chapter 25; Miscellaneous.

[111] Zico, 'Myanmar Consumer Protection Law 2019' under https://zico.group/blog/myanmar-consumer-protection-law-2019.

[112] Consumer Protection Law 2019, s 2(b).

[113] ibid, s 62.

is essential to ensure the health and satisfaction of the consumers. The Consumer Protection Law 2019 protects consumers from loss or damage arising from using goods or services that are unfit for their purpose. Moreover, associations of consumer protection[114] can be set up and take actions regarding the goods or services that are not safe for the consumer.[115] Regarding the definition of 'fraud', the Consumer Protection Law 2019 does not substantially change from the Consumer Protection Law 2014.[116] Nevertheless, the new Consumer Protection Law emphasises the protection of the consumer before the formation of the contract. The entrepreneur shall not mislead anyone purchasing goods or services by means such as combining the good quality products with lower quality products, using exaggeration in the information provided, increasing the price of the goods before sale promotion, etc.[117]

Consumer

Under the Consumer Protection Law 2019, the consumer has different rights, such as being satisfied by the goods or services provided and to be able to use these goods in a safe manner. The consumer shall be informed of the goods and services through receipts or documents, thus enabled to choose freely the goods or services on the market. In case of any damage, the consumer can receive an explanation and can complain in order to obtain remedies. The consumer has the right to live in a healthy environment.[118] The rights of consumers are more detailed in the new law than in the former one. As to the duties of consumers, they are similar to those contained in the Consumer Protection Law 2014.[119] Consumers are not the only parties who can make a complaint for any damage or loss related to the goods or services.[120] If the consumer is a victim, the victim's family, the persons concerned with the victim, the governmental organisations or the Consumer Protection Organisations can also make a complaint.[121] Therefore, the victim can obtain civil remedies in addition to any criminal penalties incurred.

Entrepreneur

The concept of entrepreneur is similar to the same concept as outlined in the Consumer Protection Law 2014.[122] However, the Consumer Protection Law 2019 extends the liability of the entrepreneur, the seller, manufacturer, the person who has the right to use the trademark, the distributor who imported from abroad and sell to local people, the reseller or the service provider providing services to local consumers.[123] The duties of the entrepreneur are more onerous under the Consumer Protection Law 2019.[124] Entrepreneurs shall provide guarantees to consumers. Indeed, an entrepreneur shall give clear and proper information on the terms and conditions and the warranties of

[114] ibid, s 2(u).
[115] ibid, s 3.
[116] ibid, s 2(g).
[117] ibid, ss 65, 66.
[118] ibid, s 19.
[119] ibid, s 20. See above at s II.C.ii.
[120] ibid, s 75.
[121] ibid, s 44.
[122] See ibid, s 2(c).
[123] ibid, s 35.
[124] ibid, ss 21, 37–39.

goods or services. Entrepreneurs shall honestly and properly treat consumers with non-discrimination in accordance with business ethics. Moreover, the goods or services traded and produced should be based on good standards and quality from the relevant government departments and government organisations. The consumer can test goods or services before purchasing. For the price, the consumer shall be aware of the additional payment before purchasing. Entrepreneurs shall not sell goods and services that can incur loss or damage to the consumer; they have to avoid any threat, speech, writing and acting which could harm the consumer through media or any other ways while the dispute is settled. The entrepreneur has to inform consumers and relevant departments on time through media or any other ways if the goods or services are not safe for them.[125] The entrepreneur may express scientific research to the relevant organisation and shall provide health and nutritional guarantees on the goods.[126]

At the same time, the Consumer Protection Law 2019 insists on the consumer's rights to claim for warranty of goods or services. Entrepreneurs shall clearly inform consumers about the quality of the goods, measurement and weight accuracy, the safety of the goods, the suitability for the consumer's needs, the similarity with the sample product, a repair or replacement of warranty goods during the warranty period or the term of use and the consistency with the description contained on the label, advertisement[127] and sale promotion.[128] If the entrepreneur fails to comply with the warranty for goods, the consumers also have the right to have the good repaired as guaranteed or to have a similar good not less than the original quality of the defective good or at least at the same value of the defective good if spare parts are not available. Consumers can also claim to replace the damaged good with the same quality of good or to disclose information if they are suffering from a failure of the entrepreneur.[129] For services, the entrepreneur shall provide accurate, consistent and complete information regarding the consumer's needs.[130] An entrepreneur who fails to provide the service during the warranty period has to compensate the loss of the consumer due to this failure and if the agreed service has not been provided during the warranty period.[131] Lawmakers also want to exercise greater control over advertisements by the entrepreneur, which shall comply with the law[132] and the conditions of sales during particular periods.[133]

Dispute Resolution

In order to reinforce the power of consumer protection institutions, lawmakers have modified the relevant administrations. Under the new law, the Consumer Protection Central Committee will be replaced with the Myanmar Consumer Protection Commission and the Consumer Dispute Settlement Bodies at regional and state level with Consumer Affairs Committees.[134] This Commission will include firstly the Union

[125] ibid, s 21(j).
[126] ibid, s 42.
[127] See ibid, s 2(i).
[128] ibid, s 23.
[129] ibid, ss 24, 25.
[130] ibid, s 26.
[131] ibid, s 27.
[132] ibid, s 63.
[133] ibid, s 64.
[134] ibid, ss 4, 17.

Minister and the Ministry Department as Chairmen, secondly, the persons who are authorised by the Officers of the government departments and organisations at the union level as members, thirdly, the experts in relation to consumer protection and representatives from consumer protection associations as members, fourthly, the chief director of the Department as the secretary.[135] The number of members in this Commission shall not exceed 29.[136]

Firstly, the Myanmar Consumer Protection Commission has the duties to submit annual reports of the consumer protection and action plan activities to the Union government. The Commission advises the Union government on consumer protection and prioritises the areas where the consumer should be protected. It decides on the issues or fines presented by the Department of Commerce and Consumer Affairs and on the appeal cases heard by the Consumer Affairs Committee. Lastly, the Myanmar Consumer Protection Commission can conduct emergency meetings when consumers are suffering serious harm or loss.[137]

Secondly, the Myanmar Consumer Protection Commission forms the Consumers' Committees in the state, region and union territory. The Committee shall be composed of five members to nine members including the chairman and the secretary.[138] The Consumer Affairs Committee aims to solve disputes between entrepreneur and consumer. The Committee can ask the inspector to investigate and examine the goods or services that may cause substantial damage to consumers. Moreover, the Committee should present the activities of the Committee to the Commission and perform duties assigned by this latter. Finally, the Consumers Committee can handle the appeal case of administrative penalty from the relevant department office.

Thirdly, the relevant department office can take actions by administrative method to entrepreneurs who fail to comply with their duties and consumer rights[139] such as warning, requesting the repair or substitution of the product or to refund the value of the loss. Therefore, the Committee can also require the entrepreneur to provide compensation for damages, impose fines, prohibit the sale of disputed goods or services for a limited period or, with the support of the government, suspend temporarily or permanently the licence of the entrepreneur.[140]

The Department of Commerce and Consumer Affairs has the duties to implement the consumer rights and interests and to inform the consumers about the protections in place. The Department can conduct research on consumer protection and assign an inspector to investigate, to report any hazardous goods or services or to remove any goods or services from the market. This inspector can also be assigned to inspect areas in order to test the safety of goods or services. From the investigation of the inspector, the Department shall settle the dispute between entrepreneur and consumer in a fair and reasonable manner.[141] The Department of Commerce and Consumer Affairs

[135] ibid, s 7.
[136] ibid, s 4.
[137] ibid, s 12.
[138] ibid, s 17.
[139] ibid, ss 21, 24, 25, 27, 52.
[140] ibid, s 53.
[141] ibid, s 46.

shall prevent any significant situation that may cause harm and loss to the consumers through the withdrawal of hazardous goods from market, the prohibition of distribution of goods or the prohibition of dangerous service.[142] Moreover, the Department is responsible for setting up consumer protection associations.[143] In brief, the Department shall collaborate with the government organisation for the safety of goods or service.[144] Finally, the Department Office can take legal action if the entrepreneur fails to comply with the provisions of the Consumer Protection Law 2019[145] and the Department can sue under criminal procedure.[146] When the Department is receiving a complaint, it must ensure the completeness of the evidence.[147]

Labelling

The Consumer Protection Law 2019 takes over the notifications of the Central Committee and it was the most important area for compliance. In fact, the new law requires the following information to be included on the label such as: trademark of the goods, type, size, number and net weight of the goods, storage instructions and usage instructions for the goods, manufacturing date and expiry date, batch number, if the goods are imported into the country, name and address of the importer, name and address of the manufacturer, manufacturing location or re-packaging location if the goods are imported into the country from abroad, name of the raw materials contained in the goods, quantity and ratio of the raw materials, description of side-effects and incompatibilities, precaution notice and information that the relevant government department has instructed to express.[148] Lastly, the entrepreneur shall provide generic name of goods, size, net weight, quantity, storage instructions, directions for use, side effects, allergy alert and/or warning in Burmese language or in the Burmese language and other languages.[149] It should be noted that Myanmar language or bilingual labelling requirements have long existed and still exist for food according to the rules of the Food and Drug Administration.[150] Hence, this law is mainly focusing on the information for consumers.

An entrepreneur who gives a false statement can be punished with imprisonment for a term not exceeding six months and/or with a fine not exceeding MMK 2 million (approximately USD 1200).[151] In the extreme, an entrepreneur who fails to provide the required label[152] can be punished with an imprisonment for a term not exceeding two years and/or with a fine not exceeding MMK 200 million (approximately USD 120,000).[153]

[142] ibid, ss 30, 31.
[143] ibid., ss 13(a), 57–61. For instance, see www.facebook.com/consumerpam.org/. In Myanmar, Facebook is currently the best way to obtain information about consumer protection.
[144] ibid, ss 28, 29.
[145] ibid, s 13(b).
[146] ibid, s 75.
[147] ibid, s 45.
[148] ibid, s 41.
[149] ibid, s 43.
[150] Directive No 1/1998 (Food Drug Administration).
[151] Consumer Protection Law 2019.
[152] ibid, s 41.
[153] ibid, s 73.

b. Implementation

The Consumer Protection Law 2019 was fully implemented on 15 March 2020 by the Department of Consumer Affairs from the Ministry of Commerce.[154] The law provides for a one-year period of grace in order to provide enough time for entrepreneurs to comply with the new rules. However, affected companies were not satisfied with the timeline proposed by the Department of Consumer Affairs and suggested a more pedagogical approach.

Notifications, orders, instructions and procedures issued by the Central Committee of Consumer Protection from Consumer Protection Law 2014 can remain valid as long as they do not contradict the provisions of the Consumer Protection Law 2019.[155] As a result, the notifications in 2018 and 2019 concerning labelling are still applicable. The label must be noticeable on the goods. It may be made with stickers or it can be printed on the user manual. For phones or laptops, it is possible to include the label inside these goods. However, for medical devices, if the product is handled by a healthcare professional, the company may not need to label the good in Burmese. By providing advice in the Burmese language, the label is not needed. Hence, the healthcare professional shall indicate to consumers the conditions of use, the conditions of storage and the side effects.

The translation can be submitted for pre-approval to the Department of Consumer Affairs. They are not obliged to reply. In fact, this procedure is optional and is not compulsory. Moreover, if the company is not sure about the qualification of the goods, the Department of Consumer Affairs recommends checking the qualification of the goods regarding the local Food and Drug Administration registration. The Department of Consumer Affairs will also publish additional lists, guidelines and indications in newspapers and on its website.[156] If companies are concerned about the future monitoring carried out by the Department of Consumer Affairs, they can check various complaints on different goods on the Department of Consumer Affairs website.[157] Nowadays, entrepreneurs can also find information on the Food and Drug Administration website.[158] Although companies have questions about the investigative powers of the Commission in order to control the implementation of the law, they can observe the complaints on the website of the Food and Drug Administration.

Intellectual Property

The implementation of the Consumer Protection Law 2019 is a great support for intellectual property law. Although laws related to intellectual property have been enacted,[159] the labelling provision helps to protect the trademark of companies and to fight against intellectual property infringement. Indeed, counterfeit goods have no labelling or have false information. In case of any misleading or unfair provisions, not only consumers

[154] ibid, s 1(b).
[155] ibid, s 82.
[156] www.doca.gov.mm.
[157] www.doca.gov.mm/en/notice.
[158] www.fdamyanmar.gov.mm/?cat=5.
[159] See Trademark Law 2019, Patent Law 2019, Industrial Design Law 2019.

but also the trademark owner can file a complaint.[160] In this regard, the Consumer Protection Law 2019 provides higher protection against trademark infringement. However, the recent judgments of commercial cases from the Supreme Court are showing the real interest of judges regarding intellectual property infringements. In practice, courts are protecting intellectual property rights.[161] It is actually important to assess how the Myanmar Consumer Protection Commission, the Consumer Committees in the state, region and union territory and the relevant department office are going to effectively protect consumers.

Labelling Controls

Controls on labelling started after 15 March 2020 using inspectors. This is the major change from the Consumer Protection Law 2014. Indeed, the inspector is now responsible for investigating the complaints and to report any goods or services that could be hazardous. He can also remove the goods or services from the market.[162] The Consumer Protection Law 2019 provides considerable powers to inspectors. The inspector can monitor local and imported goods on the market and also if the goods or services can be consumed, used or are hazardous; he can check if the label is included or not and if the information about the harmfulness of the goods is provided.[163] The inspector can ask the relevant department office to test if a good or service is deemed to be hazardous or not. If it is, he can report to the relevant department office not to distribute or to sell the good or service.[164] The inspector can advise the police in order to perform their duties.[165] In order to protect consumers, the Department of Consumer Affairs has dispatched 154 inspectors across the country to check on the labelling of products.[166]

III. Conclusion

Some actions should be undertaken in order to support the provisions of the Consumer Protection Law 2019. For instance, it will be valuable to educate and to develop the understanding of consumers about their responsibilities as consumers. For the purpose of being aware of their rights and responsibilities, consumers should have greater awareness of the Consumer Protection Association. In addition, the Consumer Committees in the state, region and union territory should increase the advertisement of their activities.

[160] F Mattei, 'Consumer Protection Law's labeling provisions finally in force to tackle IP infringement' (2020) https://rouse.com/insights/news/2020/myanmar-s-consumer-protection-law-tackles-ip-infringement.

[161] See *Myanmar Win Life Co, Ltd v Golden Poer Lamp Co, Ltd* (Civil Special Appeal 24/2017; *Daw Nan San Mon v Daw Chun Lint* (Civil Appeal 520/2017); *Myanmar Awba Group Co, Ltd v U Soe Naing Oo* (Civil Appeal 552/2018); *U Kyaw Hlaing v Knorr Naehrmittel AG* (Civil Appeal 54/2018); *Pan Asia Majestic Eagle Ltd v Amalgamated Telecom Management Co, Ltd And Others* (Civil Appeal 389/2018); *Mr Seri Somboonsakdikul v Grand Wynn Manufacturing Ltd* (Civil Appeal 444/2018); *U Bin Thit v Fm Industrial and Construction Co, Ltd* (Civil Appeal 881/2018); *Ntr Myanmar Co, Ltd v Nine Automobile Asia Co, Ltd* (Civil Appeal 118/2019).

[162] Consumer Protection Law 2019, s 14.

[163] ibid, s 2(m).

[164] ibid, s 15.

[165] ibid, s 16.

[166] H Thant, 'Govt warns manufacturers: Time is up on Myanmar labelling rule', mmtimes.com, 16 March 2020.

The enactment of the Consumer Protection Law 2019 is an excellent opportunity to modernise Myanmar private law such as the Contract Act 1872 and the Sale of Goods Act 1930. As a matter of fact, the Consumer Protection Law 2019 protects the consumer but also the weak party[167] in its legal relationship with the entrepreneur. In practice, local people are not overzealous in drafting an agreement concerning the formation and the performance of their obligations. Hence, the modernisation of the Contract Act 1872 and Sale of Goods Act 1930 could move toward the direction of protecting the weak party in any contract. In a more comprehensive way, the Consumer Protection Law 2019 could also support the creation of a Civil Code in Myanmar in order to harmonise the different laws relating to civil law.[168]

[167] JP Chazal, 'Vulnérabilité et droit de la consommation' (Conference on the vulnerability and the law organised by the University of P Mendes-France, Grenoble II, 23 March 2000).

[168] R Nguyen, 'Réflexion sur la codification du droit civil en Birmanie', PhD thesis, Université de Bourgogne-Franche Comté (2018); R Nguyen, 'The Opportunity of a Civil Code in Myanmar' (forthcoming); R Nguyen, 'Enacting a Civil Code Could Open Many Doors for Myanmar', mmtimes.com, 31 January 2020.

10

Singapore

GARY LOW

I. Overview

Singapore is a tiny island at the heart of Southeast Asia with a population of over 5.6 million residents.[1] In terms of territorial breadth, it is slightly more than half the size of Hong Kong.[2] Its GDP in 2020 stood at SGD 491 million (approximately USD 355 million), with a per capita GDP of SGD 82,500 (approximately USD 62,300). It exported SGD 515.6 billion and imported SGD 453.5 billion in goods (respectively, approximately USD 390 billion and USD 343 billion) in 2020. Its top trading partners include China, Malaysia, Hong Kong, the EU and the United States.[3] Most goods in the local market are imported from these countries. Singapore is one of the world's freest economies.

Being a former British colony, it inherited a common law legal system. As can be expected, the basis and inspiration for many of its laws was and remains English. However, since the 1990s, political traction gained by the legal autochthony movement in Singapore[4] has translated into a steady departure from the influence and embrace of English law. The country's case law and statutes have since been known to draw inspiration from other common law jurisdictions such as Australia and Canada, and also the EU.[5]

At a general level, a key plank in regulating marketplace participants remains the Sale of Goods Act,[6] which for all intents and purposes mirrors the UK's Sale of Goods

[1] Singapore Department of Statistics, Ministry of Trade and Industry, 'Population Trends, 2020' (September 2020).

[2] Singapore is approximately 719 km^2, compared to Hong Kong's 1108 km^2.

[3] Statistics obtained from the Singapore Department of Statistics: www.singstat.gov.sg/modules/infographics/singapore-international-trade.

[4] E Tan, 'The Continuing Resistance to Foreign Law in Constitutional Adjudication in Singapore' in J Neo (ed), *Constitutional Interpretation in Singapore* (London: Routledge, 2017) 293.

[5] For example, Singapore's Consumer Protection (Fair Trading) Act is based in part on a Saskatchewan statute. Singapore's Personal Data Protection Act drew inspiration from the Canadian model. Section 9A of the Interpretation Act on approaches to statutory interpretation and use of extrinsic materials is based on its Australian counterpart. Singapore's Competition Act is modelled on the UK version (which itself draws from EU competition law). NB, all cited legislation refers to Singapore, unless indicated otherwise.

[6] The Sale of Goods Act (Cap 393, 1999 Rev Ed) was originally enacted from the UK Sale of Goods Act 1979 c 54. See also the Supply of Goods and Services Act (Cap 394, 1999 Rev Ed), taken also from the UK Supply of Goods and Services Act 1982, c 29.

Act 1979 from which it is derived. Another important part of the general framework is the Unfair Contract Terms Act,[7] again, derived from the UK counterpart.[8] It will therefore not surprise the English lawyer that consumer contracts may not exclude or restrict negligence liability for death or personal injury, and whereas other contractual terms limiting or exempting liability on the part of the seller may be excluded, these are always subject to a judicial control of reasonableness.[9]

Insofar as consumer-specific legislation is concerned, the legislative landscape is historically dotted across differing market segments, types of contracts and types of goods. The reason for such fragmentation is best explained by the diffusion of ministries or regulators tasked with oversight of different parts of the economy. Notable examples include the Singapore Food Agency under the Ministry of Environment and Water Resources[10] which administers the provisions of the Sale of Food Act, Enterprise Singapore under the Ministry of Trade and Industry which oversees compliance on weights and measures[11] and the Competition and Consumer Commission of Singapore in relation to unfair business practices.

Colonial beginnings aside, the local impetus for rationalising Singapore's consumer protection regime stems from the establishment of the Consumers Association of Singapore (CASE) in 1970, a non-governmental organisation with leadership based on tripartite cooperation between academia and the national labour movement. The immediate reason why these varied interest groups coalesced into CASE was the heretofore lack of a unified front championing consumers' interests in the face of rising prices for staples like bread and pork. Whilst these segments of Singapore's economy remained tightly regulated, this role CASE played of facilitating price stability was both important and publicly visible; and with the transition to a free market lightly regulated amongst others through a competition law regime, CASE's role has similarly transitioned from price control to that of price competition. Its work is now dominated by tackling informational asymmetry and combating unfair business practices in the market.

The Consumers Association of Singapore takes a three-pronged approach to facilitating Singapore's consumer protection framework. The first focuses on the demand side of the market, in the sense of holding talks and other outreach programmes on consumer education and empowerment. Secondly, focussing on the supply side of the market, CASE collaborated with trade associations to promulgate best practices and accreditation programmes. Thirdly, through the decades, it lobbied – with apparent reasonable success – the Ministry of Trade and Industry to table bills aimed at consumer empowerment, whether in terms of information disclosure or substantive rights and remedies, and also to combat unsavoury business practices.

[7] Cap 396, Rev Ed 1994.

[8] The UK Unfair Contract Terms Act 1977, c 50.

[9] Identical to the English position, a party may not exclude liability in relation to title, and may only limit or exclude liability in relation to quality or conformity to description or fitness for purpose where it is reasonable to do so: The Sale of Goods Act, ss 6 and 55; see also the UK Unfair Contract Terms Act.

[10] This new agency came into being on 1 April 2019, having taken over the mandate for food-related matters from the now defunct Agri-Food and Veterinary Authority of Singapore.

[11] With respect to the Consumer Protection (Consumer Goods Safety) Regulations.

The fruits of this labour include the Consumer Protection (Trade Descriptions and Safety Requirements) Act of 1975,[12] and one might find parallels in its counterparts in the UK[13] and Malaysia,[14] from which it drew inspiration. This Act, as the name suggests, was primarily concerned with ensuring accurate labelling on consumer products, as well as catering for the recognition and establishment of safety related standards. In 1985, the Small Claims Tribunal Act[15] was passed, due to active encouragement from CASE to promote access to justice for consumers. From a legislative perspective, the *status quo ante* persisted for decades: that is, until the passage in late 2003 of the Consumer Protection (Fair Trading) Act,[16] through the successful lobbying of CASE since 1996.[17] What underpinned CASE in lobbying for a consumer-specific – and, indeed, -centric – piece of legislation, was a growing trend of sharp business practices, including aggressive and unethical sales tactics, across different market segments, but also across different modes of sale.[18] The occasion for the Consumer Protection (Fair Trading) Act was a root-and-branch overview commenced in 2001 by the Ministry of Trade and Industry of the legislative framework for consumer protection and which precipitated negotiation for and the signing of a Free Trade Agreement with the United States in 2003 (and which also led to the introduction of Singapore's first antitrust regime).[19]

As alluded to above, growing confidence and influence from the legal autochthony movement probably resulted in a move away from traditional English legislative influence, and the Consumer Protection (Fair Trading) Act was the product of other commonwealth jurisdictions, most notably Saskatchewan in Canada and New South Wales in Australia.[20] The latter, in particular, attracted keen interest due to the desire to empower consumers and limit the direct role of the government insofar as this segment of the market is concerned. This has the twin attraction of requiring a more limited expenditure from the government purse than it would otherwise have had to commit, as well as being in accordance with the government's approach towards citizenry self-reliance.

The successful passage of the Consumer Protection (Fair Trading) Act marked the start of cordial, formal and informal ties between CASE and the Ministry of Trade and Industry. As the Minister of State for Trade and Industry said during the second reading of the then Consumer Protection (Fair Trading) Bill of 2002:

> I would like to assure Members that we do not regard this as a once-off exercise. As several Members have said … *this is the starting point*. We want to kick-start it, we want to get it

[12] Cap 393, Act 10 of 1975.

[13] Trade Descriptions Act 1968.

[14] Trade Descriptions Act 1972.

[15] Cap 208, 1998 Rev Ed. See below at s IX.A.

[16] Consumer Protection (Fair Trading) Act 52A, Rev Ed 2009 (Informal Consolidation 2016).

[17] S Loke, 'The Changing Landscape of Consumer Law in Singapore' (Singapore Law Gazette, November 2002).

[18] Singapore Parliamentary Debate 10 November 2003, vol 76, col 3352 (Comment by The Minister of State for Trade and Industry, Mr Raymond Lim).

[19] The Act itself was the product of a joint taskforce led by CASE and MTI and comprising private and business organisations, to study the need for fair trading legislation in Singapore, and if so, what form such legislation ought to take. The suggestion to collaborate was announced by then Senior Minister of State for Trade and Industry, Mr Peter Chen, in Parliament on 8 March 2001. A delegation of CASE, MTI, AGC and industry interests visited Melbourne and Sydney to study their respective consumer protection regimes.

[20] R Chandran, 'Consumer Protection (Fair Trading) Act' (2004) *Singapore Journal of Legal Studies* 192.

> moving and *we have taken an evolving approach on consumer protection.* For us, it is a continuous learning exercise. As some of you know, MTI, at the beginning, had reservations on this Bill *but by working closely with CASE* and other associations, we have a better understanding of it.[21]

In this vein, a further update was undertaken in 2008 in order to introduce a greater range of remedies and raise the standard of consumer protection to a level comparable with that of the UK and the EU;[22] and, recently in 2016 and 2017, to strengthen governmental oversight and relevant enforcement powers especially as regards unfair commercial practices.

II. Information Duties and Right of Withdrawal

The Consumer Protection (Fair Trading) (Cancellation of Contracts) Regulations 2009[23] is the subsidiary legislative source of withdrawal rights for consumer contracts. It provides that a consumer may withdraw from a 'regulated contract' within five working days[24] after the day on which the contract was entered into or the day in which the consumer information notice (containing certain required details of consumer rights) is brought to the consumer's attention, whichever is later. Such right may be invoked without further need on the part of the consumer to provide justification. To be sure, at the time of entry into force of the regulations, the mischief aimed at was with regards to timeshare contracts. Distance selling contracts were, unlike in other jurisdictions, relatively unproblematic and therefore not included within the definition of a 'regulated contract'.

These regulations were not the first to introduce withdrawal rights for consumers; indeed such rights existed for certain types of financial products, such as insurance (14 calendar days)[25] and investment schemes (seven calendar days).[26] As the rights under these other rules were more favourable to consumers, the regulations were deliberately limited in their scope to govern only 'regulated contracts' in order to preserve the more consumer-advantageous rights found in these other types of contracts. In this vein, the regulations define a regulated contract as pertaining to unsolicited doorstep selling contracts, as well as timeshare and long-term holiday product contracts.[27] Where there is a valid withdrawal from a regulated contract, suppliers are obliged to provide a refund within 60 days of receipt of the notice of withdrawal.[28]

[21] Singapore Parliamentary Debate 11 November 2003, vol 76, cols 3463–4 (Comment by The Minister of State for Trade and Industry, Mr Raymond Lim) (emphasis added).

[22] Singapore Parliamentary Debate 9 March 2012, vol 88, cols 1764–73 (Mr Teo Ser Luck, Mr Lim Biow Chuan).

[23] Consumer Protection (Fair Trading) (Cancellation of Contracts) Regulations 2009 (GN No S 65/2009). The Act Based in turn on s 11 of the Consumer Protection (Fair Trading) Act. The original incarnation is the Consumer Protection (Fair Trading) (Cancellation of Contracts) Regulations 2003 (S 620/2003) which came into force on 1 March 2004.

[24] This was initially set at three working days, and increased to five from 15 April 2009.

[25] Insurance (General Provisions) Regulations (Cap 142, Reg 17), reg 8.

[26] Notice on Cancellation Period for Collective Investment Schemes Constituted as Investment Trusts (SFA 04/13-N01), pursuant to ss 101 and 293 of the Securities and Futures Act (Cap 289, 2006 Rev Ed).

[27] Consumer Protection (Fair Trading) (Cancellation of Contracts) Regulations 2009, reg 2.

[28] ibid, reg 5.

The differences in cooling-off period stem from the earlier-mentioned fact of fragmented market regulation, with the Ministry of Trade and Industry being inter alia in charge of consumer affairs and business practices generally, whereas the de facto central bank – the Monetary Authority of Singapore – takes point on all matters financial. No attempt has been made to equalise the differences.[29]

Informational duties and the right to withdraw are inextricably linked. According to the approach taken in Singapore, these duties and rights are to be found in discrete consumer contracts: in the same way there is no right to withdraw from consumer contracts generally, there are no general informational duties imposed at law. The Minister (of Trade and Industry) is empowered under section 11 of the Consumer Protection (Fair Trading) Act to prescribe the manner and period within which consumer contracts may be withdrawn from, and he has to-date not seen fit to do so for consumer contracts generally.

What has been done instead, is to oblige the supplier in the case of regulated contracts to communicate to the consumer (a) the name of the supplier, (b) the supplier's reference number, (c) the designated person under the employ of the supplier to whom a notice of cancellation ought to be addressed, including at least one name and at least one address or contact number. Such information is to be given in order to make it practicable for the consumer to exercise his right to withdraw. It is also the reason why, within the context of the Regulations, the withdrawal period does not start until such information has been communicated to the consumer. The supplier has thus every incentive to provide this information since a failure to do so exposes him to the continued and unnecessary extension of the consumer's right to withdraw.

The obvious point therefore is that there is no general right to withdraw, and no other informational obligations imposed on businesses save for those outlined above. A fragmented, sectoral approach to regulation has contributed to this state of affairs. The lack of a critical mass of related consumer complaints in other segments of the market has, in turn, preserved political inertia in not pushing for that general right.

III. Consumer Sales Law

A. Sale of Goods Act

The Sale of Goods Act is applicable to all, and not just consumer, contracts.[30] The Act implies into all contracts for the sale of goods terms to the effect that goods need to accord to the description provided, be of satisfactory quality and fit for purpose, and if sold by sample, must match that sample.[31] The jurisprudence of the Singapore courts in this area

[29] Aside from differences in cooling-off periods, amendments to the Consumer Protection (Fair Trading) Act in 2009 bring insurance, investment and moneylending consumer contracts within the ambit of that Act, entitling consumers to redress under the general consumer protection regime.

[30] Singapore retained the UK Sale and Supply of Goods Act 1982 c 29 (amended and retitled Supply of Goods Act 1993 Cap 394 Rev Ed 1999), which aligns the rights of contracting parties insofar as goods are concerned with that of the Sale of Goods Act. Singapore does not have specific legislation on the supply of services.

[31] Sale of Goods Act, ss 13–15.

is very much aligned with that of English law. Although cases of suppliers attempting to contract out of these implied terms are not unheard of, such a practice would have been frowned upon by a court applying the provisions of the Unfair Contract Terms Act. The aforementioned implied terms under the Sale of Goods Act are mandatory (that is, cannot be excluded or restricted) where one of the parties is dealing as a consumer.

Liability for breach of the Sale of Goods Act is strict, and not fault-based. Breach of any of these terms entitles the consumer to reject the goods and terminate the contract. The fact that a supplier has done all he reasonably could have is no defence under the Act. The right to reject is lost only where the consumer has accepted the goods; defined under the Act where (1) the consumer informs the supplier of his acceptance, (2) where the consumer acts inconsistently with the ownership of the seller, and (3) where the consumer retains the goods beyond a reasonable time without informing the supplier he has rejected them.[32]

Consumer-specific provisions are embedded within the Sale of Goods Act to give consumers added protection. Similar to its English and Hong Kong cousins, the Act defines consumer contracts as the sale of goods by a seller in the course of a business where such goods are ordinarily bought for private use or consumption, or such sale where the buyer does not buy or hold himself out as buying for a business.[33] This is important since consumers have a right to reject goods for non-conformity in sales by description,[34] sample,[35] or with reference to quality or fitness.[36] In commercial cases where 'the breach is so slight that it would be unreasonable for the buyer to reject them',[37] no such rejection is permissible at law.[38] This is the same where the seller delivers the wrong quantity of goods.[39] The Sale of Goods Act enshrines the right of the consumer to a reasonable opportunity for inspection, ensuring that such right cannot be lost by agreement or waiver or any other means an unscrupulous seller might think of.[40]

Insofar as consumers are concerned, however, the Sale of Goods Act and the Unfair Contract Terms Act are for all intents and purposes no longer the main piece of legislation regulating consumer contracts for the sale of goods. In the vast majority of consumer disputes, therefore, there is little or no practical reliance on either statute.[41]

B. Consumer Protection (Fair Trading) Act

Like many other jurisdictions of influence, like the UK, the EU and Australia, consumer protection has a dedicated legislative framework in the form of the Consumer Protection (Fair Trading) Act. It provided, for the first time, civil remedies like damages

[32] ibid, s 35(1) and (4).
[33] ibid, s 55(7).
[34] ibid, s 13.
[35] ibid, s 15.
[36] ibid, s 14.
[37] ibid, s 15(A)(1)(b).
[38] ibid, s 15(A)(1).
[39] ibid, s 30(2)(A).
[40] ibid, s 35(3).
[41] See G Low, 'Singapore Consumer Law' in H-W Micklitz and G Saumier (eds), *Enforcement and Effectiveness of Consumer Law* (Cham: Springer, 2018) for statistics on consumer disputes.

for consumers aggrieved or injured by unfair business practices.[42] Since 2008, available consumer remedies include a general right to cure, or price reduction.[43] Furthermore, there is a presumption of non-conformity of goods at the time of sale or delivery where defects are uncovered within six months of sale or delivery.[44] Beyond this six-month period, the consumer will need to prove that the defect existed at the time of delivery.

The Consumer Protection (Fair Trading) Act envisages a two-stage remedies system. Consumers may ask for repair or replacement, or reduction in price or refund of the purchase price. In any event, suppliers always have a right to offer repair or replacement in the first instance and at their choice. If on the other hand such repair or replacement is (a) not provided within a reasonable time, (b) significantly inconvenient to the consumer, (c) not possible or (d) too costly compared to other remedies, the consumer is entitled to insist on a price reduction or refund. The Act is silent as to whether the consumer may, additionally, be compensated by way of consequential damages. Presumably, on the basis that consequential damages are outside the scope of the Consumer Protection (Fair Trading) Act, any such remedy available to the consumer would be governed by general contract law principles.

Certain types of contracts remain outside the ambit of the Consumer Protection (Fair Trading) Act. These include the sale of real property[45] or contracts for the provision of domestic help,[46] indicating that the main purpose of the Consumer Protection (Fair Trading) Act, like the Sale of Goods Act, is to regulate the everyday exchange of goods in the marketplace.[47] Due to widespread problems in these areas, contracts for the sale of pets as well as those concerning second-hand vehicles were considered ripe for consumer protection and fall within the ambit of the Act.

IV. Unfair Contract Terms

Contractual terms excluding or limiting liability are controlled by means of common law rules as well as statute (that is, the Unfair Contract Terms Act).

A. Common Law

The first point of note is that the law distinguishes between an exemption clause and a term of the contract that merely seeks to define parties' legal obligations.[48]

[42] See WL Loo and E Goh-Low, 'Award of Damages under the Singapore Consumer Protection (Fair Trading) Act' (2007) 9 *The Australian Journal of Asian Law* 66.

[43] Consumer Protection (Fair Trading) Act, s 12C and s 12D.

[44] ibid, s 12B(3). This presumption is rebuttable, and for perishables, the presumption period varies depending on the shelf life of the perishable good.

[45] These are governed by the Land Titles Act (Cap 157, 2004 Rev Ed) and the Land Titles (Strata) Act (Cap 158, 2009 Rev Ed). Singapore law in the area of real property is based on English land law in that the doctrines of tenure and estates are applicable, although, different than its erstwhile colonial master, it has since 1956 adopted the Australian Torrens system for registration of interests in land.

[46] Which are, as per common sense, contracts of employment, although some might argue that these are consumer contracts in the sense that domestic services are being consumed.

[47] Consumer Protection (Fair Trading) Act, s 2.

[48] See *Emjay Enterprises Pte Ltd v Skylift Consolidator (Pte) Ltd* [2006] 2 SLR(R) 268 at [12].

Second, judicial control of exclusion clauses centred on the technicalities of contractual incorporation, thus permitting the common law courts to ostensibly avoid confronting their true objective of correcting imbalances of bargaining power or seeking substantive fairness in contractual terms. Singapore aligns its judicial position with that of England, in that respect, upholding the well-established proposition that an exemption clause contained in a document sought to be incorporated after the conclusion of the contract does not form any part of that contract.[49] This is of course an altogether different matter if the exemption clause is contained in a document signed by the parties to the contract,[50] even if the party concerned was ignorant as to the contents of that document.[51]

In addition, exemption clauses can be incorporated by the affording of reasonable notice. Insofar as notice is concerned, the law does not require actual notice (and therefore subjective knowledge), preferring instead the objective standard where reasonable steps had been taken to bring the exemption clause to the attention of the other party.[52] While this orthodoxy might appear cold-hearted and harsh to the casual reader, its rough edges have been smoothened by subsequent cases raising the standard of what reasonable notice is to very nearly requiring subjective knowledge.[53]

Finally, exemption clauses can be said to be incorporated with reference to a course of dealing as between the parties. Whether a course of dealing can be established is, like that of reasonable notice, heavily dependent on the specific facts of each case. Few judicial authorities on the matter stand out in the post-1993 local law reports,[54] and thus one is forced to refer to the English position prior to 1993, which is indicative of a high evidentiary threshold to succeed. Thus, in *Hollier v Rambler Motors (AMC) Ltd*,[55] the plaintiff's car had been repaired three or four times within a period of five years at the defendant's garage, and that had been held as insufficient to ground a course of dealing.

Even where exemption clauses are incorporated, the common law courts consistently sought to exercise judicial control over these terms. Put simply, where there is any doubt or ambiguity in the language of the term or of its scope, this will be resolved against the party seeking to rely on it. The Singapore courts have wholly adopted the English position on the *contra proferentum* rule.[56]

[49] See eg *Chapelton v Barry Urban DC* [1940] 1 KB 532; *Thornton v Shoe Lane Parking* [1971] 2 QB 163.

[50] *Cosmat Singapore (Pte) Ltd v Bank of America National Trust & Savings Association* [1992] 2 SLR(R) 195.

[51] This is quintessentially the gist of *L'Estrange v Graucob* [1934] 2 KB 394, applied in *Press Automation Technology Pte Ltd v Trans-Link Exhibition Forwarding Pte Ltd* [2003] 1 SLR(R) 712, in which the judge expressly rejected the Canadian approach in *Tilden Rent-A-Car Co v Clendenning* (1978) 83 DLR (3d) 712 that the mere presence of a signature is insufficient to constitute consensus *ad idem*.

[52] *Parker v South Eastern Railway* (1877) 2 CPD 416.

[53] [1971] 2 QB 163 at 170; see also *Tjoa Elis v United Overseas Bank* [2003] 1 SLR(R) 747 at [75].

[54] Singapore preserves and receives into its legal system the English common law in existence on the date of the Application of English Law Act, reserving to the Singapore Court of Appeal the prerogative to depart from that position as it sees fit.

[55] [1972] 2 QB 71.

[56] See *Rapsican Asia Pte Ltd v Global Container Freight Pte Ltd* [2002] 1 SLR(R) 701 at [41]; *Sunlight Mercantile Lte Ptd v Ever Lucky Shipping Co Ltd* [2004] 1 SLR(R) 171.

B. Unfair Contract Terms Act

The statutory control of exclusion clauses through the Unfair Contract Terms Act is *in pari materia* with its UK counterpart and seeks to curtail the extent to which liability for breach of contract or negligence can be excluded or limited through contractual terms. Clauses that exclude liability for death or personal injury are per se void. For all other terms purporting to exclude or limit liability, these are subject to a 'reasonableness test'. Indeed, the outcome of the test is highly fact-dependent, and amongst others, the factors the courts have taken into account include the relative bargaining position of the parties, as well as whether an inducement was offered to agree to the term. As with the English position, the reasonableness of the term is judged at the time the contract was entered into, and not when the breach arose. The law in Singapore insofar as Unfair Contract Terms Act is concerned is very much in line with the English position.

V. Product Liability

There is in Singapore only a general common law framework for an action in negligence against manufacturers of defective products.

At common law, a manufacturer owes a duty of care to the ultimate consumer of his product: *Donoghue v Stevenson* et al.[57] For decades, Singapore followed the English position unflinchingly, and departed from it only in 2007, via the Court of Appeal case of *Spandeck Engineering v Defence Science & Technology Agency*.[58] The facts of the case aside, the Appellate Court clarified that henceforth there would be a single two-stage test on the duty of care in negligence cases, based on proximity and policy considerations.[59] The concept of proximity focuses on the relationship between the manufacturer and the consumer. It encompasses physical, circumstantial and causal proximity, and any voluntary assumption of responsibility and reliance.[60] If a prima facie duty of care arises, the court must decide whether to affirm or negate such a duty by 'weighing and balancing competing moral claims and broad social welfare goals'.[61] To-date, there have been no reported cases applying the *Spandeck* test in consumer disputes.

Although it was suggested in 2015 that the Consumers Association of Singapore might lobby the Ministry of Trade and Industry to enact legislation requiring manufacturers to provide warranties for all goods sold in Singapore, this has not only yet to materialise, but there has also been no further action on the part of the Consumers Association on this issue.[62] Manufacturer's liability for defective products has therefore yet to be introduced by statute or case law. The underlying concern mitigating against such introduction appears to stem from the desire to avoid *unnecessarily* burdening

[57] [1932] AC 562.

[58] [2007] 4 SLR(R) 100.

[59] This is similar to Lord Wilberforce's formulation in *Anns v Merton LBC* [1978] AC 728, which was overruled in England in *Murphy v Brentwood DC* [1991] 1 AC 398.

[60] [2007] 4 SLR(R) 100 at [81].

[61] ibid [85].

[62] J Lim, 'CASE Wants "Lemon Law" to Include Manufacturers', Asiaone.com, 30 March 2015.

businesses with regulatory costs, thereby reducing business competitiveness, and in turn, reducing consumer welfare. Also, Singapore is a major trading hub, with imports for domestic consumption constituting the vast majority of its produce and products.

The major exception to this state of affairs is encapsulated in section 12B(3) of the Consumer Protection (Fair Trading) Act (see above discussion) that defects discovered within a six-month period are presumed to have existed at the time of purchase.[63] Although this can be seen to shift the risk of defects to sellers, in most cases these products can simply be returned to or repaired by the manufacturers on the basis of standard warranties (most of which are of a period of at least a year). The run-of-the-mill challenge is as regards complaints (and there are many) which could be characterised as wear-and-tear rather than defects – but these are invariably questions of evidence rather than substantive law.

VI. Product Safety

The main legislation regulating product safety is the Consumer Protection (Trade Descriptions and Safety Requirements) Act.[64] Two subsidiary pieces of legislation bear mentioning: first, the Consumer Protection (Safety Requirements) Regulations 2004, which gazettes 45 categories of household electrical, electronic and gas products as 'controlled goods', and requires suppliers of such goods to register with Enterprise Singapore[65] – the relevant government regulator – prior to sale; and secondly, the Consumer Protection (Consumer Goods Safety Requirements) Regulations 2011, which empowers Enterprise Singapore to oversee the safety of consumer goods generally.

Consumer goods regulated under the Consumer Protection (Consumer Goods Safety Requirements) Regulations are divided into two categories. Under the first category, consumer goods for which there are standards formulated by any one of four internationally recognised standard setting bodies[66] ought to comply with those standards as well as any additional standards Enterprise Singapore may set from time-to-time.[67] The second category covers all other consumer goods not falling within the first category. With there being no agreed international standard, Enterprise Singapore may adopt regional safety standards where available, or work with the relevant consumer, commercial, and manufacturing stakeholders to formulate domestic

[63] See above at s III.B.

[64] Consumables are regulated separately from goods, chiefly under the Sale of Food Act 1973 (Cap 283, 2002 Rev Ed).

[65] These powers used to be held by the Standards Productivity and Innovations Board (SPRING), formerly a statutory board under the Ministry of Trade and Industry. In the second quarter of 2018, it merged with another statutory board, the International Enterprise Singapore, to form Enterprise Singapore, a super-regulator focused on business regulations. Its duties in relation to consumer protection have since transferred to the Competition and Consumer Commission of Singapore.

[66] The International Organisation for Standardisation (IS), the International Electrotechnical Commission (IEC), the European Committee for Standardisation (EN standards) or the American ASTM International.

[67] Under reg 2(2), there is no requirement to comply with any provision of international safety standards deemed inappropriate for application in Singapore (for instance, in relation to different voltage and phasing for electrical goods, or where there is a failure to take into account Singapore's tropical climate, or where the provision does not specifically pertain to safety).

safety standards (Singapore Standard, or SS) for such goods. It is important to note that these standards *by themselves* have no force of law. That said, an industry standard may be used as evidence of breach of a particular hard law (as in the case of the Consumer Protection (Safety Requirements) Regulation, or reference to the Codex Alimentarius for labelling rules in the Sale of Food Act), which explains compliance for these types of standards. Compliance of all other types of standards is purely voluntary, although the fact of industry stakeholder participation in the formation of such rules makes for easier acceptance and widespread adoption.

Enterprise Singapore conducts pre- and post-market surveillance for most consumer goods within Singapore's domestic circulation. It is unclear how the regulator decides which types of products warrant pre- as opposed to post-market surveillance. It has, in recent years, concentrated on testing for children's toys and clothing, electrical products relating to lighting and haircare, as well as power banks and furniture.[68] Regardless of whether the goods are controlled or not, when they are found to be unsafe, Enterprise Singapore may notify the supplier to stop the supply of the product, and informs the public of its action. It may also require the supplier to inform consumers of the nature of the safety issues with the product. Suppliers who persist in supplying the unsafe product to the market may be fined or imprisoned or both.[69]

That having been said, there are significant exceptions to Enterprise Singapore's oversight.[70] Thus, food and beverages come under the purview of the Singapore Food Agency;[71] cosmetics, pharmaceuticals and medical devices are regulated by the Health Sciences Authority (HSA);[72] and motor vehicles are regulated by the Land Transport Authority (LTA).[73] These type of products are regulated under sector-specific laws.

VII. Adaptation to the Digital Age

The primary piece of legislation governing e-commerce in Singapore is the Electronic Transactions Act (Cap 88) of 1998,[74] and which is heavily based on the UNCITRAL Model Law on Electronic Commerce. As such, the mere fact that an agreement

[68] For example, 'Enterprise Singapore cautions consumers on safety issues with baby carriers, cots, and strollers' (5 November 2019), 'Enterprise Singapore cautions consumers on safety issues with magnetic toys for children' (2 September 2019), 'Enterprise Singapore's Market Surveillance Finds 106 Unregistered Household Products Sold Online' (2 May 2019).

[69] Consumer Protection (Consumer Goods Safety Requirements) Regulations 2011 (GN No S 113/2011), reg 3.

[70] See the schedule to the Consumer Protection (Consumer Goods Safety Requirements) Regulations 2011 for a full list.

[71] Under Rule 3 of the Wholesome Meat and Fish (Processing Establishments and Cold Stores) Rules (Cap 349A), SFA may recall or cease stocks for adulteration or deemed unfit for consumption.

[72] Pharmaceuticals are controlled under the Health Products Act (Cap 122D, 2008 Rev Ed).

[73] Motor vehicle owners need to comply with the technical requirements of the Road Traffic Act (Cap 276, 2004 Rev Ed) as spelt out under the Road Traffic (Motor Vehicles, Construction and Use) Rules, the Road Traffic (Motor Vehicles, Lighting) Rules, the Road Traffic (Motor Vehicles, Seat Belt) Rules; and also the National Environment Agency's rules regarding compliance with Euro 3/4/5 exhaust emission standards.

[74] Electronic Transactions Act (Cap 88, 1998), revised in 2011. For a general overview and background to the introduction of this Act, see J Chan, 'Legal Issues in E-Commerce and Electronic Contracting: The Singapore Position' (8th ASEAN Law Association General Assembly 2003).

is in electronic form is no bar to its recognition at law; this is also the same for the validity of electronic records in the formation of contracts as well as pre-contractual statements.[75] Electronic signatures are recognised, and the manner of proof of such signatures is prescribed.[76] The statute also deals with the security and authenticity of electronic records.[77] I will refrain from further comment on these topics raised, since they threaten to seduce the discussion into the realm of evidence and internet regulation[78] and away from the issue of consumer protection.

Three further points need be raised. First, the mere fact that contracts are concluded electronically is no bar to the recognition and enforcement of consumer rights.[79] Second, legislation on financial products or advertising apply to the online environment as they would to the brick-and-mortar world. Third, there is no specific consumer legislation regulating digital products:[80] this is perhaps an indication either that in the eyes of the policy maker, digital products are no different than real world products, or that the likely impact of digital products in the Singapore market is at present not significant enough to warrant legislative attention. That having been said, when Singapore assumed the Chairmanship of ASEAN in 2018, it focussed its efforts on realising the bloc's digital single market. Member State-level agreements have therefore been reached regarding creating common rules or comparable standards for consumer protection and data protection insofar as these affect intra-ASEAN digital trade in goods and services.[81]

Singapore itself has in place rules regulating the flow of information. As can be expected, these include legislation aimed at protecting the collection and use of personal data. The Personal Data Protection Act entered into force in 2012, and established the statutory Personal Data Protection Commission (PDPC) as the body charged with regulating all matters pertaining to personal data.[82] The primary basis for consumer data protection is consent,[83] and the Personal Data Protection Act requires consumers' consent be obtained before personal data may be collected and used.[84] Consumers may revoke consent at any time,[85] and if so revoked, their personal data must be destroyed and proof of destruction furnished.[86] The Personal Data Protection Act is notable in that it establishes a nationwide Do-Not-Call Registry,[87] which obliges telemarketers

[75] Electronic Transactions Act, s 2.
[76] ibid, s 8.
[77] ibid, s 13.
[78] For instance, the regulation of certification authorities who provide private and public encryption keys under the Electronic Transactions (Certification Authority) Regulations; and the security of internet transactions through soft law such as the Internet Banking Technology Risk Management Guidelines spearheaded by the Monetary Authority of Singapore or the self-regulatory TrustSG security and privacy standards of Singapore's National Trust Council.
[79] In *Chwee Kin Keong and ors v Digilandmall.com* [2004] 2 SLR 594, the court did not distinguish between online and offline contracts: the same principles of contract law applied regardless.
[80] There is no agenda tabled by the government on this issue, and, indeed, no discussion at present on the need to regulate digital products.
[81] eg 'The ASEAN Framework on Digital Data Governance' and the 'ASEAN Agreement on Electronic Commerce'.
[82] Personal Data Protection Act 2012 (Act 26 of 2012), s 5.
[83] ibid, s 13.
[84] ibid, ss 14 and 15.
[85] ibid, s 16.
[86] ibid, s 16 read with s 25.
[87] ibid, Part IX.

to check whether a consumer's telephone number is listed under the registry, before cold-calling.[88] In a move to safeguard against Singapore becoming a haven for spam, the government is looking into the possibility of including instant messaging services within the ambit of the Do-Not-Call Registry.[89]

Personal data is also regulated through sector-specific legislation such as the Statistics Act, the Banking Act, as well as the Official Secrets Act. It should also be noted that the Personal Data Protection Act specifically exempts[90] public institutions from complying with its obligations. This indicates that the statute is solely intended to regulate data within the private sphere. Taking its cue from the developed West,[91] Singapore has established standards for data portability, giving consumers greater control over personal data collected by businesses.[92]

VIII. Unfair Commercial Practices

Part II of the Consumer Protection (Fair Trading) Act regulates unfair practices. The approach taken is to define unfair practices generally. Thus, it constitutes an unfair practice to say or do anything or to omit to do or say anything such as to reasonably deceive or mislead a consumer, to make a false claim or to take advantage of a vulnerable consumer.[93] The general test of whether a supplier has engaged in an unfair practice is that of reasonableness, in that the reasonableness of the actions of the supplier in those circumstances must be considered.[94] The Consumer Protection (Fair Trading) Act provides, under Schedule Two, a blacklist of 20 specific practices deemed unfair, such as the concealment of onerous or material terms in small print, and the warranting to consumers that a particular good has a quality or grade that is known not to have.

One important consequence of this is to bring false or misleading advertising within the ambit of the Consumer Protection (Fair Trading) Act. However, a false or misleading advertisement is not per se actionable under the Act unless brought by a consumer who has entered into a consumer contract involving that unfair practice.[95] The alternative is for the Competition and Consumer Commission of Singapore of its own volition

[88] ibid, s 43.

[89] See PDPC, 'Public Consultation for Managing Unsolicited Commercial Messages and the Provision of Guidance to Support Innovation in the Digital Economy' (27 April 2018). Available under www.pdpc.gov.sg/Guideline-and-Consultation-Menu under 'public consultations'.

[90] Personal Data Protection Act 2012, s 4. While the Act does not apply to public agencies, these agencies are subject to similar data protection obligations under the Singapore Government Instruction Manual.

[91] See for instance Article 20 of the Regulation (EU) 2016/679 of the European Parliament and of the Council of 27 April 2016 on the protection of natural persons with regard to the processing of personal data and on the free movement of such data (General Data Protection Regulation), OJ 2016, No L119, p 1.

[92] See the Speech by Dr Koh Poh Koon – the then Senior Minister of State for Trade and Industry and National Development – at the Official Launch of the Competition and Consumer Commission of Singapore (9 April 2018) at [19]–[21], accessed at the 'newsroom–speeches' section under www.mti.gov.sg; PDPC, 'Response to Feedback on the Public Consultation on Proposed Data Portability and Data Innovation Provisions' (20 January 2020). The Personal Data Protection Commission was amended in 2020 to allow for data portability to businesses established within Singapore.

[93] ibid, s 4.

[94] ibid, s 5(3)(a).

[95] ibid, s 6.

to apply under section 9 of the Consumer Protection (Fair Trading) Act for a declaration that an advertisement is false or misleading or an injunction for that practice to be halted. The cases that make it to court are few and far between.

Perhaps one of the reasons for paucity in cases is due to the existence of the Advertising Standards Authority of Singapore (ASAS),[96] a quasi-self-regulatory body made up of representatives from the Consumers Association of Singapore as well as mainstream media groups, advertising organisations and the Infocommunications and Media Development Authority (IMDA).[97] The Advertising Standards Authority publishes and enforces the Singapore Advertising Code of Practice, a soft law instrument developed in consultation with industry players. Although this code has no force of law, offending advertisers are sanctioned by media owners withholding of advertising space. This sanction effectively ensures compliance.

Sanctions, however, are not always effective. Consider the rising importance of social media as an alternative to mainstream media. Increasingly, advertising is conducted not on television screens or printed in magazines, but on blogs or posts by social media influencers, and occasionally in a way not apparent to the consumer that the influencer has been paid to promote a good or service. Traditional sanctions are ineffective since influencers are not dependent on mainstream media's advertising space. The Advertising Standards Authority has responded by engaging social media agencies and adapting guidelines for their use.[98] In other words, relying on co-ownership of the guidelines by social media influencers rather than the threat of sanctions to ensure compliance.

A related development on unfair commercial practices to take note of is that of drip pricing and pre-ticked boxes, which is conceivably misleading. Shortly after the Competition and Consumer Commission of Singapore was empowered to enforce the Consumer Protection (Fair Trading) Act, it launched a months-long investigation into this practice in the online sphere, resulting in a comprehensive report and guidance on what is permissible and what is not. It then reached out to several major online stakeholders to implement the guidelines. The approach appears to be that of co-regulation: the engagement and co-option of private stakeholders to voluntarily comply with the soft law it promulgates, with the level of compliance corelative to its conviction to apply its investigative and enforcement powers under the Consumer Protection (Fair Trading) Act. It has to this date not been required to go down this latter route.

IX. Access to Justice

Although Singapore has made inroads in modernising and raising standards in its consumer protection regime, it is important to bear in mind that the principle of *caveat emptor* remains the guiding approach insofar as law and policy in this area is concerned. This is partly due to the seeming unwillingness to burden businesses

[96] Of which this author was a council member between 2018 and mid-2019.

[97] IMDA is a statutory board under the Ministry of Communications and Information, and is amongst others charged with regulating broadcast media.

[98] ASAS, 'Guidelines on Interactive Marketing Communications & Social Media' (2016).

unnecessarily, and also because of the prevailing attitude that consumers are expected to take personal responsibility not only for deciding whether to enter into a transaction, but also in seeking redress should problems arise. The majority of remedies listed in the main consumer protection legislation – the Consumer Protection (Fair Trading) Act – are therefore private in nature, whether addressed through self-help or with assistance from the courts.

A. Small Claims Tribunal

Many consumers do in fact attempt to seek redress directly with the traders involved, though it is a separate question whether the formal court system is utilised to resolve consumer disputes. As the sums involved tend to be modest, virtually all consumer disputes fall within the monetary jurisdiction of the State Courts[99] rather than that of the Supreme Court (which deals with disputes of a value of at least SGD 250,000 (approximately USD 185,000)).[100] Within the State Courts structure, the majority of disputes are dealt with by the Small Claims Tribunal (which deals with disputes of a value of up to SGD 20,000 (approximately USD 15,000)).[101] In fact, the Small Claims Tribunal was set up in 1985 with the specific purpose of resolving consumer disputes, property damage claims and short-term residential lease disputes.

A concerted effort has been made, over the last three decades, to streamline the judicial process and to attempt to ensure costs are not prohibitive. The result is a fast-tracked and relatively cheap procedure, at least insofar as the Small Claims Tribunal is concerned. Thus consumer disputes within the value of SGD 5000 (approximately USD 3750) require only a lodgement fee of SGD 10 (approximately USD 7.50), and SGD 20 for claims between SGD 5000 and SGD 10,000. Information on how to commence claims and to enforce judgments is readily available in electronic and hard-copy format. Most if not all are adjudicated without legal representation, thus keeping costs down.

Hearings before the Small Claims Tribunal are largely documentary affairs, and although formally a court procedure, the Tribunal Referee usually conducts matters as informally as possible; and as a matter of judicial policy, encourages parties to settle their dispute amicably, stepping in to adjudicate only as a last resort. Decisions of the Small Claims Tribunal are enforceable as court orders, and claimants may avail themselves of general enforcement mechanisms like writs of seizure and sale, garnishee orders or examination of judgment debtors. Like any other country, sometimes the costs of enforcement vis-à-vis the value of the debt dissuade (would-be) creditors (whether consumers or businesses) from going down this route: this is especially true of many consumer disputes since the values tend to be small.

[99] Small Claims Tribunal Act, s 2.

[100] State Courts Act (Cap 321, 2007 Rev Ed), s 2.

[101] This sum can, by consent of parties to the dispute, be increased to a maximum of SGD 60,000 (approximately USD 45,200): Small Claims Tribunal Act, s 5(4).

B. Mediation

A key approach to domestic dispute resolution in Singapore, perhaps in a nod to Confucian influences, is to encourage mediation rather than litigation.[102] As such, once a claim is lodged, and if it is one that does not involve personal injury (as the run-of-the-mill consumer disputes tend not to), action is stayed in favour of state-supported mediation. Mediation typically occurs within 14 days of a claim being lodged, and if it is not resolved before the State-appointed mediator, is thereafter fixed for a hearing within 10 days of the failed mediation session. As tourism is a major contributor to the Singapore economy, an even faster-track is put in place for tourist disputes. Mediation and/or a hearing may be fixed within 24 hours of a claim being lodged.

C. Financial Industries

Insofar as the financial sector is concerned, Singapore's de facto Central Bank – the Monetary Authority of Singapore – worked together with stakeholder banks and other financial institutions to set up the Financial Industries Dispute Resolution Centre (FIDReC).[103] This Centre has been in operation since 2003, offers a fast-track arbitration process to deal with complaints between consumers (often retail investors) and financial institutions. Its attractiveness lay in the fact that it offered something for everyone – defendants received the confidentiality they wanted, and both parties could avail of a speedy process. Its caseload ballooned in the wake of the 2008 global financial crisis, especially since a sizeable number of consumers purchased instruments linked to the now-defunct Lehman Brothers.

D. Consumers Association of Singapore

An important *facilitator* of the private enforcement of consumer rights is the Consumers Association of Singapore (CASE). Although the Association cannot represent consumers in private actions against firms, it can and often uses its clout to attempt to reach an amicable agreement. Like many of its counterparts across the developed world, CASE is non-governmental and membership-based. Akin, for example, to the UK's Which?, its articles of association restrict its capacity to act in consumer disputes to those on its membership. Due in part to historical buy-in from the national labour movement, it must be said, it does represent a large swathe and cross-section of the domestic consumer population. Furthermore, to get around this formality, membership fees for individuals are kept deliberately affordable: non-members who approach CASE regarding their disputes may enrol for a very small amount of money to take advantage of

[102] See for instance J Lee and H Teh (eds), *An Asian Perspective on Mediation* (Singapore: Academic Publishing 2009) 54–55; S Menon, 'Building Sustainable Mediation Programmes: A Singapore Perspective' (2015) *Asian Journal on Mediation* 1.

[103] See www.fidrec.com.sg.

CASE's professional expertise and leverage with the trading community, or otherwise, engage CASE to assist in drafting preliminary correspondence with the trader in question to commence negotiations over redress.

E. Case Examples

What is striking about the Singapore model (of access to justice) is the dearth of consumer case law. Indeed, a check on the local case law repository is likely to throw up commercial cases on the Sale of Goods Act or Unfair Contract Terms Act, and very little on the Consumer Protection (Fair Trading) Act. This is likely for the following reasons: first, the relatively small sums involved in the bulk of disputes compared to the cost of formal resolution tends to dissuade parties from seeking redress. Second, the cases that do go through formal adjudication are cleared through the Small Claims Tribunal, and such cases do not result in grounds being published. Rare is the opportunity, therefore, for Singapore courts to develop consumer law jurisprudence. Finally, many of the more egregious unfair trading practices are halted through behind-the-scenes work involving CASE and the signing of voluntary compliance agreements usually undertaking not to commit similar breaches in the future and to recompense consumers.[104]

CASE maintains a blacklist of businesses who are the subject of numerous complaints. This list is published on their website. At the height of a recent problem involving errant traders at a local shopping mall, CASE also published a specific list of those traders at the shopping mall itself. This type of reputational sanction is a classic tool of regulators. The reasons why it is not used as widely as it is, is perhaps due to the spectre of Singapore's strict defamation laws as well as the recent criminalising of 'doxing',[105] thus requiring CASE to balance the need to inform consumers about potential unfair practices against the risk and costs associated with litigation by businesses thus affected.

X. Changes to the Regulatory Scene

Until December 2016, the Consumer Protection (Fair Trading) Act provided for CASE, together with the Singapore Tourism Board, as 'specified bodies' to advance the interests of consumers and tourists to the country.[106] As 'specified bodies' under the Act, CASE and the Singapore Tourism Board were empowered to negotiate with firms who are or appear to be engaging in unfair trading practices with a view to changing

[104] Even these have limits: firms in the past that breach or refuse to sign VCAs and have court injunctions served against them simply close the business and start over. There is no general Directors Disqualification Act like in the UK. There are provisions in statutes to bar persons from being directors, but these require the involvement of specific sectoral regulators such as the Accounting and Corporate Regulatory Authority (ACRA) (Companies Act) or the Monetary Authority of Singapore (MAS) (Financial Advisors Act or the Securities and Futures Act).

[105] 'Doxing' refers to the malicious publishing online of an individual's private or identifying information. See Protection from Harassment Act (Cap 256A, 2015 Rev Ed), s 5.

[106] Consumer Protection (Fair Trading) Act, s 8(10).

their behaviour. If an agreement is reached, it can be concretised in a Voluntary Compliance Agreement (VCA), which inter alia may contain a commitment from the firm to compensate consumers who have already suffered a loss as a result of the firm's behaviour. If the firm is unwilling to enter into a VCA or breaches it, the specified body could, on approval from the Injunctions Proposals Review Panel (as appointed by the Minster for Trade and Industry), make an application before the courts for an injunction on pain of contempt of court to restrain the firm in question from persisting in its behaviour.[107]

Whilst the right to commence injunction proceedings have been used on occasion, neither CASE nor the Singapore Tourism Board had seen fit to use it frequently for the following reasons. First, the costs incurred are inevitably not recovered – either because the law rarely allows recovery on a complete indemnity basis, or because of impecuniosity of the defendant firm – and therefore the decisions on whether to proceed with an injunction invariably involve questions of where the scarce resources of a not-for-profit organisation ought best to be employed. Second, the facilitative efficiency of Singapore's company laws means that a firm that is or is about to be served with an injunction can simply wind-up, and the errant trader can swiftly set up a new company in order to circumvent the order. Most disputes are therefore resolved through the signing of VCAs, direct legal action by consumers, or invoking extra-legal reputational sanctions like naming-and–shaming on (social) media.

A review by the Ministry of Trade and Industry in 2015 led to changes to the enforcement regime under the Consumer Protection (Fair Trading) Act in early December 2016. The power to initiate injunctive proceedings was transferred from the non-governmental CASE to the statutory Standards Productivity and Innovations Board (SPRING), under the purview of the Ministry for Trade and Industry. In addition, SPRING was accorded investigative powers to enter suppliers' premises and seize documents and to preserve evidence, in line with the powers it already possesses in relation to the Weights and Measures Act,[108] and identical to the Competition Commission of Singapore's investigative powers vis-à-vis the Competition Act.

Then, barely a year later, the Ministry for Trade and Industry announced a further consolidation of market regulatory agencies by mid-2018, with SPRING to cease to exist in its current form. Insofar as product safety and weights and measures are concerned, these are transferred to a business-focussed regulator known as Enterprise Singapore. As for its consumer protection obligations and powers under the Consumer Protection (Fair Trading) Act, these have since been transferred to the Competition Commission of Singapore, renamed as the Competition and Consumer Commission of Singapore from April 2018. This appears to be part of a wider worldwide trend, where market regulators are entrusted with both competition and consumer portfolios. Open questions remain as to what the Commission's policy position is on the interface between competition and consumer protection. Also, it is premature to anticipate how the Commission will conduct itself in pursuit of consumer protection, and, amongst others, much may depend on how the former consumer protection division within SPRING is structured

[107] ibid, s 10.
[108] Weights and Measures Act (Cap 349, 1985 Rev Ed), s 30.

within the new Commission, leading to a preservation and integration of substantive knowhow or processes, or an unfortunate loss of institutional knowledge and standing ties with other stakeholders in the market, like CASE.

Finally, although the modern approach to consumer regulation entails encouraging consumer self-help and market competition, regulators have not shied away from direct intervention when it is apparent that the market cannot quickly enough correct undesirable business practices. When Singapore was dealing with the spread of Covid-19, certain retailers raised manifold the otherwise ordinary price of surgical masks. In response to public outcry of alleged profiteering, the Ministry of Trade and Industry intervened under the Price Control Act[109] to require these retailers to justify the basis for their raising of prices, to the extent of inspecting retailers' premises and books.[110]

XI. Conclusion

Consumer protection, like many areas of law, can be best characterised *crescit eundo* – it grows as it goes. Many improvements to the consumer protection framework can be traced to the non-governmental CASE's successful lobbying of the Ministry of Trade and Industry, or reactions to sharp practices widely publicised in mainstream or social media. Where changes have occurred, these are the product of a fair amount of comparative legal study in order to find out best practices in consumer protection.

Like Hong Kong, it provides an example of light-touch regulation in the context of one of the world's freest economies. Singapore, as a country with a small domestic hinterland and which imports almost all its consumption needs, is sensitive to the fact that consumer protection standards could conceivably impose unnecessary costs on businesses, costs which potentially render domestic firms uncompetitive or act as a barrier to entry to foreign firms. In that sense, the main functions of consumer law in Singapore appears not dissimilar to its counterpart in the EU – ensuring the competitiveness of firms and equal market access to all.[111]

[109] The Act itself originated as the Price Control Ordinance of 1950, during a period of post-war scarcity and rationing of staples like rice and sugar (see lii and liii, Minutes of Proceedings of the Colony of Singapore Legislative Council of 19 October 1949). Powers under the Price Control Act have only been utilised twice before. Once in 1973 to regulate the import and export of rice, and in response to panic buying due to price uncertainty in the wake of the global oil shocks. The second in 1990 in response to market manipulation by large volume pork importers.

[110] Ministry of Trade and Industry Press Release, 'Issuance of letters by Price Controller to sellers that have received consumer complaints' (30 January 2020); 'Price Control Act letter of demand issued to retailer 3 Stars' (10 February 2020); 'Inspection of 3 Stars Premises under the Price Control Act' (17 February 2020).

[111] In addition to EU consumer law's goals of protecting consumers and strengthening the internal market.

11

South Korea

SHINDONG JUNG

I. Introduction

Until the 1990s, consumer issues in South Korea did not receive much attention. The government's policy and public opinion were usually focused on industrial promotion, making South Korea's economy one of the world's fastest-growing from the early 1960s to the late 1990s.[1] At that time, most consumer issues were regulated by consumer public law, and consumers were considered just as the subjects of protection. This paradigm was changed with the fully revised Consumer Protection Act 1980,[2] which entered into force on 28 March 2007.[3] The government reorganisation in February 2008 introduced a unified implementation system for consumer policies. As a result, the powers to establish and review consumer policy plans[4] and enact and amend various pieces of legislation regarding consumer issues were transferred from the former Ministry of Finance and Economy to the Korea Fair Trade Commission (KFTC).[5] In addition, the Korea Consumer Protection Agency was renamed as the Korea Consumer Agency[6] and the Korea Fair Trade Commission took over the power to govern the agency. This paradigm shift was aimed at strengthening the position of consumers as the ones who exercise sovereignty, not just as the subjects of protection.

[1] South Korea recorded the fastest rise in average GDP per capita in the world between 1980 and 1990. See 'GDP per capita growth (annual %) – Korea, Rep.' https://data.worldbank.org/indicator/NY.GDP.PCAP.KD.ZG/?locations=KR.

[2] Act No 3257 (Enforcement Date 13 September 1982).

[3] The Korea Consumer Protection Act was renamed as the Korea Framework Act on Consumers.

[4] The provisions for the establishment of Master Plan were recently added to the Framework Act on Consumers 2008 to regulate a mid- and long-term Master Plan for Consumer Policy. This master plan is established every three years with the purpose of implementing consumer policies. See KFTC, 'Consumer Policy of KFTC', p 3. Available from the publications (others) section of the KFTC website: www.ftc.go.kr/eng/index.do.

[5] This committee is a ministerial-level central administrative organisation under the authority of the Prime Minister and also functions as a quasi-judicial body. It is committed to four main mandates: promoting competition, strengthening consumers' rights, creating a competitive environment for SMEs and restraining concentration of economic power. For details consult the KFTC website, ibid.

[6] This agency is a public organisation established in 1987 in accordance with the Consumer Protection Act in order to effectively implement Korean consumer protection policies.

Furthermore, since the 2000s, private law or consumer contract law have been attracting attention to solve various consumer issues. The following Acts can be mentioned as such core legislation in the area of consumer private law: 'Act on the Consumer Protection in Electronic Commerce, etc', 'Act on Door-to-Door Sales, etc', 'Act on the Regulation of Standard Business Terms', 'Product Liability Act' and the 'Framework Act on Consumers', which regulates alternative dispute resolution. Concerning revision and interpretation of those Acts, European consumer law, particularly German consumer law, has recently been used as comparative law materials to assist in reforms.[7]

This contribution starts with issues concerning consumer contract law in Korea. It then moves to the problem of product liability and product safety, to the topics of unfair trade practices and to the question of e-commerce transactions, which have received much attention due to the rapid growth of the 'platform economy'. The contribution then deals with alternative consumer dispute resolution in Korea.

II. Information Duties and Right of Withdrawal

A. E-Commerce

In South Korea, the 'Act on the Consumer Protection in Electronic Commerce, etc' (hereinafter: 'E-Commerce Act')[8] entered into force on 1 July 2002 to protect the rights and interests of consumers and enhance market confidence by prescribing matters relating to the fair trade of goods or services by means of electronic commerce transactions. This Act defines three important terms in relation to its scope: Electronic commerce transaction, Mail order and Mail order brokerage[9] First, the term 'Electronic commerce transaction' means any commercial transaction of which the whole or part of goods or service is made through electronic documents[10] in transactions for goods or service. According to this definition, 'electronic commerce transaction' has a very broad meaning in the Korean legal system, thus this Act uses the concept of 'mail-order' for regulations related to consumer protection in non-face-to-face transactions. It defines 'Mail order' as selling goods or services by providing information on the sale and receiving a consumer's order by means of mail, telecommunications or other methods. This is wider than simply those using the postal services. In addition, with respect to online intermediary platforms, the term 'Mail order brokerage' is used in this Act. It means the act of intermediating a mail order between both parties to a transaction by allowing the use of a cybermall.[11] These definitions have received criticism for being too

[7] The German Civil Code (*Bürgerliches Gesetzbuch*; BGB) served as a template in the civil law of South Korea.

[8] Act No 6687 (Enforcement Date 1 July 2002). English translations of South Korean legislation, including the legislation referred to in this contribution, are available from the website of the Korean Ministry of Government Legislation at www.law.go.kr/LSW/eng/engMain.do.

[9] E-Commerce Act, Art 2.

[10] According to the 'Korean Electronic Documents and Transactions Act', 'electronic document' refers to any information that is processed, sent, received or stored in electronic form by the information processing system. The E-Commerce Act uses this definition of the electronic document without any modification.

[11] The Cybermall refers to a virtual shopping mall established to transact goods, etc using computers, etc and information communications facilities, see E-Commerce Act, Art 2(4).

unfamiliar when compared to everyday usage. Accordingly, there is a movement in the Korean National Assembly to revise the terminology in the e-commerce law based on the core concept of online platform.[12]

i. Information Duties of the Mail Order Distributor

In Korean consumer contract law, the resolution of information asymmetry is of the utmost importance. The central consumer protection measures under the Korean E-Commerce Act are therefore information duties and the right of withdrawal. It can be said that these two means of protection under consumer contract law were partially influenced by European Union law and German law.

First, Article 13 of the E-Commerce Act regulates the duties to provide information on the identity of sellers and transaction conditions in online transactions. Under this provision, a mail order distributor shall include therein each of the following in placing indications or advertisements to take orders for a transaction of goods or services: trade name and name of the representative, address, telephone number and e-mail address. This duty to provide information on the identity of sellers goes beyond the meaning of contract law obligations and is also subject to penalties. In practice, if the seller provides false identification information, the seller can be punished by a fine of up to 10 million won (approximately USD 8,900).[13] Furthermore, a seller shall indicate, advertise or notify the transaction conditions (contents, method of supply, requirements and procedures for exchange, return and guarantee of the goods or services etc)[14] in an appropriate manner so that consumers can clearly understand the terms of a transaction of goods or services, before concluding a contract, and therefore sign a deal without any error or discrepancy. The Korean Fair Trade Commission may determine and publicly notify the matters concerning contents and methods of indication, advertisement and announcement of the information on goods or services and transaction conditions.[15]

ii. Right of Withdrawal in Mail Order Sales

Articles 17 and 18 of the E-Commerce Act regulate the right of withdrawal in mail order sales, namely the general and the special right of withdrawal. A consumer who has concluded a contract with a mail order distributor for the purchase of goods or services can, in principle, withdraw the contract within a period of seven days from the date of receipt of a document on the content of the contract (the general withdrawal from

[12] See S Jung, 'Law to Be Enacted for Fair Online Platform Transactions', BusinessKorea.co.kr, 29 September 2020.

[13] E-Commerce Act, Art 43.

[14] Additionally, matters regarding method of exercise, and effect of withdrawal, technical matters necessary for the electrical transmission, installation, etc, of the goods, matters concerning compensation for damage, settlement of complaints against the goods and resolution of disputes between consumers and traders shall be notified, see ibid, Art 13(2).

[15] See KFTC, 'Public notification on provision of information of goods, etc. in electronic commerce transactions'. Available from the Laws and Guidelines (consumer: e-commerce) section of the KFTC website: www.ftc.go.kr/eng/index.do.

distance contracts). For mail order contracts, such right of withdrawal is justified as the consumer is not able to see the goods before concluding the contract. However, certain exceptions to such right of withdrawal exist for mail order sales. First, the consumer's right of withdrawal is excluded where the goods have been destroyed or damaged due to a cause attributable to the consumer.[16] This shall not apply where the package has been damaged to check the contents of the goods. It means that the consumer should be allowed to test and inspect the goods to the extent necessary to establish their nature, characteristics and the functioning, since in the case of mail order the consumer is not able to see the goods before concluding the contract. While in similar cases the EU consumer under the EU Consumer Rights Directive should not lose the right to withdraw but should be liable for any diminished value of the goods,[17] the E-Commerce Act does not make such provision for liability for diminished value of the goods resulting from the handling of the goods. Rather, in South Korea it is only a question of the exclusion of the rights of withdrawal.

Secondly, where the value of the goods has substantially decreased due to the consumer's use or partial consumption or where the value of the goods has substantially decreased due to the lapse of time, making resale difficult or impossible, the consumer cannot exercise the right of withdrawal.[18] With regard to this reason for exclusion, contracts as regards the provision of accommodation other than for residential purpose and transport service (for example flight booking) are discussed. In contrast to the legal situation in the EU,[19] the right of withdrawal of consumers under Korean law may also be exercised in principle for the passenger transport service contract and accommodation contract.[20] However, according to the Korean courts,[21] it must be examined whether a case where the consumer made a reservation through mail-order sales with a lodging business or a travel business but intends to withdraw the order falls under this reason for exclusion (where the value of goods, etc is significantly reduced to the degree that resale is impracticable due to the lapse of time).[22]

Third, the right of withdrawal cannot be exercised where the packaging of copyable goods is opened or unsealed as withdrawal is inappropriate due to the nature of the goods. This exception of withdrawal applies, for example, if digital content is supplied on a tangible medium, such as a CD or a DVD.

Finally, where the provision of services or digital content has commenced, the consumer cannot exercise the right of withdrawal. However, this shall not apply to the portion for which the provision of such services or digital content has not commenced

[16] E-Commerce Act, Art 17(2) No 1.

[17] See Directive 2011/83/EU of the European Parliament and of the Council of 25 October 2011 on consumer rights, OJ 2011 No L304, p 64, Art 14(2) and recital 47.

[18] E-Commerce Act, Art 17(2) Nos 2 and 3.

[19] See eg Consumer Rights Directive (EU), Art 3(3)(k) and recital 27.

[20] According to Art 3(4) of the E-Commerce Act, only transactions of securities by investment traders and investment brokers under the Korean Financial Investment Services and Capital Markets Act and transactions of financial instruments by financial companies are excluded from the scope of this Act.

[21] Seoul Central District Court Decision 2018Na29442, 24 October 2020.

[22] Accordingly, the KFTC 'Guidelines for consumer protection in electronic commerce, etc' lay down the right of withdrawal in contracts for accommodation other than for residential purpose and transport service. Available from the Laws and Guidelines (consumer: e-commerce) section of the KFTC website: www.ftc.go.kr/eng/index.do.

in cases of a contract comprising divisible services or divisible digital content.[23] For services, this seems to be a big difference between Korean and EU consumer law, because in the EU the consumer should benefit from his right of withdrawal even in cases where the provision of services has been requested before the end of the withdrawal period.[24] However, it does not make much difference in practice because the consumer concludes mainly the contract comprising divisible services (for example contracts for the provision of accommodation). In other words, although the Korean consumer may exercise the right of withdrawal in the case of divisible services, the trader (the mail order distributor) is assured to be adequately paid for the service provided, thereby it is similar to the position in the EU.

Significant differences between South Korea and the EU exist in relation to contracts for digital content[25] which is not supplied on a tangible medium. In the EU, the consumer has the right of withdrawal for such contracts only if there is no consent to the beginning of the performance during the withdrawal period and the consumer has not acknowledged that, in consenting, the right to withdraw from the contract is lost.[26] In contrast to this approach, in Korea the consumer may exercise the right of withdrawal despite the fulfilment of such information duties by the trader, as long as the exercise of the right relates only to the portion for which the provision of divisible digital contents has not commenced.[27] It means that in cases of a contract comprising divisible digital content the consumer should be able to terminate the obligation of the contracting parties to perform the contract and the trader (the mail order distributor) should be adequately paid for the digital content provided.

Furthermore, the E-Commerce Act regulates a different, special type of right of withdrawal for mail order sales, which does not affect the aforementioned general right of withdrawal (the special withdrawal from distance contracts). According to Article 17(3) of the E-Commerce Act, where the contents or characteristics of the goods or services are different from what was indicated or advertised, or have been performed differently from the terms of the contract, the consumer can exercise the right of withdrawal in the cases of the mail order sales within three months from the date of receiving the goods or within 30 days from the date they knew or could have known such fact. The provisions on the exceptions to the general right of withdrawal do not apply to this special right of withdrawal.

This special right of withdrawal is very similar in terms of its requirements to the general revocation for performance not in conformity with the contract under the Civil Code of South Korea.[28] If, in the case of a reciprocal contract, the obligor does not

[23] E-Commerce Act, Art 17(2) No 5.

[24] See eg Consumer Rights Directive (EU), Art 14(4)(a) and recital 50.

[25] According to the 'Act on the Promotion of Cultural Industries', the term 'digital content' means materials or information, such as codes, letters, diagrams, colours, voices, sound, images or videos (including the combination thereof), which are manufactured or processed in the digital form so as to enhance the usefulness of the preservation or utilisation thereof. The E-Commerce Act uses this definition of digital content without any modification.

[26] See eg Consumer Rights Directive (EU), Art 14(4)(b) and recital 19.

[27] In relation to this provision, there has recently been a discussion about when the provision of digital content commences in sales contracts for online game items.

[28] In this context, the special right of withdrawal is also known as revocation of the contract for consumer protection.

render an act of performance which is due in conformity with the contract, then the obligee may revoke the contract according to the Civil Code, if he has specified, without result, an additional period for performance or cure. However, this special right of withdrawal in Article 17(3) of the E-Commerce Act differs from the general revocation in the Civil Code in that the consumer may terminate the obligation of the contracting parties to perform the contract, where the contents or characteristics of the goods are different from what was advertised. Since what was advertised does not always mean the content of the contract,[29] the consumer is better protected by the special right of withdrawal than by the general revocation for performance not in conformity with the contract.

There is no difference between the general and the special withdrawal of the consumer in terms of legal consequences of withdrawal from distance contracts in the E-Commerce Act. In the event that the consumer withdraws from the contract, the mail order distributor should reimburse all payments received from the consumer.[30] The reimbursement can be made by voucher if the consumer has used vouchers for the initial transaction or has expressly accepted them. For the cost of returning the goods, the E-Commerce Act distinguishes between the general and the special withdrawal of the consumer. In cases of the general withdrawal, the consumer shall bear the cost of returning the goods; in cases of the special withdrawal, the mail order distributor shall bear the cost.[31] However, unlike EU law,[32] there is no provision on the question of the expenses borne by the trader to deliver goods to the consumer. As is common practice in South Korea, the consumer usually bears the expenses borne by the trader to deliver goods to the consumer,[33] regardless of whether the consumer chooses a common and generally acceptable type of delivery offered by the mail order distributor or a certain type of delivery, that would have incurred higher delivery costs.[34] Regarding this problem, it is criticised that the provisions on the legal consequences of withdrawal from distance contracts in the E-Commerce Act do not make an adequate contribution to consumer protection.

B. Off-premises Contracts

On 1 July 1992, the 'Act on Door-to-Door Sales, etc (hereinafter: 'Door-to-Door Sales Act')'[35] entered into force in South Korea to protect the rights and interests of consumers and raise market confidence by providing for matters regarding fair transactions of goods and services through door-to-door sales, telemarketing and recurring transactions etc.

[29] See eg Supreme Court Decision 2005Da5829,5836, 9 June 2020.
[30] E-Commerce Act, Art 18(2). According to this provision, the mail order distributor (seller) shall make a refund of the price of goods, within three business days from the date the goods are returned.
[31] ibid, Art 18(9) and (10).
[32] See Consumer Rights Directive (EU), Art 13(1).
[33] KFTC, 'Guidelines for consumer protection in electronic commerce, etc' provides in accordance with the custom in practice.
[34] See eg Consumer Rights Directive (EU), recital 46.
[35] Act No 4481 (Enforcement Date 1 July 1992).

According to the definition of the Door-to-Door Sales Act, the term 'door-to-door sales' means that a person engaging in the business of selling goods or services sells goods or services by soliciting consumers at any place, other than the sales office, distribution shop etc to receive an offer for a contract or conclude contracts. In other words, the off-premises contract between the trader and the consumer is the core of the door-to-door sales concept. This definition of door-to-door sales has been extended to provide sufficient consumer protection – it also includes situations where a trader solicits consumers at any place, other than a place of business by making recommendations to receive an offer for a contract or to enter into contracts on the business premises of the trader.[36]

In the case of door-to-door sales (as in the case of e-commerce transactions), the trader must perform his information duties and the consumer has a right of withdrawal. First, Article 7 of the Door-to-Door Sales Act establishes rules on information to be provided for off-premises contracts. In other words, it regulates the duties to provide information on the identity of sellers and transaction conditions in door-to-door sales. According to this provision, the door-to-door seller shall explain the following matters to the consumer: trade name and name of the representative, address, telephone number and e-mail address, contents of the goods or services and method to supply, procedures for exchange, return and guarantee of the goods or services etc. The door-to-door seller should give the consumer clear and comprehensible information before the consumer is bound by the off-premises contract.

This duty to provide information goes beyond contract law obligations and (as in the case of e-commerce transactions) is also subject to penalties. The door-to-door seller, who issues a contract with a false statement written therein, can be punished by a fine of up to 10 million won (approximately USD 8,900).[37]

Furthermore, the right of withdrawal in off-premises contracts also contributes to a high level of consumer protection in South Korea. According to Article 8 of the Door-to-Door Sales Act, the consumer can in principle withdraw from the off-premises contract within a period of 14 days from the date of receipt of a document on the content of the contract.[38] The right of withdrawal in the Door-to-Door Sales Act is justified due to the potential surprise element or psychological pressure on the consumer. In comparison with the E-Commerce Act, the withdrawal period of the Door-to-Door Sales Act is 14 days, not seven, extending the consumer consideration period for door-to-door sales, yet there are no reasonable reasons for the difference.

The relevant provisions on the exceptions to the consumer's right of withdrawal are very similar to those in the E-Commerce Act. First, the consumer's right of withdrawal is excluded where the goods have been destroyed or damaged due to a cause attributable to the consumer. However, this exception does not apply where outer packaging is damaged in the course of verifying the content of goods or services. Secondly, where

[36] This definition of door-to-door sales is very similar to the definition of off-premises contract pursuant to the Consumer Rights Directive (EU), Art 2 No 8.

[37] Door-to-Door Sales Act, Art 63.

[38] Furthermore, the consumer can withdraw from the off-premises contract within a period of fourteen days from the date on which hindrance ends, where the door-to-door seller hinders withdrawal of the consumer, ibid, Art 8(1) No 4.

the value of the goods has substantially decreased due to the consumer's use or partial consumption or where the value of the goods has substantially decreased due to the elapse of time, making resale difficult or impossible, the right of withdrawal cannot be exercised. Third, where the packaging of copyable goods is opened, the right of withdrawal cannot be exercised. In contrast to the E-Commerce Act, there is no provision on the question of the exceptions to exercising the right of withdrawal in cases of the provision of services or digital content.[39] Therefore, the necessity of exceptions to the consumer's right of withdrawal in relation to the provision of services or digital content and the corresponding amendment to the Door-to-Door Sales Act are discussed.

In addition, the relevant provision of the Door-to-Door Sales Act sets out the consumer's special right of withdrawal, which in terms of requirements is similar to Article 17(3) of the E-Commerce Act. According to the Door-to-Door Sales Act, where the contents or characteristics of the goods or services are different from what was indicated or advertised, or have been performed differently from the terms of the contract, the consumer can exercise the right of withdrawal in the cases of the door-to-door sales within three months from the date of receiving the goods or within 30 days from the date he knew or could have known such fact.[40]

Concerning legal consequences of withdrawal, there is almost no difference between distance contracts and the off-premises contracts: in the event that the consumer withdraws from the contract, the door-to-door seller shall reimburse all payments received from the consumer.[41] However, the Door-to-Door Sales Act does not distinguish between the general and the special right of withdrawal for the cost of returning the goods: the door-to-door seller shall bear the costs of returning the goods.[42] In this point, the consumer is better protected under off-premises contracts than under distance contracts.

C. Telemarketing

The Door-to-Door Sales Act regulates the protection of the consumer in telemarketing, defined as selling goods or services by making recommendations to consumers by telephone or by inducing consumers to respond to a call.[43] The provisions regarding the door-to-door sales apply to telemarketing except for certain matters provided by the Act. For example, the Door-to-Door Sales Act stipulates the telemarketer's duty to keep records of conversations.[44] However, the provisions on the information duties of the

[39] This is presumed because almost no contracts for digital content, which is not supplied on a tangible medium, had been concluded via door-to-door sales.

[40] Door-to-Door Sales Act, Art 8(3). As in the E-Commerce Act, the special withdrawal from off-premises contract does not affect the general right of withdrawal and the provisions on the exceptions to the general right of withdrawal do not apply to this special right of withdrawal.

[41] ibid, Art 9(2). According to this provision, the door-to-door seller shall make a refund of the price of goods, within three business days from the date the goods are returned.

[42] ibid, Art 9(9).

[43] ibid, Art 2(3).

[44] The consumer can request the telemarketer to allow him to inspect the records of conversations preserved by visits, telephone, facsimile, e-mail or any other means and the telemarketer so requested shall comply with such request, ibid, Art 7-2(2).

trader and the consumer's right of withdrawal in the off-premises contract also apply to telemarketing sales.

The distinction between 'telemarketing' in the Door-to-Door Sales Act and 'mail order' in the E-Commerce Act is not easy to draw, since the term 'mail order' not only means selling goods or services on the Internet, but also includes selling by telephone. In practice, this problem is solved by the criterion of whether the consumer initially had an intention to purchase or was induced to purchase by the solicitation of the seller.[45] Although the consumer in the mail order sales can in principle withdraw the contract within a period of seven days from the date of a document on the contract, the withdrawal period for the telemarketing sales is 14 days.[46]

III. Termination of Contract in Recurring Transactions

The Korean Door-to-Door Sales Act regulates a type of special sales called 'recurring transactions' for consumer protection, which is an important exception to the principles of the Korean Civil Code.[47] 'Recurring transactions' means transactions made under a contract for providing goods or services continuously or on an irregular basis during not less than one month,[48] which falls under the term 'contracts for the performance of a continuing obligation' in the general contract law of South Korea. Under the Korean Civil Code, each party can in principle terminate a contract for the performance of a continuing obligation for a compelling reason if a contract period has been fixed by the parties. In other words, a party can in principle only terminate a contract for a definite period of time if there is a justified interest in the termination of the contract. Nevertheless, for contracts for recurring transactions concluded pursuant to the Door-to-Door Sales Act, the consumer may terminate the contract with the trader at any time during the contract period. This means that in cases of consumer contracts there is a statutory right to terminate the contract without giving a reason (as with the consumer's right of withdrawal), even though a specific contract period was agreed. In practice, this legal right to terminate the consumer contract carries an important meaning especially with regard to gym contracts in South Korea, for which a contract period of one year is normally agreed. Regarding those provisions on recurring transactions, there is a critical view that it unreasonably burdens the trader. Accordingly, the Door-to-Door Sales Act lays down that the statutory right of termination shall not apply where any other Act provides otherwise or where specified by Presidential Decree.[49]

[45] See KFTC, 'Guidelines for consumer protection in extraordinary sales'. Available from the Laws and Guidelines (consumer: Door-to-door sales) section of the KFTC website: www.ftc.go.kr/eng/index.do.

[46] This is because the provisions on the consumer's right of withdrawal in an off-premises contract apply to telemarketing sales.

[47] Act No 471 (Enforcement Date 1 January 1960).

[48] Door-to-Door Sales Act, Art 2(10).

[49] For example, the statutory right of termination can be excluded, where goods or services are to be produced specially in accordance with the order of a consumer and the relevant trader in recurring transactions is likely to sustain a severe and irrecoverable loss if the consumer is allowed to withdraw contract, Enforcement Decree of the Door-to-Door Sales Act, Art 40.

IV. Non-conformity of Goods with the Contract

Although the main source of disputes between consumers and sellers concerns the non-conformity of goods with the contract, there is still no specific legislation on the sale of consumer goods in Korea. Therefore, the difficulties encountered by consumers regarding non-conformity with the contract must in principle be resolved by the Korean Civil Code.[50] There is thus criticism that there is a loophole in consumer private law and special rules are needed governing the sale of consumer goods.

The Korean Civil Code undoubtedly recognises the principle that the goods must, above all, conform with the contractual specifications. For defective goods, the buyer may demand cure,[51] for which the buyer may choose that the defect is remedied or a good free of defects is supplied. Furthermore, in the case of non-conformity of the goods with the contract the buyer can demand damages or revoke the agreement.[52] However, the buyer is not entitled to have the contract revoked if the lack of conformity is minor, but only if the objective of the contract is not unattainable thereby. It is still unclear whether for defective goods the buyer is entitled to have the price reduced under the Civil Code.[53]

The parties to the sales contract may, by common consent, restrict or waive the rights granted to the buyer according to the Civil Code, because it regulates only the legal relationships between private individuals as the codification of general private law. This means that legislation on the sale of consumer goods is required in Korea.

However, the fact that there is still no specific legislation on the sale of consumer goods in Korea does not mean that a high level of consumer protection cannot be ensured in practice. The Fair Trade Commission publishes the Regulations on Consumer Dispute Resolution providing the detailed criteria for the settlement of consumer disputes, such as repair, exchange, refund or compensation issues.[54] It can be the criteria for any agreement or recommendation on the settlement of disputes, unless there is any separate agreement as to the method of settlement between the parties in dispute. In practice, the criteria are used by many traders for the settlement of consumer disputes regarding the non-conformity of goods with the contract. Most consumer organisations and the Korea Consumer Agency also use the criteria for consumer dispute resolution.[55] Thus, the Regulations on Consumer Dispute Resolution, which ensures a higher level of consumer protection compared to the Civil Code, have proven to be effective even though they are non-mandatory.

[50] In addition, for certain categories of goods (eg electronics), it is current practice for sellers and producers to offer guarantees on goods against any defect which becomes apparent within a certain period.

[51] Civil Code, Art 581(2).

[52] ibid, Art 581(1).

[53] Art 582 of the Civil Code provides for a limitation on the period during which buyer can exercise their rights, because it is necessary to limit in time the period during which the seller is liable for any lack of conformity. So, the rights mentioned shall be exercised by the buyer within six months from the time when he was first aware of the fact, that the relevant good is defective.

[54] Available from the Laws and Guidelines (consumers: consumers) section of the KFTC website: www.ftc.go.kr/eng/index.do.

[55] In South Korea, consumer disputes are rarely handled by courts. They are mainly handled by official consumer ADR bodies.

V. Unfair Contract Terms

In South Korea, the 'Act on the Regulation of Standard Business Terms' (hereinafter: 'Standard Business Terms Act')[56] came into force on 1 July 1987 to protect consumers by preventing traders from preparing unfair terms and conditions and using them in transactions.[57] The Act covers four important points regarding its purpose and scope: definition of standard business terms, incorporation of standard business terms into the contract, interpretation of standard business terms and test of reasonableness of contents.[58]

A. Definition of Standard Business Terms

'Standard business terms' are defined as all contractual terms pre-formulated for multiple other parties which one party to the contract presents to the other party upon the entering into of the contract. It is irrelevant whether the provisions take the form of a physically separate part of a contract or are made part of the contractual document itself, what form the contract takes, what typeface or font is used for them or what their volume is. However, contract terms do not become standard business terms if they have been negotiated in detail between the parties.[59]

B. Incorporation of Standard Business Terms into the Contract

It must be checked whether the legal requirements for incorporation of standard business terms into the contract are met. According to Article 3(2) of the Standard Business Terms Act, standard business terms only become a part of a contract if the trader, when entering into the contract, refers the consumer to them clearly and in a manner that is generally to be expected for the type of contract in question, when the trader, upon the request of the consumer, provides a copy of the standard business terms and when the trader explains important details provided in the standard business terms.[60] However it is irrelevant for the incorporation of standard business terms into the contract whether the other party to the contract (consumer) agrees to their applying.[61] If the three requirements are not met, the trader cannot claim that provisions in standard business terms form part of the contract.

If standard business terms in whole or in part have not become part of the contract, the remainder of the contract remains in effect. This does not apply where it is

[56] Act No 15697 (Enforcement Date 1 July 1987).

[57] German law served as a template for Act on the Regulation of Standard Business Terms.

[58] See KFTC, 'Consumer Policy of KFTC', p 21.

[59] Standard Business Terms Act, Art 4 lays down, that individually agreed terms take priority over standard business terms (Priority of individually agreed terms).

[60] According to Art 3 of the Standard Business Terms Act, this does not apply where it is considerably difficult to explain them due to the nature of the contract.

[61] On the contrary, according to the German Civil Code, § 305(2), standard business terms can only become a part of a contract if, inter alia, the other party (consumer) to the contract agrees to their applying.

impossible to achieve the purpose of the contract with only the effective parts or such effective parts are unreasonably unfavourable to one party. This legal consequence of non-incorporation is a special rule against the principle of partial ineffectiveness in general contract law of South Korea. In the Civil Code, it is provided as a general principle that, if a part of a contract is ineffective, the entire contract is ineffective, unless it is to be assumed that it would have been undertaken even without the ineffective part.[62]

C. Interpretation of Standard Business Terms

The Standard Business Terms Act lays down the rules for the interpretation of standard business terms. First, Article 5(1) provides, as a general principle of interpretation, that the standard business terms shall be construed impartially in accordance with the principle of trust and good faith, and shall not be construed differently depending on consumer. Second, if the meaning of terms and conditions is not clear (ambiguous clauses), it shall be construed in favour of the consumer. Therefore, any doubts in the interpretation of standard business terms are resolved against the trader.

D. Test of Unfairness of Contents

The main purpose of the Standard Business Terms Act is to ensure that contracts concluded with consumers do not contain unfair terms. Accordingly, the Standard Business Terms Act stipulates that provisions in standard business terms are ineffective if, contrary to the requirement of good faith, they unreasonably disadvantage the consumer (test of unfairness of contents).[63] According to Article 6(2) of the Standard Business Terms Act, any of the following in terms and conditions shall be presumed to be unfair: clauses unreasonably unfavourable to consumers, clauses which consumers would have difficulty anticipating in light of various circumstances, including the type of transaction, clauses which are so restrictive of essential rights under a contract that the purpose of the contract may not be achieved. Taking into account these principles, the Standard Business Terms Act lays down detailed criteria as to whether or not there is an unreasonable disadvantage, for example regarding fictitious receipts, reversal of contracts, lump-sum claims for damages, contractual penalty, exclusion of liability, prohibition of set-off, liability of an agent with power to enter into a contract, etc.[64]

[62] Civil Code, Art 139.

[63] The test of unfairness of contents can be conducted in courts and in the Korea Fair Trade Commission. The examination of terms and conditions by the Commission does not require a specific contractual relationship as a prerequisite, but focuses only on the fairness of the Terms and determines their validity. In comparison, the court examines the validity of the terms as a matter for a prior decision to confirm the rights and obligations of the relevant parties, in an actual contractual relationship, and the effect of such confirmation has ex post facto effect only on the persons who bring the individual case to the court.

[64] See 'Guidelines for Examination of Terms and Conditions' announced by KFTC and available from the Laws and Guidelines (consumers: terms and conditions) section of the KFTC website: www.ftc.go.kr/eng/index.do.

If the standard business terms in whole or in part are ineffective, the remainder of the contract remains in effect. This does not apply where it is impossible to achieve the purpose of the contract with only the effective parts or such effective parts are unreasonably unfavourable to one party. The legal consequence is a special rule against the principle of partial ineffectiveness in general contract law of South Korea, and has already been mentioned with regard to the legal consequence of non-incorporation.

VI. Product Liability

To protect the injured persons by providing for the liability of producers for damages caused by the defects of their products, the 'Product Liability Act'[65] came into force on 1 July 2002. Since the increased liability on the part of the manufacturer can be the sole means of adequately solving the problem of a fair apportionment of the risks inherent in modern technological production, the Product Liability Act provides for liability without fault, and punitive damages. In practice, cases involving product liability are rarely handled by courts, but considerable significance is given to the preventive function pursued by the Product Liability Act.

First, Article 3(1) of the Product Liability Act provides that the producer shall compensate for damages to the life, body or property of a person caused by a defect of a product (excluding damages inflicted only to the relevant product).[66] In such cases, the producer has an obligation to compensate the injured person for the resulting damage, regardless of their fault.

Second, the provision on punitive damages sets out that, if a producer causes serious damage to the life or body of a person as a result of not taking necessary measures against a defect of a product despite the producer's knowledge of such defect, the producer shall be liable up to three times the damage sustained by the person.[67] In such cases, the court shall consider certain factors (degree of intentionality, severity of damage caused due to the defect of the relevant product, financial gains obtained by the producer from supplying the relevant product, period during which the relevant product is supplied and supply volume, etc) when determining damages.[68] South Korean courts originally did not award punitive damages and foreign punitive damages were considered as a violation of public order.[69] In the meantime, legislation on punitive damages was urgently requested due to the so-called 'humidifier disinfectants scandal'[70] in 2016: the pulmonary toxicity of PHM[71] was discovered due to an outbreak of severe lung disease and humidifiers containing PHMG that were widely used in South Korea.

[65] Act No 14764 (Enforcement Date 1 July 2002).

[66] Provisions on material defects in the Korean Civil Code shall apply to damages inflicted only to the relevant product.

[67] Product Liability Act, Art 3(2).

[68] In addition, the court can consider financial status of the producer and efforts made by the producer to repair the damage.

[69] See eg Seoul Eastern District Court, Decision 93Gahab19069, 10 February1995.

[70] See H Lee, 'Oxy suspected of watering down report', koreaherald.com, 24 April 2016.

[71] Polyhexamethylene guanidine (PHMG) is a guanidine derivative that is used as a biocidal disinfectant.

Today, punitive damages carry an important meaning, especially for violations of the Product Liability Act that are hard to detect.

The Product Liability Act applies only to movables which have been industrially produced. Accordingly, Article 2(1) states that 'product' means all movables, even though incorporated into another movable or into an immovable. The term 'defect' within the meaning of this Act is defined as all defects of a product with regard to manufacturing, design or indication or lack of safety ordinarily expected of a product.[72]

Furthermore, the term 'producer' is defined very broadly as the protection of the consumer requires that all producers involved in the production process should be made liable, in so far as their finished product, component part or any raw material supplied by them was defective. In this context, importers of products into South Korea and to persons who present themselves as producers by affixing their name or trade mark, fall under the term 'producer' within the meaning of the Product Liability Act.[73] For the similar reason, the product liability also extends to persons who supply a product the producer of which cannot be identified, although they do not fall under the term 'producer'.[74] Due to this broad definition, several persons can be liable for the same damage. In these situations, the protection of the consumer requires that the injured person should be able to claim full compensation for the damage from any one of them. Accordingly, Article 5 of the Product Liability Act lays down, that, where not less than two persons are liable for the same damages, they shall be liable jointly.

In the context of fair apportionment of risk between the injured person and the producer, the producer's liability obligation under the Product Liability Act is excluded in certain cases in order to reduce the burden on the producer. According to its Article 4, the producer shall be exempted from any liability for damages under the Product Liability Act, where the producer who is liable for damages can prove certain facts, for example that the producer did not supply the product, that the existence of the defect could not be identified by the state of scientific or technical knowledge of the time when the producer supplied the product, that the defect is attributable to the producer complying with the standard prescribed by any Act or subordinate statute of the time when he supplied the product or that the defect is attributable to the design or the instruction on manufacturing by the producer of the product made of the relevant raw materials or components. The producer can thus free himself from liability by furnishing proof as to the existence of certain exonerating circumstances.

VII. Product Safety

Consumer issues concerning product safety are mainly regulated in South Korea by consumer public law. For example, the 'Electrical Appliances and Consumer Products Safety Control Act'[75] deals with the matters related to safety control of electrical

[72] The term 'defect' can cover three types of defect: defect in manufacturing, defect in design and defect in indication, Product Liability Act, Art 2(2).

[73] ibid, Art 2(3).

[74] ibid, Art 3(3).

[75] Act No 2674 (Enforcement Date 1 July 1974).

appliances and other manufactured products for consumers. Above all, the Act regulates the safety certification and the safety verification, which are important measures for product safety. According to its Article 19, no producer, importer or distributor of products subject to safety verification shall sell or rent such products without the safety verification mark.

Specific legislation concerns the safety of products for children, namely the 'Special Act on the Safety of Products for Children'.[76] For example, Article 6 of this Act provides that the Minister of Trade, Industry and Energy may investigate the safety, where the relevant product for children causes, or is likely to cause, harm to children's safety or health. In this case, the Minister may publicise results of safety investigations and issue an order for collecting, destructing, repairing, exchanging, refunding, improving or prohibiting the manufacture or distribution thereof to the relevant trader.

VIII. Unfair Trade Practices

To prevent any abuse of market-dominating positions by traders and any excessive concentration of economic power, and to regulate undue collaborative acts and unfair trade practices, the 'Monopoly Regulation and Fair Trade Act'[77] (hereinafter: 'Fair Trade Act') entered into force on 1 April 1981. This Act mainly regulates the prohibition of abuse of market-dominating position and the restriction on combination of enterprises, etc, but also provides for unfair trade practices regarding consumer protection. It also covers the provisions on unfair trade practices which harm only competitors' economic interests or which relate to a transaction between traders. However, the contribution only introduces the relevant provisions on unfair trade practices that directly harm consumers' economic interests and thereby indirectly harm the economic interests of legitimate competitors.

Trade practices directly related to influencing consumers' transactional decisions are regulated by three provisions. First, due to the harm to the normal process of competition in the market and reduced market efficiency, Article 23(1) No 1 of the Fair Trade Act stipulates that no trader may unfairly discriminate against a certain transacting partner. The prohibition of price discrimination carries an important meaning with regard to consumer protection. Price refers to the total cost actually paid by the consumer and conditions that directly affect the price (for example discount rate) are also included. Second, pursuant to Article 23 No 2, no trader may unfairly induce customers of competitors to deal with himself. In particular, two types of acts are prohibited regarding consumer protection, namely unfair incentives and fraudulent inducement. It also covers unfair advertising, but the issue is mainly regulated by other relevant legislation in Korea. Third, Article 23(1) No 3 deals with the problem of forced trade as otherwise the trader can reinforce its market power and restrict choices for consumers by forcing the counterparty to purchase certain goods. For example, tie-in sale is regulated as a form of forced trade.

[76] Act No 12733 (Enforcement Date 4 June 2015).
[77] Act No 3320 (Enforcement Date 1 April 1981).

As already mentioned, the problem of unfair advertising is mainly solved by separate legislation, namely this 'Act on Fair Labelling and Advertising' (hereinafter: Fair Advertising Act).[78] The Act, which entered into force on 1 July 1999 to prevent unfair labels and advertisements for products and services that deceive or mislead consumers, regulates four types of unfair advertising (Article 3(1)): advertising falsely, or by way of inflating facts ('false or exaggerated advertising'), advertising through methods such as concealment or understatement of facts ('deceptive advertising'), advertising oneself or his product as being superior or advantageous in comparison with another trader or product of another trader without clearly stating the subject or standards of comparison, or without providing objective grounds ('unfairly comparative advertising') and slandering another trader or the product of another trader by advertising them with contents having no objective basis or slandering them by advertising unfavourable facts only ('slanderous advertising'). No trader shall place any of the unfair advertising that is likely to undermine fair trade by deceiving or misleading consumers. As a means to combat unfair advertising, strict liability is prescribed under this Act. According to Article 10 of the Fair Advertising Act, a trader shall compensate for damages to the body or property of a person caused by unfair advertising, even in the absence of fault or tortious intent. Furthermore, the Fair Trade Commission may issue adequate measures (for example suspension of the relevant violation, publication of the fact that a corrective order has been issued to the relevant trader or corrected advertising) to the relevant trader to correct the unfair advertising.[79]

IX. Regulatory Framework for Online Intermediary Platforms

In South Korea, the question of rights and duties in the triangular relationship between consumers, suppliers (mail order distributor) and traders who operate a platform (mail order broker) had already been approached before the E-Commerce Act came into force in 2002. Although this topic was discussed before the rapid growth of the 'platform economy', some meaningful legislation was passed in the early 2000s. Of course, the recent rise of online platforms has again triggered the debate whether the regulatory framework has to be adjusted in order to adequately reflect the changing market structure. Accordingly, there is a movement in the Korean National Assembly and the Korean Fair Trade Commission to revise the e-commerce law.[80]

[78] Act No 5814 (Enforcement Date 1 July 1999).

[79] Fair Advertising Act, Art 7. The 'Act on Labelling and Advertising of Foods' (Act No 15483, Enforcement Date 13 March 2019) provides for unfair advertising of foods as a special law. For example, advertising a food to mislead consumers into believing that the food is effective in preventing, treating or curing any disease is prohibited.

[80] See H Lee, Korea JoongAng Daily, 'New legislation on online shopping proposed by FTC', korea joongangdaily.com, 28 September 2020.

A. Duty to Inform about the Role of the Mail Order Broker

As already mentioned, the terms 'Mail order brokerage' and 'Mail order broker' are used for online intermediary platforms[81] in the current E-Commerce Act. The Act expressly defines the term 'Mail order brokerage' as the act of intermediating a mail order between both parties to a transaction by allowing the use of a cybermall and regulates the duty to inform about the role of the mail order broker: according to Article 20(1) of the E-Commerce Act, the mail order broker shall notify beforehand that he is not a party to the mail order, so that consumers can easily recognise such fact. This duty of the mail order broker to report its role as an intermediary will help avoid any confusion about contractual roles. As the information must be available throughout the entire 'customer journey', the Prime Minister's Ordinance[82] on the E-Commerce Act accordingly prescribes a specific notification method: the notification should be given on the initial homepage of cybermall operated by the mail order broker and on the first page of advertising media or directly before the conclusion of the supplier-customer contract.[83] In addition, the mail order broker must inform the customer in a prominent manner that the consumer will be entering into a contract with a mail order distributor and not with the mail order broker. The relevant provision of the Prime Minister's Ordinance therefore requires that the font size for the information about the role of the mail order broker shall be equal to or larger than the font size indicating the contract parties.[84]

A mail order broker in violation of the information duty shall have joint liability with the seller in paying compensation for the damage caused intentionally or negligently by the latter to the consumer's property.[85] With regard to this liability of mail order brokers, it is criticised that the consumer should be able to exercise the rights and remedies available against the seller under the distance contract, and also against the mail order broker; this has been highlighted as creating confusion about contractual roles.[86]

B. Duty of the Mail Order Broker to Inform about the Supplier

It is not sufficient that the consumer merely knows about entering into a contract with a third-party supplier – the consumer also needs to be informed of the identity and the address of the third-party mail order distributor. Article 20(2) E-Commerce Act therefore requires the mail order broker to confirm the name (where the trader is a

[81] 'Coupang', 'Gmarket' and 'Naver Shopping' etc can be mentioned as South Korea's leading online platforms. Naver is the dominant portal in South Korea, with 30 million people using its website daily. In October 2020, the Korea Fair Trade Commission imposed a 26.5 billion won fine (approximately USD 23.7 million) on Naver for manipulating algorithms to give greater exposure to sellers affiliated with its shopping platform.

[82] 'Enforcement Rule of the Consumer Protection in the Electronic Commerce Transactions, etc' (Ordinance of the Prime Minister No 991).

[83] ibid, Art 11-2(1).

[84] ibid, Art 11-2(2).

[85] E-Commerce Act, Art 20-2(1).

[86] See European Law Institute (ELI), 'Model Rules on Online Platforms' (2019), Art 19.

corporation, its name and the name of its representative), address, telephone number, etc and to provide them to consumers before the conclusion of the distance contract. In South Korea, such information is required before the distance contract is concluded, not afterwards. As such, the E-Commerce Act does not take into account that the mail order broker may have a legitimate interest in not disclosing the identity of the third-party mail order distributor before the conclusion of the contract, in order to protect its business model as an intermediary.[87] For the duty to inform about the supplier, the mail order broker shall confirm and ensure that the identification information of the third-party supplier is correct. The principle that the platform operator can generally rely on the information provided by the third-party supplier thus does not apply in South Korea.[88]

A mail order broker in violation of this information duty shall have joint liability with the third-party supplier for the damage caused to the consumer's property by failing to provide information or by providing false information. However, this does not apply if the mail order broker paid due attention to prevent any damage to the consumers.[89]

C. Liability of the Mail Order Broker with Predominant Influence?

Concerning the rapid growth of the 'platform economy', recent discussions in South Korea have questioned whether, in addition to the liability of the mail order broker for lack of transparency, the mail order broker having a predominant influence over the mail order distributor (supplier) may be liable in certain cases towards the consumer. Such a predominant influence of the mail order broker is already taken into account in the current E-Commerce Act by the term 'mail order broker who perform important elements of mail orders': in provisions for regulation of the online intermediary platforms, the term 'mail order broker who performs important elements of mail orders' is used where the distance contract is concluded through facilities provided on the platform, or the mail order broker uses payment systems which enable the mail order broker to withhold payments made by the consumer to the mail order distributor.[90] However, the relevant provisions only set out certain rules for formal requirements concerning the intermediary role, do not lay down, for example, rights and remedies the consumer can exercise against the mail order broker in case of non-performance of the distance contract. In this context, the necessity of increased liability of the mail order broker with predominant influence and the corresponding amendment to the E-Commerce Act are discussed in the Korean National Assembly and the Korean Fair Trade Commission.[91]

[87] ibid, Art 14(2). The provision lays down, that not later than immediately after the conclusion of a contract, the platform operator must inform the customer about the identity of the supplier, and must enable communication between the supplier and the customer.

[88] ibid, Art 14(3).

[89] E-Commerce Act, Art 20-2(2).

[90] ibid, Art 20-3(1) and (2).

[91] Especially Art 20 of the ELI Model Rules on Online Platforms is used as material for the legislation.

X. Consumer Dispute Resolution

Today, it is necessary to ensure access to simple, efficient, fast and low-cost ways of resolving consumer disputes, arising from sales or service contracts and such access should apply to online as well as to offline transactions. In this context, the Framework Act on Consumers 2007[92] regulates alternative dispute resolution (ADR) by official consumer ADR bodies (Korea Consumer Agency and Korean Consumer Dispute Settlement Commission) and offers a simple, fast and free out-of-court solution to disputes between consumers and traders. Most consumers and traders in South Korea are aware of such free out-of-court redress mechanisms by official consumer ADR bodies and know how to file a complaint with an ADR entity.[93] Although consumer disputes are rarely handled by courts and by private consumer mediation bodies, they are handled effectively by official consumer ADR bodies.

The consumer dispute resolution by official ADR bodies has three steps. First, '1372 Consumer Counselling Centre' offers a free counselling service for the consumer experiencing any inconvenience or damage in the process of using the products and services provided by the trader. This centre is a nationwide integrated consumer call centre operated by the Korean Fair Trade Commission with participation from the Korean Consumer Agency, consumer organisations and local governments.

Second, the consumer can apply for consumer mediation by the Korean Consumer Agency through personal visits, postal mail, fax or the Internet, if problems are not resolved through consumer counselling. Once an application for the consumer mediation is received, the trader will be notified. The trader should then explain how the dispute has occurred and what his stance is on the case. The Korean Consumer Agency recommends possible solutions to both parties based on the results of the fact-finding investigation, related laws and regulations. If the parties agree to a settlement, a contract of settlement within the meaning of the Korean Civil Code is concluded.[94] By way of mutual concession, the contract is concluded by which a dispute of the parties with regard to a legal relationship is remedied.

Third, if parties fail to reach a contract of settlement, they can request a free conciliation by the Consumer Dispute Settlement Commission, which is composed of 150 or fewer members. The Commission shall make a proposal to the parties to resolve the dispute (conciliation proposal), which is based on applicable law and the facts resulting from the dispute resolution procedure.[95] If the parties accept the proposal – in other words, a settlement through conciliation is reached – the Commission shall transmit the result of the dispute resolution procedure to the parties in text form with the required explanations. This notification is as equally binding as a 'Settlement in Court' (with the

[92] Act No 7988 (Enforcement Date 27 March 2007).

[93] See several consumer dispute settlement cases www.kca.go.kr/eng/sub.do?menukey=6012.

[94] Civil Code, Art 731.

[95] There are two types of Consumer Dispute Settlement Commission meetings: plenary mediation session and partial mediation session. Plenary mediation session consists of the chairman, standing commissioners and five to nine members designated by the chairman and the partial mediation session consists of the chairman or standing commissioners and two to four members designated by the chairman. The meetings are held one to three times every week.

same effects as a final ruling made under the Civil Procedure Act).[96] In this context, the Consumer Dispute Settlement Commission is referred to as a quasi-judicial body that deliberates and decides on consumer dispute cases.

XI. Conclusion

Concerning the paradigm shift aimed at strengthening the position of consumers as the ones who exercise sovereignty, not just as the subjects of protection, consumer private law has recently attracted attention in South Korea. It also means a shift from the era when most consumer problems were regulated by consumer public laws. In this context, there is also an emphasis on cooperation between the Korean Fair Trade Commission and consumer organisations[97] on consumer issues. Furthermore, the Fair Trade Commission, which deals with competition policies, also deals with consumer policies and has the authority to enforce consumer laws in South Korea. Both competition policy and consumer policy are closely related insofar as they deal with the 'market' and have the ultimate goal of increasing 'consumer welfare'. However, how to effectively implement competition and consumer policies is a future challenge in South Korea.

Recently, the rise of platforms has triggered a debate over new legislation in light of the many new legal issues that have arisen in relation to the new market conditions of the 'platform economy'. Especially in relation to Peer-to-Peer transactions on sharing economy platforms or social network platforms and the online review manipulation problem, appropriate and meaningful legal solutions are expected.

[96] Art 67(4) of the Framework Act on Consumers provides that if the parties accept or are considered to have accepted the contents of the dispute settlement pursuant to paragraph (2), the contents of the dispute settlement shall have the same effect as a judicial compromise.

[97] eg Korea Green Consumers Network, Korea Consumers Union and Consumer Affairs Institute. See www.consumer.or.kr/english/partner/p_main.html.

12

Taiwan (Republic of China)

JERRY G FONG

I. Introduction

Taiwan (Republic of China), an island of 35,882.6 km^2 and with a population of over 23.5 million, is one of the world's important exporters of semiconductors, IT and other high-tech products. Taiwan is also the most democratic Republic in the long-running traditional Chinese society. With the endeavour of well-educated and hardworking people for the past several decades, Taiwan not only has established a rule-of-law democratic society but has also developed into a prosperous society with a robust economy.

As a rule-of-law society, Taiwan not only inherited the long-lasting Chinese legal tradition but also adopted a basic legal framework and principles from major civil law countries, such as Germany, Switzerland and Japan, since the founding of the Republic of China in 1911. Following the civil war between the Nationalist Party (Kuomintang) and the Communist Party, the Nationalist government moved to Taiwan in 1949, but the civil law legal system remains until today.

Taiwan is also a country based on written law. Only legislation passed by the Legislative Yuan (Congress) is the law of the land.[1] In addition to the legislation passed by the Legislative Yuan, the competent authorities in the central government can promulgate Enforcement Rules for the laws within their jurisdiction and can also draft regulations, rules and issue interpretive letter rulings to facilitate the implementation of the law.

With a stable political and legal system, and with the fast-expanding and stable economic environment, even though Taiwan maintains diplomatic relationships with

[1] Before 1 July 2018, court decisions, unless adopted as judicial precedents by the Supreme Court, do not have a legally binding effect (Court Organic Act, Art 57). However, after adopting the so-called 'Big Court' system by the Court Organic Act on 7 December 2018, all decisions made by courts will have certain legal effects. This revision makes Taiwan's court decisions have similar legal effects as the *stare decisis* principle in the common law.

just over a dozen countries,[2] it still retains a very close economic relationship with most of the countries around the world.[3] According to the World Trade Organization, Taiwan was the 16th largest exporter and 28th largest importer of merchandise in 2017.[4]

In fact, with a solid economic development base and strong industry position, Taiwan's economy has not been negatively affected by the protracted trade war between the United States and China that impacts the whole world. According to a study released by the United Nations Conference on Trade and Development (UNCTAD), Taiwan is the biggest winner of this Sino-American trade war with a gain of USD 4.2 billion export increase for the first six months of 2019.[5]

Thanks to the trade diversion effects, Taiwan's economic performance is even better than before. According to the economic figures compiled by the government, Taiwan's GDP grew 2.6 per cent in 2018 and stood at USD 589,391 million. The GDP per capita also reached USD 25,005 in 2018.[6] In 2019, while the whole world was facing the uncertainty caused by the prolonged US-China trade war, Taiwan's economy was still robust. For example, Taiwan's GDP grew 0.78 per cent and 0.67 per cent in the first and second quarters of 2019, respectively.[7] In the third quarter, due to Taiwanese business returning production from China, US buyers shifting their orders to Taiwan to avoid higher US tariffs and the increasing domestic consumption, the GDP grew 2.91 per cent, the fastest pace since Q2 2018 and the fourth consecutive quarterly growth.[8]

Concerning export/import trading, according to the exports and imports statistics compiled by the Ministry of Finance,[9] the total exports figure for 2020 was NTD 9,423,676 million (USD 318,897 million), whereas the total imports were NTD 8,430,172 million (USD 285,116 million). These figures indicate that imported consumer goods are supplemental to domestic consumer goods. This can also be evidenced by the fact that most consumer disputes are related to local business operators and domestic goods.

[2] On the political field, Taiwan presently maintains diplomatic relationships with only 17 countries, including the Holy See. For a list see the Ministry of Foreign Affairs' website under 'embassies and missions' at https://en.mofa.gov.tw.

[3] ibid. Taiwan sets up unofficial representative offices in 74 countries, including the European Union. Besides, 56 countries also have economic or business representative offices in Taiwan.

[4] For details on Taiwan's economy see www.taiwan.gov.tw/content_7.php.

[5] The UNCTAD study, 'Trade and Trade Diversion Effects of United States Tariffs on China', was released on 5 November 2019. According to this study, the biggest fallout of the trade war has been the trade-diversion effect. The paper puts the trade diversion effects for the first half of 2019 at about USD 21 billion. Trade diversion effects have brought substantial benefits for Taiwan (the paper called 'province of China'), Mexico and the European Union. In the first six months of the 2019 financial year, Taiwan's export to the United States gained by USD 4.2 billion. This is the highest among countries that have recorded increases in exports to the United States after its trade-war resulted in the reduction of Chinese exports. UNCTAD Research Paper No 37, 6 November 2019, https://unctad.org/webflyer/trade-and-trade-diversion-effects-united-states-tariffs-china.

[6] See https://countryeconomy.com/gdp/taiwan.

[7] GDP Growth Rate in Taiwan averaged 1.25 per cent from 1981 to 2019, reaching an all-time high of 5.64 per cent in the fourth quarter of 1990 and a record low of -5.07 per cent in the fourth quarter of 2008. See https://tradingeconomics.com/taiwan/gdp-growth.

[8] 'Taiwan economy grows 2.91% y/y in Q3, best pace in more than a year', reuters.com, 31 October 2019.

[9] Ministry of Finance, Trade Statistics Database, accessible under www.mof.gov.tw/Eng/htmlList/6688.

II. The Consumer Law Framework

A. Background

Since the 1980s, Taiwan's economy has boomed and has been accompanied by the need for a comprehensive consumer protection regime. Even if many laws were relevant to consumer protection, Taiwan lacked a fundamental legal foundation for a comprehensive consumer protection framework. Moreover, consumers were not concerned about their rights. Most importantly, local business groups were opposed to enacting specific legislation for fear of increased costs or impediments to their business. Under such circumstances, the government took a very conservative approach, only using administrative measures to supplement the deficiency of consumer protection.

Without basic legislation to lay the legal foundation for protecting the welfare and interests of consumers, aggrieved consumers could only rely on other relevant laws, such as the Civil Code and Criminal Code to seek justice, or depend on different authorities to develop administrative measures. Such remedies, even if available, were indirect and not necessarily working well for consumer protection.

To establish the legal foundation for a stronger and more effective consumer protection regime in Taiwan, starting from the early 1970s, many social activists and scholars began to campaign for a dedicated statute to protect consumers. Such initiatives failed to produce the desired result. Although several tragic events occurred in the 1980s that attracted the attention of the whole society and government, it took another decade to finalise the 'the constitution of consumers', that is, the Consumer Protection Act[10] in 1994.

With the enactment of the Consumer Protection Act as the ultimate legislation for consumer protection, and along with more than two decades of government efforts, consumer protection organisations/groups and the growing awareness of consumers, consumer protection has achieved a consensus in Taiwan. Over the years, many new consumer-related laws have appeared. Coupling with various pre-existing legislation and amendments thereafter,[11] together with the Consumer Protection Act, there is a broad and expansive consumer protection legal framework in Taiwan.

More importantly, after more than two decades of continuous efforts since the enactment of the Consumer Protection Act, consumer protection thinking has rooted deeply in the genes of government, and consumer awareness is also on the rise.

Nevertheless, even with such vast improvement in the past decades, many deficiencies remain, such as how to effectively handle increasing disputes arising from online transactions; how to deal with false and misleading advertisements; whether strict liability shall apply to healthcare services; whether the present remedies suffice; and how to promote consumer protection groups. This chapter will first introduce the legislative history, consumer protection legal framework and supporting administrative regime. Thereafter, the focus is on the special issues affecting Taiwan.

[10] An English version of the legislation is available from the 'Laws & Regulations Database of The Republic of China': https://law.moj.gov.tw/ENG/Index.aspx.

[11] Please see below ss II.B and III for further discussion.

B. Establishing and Perfecting the Consumer Protection Legal Regime

Before 1980, consumer protection was not a priority issue on the government's agenda because many relevant laws, regulations and policies already existed, although they were fragmented. The government took a conservative attitude to consumer protection. This approach faced increasing challenges, especially after several widely publicised events in which defective products severely damaged consumers' health and even caused death. One of the most serious incidents were the polychlorinated biphenyls contaminated edible oils from which 2,000 suffered irrecoverable harm in 1979. This and other events raised strong concerns from the general public, media and key opinion leaders, and led to the founding of Taiwan's first consumer protection group, the Consumers' Foundation Chinese Taipei in November 1980.

After realising the severity of the public outcry, the then Premier of Executive Yuan (Taiwan's Cabinet) officially proclaimed in 1982 that the protection of consumers is an indispensable responsibility of the government. Thereafter, the Executive Yuan instructed the Ministry of the Interior and the Ministry of Economic Affairs to study and evaluate with local scholars the question of whether Taiwan should adopt basic consumer legislation, or a 'consumer constitution' advocated by local scholars.

Following Cabinet instructions, the agencies drafted the first version of the Consumer Protection Act in 1983. However, internal disputes, especially on whether the Consumer Protection Act should be consolidated with the Fair Trade Act or be separate legislation, stalled the legislative process. After almost a three year impasse, the government finally determined to proceed with the *sui generis* approach and restarted the legislative process in 1986.

During the interim, the Executive Yuan formulated a 'Consumer Protection Program' as the policy guidance for related government agencies. Under such a Program, the government adopted new policies to strengthen the protection of consumers. Among the policies, some are worth special attention, such as promoting the Good Pharmaceutical Manufacturing (GMP) standards; encouraging hospitals and clinics to charge reasonable fees; regulating labelling for drugs, infant milk powder and cigarettes; and setting up a consumer protection task force in local District Attorney's Offices.

However, because the Program was an ad hoc administrative policy, it did not have strong legally binding effects, especially as regards enforcement. Moreover, since it was difficult to make an independent assessment about the effectiveness of the implementation, coupled with other problems, such as many agencies having overlapping authority and the lack of specific measures to resolve issues that were strongly concerning the consumers, the Program failed.[12]

Recognising that the Program was not sufficient to resolve essential consumer protection issues and that consumers' interests needed a better protection scheme, the government finally restarted the legislative process in 1987 by redrafting the Consumer Protection Act. Many active legislators at the Legislative Yuan, however, were not

[12] Even though the Program listed 43 consumer protection approaches, most of them were policy statements and without concrete implementing measures.

satisfied with the administrative branch's draft because it failed to address many core consumer issues. With help from the Consumers' Foundation Chinese Taipei and scholars, the legislators countered with their version of the draft which adopted international consumer protection principles and rules in other countries, such as Germany, Japan, Sweden and the United States, as well as the EU.

After much delay, the Consumer Protection Act was formally promulgated on 11 January 1994, almost 12 years after the proclamation in 1982. The Fair Trade Act,[13] which initiated its legislative process later than the Consumer Protection Act, had already gone into effect in 1991. In comparison with the Fair Trade Act or other laws, the legislative journey of Taiwan's Consumer Protection Act is definitely more challenging than other laws.

To fulfil the legislative purposes of the Act and to cope with the fast-changing society, technology and business environment, the Act was revised in 2003, 2005 and 2015. The 2003 revisions included revamping the consumer dispute complaint and mediation procedures, reinforcing the consumer mediation committee's authority in handling consumer disputes and increasing penalties for business operators who fail to cooperate with the competent authorities. The 2005 revision only dealt with instalment transaction-related credit issues, such as disclosing annual percentage rates and all the costs of borrowing.[14]

The 2015 revision is the most important. It made the statute more comprehensive as regards to 'standard contracts', 'mail order purchases' and 'door-to-door purchases' and to cope with the changes ushered in by the advancement of technology and the popularity of e-commerce. To resolve practical disputes, it introduced group litigation (class action) and punitive damages.

The competent authority in the central government in charge of consumer protection affairs has also gone through extensive restructuring. The original Consumer Protection Commission, which ceased to exist from 1 January 2012, and responsibility for consumer protection was transferred to the Executive Yuan so as to implement the Fair Trade Act more effectively. The Executive Yuan set up two new divisions on 1 January 2012: the Consumer Protection Committee and the Department of Consumer Protection.[15]

After the re-organisation, the Consumer Protection Committee is responsible for consumer protection policies, regulations, mechanisms and evaluating implementation results. The Department of Consumer Protection, on the other hand, is responsible for the revision and interpretation of the Consumer Protection Act, drafting regulations and mandatory and prohibitory provisions for standard contracts.[16]

[13] The Fair Trade Act unequivocally proclaims in its Art 1 that 'protecting consumers' interests' is one of its legislative purposes.

[14] Only one provision, Art 22-1, was added in 2005 revision which provides that '[t]rader shall express the annual percentage rates of all the costs of borrowing over the term of the credit in their advertisements when engaging in credit transactions'.

[15] According to Art 41 of the Consumer Protection Act, the Executive Yuan is responsible for the promotion of consumer protection matters. However, the Executive Yuan enacted the Regulations Governing the Establishment of the Consumer Protection Committee in 2012 and delegated its responsibility under the Consumer Protection Act to the Consumer Protection Committee.

[16] The Department of Consumer Protection's other powers include supervision, coordination and assessment of consumer protection policy execution; coordinating and reviewing of consumer protection policies, plans, programmes and measures; supervision of consumer ombudsman.

III. The Consumer Protection Act

A. Overview

The enactment of the Consumer Protection Act laid the groundwork for the consumer protection legal framework in Taiwan. However, in addition to the Consumer Protection Act, its Enforcement Rules and relevant regulations,[17] there are diverse laws and regulations also related to consumer protection under different agencies' authorities, particularly under the Ministry of Health and Welfare. Together, they comprise the comprehensive consumer protection regime in Taiwan. This section will discuss the Consumer Protection Act; the following section will discuss other consumer-related laws, such as the Fair Trade Act and the Financial Consumer Protection Act.

The Consumer Protection Act sets forth the legislative goals and groundwork of consumer protection, as well as the relationship between the Consumer Protection Act and other consumer laws.[18] It also provides basic definitions that delineate the boundary and application of the Consumer Protection Act and other laws, such as 'consumer', 'business operator' (or 'trader' as used in the official translation), 'consumer relationship', 'consumer transaction', 'consumer litigation', 'standard terms and conditions', 'standard contract', 'distance sales', 'door-to-door sales' and 'instalment sales'.[19] It further provides the measures that the government, business operators and consumers should take to achieve the goals of this law.[20]

Moreover, the Consumer Protection Act explicitly recognised certain legitimate consumer interests, and how to safeguard such interests, including: health and safety safeguards;[21] standard contracts;[22] special transactions, such as distance sales, door-to-door sales and instalment sales;[23] and consumer information, covering advertising, costs of borrowing, labelling for goods or services, written warranties and packaging.[24] Such provisions are the main substances of the Act since they provide the minimum protection for consumers' health and safety, establish rules for fair trading, ensure the consumers can obtain full and accurate information and provide the basis for consumers to claim their rights.

The Act further stipulates the fundamental rules for the operation, promotion and missions of the consumer protection groups[25] that covers consumer protection groups' qualifications, founding purpose, duties and limitations. To ensure the proper implementation of consumer protection, the Consumer Protection Act also sets forth rules for administrative supervision[26] by delegating the government with

[17] Such as Regulations regarding Consumer Dispute Mediation (1993), Regulations regarding Consumer Ombudsman Appointment and Authorities (2018). Most of the regulations do not have an English translation.
[18] Consumer Protection Act, Art 1.
[19] ibid, Art 2.
[20] ibid, Arts 3–5.
[21] ibid, Arts 7–10-1.
[22] ibid, Arts 11–17-1.
[23] ibid, Arts 18–21.
[24] ibid, Arts 22–26.
[25] ibid, Arts 27–32.
[26] ibid, Arts 33–42.

investigative powers and powers to handle emergencies, set up a consumer ombudsman and consumer service centres.

To resolve consumer disputes effectively and rapidly, the Consumer Protection Act establishes consumer disputes resolution mechanisms[27] by adopting a bifurcated procedure, that is, complaint and mediation procedures for consumer disputes[28] and consumer tort actions.[29] Finally, the Act also stipulates the penalties, including punitive damages, to be imposed on business operators who violate the provisions[30] and delegates the competent authority that may, depending on the situation, impose administrative fines or order the suspension of the business.

B. Information Duties and Right to Withdraw

One of the most important breakthroughs of the Consumer Protection Act is it obliges business operators to provide consumers with the necessary information and confers on consumers a statutory right to withdraw from certain specific contracts, namely distance sales and door-to-door sales, within a statutory period (seven days).[31] Compared with other laws, the Consumer Protection Act was not the first law to introduce withdrawal rights for consumers; Article 88 of the Civil Code and other laws (such as the Insurance Law) also provide revocation rights, but the right to withdraw under the Consumer Protection Act is the most powerful, influential and commonly invoked right, especially as the original Act failed to allow any exception from such withdrawal rights. Moreover, the definitions of specific (or regulated) contracts were also problematic, particularly on whether and how such provisions are applicable to online transactions.

With so many disputes exposed, the 2015 Revision of the Consumer Protection Act, not surprisingly, focused on the information duties of the business operators, but at the same time, kept the consumers' withdrawal right intact. The major changes include: changing 'mail order purchase' and 'door-to-door purchase' to 'distance sales' and 'door-to-door sales', respectively; extending the distance sales' reach to cover Internet-related sales;[32] obliging business operators to provide buyers-consumers with more comprehensive information of the seller and terms of the transaction;[33] and providing an exception for the withdrawal right to balance the interests of the consumers and the business operators.

To resolve the original regulatory deficiencies, when drafting the 2015 revision, the drafters consulted the EU Consumer Rights Directive of 2011[34] and Japan's Specified Commercial Transactions Act heavily, particularly in drafting Articles 18, 19 and 19-2.

[27] ibid, Arts 43–55.
[28] ibid, Arts 43–46.
[29] ibid, Arts 47–55.
[30] ibid, Arts 56–62.
[31] ibid, Arts 18–21.
[32] Art 2(10) defines 'Distance sales' as the transaction is made via radios, television broadcasts, telephones, facsimiles, catalogs, newspapers, magazines, *the Internet*, flyers or any other similar channels, which consumer does not have opportunity to review the goods or services' (emphasis added).
[33] Legal consequences for violating this duty to inform (Arts 18, 22(2)) are also established.
[34] Directive 2011/83/EU of the European Parliament and of the Council of 25 October 2011 on consumer rights, OJ 2011 No L304, p 64.

For example, Article 18 of the 2015 Amendment draws closely on Articles 6–8 of the Consumer Rights Directive and Article 4 and Article 10 of Japan's Specific Commercial Transaction Act. Thus, the present Article 18 explicitly requires the business operators of distance sales or door-to-door sales to provide pertinent transaction information, in a clear and conspicuous written format, to consumers.[35] In distance sales made via the Internet, the business operator shall provide the consumer with recoverable and saveable information in electronic format.

The other major amendment is to redress the problem of how to deal with digital products, exposed by the litigation between the Taipei City Government and a well-known local e-commerce platform.[36] Hence, after consulting Article 10 of the Consumer Rights Directive, Article 19 added Paragraph (3) which states that

> [w]hen business operators failed to provide consumers with information on matters related to the consumer's right to rescind contracts upon receipt of goods or services, the seven day period shall not be counted until the date the information is provided. The right to rescind would be lost if the seven day period (as set forth in the first paragraph) has lapsed for four months.

A new Paragraph (4), inspired by Article 11 of the Consumer Rights Directive and Article 9(2) of Japan's Specific Commercial Transaction Act, explicitly states that the contract would be deemed rescinded when consumers have delivered or issued in writing within the period prescribed in the first Paragraph (seven days) and third Paragraph (extended seven days period, or four months). Following the consumer's notification of withdrawal to business operators in writing according to Article 19, the business operators must retrieve the goods within 15 days and make a refund within 15 days after receiving the goods.[37]

Article 19 of the Consumer Protection Act also follows Articles 16 and 19 of the Consumer Rights Directive, by providing a 'reasonable matters' exception to the distance sales rule of Article 18 and authorises the Executive Yuan to decree such reasonable

[35] The information to be provided includes the following:

(1) The name of the traders, representatives, firms or place of business, phone number or email and contact information in which consumers can get rapid and effective communication.
(2) The contents, prices, payment dates, payment methods, delivery dates and method of delivery.
(3) The period and procedure for consumers to exercise the right to rescind in accordance with Art 19.
(4) The right to rescind, prescribed in the first paragraph of Art 19, cannot be exercised upon the application of provisions prescribed in accordance with the second paragraph of Art 19.
(5) Consumer complaint handling the procedure.
(6) Any other matters proclaimed by the competent authorities.

[36] In 2011, the Taipei City Government ('TCG') accused the platform's return policy, ie, rejecting any unsealed or unpacked software, such as Windows CD ROM and other digital products, of violating Article 19 of the Consumer Protection Act and ordered the platform to revise its return policy or face stiff administrative fines. The platform brought a suit against TCG and the Supreme Administrative Court ruled in its favour in two separate decisions, 101 Nien Du Pan Tse Di 707 (9 August 2012) and 101 Nien Du Pan Tse Di 272 (22 March 2012). This case exposed the problems of the Consumer Protection Act in lacking proper provisions to regulate the sale of digital products and supply of services.

[37] Consumer Protection Act, Art 19-2. Moreover, after rescinding the contract, the restitution provision shall be null and void if it is more adverse to the consumers than the provision prescribed in Art 259 of the Civil Code.

exception matters.[38] The Executive Yuan finalised 'The Regulations on Reasonable Matters as Exceptions to Rescind the Distance Sales' in December 2015.[39] Contrary to the Consumer Rights Directive's 13 exceptions, Taiwan's version only permits the following seven exceptions for the distance and door-to-door sales:

- The supply of goods which are liable to deteriorate, with fairly short shelf life, or expire rapidly.
- The supply of goods or services made to the consumer's specifications or personalised.
- The supply of newspapers, periodicals or magazines.
- The supply of sealed audio, video recording or computer software which have been unsealed after delivery.
- The supply of digital content which is not supplied on a tangible medium, or online services which would be fully performed once begun, with the consumer's prior consent.
- The supply of sealed personal hygiene products which have been unsealed after delivery.
- The supply of international airline passenger services.

While providing the above exceptions, the Department of Consumer Protection, in a 2017 Interpretative Letter, effectively limited the application of such exceptions. In that Letter the Department of Consumer Protection underscored the importance of the business operators' information duties by stating that the provision of the necessary information to the consumers is the prerequisite requirement for the exceptions. If the business operators failed to provide such information as required by the Consumer Protection Act, even if the products or services fall into the above seven exceptions, the withdrawal right will remain, and the consumers can still exercise their rescission rights.[40]

C. Consumer Sales Contract

Under the civil law tradition, Taiwan does not have 'consumer sales contract' terminology, rather, the Consumer Protection Act uses 'consumer relationship' and 'consumer dispute' to determine whether the Consumer Protection Act or the Civil Code shall apply. Pursuant to the Consumer Protection Act, the 'consumer relationship' means the legal relationship arising between consumers and the business operators for the sale of goods or provision of services. 'Consumer dispute' refers to any dispute arising from the sale of goods or provision of services between consumers and traders. As long as there is

[38] Art 19(1) clearly states that '[c]onsumers of distance sales or door-to-door sales may return the goods or rescind the contract in writing within seven days upon receipt of goods or services without stating the reasons or be responsible for any expenses or costs, except in the case of distance sales with reasonable matters'. 'Reasonable matters prescribed in the previous paragraph shall be proclaimed by the Executive Yuan'. (Art 19(2)).

[39] This Regulation went into effect on 1 January 2016.

[40] Department of Consumer Protection, Yuan Tai Shao Bao Tse Di 1060168772, 8 March 2017.

a consumer relationship or a consumer dispute, no matter whether it is the sale of goods or the provision of services, as *lex specialis* the Consumer Protection Act overrides the Civil Code.

While the Consumer Protection Act deals with the special regulated sales, that is, distance sales, door-to-door sales and instalment sales, it does not cover contract formation, right to cure or reduction of price and many other basic contractual matters. The Civil Code still has a final say in resolving the basic contractual issues, such as warranties, and the right of rescission as stipulated in Articles 354–66.

Compared to the Civil Code's general sales of goods regulation, the application of the Consumer Protection Act is limited to 'consumer relationship' and also limited to the above-discussed special regulated sales. Obviously, the Consumer Protection Act offers consumers a unique privilege, both with respect to the business operators' information duties and the right to withdraw, under such special contracts that are otherwise unavailable for other contracts.

D. Product Liability

i. *Standard of Liability*

The Consumer Protection Act made a sharp departure from the traditional Civil Code's negligence-based liability principle. To protect consumers' interests, with respect to product liability, the Act embraced strict liability, which is applicable to both the sellers of goods and the providers of services, for the first time in Taiwan's legislative history. All business operators who engage in designing, producing or manufacturing goods or who provide services shall ensure that goods or services provided 'meet and comply with the contemporary technical and professional standards with reasonably expected safety requirements when placing the goods into the stream of commerce, or at the time of rendering services'.[41]

Moreover, the Consumer Protection Act further forces joint tortfeasors, distributors and marketers to be jointly and severally liable with the business operators.[42] To be exempt from such strict liability, the business operators have the burden of proving the goods or services provided complied with the contemporary technical and professional standards of reasonably expected safety requirements when placing the goods into the stream of commerce, or at the time of rendering services.[43] By adopting strict liability, the Consumer Protection Act attempts to eliminate the disadvantages created by the negligence-based liability principle under which consumers usually were unable to satisfy the burden of proving the business operator's gross negligence and causation.

Due to the strict liability principle, any business operator who engages in designing, producing or manufacturing of goods or in the provisions of services, has the

[41] Consumer Protection Act, Art 7(1).

[42] ibid, Arts 7(3) and 8. The only exception is those who bear the joint and several liabilities 'can prove that they have not been negligent'. Even if no negligence has proved, according to Art 8, the court may only reduce damages.

[43] ibid, Art 7-1.

responsibility to ensure that goods or services provided comply with the 'contemporary technical and professional standards'. Besides, all safety warnings and emergency response manuals shall also be marked or labelled conspicuously on any goods or services which may cause harm to the lives, bodies, health or properties of consumers.[44] Business operators who import goods or services must also be responsible for the goods or services imported.[45]

ii. Services

One significant issue arises from expanding the strict liability to services: whether providers of healthcare services are also subject to such strict liability. In fact, the first case appeared immediately after the enactment of the Consumer Protection Act in 1994. The plaintiff, Ms Tan, gave birth in the Mackay Memorial Hospital in December 1994. Unfortunately, the infant's right arm suffered irreparable injury due to dystocia of the shoulder. Ms Tan invoked strict liability under Article 7 of the Consumer Protection Act and asserted the service provider (Mackay Memorial Hospital and the physician) should be liable and demanded NTD 1,000,000 (USD 330,000) in damages. The Court ruled for the plaintiff, finding that the doctor did not pay attention to the important information given by the patient, and also failed to fulfil the obligation to explain the risk of shoulder dystocia.[46]

This decision immediately triggered a major debate in the medical profession and the judiciary in Taiwan on whether or not medical services shall be subject to strict liability under the Consumer Protection Act. After a decade of debate, the government finally revised the Medical Care Act in 2004 by adding a new Article 82(2), which states that medical personnel will be responsible only in the event of intentional or negligent conduct.

However, a 2017 Taiwan Supreme Court decision re-ignited the dispute by asking the healthcare service providers to prove the medical treatment provided can satisfy 'the contemporary technical and professional standards'. The Court, using the shifting of the burden of proof approach, effectively re-applies Article 7 to healthcare services, despite the 2004 revision of the Medical Care Act. In the case in question, the family of a deceased patient filed a lawsuit against two physicians and the hospital according to the strict liability rule under the Consumer Protection Act.[47] The Taipei District Court ruled for the plaintiff and ordered the hospital to pay damages of NTD 150,000 (USD

[44] ibid, Art 7(2).

[45] ibid, Art 9. In line with the strict liability principle, Art 10 of the Consumer Protection Act further stipulates that the business operator shall also be responsible for recycling, providing a warning sign and the emergency handling methods.

[46] The District Court decision was later upheld by the Taiwan High Court in 1998 (87 Nien Du Shang Tse Di 151).

[47] In this case, the patient fell and injured her head. After the patient was sent to the National Taiwan University Hospital for treatment, she was treated with regular wound treatment, but did not have a CT scan. Several hours later, the patient lost consciousness. After an emergency CT scan, the doctors found that the patient had suffered a skull fracture which caused an epidural haematoma and with an intracranial haemorrhage of 100 cc. After performing epidural haematoma evacuation, the patient remained in a coma and later died.

5,000). On appeal, the court reversed the decision and held there was no negligence. After careful deliberation, the Supreme Court reversed the High Court's decision and remanded the case for a retrial.[48] According to this Supreme Court ruling, particularly with the shift of the burden of proof remaining, it seems that healthcare services in Taiwan are still not out of the woods yet.

iii. Product Safety: Recall

The Consumer Protection Act also requires the business operators to immediately recall the goods or discontinue the services provided when there are sufficient facts to support that such goods or services may present potential dangers to the health and safety of the consumers, except where the business operators have adopted necessary measures sufficient to remove or prevent such harm or danger.[49] The Consumer Protection Act also forbids the business operators to exclude or restrict their liability as against consumers or third parties.[50]

E. Unfair Terms and Standard Contracts

To maintain the fairness and equality of transactions and to prevent the abuse of standard contracts by business operators,[51] the regulation of the standard contracts is another key revision from 2015. For example, although Article 11 of the Consumer Protection Act still requires the business operator to provide 'a reasonable period, not longer than thirty days', for consumers to review all contract clauses, before entering into a standard contract, it added a new Paragraph (2) which explicitly states that the terms and conditions adopted by business operators in standard contracts that provide for consumers to waive the right 'shall be invalid'. Moreover, to alleviate the consumers' burden of proof, in addition to providing consumers with copies of the standard contracts,[52] Article 13 further demands the business operators provide consumers with the original copies of standard contracts that have been signed or stamped by the consumers.

i. Effect

The powers of competent central government authorities to set mandatory or prohibitory provisions of standard contracts for certain industries are also unchanged, but

[48] Taiwan Supreme Court, 106 Nien Du Tai Shang Tse 227, 29 March 2017. The Court stated that, according to traditional negligence theory, the victim should prove the causal relationship between the negligence of the medical treatment and the death of the patient. However, the Court noted that when the causal relationship is difficult to clarify, and considering the fact that inequality exists between the medical profession and patients, the 'manifestly unfair' exception in the proviso of Art 277 of the Code of Civil Procedure shall apply and held that the burden of proof shall shift to the physician.

[49] Consumer Protection Act, Art 10.

[50] ibid, Art 10-1.

[51] ibid, Art 11 provides that the terms and conditions adopted in the standard contracts shall conform to the principles of equality and reciprocity.

[52] The only exception for such requirement is 'when it is obviously difficult to provide due to the nature of the contract'. The proviso of Consumer Protection Act, Art 13(2).

a new paragraph is added which states that where the contract is in violation of the mandatory or prohibitory provisions, it shall be null and void. Moreover, in order to clarify the validity of the standard contract used by the business operators, the 2015 revision specifically provides the basic terms of the mandatory or prohibitory provisions shall to be considered.[53]

In addition to the above mandatory invalidation rule under Article 17, Article 12 also stipulates that 'any standard terms and conditions in violation of the good faith requirements are unconscionable to consumers, shall be rendered null and void'. The Consumer Protection Act also expressly provides that, where the terms and conditions provided in standard contracts fall within the following three categories, such standard contracts are presumed unconscionable:[54]

- Where the terms and conditions of the contracts are in violation of the principle of equality and reciprocity.
- Where the terms and conditions of the contracts of the arbitrary rules are obviously contradictory to legislative intent.
- Where the purposes of the contracts cannot be achieved due to the major rights or obligations of the contracts being restricted by such terms and conditions.

ii. Interpretation and Inclusion

To strengthen the protection of the consumers, other provisions also treat consumers favourably. For example, if the provisions of the standard contract are ambiguous, the Consumer Protection Act stipulates that the provisions shall be interpreted in favour of consumers;[55] terms and conditions not specified in standard contracts and not foreseeable by the consumers under normal circumstances shall not constitute a part of the contract.[56] Article 13 further requires business operators to express the standard terms and conditions in full. Where it is difficult to meet with the requirements, the business operators shall use other conspicuous methods to put the terms and conditions on public notice, so they constitute a part of the contract upon the consumer's consent.[57]

iii. Mandatory or Prohibitory Provisions

To provide clear guidelines to the business operators as to what provisions shall and shall not be included in the standard contracts, Article 17 delegates the Executive Yuan to set forth 'Mandatory or Prohibitory Provisions of Standard Contracts' for

[53] ibid, Art 17(3).
[54] ibid, Art 12(2).
[55] ibid, Art 11.
[56] ibid, Art 14.
[57] In addition, the Consumer Protection Act further requires the business operators shall provide consumers copies of the standard contracts except for when it is difficult to provide due to the nature of the contract.

certain industries. Under the delegation of the Consumer Protection Act,[58] the Department of Consumer Protection and Consumer Protection Committee approved a total of 91 standard contracts[59] and 87 'Mandatory and Prohibitory Provisions' to deal with prejudicial and unfair terms.[60] Those standard contracts and the mandatory and prohibitory provisions not only safeguard consumer welfare but also provide the basic guidelines for both the consumers and business operators. They cover a wide range of consumer transactions, ranging from ISP services to travelling, from tutoring to wedding photography. In fact, they cover most consumer transactions.

Following the 2015 revision,[61] the Department of Consumer Protection further revised the 'Online Retail Transaction Mandatory and Prohibitory Provision' in April 2016[62] by deleting the original provisions that allowed revocation for reason,[63] and replaced it with a contract confirmation and performance mechanism in Section 5. Pursuant to this change, the business operator shall provide the confirmation mechanism for the type, quantity, price and other important matters of the merchandise before the consumer enters into the contract. Once the contract has been made, the business operator shall fulfil the contents of the advertisements.[64]

F. False and Misleading Advertisements, Unfair Commercial Practices

To enable consumers to obtain sufficient and correct information and to avoid exaggerated or false advertisements that would mislead consumers, in addition to the provision of information duties as illustrated in Article 18, the Consumer Protection Act further provides special provisions regarding consumer information. Such provisions are conspicuously different from the general provisions on advertising and guarantees

[58] Art 17 of the Consumer Protection authorises the central government's competent authority, ie, the Department of Consumer Protection and Consumer Protection Council, to 'set, mandatory or prohibitory provisions of standard contracts which required certain industries to apply after approved by the Executive Yuan and proclaimed by the competent authorities'. If the standard contract violates such mandatory or prohibitory provisions, the Consumer Protection Act specifically stipulates that such a contract 'shall be null and void' (Art 17(3)).

[59] Examples of standard contracts examples (only in Chinese) are available from www.ey.gov.tw/Page/37D1D3EDDE2438F8.

[60] All Mandatory and Prohibitory Provisions for standard contracts (only in Chinese) are available from www.ey.gov.tw/Page/2285E9A14973DE75.

[61] The 2015 amendment unequivocally prescribes the purpose, content, scope and legality of authorised public notices. To ensure consistent implementation of this stipulation, complementary measures on administrative penalties are also appended (Arts 17 and 56-1).

[62] The reason for such an amendment is that, according to the Civil Code, as long as the buyer and the seller have a meeting of the minds, the contract is formed and the business operator cannot terminate the contract at will.

[63] The original provision of 2011 permits the business operator to refuse the consumer's order, if with a valid and reasonable reason, within two working days after the parties entered into a contract (section 2). It also stipulated that only when a consumer who has paid the price will be deemed as enter into a contract (section 3). These two sections were both deleted in 2016.

[64] Such language is similar to Article 22(2) ('After the contract is made and entered between business operators and consumers, business operators shall fulfil the contents of the advertisements of goods or services').

in the Civil Code. For example, the legal nature of an advertisement is changed from 'invitation to offer' to 'offer'. Thus, when a consumer commits to the advertisement, a contract is validly entered based on the advertisement.[65] The Consumer Protection Act further stipulates that if the media that publishes the advertisement knew or had reasonable reason to know of its falsity, it shall also be responsible to the consumer.[66] Also, the Act further requires that all products shall have Chinese instructions and, if the product is accompanied by a warning label in the country of origin, the product must also have a Chinese warning label, and its content must be comparable with the original.[67] If the business operator guarantees the quality of the goods or services to consumers, it should provide a written guarantee that complies with the requirements of the Consumer Protection Act to ensure the correctness of the information obtained by the consumers.[68]

It is worth noting that with respect to false and misleading advertisements, business operators may be under the dual jurisdiction of the Consumer Protection Act and the Fair Trade Act. Contrary to the latter, the Consumer Protection Act only deals with false or misleading advertisements per se. On the contrary, in addition to false, untrue or misleading advertisement,[69] the Fair Trade Act also deals with pyramid sales (multi-level marketing),[70] and other deceptive or unfair conduct.[71]

The Taiwan Fair Trade Commission also publishes various regulations,[72] guidelines and standard contracts as the guidance for the business operators. Any violation of such regulations or guidelines will be subject to fines ranging from NTD 50,000 to 25 million (approximately USD 1750 to 895,000).[73]

Under such dual regimes, the Taiwan Fair Trade Commission takes a proactive role in dealing with false, untrue or misleading advertisements and pyramid sales. For example, from 2015 to 2018, the Commission decided 178 cases relating to false, untrue or misleading advertisements, 114 cases on improper multi-level pyramid sales cases and 42 other deceptive or unfair conduct cases.[74]

[65] It is because Art 22 specifically requires that the business operator shall ensure the authenticity of the advertising content, and 'its obligations to the consumer shall not be lower than the content of the advertisement'. Such strict requirements also sparked a variety of litigation regarding the mislabelling of prices in online transactions.

[66] Consumer Protection Act, Art 23.

[67] ibid, Art 24.

[68] ibid, Art 25.

[69] Art 21 of the Fair Trade Act provides that '[n]o enterprise shall make or use false or misleading representations or symbols on the matter that is relevant to goods and is sufficient to affect trading decisions on goods or in advertisements, or in any other way make it known to the public'.

[70] Multi-level marketing related laws and regulations can be found at Taiwan Fair Trade Commission's English version under the 'Laws & Regulations' section of www.ftc.gov.tw/internet/english.

[71] In addition, Art 25 of the Fair Trade Act has a catch-all provision that prohibits 'any deceptive or unfair conduct that can affect trading order'. Pursuant to this mandate, the Taiwan Fair Trade Commission publishes various guidelines, ranging from selling pre-sale houses to overseas resort member cards.

[72] Regarding false and misleading advertisements, the Taiwan Fair Trade Commission also promulgates many guidelines on topics ranging from endorsements and testimonials advertisement to real estate, weight loss and body care advertising. All relevant guidelines are available under the 'Laws & Regulations' section of www.ftc.gov.tw/internet/english.

[73] Fair Trade Act, Art 42.

[74] '2018 Statistical Yearbook of Fair Trade Commission'.

G. Administrative Liabilities

In addition to the aforementioned protective provisions, the Consumer Protection Act further adopts administrative measures to strengthen the implementation of consumer protection. For instance, in terms of measures to protect the health and safety of consumers, the Act authorises the competent authorities with more effective administrative supervision powers, such as the right to conduct an investigation.[75] If the authorities, after investigation, believe that the goods or services harm the consumers' lives, health or property, they have the right to order the business operators to redress the situation within a certain time frame, or to improve, recycle or destroy goods; where necessary, the authorities can also order the business operator to stop providing goods or services immediately, or take other necessary actions.[76] Such authorisation, plus the proactive action taken by local governments, has invoked some intense disputes between the Taipei City Government and commercial platform providers, such as Google[77] and PChome.

For any violation under the Consumer Protection Act, the competent authority can either impose administrative fines or suspend the business operation against the business operators. For instance, if the competent authority believes that consumer welfare is at risk because of the goods or services provided by the business operator, the competent authority may suspend the business operation and request consumer protection groups to bring a lawsuit to protect consumers.[78] Such suspension of business operations is probably more effective than administrative fines.

IV. The Financial Consumer Protection Act and Other Consumer Protection Related Laws and Regulations

In addition to the Consumer Protection Act, many laws and regulations in Taiwan are also relevant to consumer protection. To integrate such legislation, the Consumer Protection Act specifically prescribes in its Article 61 that other laws and regulations shall also be applied if they are more favourable or can better protect consumers.[79]

[75] Consumer Protection Act, Art 33.

[76] ibid, Art 36. If needed, the authorities can also publicise the name, address, goods, services, or other necessary information of the business operator through the mass media, or take other necessary actions (Art 37).

[77] The Taipei City Government found Google's returning policy, ie, consumers can only cancel the Apps purchased within 15 minutes after downloading, violated the seven day statutory period under Art 19 and right to withdraw. After Google refused to correct such violation following the City Government's order, the City Government fined Google NTD 1,000,000 (approximately USD 333,000). Google thereafter appealed to the Taipei High Administrative Court and the Court reversed the City Government's administrative decision. Taipei High Administrative Court, 101 Nien Du Su Tse Di 495, 6 December 2012.

[78] Consumer Protection Act, Art 60.

[79] According to Art 61 of the Consumer Protection Act, if the violation constitutes a criminal offence under other laws, the case shall immediately be forwarded to District Attorney for a criminal investigation.

Business operators are therefore not only under the jurisdiction of the Consumer Protection Act but are also subject to administrative or criminal punishment under other laws relevant to consumer protection.

Before the enactment of the Consumer Protection Act, many pre-existing statutes were already playing a pivotal role in protecting consumer interests, such as the Civil Code, the Criminal Code, the Pharmaceutical Affairs Act, the Cosmetic Hygiene and Safety Act, the Act Governing Food Safety and Sanitation, the Medical Care Act, the Commodity Labelling Act and the Fair Trade Act.

After the promulgation of the Consumer Protection Act, the Legislative Yuan continued to pass laws related to consumer welfare, such as the Multi-Level Marketing Supervision Act (2014), the Financial Consumer Protection Act (2011), the Consumer Debt Clearance Act (2007), the Health Food Control Act (1999) and the Computer-Processed Personal Data Protection Law (1995). The total of these laws, plus many other regulations declared by the competent authorities,[80] constitute the present comprehensive consumer protection legal framework in Taiwan.

Among all relevant laws with respect to consumers, one statute is particularly important: the Financial Consumer Protection Act.[81] Taiwan adopted specialised financial consumer protection legislation due to the consumer disputes caused by the financial crises between 2004 and 2008, especially the economic tsunami caused when Lehman Brothers filed for bankruptcy in September 2008, which caused the value of its credit-linked notes to plummet and consumer disputes to erupt. In the event of a financial dispute, as demonstrated by the credit card debts and linked debts, judicial relief usually comes too little, too late, and the cost incurred is also not in line with the economic benefits of going to court.

As a result, Taiwan passed the Financial Consumer Protection Act in 2011 to tackle these newly emerging issues. Contrary to the Consumer Protection Act that applies to all types of consumer-related transactions and services, the Financial Consumer Protection Act has exclusive jurisdiction over any dispute arises out of financial and investment transactions. By creating such a special dispute resolution system to tackle those often complex and unconventional consumer disputes, Taiwan is able to resolve those thorny issues more efficiently.

V. Consumer Dispute Resolution

A. Consumer Protection Act

When facing consumer disputes, both the Consumer Protection Act and Financial Consumer Protection Act deal with consumer dispute resolution directly. However,

[80] For example, there are seven regulations that deal with food safety, and four dealing with cosmetic products.

[81] The Financial Consumer Protection Act was promulgated by the Legislative Yuan (Congress) on 29 June 2011, and took effect on 30 December 2011.

they have independent resolution mechanisms and as a result the present consumer disputes resolution structure in Taiwan can be divided into: (1) general, non-financial consumer disputes under the jurisdiction of the Consumer Protection Council and Department of Consumer Protection in central government and various consumer protection authorities in every county or municipality, such as consumer ombudsman and consumer service centres; (2) financial related disputes under the jurisdiction of the Financial Ombudsman Institute and supervised by the Financial Services Commission.

The present general scheme adopts a 'two-track, three-level' consumer dispute resolution system. When any consumer dispute arises from the consumer transactions between consumers and business operators, or consumers suffer any damage or harm, consumers can choose between (1) filing a lawsuit with the court directly (the 'consumer litigation' under the Consumer Protection Act),[82] and (2) utilising the administrative remedy procedure provided by the local government.

If consumers elect to use the administrative remedy procedure, they can choose to file their complaint with the business operators or consumer protection groups (such as the Consumers' Foundation Chinese Taipei). Where a consumer chooses to file a complaint with the business operator, it shall resolve such consumer complaints within 15 days. If there has not been a proper response to the complaint, a further (second) complaint can be filed with the ombudsman or consumer service centres of the municipal or the county governments. If the consumer complaint is still not properly resolved, such complaint will go into mediation phase which can be made with the Consumer Dispute Mediation Commission of the municipal or the county governments. If all such remedies failed to reach a settlement, the aggrieved consumer can still file a civil lawsuit with a local court.

To ease the filing of a proper complaint, the Consumer Protection Council devised three different channels: (1) file an online complaint through the webpage[83] set up by the Consumer Protection Council; (2) go to one of the local government consumer service centres to fill out the complaint form; (3) download the Consumer Dispute Registration Form online, fill it out and fax or post it to the consumer service centres where the consumer resides. Consumers can call the national consumer service line ('1950') to receive consumer consultation services.

Pursuant to the most updated statistics compiled by the Consumer Protection Council,[84] all levels of government received a total of 58,962 consumer complaints in 2018, which represents an increase of 8.67 per cent compared with 54,255 complaints in 2017. Among all the complaints, the first level of complaints reached 46,471 cases, which accounts for 78.81 per cent of all the registered complaints in 2018 and an increase of 8.53 per cent or 3,641 cases compared with 2017. The second level complaints have 10,023 cases, representing an increase of 896 cases or a 9.81 per cent increase. About

[82] 'Consumer litigation' under the Consumer Protection Act means 'any legal action pursued to the court arose from consumer relationship'.

[83] The English version of the online complaint form is at https://appeal.cpc.ey.gov.tw/EN/step_three_2_en.aspx.

[84] The recent statistics compiled by the Consumer Protection Council were published on 18 March 2019 for the full year of 2018.

80 per cent of cases were resolved in the first level of dispute resolution mechanism. Among all the cases, only 2,468 cases went into mediation proceedings, which accounts for only 4.18 per cent of all the complaints during 2018. These numbers demonstrated that the present scheme of the consumer dispute resolution is working well for the purpose of resolving consumer disputes.

The aggrieved consumer can decide to file consumer litigation directly, or when the complaint-mediation procedure has failed to produce any resolution, the consumer can still file a consumer claim. Under the Consumer Protection Act regime, consumer litigation has a significant difference from the typical civil litigation. For example, in filing civil litigation, the consumer shall be the plaintiff. On the contrary, in addition to the aggrieved consumer, the Consumer Protection Act also delegates the consumer ombudsman and consumer protection group to file consumer litigation on behalf of the aggrieved consumers. In addition, the Consumer Protection Act also provides other assistance for filing consumer litigation, for instance, the plaintiff only needs to pay a reduced court fee, and the court can waive all court fees in filings for an injunction or allow the consumer protection groups to post no bond for preliminary injunction execution.[85] Moreover, in consumer litigation, the Consumer Protection Act permits the plaintiff to claim for punitive damages up to five times the amount of the damages.[86]

B. Financial Consumer Protection Act

Any dispute arising out of financial transactions is subject to the dispute resolution mechanism under the Financial Consumer Protection Act and shall be handled by the Financial Ombudsman Institute.[87] To carry out its authority in handling the financial dispute cases, the Financial Ombudsman Institute establishes an Ombudsman Committee.[88] Committee members are divided into three groups in line with their expertise; banking, insurance and securities and futures.[89]

The financial consumer dispute resolution procedure starts when a financial consumer files a complaint with the Financial Ombudsman Institute. The Financial Ombudsman Institute will first seek to institute mediation proceedings.[90] When the mediation procedure achieves a resolution, a mediation statement shall be prepared and sent to a court of law for approval. Once approved, such a mediation statement shall have the same force and legal effects as a final and irrevocable civil judgment and the parties to the dispute shall not again institute legal proceedings, nor file a

[85] Consumer Protection Act, Art 48.

[86] ibid, Art 51.

[87] The Financial Ombudsman Institute was formally inaugurated on 2 January 2012. To maintain independence, the whole funding for Financial Ombudsman Institute, NTD 1 billion (approximately USD 33 million), was from government budget and all services provided by the Ombudsman to financial consumers are free of charge.

[88] All board members' nominations need to be submitted to and approved by the FSC.

[89] According to Art 17 of the Financial Consumer Protection Act, the Ombudsman Committee shall consist of 9–25 members. Currently, it has 19 Committee members, one of whom is the Committee Chair.

[90] ibid, Art 23.

complaint or apply to institute an ombudsman case under the Financial Consumer Protection Act.[91]

However, if any party to the financial dispute does not agree to participate in mediation proceedings, or if mediation proceedings fail to achieve a resolution, then the consumer must apply to institute an ombudsman case within 60 days of the date on which the mediation failed. Once the aggrieved financial consumer files a complaint with the Financial Ombudsman Institute, and the complaint satisfies all requirements under Article 24 of the Financial Consumer Protection Act, the ombudsman case will commence.

After the Financial Ombudsman Institute institutes an ombudsman case, the chairperson of the ombudsman committee shall appoint at least three committee members as pre-examiners to inspect the case and prepare an inspection opinion. The procedure for an ombudsman case can proceed without holding a hearing. However, in special cases or as the committee deems necessary, it can also be conducted with oral argument. In such a case, the parties to the dispute shall be allowed to state their causes and opinions before the committee.[92]

Pre-examiners shall submit an inspection opinion to the ombudsman committee. The ombudsman committee can adopt the inspection opinion as an ombudsman decision by a simple majority vote. The Financial Ombudsman Institute then prepares the decision, in the name of the Institute, as an ombudsman statement that is served upon the parties. The parties shall notify the Institute in writing, before the time limit prescribed in the ombudsman statement, whether they accept or reject the decision. Once both parties accept it, the ombudsman case is resolved.

A financial consumer may, within 90 days from the Institute adopting the ombudsman statement, apply for the Institute to send the ombudsman statement to a court for approval.[93] Except for certain special cases, the court, after approving the statement, shall have the approved ombudsman statement served upon the parties to the dispute and their counsel. A court-approved ombudsman statement has the same force as a final and irrevocable civil judgment, and the parties to the dispute shall not again institute legal proceedings, nor shall they file a complaint or application to institute an ombudsman case under the Financial Consumer Protection Act.[94]

VI. Conclusion

For the two decades following the enactment of the Consumer Protection Act, Taiwan has been diligently perfecting the consumer protection regime by proactively adopting

[91] According to Art 23(5) of the Financial Consumer Protection Act, the provisions of Art 28 and Art 30, which deal with the preparation, service, approval and validity of the ombudsman statement, shall apply mutatis mutandis to the mediation statement.

[92] ibid, Art 26.

[93] According to Art 29, the Financial Ombudsman Institute shall forward the ombudsman statement and the associated case files, within five days, for approval by the district court with jurisdiction in the locality where the offices of the ombudsman body are located.

[94] Where there are legal grounds to consider a court-approved ombudsman statement invalid or voidable, a party to the dispute may file suit in the district court of jurisdiction to request that the ombudsman case be declared invalid or void.

various measures. For example, amending the Consumer Protection Act, strengthening consumer protection through existing or new legislation, promoting the competent central government authority to the level of Executive Yuan, adopting new consumer protection related policies, proclaiming regulations and making necessary administrative interpretations. Even with such efforts, the above discussion clearly shows that such endeavours are not enough to resolve all the problems or disputes, especially in the online environment, where advertising, online shopping or providing services all pose new challenges or raise new disputes along with the fast-growing business activities and new business models.

If we take a comprehensive approach and evaluate consumer-related legislation in Taiwan, there is no doubt that the Consumer Protection Act is the most important statute for perfecting consumer protection in Taiwan. With the enactment of the Consumer Protection Act, the competent authorities in the central government and local governments finally have a legal basis to take active approaches to protect consumer welfare and interests, for example by promulgating 91 standard contracts and 87 mandatory and prohibitory provisions for different industries. Even though in some cases, local governments moved too quickly or were too assertive, such as the Taipei City Government, all actions taken by different governments have significantly improved the overall conditions concerning consumer protection.

Moreover, enacting the Financial Consumer Protection Act to focus on finance-related consumer disputes and setting up Financial Ombudsman Institute to handle financial consumer disputes also demonstrates a special approach in protecting consumers.

Looking ahead, fast-moving technologies, such as 5G, Artificial Intelligence, Blockchain, Internet of Things and ubiquitous mobile applications, will bring further challenges to consumer protection. Although Taiwan's present consumer protection framework, including the bifurcated consumer dispute resolution mechanism between the Consumer Protection Act and Financial Consumer Protection Act, is capable of handling most of the consumer-related matters, it still needs further refinement.

To use baseball terminology, Taiwan's consumer protection efforts for the past two decades is just reaching the second base, it still has a long way to go to reach home plate. In addition to proactive action from all levels of governments and consumer protection groups, consumer awareness also needs further strengthening. Only with the cooperation from both the consumers and the government can the legislative goals of the Consumer Protection Act of protecting consumer interests, facilitating safety and improving the quality of life of the consumers finally be achieved.

13

Thailand

AIMPAGA TECHAAPIKUN

I. Overview

The Kingdom of Thailand has approximately 66.19 million inhabitants.[1] With a GDP of approximately USD 326 billion in 2020, it is one of the largest economies in Southeast Asia.[2]

Thailand previously used customary laws and local statutes. However, due to the issue of extra-territorial and foreign pressure in the nineteenth century,[3] Thailand has undergone a judicial and legal reform. Consequently, current Thai law is influenced by civil law jurisdictions such as Germany, France, Belgium, Switzerland and Japan and common law countries such as the United Kingdom and the United States. The civil law influence over Thai law can be seen in its four principal codes: the Penal Code, the Civil and Commercial Code, the Criminal Procedure Code and the Civil Procedure Code. At the same time, common law has essential roles to play. For instance, Thai criminal procedure adopts in general the accusatorial, as opposed to inquisitorial, model of trial. In addition, even though previous rulings given by the Supreme Court are not regarded as strictly binding on lower courts, they are immensely influential and considered as precedent that later decisions should follow.

The judicial system of Thailand consists of the four courts which serve different responsibilities: the Constitutional Court, the Courts of Justice, the Administrative Court and the Military Court. The Constitutional Court renders judgments or decisions on the constitutionality of the provisions of law and other powers as provided for in the Constitution and other laws.[4] The Administrative Court decides the administrative disputes between a state organisation exercising admirative power and another party which can be a private party or another state organisation, the private sector and state organs. The Military Court adjudicates cases involving military personnel within its jurisdiction as prescribed by the Act for the Organisation of the Military Court.[5] The Courts of Justice have the power to adjudicate all cases except those specified by

[1] Bank of Thailand, 'Thailand's Macro Economic Indicator' accessible online under www.bot.or.th.
[2] ibid.
[3] RH Hickling, 'The Legal System of Thailand' (1972) 2 *Hong Kong Law Journal* 8.
[4] Constitution of The Kingdom of Thailand, Chapter X Part II.
[5] BE 2498 (1955).

law to be within the jurisdiction of other courts. The Court of Justice are, in principle, divided into three levels; the courts of first instance, the appellate courts and the Supreme Court.[6]

Consumer rights have been enshrined in and are thus protected by the Constitution.[7] Moreover, the right to form an independent organisation for safeguarding the rights of consumers has been specified in the same provision. The existence of consumer rights in the Constitution reflects that Thailand has considered the issue of consumer protection and policy as one of the pivotal keys to develop the country. As consumer protection is entangled with many matters, at the national level, several ministries which are involved. Whereas the Prime Minister's Office is tasked with the duty to make consumer protection policy in general,[8] the Ministry of Public Health is responsible for foods,[9] drugs,[10] cosmetics[11] and all products related to health and medical services,[12] and the Ministry of Commerce is in charge of competition,[13] price control[14] and weights and the measures of goods.[15]

With regard to the laws relating to consumers, the concept of the need for consumer safeguards has existed in the Thai legal system for nearly a decade.[16] Presently, there are three categories of protection laws. The first is the general law not designed specifically to protect consumer rights, such as the Civil and Commercial Code and the Penal Code. Although these laws were not created for the purpose of tackling consumer protection issues, these laws can, to some extent, prevent the infringement of consumer rights. For instance, a seller who lies about the quality or origin of their product can be charged with fraud in violation of section 341 of the Penal Code.

Secondly, there are laws specifically enacted to promote the consumers' economic interests as suggested by the UN Guidelines for Consumer Protection.[17] The Consumer Protection Act[18] is the first piece of Thai legislation explicitly providing consumer protection measures. This legislation has its roots in the demand originally promoted by the National Council of Women of Thailand for legal measures to protect the economic interests of consumers.[19] Since then, the government has always considered consumer protection to be an essential matter. Several pieces of legislation have been promulgated to promote the rights of consumers, including in the areas of unfair contract terms,[20] product liability,[21] as well as direct sales and direct marketing.[22]

[6] Constitution of The Kingdom of Thailand, Chapter X Part I.
[7] ibid, s 46.
[8] Consumer Protection Act BE 2522 (1979), s 8.
[9] Food Act BE 2522 (1979), s 5.
[10] Drug Act BE 2510 (1967), s 5.
[11] Cosmetic Act BE 2558 (2015), s 5.
[12] Medical Products Act BE 2551 (2008), s 5.
[13] Competition Act BE 2560 (2017), s 6.
[14] Price of Goods and Services Act BE 2542 (1999), s 6.
[15] Weights and Measures Act BE 2542 (1999), s 6.
[16] S Supanit, *Explanation of Development of Thailand Consumer Protection Law* (Bangkok: Chulalongkorn University Press 2011) 5–10 (in Thai).
[17] Available online under https://undocs.org/en/A/RES/39/248.
[18] BE 2522 (1979).
[19] Supanit, 'Explanation of Development', 5.
[20] Unfair Contract Terms Act BE 2540 (1997).
[21] Product Liability Act BE 2551 (2008).
[22] Direct Sales and Direct Marketing Act BE 2545 (2002).

Lastly, the laws belonging to the third category are those related to particular goods or services. The nature of businesses connected to these goods or services are complex and therefore need to be controlled by specific legislation. These goods and services are, for example, telecommunication services,[23] banking and finance[24] and insurance services.[25] The official bodies established by these kinds of laws are empowered and assigned not only to promote and protect consumer rights but also other administrative matters concerning the relevant businesses. Although consumer protection remains important for such bodies, it may not necessarily be their highest priority.

II. The Structure of Consumer Protection Law in Thailand

Among several statutes concerning consumer protection, the Consumer Protection Act is considered the foundation of consumer protection policy, as it addresses the five basic rights of consumers recognised in the UN Guidelines for Consumer Protection 1999:

(1) The right to receive correct and sufficient information and descriptions as to the quality of goods or services;
(2) The right to enjoy freedom in the choice of goods or service;
(3) The right to expect safety in the use of goods or services;
(4) The right to receive a fair contract; and
(5) The right to have an injury considered and compensated.

The Consumer Protection Act provides protection in four main fields: advertisements, labels, contracts and product safety. These main matters are primarily supervised by special committees commissioned under the Act, save for being provided otherwise in other laws.[26] In cases where specific legislation directly governs such matters (such as food[27] or drugs),[28] the Consumer Protection Act applies only insofar it is not a repetition or contrary to those special laws.[29]

To achieve the objectives mentioned above, the Consumer Protection Act also established the following governmental organisations: the Consumer Protection Board (CPB)[30] and the Ad Hoc Committees consisting of the Committee on Advertisements, the Committee on Labels, the Committee on Contracts and the Committee on Products and Services Safety.[31] Violation of the rules or the orders of the Consumer Protection Board and the Ad Hoc Committees may lead to criminal and administrative sanctions.[32]

[23] Telecommunications Business Act BE 2544 (2001).
[24] Financial Institutions Businesses Act BE 2551 (2008).
[25] Life Insurance Act BE 2535 (1992) (Amended by Life Insurance Act (No 2) BE 2551 (2008) and (No 3) BE 2558 (2015)) and Non-Life Insurance Act BE 2535 (Amended by Life Insurance Act (No 2) BE 2551 (2008) and (No 3) BE 2558 (2015)).
[26] Consumer Protection Act, s 14.
[27] Food Act BE 2510 (1967).
[28] Drug Act BE 2522 (1979).
[29] Consumer Protection Act, s 21.
[30] ibid, s 10.
[31] ibid, ss 14, 21.
[32] ibid, ss 45–62.

Even though the law imposes both imprisonment and fines as possible punishments, in practice, a businessman breaking the rules, notifications or orders will be fined rather than imprisoned. Although criminal and administrative penalties are in place, the Consumer Protection Act does not contain a provision relating to civil remedies. This means that a consumer whose rights have been violated has to seek redress and compensation, if available, from another law indirectly regulating the issue, such as the Civil and Commercial Code, the Consumer Cases Procedure Act,[33] the Product Liability Act, or even the Direct Sales and Direct Marketing Act.[34]

Moreover, the Consumer Protection Act also founded a body to administer day-to-day consumer protection affairs: the Office of the Consumer Protection Board. It has the powers, and duties, inter alia, to oversee and receive complaints from consumers and to encourage or conduct research on problems concerning consumer protection issues.[35] This body, being under the supervision of the Secretariat of the Prime Minister, has an essential role in coping with infringements of consumer rights.[36]

In addition to the Consumer Protection Act, other legislation also tackles consumer problems. For example, the Unfair Contract Terms Act[37] provides Thai courts with guidelines to judge the unfairness of contracts or juristic acts. Under this statute, the courts are equipped with the power to decide that a contract or an agreement which is unfair can be enforced only to the extent that is appropriate and fair. Similarly, the Direct Sales and Direct Marketing Act was passed exclusively to address direct sales and direct marketing transactions. The latter law establishes the Direct Sales and Direct Marketing Commission. This Commission controls the application of this law in the same way as the Consumer Protection Board (CPB) under the Consumer Protection Act. The Product Liability Act provides the regulations imposing liability for dangerous products on manufacturers, sellers, importers and other related parties in the distribution chain. The Consumer Case Procedure Act is primarily a procedural law which aims to simplify the exercise of consumer claims. This Act changes some rules of the Civil Procedure Code which are considered as an enormous obstacle for accessing to the right to have the harm examined and compensated through the legal system.

The Personal Data Protection Act[38] and the Establishment of Consumer Council Act[39] are two recent pieces of legislation. The Personal Data Protection Act, following the EU General Data Protection Regulation,[40] was passed to increase the protection of privacy. Although a significant proportion of this law has not yet been enforced, it has nonetheless affected some practices of business sectors, pushing businesses to treat consumers' privacy with greater care. The Establishment of the Consumer Council Act

[33] BE 2551 (2008).

[34] S Supphanit, *Consumer Protection Law* (Bangkok: Chulalongkorn University Press, 2014) vol IX, 8 (in Thai).

[35] Consumer Protection Act, ss 19–20.

[36] N Navathakulphisut, *Consumer Protection Law* (Bangkok: Faculty of Law Thammasat University, 2019) vol I, 37 (in Thai).

[37] BE 2540 (1997).

[38] BE 2562 (2019).

[39] BE 2562 (2019).

[40] Regulation (EU) 2016/679 of the European Parliament and of the Council of 27 April 2016 on the protection of natural persons with regard to the processing of personal data and on the free movement of such data, and repealing Directive 95/46/EC, OJ 2016 No L119, p 1.

provides the framework for setting up the Consumer Council and details the rules of its scope, power, resources and management. At the time of writing, the Council has not yet been sucessfully formed, which is a challenge to the success of consumer protection regime in Thailand. Apart from all legislation mentioned, a Bill on defective goods is in the pipeline to be scrutinised by Parliament.

In general, each law is promulgated to serve different matters so the consumers can apply the rule which responds to their needs. The Consumer Protection Board takes on the essential role as the centre for receiving consumer complaints, advising consumers whose rights have been violated, and appointing the officer who has power to order, sanction and conduct mediation.

III. Information Duties and Right of Withdrawal

A. Information Duties

The right to be informed is well established in Thailand as it is enshrined in the Consumer Protection Act.[41] If the consumer is not properly informed, such contract cannot be considered to be fair. The rule of contract law and obligations under the Thai Civil and Commercial Code will be applied in this case, according to which the consumer can ask for nullity of the contract because of fraud, misrepresentation or mistake.[42]

Besides the Thai Civil and Commercial Code, the Consumer Protection Act sets the rules for controlling information in the form of advertisements, labels and standard contracts. For example, advertisements may not contain any statement which is unfair to the consumer such as where the statement is false, exaggerated or will cause misunderstanding in the essential elements of such product or harm the society as a whole.[43]

In addition to the control of advertisements, the Consumer Protection Act prescribes that all goods manufactured for sale under the law on factories and goods imported into Thailand for sale must have a label complying with all requirements specified by this law.[44] This method compels almost all businesses to declare essential information to consumers to allow for an informed choice.[45] The label of the controlled goods shall contain truthful statements and have no other statements which may induce misunderstanding regarding the material facts about such goods. Moreover, it must contain some basic information required by law, such as the name or trademark of the manufacturer or the importer, the place of manufacturing or the place of operation of the import business, price, quantity, usage, recommendation, warnings and expiry date. Violation of this law leads to criminal sanction such as a fine or imprisonment.[46] The Committee

[41] Consumer Protection Act, s 4.
[42] Thai Civil and Commercial Code, ss 156–57 and ss 159–60.
[43] Consumer Protection Act, s 22.
[44] ibid, s 30.
[45] Navathakulphisut, 'Consumer Protection Law', 60.
[46] Consumer Protection Act 1979, ss 45–62.

on Labels has announced a considerable number of notifications concerning labels of products such as gas water heaters,[47] cases for mobile phones or tablets which contain a chemical liquid,[48] motorcycles,[49] bathtubs for children,[50] etc. The labels of these products and services are not governed by any other laws.

The control of contracts by the Committee on Contract is another measure connected with pre-contractual information. This body has the power to set the standard conditions or model clauses which must be included in the contract in form of the notifications as the same model for advertisements and labels. This measure guarantees the consumers the right to be informed as well as the right to access to a fair contract. Businessmen who violate or fail to comply with these duties included in the Consumer Protection Act may be subject to a fine or imprisonment.[51]

B. Right of Withdrawal

In general, Thai law does not provides consumers with the right to withdraw from a contract without giving any reason, except in the case of direct sales and direct marketing. The lack of a proper opportunity to inspect goods or the various techniques of direct sales may place pressure on consumers to purchase without a carefully and comprehensively considered decision.[52] For this reason, the Direct Sales and Direct Marketing Act grants the consumer the right to terminate a contract. Consumers who buy goods online or by post from registered merchants can therefore exercise this right without giving any reason.[53] However, this right is available only for a period of seven days starting from the receipt of the goods. The consumer shall return the purchased goods to the seller, and the latter is obliged to refund the consumer with the full amount of money paid to him.[54] The refunding process of the full amount must be completed within 15 days, save for the case that the goods are damaged or lost when they are the consumer's responsibility.[55] Where the consumer is responsible for the damage or the loss of goods, the consumer is still entitled to withdraw from the contract and may claim for the refund, but has to pay for or be partially responsible for the damage or loss caused.[56] For disposable goods, the consumer has to return the remaining part before they exercise the right to terminate the contract.[57] Furthermore, this Act stipulates that the terms and conditions of returning the goods and services must comply with the Ministerial Regulations,[58] which so far have not yet been imposed.

[47] BE 2562 (2019).
[48] BE 2561 (2018).
[49] BE 2560 (2017).
[50] BE 2556 (2013).
[51] Consumer Protection Act, ss 45–62.
[52] Thirawat, 'Consumer Contract', 169–70.
[53] Direct Sales and Direct Marketing Act, s 27.
[54] ibid, s 33.
[55] ibid, s 36.
[56] ibid, s 35.
[57] ibid, s 34.
[58] ibid, s 34.

IV. Unfair Contract Terms

A. Scope

As mentioned above, both the Consumer Protection Act and the Unfair Contract Terms Act cope with the problem of unfair contract terms by adopting different approaches. The Consumer Protection Act entitles the Committee on Contract to consider some businesses to be a controlled contract business. A control mechanism will be needed only when such contracts are required by law or custom to be made in writing.[59] In short, only written contracts could fall into the scope of the law. In marked contrast, it seems that the Unfair Contract Terms Act is applicable in every case of unfair contract terms. All forms of contracts between consumers and businessmen are governed by this piece of legislation, regardless of whether they are in writing or not. Furthermore, as the legislation applies to all standard form contracts, its scope of application is not limited to consumer contracts but also applies to commercial contracts, that is, between businesses.[60]

B. Consequences

Turning back briefly to the Consumer Protection Act, the Committee on Contract can prescribe terms, conditions and forms of contracts of a controlled business. If a contract in question has a prohibited term, it shall be deemed that such term does not exist. At the same time, some terms or conditions are required.[61] In such case, a contract which is concluded without such required terms or conditions, or is done in a non-conforming fashion, then, with the prescription of the Committee, that contract shall be deemed as automatically having the stipulated terms or being done under the stipulated conditions, as the case may be.[62]

There are several contracts which have been controlled by the Committee of Contract since consumers in these contracts normally need assistance for unfair terms. These contracts include agreements on apartment rental,[63] used car purchase,[64] vehicle and motorcycle hire purchase,[65] construction,[66] fitness club membership[67] and consumer credit, etc.[68]

On the part of the Unfair Contract Terms Act, the courts are granted powers to consider which contract or juristic act is too unfair. If the courts decide that is the case,

[59] ibid, s 35 bis.
[60] Unfair Contract Terms Act, s 4.
[61] Consumer Protection Act, s 35 quarter.
[62] ibid, s 35 ter.
[63] Notification of the Committee on Contract concerning the Apartment Room for Rent BE 2562 (2019).
[64] Notification of the Committee on Contract concerning the Sale of Used Cars BE 2562 (2019).
[65] Notification of the Committee on Contract concerning the Hire Purchase on a Vehicle or a Motorcycle BE 2561 (2018).
[66] Notification of the Committee on Contract concerning the Residential Construction Agreement BE 2559 (2016).
[67] Notification of the Committee on Contract concerning the Fitness Club Membership BE 2554 (2011).
[68] Notification of the Committee on Contract concerning Consumer Credit BE 2544 (2001).

they can order such unfair contract to be effective and enforceable only to the extent that the contract is deemed appropriate and fair.[69] The decision shall be made on a case-by-case basis, depending upon the facts of the case and the Court's discretion. This measure is very exceptional for a civil law system such as Thailand which normally prioritises the free will of parties, and thus the courts would respect the contract and not intervene.

Being different from the mechanism provided under the Consumer Protection Act, the economic interests of the consumer vis-à-vis the contract will be protected on a case-by-case basis. Engagement in a lawsuit is a necessary condition for determining the fairness or unfairness of a contract. Thus, this approach can be defined as the measure of redress which is different from the preventive measure applied by the Commission on Contracts under the Consumer Protection Act. In practice, the judges usually interpret the unfairness of the contract by following the regulations of the Commission under the Consumer Protection Act. This situation means that if such contract follows the regulation of contracts under the Consumer Protection Act, such contract is deemed not to be an unfair contract.[70]

C. Assessment

The principle of good faith is a criterion for the courts to determine the fairness and enforceability of contracts.[71] Other criteria stipulated include the parties' bargaining power, economic status, knowledge and understanding, adeptness, anticipation, guidelines previously observed, other alternatives and all advantages and disadvantages of the contracting parties. The benefits and drawbacks of the parties will be determined according to the actual conditions and ordinary usages applicable to such a kind of contract, the time and place of making the contract or performance of the contract and the much heavier burden borne by one contracting party when compared to that of the other party.[72]

D. Unfair Contract Criteria

i. List

To implement the law effectively, a non-exhaustive list is provided as a guideline for the courts to determine the fairness of a contract.[73] For instance:

- In the case of doubt, it shall be interpreted as a standard-form contract in favour of the party that does not prescribe the said contract.[74]

[69] Unfair Contract Terms Act, s 4(1).
[70] Thai Supreme Court Decision No 14578/2557.
[71] Thirawat, 'Consumer Contract', 126.
[72] Consumer Protection Act, s 10.
[73] Unfair Contract Terms Act, s 4(3).
[74] ibid, s 4(2).

- The terms excluding or restricting liability arising from a breach of contract shall be considered as the terms rendering an advantage over the other party.
- The terms rendering the other party to be liable or to bear more burden than that prescribed by law shall be considered as terms that render an advantage over the other party.
- The terms granting the right not to comply with any clause of the contract or to comply with the contract within a delayed period without a reasonable ground shall be considered as the terms rendering an advantage over the other party.
- The term in a contract of sale with a right of redemption whereby the buyer fixes the redeemed price higher than the selling price plus a rate of interest exceeding 15 per cent per year shall be considered as the term that renders an advantage over the other party.
- The term in a hire-purchase contract which prescribes an excessive hire-purchasing price or which imposes unreasonable burdens on the part of the hire-purchaser.[75]

Apart from the non-exhaustive list above, the Unfair Contract Terms Act also provides some provisions establishing rules on certain conditions and terms of contracts, including:

- In a contract which prescribes that something is given as a deposit, if there occurs a case that the to-be-forfeited deposit is disproportionately high, the Court may order that the forfeiture must be reduced to the actual damage which occurred.[76]
- Terms, announcement or notices made in advance to exclude or restrict liability for a tort or a breach of contract respecting loss of life, body or health of another person as a result of an action deliberately or negligently committed by the person making the terms or an announcement or notice by another person for which the person making the terms, announcement or notice shall also be liable, shall not be raised as an exclusion or restriction of the liability.[77]
- The agreement or consent of the injured party to an action explicitly prohibited by law or which is contrary to public order or good morals shall not be raised as a defence to exclude or restrict the tortious liability.[78]

ii. Examples

The Supreme Court has held the following terms to be unfair:

- A term requiring the buyer to pay the full price of the apartment as specified by the contract even if the size of the room is bigger or smaller than the actual size of the room.[79]

[75] ibid, s 4(3).
[76] ibid, s 7.
[77] ibid, s 8.
[78] ibid, s 10.
[79] Thai Supreme Court Decision No 4566/2561.

- A term requiring the hire purchaser to pay the same amount of compensation in case that there is a breach of contract without distinguishing the culpability of the purchaser or the types of contract breach.[80]
- A term requiring the credit card holder to pay the entire amount spent in the case that the card is used by a third person without the consent of the cardholder after the card is lost or destroyed.[81]

V. Sale of Goods

A. Non-conformity

At present, there is no specific statute prescribing the rule of non-conformity for consumer goods. The provisions of obligation and sales contracts under the Civil and Commercial Code are generally applied in this case. The application of these conventional and general rules has not been changed since the introduction of the Civil and Commercial Code in 1924. The Code is influenced by several European national laws with a mixture of English law.[82] Under the law on sales contracts, the seller is liable under an implied guarantee for any defect in the goods sold which impairs either its value or its fitness for ordinary purposes, or for the purposes of the contract. The liability is applicable even if the seller did not know of the existence of such defect.[83] To claim compensation or remedies, the buyer is to prove that the defect existed before the conclusion of the contract or at least at the moment of delivery.[84] This condition usually challenges access to a remedy of the buyer and may create an obstacle to sue the seller.[85]

A buyer can only sue the seller. They cannot sue other persons who are not parties to the contract. In the same vein, another person who is not the purchaser (despite being the user of such goods) has no right to claim for compensation on the grounds of defect.[86]

To seek compensation, a buyer has to prove that the defect existed before the sale or at least at the delivery of the goods. The buyer must institute a proceeding within one year after the discovery of the defect.[87] The seller's obligation can be excluded where the buyer knew of the defect at the time of sale, or would have known of it had they exercised such care as might be expected from a person of ordinary prudence;

[80] Thai Supreme Court Decision No 4340/2559.
[81] Thai Supreme Court Decision No 1989/2552.
[82] K Prokati, *The Responsibility of the Seller for Defective Goods under Sale Contract* (Bangkok: Thammasat University Publisher, 1989) 15 (in Thai).
[83] Thai Civil and Commercial Code, s 472.
[84] P Ekchariyakorn, *Law on Sale, Exchange and Gift* (Bangkok: Winyuchon Press, 2018) 125 (in Thai).
[85] Thai Supreme Court Decision No 1223/2545.
[86] Thai Supreme Court Decision No 17095/2555.
[87] Thai Civil and Commercial Code, s 474.

where the defect was apparent at the time of the delivery, and the buyer accepted the property without reservation; and where the property was sold at a public auction.[88]

B. Limitations or Exclusions of Liability

The Unfair Contract Terms Act prescribes that terms excluding or restricting the liability of the business operator for a defect in a consumer contract are void, except for the case where the consumer knows of the defect at the time of making the contract. In this case, the terms excluding or restricting the liability shall only be enforceable to the extent that they are fair and reasonable according to such circumstances.[89] According to the Thai Supreme Court, the contract term excluding the liability from defective car after delivery was not effective as it exploited the right of the consumer.[90] The Court also specified that the finance company could not deny liability since it is the party to the car leasing agreeement even if the consumer is not the owner of such defective car.

C. Remedies for Non-conformity

In cases of non-conformity, the buyer can refuse to pay or ask for remedies provided by the Civil and Commercial Code, such as damages[91] or the termination of the contract.[92] Moreover, the Consumer Case Procedure Act also recognises the right to repair and the right to replace consumer goods. Even if Thai consumer protection laws provides for the right to replace, this right is used with limited conditions such as where the defect cannot be reparable in normal working condition or the repair may cause danger to life, body or the health of the consumer using such good.

Moreover, when granting the right to replace instead of the right to repair, the Court must consider all relevant factors such as the nature of the goods, the behaviour of the business operator, as well as the honesty of the consumer. In the case that the consumer has benefited from such goods or caused damage to the goods, the consumer has to be responsible for the use or damages as it is deemed appropriate.[93]

Additionally, the Consumer Case Procedure Act also stipulates that the Court has the power to order the producer or the importer into a case and to adjudicate such person to be jointly liable for the defect.

D. Implied Warranty

Apart from the rule of implied warranty on defective goods, under the Thai Civil and Commercial Code, a seller is bound to deliver goods corresponding to their

[88] ibid, s 473.
[89] Unfair Contract Terms Act, s 6.
[90] Thai Supreme Court Decision No 2767/2560.
[91] Thai Civil and Commercial Code, s 222.
[92] ibid, ss 387–89; the Thai Supreme Court Decision No 2767/2560.
[93] Consumer Case Procedure Act BE 2551 (2008), s 41.

description.[94] This liability is applied in the cases where such transaction is determined to be a sale by description, which is not clearly defined by the law. A sale by description is the sale in which a buyer decides to buy goods because of the description made/given by the seller. If the buyer can prove that the purchase decision was based on believing the seller's description and it appears that the goods delivered do not comply with such description, the buyer can bring a claim against the seller but must do so within one year from the date of delivery.[95] It should be noted that this period of prescription is different from the case of defective goods which may be longer because time only starts counting for that prescription from the time of the discovery of the defect.[96] As the law of sale by description does not mention distinctively the remedies available to consumers, the general rules of obligation and contract law are still applied – a buyer can claim for damages, a rescission of contract or a new performance of the obligation to deliver the goods corresponding to the description.[97]

E. Non-delivery

In the case of non-delivery of goods sold in a time-specific contract, the buyer has a right to terminate the contract and/or claim for damages arising or has the right to request a new performance of the seller's obligation to deliver the goods. However, the right to repudiate the contract can only be used under the condition that the buyer has fixed a reasonable period and notified the seller to perform the obligation to deliver goods in that period; the buyer may rescind the contract if there is no delivery within such period.[98] Nevertheless, the buyer may rescind the contract without the notification if it appears that the object of the contract according to its nature or to the intention declared by the parties can be accomplished only by the performance at a fixed time or within a fixed period, and such time or period has passed without the performance of the seller.[99]

F. Commercial Guarantee

Concerning the question of a commercial guarantee, there is currently no law explicitly governing this issue. The law on direct sales and direct marketing only stipulates that a commercial guarantee must be written in the Thai language and must be easy to understand.[100] Thus, the general rules of contract law under the Thai Civil and Commercial Code, including the law of unfair contract terms, are applied to the case of a commercial guarantee. When the commercial guarantee is misleading or overlaps with the legal warranty, the Court has the power to intervene into the content of such

[94] Thai Civil and Commercial Code, s 503.
[95] ibid, s 504.
[96] ibid, s 474.
[97] Ekchariyakorn, *Law on Sale, Exchange and Gift*, 148.
[98] Thai Civil and Commercial Code, s 387.
[99] ibid, s 388.
[100] Direct Sales and Direct Marketing Act, s 37.

commercial guarantee and order the application of its terms and the condition as is fair and reasonable according to the circumstances.[101]

In 2018, the Thai Supreme Court decided that a hire-purchaser has the right to seek and recover damages from the seller and automobile importer under the business commercial guarantee offered in the event of a defective car. This kind of guarantee was considered as one type of contract which bound the seller and the car importer. The Supreme Court in this case orderd the seller and the car importer to compensate the consumer by citing the rules of the Consumer Case Procedure Act.[102] However, the Court did not state whether or not the law of defective goods would apply in this case. This point raises concerns about the legislation on defective goods being limited to contractual parties and not to other persons. Nonetheless, according to Thai Supreme Court precedents, the law of defective or non-conformity of goods sold could be applied only by the contract parties. In case of hire purchase, the consumer is not recognised as the party to the sale contract, but may ask for the remedy from the finance company by the rule of defective or non-conformity of goods.[103] However, if there is a commercial guarantee provided by the business operators, such consumer can apply the general rule of contract law to sue the business operators as there is a contractual relationship created by the guarantee.

VI. Product Liability

Prior to 2008, a person injured by a dangerous product or who had property that was damaged by such product could claim for damages through either of two conventional ways, namely contractual obligation or tort law. However, since the introduction of the Product Liability Act,[104] the victim has been equipped with the new measure for claiming damages on the ground of strict liability pronounced by the new legislation.[105] Following the trend of the laws of European Union countries and the United States, the Product Liability Act stipulates new rules for considering the liability of an entrepreneur arising from its unsafe products distributed in the market.[106] Also, the law facilitates the right to remedy the injured person. To do so, this Act imposes that all entrepreneurs shall be jointly liable for damages occurring to the damaged party from an unsafe product sold to the consumer.[107]

A. Scope of Application

The Product Liability Act gives a broad definition of entrepreneurs which includes a producer or a party authorising the production, an importer, a seller of the product

[101] Unfair Contract Terms Act, s 4 and s 6.
[102] Thai Supreme Court Decision No 4567/2561.
[103] ibid.
[104] BE 2551 (2008).
[105] S Thanitcul, 'Thailand' in L Nottage and S Thanitcul (eds), *ASEAN Product Liability and Consumer Product Safety Law* (Bangkok: Winyuchon, 2016) 250–51 (in Thai).
[106] ibid.
[107] Product Liability Act, s 5.

who cannot identify its producer, a party authorising the production, or importer, and a party using a name, trade name, mark, message or other means which may be understood by the consumer as being the producer, the party authorising the production or the importer.[108]

This broad definition of 'product' covers all type of assets. Any physical thing, including electricity, could be the 'product' regardless of being locally produced or imported for sale. There are three exceptions to this vast definition. First, a ministerial regulation could exempt a substance from being a 'product'. Second, agricultural commodities are not deemed as a 'product' according to the Act. Lastly, drugs and medical devices produced for individual use by a medical professional also fall out of the scope of the definition.[109]

The Product Liability Act classifies three differents categories of unsafe products: products suffering from a production defect, products of defective design and products which are unsafe because of inadequate warning of danger or instructions for safe use.[110]

B. Requirements

To lodge a claim, the victim must prove that damages were sustained from the product of the entrepreneurs, and the use or storage of the product was done in the usual manner. There is no requirement to prove that the damage was caused by an intentional or negligent act of the entrepreneurs.[111]

C. Exclusions of Liability

The defendant is not liable if – upon furnishing evidence – the product is not unsafe, the injured victim knew that the product was unsafe or the loss was caused by the victim, such as using the product incorrectly or a failure to follow any warning or ignoring information concerning the product given by entrepreneurs.[112]

Moreover, a party producing products by order will not be liable if it can prove that the danger was unexpected and caused by the designs or instructions of the party authorising the production.[113] The producer of the product components shall not be liable if it can be proved that the danger of the products was caused by the designs, or instructions for usage and storage, or the warning, or product information provided by the party producing the product.[114]

This Act also provides that an agreement between a consumer and an entrepreneur made in advance for exempting or limiting liability occurred by an unsafe

[108] ibid, s 4.
[109] ibid.
[110] ibid.
[111] ibid, s 6.
[112] ibid.
[113] ibid, s 8(1).
[114] ibid, s 8(2).

product, cannot be used to exclude or restrict the liability of such entrepreneur.[115] It is important to note that the defences of development risk and state of the art are not recognised by the Thai law, since Thai legislators would like to completely promote the rights of consumers.

D. Damages

The Act not only shifts the burden of proof to the entrepreneur but it also introduces new types of damages which are not recognised by the Civil and Commercial Code. A person injured by an unsafe product can claim damages for emotional distress, which is not established in the general law.[116] Plus, if an injured person dies, certain relatives or an heir can claim for this type of damages.[117] Moreover, the courts can award some punitive damages if the entrepreneur knows that the product is unsafe but failed to take proper action to prevent the damage, or failed by gross negligence to recognise the fact. However, the award of such punitive damages cannot exceed twice the amount of the actual compensation.[118] The right for demanding damages will expire after three years from the date that the injured person learns of the unsafe nature of the product and knows the identity of the business operator liable for the loss or damage. The injured person also loses the right to claim for damages if 10 years have passed after the date of sale of the product.[119] However, if the loss of life, body, health or hygiene is the result of an accumulation of chemicals in the body, and the symptom appears after the said period, the victim is still entitled to claim damages. In such case, the claim must be made within three years from the date the victim becomes aware of the damage and the identity of the entrepreneurs responsible. Again, nonetheless, it cannot excede 10 years from the date the victim became aware of the damages.[120]

Apart from the rules and conditions mentioned above, the Product Liability Act also authorises the Consumer Protection Board and associations or foundations certified under the Consumer Protection Act to file a legal proceeding for compensation on behalf of the damaged party.[121] Moreover, if the injured person is entitled to ask for other benefits recognised by other laws, the proceeding according to this Act does not impair his right to claim further damages.[122]

E. Litigation

Up to now, there is one Supreme Court ruling concerning product liability. The case was conducted by the Consumer Protection Board on behalf of the consumer. In this case, the Supreme Court decided that the manufacturer of jasmine rice (the defendant) was

[115] ibid, s 9.
[116] ibid, s 11(1).
[117] ibid.
[118] ibid, s 11(2).
[119] ibid, s 12.
[120] ibid, s 12(2).
[121] ibid, s 10.
[122] ibid, s 14.

not liable for the contamination of some fungus in the bag of rice in question. According to the Supreme Court, the defendant could prove that the manufacturing process complied with acceptable standards defined by many organisations. The defendant also made an argument that a problem in the manufacturing process would have resulted in more contaminated rice. However, in this case, there was only one bag of contaminated rice. The Court stated that the plaintiff had a duty to disprove the defendant's argument for showing that there was a defect in the manufacturing process.[123] According to the Court, the plaintiff could not shift the burden of proof as they were the only one who claimed such a contamination. It would be unfair for the defendant to bear the duty to establish the cause of the contamination and the person responsible for such contamination. The Court also pointed out that there might be more causes of such defect to which the defendant might not be responsible for. Accordingly, the Court decided that the defendant was not liable for this contamination. Due to the Court's interpretation, the plaintiff still had a burden of proof because the defendant had to first establish that the process of manufacturing had no defect or was not unsafe. This duty of the plaintiff did not contradict section 6 of the Product Liability Act. This decision leads to the new challenges for consumers: how should the Thai Court define the scope of the burden of proof?

VII. Product Safety

For the product safety issue, the Consumer Protection Act provides the general guidelines.[124] However, some categories of products have their own laws governing product safety. These products include foods, drugs, medical devices, cosmetics, industrial products and agricultural products. Each piece of legislation sets up a government body to oversee and control the standards of relevant products to meet the relating international standards such as the CODEX or the ISO.[125]

Industrial goods are controlled by the Industrial Products Standards Act,[126] which sets up the Industrial Product Standard Council and the Industrial Product Standard Institute. Presently, there are more than 3,000 industrial products that are regulated by this law including electronic products, electrical products, toys, vehicles, food, furniture, etc.[127] A standard mark (TIS mark) will be displayed on an industrial product that conforms to the standards announced by the Ministry of Industry. To receive such mark, the producer or the supplier of the product must surrender the product to be inspected by a competent officer, and if successful, the Industrial Product Standard Council will issue a licence to the relevant producer or the supplier.[128] A criminal penalty will be imposed for those distributing an unlicensed product.[129]

[123] Thai Supreme Court Decision No 4829/2558.
[124] Consumer Protection Act, s 36.
[125] Thanitcul, 'Thailand', 242.
[126] BE 2511 (1968).
[127] See the list of Industrial Product Standards in the Website of Thai Industrial Standards Institute at www.tisi.go.th/list-tisi.
[128] Industrial Products Standards Act, s 16.
[129] ibid, ss 54 and 55.

Agricultural commodities are regulated by the Agricultural Products Standard Act,[130] which grants powers to the Committee on Agricultural Product Standards to submit the recommendations to the Ministry of Agriculture and Cooperative to issue a Ministerial Regulation or Notification concerning the standards of the agricultural product.[131] Food safety and drugs are regulated by the Food Act[132] and the Drugs Act,[133] respectively.

The Consumer Protection Act was recently updated to include a new Part 1/1 on product safety. This new part of the Act sets up a framework for regulating the sale of dangerous goods and services. The Consumer Protection Act gives power to the Committee on Products and Services Safety to order any businessman to have his goods examined or verified, if the issue of safety is in doubt. If the business fails to have the test or verification, or delays in so doing without justification, the Committee may arrange for the verification at his cost.[134]

If it is determined that such commodities are dangerous and the danger to consumers cannot be avoided through labelling regulation, the Committee has the authority to prohibit the business from making, importing, or selling the goods or services. The Committee also could require the business to adapt or improve or to destroy or return such unsafe goods/services to the country which shipped the commodities into the Kingdom of Thailand, as deemed fit.[135]

To achieve this task, the Unsafe Product Verification and Alert Centre was established for facilitating the testing of the products in question. This body is attached to the Office of the Consumer Protection Board and works as the administrator in the scope of unsafe products. Furthermore, it has to cooperate with other organs and academic institutes to conduct research, to study and gather all claims of consumers concerning unsafe product and to undertake random inspections.[136]

VIII. Consumer Protection Law in the Digital Age

Concerning the issue of protecting the rights of consumers in e-commerce, the legal measures adopted are governed by the consumer protection laws already mentioned above, such as the Consumer Protection Act, the Unfair Contract Terms Act and the Direct Sale and Direct Marketing Act. There are two further laws which have been promulgated and are essential for regulating electronic transactions and electronic commerce: the Electronic Transactions Act[137] and the Decree of Ministry of Commerce on the Registration of the E-commerce.[138] These two statutes provide conditions and

[130] BE 2551 (2008).
[131] Agricultural Products Standard Act, s 15.
[132] BE 2522 (1979).
[133] BE 2510 (1967).
[134] Consumer Protection Act, s 29(8).
[135] ibid, s 29(9).
[136] See also the website of the Unsafe Product Verification and Alert Center: Thailand Consumer Alert System http://thaicas.ocpb.go.th.
[137] BE 2544 (2001). The Act has been amended several times; the most recent amendment was in 2019.
[138] The Decree of Ministry of Commerce on the Registration of the E-commerce was promulgated in virtue of the Commercial Registration Act BE 2553 (2010).

obligations of the electronic transaction service provider and the businessmen who conduct their business online.

The Electronic Transaction Act is the primary statute which sets out the legal frameworks for the validity of electronic signatures and electronic transactions. This legislation includes a mix of provisions from several international models, but the key sections follow the UNCITRAL Model Law on Electronic Commerce.[139] The Act establishes the Commission on Electronic Transactions to supervise its application.[140] This authority holds powers to propose to or counsel the Minister of the Information and Communication Technology on the enactment of the Royal Decrees relating to the electronic transactions.[141] Nowadays, there are laws guaranteeing the security of consumers in electronic transactions, especially in the case of electronic payments. Those laws are, for example, the Royal Decree on Regulating of Electronic Payment Services,[142] the Royal Decree on Security Procedures in Electronic Transactions[143] and the Royal Decree on Regulating of Electronic Payment Services of Certain Financial Institutes.[144]

Apart from the Electronic Transaction Act, a businessman who wishes to conduct business via electronic transactions is required to register the business with the Ministry of Commerce by the provision of the Decree of Ministry of Commerce on the registration of the e-commerce.[145]

IX. Unfair Commercial Practices

Thailand has no specific law dealing with unfair commercial practices. Certain types of commercial practices are regulated by different rules depending on their nature. For example, for misleading advertisements or fake labels, the Consumer Protection Act applies.[146] For doorstep selling or a pyramid selling scheme, the Direct Sales and Direct Marketing Act will apply. Or, in the case of aggressive or harassing commercial practices, certain provisions of the Thai Criminal Code such as extortion[147] or fraud[148] will be invoked.

Advertising

The Consumer Protection Act provides a broad definition of advertisements and requires that the applicable advertisements do not contain any statement which is

[139] National Electronics and Computer Technology Center, 'The Electronic Transaction Act BE 2544' (in Thai).
[140] Electronic Transactions Act, s 36.
[141] ibid, s 37.
[142] BE 2551 (2008).
[143] BE 2553 (2010).
[144] BE 2559 (2016).
[145] Decree of Ministry of Commerce on the registration of the e-commerce BE 2553, s 5.
[146] Consumer Protection Act, Chapter 2.
[147] Thai Criminal Code, s 337.
[148] ibid, s 341.

considered as unfair to consumers or which may harm society as a whole. In addition, said advertisements shall not be implemented by a method which may be harmful to health or cause physical or mental harm or annoyance to consumers. In the case that a businessman deems that an advertisement might be in violation or might not be in conformity with the standards set by the Consumer Protection Act, the businessman may apply to the Committee on Advertisements for a consultation to consider whether or not the advertisement follows the law and rules. The businessman may make such an application before broadcasting or distributing the advertisement. Although a discussion of foods and medicines would exceed the scope of this chapter, it is nonetheless to be noted that advertisements relating to food and drugs are to be submitted for consultation before broadcast or distribution.

Advertisements are controlled by both the Office of Prime Minister and the Committee on Advertisement. The Office of Prime Minister has, for instance, announced regulations constraining the sale of a condominium unit,[149] advertisements concerning premium, gift or prize giving for sales tactics[150] and advertisements stating some texts relating to the King and the Royal Family.[151] The Committee of Advertisement has so far announced the Notification on the Guideline on Sale Marketing by Price Discount,[152] the Notification on the Guideline for Proving the Fact of Advertisements[153] and the Notification on Advertisements using a Statement which is Difficult to Prove.[154]

i. Sale Marketing by Price Discount

The Notification on the Guideline on Sale Marketing by Price Discount requires that the business operators have to specify the rules, conditions and the periods of price reduction and the period of price discount. In addition, the numbers, quantities or volumes of products or services which will be discounted must be clearly stated. Furthermore, the final price with a discount should be calculated from the normal price.

ii. Genuine Nature

The Notification on the Guideline for Proving the Fact of Advertisements specifies that where the Committee so requires, the business operators shall prove the genuineness of their advertisement. The operators shall complete the task in the period specified in the guideline. If statistics or numbers have been claimed in the advertisement, the business operators are obliged to show a report or any supporting documents proving the authenticity of the statistics or numbers.

[149] Ministerial Regulation on the Advertisement of the Sale of Condominium Unit BE 2538 (1995).

[150] Ministerial Regulation on the Advertisement concerning Sales Tactics by Premium, Gift or Prize BE 2534 (1991).

[151] Ministerial Regulation on the Advertisement on the Statements relating to the King and Royal Family BE 2526 (1983).

[152] BE 2555 (2012).

[153] BE 2535 (1992).

[154] BE 2526 (1983).

iii. Statements That are Difficult to Prove

The Notification on the Advertisement using a Statement which is Difficult to Prove concerns statements such as '100 per cent', 'the greatest' or 'the first'. Such statements are difficult to prove and should only be used where proof of their accuracy can be furnished.

In practice, a consumer facing the problem of misleading or fake advertisements, the lack of label required or an unfair contract, can notify the Office of the Consumer Protection Board who will assist the consumer as a mediator in order to receive a remedy. If the mediation fails, the Office can sue the business operators on behalf of the consumer and a public prosecutor will be the consumer's legal counsel. Apart from such convenience, however, the law does not make the trial process any easier. The plaintiff still needs to rely on the law of contract[155] or tort[156] under the Civil and Commercial Code to receive compensation or to terminate a contract. For example, Mrs Y buys a second hand car and she later finds out that the seller made a fake advertisement in respect of the car she has bought. In this case, Mrs Y may either sue the seller by herself or make a petition to the Office of the Consumer Protection Board. In the latter instance, the Office will conduct an investigation and initiate the mediation for remedy. If the mediation is not successful, an officer of the Office of the Consumer Protection Board, under the approval of the Consumer Protection Board, will sue the seller on behalf of the buyer.

For the control of direct sale and direct marketing, the Direct Sales and Direct Marketing Act specifies several measures which were motivated by the EU Distance Selling Directive.[157] Firstly, the businesses in direct sales and marketing must be registered.[158] Secondly, pyramid sale schemes are no longer allowed in Thailand and are explicitly prohibited.[159] Thirdly, it is the duty of the business to provide consumers with information in the form of purchase documents.[160] Additionally, the modes of offering or proposing goods or services for sale are controlled by law.[161] Lastly, it is recognised that consumers have the right to freely terminate contracts within seven days from the day they receive said goods or services.[162] The Act provides the Direct Sales and Direct Marketing Commission with the powers and duties to consider complaints from the consumer who was affected or damaged by the practice of a business operator, to warn the consumer about the product or service which may cause harm or damage, to control the operation of the direct sale operator or direct marketing operator, to stipulate regulations and notifications regarding this Act and to control and supervise the performance of the officers to comply with this law. An example of the Commission's mission for consumer protection was its 2017 announcement of the order sanctioning

[155] Thai Civil and Commercial Code, s 156.
[156] ibid, s 420.
[157] Directive 97/7/EC of the European Parliament and of the Council of 20 May 1997 on the protection of consumers in respect of distance contracts, OJ 1997 No L144, p 19.
[158] Direct Sales and Direct Marketing Act, ss 20, 27.
[159] ibid, s 19.
[160] ibid, ss 30–32.
[161] ibid, s 24
[162] ibid, ss 33–34. See above s III.B.

the company who made the misleading advertisement on the price of a cooking pan in the form of dubious discounts or fake original price. The company in question was required to suspend all advertisements concerning the fake original price and was fined.[163] However, the Commission did not order the company to refund the price to the buyers.

Consumers who have suffered from different unfair commercial practices mentioned above may claim a remedy such as damages or the termination of the contract. However, as there is no specific law governing the issue, those consumers have to base their arguments on the general rules of contract law and tort law according to the Thai Civil and Commercial Code.[164] Punitive damages may be awarded by the court if it appears that the business operators intentionally mislead or deceive the consumers.[165]

Apart from these consumer laws, the recently enacted Competition Act[166] may be applied in respect of the rule of unfair trade practices.[167] Under this Act, business operators cannot distort other competitors by unfair commercial practices mentioned therein. Even though this Act mainly focuses on the rights of competitors, it also provides consumers with a chance to claim compensation from business operators who violate the law.[168]

X. Personal Data Protection

Under the significant influence of the European General Data Protection Regulation, the Personal Data Protection Act[169] is designed to protect personal data protection from use by government and business sectors.[170] This new law creates the Personal Data Protection Committee which is responsible for enforcing the law and drafting the guidance to assist organisations in ensuring compliant practices.[171] At the same time, the Office of Personal Data Protection Committee is set to be established for supporting and facilitating the Personal Data Protection Committee in the area of administrative and academic tasks.[172]

The new law sets some standards for organisations for the collection and use of personal information such as a valid consent for collecting, using and disclosing personal data (except where the law permits otherwise),[173] the application of appropriate

[163] The Order of the Direct Sales and Direct Marketing Commission No 1/2560 concerning the Ban of Advertisement of Product, 30 May 2017.

[164] Thai Civil and Commercial Code, ss 215, 222, ss 387–89, s 420.

[165] Consumer Case Procedure Act BE 2551(2008), s 42.

[166] BE 2560 (2017).

[167] Competition Act, s 57.

[168] ibid, s 69.

[169] BE 2562 (2019). Personal data means any information relating to a natural person, which enables the identification of a person, whether directly or indirectly but does not include the information of a deceased person, s 6.

[170] Although the Act was published in Thailand's Government Gazette on 27 May 2019, the Personal Data Protection Act has not yet been implemented in full.

[171] Personal Data Protection Act, s 8.

[172] ibid, ss 43–45.

[173] ibid, s 19.

security measures[174] and a duty to notify the Office of Personal Data Protection Committee of any data breach within 72 hours after becoming aware thereof. In the case that the breach is likely to pose a high risk to the rights and freedoms of the data subject, the data subject must be notified without delay.[175] Violation of this new law may lead to administrative sanctions, fines,[176] civil damages[177] and also criminal sanctions.[178]

Even if this law has not been fully enforced at this time, it appears that some business sectors are aware of this new legislation due to the many publications, training courses and seminars about the Personal Data Protection Act made by some stakeholders regularly.[179]

XI. Access to Justice

Instead of establishing a special tribunal, the Thai Parliament opted to introduce a new law on procedure exclusively for the case of consumer claims in 2008 – the Consumer Cases Procedure Act[180] – and the law for application of the class action lawsuit in 2015 – the Class Action Act.[181] Both laws are now essential tools for consumers to wield in order to get justice, with different approches.

A. Consumer Cases Procedure Act

The Consumer Cases Procedure Act creates an expressway in the same pyramid of justice by facilating consumers to fight for their rights. This law stipulates many plaintiff-friendly provisions such as:

- The ability of the plaintiff to institute the proceeding orally or with the assistance of a competent case official who will help plaintiffs in drafting their claims and conduct discovery-like activities.[182]
- Reducing the burden of proof of the plaintiff by simplifying the rules of evidence.[183]
- The ability to amend damages over time: where there is a physical injury, and it is impossible to know the exact amount of actual damages when the judgment is issued, the Court may provide in its judgment that the judgment may be amended within a specified period (which may not exceed 10 years) to cover any additional damages that become apparent during the specific timeframe.[184]

[174] ibid, s 37.
[175] ibid, s 37(4).
[176] ibid, ss 82–90.
[177] ibid, ss 77–78.
[178] ibid, ss 79–81.
[179] There are many papers, articles and clip videos concerning the Act available on the website of the Electronic Transactions Development Agency (ETDA) and website of the Office of the Personal Data Protection Committee, see www.etda.or.th/content/personal-data-protection-by-etda.
[180] BE 2551 (2008).
[181] BE 2558 (2015).
[182] Consumer Cases Procedure Act, ss 4 and 20.
[183] ibid, ss 10, 11 and 29.
[184] ibid, s 40.

- Introducing new types of damages and remedies awarded to consumers, such as punitive damages[185] or the right to repair and to replace the defective goods.[186]

As this law provides special rules which are different from the law on civil procedure, there are some problems about the application of this law especially at the beginning of the implementation.

i. 'Consumer Case'

Due to the interpretation of the courts, the case that was originally launched by the business operator against a consumer is also recognised as a consumer case under this law.[187] Thus the business operator also receives some advantages from this Act. This interpretation is criticised by some scholars and the consumer organisations who consider that the business operators take more benefit from this Act than real consumers. For example, banks usually apply the rules of consumer cases for suing against consumers in credit cases.[188]

Moreover, the courts have ruled that a case between business operators or between legal persons can also be a consumer case.[189] This interpretration draws heavy criticism from both scholars and practitioners alike.

ii. The Lack of Consumer Case Officials

Even though the law appoints the consumer case officials for assisting the court in the consumer cases,[190] in practice there are only one or two case officials on duty per court.[191] The lack of an appropriate number of case officials in each court nowadays shows the imbalance between the workload and the number of responsible persons. This is the crucial factor which may delay justice for consumers and failure in enforcing the law.

iii. The Lack of Knowledge and Understanding

Being different from the classic rules of civil procedure law, some practitioners have difficulties in interpreting and applying the law. For example, consumer lawyers apply the rules of accusatorial procedure instead of the inquisatorial procedure as the law states, the court does not take sufficient roles following the rules of inquisitorial procedure and there are some doubts concerning the determination of punitive damages.[192]

[185] ibid, s 42.
[186] ibid, s 41.
[187] The Ruling of the President of the Court of Appeal No. 50/2551, No 56/2551 and No 33/2552.
[188] N Nawatrakulpisut, 'Amendment of the Consumer Protection Law: Important Steps Forward for Improvement towards More Efficient Protection' (2020) 49 *Thammasat Law Journal* 178–83 (in Thai).
[189] The Ruling of the President of the Court of Appeal No 50/2551.
[190] Consumer Cases Procedure Act, s 4.
[191] S Prapainop, 'Development of the Consumer Case Management System', PhD Thesis, Thammasat University (2017), 280 (in Thai).
[192] ibid, 11–16, 212–52.

Some of the problems mentioned above show that practitioners must gain more knowledge and understanding of the law, while the development of the additional tools or mechanisms is still needed for promoting the application of Act.

iv. Class Action

According to the Act Amending the Civil Procedure Code of Thailand,[193] for the first time consumers have the possibility to commence class action lawsuits before the civil court. This action is recognised as one of the tools for the small claims plaintiff to seek redress as a group. Under the law of class action, the eligible claim for the class action must be based on the same common fact and the same principle of law. Moreover, this law is not limited to the consumer cases only – the plaintiffs may bring the class action lawsuits for other types of claims, such as concerning the environment or employment. Some examples of cases which applied the rule of class action recently are:

- The order for a car manufactuer to pay 291 car owners compensation ranging from THB 20,000 to 200,000 (THB 23 million in total = approximately USD 730,000) for the sale of substandard vehicles in 2018.[194]
- Unfair mobile contracts concerning the mode of price calculation.[195]
- Unsafe cosmetic product causing disfiguration to the consumers.[196]

Alongside the Consumer Cases Procedure Act and the Class Action Act, the Consumer Protection Act provides some legal measures for facilitating the rights of consumers to access the courts by:

- Instituting civil and criminal proceedings in the Court against the persons infringing the consumer's rights by order of the Consumer Protection Board, if the Consumer Protection Board deems it fit for protecting the right of consumers as a whole.[197]
- Authorising the associations recognised by the Consumer Protection Board to institute civil and criminal proceedings or to sue for recovery of damages on behalf of its member if it has obtained the power of attorney to claim damages from its member.[198]
- Initiating negotiation or the mediation between the consumers and the businessmen with the support of the Office of the Consumer Protection Board.

In practice, when the consumer is faced with a problem and is unable to ask for compensation from or negotiate with the businessman, that consumer may prefer to

[193] This Act was effective in December 2015.
[194] Judgment of the Civil Court Black No. 492/2560.
[195] Three cases have been launched by the NGOs (the Foundation for Consumers) against three mobile operators in 2018. During the mediation, one operator agreed to compensate the consumers. The cases against the others two operators are still in the court consideration. The Foundation for Consumer, 'The Against three Operators', consumerthai.org, 10 June 2020 (in Thai).
[196] Judgment of the Satun Provincial Court Red No 3550/2561.
[197] Consumer Protection Act, s 39.
[198] ibid, s 40.

ask for assistance from the Office of the Consumer Protection Board or other consumer organisations including NGOs.[199] According to the statistics reported by the Office in 2019, there were 7,676 requests for assistance, the three first types of cases concern housing and real estate (31.06 per cent), consumer goods (28.95 per cent) and services (22.43 per cent).[200]

XII. Right to Consumer Participation: Consumer Council

In 2019, after a long debate following the 2017 Constitution, Parliament passed new legislation which assures consumers the right to participate: the Establishment of Consumer Council Act.[201] This Act focuses on promoting public awareness, offers knowledge about consumer rights and public participation. Moreover, the Consumer Council, an independent organisation, was established by the Act to represent consumers.[202] This new Council cannot be controlled or intervened by the government, any public authorities, any political parties, any entrepreneurs or any employees of the business sectors.[203]

To set up the Consumer Council, at least 150 consumer organisations must send their requests to the Central Registrar showing their valid consent for establishing said Council.[204] With the sufficient amount of consent from certified consumer organisations, the Central Registrar will announce the establishment of the Consumer Council. Its members must then select the commissions and draft all relevant regulations.[205] At the first stage, this new type of consumer organisation will receive government subsidies for running their tasks (approximately THB 350 million = approximately USD 11 million).[206]

According to the new law, the Consumer Council has many powers such as:

- making and proposing recommendations concerning consumer protection issues to the government;
- supporting, conducting, examining and monitoring the problems of goods and services;
- warning consumers in case goods or services are not safe or may prejudice consumers;
- promoting consumer education and consumer research;
- assisting some consumer organisations for safeguarding the rights of consumers and promoting the consumers' right to participate at the local level; and

[199] ibid, s 41.
[200] Office of the Consumer Protection Board, 'Report of the consumers' complaints from October 2018–September 2019'.
[201] BE 2562 (2019).
[202] Establishment of Consumer Council Act, s 9.
[203] ibid, s 10.
[204] ibid, s 9.
[205] ibid, s 11.
[206] ibid, s 19.

- facilitating and assisting the members in case of negotiating or settling a dispute before/after the court proceeding.[207]

This Council can file a case before the court as the agent of the consumer. If the business is guilty and liable for damages, the Council may receive some commission – at least 25 per cent of indemnity ordered, but not more than a half of the indemnity paid to the consumer. However, the Council may ask for higher commission in some exceptional cases.[208]

In the eyes of consumer activists, the creation of this Council is still a thorn for the future as the law requires too many processes to be complied with. These requirements create some obstacles for setting up the Council. Some of the problems that are now anticipated are the lack of consensus between members or the presence of fake consumer organisations which will disrupt the works of the Council.[209]

XIII. Conclusion

As we have now seen an overview of consumer protection laws in Thailand, it is essential to note that Thailand has several substantive laws covering almost every area of the protection of consumer rights. These laws per se are not deemed to be below the international standard, especially now Thailand has passed the recent new law on personal data protection and product safety which are motivated by the famous EU laws and other developed countries. This fact shows that Thailand does have a good response to the issue of consumer protection.

This demonstrates that Thailand has a strong commitment to consumer protection, even though specific sectors still require particular legislation, such as unfair commercial practices, non-conformity of goods and commercial guarantees, and the law on consumer protection in online transactions. It appears that Thailand's current e-commerce rules are incapable of resolving all consumer complaints online, given the growth of e-commerce in recent years and the various different types of consumer complaints.

The issue of vulnerable consumers is also a critical issue for Thailand. It must address quickly, particularly in the case of elderly persons who may be hesitant to use the Internet and digital technology and thus become victims of rights violations. A proportionately large number of persons over the age of 60 will allow for use of the term 'grey society'. Children and the disabled require additional assistance in all areas, including access to justice. Thai regulations appear to be less aware of these vulnerable consumers as no special rules are currently in place.

Apart from the need for additional laws and regulations, we should understand that Thailand has clearly separated consumer protection and competition by dividing the

[207] ibid, s 14.
[208] ibid, s 13.
[209] Foundation for Consumers, 'One year lost, the delay of the Consumer Council', consumerthai.org, 22 July 2020 (in Thai).

state agencies and laws to respond to these issues separately. At the same time, numerous state agencies are mandated by other legislation to address consumer protection issues in very particular areas, such as telecommunications, food and drugs, financial services, etc. The establishment of many agencies may occasionally result in inconsistencies or incoherence in the enforcement and interpretation of the law, as well as duplicating tasks, which pose new obstacles for businesses and consumers alike. The promotion of the cooperation of all state agencies, including the competition agency and authority reform, are still required for Thailand, while the issue of consumer law enforcement by all relevant parties, including lawyers, judges and consumers' right to self-protection, must continue to be pushed.

14

Vietnam

NGUYEN VAN CUONG

I. Introduction

Vietnam is a country in South East Asia with a population of 96.5 million (in 2019).[1] It had a GDP per capita of VND 6 billion in 2019 (approximately USD 266.7 billion).[2] Vietnam is a large producer of agricultural products such as rice, coffee, rubber, tea, pepper, soybeans, cashews, pork, poultry and seafood. Vietnam also hosts many manufacturers of consumer goods such as clothing, shoes, mobile phones, smart televisions, etc. It also imports many types of consumer goods from abroad, such as mobile phones, laptops, cars, luxury clothing, etc.

Due to its history as a former French colony (gaining independence in 1945, however, the North and South of Vietnam were reunified as a country only in 1975), a socialist country adopting a central planning economy until 1986 then transiting to a market economy from 1986,[3] Vietnam has a legal system with many aspects of both civil law and socialist tradition. Laws or legal codes adopted by the National Assembly are its main source of law. However, laws usually provide only frameworks for the Government (Cabinet) and its ministries to issue detailed guidance (under the form of Government Decrees or Ministry Circulars). With the adoption of its Constitution of 1992, Vietnam embraced more and more market-oriented legal rules into its legal system. As a result, Vietnam adopted its first Civil Code in 1995, its first Commercial Law in 1997[4] and its first Competition Law in 2004. Vietnam also joined the World Trade Organization (WTO) in 2007. In 2013, Vietnam adopted its new Constitution to provide a constitutional basis to push its reform to a more open and competitive market economy. Consequently, Vietnam's National Assembly comprehensively revised its current laws and adopted various new laws regulating market relations such as the

[1] General Statistics Office, *Statistical Yearbook of Vietnam 2019* (Hanoi: Statistical Publishing House, 2020) 93, available under www.gso.gov.vn/en/statistic-book/.

[2] ibid, 198.

[3] A Fforde and S de Vylder, *From Plan to Market: The Economic Transition in Vietnam* (Oxford: Westview Press, 1996) 144.

[4] Its current Commercial Law was adopted in 2005.

Civil Code of 2015, the Corporate Law of 2014 and 2020, the Investment Law of 2014 and 2020 and the Competition Law of 2018, etc. Responsibility for consumer policy lies with the Vietnam Competition and Consumer Authority of the Ministry of Industry and Trade.

As a civil law country, transactions between traders and consumers are regulated by various laws and guiding documents in Vietnam. Among these sources of consumer protection law, the Law on Consumer Protection in 2010[5] is regarded as a main source. The Law on Consumer Protection of 2010 is also the first special law to deal with transactions between traders and consumers in Vietnam. However, other legal documents such as the Civil Code of 2015 (formerly, Civil Code of 2005), the Law on Dealing with Administrative Violation of 2012 and the Criminal Code of 2015 (as amended in 2017)[6] are also regarded as supplementary sources for consumer protection in Vietnam. The Civil Code of 2015 provides supplementary legal rules for regulating contracts between traders and consumers in addition to legal rules found in the Law on Consumer Protection. This Civil Code also provides additional compensation legal rules in addition to product liability rules found in the Law on Consumer Protection of 2010. The Criminal Code of 2015 (as amended in 2017) provides legal rules to prosecute traders for seriously infringing upon consumer rights, such as crimes related to counterfeit goods, false advertising and deceiving customers.[7] In addition to these statutes, the Vietnamese Government also issued some guiding documents concerning, for example, the protection of consumer rights,[8] administrative violations in commercial activities[9] and a list of essential goods and services.[10]

It is worth noting that the Law on Consumer Protection of Vietnam was adopted at the time marking 25 years of consumer experience in an emerging market economy with a legal system based upon an assumption of equality between producers or traders and consumers. Vietnam's membership in the WTO had been three years. The Civil Code of 2005 and the Commercial Law of 2005 (in force at that time) were drafted upon the contractual freedom ideal. Consumers were not explicitly considered as a weaker party in relation with traders or producers. After 25 years of experiencing market relations, Vietnamese consumers found that they had more opportunities and choices to access various goods and services available on the market, including those locally produced or those imported from Vietnam's trading partners in East Asia, South East Asia and other continents such as from North America and Europe. However, they also soon found that they were not truly equal in relation with traders or producers and that they needed more legal tools to ensure fairer treatment from producers or traders. The Vietnamese

[5] Literally, this Law is named as 'the Law on Protection of Consumers' Rights and Interests'.

[6] This Code entered into force on 1 January 2018.

[7] Criminal Code of 2015, Arts 192, 197 and 198.

[8] Decree 99/2011/ND-CP dated 27 October 2011 detailing and guiding a number of articles of the Law on Protection of Consumer Rights.

[9] Decree 185/2013/ND-CP dated 15 November 2013 providing the sanctions on administrative violations in commercial activities, production of, trading in counterfeit or banned goods, and protection of consumer rights. The Decree was amended by Decree 124/2015/ND-CP dated 19 November 2015.

[10] Decision 02/2012/QD-TTg dated 13 January 2012 promulgating the List of essential goods and services for which standard form contracts must be registered. This Decision was revised by Decision 35/2015/QD-TTg dated 20 August 2015 and Decision 38/2018/QD-TTg dated 5 September 2018.

National Assembly met this demand by adopting the Law on Consumer Protection in 2010 to enhance the position of consumers in relation to traders or producers by offering more legal rights to consumers and placing more burdens upon traders or producers.

Although certain forms of case law have been recently recognised in the Vietnamese legal system,[11] case law does not seem to play any significant role in consumer protection in Vietnam. Self-regulation is not officially regarded as a source of laws for consumer protection in Vietnam. As for the legal transplantation perspective, the main influences for Vietnam's Law on Consumer Protection of 2010 include the UN Guidelines on Consumer Protection, EU law, North American laws, and some Asian countries including Japan, South Korea and China. As for enforcement, the national authority to enforce the Law on Consumer Protection is the Vietnam Competition and Consumer Authority – an agency under the Ministry of Industry and Trade. The Vietnam Competition and Consumer Authority consists of one administrative office; one centre for information, consultation and training; and five divisions (Merger Control, Unfair Competition Investigation, Antitrust, Consumer Protection and Standard Contract and General Conditions Control). Consumer protection activities conducted by the Vietnam Competition and Consumer Authority are mainly initiated by the Consumer Protection Division and the Standard Contract and General Conditions Control Division. These two divisions have a quite limited number of officials (approximately 12). However, the courts and provincial Department of Industry and Trade are also directly involved in the implementation of this Law.

II. Information Duties and Right to Withdraw

A. Pre-contractual Information Duties

Even before the Law on Consumer Protection of 2010, Vietnamese laws had some provisions on the pre-contractual information duties owed by the seller to the purchaser in a sales contract. Article 442 of the Civil Code of 2005[12] stated that a seller has the obligation to provide a purchaser with necessary information on the property for sale and instructions on the use of the property. If the seller fails to perform this obligation, the purchaser has the right to require the seller to perform such obligation within a reasonable time limit and, if the seller still fails to perform such obligation that prevents the purchaser from achieving the purposes of entering into the contract, the purchaser has the right to cancel the contract and demand compensation for damage. However, the Law on Consumer Protection of 2010 broadens the pre-contractual information duties of traders. Article 12(6) of the Law on Consumer Protection of 2010 states that traders shall 'inform accurately and fully to consumers of the standard form

[11] Resolution 03/2015/NQ-HDTP dated 28 October 2015 issued by the Supreme People's Court's Council of Justices on the process for selecting, publishing and adopting precedents.

[12] Now Art 443 of the Civil Code of 2015.

contracts before the transaction'. Article 14(6) of the Law on Consumer Protection of 2010 states that where the contract between traders and consumers is concluded by electronic means, 'traders shall let consumers check the entire contract before signing'.

There is also a general information obligation in consumer contracts. Article 8(2) of the Law on Consumer Protection of 2010 states that the consumer is entitled to be provided 'accurate and complete information about traders; contents of contract; the source and origin of goods; ... and other necessary information about goods and/or services that the consumer purchases and/or uses'. Furthermore, Article 10 of the Law on Consumer Protection of 2010 explicitly prohibits traders from deceiving or misleading consumers via advertising activities, or hiding or providing information that is incomplete, false or inaccurate about one of the following details: goods and/or services that traders provided; reputation, business ability and ability to provide goods and/or services of traders; the contents and characteristics of the transaction between consumers and traders.

Breach of information duties shall be sanctioned with monetary fines. Article 66 of Decree 185/2013/ND-CP states that a fine of between VND 10–20 million (approximately USD 430–860) shall be imposed on traders who have one of the following violations concerning providing information on goods or services for consumers:

(1) No warning on the capacity that goods and services have adversely to affect health, life and property of the consumer and the precautions prescribed;
(2) Not providing information about the supply and availability of replacement spare parts, accessories of goods as prescribed;
(3) Failure to supply instructions or failure to supply information about the conditions, duration, location of warranty procedures in cases where the goods or services are covered by a warranty as prescribed;
(4) Failure to notify exactly or fully consumers about model contracts or general transaction conditions before conducting transactions as prescribed;
(5) Concealing information, or providing incomplete, false or inaccurate information to consumers as prescribed.

According to Articles 126 and 127 of the Civil Code of 2015,[13] consumers can request the court to invalidate the contract concluded by showing that they were mistaken or deceived by traders. Pursuant to Article 126(1), if there is a misunderstanding in a civil transaction that makes a party or the parties fail to meet the objectives of the transaction establishment, the mistaken party shall have the right to request a court to declare such transaction invalid. Article 127 states that any party entering into a civil transaction as a result of deception[14] has the right to request a court to declare such transaction invalid.

[13] Similar provisions are also found in the Civil Code of 2005.

[14] Deception in a civil transaction means an intentional act of a party or a third person to mislead the other party as to the subject, the nature of the entity or contents of the civil transaction which has caused the other party to enter into such transaction, Civil Code of 2005, Art 127.

B. Right to Withdraw

In principle, consumers in Vietnam do not have the right to withdraw from contracts without giving reasons. However, door-to-door sale contracts are an exception. Article 19(3) of Decree 99/2011/ND-CP states that within three working days after concluding a door-to-door sale contract, consumers may request unilaterally to terminate that contract and should notify such in writing to the trader. Before this time limit expires, a door-to-door salesperson may not request the consumer to make any payments or perform the contract, unless otherwise provided by law. The period of three working days is regarded as a cooling-off period for consumers to prevent sellers from abusing their skills and professionalism to lead consumers to make unwise decisions.

III. Consumer Sales Law

A. Non-conformity

From the outset it is worth noting that, for (non-)conformity, most of the provisions of the Civil Code of 2015 were already stipulated in the Civil Code of 1995 and 2005.[15] The Civil Code of 2015 requires that the property in a transaction must, inter alia, match the description or the sample, be reasonably fit for the purpose for which they were sold, and be of merchantable quality and durability. More concretely, Article 445(2) of the Civil Code of 2015[16] expressly states that 'a seller must assure that an object for sale corresponds to descriptions on any package, to any trademark or to any sample selected by the purchaser'.

Articles 436–38 of the Civil Code allow buyers to refuse to accept the delivery of goods which do not conform with the description in the contract. Where goods exhibit defects which cause a loss in value or utility, Article 445(1) of the Civil Code states that the buyer must notify the seller immediately of such defects. Furthermore, this same provision states that the buyer has, in principle, the right to require the seller to repair or replace the defective object, to reduce the price and to compensate for damage. However, the seller will not be liable for defects where the buyer knew or must have known about the defect when purchasing the object, the object was auctioned or sold at a second-hand shop or the buyer is at fault in causing the defects.

In practice, based upon these provisions of the Civil Code and relevant rules in the Law on Consumer Protection of 2010, several consumers submit their complaints to the Vietnam Competition and Consumer Authority to ask for assistance. For example, as reported by the Vietnam Competition and Consumer Authority in 2019, consumers complained that they purchased goods on Lazada.vn (a popular trading platform)

[15] See Civil Code of 2005, Arts 423 and 437, in Baker & McKenzie & Clifford Chance, *Civil Code of the Socialist Republic of Vietnam* (Hong Kong: Asia Information Associated, 1996) 146–50.

[16] Similar provisions were found in the Civil Code of 2005, Art 444(2).

but received goods that did not correspond with the advertisement. When contacted, Lazada explained to the consumers that the transactions were made outside the Lazada platform system, and thus they were not entitled to Lazada's return/refund policy. This position changed after complaints were submitted to the Vietnam Competition and Consumer Authority, which worked with Lazada to resolve the complaints. Accordingly, Lazada punished the sellers that violated the Consumer Protection Law and compensated consumers eligible for the Lazada's return/refund policy.[17]

B. Warranty

Articles 446–49 of the Civil Code of 2015 concern the obligations concerning warranties. If agreed by the parties or provided by law, a seller has the obligation to provide a warranty for the object for sale and purchase for a certain period that is calculated from the time when the purchaser has the obligation to accept the object.[18] A purchaser who discovers a defect during the warranty period has the right to require the seller to repair the object free of charge, or reduce its price or replace it with another object, or it has the right to return the object in exchange for a refund.[19]

Article 448 concerns the repair obligation. According to this provision, a seller must not only repair a defective object and assure that it satisfies the quality standards or characteristics as undertaken but shall also pay the costs for repair and for transporting it to and from the place of residence or head office of the purchaser to the place of repair. A buyer has the right to require the seller to complete the repairs within a time limit agreed by the parties or within a reasonable time. If the seller is not able to make or complete the repairs within such time, the buyer has the right to demand a price reduction or replacement of the defective object with another object, or it has the right to return the object in exchange for a refund.

In addition to demanding the performance of warranty obligations, the buyer may also demand compensation from the seller for damage caused during the warranty period due to technical defects of the object, unless the seller can prove that the damage was caused due to the fault of the buyer and with reduction in the amount of compensation where the buyer has not availed of all necessary measures available to it to mitigate the damage.[20]

The Civil Code features a shortcoming with regard to voluntary warranties insofar as it does not explicitly cover the relationship in which a manufacturer offers a warranty to a consumer. However, Article 21 of the Law on Consumer Protection of 2010 fills this gap with supplementary and extensive rules which provide that where goods, components or accessories are warranted, traders shall fully comply with warranty obligations for goods, components or accessories supplied by them.

[17] Vietnam Competition and Consumer Authority, 'Annual Report of 2019', p 4, available from the homepage of the Ministry of Industry and Trade under 'publications': http://en.vcca.gov.vn.

[18] Civil Code of 2015, Art 446.

[19] ibid, Art 447.

[20] ibid, Art 449.

In addition, traders shall provide consumers with the receipt of the warranty, clearly stating its duration. The period for implementation of the warranty is not included in the warranty duration for the goods, components and accessories. Where traders replace components, accessories or exchange commodities, such warranty duration for components, accessories or goods are calculated from the time of replacing components, accessories or of exchanging new commodities. Further obligations also include the provision of similar goods, components or accessories to the consumer for temporary use; to exchange for new similar goods, components or accessories, or refund money to the consumer where the defect has not been repaired in the warranty period or where there have been three failed attempts; to bear the cost or repair and transport; and to bear responsibility for the warranty, even when a third party undertakes repairs.

IV. Unfair Terms

A. List of Unfair Terms

One of the purposes of the Law on Consumer Protection of 2010 is to promote fair treatment extended by enterprises (traders) to consumers. As a result, the unfairness of contractual terms becomes one of the important focal points of this legislation. Instead of providing a general standard to assess a certain contractual term as fair or unfair, the Law on Consumer Protection of 2010 specifies a list of contractual terms deemed as unfair. This technique of legislative drafting has both advantages and disadvantages. This technique can provide clear guidance for consumers and consumer protection authorities to recognise certain contractual terms as unfair by simply comparing these contractual terms with the list. However, this technique may ignore contractual terms that require a deeper analysis to certify that they are unfair. Despite the fact that the EU Unfair Terms Directive[21] was a source for reference during the drafting process of Vietnamese legal rules on consumer contracts in the Law on Consumer Protection of 2010, the Vietnamese Law does not follow the approach under the EU Directive by adopting a general standard of unfairness.[22] Vietnamese lawmakers were perhaps concerned that a general standard of unfairness may undermine the transparency of legal rules in the Law on Consumer Protection of 2010. However, similar to the annex of the EU Unfair Terms Directive, Article 16 of the Law on Consumer Protection of 2010 provides for a list of contractual terms considered as unfair (and invalid):

(1) Terms that exclude liability of traders to consumers as prescribed by laws;
(2) Terms that restrict or exclude the right to complain and take lawsuits by consumers;

[21] Council Directive 93/13/EEC of 5 April 1993 on unfair terms in consumer contracts, OJ 1993 No L95, p 29.
[22] On the general fairness test see Unfair Terms Directive (EU), Art 4.

(3) Terms that allow traders to unilaterally change the conditions of the contract agreed in advance with the consumer or the rules, regulations for the sale of goods or service supply applies to consumers when buying and using goods and/or services do not specifically indicate in the contract;
(4) Terms that allow traders to unilaterally determine if the consumer fails to perform one or more obligations;
(5) Terms that allow traders to set forth or change the price at the time of delivery of goods or providing of services;
(6) Terms that allow traders to explain the contract in case of different interpretation of the terms;
(7) Terms that exclude liability of traders in cases where traders sell goods or provide services through a third party;
(8) Terms that force consumers to comply with obligations even if the traders have not fulfilled their obligations;
(9) Terms that allow traders to transfer rights and obligations to third parties without the consumer's consent.

These controls apply to all consumer contracts, including standard form contracts. Consumers who find their consumer contracts to contain such provisions can request the court to declare these provisions invalid.

B. Standard Form Contracts

The Law on Consumer Protection of 2010 states that standard form contracts involving certain essential goods and services[23] shall be registered with the Vietnam Competition and Consumer Authority before being used. As reported by the Vietnam Competition and Consumer Authority, in 2016, there were 1,342[24] dossiers regarding standard form contracts filed by enterprises to this Authority for registration, of which 885 contained clauses harmful to consumers.[25] In recent years, the number of dossiers filed for registration has decreased: 857 (2017), 541 (2018) and 254 (2019). dossiers regarding standard form contracts filed by enterprises to the Vietnam Competition and Consumer Authority for registration.[26]

Enterprises using standard form contracts involving certain essential goods and services[27] without the approval of the Vietnam Competition and Consumer Authority shall be sanctioned with an administrative fine. Pursuant to Article 68 of Decree 185/2013/ND-CP, sanctions for the violation of rules concerning the

[23] Such as the supply of electricity or clean water for residential consumption; pay-TV; fixed telephone subscription; mobile phone subscription; Internet connection; air transport of passengers; rail transport of passengers; purchase and sale of apartments; life-insurance policy; issue of debit cards.

[24] Banks: 921; real estate companies selling apartments: 304; insurance companies:171; telecommunication providers: 40; water companies: five; electricity companies: one.

[25] Vietnam Competition and Consumer Authority, 'Annual Report of 2016', p 28.

[26] Vietnam Competition and Consumer Authority, 'Annual Report of 2017', p 33; Annual Report of 2019', p 47.

[27] See n 23.

registration of standard form contracts can be monetary fines and additional forms of penalties. Failing to comply with the requests of competent state agencies on cancellation or modification of the contents of standard form contracts that violate laws on the protection of consumer rights or are contrary to general principles on concluding contracts is punishable with a fine between VND 20–30 million (approximately USD 860–1300). In contrast, a fine between VND 30–50 million (approximately USD 1300–2160) shall be imposed on an enterprise that fails to register or re-register standard form contracts with the competent state management agency to protect the rights of consumers under regulations or fails to notify consumers about changing standard form contracts as prescribed.

Additional forms of penalties may also be imposed, such as depriving the violator of the business licences from one month to three months, or suspending the violator from operations from one month to three months.

Enterprises signing contracts with consumers which have unfair terms shall also be sanctioned with an administrative fine between VND 20–30 million in cases of using standard form contracts or from VND 10–20 million for other cases.[28] Enterprises operating in Hanoi and Ho Chi Minh city shall be even sanctioned with an administrative fine from VND 40–60 million in cases of using standard form contracts containing unfair terms or from VND 20–40 million for other cases.[29] In addition, violators are requested to pay back illicit gains from committing violations. In practice, no enterprises have been publicly reported to have had monetary fines imposed for signing contracts with consumers which have unfair terms.

V. Product Liability

Prior to the Law on Consumer Protection of 2010, consumers only had the right under the Civil Code of 2005 to claim in negligence compensation for damage caused by defective goods. Sales law does not explicitly cover losses of life (death) and personal injury. The Law on Consumer Protection of 2010 strengthens product liability law in Vietnam by applying strict liability for defective products. The EU Product Liability Directive[30] was certainly a source of reference and aspiration for Vietnamese lawmakers to design legal rules on product liability in the Law on Consumer Protection of 2010.

Article 23 of the Law on Consumer Protection of 2010 states that in principle 'traders'[31] shall be liable for damages in the case where defective goods, which are

[28] Decree 185/2013/ND-CP, Art 71.

[29] ibid.

[30] Council Directive 85/374/EEC of 25 July 1985 on the approximation of the laws, regulations and administrative provisions of the Member States concerning liability for defective products, OJ 195 No 210, p 29.

[31] Traders include (1) organisations or individuals producing goods; (2) organisations or individuals importing goods; (3) organisations or individuals attaching their trade name to goods or using the trademark or commercial instruction, by which organisations or individuals producing or importing goods are identified; (4) organisations or individuals directly providing defective goods to consumers in case of failure to identify organisations or individuals responsible for damages as prescribed in points a, b and c.

supplied by them, cause damage to life, health, properties of consumers, even if the defects are not known to or not caused by those organisations or individuals. Based on this provision, it is fair to state that personal injury or property damage caused by dangerous products can be recovered in strict liability. However, only 'actual damage' is compensated; punitive damage are not recognised in Vietnamese laws.

As for determining a 'defect', Article 3(3) of the Law on Consumer Protection of 2010 explains that 'defective goods' are goods that do not ensure the safety of consumers, which are likely to cause damage to the life, health and property of consumers, even though such goods are manufactured under current technical standards or norms, with no defects being detected at the time the goods are supplied to consumers. These include mass-produced goods with defects arising from an engineering design; single goods with defects arising from the production, processing, transportation and storage; and goods with the potential to deteriorate in safety during use, but with no adequate instructions or warning having been provided to consumers.

There are certain defences available to producers to exempt their liability. Article 24 of the Law on Consumer Protection of 2010 states that 'traders specified in Article 23 of this Law shall be exempt from compensation if they can prove that the defects of the good could not be detected with the scientific and technical knowledge at the time traders supplied the defective good to consumers'. This is the famous development risks defence that was made optional under the EU Product Liability Directive.[32]

Unfortunately, there are no cases before the courts in Vietnam in which the said provisions on product liability were applied.

VI. Product Safety

In the Vietnamese legal system, the 'Law on Quality of Goods and Products of 2007' provides for safety regulations for products. Articles 5 and 10 of this Law state that producers shall be responsible for the safety of their products. Producers shall inform distributors and consumers of the possibility that products may cause risks to their lives, health or property.

The Ministry of Science and Technology shall, in cooperation with other ministries, be responsible for maintaining the standards for the safety of products. However, the Ministry of Industry and Trade shall monitor the voluntary and mandatory recall of unsafe consumer goods (through the Vietnam Competition and Consumer Authority) and the Ministry of Public Health shall monitor the voluntary and mandatory recall of unsafe pharmaceutical products (through the Drug Administration of Vietnam).

As for the recall of unsafe/defective goods, Article 22 of the Law on Consumer Protection of 2010 states that upon detection of defective goods, producers or importers of the goods shall:

(1) Promptly take all necessary measures to stop the supply of defective goods in the market;

[32] Product Liability Directive (EU), Art 7(e).

(2) Inform publicly about the defective goods and the recall of the goods by placing notices in at least five consecutive issues of a daily newspaper or five consecutive days through the radio or television in the area where such goods are circulated with the following details:
   (a) Description of the goods to be recalled;
   (b) Reasons for recall of the goods and warning on the risk of damage caused by the defects of the goods;
   (c) Time, place and means of recall of the goods;
   (d) Time and mode of overcoming the defects of the goods;
   (e) The measures necessary to protect the interests of consumers in the course of recall of the goods;

(3) Implement the recall of the defective goods in line with the publicly-informed content and bear the expenses incurred in the recalling process;

(4) Report the results to the provincial Department of Industry and Trade after completion of the recall, in the case where the recall of the defective goods is conducted on the territories of two or more provinces, the results shall be reported to the Vietnam Competition and Consumer Authority.

As reported by the Vietnam Competition and Consumer Authority, in 2016, there were 33 voluntary recalls of unsafe consumer goods in Vietnam such as smartphones, laptops and cars, etc.[33] In 2017, there were 15 voluntary recalls of unsafe consumer goods in Vietnam such as motorbikes and cars.[34] In 2018, there were nine voluntary recalls of unsafe consumer goods in Vietnam such as laptops and cars, etc.[35] In 2019, there were four voluntary recalls of unsafe consumer goods in Vietnam such as laptops, cars and life jackets for children.[36]

VII. Adaption to the Digital Age

The Vietnamese legal system has certain special rules regarding consumer protection in e-commerce. Decree 52/2013/ND-CP dated 16 May 2013 provides special rules concerning consumers' personal information. Accordingly, where a trader engaged in e-commerce business activities authorises a third party to collect and store personal information of consumers, the contract between the two parties must clearly define the responsibility of each party to comply with the Decree 52/2013 and relevant regulations on the protection of personal information. If the contract between the two parties does not clearly define the responsibility of each party, the trader engaged in e-commerce business activities shall take full responsibility in case the collection, storage and use of personal information of consumers by the third party violates the Decree 52/2013 and relevant regulations on protection of personal information. In addition, traders

[33] Vietnam Competition and Consumer Authority, 'Annual Report of 2016', pp 24–27.
[34] Vietnam Competition and Consumer Authority, 'Annual Report of 2017', p 32.
[35] Vietnam Competition and Consumer Authority, 'Annual Report of 2018', p 38.
[36] Vietnam Competition and Consumer Authority, 'Annual Report of 2017', p 44.

that collect and use personal information of consumers shall formulate and announce their personal information protection policy with details on, inter alia, the purpose(s) of collection of personal information, the scope of information use, the duration of information storage, persons or organisations that may access such information, and the method and tools for consumers to access and modify their personal data on the e-commerce system of the information collection unit, etc. These details must be clearly displayed to consumers before or at the time of information collection. If the information collection is conducted through e-commerce websites of information collection units, the personal information protection policy must be publicly displayed at an easy-to-spot position on these websites.

Article 70 of the Decree 52/2013 also states that:

(1) Except for the cases specified in Clause 4 of this Article, traders … that collect and use personal information of consumers on their e-commerce websites ('information collection units') shall obtain the prior consent of consumers to have such information ('information subjects').
(2) Information collection units shall develop a mechanism for information subjects to express their consent explicitly through online functions on their websites, emails, messages, or otherwise as agreed upon by the two parties.
(3) Information collection units shall develop a separate mechanism for information subjects to choose to permit or not to permit the use of their personal information in the following cases:
    (a) Sharing, disclosure, or transfer of information to a third party;
    (b) Use of personal information for sending advertisements, product introductions, and other commercial information.
(4) Information collection units are not required to obtain the prior consent of information subjects in the following cases:
    (a) Collection of personal information already published on e-commerce websites;
    (b) Collection of personal information for concluding or performing goods and service purchase and sale contracts;
    (c) Collection of personal information for calculating prices or charges for use of information, products and services online.

Article 71 of the Decree 52/2013 requires information collection units shall use personal information of consumers for purposes and within the scope already notified, except in the following cases: (1) they have separate agreements with information subjects on the use, purpose, and scope other than those they have notified; (2) to provide services or products at the request of information subjects; (3) to perform the obligations prescribed by law. The use of information prescribed in this Article includes sharing, disclosure and transfer of personal information to third parties.

Violations related to consumers' personal information such as illegal collection and storage of consumers' personal information shall be fined up to VND 30 million per violation (as stipulated in Article 84 of the Decree 15/2020/ND-CP dated 3 February 2020 dealing with administrative violations against regulations on postal services, telecommunications, radio frequencies, information technology and electronic transactions). In practice, very few cases of handling violations of consumers' personal information are reported by the public media except for one case in Hanoi recently reported by a Vietnamese newspaper in which a person was fined VND 7.5 million (approximately USD 325) for collecting consumers' personal information without their prior consent.[37]

As for e-contracts and e-signature, Vietnam adopted the Law on Electronic Transactions in 2005 to facilitate electronic transactions. This Law is modelled on the UNCITRAL Model Law on Electronic Commerce of 1996. Accordingly, information in data messages cannot have its legal validity disclaimed for the sole reason that it is expressed in the form of messages. Where the law requires information to be in writing, a data message shall be considered having met this condition if the information contained therein is accessible and usable for reference when necessary. However, as for internet sales, the Vietnamese legal system does not offer any special rights for relevant parties, including consumers.

As for digital products, Vietnamese laws regarding this issue seem to be in a very early stage of development. There are almost no special rules regulating digital products.

VIII. Unfair Commercial Practices

The Vietnamese legal system does not offer a general unfairness standard to classify certain commercial practices as unfair. Instead, it lists specific commercial practices as unfair, especially misleading, or coercive. Unfair commercial practices are currently stipulated in Article 10 of the Law on Consumer Protection of 2010:

(1) Traders shall not deceive or mislead consumers by means of advertising or by hiding information or providing inadequate, inaccurate, or distorted information about any of the following:
   (a) goods and/or services supplied by those traders;
   (b) reputation, business capacity, or capacity to provide goods and/or services of those traders;
   (c) terms and characteristics of the transaction between consumers and those traders.
(2) Traders shall not harass consumers by means of marketing goods and/or services against the will of consumers on more than one occasion and shall not prevent consumers from carrying on the normal course of their work or lives.
(3) Traders shall not coerce consumers by means of the following behaviours:
   (a) employing force or threatening to use force or other means to cause harm to life, health, reputation, dignity, or property of consumers;
   (b) taking advantage of difficult circumstances of consumers or taking advantage of natural calamities or epidemics to coerce consumers into transactions.
(4) Traders shall not carry out trade promotion activities, or make offers to directly transact with persons having no civil capacity as stipulated by the civil laws.
(5) Traders shall not request consumers to pay for unsolicited goods and/or services.

[37] 'Xu phat 4 ca nhan, to chuc dung thong tin cua nguoi khac de quang cao' ('Imposing fines upon 4 individuals and organizations for using personal information for advertising'), thanhtra.com.vn, 10 September 2020.

The Law on Consumer Protection of 2010 allows consumers and consumer protection organisations to challenge unfair commercial practices.[38] However, this Law fails to see competitors as having any specific role in the enforcement of the Law on Consumer Protection.[39]

Unfair commercial practices are often sanctioned by administrative fines. For example, traders providing misleading information regarding their products or services shall be fined VND 20–30 million (approximately USD 870–1300) as stipulated by Article 66(2) of Decree 185/2013/ND-CP dated 15 November 2013. Traders conducting false advertisements can even be sanctioned with criminal penalties as stipulated in Article 197 of the Criminal Code of 2015 (with a maximum penalty of imprisonment for a term of three years). Traders who coerce consumers by employing force or threatening to use force or other means to cause harm to life, health, reputation, dignity or property, or who take advantage of difficult circumstances, natural disasters or epidemics will violate Article 10(3) of the Law on Consumer Protection of 2010 and shall be fined VND 10–30 million.[40]

In practice, several traders have been fined for conducting false advertising, or misleading advertising. For example, in 2017, the Vietnam Competition and Consumer Authority handled eight cases in which traders committed misleading advertisements.[41] In 2018, a company was fined VND 110 million (approximately USD 90,500) for misleading their consumers about their products (which were made in China, but stated as being made in Korea).[42]

IX. Access to Justice

Improving consumers' access to justice is one of the key purposes of drafting the Law on Consumer Protection of 2010 in Vietnam. Of the 51 articles in the Law on Consumer Protection of 2010, 17 stipulate channels for resolving disputes between consumers and traders. This significant number clearly shows the intention of the drafters of the Law on Consumer Protection to design a better self-help system for consumers in Vietnam. According to Article 30(1) of the Law on Consumer Protection 2010, disputes between consumers and traders can be resolved through four channels, namely, negotiation, mediation, arbitration and litigation.

[38] Law on Consumer Protection 2010, Arts 25, 31 and 41.

[39] However, it should be noted that, according to Art 58(1) of Vietnam's Competition Law of 2004, enterprises are entitled to lodge complaints with the Vietnam Competition and Consumer Authority when they deem their interests have been infringed by their competitors' violations of the Competition Law. Unfortunately, among unfair commercial practices prohibited by the Law on Consumer Protection of 2010, based on Art 45(3) of the Competition Law of 2004, enterprises can only lodge a complaint with the Vietnam Competition and Consumer Authority when they deem their interests have been infringed by their competitors' false or misleading advertisements.

[40] Art 79, Decree 185/2013/ND-CP.

[41] Vietnam Competition and Consumer Authority, 'Annual Report of 2017', p 17.

[42] ibid, p 27.

A. Negotiation

Article 31 of the Law on Consumer Protection of 2010 concerns negotiation. According to this provision, consumers have the right to submit a request to traders to negotiate when their legitimate rights or interests are deemed to be infringed upon. Traders are obliged to receive and negotiate with consumers for a period not exceeding seven working days after receipt of the request. The result of a successful negotiation between the traders and consumers shall be made in writing unless the parties otherwise agree.

B. Mediation

Traders and consumers have the right to agree to select a third party (an individual or organisation) to perform the mediation.[43] Mediation shall be conducted in the manner of objectivity, honesty, goodwill, and without use of force or deceit. Unless agreed otherwise or provided by law, the parties participating in the mediation must ensure confidentiality of information relating to the mediation. Minutes of the mediation must contain the following principal contents: names and addresses of the mediators, the parties, content, time and place, the opinions of the parties, the results of the mediation as well as the duration for their implementation. The minutes of mediation must be signed by the parties and the signature for confirmation of the organisation or individual conducting the mediation. The parties are responsible for implementing the results of successful mediation within the agreed period prescribed in the minutes of the mediation; in cases where one party does not implement voluntarily, the other party shall have the right to sue in court for settlement in accordance with laws.[44]

In practice, several disputes between consumers and traders are submitted to local consumer protection associations or the national consumer association (Vietnam Consumers Protection Association – VICOPRO) for mediation. According to Mr Nguyen Manh Hung (chairman of Vietnam Consumers Protection Association), from 2011 to 2017, local consumer protection associations and VICOPRO (formerly VINASTAS) received 10,745 consumer complaints. Approximately 80 per cent of these complaints were successfully settled through mediation (between consumers and traders) offered by consumer protection associations.[45]

C. Arbitration

Article 38 of the Law on Consumer Protection of 2010 acknowledges that disputes between consumers and traders can be resolved through arbitration.[46] Arbitration

[43] Law on Consumer Protection, Art 33.

[44] ibid, Art 37.

[45] Truong Duc Nhan, 'Nang cao ky nang giai quyet khieu nai cua nguoi tieu dung' ('Enhancing skills for handling consumer complaints'), sct.bacgiang.gov.vn, 29 October 2019.

[46] It is worth noting that arbitration is currently governed by the Law on Commercial Arbitration (which replaced the Ordinance on Commercial Arbitration of 2003). According to Arts 24 and 25 of this Law, arbitration centres have to receive advance permission from the Minister of Justice for establishment and they can only start to operate upon registration with provincial Departments of Justice.

clauses in standard form contracts are not binding on consumers, however.[47] At present, there are no reports by the public media or Vietnamese authorities of disputes between consumers and traders that have been resolved through arbitration.

D. Litigation

The Law on Consumer Protection features two major new provisions which are seen as being favourable to consumers.[48] The first is the provision of a 'simplified civil procedure' applicable to a number of simple lawsuits brought by individual consumers. The second is the provision on the right of consumer protection organisations (or social organisations participating in consumer protection activities) to bring legal actions against offending traders without express written authorisation from consumers.

The introduction of a 'simplified civil procedure' applicable to a number of lawsuits brought by individual consumers is seen as an effort to remove unreasonable legal barriers and enhance consumers' access to justice. Article 41(2) of the Law on Consumer Protection 2010 stipulates that simplified civil procedure will be applied to lawsuits brought by consumers when these lawsuits meet all three of the following conditions:

(1) The plaintiff is an individual consumer and the defendant is a trader directly supplying goods and/or services to the plaintiff;
(2) The lawsuits are simple, with clear evidence; and
(3) The value of the transaction is equal to or less than VND 100 million (approximately USD 4,500).[49]

Given the above-mentioned provision, the Law on Consumer Protection does not create a new specialised court within the current court system. Instead, the current court system still assumes the task of resolving disputes between consumers and traders. However, in lawsuits meeting the above three conditions, a simplified rather than normal civil procedure will be applied, with the hope that this simplified procedure will help resolve lawsuits more swiftly. Unfortunately, 'simplified civil procedure' is not found in the Code of Civil Procedure of 2004 (as amended in 2011). The said provisions were not put into operation until the new Code of Civil Procedure of 2015 came into force on 1 July 2016. However, after four years from the time at which the Code of Civil Procedure of 2015 took effect (that is, 1 July 2020), there were no cases brought by consumers to the court system by applying the simplified civil procedure.

[47] Law on Consumer Protection, Art 38. A similar provision can also be found in Art 17 of the Law on Commercial Arbitration of 2010.

[48] Other important provisions include the provision to exempt plaintiffs in lawsuits brought by consumers from the obligation to advance court fees, and the provision to shift the burden of proof from plaintiffs (consumers or consumer protection organisations) to defendants (accused offending traders). Specifically, Art 43(2) of the Law on Consumer Protection states that 'consumers bringing lawsuits to protect their rights and legitimate interests are exempted from advancing the court fees'. In addition, Art 42(2) of the Law on Consumer Protection (Vietnam) states that 'traders shall prove to be faultless in causing damage to consumers'.

[49] Law on Consumer Protection, Art 41(2).

As for lawsuits initiated by consumer protection organisations/associations, Article 44 of the Law on Consumer Protection of 2010 states that consumer protection organisations shall be responsible for informing publicly by appropriate forms of legal action and shall take responsibility for the information they publish, ensuring no impact on the normal operation of organisations or individuals trading goods and/or services. Information is to be provided on the consumer protection organisations initiating the lawsuits, the traders being sued, the legal basis and the procedures and deadline for registering to join the case. Within three working days after the case is filed with the court, the court shall publicly post at the courthouse the information about this filing. According to Article 45 of the Law on Consumer Protection of 2010, verdicts and decisions by the Court to settle the civil case being brought by consumer protection organisations must be publicly posted at the office of the Court and publicised on the mass media using appropriate forms. Money in compensation for damages in civil cases being brought by consumer protection organisations by virtue of the public interest shall comply with the verdict or decision of the Court.

The legislative wisdom of drafting provisions in the Law on Consumer Protection promoting the use of the court system by consumers and consumer protection organisations to assert their rights against offending businesses is still a matter of debate. As many previous studies show, litigation is generally not a preferred method of dispute resolution in Vietnam.[50] The lengthy and time-consuming litigation system has perhaps not won over Vietnamese consumers to bring their cases to be settled before the court, especially for consumer goods of low monetary value. In addition, as the current court system has several problems in terms of both its caseload and its competence, whether this legislative decision actually benefits consumers is doubtful. It is not surprising that at present, almost no disputes between consumers and traders were reported to be settled before the courts. Consumer associations have not initiated any legal suits to challenge offending traders.

X. Conclusion

It is reasonable to conclude that consumer protection laws have been strengthened in Vietnam in recent years, especially since 2011. The establishment of a mechanism for control of standard form consumer contracts from 2012 and several other activities conducted by the Vietnam Competition and Consumer Authority (especially handling hundreds of consumer complaints each year) are signals of better consumer protection in Vietnam. In addition, the number of consumer complaints reported to the Vietnam Competition and Consumer Authority has recently increased. For example, this Authority received only approximately 200 consumer complaints in 2013, but 1,313 in 2017.[51] However, weak enforcement remains a fact. Many consumers still feel that

[50] See P Nicholson, *Borrowing Court Systems: The Experience of Socialist Vietnam* (Leiden: Martinus Nijhoff, 2007) 269–72.

[51] Vietnam Competition and Consumer Authority, 'Annual Report of 2017', p 29.

their problematic experiences in markets have not been fully addressed by the current legal system and the effort from the competent authorities. The low rate of lawsuits and complaints officially lodged by consumers before the courts and the Vietnam Competition and Consumer Authority also shows that consumers have not placed their high trust in these formal institutions as an effective means of protecting their interests. This shows that an effective consumer protection system in Vietnam is still in a very early stage of development. The use of administrative fines and control for transactions between traders and consumers is also a visible feature of the current consumer protection system in Vietnam.

PART 3

Comparative Analysis

15

Information Duties and the Right of Withdrawal

MEIKA ATKINS AND EILEEN WEBB

I. Introduction

Regulatory regimes focused on consumer contracting express core social values of fairness and liberalisation; they support market efficiency by promoting trust and honesty between consumers and traders in the consumer market. The opening of a globalised consumer market and the increased use of standardised contracts has seen the emergence of a series of market inefficiencies, including an 'information asymmetry'[1] between consumers and traders, and increasing use of novel marketing techniques that impact consumer rights and decision-making.[2] To address these inefficiencies, many countries have enacted reforms that seek to mandate the disclosure of information to consumers ('consumer information laws'); and empower consumers to withdraw from particular contracts ('withdrawal rights').

Throughout Asia, the last decade has witnessed a considerable uplift in economic integration both between ASEAN member states and other economies in the Asian region and beyond. Particularly within ASEAN, this has seen some degree of harmonisation of minimum standards of consumer protection laws. However, as Nottage notes, 'diversity among member states (demographics, economic development, legal and political systems, NGOs and press freedom) can influence the timing and extent of consumer law reform and implementation in each country'.[3] This statement applies equally to other non-ASEAN nations discussed in this book. As such, while there are many parallels between consumer protection laws of the nations under consideration – and, indeed, some mirroring among some the ASEAN member states – consistent implementation of consumer protection regimes will depend

[1] G Straetsman, 'Introduction' in G Straetsman (ed), *Information and Disinformation* (Cham: Springer, 2019) 6.

[2] For example, the rise of e-commerce and direct sales has identified shortcomings in some consumer protection legislation.

[3] L Nottage, 'Introduction: Backdrop and Overarching Perspectives' in L Nottage et al (eds), *ASEAN Consumer Law Harmonisation and Cooperation: Achievements and Challenges* (Cambridge: Cambridge University Press, 2019) 52.

on the particular nation's competing economic priorities. It is therefore likely that laws will continue to differ between jurisdictions in terms of content, standards and recourse.[4]

This chapter discusses the key consumer information laws and withdrawal rights that emerge from the national consumer frameworks considered in this book. The body of the chapter commences by discussing the rationale underpinning consumer information laws and withdrawal rights (Section II). The chapter then evaluates the formulation and operation of the key consumer information laws and withdrawal rights emerging in the relevant national frameworks (Sections III–V). The chapter will then conclude with some general observations about future challenges ahead (Section VI).

II. The Rationale for Information Duties and Rights of Withdrawal

A. Information Duties

In an age of standard form contracts, consumers are invariably at a disadvantage in relation to bargaining power and information regarding a product or service. The rationale for information duties is based on fairness and convenience; a consumer should have the opportunity to make an informed choice in relation to a purchase, and the supplier (having a considerable depth of knowledge about its own product or service) is best placed, from a perspective of efficiency and convenience, to provide this information.[5] The aspiration to balance this asymmetry, so far as is possible, can be addressed through mandatory information duties within the legislation of particular jurisdictions. In other cases, terms may be incorporated expressly within the contract or implied into the terms of the contract by legislation. Information laws cannot be precisely attributed to any single intended policy objective.[6] Some consumer information laws – such as those emerging in the context of product safety and liability, and misleading and deceptive conduct – clearly point to individual policy objectives of protecting consumers from harmful or hazardous products and the provision of misleading information, respectively. Other consumer information laws – such as those emerging in specific contexts and industries – seek to promote a broader, more complex range of policy objectives which are often dependent on the individual challenges facing each jurisdiction.[7]

[4] J Paterson, 'Regulating Consumer Contracts in ASEAN: Variation and Change', in Nottage et al, ibid, 205 et seq.

[5] E Tscherner, 'Can Behavioral Research Advance Mandatory Law, Information Duties, Standard Terms and Withdrawal Rights?' (2014) 1 *Austrian Law Journal* 144 at 148.

[6] Paterson, 'Regulating Consumer Contracts', 210 et seq.

[7] For example, as highlighted by H Hirose, KF Lenz and T Shiraishi, 'Japan', in this volume. Japan's recognition of pre-contractual information duties emerged as a government initiative aimed at protecting Japan's aging population; and the rising number of ordinary consumers entering the speculative financial market.

B. Withdrawal Rights

Despite information disclosure obligations, products simply may not meet expectations, not function as anticipated (or at all) or for some other reason the consumer may seek to withdraw from the contract and obtain a refund of the purchase price. In some contexts, they may have felt pressured by selling techniques to enter into the contract, this is often considered problematic in the context of doorstep selling. In the past, and in some jurisdictions even today, there is no obligation to permit the consumer to withdraw from the contract unless permitted to do so by contract. In other cases, withdrawal can only be effected where, for example, the goods are faulty or in need of repair, not because of aesthetic preferences or a consumer's change of mind. Depending on the nature of the product, there may be a cooling-off period or a contractual or statutory provision providing that goods can be returned within a particular time frame and a refund obtained.[8]

III. General Information Duties and Rights

While most consumer law legislation in the jurisdictions considered in this book provide for general obligations and prohibitions in relation to the supply of information, several jurisdictions, particularly within ASEAN, have adopted a dichotomy similar to that utilised in the Australian Consumer Law. Therefore, as well as a general provision against providing misleading information, several jurisdictions list specific 'variations on the same theme' being more discrete forms of misrepresentation. Furthermore, some types of transactions are regarded as requiring targeted provisions to address shortcomings in information provision. Examples include food labelling, product warnings and direct sales. For varying reasons, such transactions are regarded as requiring a special focus in legislation to address the importance of the areas from a health and safety perspective or simply to ensure that the law has 'caught up' with new forms of commerce.[9]

Table 1 Trader information duties in consumer contracts

General	*Specific*	*Specific*
	In relation to varied scenarios that may amount to misleading or unfair conduct	Legislative provisions that focus on particular conduct or industries

[8] China, Japan, Malaysia, Singapore, Taiwan, Thailand and Vietnam have each introduced some form of statutory withdrawal right into their consumer frameworks; other countries, such as India, Indonesia, Hong Kong, Macau and Myanmar are still yet to enact any statutory rights of withdrawal. Even where countries have enacted specific withdrawal rights, the availability, requirements and prescribed cooling-off periods differ considerably between jurisdictions. See s V for discussion.

[9] S Galasintu, S Supanit and C Chaiittivej, 'The Issue of Direct Sales and Direct Marketing Law and Enforcement in Thailand: A Comparative Study of the Relevant UK and Malaysia Laws' (2018) 39(2) *Kasetsart Journal of Social Sciences* 328 at 329.

The general and specific dichotomy has been adopted in several jurisdictions. Therefore, while there may be a general 'catch-all' provision, many jurisdictions also provide a 'checklist' – of varying length and complexity – listing specific examples of misleading or unfair conduct. Other legislation goes further and addresses discrete conduct or industries.[10] See Table 1. There is no example of a broad duty to provide information in all contexts as found in European law.[11]

A. Recognised Pre-contractual Duties

Pre-contractual information duties and labelling regulations are some of the earliest information obligations adopted to protect consumers. These laws, together with the prohibition of misleading, or in some cases, unfair conduct and contract transparency provisions, seek to protect consumers by preventing businesses from engaging in dishonest and deceptive behaviour. Broadly speaking, the most widely recognised pre-contractual duties emerge from the various misleading and unfair conduct provisions and product information requirements.

i. Misleading and Unfair Conduct

As Straetsman notes, 'prohibiting misleading information and informing consumers with correct information lies at the core of the so-called information paradigm which resulted in consumer information models across the world'.[12] As such, many countries discussed in this book have legislated to impose restrictions on traders engaging in misleading or unfair conduct provisions, either through direct prohibition[13] or affirming a consumer's right to receive accurate and truthful information.[14] Such provisions may be general in nature, for example, a broad prohibition of misleading or unfair practices. General information duties are commonly used to assist in filling the gaps in developing frameworks and pre-emptively allow for new and increasingly complex cases.[15] Even so, some jurisdictions are yet to enact any laws that direct information provision; however, the provision of information in those jurisdictions is still guided

[10] The scope of this chapter prevents a complete examination of all examples in this category. Some areas regarded as of considerable significance will be outlined.

[11] See Art 5 of Directive 2011/83/EU of the European Parliament and of the Council of 25 October 2011 on consumer rights, OJ 2011 No L204, p 64. Whereas Art 6 contains the information requirements for distance and off-premises contracts, Art 5 concerns the information requirements for contracts other than distance or off-premises contracts.

[12] Straetsman, 'Introduction', 6.

[13] Consumer Protection Act 1999 (Malaysia), ss 9–10; Consumer Protection Law 2014 (Myanmar), ss 9–14; Consumer Protection (Fair Trading) Act (Singapore), s 4(a); The Law on the Protection of Consumer Rights and Interests 2013 (China), Art 20; Law on Protection of Consumer Rights 2010 (Vietnam), Art 10.

[14] Law No 8 of 1999 on Consumer Protection (Indonesia), Arts 7, 9–11; Consumer Protection Law 2014 (Myanmar), s 6(a)(iii); Consumer Protection Act 1979 (Thailand), ss 4(1), 22; Law on Protection of Consumer Rights 2010 (Vietnam), Arts 8, 10.

[15] See, eg, Consumer Protection Act 1999 (Malaysia) and the Competition and Consumer Act 2010 (Cth) (Australia), Schedule 2.

by the general principles of contract law, which are generally understood to comprise a duty of information.[16]

While some jurisdictions have developed discrete consumer laws crafted for the unique requirements of a particular nation,[17] most consumer law in jurisdictions discussed in this chapter is a hybrid mix of civil[18] or common law received through colonial occupation[19] or through adoption of legal influences after consideration of external legal systems,[20] responses to internal and regional events and specific consumer law precedent drawn primarily from the European Union and Australia. This can be seen in the varying use of some fundamental terminology across the jurisdictions. Indeed, Paterson highlights that the common law interpretation on the prohibitions on misleading conduct in Singapore draw extensively from Australian case law[21] while the term 'unfair practices' resembles the threshold requirement set out in the EU Unfair Commercial Practices Directive.[22]

Australia has adopted a general provision that addresses misleading or deceptive conduct in trade or commerce.[23] There are also general provisions regarding unconscionable conduct that encompass consumer transactions.[24] The Australian Consumer Law also includes specific prohibitions of discrete forms of false or misleading conduct in a variety of circumstances that will be discussed in Section IV.A below.[25] This has been adopted in several jurisdictions. Consumer protection laws in Malaysia[26] and Myanmar[27] contain a general provision addressing misleading or deceptive conduct which reflects provisions found in the Australian Consumer Law.[28] In Japan, the Act Against Unjustifiable Premiums and Misleading Representations prohibits misleading and deceptive claims that induce the purchase of goods.[29]

[16] For example, Macau's current consumer framework is in its early stages and is less comprehensive than neighbouring jurisdictions. Macau's current framework is still in its early stages and has not yet expressed any direct information obligations or rights, however, the provision of Macau's consumer laws are underscored by the contract law general principle of good faith provided for in Article 219 of the Civil Code 1999.

[17] For example, China.

[18] Examples include Dutch settlement in Indonesia and French settlement in Thailand that introduced civil law. When Japan 'opened' to the West during the Meiji Restoration commencing in 1868, representatives examined several prospective legal systems and primarily, adopted the French model for civil law.

[19] For example, the British common law influence in Hong Kong. It is important to note that not all jurisdictions experienced colonial rule, for example, Japan.

[20] For example, during the Meiji Restoration (1868), Japanese officials travelled abroad and considered a variety of legal systems with a view to adopting systems best suited to an independent nation. These representatives examined and introduced European (primarily French and German, but also some British) elements into the legal system.

[21] Paterson, 'Regulating Consumer Contracts', 213 with reference to *Freely Pte Ltd v Ong Kaili* [2010] 2 SLR 1065.

[22] See Art 5 of Directive 2005/29/EC of the European Parliament and of the Council of 11 May 2005 concerning unfair business-to-consumer commercial practices in the internal market, OJ 2005 No L149, p 22.

[23] Competition and Consumer Act 2010 (Cth) (Australia), Schedule 2, s 18. For detail see G Pearson, 'Australasia', in this volume.

[24] ibid, ss 20–21.

[25] ibid, s 29.

[26] Consumer Protection Act 1999 (Malaysia), Part II, ss 8–9.

[27] Consumer Protection Law 2019 (Myanmar), ss 9–10 and 13–14.

[28] Note that these provisions also refer to unfair practices.

[29] It seems that there was far less Australian influence in the design of the Japanese legislation: M Morimoto, 'Japanese Consumer Rights' in P Haghirian (ed), *Routledge Handbook of Japanese Business and Management* (London: Routledge, 2016) 251.

However, the term 'unfair' is also used widely in the sense of 'unfair practices' either in addition to references to misleading conduct or as a discrete element.[30] This is significant because the concepts of 'misleading' and 'unfair' can differ and, in Australia at least, there has been resistance to the use of the term 'unfair' because of concerns regarding certainty.[31] Nevertheless, in practice, the conduct to which the terms apply seem to be used interchangeably. For example, in Brunei, Article 4 of the Consumer Protection (Fair Trading) Order 2011 defines an unfair practice as including, inter alia, references to the consumer being misled or deceived or the supplier making false claims.[32] Similarly, Singapore's Consumer Protection (Fair Trading) Act provides that an unfair practice includes conduct that misleads, deceives or is false.[33] Unfairness can also be demonstrated in the Malaysian legislation, inter alia where the circumstances under which the contract was entered into results in unjust advantage to a supplier or unjust disadvantage to a consumer.[34] Other terms used within the legislation in various jurisdictions include information that is false,[35] aggressive or incorrect.[36] Japan's Consumer Contract Act refers to aggressive practices that are specifically defined, for example, duress.[37]

Of course, conduct may also mislead or be unfair to a consumer where there is a lack of disclosure rather than an overt misrepresentation. Therefore, liability for omissions or non-disclosure is often expressly embedded in consumer legislation.[38]

In this respect, Singapore has explicitly prohibited omissions which amount to misleading and deceptive conduct.[39] Furthermore, Singapore's legislation also implies liability for omissions in Schedule II by, inter alia, prohibiting the concealment of onerous or material terms in small print.[40] Similarly, Hong Kong's Trade Descriptions Ordinance contains an obligation not to omit or conceal material information, fail to identify material information or fail to identify commercial intent.[41]

[30] For example, proposed legislation in Macau also refers to 'aggressive practices'.

[31] Consumer Action Law Centre, 'Unfair trading and Australia's Consumer Protection Laws', Discussion Paper (July 2015), 4.

[32] Consumer Protection (Fair Trading) Order 2011 (Brunei). Note that Schedule 2 of this Act lists specific unfair practices similar to those found in the Australian Consumer Law.

[33] Consumer Protection (Fair Trading) Act (Singapore), s 4. See *Freely Pte Ltd v Ong Kaili* [2010] 2 SLR 1065 where the Australian interpretation of 'misleading' conduct was applied by the court.

[34] Consumer Protection Act 1999 (Malaysia), s 24C.

[35] Contract Law of the People's Republic of China, Art 42(2).

[36] See for example Law No 8 of 1999 on Consumer Protection (Indonesia), Part IV.

[37] Consumer Contract Act (Japan), s 4(3): 'A consumer may rescind …, if the consumer manifested that intention as a result of being overwhelmed by any of the following acts taken by the trader in soliciting the consumer to enter into the consumer contract. The provisions then list prohibited acts of the trader, for example s 4(v): while knowing that a consumer is overly worried about maintaining their current life with respect to livelihoods, health and other matters because their decision-making capacity is extremely low due to aging or mental and physical disorders, the trader takes advantage of the situation, prompts their fears and although there are no reasonable grounds for supporting solicitation nor any other rational basis, the trader states that it will be difficult for the consumer to maintain their current life unless the consumer enters into the contract'.

[38] It is noteworthy that Macau's legislation imposes liability for omissions only in the context of food labelling, Decree-Law No 50/92/M, Art 19(3).

[39] Consumer Protection (Fair Trading) Act (Singapore), s 4(a).

[40] ibid, Schedule II, No 20.

[41] Trade Descriptions Ordinance (Hong Kong), s 13E.

Some legislation differs in relation to deliberate rather than inadvertent omissions. In Brunei, an unfair practice in relation to a consumer transaction includes to do or say anything or omit to do or say anything if, as a result, a consumer might be deceived or misled.[42] Again, this would appear to include circumstances where the omission was inadvertent. However, under India's new Consumer Protection Act 2019, the definition of the term 'deficiency' was extended with the addition of 'any act of negligence or omission or commission by such person which causes loss or injury to the consumer; and deliberate withholding of relevant information by such person to the consumer'.[43] Therefore, prohibiting intentional omissions of relevant details, or any omission that damages consumers. Similarly, under Chinese law, a party may be liable for damage if, in concluding a contract and causing losses to the other party, the first party deliberately concealed important facts relating to the conclusion of the contract.[44] These provisions impose liability on parties who intentionally omit to provide important details; however, it does not appear to extend to unintentional omissions.[45] Pursuant to reforms in 2018, Japan's Consumer Contract Act provides that a consumer can revoke their obligations under the contract where there has been gross negligence on the part of the trader.[46]

Article 10 of Vietnam's Law on Consumer Protection of 2010 seems to consider the circumstances in which the omission occurred. Article 10 explicitly prohibits traders from 'hiding or providing information that is incomplete, false, or inaccurate about one of the following details: (a) the goods or services offered; (b) reputation, business ability, and ability to provide the goods or services offered; (c) the contents or characteristics of the contract'.[47] The term 'hiding' impliedly prohibits traders from intentionally or fraudulently omitting information. Prohibiting the provision of 'incomplete, false or inaccurate' information effectively prohibits traders from making representations which might be half-true, completely untrue or otherwise mislead consumers, even when done so unintentionally.[48]

Some jurisdictions focus specifically on advertising rather than conduct generally. For example, the pertinent provisions in Chinese legislation prohibit false or misleading advertising and explicitly recognise the pre-contractual duties required of advertisers.[49] This includes an obligation on advertisers to provide correct information in advertisements in relation to the goods' function, origins, usage, quality, ingredients and price.[50] As Jing notes in the Chinese national report, Article 20 of the Law on the Protection of Consumer Rights and Interests 2013 is one of the most widely applied articles in consumer contract disputes, according to case data from the PKU Law Database,

[42] Consumer Protection (Fair Trading) Order 2011 (Brunei), s 4.
[43] Consumer Protection Act 2019 (India), s 2(11).
[44] Contract Law of the People's Republic of China, Art 42(2).
[45] ibid, Art 42(2).
[46] Note that prior to this reform, fraudulent concealment or deceit was required: Morimoto, 'Japanese Consumer Rights', at Section 4.
[47] Law on Consumer Protection of 2010 (Vietnam), Art 10. See also Law No 8 1999 (Indonesia) which sets out a range of more specific provisions addressing misleading advertisements.
[48] ibid.
[49] Law on the Protection of Consumer Rights and Interests 2013 (China), Art 20.
[50] ibid, Art 10.

showing that pre-contractual information liability is an important factor of consumer disputes in judicial practice.

In Thailand, the Consumer Protection Act 1979 provides a broad definition of 'advertisements'[51] requiring that applicable advertisements not contain any statement which is considered to be unfair to consumers or which may harm society as a whole.[52] Vietnam has a similar provision set out in Article 10 of the Law on Consumer Protection of 2010 which explicitly prohibits traders from deceiving or misleading consumers via advertising activities, or hiding or providing information that is incomplete, false or inaccurate about one of the following details: (a) goods and/or services that traders provided; (b) reputation, business ability, and ability to provide goods and/or services of traders; and (c) the contents and characteristics of the transaction between consumers and traders.[53]

Complementary, but more specific, regulation can be found in Vietnam's Law on Advertising 2012.[54] In India, the unfair trade practices provisions discussed above are complemented by quite specific prohibitions regarding false and misleading advertisements.[55] Indonesia's Law No 8 specifically regulates advertising in relation to the production of misleading, incorrect or exploitative advertisements. This is also applicable to the advertisement of medicine or health-related products in stipulated circumstances.[56] Furthermore, in South Korea, the Act on Fair Labelling and Advertising prohibits advertisements for products and services that deceive or mislead consumers.[57] Four categories of unfair advertising are addressed being false or exaggerated advertising, deceptive advertising, unfairly comparative advertising and slanderous advertising.[58]

ii. *Duty to Inform/Right to be Informed*

Article 8 of China's Law on the Protection of Consumer Rights and Interests gives consumers the right to 'obtain true information' about the goods or services they receive and 'demand from business operators' information on a range of matters relating to the price, manufacture, production and operation of the goods and services. Article 13 also gives consumers the right to obtain education.[59] This is defined separately in Chapter II of the legislation, and indirectly provides consumers with the right to be provided relevant information.[60] Articles 20 and 21 of the Law on the Protection of Consumer Rights

[51] Consumer Protection Act 1979 (Thailand), s 3.
[52] ibid, s 22.
[53] See also Law No 8 of 1999 on Consumer Protection (Indonesia), Arts 9–11 which includes a range of more specific provisions addressing misleading advertisements.
[54] Law on Advertising 2012 (Vietnam).
[55] Consumer Protection Act 2019 (India), ss 2(1) and (28).
[56] For example, where the goods or services are promoted by the promise of certain prizes.
[57] Act on Fair Labelling and Advertising Act (South Korea), Art 3(1).
[58] The characteristics of each of these categories is discussed in the South Korean national report in this volume.
[59] Law on the Protection of Consumer Rights and Interests 2013 (China), Art 13.
[60] Q Lu, 'The Information Duties of Consumer Protection Law' (2014) 8 *Tsinghua University Law Journal* 156.

and Interests 2013 address the most commonly invoked – pre-contractual information duties in the Law. Article 20 explicitly lists the important types of pre-contractual information in practice, including but not limited to information on the quality, performance, use and validity period of goods or services. Information provided by sellers must be true and also provides for comprehensive information to be provided to consumers.[61]

Similarly, India's Consumer Protection Act 2019 provides consumers with 'the right to be informed' about the quality, quantity, potency, purity, standard and price of goods or services.[62] India also has various pieces of specific legislation addressing specific products and sectors of the economy. The legislation provides detail on mandatory information that, in such instances, must be disclosed to the consumer.[63] Similarly, Taiwan addresses the provision of general consumer information in Articles 22–26 of the Consumer Protection Act in relation to inter alia advertising, and labelling. There are also specific disclosure provisions in relation to health and safety,[64] standard contracts[65] and door to door sales.[66]

In Myanmar, general information obligations are expressed as duties of the seller or entrepreneur. Section 21 of the Consumer Protection Law 2019 states that entrepreneurs must give clear and proper information on conditions and warranties of goods or services and letting the consumer know the additional payment relating to goods or services before purchasing.[67] Though largely general in nature, Myanmar's consumer law reflects duties similar to the express rights exhibited in Vietnam. Vietnam's Law on Consumer Protection of 2010 provides that consumers have a general right to receive 'accurate and complete information about traders; contents of contract; the source and origin of goods; … and other necessary information about goods and/or services that the consumer purchases and/or uses'.[68] This imposes an implied obligation on sellers to ensure the accuracy of information in relation to those subject matters; and to provide consumers with any information that might be material, both pre-contractually and once the contract has been entered into.[69]

In comparison, Thailand's Consumer Protection Act explicitly acknowledges the right to be informed and the right to a fair contract.[70] For the right to be informed before the conclusion of a contract, the Consumer Protection Act provides a broad definition of advertisements and requires that advertisements not contain any statement considered unfair to consumers or which may adversely affect society as a whole. Plus, said advertisements shall not be implemented by a method which may be harmful to health or cause physical or mental harm or annoyance to consumers. Thirdly, it

[61] Law on the Protection of Consumer Rights and Interests 2013 (China), Art 20.
[62] Consumer Protection Act 2019 (India), s 2(9), (47).
[63] ibid.
[64] Consumer Protection Act (Taiwan), Arts 7–10-1.
[65] ibid, Arts 11–17-1.
[66] ibid, Arts 18–21.
[67] Consumer Protection Law 2019 (Myanmar), s 21.
[68] Law on Consumer Protection of 2010 (Vietnam), Art 8(2).
[69] Post-contractually, it is likely this obligation would most likely arise when a product is found to be defective.
[70] Consumer Protection Act (Thailand), s 4.

is the business's duty to provide consumers with information in the form of purchase documents.[71] Furthermore, the Committee on Contract has the power to issue the rules prescribing terms, conditions and forms of contracts. The Thai Consumer Protection Act explicitly acknowledges the right to be informed and the right to a fair contract.[72]

Indonesia's Law No 8 protects the right of consumers to obtain correct, clear and honest information on the condition and warranty of the goods and/or services.[73] Further, the Law provides for additional responsibilities on a business actor, for example, a manufacturer/importer that sells goods to other business actors such as retailers/sellers, to ensure accordance with the sample, quality and composition originally stated.

Finally, in Japanese private law, there is a basic principle of private autonomy with the idea of self-responsibility that has been assumed under the Civil Code.[74] Therefore, no general contract law provisions on 'duty to inform' are provided in the Civil Code. The Consumer Basic Act 2004 seeks to provide for consumer rights with regard to the provision of information by suppliers and marketers.[75] Some provision for information duties can also be found in the public law. For example, the Act against Unjustifiable Premiums and Misleading Representations provides for regulations against misleading advertising and representation practices relating to quality and content, price and other misleading, designated representations.[76]

IV. Specific Information Duties and Rights

A. Misleading or Unfair Conduct

Chapter 3 of the Australian Consumer Law refers to specific protections with Part 3-1 referring to unfair practices. Section 29(1)(a)–(n) enumerates specific types of false or misleading representations that may contravene the legislation.[77] Other more specific representations are identified in relation to land,[78] employment,[79] the nature of goods or services,[80] bait advertising[81] and incentives such as rebates and prizes.[82]

Some jurisdictions have adopted provisions that more or less adopt some or all of these provisions, in particular, the factors identified in section 29 of the Australian

[71] Direct Sales and Direct Marketing Act (Thailand), ss 30–32.
[72] Consumer Protection Act (Thailand), s 4.
[73] Law No 8 of 1999 on Consumer Protection (Indonesia).
[74] The reformed Civil Code of 2017 stipulates the principle more clearly in Art 521.
[75] Morimoto, 'Japanese Consumer Rights', at Section 4.
[76] Act against Unjustifiable Premiums and Misleading Representations (Japan), Art 5.
[77] Note that there are other elements that must be established, for example that the transaction must be in trade or commerce and that the conduct involves the promotion or supply of goods or services.
[78] Competition and Consumer Act 2010 (Cth) (Australia), Schedule 2, s 30.
[79] ibid, s 31.
[80] ibid, ss 33–34.
[81] ibid, s 35.
[82] ibid, s 32.

Consumer Law. For example, Malaysia's Consumer Protection Act 1999 and Indonesia's Law No 8 have specific misleading and deceptive conduct provisions which reflect those found in the Australian Consumer Law.[83] Similarly, Myanmar features a number of provisions targeted at misleading and deceptive conduct,[84] including misleading consumers about the price or quality of their goods[85] or selling substituted goods[86]

In Brunei, an unfair practice is defined as including, inter alia, references to the consumer being misled or deceived or the supplier making false claims.[87] Schedule 2 lists specific unfair practices similar to those found in the Australian Consumer Law. Similarly, Singapore's Consumer Protection (Fair Trading) Act provides the meaning of an 'unfair practice'.[88] In this context, an unfair practice includes conduct that misleads, deceives or is false. Schedule 2 of this Act also provides a blacklist of 24 specific unfair practices. Such practices include: misrepresenting particular characteristics of the goods or services, including with respect to: quality,[89] origin,[90] condition[91] or price;[92] and making false or misleading representations concerning the need for any goods or services.[93] Most recently, India's Consumer Protection Act 2019 has enhanced protections in relation to various unfair trade practices.[94] Like Singapore, this includes promotion of the sale, use or supply of any good or service including matters such as quality, price, standard and composition.[95]

B. Product Labelling

Accurate and adequate information on product labels is an essential safeguard for consumers in order to provide choice and safeguard health and safety. Misleading information on labels are subject to the reach of the general and specific on unfair representations although some jurisdictions, for example, South Korea, refer specifically to misleading information in product labelling.[96] While some jurisdictions require that general requirements be applied to all labelling,[97] some simply place requirements within broader disclosure requirements[98] or provide for labelling specific to discrete

[83] Consumer Protection Act 1999 (Malaysia), Part II; Paterson, 'Regulating Consumer Contracts', 214.
[84] Consumer Protection Law 2019 (Myanmar), ss 9–10 and 13–14.
[85] ibid, ss 9(a) and 14(a).
[86] ibid, s 13.
[87] Consumer Protection (Fair Trading) Order 2011 (Brunei), Art 4.
[88] Consumer Protection (Fair Trading) Act (Singapore), s 2.
[89] ibid.
[90] ibid.
[91] ibid, s 3.
[92] ibid, s 5.
[93] ibid, s 1B. See also the definition of 'unfair practice' in Brunei's Consumer Protection (Fair Trading) Order 2011, s 4.
[94] Consumer Protection Act 2019 (India), s 2(47). The legislation commenced on 20 July 2020.
[95] ibid, s 2(47)(i).
[96] Act on Labelling and Advertising (South Korea), Art 3(1). More specifically, see Act on Labelling and Advertising of Foods (South Korea).
[97] See the discussion of the recent amendments to Myanmar's Consumer Protection Law 2019 below.
[98] For example, Chapter IV of the Indonesian legislation addresses labelling within regulation of promotion of goods generally.

products such as foodstuffs and pharmaceuticals.[99] It is encouraging, however, that some jurisdictions are engaged in promoting general labelling protections.

In Japan, the Act against Unjustifiable Premiums and Misleading Representations[100] seeks to regulate against misleading advertisements and representations in relation to superiority of quality or content, a misleading advantage of price or other conditions and other misleading designated representations.[101] More recently, Myanmar introduced sweeping legislative amendments to the Consumer Protection Act in 2020. This includes a requirement that labelling of information or directions related to a product's usage must be in either the Myanmar language or have a bilingual label that includes the Myanmar language. These requirements extend to information about product safety, usage and storage instructions, and warnings in relation to allergic reactions and potential side effects.[102] Sections 41–43 provide a comprehensive list of factors that must be included on the labelling, including in relation to health and nutritional guarantees. Similarly, in Thailand, the Committee on Labels, an ad hoc committee, established pursuant to the Consumer Protection Board, can define what kind of goods are considered to be unsafe products and, in such circumstances, a particular label is required.[103]

In several jurisdictions, the failure to provide this information would be caught by the general or specific unfair or misleading conduct provisions. Indonesia's Law No 8 notes that it is an unfair practice to not conform to standards, laws or label information.

C. Product Safety and Defective Goods

A specific information obligation imposed expressly or impliedly in several jurisdictions is the duty to inform, or the right to be informed, where a product is defective.[104] In most cases, such provisions will also attract the more general disclosure obligations. In adopting these protections, the generality of the provision determines whether such information obligations extend to other circumstances – such as when health concerns eventuate or other material considerations are discovered.[105]

[99] These provisions are discussed under specific provisions below: 'ASEAN Labelling Requirements' (2007), available under www.asean.org/storage/images/archive/20605.pdf.

[100] See also Household Goods Quality Labeling Act (Japan).

[101] Act against Unjustifiable Premiums and Misleading Representations (Japan), Art 5.

[102] The requirement for Myanmar language labels was introduced with effect on 26 April 2019 by virtue of Notification 1/2018 of the Central Consumer Protection Committee. It has been postponed as the corresponding chapter on labelling (Chapter 18) will only enter into force one year after the enactment of the new law. It should be noted that Myanmar language or bilingual labelling requirements have long existed and still exist for food by virtue of Food and Drug Administration Directive No 1/1998. Hence, this law is mainly focusing on the information for consumers.

[103] Consumer Protection Act (Thailand), ss 14, 21 and 36.

[104] See generally L Nottage and S Thanitcul (eds), *ASEAN Product Liability and Consumer Product Safety Law* (Bangkok: Winyuchon Publication House, 2016); L Nottage and J Paterson, 'Product Safety Law and Consumer Contracts in Southeast Asia: Partly Trading Up?' in P Hsieh and B Mercurio (eds), *ASEAN Law in the New Regional Economic Order* (Cambridge: Cambridge University Press, 2019) 392–414.

[105] ibid.

In several jurisdictions the European influence is evident with provisions of the EU General Product Safety Directive[106] being adopted in Macau and Hong Kong. Furthermore, the UK's Consumer Protection Act 1987 is restated in Malaysia's Consumer Protection Act 1999.[107] Though Malaysia's Consumer Protection Act 1999 does not impose a general information right or obligation with respect to consumer products, the legislation does impose a general right to information where goods are found to be, or may otherwise be unsafe.[108] According to the Act, a 'defect' exists if the 'safety of the product is not such as a person is generally entitled to expect'.[109] In Myanmar, entrepreneurs must also give notice to consumers and relevant departments in time by media or by other methods if produced goods or services are not safe by themselves or otherwise and complying with the decision of the relevant department.[110]

Although occurring at the post contractual stage, it is instructive to note that in some jurisdictions information duties are imposed on suppliers to notify consumers when products are found to be unsafe and need to be recalled. Japan's Food Labeling Act provides for positive obligations with regard to labelling upon persons operating food-related businesses.[111] Penalties can be imposed on businesses that do not comply, including recalls.[112] India has only recently introduced mandatory general product recall provisions. Prior to the 2019 legislation, only food and nutrition products could be compulsorily recalled. Otherwise, any recall was voluntary. Section 20 of the Consumer Protection Act 2019 provides that the relevant government authority to order the recall of goods or withdrawal of services where such goods or services are dangerous, hazardous or unsafe.[113]

Other jurisdictions are less specific but the operation of more general provisions would catch information provision regarding unsafe goods. Indonesia's Law No 8 of 1999 on Consumer Protection does not explicitly impose an information obligation with respect to defective products but such an obligation is effectively implied through the relatively comprehensive recall provisions.[114] A product must be recalled by a producer or distributor where the product is found to be 'defective, polluted, or otherwise violates applicable standards or is fraudulently marketed'.[115] It should be noted too that producing goods that do not conform to appropriate or stipulated safety standards may be deemed to be an unfair practice. China's recall obligations are narrower; for a product to be 'defective', the product has to endanger personal or property safety, limiting the scope of a seller's information obligations.[116] Once a product or service has overcome

[106] Directive 2001/95/EC of the European Parliament and of the Council of 3 December 2001 on General Product Safety, OJ 2001 No L11, p 4.

[107] J Malbon and L Nottage, 'Theoretical Perspectives on ASEAN and Consumer Law Developments' in Nottage et al, 'ASEAN Consumer Law', 118.

[108] Consumer Protection Act 1999 (Malaysia), s 21A.

[109] ibid, s 67(1).

[110] Consumer Protection Law 2019 (Myanmar) s 21(j), (k).

[111] Food Labeling Act (Japan), Art 5.

[112] ibid, Arts 6–8, 11–12.

[113] Consumer Protection Act 2019 (India), s 20.

[114] Law No 8 of 1999 on Consumer Protection (Indonesia), Art 8.

[115] ibid.

[116] See Law on the Protection of Consumer Rights and Interests 2013 (China), Art 19.

this hurdle, however, the Law on the Protection of Consumer Rights and Interests 2013 imposes a broad range of information obligations on business operators to: report the defect to the relevant administrative departments; take measures such as cessation of sale; inform consumers; issue warnings; and ultimately, take adequate steps to recall, destroy or cease sale of the defective good.[117]

Although as more of a general information obligation, Vietnam's Law on Consumer Protection of 2010 requires sellers to inform consumers of any necessary information about goods and/or services that the consumer is using.[118] This would seem to imply an obligation on sellers to advise consumers regarding safety warnings or defective goods.[119]

At the time of writing, Brunei does not have specific legislation addressing product safety information although there are discrete laws addressing information in relation to certain medicines[120] and foodstuffs.[121]

D. Door-to-Door and Direct Sales

Special provisions may apply to the ubiquitous door to door sales and to the more recent development of 'direct sales'. The Indian legislation defines direct selling as the marketing, distribution and sale of goods or provision of services through a network of sellers, other than through a permanent retail location.[122] Several jurisdictions, for example Malaysia, have taken steps to address direct sales with the requirement that all distance, mail order or door-to-door sales must be in writing.[123] The sales contract is required to provide information on the cooling-off period in 18 point font, and signed both by the vendor and purchaser.[124] Moreover, during the cooling-off period no goods or services will be performed until the period expires, unless the consumer makes a written request for performance.[125] India's recent Consumer Protection Act 2019 broadened the definition of consumer in order to include persons who purchase goods online, by any electronic means, teleshopping, direct selling or multi-level marketing.[126] Although

[117] However, as Jing explains in the China national report, China's product recall system suffers from a lack of industry coordination at all levels. While China's provisions are a step in the right direction; the current defective product recall system has a relatively low level of legislation, with only one administrative regulation, and the rest imposed through departmental rules. As contended by Jing, from a practical perspective, these rules suffer from a lack of coordination amongst industries of different provinces. For example, the time requirements of the product recall system itself are contrary to each other, resulting in inadequate protection of consumers.

[118] Law on Consumer Protection of 2010 (Vietnam), Art 8(2).

[119] It would seem similar comments can be made regarding the various discrete product liability and product safety statutes in South Korea: See, for example, Product Liability Act; Electrical Appliances and Consumer Products Safety Control Act; Special Act on the Safety of Products for Children Act.

[120] Medicines Order 2007 (Brunei).

[121] Public Health (Food) Act 2000 (Brunei).

[122] Consumer Protection Act 2019 (India), s 2(14).

[123] Direct Sales and Anti Pyramid Scheme Act 1993 (Malaysia), s 23(1)(a).

[124] ibid, s 23(1)(b) and (c).

[125] ibid, s 25(1) and (2).

[126] Consumer Protection Act 2019 (India), s 2(7).

direct selling and e-commerce seems to be adequately addressed within the 2019 Indian legislation, it seems to foreshadow more legislative intervention in this area by stating that the Central Government may take such measures in the manner as may be prescribed for the purposes of preventing unfair trade practices in e-commerce, direct selling and also to protect the interest and rights of consumers.[127]

In Japan, abusive selling methods, for example door-to-door sales, telemarketing and multi-level marketing have been addressed by the Act on Specified Commercial Transactions 2016. The Act provides that the main elements of the contract must be disclosed at (and often prior to) the conclusion of the contract. This generally requires a mandatory written document. Similarly, in 2015, Taiwan made further revisions to its Consumer Protection Act, which focused on the information duties of the business operators. In this amendment, the words 'mail order purchase' and 'door-to-door sales' to 'distance sales' and 'door-to-door sales' respectively extend the reach of 'distance sales' reach to cover internet-related sales;[128] and obliging business operators to provide consumers with more comprehensive information of the seller and terms of the transaction.[129] As noted by Fong in the Taiwan national report:

> … thus the present Article 18 explicitly requires the business operators of distance or door to door sales to provide pertinent transaction information, in a clear and conspicuous written format, to consumers. If distance sales are made via the Internet, the business operator shall provide the consumer with recoverable and saveable information in electronic format.

South Korea's Act on the Consumer Protection in Electronic Commerce provides for comprehensive regulation regarding information duties and the right of withdrawal with respect to electronic commerce transactions.[130] Moreover, Article 12(6) of Vietnam's Law on Consumer Protection of 2010 states that traders shall 'inform accurately and fully to consumers of the standard form contracts before the transaction'. Article 14(6) states that where the contract between traders and consumers is concluded by electronic means, 'traders shall let consumers check the entire contract before signing'.[131] Unfortunately, some other jurisdictions such as Thailand remain reliant on laws that do not, arguably, address this new paradigm of sales to consumers.[132]

[127] ibid, s 94 (India). See too the use of discrete legislation in South Korea, for example, Door to Door Sales Act No 4481 and, in the case of e-commerce transactions the Act on the Consumer Protection in Electronic Commerce, No 6687.

[128] Such extension of the application can be clearly evidenced by the revised definition of the Distance Sales. According to the Consumer Protection Act (Taiwan), Art 2(10), 'Distance sales' means the transaction is made via radios, television broadcasts, telephones, facsimiles, catalogues, newspapers, magazines, the Internet, flyers or any other similar channels, which consumer does not have opportunity to review the goods or services.

[129] ibid, Arts 18 and 22. Business operators of distance sales and door-to-door sales are obligated to provide buyers-consumers with comprehensive information of the sellers and terms of purchase. Legal consequences for violating this duty to inform are also established.

[130] Act on the Consumer Protection in Electronic Commerce (South Korea), Arts 13–14.

[131] Law on Consumer Protection of 2010 (Vietnam), Art 14(6).

[132] Galasintu, Supanit and Chaiittivej, 'The Issue of Direct Sales', 329.

E. Financial and Like Services

Most jurisdictions provide separately for information disclosure obligations with regard to financial services. For the purposes of this chapter, however, it is noteworthy that, in Singapore, contracts involving financial instruments or services were initially excluded from the application of the Consumer Protection (Fair Trading) Act, since these were regulated by way of specific legislation. Since the recent global financial crisis gave rise to many complaints regarding the behaviour of financial institutions in the marketing of such products and the rendering of advice, the Singapore government felt the need to safeguard the interests of retail investors. This resulted – speedily, one might add – in an important amendment in 2008 to the Act to extend it to financial products and services insofar as financial institutions committed unfair practices, specifically including the application of undue influence or unconscionable conduct.[133] Japan has introduced specific information duties regarding ventures such as 'Specified Continuous Services', for example beauty-treatment clinics and businesses claiming to enhance student examination performance, because consumers lack information on the actual effects or results in the future and cannot be properly informed. This also applies to other transactions such as insurance,[134] or speculative ventures[135] such as forward trading or derivatives.[136] Since 2017, Malaysia has included consideration of credit sale agreements within the Consumer Protection Act 1999.[137]

F. Food and Beverages

The introduction of Japan's Food Labeling Act unified several food labelling systems that had previously been the subject of discrete legislation and oversight while also enhancing consumer protections. The legislation provides for positive obligations with regard to labelling upon persons operating food-related businesses.[138] Article 4(1) stipulates the information that must be provided on labels such as an expiration date, country of origin, ingredients and additives. Penalties can be imposed on businesses that do not comply, including recalls.[139] Other legislation, for example the Food Sanitation Act, provides for prohibition of false or misleading statements and advertisements in relation to food and related items that may cause harm to public health.[140] In response to concerns regarding

[133] Consumer Protection (Fair Trading) Amendment Act 2008 (Singapore), s 2.

[134] Insurance Business Act 1995 (Japan) stipulates pre-contractual information duties with administrative and criminal sanctions.

[135] Act on Specified Commercial Transactions 2016 (Japan), Chapter 4 regulates Specified Continuous Services such as a beauty-treatment clinic or cram school. See also Act on Specified Commercial Transactions 2016 (Japan), Chapter 5 regulates 'Business Opportunity Sales Transactions'.

[136] See eg Financial Instruments and Exchange Act 2017 (Japan); Commodity Derivatives Act 2017 (Japan); Golf-club Membership Act 1992 (Japan), all of which are controlled by the administrative rules on information disclosures.

[137] Consumer Protection Act 1999 (Malaysia), Part IIIB.

[138] Food Labeling Act (Japan), Art 5.

[139] ibid, Arts 6–8, 11–12.

[140] Food Sanitation Act (Japan), Arts 19–20.

unsafe ingredients in food and beverages in Myanmar, amendments passed in 2013 now stipulate that a person who produces, imports, exports, stores, distributes or sells food shall strictly abide by any order, directive and conditions issued by the relevant Government department or organisation or Board of Authority with respect to quality assurance of food, labelling and advertising.[141] Where circumstances necessitate a recall, the supplier is obliged to inform consumers of the reasons for the withdrawal.[142] Macau's legislation imposes liability for omissions only in the context of food labelling. Those who display, possess or sell 'foodstuffs intended for public consumption' may be liable where 'labelling is omitted, inaccurate or deficient, have been altered or deleted or are not in accordance with their actual content'.[143] Additionally, for those who have on display for sale 'foodstuffs intended for public consumption whose indication of the date of minimum durability is concealed or covered up by an overlapping label or by another means of hindering or preventing their reading by the consumer'.[144]

G. Pharmaceuticals

Again, the general and the more discrete unfair or misleading conduct provisions would seem to catch circumstances where there is inadequate or inappropriate information provided with regard to pharmaceuticals. However, given the dangers of no or inaccurate information regarding pharmaceuticals, some jurisdictions provide specifically for information obligations. For example, following the 2014 amendment to the National Drug Law 1992, the Myanmar Food and Drug Board of Authority was formed to help ensure the quality, safety and effectiveness of pharmaceuticals and to systematically control and regulate manufacture, import, export, storage, distribution and sale of food and drugs.[145] This model is similar to the food model and requires that licences,[146] quality assurance,[147] labelling and advertising[148] are necessary for a person who desires to manufacture, import, export, store, distribute or sell drugs. Similarly, Indonesia prohibits traders from supplying faulty 'pharmaceutical or food products with or without providing complete and correct information'[149] while Thailand's Product Liability Act 2008 seeks to protect consumers through addressing inadequate warnings or failure to warn in relation to products.[150] This would seem to extend to pharmaceuticals.

[141] National Food Law 1997 (Myanmar), s 18.

[142] Food Safety and Standards Act 2006 (Myanmar), s 28(1), (2).

[143] Decree-Law No 50/92/M (Macau), Art 19(1).

[144] ibid, Art 19(3).

[145] National Drug Law 1992 (Myanmar), s 3.

[146] ibid, s 8: 'A person desirous of manufacturing, storing, distributing and selling pharmaceutical raw material or registered drug shall apply for a licence in the prescribed manner'.

[147] ibid, s 9: 'A person who has been granted the right to manufacture, import, export, store, distribute or sell pharmaceutical raw material or registered drug shall abide strictly by the order, directive and conditions issued by the Board of Authority in respect of quality assurance of the drug'.

[148] ibid, s 10: 'A person who has been granted registration of the drug or who has obtained a licence shall abide strictly by the order, directive and conditions issued by the Board of Authority in respect of labelling and advertising'.

[149] Law No 8 of 1999 on Consumer Protection (Indonesia), Art 8(3).

[150] Nottage, 'Introduction', 51.

In Japan, like in relation to food labelling, both positive and negative obligations are imposed in relation to the marketing of pharmaceuticals. Therefore, Articles 50–53 of the Act on Securing Quality, Efficacy and Safety of Products Including Pharmaceuticals and Medical Devices provides that certain information and in some cases warnings must be described on the immediate container or capsule of a pharmaceutical.[151] Specific requirements are addressed regarding external information and package inserts.[152] Such information must be readily visible and written in easily understandable terms.[153]

V. Rights of Withdrawal

Alongside wider recognition of the information imbalance between consumers and sellers; more intrusive rules have been developed in many jurisdictions that provide consumers with the right to withdraw from certain consumer contracts without reason.[154] This form of withdrawal right commonly operates through the designation of a specific cooling-off period, within which consumers are able to cancel the contract without penalty.[155] It should be noted that many jurisdictions have enacted mandatory withdrawal rights for certain industry-specific contracts (commonly, financial and insurance products) which are not discussed in this chapter.[156]

Broadly speaking, withdrawal rights recognise the need to protect consumers from 'unscrupulous sellers, high-pressure tactics, and their own irrational impulses',[157] while simultaneously incentivising consumers to enter contracts that might otherwise be considered too risky. As such, withdrawal rights have been introduced to provide an added layer of protection where the ability of a consumer to make an informed decision is likely to be compromised. Most commonly, this includes where consumers are not able to examine the goods beforehand, such as distance sales or mail-order sales (for example sales occurring via the Internet, email, regular mail or phone), or where consumers might feel pressured into making hasty or unconsidered decisions (for example door-to-door sales and other forms of direct marketing).

[151] Act on Securing Quality, Efficacy and Safety of Products Including Pharmaceuticals and Medical Devices (Japan), Art 50.
[152] ibid, Arts 51 and 52.
[153] ibid, Art 53.
[154] Straetsman, 'Introduction', 6.
[155] R Steennot, 'The Right of Withdrawal under the Consumer Rights Directive as a Tool to Protect Consumers Concluding a Distance Contract' (2013) 29 *Computer Law & Security Review* 105.
[156] For example, Singapore has mandated consumer withdrawal rights for the provision of insurance and investment scheme contracts. See Insurance (General Provisions) Regulations, reg 8 and Notice on Cancellation Period for Collective Investment Schemes Constituted as Investment Trusts (SFA 04/13-N01), pursuant to ss 101 and 293 of the Securities and Futures Act.
[157] P Sánchez Abril, F Oliva Blázquez and J Martínez Evora, 'The Right of Withdrawal in Consumer Contracts: a comparative analysis of American and European law' Research Paper No 18–13, University of Miami Business School (4 October 2018), 6.

While the general rationale underpinning the provision of withdrawal rights remains relatively consistent amongst the countries examined in the book; the nuances of each jurisdiction's statutory withdrawal rights differ considerably. Table 2 provides a brief description of these distinctions, with further detail and explanation provided in the corresponding national reports.

Table 2

Jurisdiction	Availability	Relevant Provision	Cooling-Off Period	Requirements
China	Distance sales, door-to-door sales, direct sales and other off-premises sales	Law on the Protection of Consumer Rights and Interests 2013, Art 25	Within 7 days of receiving the goods	Consumers must return the goods to the seller, assuming the cost of freight unless otherwise agreed
Japan	Door-to-door sales, telemarketing sales, multi-level marketing transactions, business opportunity sales contracts	Act on Specified Commercial Transactions, Arts 9, 9-2, 40(1), 58	From the day of receiving the contract from the enterprise: Door-to-door sales and Telemarketing Sales (8 days); multi-level marketing transactions (20 day cooling off + 20 additional days to terminate); Business Opportunity Sales (20 days)	Must notify the seller in writing
Malaysia	Direct sales (including door-to-door sales and mail order sales)	Direct Sales and Anti Pyramid Scheme Act 1993, s 26	10 days from the date of purchase	Must serve notice on the seller in writing
Singapore	Door-to-door sales, timeshares and long-term holiday product contracts (referred to as 'regulated contracts')	Consumer Protection (Fair Trading) (Cancellation of Contracts) Regulations 2009, reg 5	Within 5 working days after the day on which the contract was entered into or the day in which the consumer information notice is brought to the consumer's attention (whichever is later)	Suppliers are obliged to provide a refund within 60 days of receipt of the notice of withdrawal

(continued)

Table 2 ***(Continued)***

Jurisdiction	Availability	Relevant Provision	Cooling-Off Period	Requirements
South Korea	Mail-order sales, Door to door sales	Act on the Consumer Protection in Electronic Commerce, Arts 17 and 18; Door to Door Sales Act, Arts 7 and 8. Note too the consumers special right of withdrawal, Art 8(3).	Within 7 days of the written terms of the contract being received or within 7 days from the day the product was delivered; 14 days from the date of receipt although pursuant to the special right of withdrawal within three months from the date of receiving the goods or within 30 days from the date the consumer knew or could have known such fact.	Distributors are required to provide a refund within 3 days of cancellation; The door-to-door seller must reimburse all payments received from the consumer. The door-to-door seller is responsible for the costs of returning the goods.
Taiwan	Door-to-door and distance sales	Consumer Protection Act, Art 19	Within 7 days of receiving goods	Does not apply to distance sales of 'reasonable matters'
Thailand	Direct sales contracts	Direct Sales and Direct Marketing Act, ss 33–34	Within 7 days of receiving goods	Must notify the seller in writing
Vietnam	Door-to-door sales contracts	Decree 99/2011/ND-CP, Art 19(3)	Within 3 working days of concluding the contract	Consumers must notify the seller in writing that they wish to unilaterally terminate that contract

As indicated in Table 2, the prescribed cooling-off periods for door-to-door sales contracts range from three and 10 days between jurisdictions, while direct and distance sales cooling off periods range from between seven and 10 days. Japan's multi-level marketing and business opportunity contracts generally attract a 20-day cooling-off period to reflect the relative complexity of those contracts.[158] However, the date in

[158] Note also, the Act on Specified Commercial Transactions (Japan) has an additional 'termination' measure for products purchased in multi-level marketing transactions.

which the cooling-off period is triggered may be of specific interest in some cases. For example, Malaysia's cooling-off period is triggered on purchase which might be inappropriate for mail order sales given the variable length of time it takes consumers to receive the goods.

In addition to mandatory withdrawal rights, some countries have enacted alternative methods for cancellation. In Japan, for example, the Act on Specified Commercial Transactions does not prescribe a mandatory withdrawal right for mail order contracts. Instead, Article 15-2 sets out a default provision allowing consumers to cancel the contract by returning the goods within eight days of delivery.[159] However, the non-mandatory nature of this provision means sellers can contract out of the provision by expressly setting out the terms of cancellation in the sales contract.

India, Indonesia, Hong Kong and Myanmar are still yet to enact any statutory rights of withdrawal. In those jurisdictions, a consumer's right to withdraw from a consumer contract is governed by the terms of the contract itself and, therefore, falls almost entirely within the seller's control. In Hong Kong, despite numerous reform proposals for the introduction of mandatory withdrawal rights over the past two decades, such reforms have been strongly (and successfully) opposed by corporate lobbyists. Even so, reform proposals to enact statutory withdrawal rights are currently being considered in Hong Kong and Myanmar.

VI. Conclusion

This chapter has considered information duties and rights of withdrawal as pertinent to several jurisdictions discussed in this book. While the design and regulation of these consumer laws remain the national responsibility of the respective countries, the central objectives underpinning the national consumer protection laws reflect various international frameworks, including the United Nations Guidelines for Consumer Protection which include protecting consumers against fraudulent, deceitful, or misleading information, advertising, labelling or other practices and ensuring consumers are made aware of all information required to make informed choices. Of course, nations within ASEAN are working towards minimum harmonisation of consumer laws and several ASEAN nations, such as Singapore and Malaysia, already demonstrate best practice provisions in the provision of information to consumers and withdrawal rights. Other nations are at varying stages in development of their consumer laws, but most jurisdictions have adopted a comprehensive suite of laws regulating the provision of information and rights of withdrawal. New developments are occurring all the time, most recently in Taiwan, India and Myanmar, that have significantly enhanced existing laws and, importantly, addressed issues relating to new kinds of sales techniques such as direct and online sales.

[159] ibid, Art 15-2.

16

Sale of Goods: A Comparative Perspective

GAIL PEARSON

I. Introduction

From the standpoint of the buyer, Sale of Goods law is to solve a number of interlocking problems: transfer of property; obtaining the goods for which the buyer has already paid – the delivery problem; issues with the nature of the goods themselves – the conformity or defectiveness problem; and what can be done – the remedies problem. E-Commerce exacerbates these problems. An earlier challenge was assimilating the concepts of goods and of services. This issue arises again with digital products and financial services.

II. Origins, Jurisdiction, Borrowings

There is underlying coherence in sales law through the fundamental principles of both the civil and common law systems. Sales law in Asia is heir to these and other ancient traditions such as the *Arthashastra* of India. The importance of a market economy in contemporary Asia is explicit in some countries as is the case of Indonesia as seen in its constitutional provisions.

Jurisdiction presents a problem for Asian countries, particularly those in the ASEAN region which have an economic integration strategy.[1] The underlying coherence of principle is not always reflected in the detail of rules, in part due to the impact of diverse colonial influences still evident in the form that sales law takes in a number of countries. This is not surprising as notwithstanding centralisation in Europe in the form of EU directives, the main dimension of consumer law in Europe remains national differences.[2]

[1] L Nottage et al, *ASEAN Consumer Law Harmonisation and Cooperation* (Cambridge: Cambridge University Press, 2019).

[2] S Nessel, 'Consumer Policy in 28 EU Member States: An Empirical Assessment in Four Dimensions' (2019) 42 *Journal of Consumer Policy* 455.

Sales law per se lies at an intersection of property law and the law of obligations – in contract or in tort – and codified in statute or code, depending on the common law or civil law tradition.[3] The chapters in this book are primarily though not exclusively concerned with contractual obligations as consumer sales issues tend to focus more on conformity than ownership. If the law involves implication of terms into a contract, this will include a term as to good title, as in Singapore. If the law provides for a mandatory guarantee of quality as in Australia, this could be seen as quasi tortious. The chapters also touch on enforcement and remedies available to consumers if the goods fail to meet their legal requirements.

There are different generations of sales law. Broadly put, the nineteenth century with the European industrial revolution focused on a contract model to resolve transactions between a buyer and a seller. The mid-twentieth century infused tort-oriented approaches in addressing representations about goods and the liability of manufacturers. The early twenty-first century has seen a further move away from a contract model in some jurisdictions.[4] These developments in sales law continue to track movements in the consumer economy and most recently the challenges of the digital economy.

Some countries make no distinction between consumers and other buyers in sales legislation. Special legislation for consumers is a later twentieth century development. For example, Singapore (1975), Thailand (1979), India (1986), China (1993), Malaysia (1999), Indonesia (1999) and Vietnam (2010) all introduced consumer protection acts. New legislation updated some of these statutes as in Singapore (2003), China (2013) and India (2019). But not all of these consumer protection acts are the chief source of law for consumer buyers as older sales law or civil codes may still predominate. This is the case for Malaysia where the consumer law does not address sales. Others have undertaken specific updates to laws including sales law, often specifically to address remedies.

Most Asian countries within the common law tradition modelled their sale of goods obligations on English legislation. The mid-nineteenth century Indian Contract Act (1872) influenced the UK Sale of Goods Act 1893, which in turn was the model for the Indian Sale of Goods Act 1930. The Indian Sale of Goods Act influenced the Malaysian Sale of Goods Act 1957. The Singapore Sale of Goods Act 1999 is modelled on the UK Sale of Goods Act 1979[5] and the Singaporean Consumer Protection (Fair Trading) Act 2007 is influenced by Canadian and Australian (more specifically New South Wales) law. Since that time, Australia overhauled its consumer law, bringing it in line with New Zealand law.

Countries with a civil law approach include Indonesia, Japan, Macau, Taiwan and Vietnam. Thailand's Civil and Commercial Code was influenced by both European and English law. This should not be surprising as the nineteenth-century systematisation

[3] Mackenzie Chalmers, the progenitor of UK codified Sales law via the Sale of Goods Act 1893 acknowledges his debt to Pothier and the civil law tradition. M Chalmers, *The Sale of Goods Including the Factors Act, 1889* (London: William Clowes and Sons Limited, 1890).

[4] See Australia and New Zealand.

[5] Note that the Consumer Rights Act 2015 (UK) has in part replaced the Sale of Goods Act 1979 (UK) for consumer contracts.

of sales law involved the treatise writers and codifiers of both England and Europe. The newer generation consumer protection laws can fill gaps in Civil Codes as in the case of voluntary guarantees in Vietnam. International law, namely the Convention on the International sale of Goods (CISG) and the Uniform Principles of International Commercial Contracts (UPICC), influenced the Japanese 2017 Civil Code which introduced new remedies into Japan for non-conforming goods. Thailand and Vietnam refer to the United Nations Guidelines on Consumer Protection (UNGCP).

There are borrowings and influences within Asian sales law. We have already mentioned the important influence of the Indian Contract Act and the subsequent Sale of Goods Act of India. In revising its law to incorporate distance selling, China analysed laws of the EU, Japan and South Korea. Contemporary developments in laws on sale seem to be less influential. For instance the European Consumer Sales Directive,[6] the Australian Consumer Law[7] and the UK Consumer Rights Act 2015 do not appear as an explicit influence. An exception is the proposed consumer law for Macau which has drawn from the EU Consumer Sales Directive.

The law has not always moved along in step with amendments to the original or been innovatively updated. For instance, the post-1979 and later changes to UK sales law have not been followed in Malaysia or India. Australia is an example of a common law country that has successively adapted sales law, first in the now repealed Trade Practices Act 1974 and in subsequent amendments to that Act, and then in the Competition and Consumer Act 2010. It is too early to canvas any influence of the two recent EU Directives to foster the strategy of a European single digital market.[8]

There are special laws to address standards for different types of goods such as food, pharmaceuticals and electrical appliances, in most countries. With three types of laws, sale of goods law, consumer protection laws and specialist laws, in some countries there is a risk of overlap. We can see this in India in the overlapping notions of 'defect' in the Consumer Protection Act and the implied terms in the Sales Act. Lack of systematisation of law for consumers is a problem in a number of jurisdictions. Some places, such as Macau, have made efforts to consolidate laws to protect consumers.

This multiplicity of laws can result in fragmentation in the coherence of the law on the sale of goods to consumers. In a number of jurisdictions, the fundamental question of applicable law for a sale or supply of goods to a consumer is problematic. In Taiwan this may require a complex determination to decide if it is the Civil Code or the Consumer Protection Act. Taiwan does not use the language of contract or sale but consumer relationship and consumer dispute. In Singapore some remedies for sales are available under the Sale of Goods Act and some under the Consumer Protection Fair Trading Act.

[6] Directive 1999/44/EC of the European Parliament and of the Council of 25 May 1999 on certain aspects of the sale of consumer goods and associated guarantees, OJ 1999 No L171, p 12.

[7] Competition and Consumer Act 2010 (Cth), Schedule 2.

[8] Directive (EU) 2019/770 of the European Parliament and of the Council of 20 May 2019 on certain aspects concerning contracts for the supply of digital content and digital services, OJ 2019 No L136, p 1; Directive (EU) 2019/771 of the European Parliament and of the Council of 20 May 2019 on certain aspects concerning contracts for the sale of goods, OJ 2019 No L136, p 28.

III. Consumer Sales

In most jurisdictions, the substantive law applies to a generic concept of goods. Additional laws may impose further requirements for particular goods such as food or pharmaceuticals. China is a little different as the focus is on remedial law more than the initial obligation. The evolution of remedies in tandem with the concept of 'three guarantees' did not apply to goods in general but only to particular types of consumer goods being produced in a planned economy, for example televisions and refrigerators. China does not appear to have a hard distinction between goods and services and uses the term commodities. Indonesia also differentiates between goods, the distinction being between those 'vital' to the State therefore to be controlled by it, and those not vital, which can be left to the community. A big question is the taxonomy of digital products.[9] For example, in Hong Kong the concept of goods does not incorporate intangible digital products such as downloads, but in Australia it does. This will be an ongoing issue for e-commerce transactions involving tangibles and software.

Not all jurisdictions have laws that apply specifically to sales to a consumer, as seen in Table 1. In some, particularly those retaining only the first generation sale of goods legislation, the law applies to both commercial and consumer sales. Some of those laws, as in the Australian State of New South Wales, were amended to bolt on additional provisions particular to consumers. There are some similarities in the concept of the consumer as a denominator of special provisions in sales contracts. In Indonesia for instance the notion of the consumer is linked to the use of the goods. Interestingly it excludes goods that are not already in the market (presumably goods still to be made). Use for domestic purposes is linked to the antithesis of use for a business or on-sale purpose. The definition of a consumer in India still refers to the doctrine of consideration. It excludes obtaining goods for commercial purposes but this exclusion does not extend to goods bought and used to earn a livelihood by self-employment.[10] There is room for conversations about who falls within or outside laws to protect consumer acquirers of goods and services. A number of jurisdictions exclude certain types of transactions such as sales by auction or of second-hand goods from consumer protection rules.

In nearly all jurisdictions the substantive obligations with respect to the goods themselves are enscribed by way of the contract. This is the case for all those countries which have Sale of Goods legislation as this includes a regime for implying terms (conditions or warranties) into the contract. It is also the case for the 'conformity' with the contract obligations in the many countries with a civil law approach. This presents a particular difficulty as without more, it may be possible to use the contract to specifically exclude those obligations which impose duties on the seller regarding the nature per se of the goods. Some jurisdictions, such as Singapore, have addressed this by providing that

[9] On the adaptation to the digital age see the contribution by A De Francheschi, in this volume.
[10] Consumer Protection Act 2019 (India), s 2(7) ('consumer').

an implied term imposing such obligations cannot by excluded by the contract if the contract is with a consumer.

In Australia under the Australian Consumer Law and in New Zealand under the Consumer Guarantees Act 1993, the seller's obligations regarding the goods arise without recourse to the contract. The obligations do not take the form of a term of the contract. The mandatory obligations arise by reason of the supply of goods to a consumer. There are also mandatory obligations in China under the old three guarantees.

Methods of selling, by electronic means, door-to-door, distance and e-commerce are addressed in different ways and to different degrees in the various countries. New forms of transactions, such as consumer leases in the 'circular economy' for household items such as clothes or furniture do not appear to be considered. Transactions associated with a sale that may influence the decision to buy such as the provision of credit are addressed in some countries as with instalment credit in Vietnam.

Table 1 Distribution of sources of law on sales

Jurisdiction	**Chief Sales Law**	**Major influence: civil law, common law, other**	**Is sales in a general law, consumer law, or other?**	**Special laws for particular goods?**	**Special rules for different methods of selling?**	**Special laws for selling financial products?**
Australia	Competition and Consumer Act 2010 (ACL) Sale of Goods Acts	Common law	Consumer law	Yes	Yes ACL: distance selling; no special e-commerce	Yes
China	The Law on the Protection of Consumer Rights and Interests (CRL) 1993 and as amended	Sui generis	Consumer law	Yes (Food Safety Law)	Yes in CRL	
India	Sale of Goods Act 1930	Common law	General law. Some aspects in Consumer Protection Act, 2019	Yes eg Food Safety and Standards Act, 2006	See Consumer Protection Act, 2019	

(continued)

Table 1 *(Continued)*

Jurisdiction	Chief Sales Law	Major influence: civil law, common law, other	Is sales in a general law, consumer law, or other?	Special laws for particular goods?	Special rules for different methods of selling?	Special laws for selling financial products?
Indonesia		Civil law				
Japan	Civil Code	Civil law	General law.		Act on Specified Commercial Transactions	Yes
Macau	Civil Code 1999	Civil law	No special law on b2c sales			
Malaysia	Sale of Goods Act 1957	Common law		Yes		
Singapore	Consumer Protection (Fair Trading) Act 2007 Sale of Goods Act 1999	Common law		Yes eg Sale of Food Act		Yes
Taiwan	Civil Code	Civil law	Also Consumer Protection Act	Yes	Mail order Door-to-door sales	Financial Consumer Protection Act 2011
Thailand	Civil and Commercial Code 1924	Civil law and Common law		Yes	Direct Sales and Direct Marketing Act	Yes
Vietnam	Civil Code 2015	Civil law				

Table 2 Conformity and other obligations for consumer sales (*L = in law; Non-ex = non-excludable in consumer sale)*

Jurisdiction	Conformity with the contract	Term implied in contract	Obligation independent of the contract; rebuttable presumption of defect	Quality; Value	Fitness for purpose; Utility	Description	Conformity with sample	After sale obligations (eg availability of spare parts)
Australia	L	L Non-ex in some States	L Non-ex	L Non-ex (includes durability and safety)	L Non-ex	L Non-ex	L Non-ex	L Non-ex
China	L			L Non-ex	L Non-ex	L Non-ex	L Non-ex	
India	L	L		L	L	L	L	
Indonesia								
Japan	L							
Macau								L
Malaysia	L	L		×	×	×	×	
Singapore	L	L Non-ex	L Non-ex	L Non-ex	L Non-ex	L Non-ex	L Non-ex	
Taiwan	L							
Thailand		L		L	L	L		
Vietnam			L	L (includes durability)	L (+instructions for use)	L	L	

IV. Contractual Obligations

The first obligation in a sales contract is to deliver the goods in accordance with the corresponding obligation to pay the price for those goods. For consumers two problems may arise: they pay the price and the goods are never delivered; or the goods are delivered yet they do not meet the expectations of the consumer. These expectations of the goods may be established by contract, or by law, or by a combination of the two.

A. Approach

Within the common law tradition, contractual terms are implied into a contract of sale of goods by law. Provided the preconditions of the statutory provision are met, the requisite term is automatically implied and becomes part of the contract between the seller and the consumer. There is a proviso to this (to be explored later), which is whether the seller has the ability or exercises that ability to specifically exclude from the contract those terms that would otherwise by implication become part of the contract. There is an implied terms regime in parts of Australia, Hong Kong, India, Malaysia, Singapore and Thailand. To gain a remedy, the consumer must establish that the implied term is part of the contract and that the term has been breached, resulting in breach of contract.

The expectations of the goods are established in a different fashion in other systems. In Vietnam in the new 2015 Civil Code the seller's obligations involve a mixture of contractual agreement and mandatory assurances. For instance, quality of goods can be determined by the agreement of the parties, a standard of a competent authority, normal standards or standards as per consumer law.[11] In China, while the old three guarantees established liabilities, there was an underlying mandatory obligation to meet administrative standards. The new three guarantees involve both contractual arrangements and mandatory obligations. In Macau there is a presumption that mandatory government standards are guaranteed by the seller.

In Australia and New Zealand, the new generation statutory consumer guarantees exist independently of the contract. Yet they build on the conceptual framework of the pre-existing implied contractual terms. There are some differences in the content of the consumer guarantees and the terms implied by law into consumer contracts for the supply of goods.

The form taken to ensure sellers have obligations to consumers with respect to the nature of the goods supplied may have little import except for two questions: can the obligation be excluded?; what form does the remedy for failing to meet the obligation take?

In the common law countries with Sale of Goods Act legislation a seller and buyer can agree that one or all of the implied terms are not part of the contract. This is still the situation in India and Malaysia. In other countries such as Australia, certain States

[11] Civil Code 2015 (Vietnam), Art 432.

amended the Sale of Goods Act to make any such exclusion void if it were a sale to a consumer. In some jurisdictions for example Singapore, exclusion clauses are restrained by unfair contract terms legislation. If failure to meet the obligation is a breach of contract, this will not require a fault element, as pointed out for Singapore.

Some countries explicitly regulate voluntary or commercial guarantees. Singapore regulates voluntary guarantees. Thailand does not do this, though unfair terms provisions apply under the Unfair Contract Terms Act. In India a warranty or guarantee is covered by unfair trade practices.[12]

B. Content

In general, all jurisdictions have rules governing what a consumer (either specifically or as a sub-genus of the buyer) can expect of the goods, as seen in Table 2.

Description usually invokes the kind of goods at issue. A breach of the implied term of correspondence with the description of the goods is said to involve a difference in kind or identity not a difference in quality. Taiwan appears to use kind rather than description. A question may arise as to what is entailed in the description of the goods. Vietnam includes the description on packaging and trademarks. In China the obligation is linked to the quality that goods of such description should have.[13]

Quality is a concept with multiple meanings. The traditional sales term of 'merchantable quality' was linked to saleability but not saleability at any price, hence the notion of value (as price) was built into the concept of merchantable quality. Over time, the idea of merchantable quality evolved to invoke attributes of the goods linked to value as something of worth not so closely linked to price. Here, the language changed from merchantable quality to satisfactory quality (as in Singapore) and acceptable quality (as in Australia) and included not only performance characteristics but also aesthetic characteristics. More recent iterations include durability. Vietnam and Australia specifically include durability as an aspect of quality. Australia also includes safety. In India the concept of a defect in the Consumer Protection Act includes faults in quality, but the liability action does not include economic loss.[14]

Purpose and fitness for that purpose or for an ordinary purpose is a common requirement for goods. This is the case in Vietnam, Thailand, Singapore, Malaysia and India.

V. Remedies

A. Non-delivery

In traditional sales law, the obligation to pay and the obligation to deliver are co-terminus. Failure by the seller to deliver to the consumer or delays in delivery can

[12] Consumer Protection Act 2019 (India), s 2(47).
[13] The Law on the Protection of Consumer Rights and Interests (China), Art 22.
[14] Consumer Protection Act 2019 (India), s 2(10), (22), (35).

become particularly contentious in distance or e-commerce transactions that typically require payment prior to delivery. In Thailand under the Thai Civil and Commercial Code, the buyer's rights to end the contract for failure to deliver depend on whether there was a fixed time for delivery and if not reasonable notice to the seller. Unsolicited goods present a different problem. If goods not requested by the consumer are delivered and an assertion for payment made, Macau, for instance, expressly provides that consumers have a right not to pay for such goods.

B. Non-conforming Goods

A consumer (or any buyer) can refuse to accept delivery if when being delivered the goods do not conform with the contract description, as illustrated in the case of Vietnam's Civil Code. Under the Thai Civil and Commercial Code conformity with the contract description is treated differently from other conformity obligations as the buyer has only one year from the date of the contract to seek a remedy, compared with time running from the discovery of a defect.

In most jurisdictions a buyer must establish some lack of conformity, breach of an implied contractual term or failure to meet a statutory guarantee in order to return goods that have been delivered. The implied guarantee under the Thai Civil and Commercial Code seems similar to the implied term. In China, following a 2013 amendment there is a right to return without reason for some goods. This applies to distance sales and e-commerce and other 'non- traditional' sales. Return without reason does not apply to perishable goods, digital products and the like, newspapers that have been delivered, or goods that have been custom made. If at the time of the sale the consumer says the goods are not suitable for return without reason the goods cannot be returned. It is not clear whether this is used by sellers in a similar fashion to an exclusion clause.

The remedies available to a consumer who receives non-conforming or defective goods depend in part on the form that the underlying obligation takes. If the obligation is to deliver goods that meet the contract, the remedy will be for breach of contract. In common law countries this will depend on whether the obligation is in the form of a condition within the contract or a warranty, breach of the first giving a right to reject the goods and terminate the contract and of the second to damages only. There are modifications of this distinction. In India, under the new Consumer Protection Act, it is an unfair trade practice if a seller refuses to take back or make a refund on a defective good.

i. Cure

Curing a non-conforming delivery may involve retendering the goods, repair of the goods or replacement with substitute goods. If the time for delivery has not yet arrived, the seller can in general redeliver conforming goods. In common law countries traditionally, the seller does not have a right to cure. This is no longer the case for consumer sales in Australia and New Zealand, both of which have mandatory consumer guarantees where the remedy is for the seller's failure to meet the statutory guarantee not breach of contract. The seller does not have the right to cure if the buyer has the right to reject for a major failure to meet the statutory guarantee. In Singapore, the seller has the right to offer to repair or replace but the consumer can claim a price reduction or refund if among others, the repair is not convenient for the consumer. In Japan the right of a price reduction depends on an unsuccessful or impossible cure.

In Japan the seller's obligation to cure a defective sale includes repair and delivery of missing items as well as a substitute delivery. This is akin to an obligation to replace the goods. A buyer can first choose one of these methods but a seller can undertake a different method, provided this does not disproportionately burden the buyer.[15] For instance, the buyer may choose the repair of a new car, but the seller may choose to deliver a substitute new car of the same type. There is a complex system for repairing and replacing goods in China. In Thailand the Consumer Case Procedure Act provides for repair and replacement of consumer goods. The limitations on the seller's right to repair depend on the efficacy of the repair. Macau also distinguishes between the buyer's rights to repair or to replacement, the latter depending on necessity. Indonesian law appears to refer to replacement or refund, but not to repair.

ii. Termination

Generally, the buyer's right to bring the contract to an end will depend on the categorisation of the lack of conformity: a breach of a condition of the contract, or a major failure. The principle of the seriousness of the breach as the basis for termination is also incorporated in the new Japanese law. In Vietnam the right of repair, replace, price reduction or return and refund appear to be alternatives. In Singapore escalation from cure to price reduction or refund is predicated on the consumer's convenience, time and cost. In China the right of rescission does not depend on repair or replacement as a prior remedy. In all jurisdictions it is worth considering the sequence of remedies question.

iii. Damages

Damages for non-conforming goods are available in most systems. In China, this would be under the General Principles of the Civil Law, the Contract Law. Whether damages requires a fault element under the Japanese Civil Code is still an open question. Foreseeability of harm plays a role in the liability of a seller for damages in Japan. This is assessed not at the time of entry into the contract but at the time of non-performance. This is unique to Japan. In Singapore the Consumer Protection (Fair Trading) Act does not address damages. It is argued that they would be available under general contract law. The Civil Code in Vietnam provides for damages as a remedy in addition to other remedies from the seller pursuant to the seller's performance obligations. In Taiwan damages are available for quality failures but not if asking for termination or a price reduction. In some places such as China, punitive damages are available for certain contraventions.

[15] (New) Civil Code of 2017 (Japan), Art 562(1).

iv. Time Limits and Burden of Proof

To pursue a remedy, at what point does the consumer have to establish that the goods do not meet the requirements of the contract or the requirements of guarantees? In Thailand, the buyer has to establish the defect existed prior to the contract or at least up to the point of delivery and must commence proceedings within one year of discovering the defect. By contrast, in Singapore there is a presumption that goods did not conform at the time of delivery, if the defect is discovered within six months of the sale or delivery. After the six months, the consumer must establish the lack of conformity at the time of delivery. In Macau the proposed Consumer Protection Law of 2019 includes something similar with a rebuttable presumption of six months.

Under the Australian Consumer Law, the time for a remedy (such as repair) is not set by the time of delivery of the goods but by a reasonable time to both the consumer and the supplier.[16] The rejection period for goods that fail to meet a statutory consumer guarantee in Australia is not governed by time from supply (or delivery) but by reasonableness. It runs until the time it would be reasonable for the relevant defect to become apparent having regard to the type and use of the goods.[17] Thus once a defect becomes apparent, a consumer should act promptly.

v. Summary

The summary of remedies is shown in Table 3.

Table 3 Showing Remedies

Jurisdiction	Delivery	Repair	Replace	Reject/Return/ Terminate/ Withdraw/ Refund	Price Reduction	Damages / Compensation
Australia	x	x	x	x	x	x
China				x		x
India	x			x		x
Indonesia						
Japan	x	x	x	x	x	x
Macau		x	x	x		x
Malaysia						
Singapore		x	x		x	
Thailand		x	x	x		x
Taiwan						
Vietnam		x	x	x	x	

[16] Australian Consumer Law, s 259(2)(a).
[17] ibid, s 262(2).

VI. Conclusions

Throughout Asia there are common underlying principles that in a sale or supply of goods to a consumer, the consumer should receive what they have been promised by either contract or law. There is scope for further systematisation of the law in all jurisdictions to make what they are entitled to clearer to consumers. There is less coherence within and between countries in remedial regimes for failures in the sale or supply of goods to a consumer. Asian countries have actively developed legal rules to protect consumers of goods. As in all jurisdictions, they have borrowed and adapted from each other and around the world to suit their own circumstances. If one believes there is scope for a model law for consumers, sales law would not be a bad place to continue.

17

A Comparative Analysis of the Regulation of Unfair Terms in Asia

JAMES P NEHF

I. Introduction

The country reports on unfair terms in consumer contracts presented a variety of approaches to very similar concerns across borders. All of the reports revealed a multi-faceted approach to policing the consumer marketplace and guarding against traders who take unfair advantage of their customers. To varying degrees, each country utilised state actors to regulate unfair terms but also allowed individual consumers to challenge the enforceability of unfair terms in private actions. Several reports also highlighted a more pro-active approach, referencing various methods by which regulatory bodies pre-approve standard terms in consumer contracts before they are put into use.

The comparative analysis in this chapter proceeds in four parts and draws some comparisons with the regulation of unfair terms in the United States. The first part examines the role of general doctrines of unfairness, specifically the unconscionability and good faith doctrines, as a check on unfair contract terms. The second part looks at the various ways in which the reporting countries address procedural unfairness in consumer contract formation. The third part is a partial taxonomy of the wide variety of substantive terms that are deemed to be unfair in countries across the region. The fourth part discusses the available remedies when a trader includes unfair terms in consumer contracts, ranging from nullifying the unfair term to possible criminal penalties.

In the typical merchant-consumer transaction, standard terms are of course the norm. Consumer transactions are documented by contracts of adhesion where most, if not all, of the terms are drafted by the merchant and are not negotiable. Even if they were negotiable, the vast majority of consumers will either not be aware of this possibility or, quite reasonably, will conclude that they cannot bargain effectively over terms either because they do not understand their legal import or they cannot envision alternatives that would better serve their interests.

Sometimes those standard terms are so one-sided in favour of the merchant that they inflict unfair hardship on the consumer. In the United States there is no omnibus law on unfair contract terms that applies uniformly throughout the country. Common law doctrines offer limited consumer protection against unfair terms.[1] Regulation of unfair terms at the statutory level is addressed piecemeal, with limited protection in certain sectors at the federal level and most of the regulatory norms imposed by the individual states.[2] While they can vary widely from state to state, there are some parallel themes.[3]

Other countries (including several of the reporting countries in this study) may take a different approach and include among their consumer laws a general or omnibus statute or regulation that prohibits certain unfair terms explicitly, either declaring them void per se or including them on a list of candidates that can be deemed unfair depending on the circumstances. The reader will see some recurring themes among the national approaches discussed below. In drafting their statutes, some of the countries were likely influenced by the European Unfair Contract Terms Directive.[4] Article 3(1) of the Directive provides that contract terms are unfair and therefore not binding on consumers if they are contrary to principles of good faith or cause significant imbalance in the parties' rights and obligations to the detriment of the consumer. A list of examples of terms that may be regarded as unfair appears in the Annex to the Directive. Several of the EU listed prohibitions, such as insulating the trader from liability, one-sided cancellation rights and limiting a consumer's right to dispute resolution, are present in the national reports and are discussed in Section III of this Chapter.

[1] At the centre of common law regulation are the two most important common law doctrines of unconscionability and good faith. Those two doctrines have played an important but limited role in regulating unfair terms in consumer contracts over the years throughout much of the world. They are discussed in the first part of this chapter.

[2] Over the years, states and municipalities have adopted laws addressing a wide variety of consumer contracting situations including consumer credit, distance selling, payday loans and numerous others. Often these enactments, whether state or federal, dictate that certain terms must be included in consumer contracts (particularly disclosure requirements), and often they dictate that certain unfair terms not be included in consumer contracts. These statutes may prohibit certain merchant conduct (eg pyramid schemes, door-to-door selling, 'bait and switch' advertising), while others provide a regulatory framework for a particular type of commercial activity or industry (eg rent-to-own contracts or the timeshare industry).

[3] In the 1970s the National Conference of Commissioners on Uniform State Laws (NCCUSL), as well as the Federal Trade Commission (FTC), drafted model statutes and strongly encouraged states to adopt one of the forms. The NCCUSL proposed two model laws. The Uniform Deceptive Trade Practices Act prohibited eleven specific deceptive trade practices along with a general prohibition of 'any other conduct which similarly creates a likelihood of confusion or misunderstanding'. The Uniform Consumer Sales Practices Act prohibited deceptive acts and practices generally and also enumerated specific types of deceptive conduct and unconscionable acts. The FTC proposed three alternative versions of an Unfair Trade Practices and Consumer Protection Law. The first alternative mimicked the FTC Act and prohibited 'unfair methods of competition and unfair or deceptive acts or practices in the conduct of any trade or commerce'. The second alternative enjoined 'false, misleading, or deceptive acts or practices in the conduct of any trade or commerce'. The third alternative was similar to the Uniform Deceptive Trade Practices Act and included a list of specific prohibited practices. None of the initiatives took hold.

[4] Council Directive 93/13/EEC of 5 April 1993 on unfair terms in consumer contracts, OJ 1993 No L95, p 29. On 22 July 2019, the European Commission adopted a 'Guidance Notice on the interpretation and application of Directive 93/13/EEC', OJ 2019 No C323, p 4. The main purpose of the Guidance Notice was to present the body of case law from the Court of Justice in a structured manner in order assist the Member States, consumer representatives and the business community in applying the Directive.

II. General Standards of Unfairness

A. Unconscionability

Several reporters stated that general standards of unfairness can be applied to limit or void unfair contract terms, particularly the doctrine of unconscionability. The unconscionability doctrine is one of the few doctrines that allows a consumer to avoid harsh contract terms to which it has technically agreed either by signing, clicking or manifesting some other form of assent to those terms. It seems to have universal usage throughout the world in one form or another. In its most common form, the doctrine requires proof of both procedural defects and substantive unfair terms, although in the vast majority of consumer contracts there will be procedural defects (absence of meaningful choice) since most consumer contracts are not negotiable and terms are dictated by the trader, usually on standard forms that all consumers must sign. Moreover, in most consumer settings there is not sufficient time to read through the trader's standard contract, and most consumers would not understand many of the terms if they took time to do so.

The substantive element, however, is often contested in consumer cases. Several of the reporting countries noted that a term is substantively unconscionable if it (1) excludes or limits the consumer's remedies for death or personal injury caused by a wrongful act of the business, or for loss caused by an intentional or negligent act of the business, (2) unreasonably expands the business's remedies or its enforcement powers or (3) unreasonably limits the consumer's ability to seek reasonable redress for a violation of a legal right. These are discussed in more detail in the fourth part of this chapter.

Courts have, generally speaking, found terms unconscionable if they have an unreasonably adverse effect on a consumer's justifiable expectations in the context of the transaction. Examples of terms held to be unconscionable in the United States include a term whereby a consumer receives a product that does not work but is barred from a refund by a warranty disclaimer,[5] clauses that require arbitration in a foreign jurisdiction or where the filing fee greatly exceeds the amount of the claim[6] and a term that gives the merchant the unfettered power to act unilaterally, such as where the agreement includes open terms and the seller has the right to fill in any term it chooses.[7] A similar list of specific unfair practices in various country reports can be seen in the fourth part of this chapter.

[5] See *Universal Leasing Servs, Inc v Flushing Hae Kwan Restaurant*, 169 AD2d 829, 565 NYS2d 199 (2d Dep't 1991); *Industralease Automated & Scientific Equipment Corp v RME Enterprises, Inc*, 58 AD2d 482, 396 NYS2d 427 (2d Dep't 1977).

[6] *Brower v Gateway 2000, Inc*, 246 AD2d 246, 676 NYS2d 569 (1st Dep't 1998); *Teleserve Sys, Inc v MCI Telecomm. Corp*, 230 AD2d 585, 659 NYS2d 659 (4th Dep't 1997).

[7] *Sunbeam Farms, Inc v Troche*, 110 Misc 2d 501, 442 NYS2d 842 (Civ Ct, Bronx Co 1981); cf *Nalezenec v Blue Cross of W NY*, 172 AD2d 1004, 569 NYS2d 264 (4th Dep't 1991); *Zuckerberg v Blue Cross & Blue Shield*, 119 Misc 2d 834, 888, 464 NYS2d 678 (Sup Ct, Nassau Co 1983), rev'd on other grounds, 108 AD2d 56, 487 NYS2d 595 (2d Dep't 1985), aff'd, 67 NY2d 688, 499 NYS2d 920 (1986).

With respect to unconscionability, the Malaysia report presented a detailed list of factors a tribunal will consider when assessing procedural and substantive unfairness. These factors would likely be considered in most countries when examining the unfairness of a consumer contract term so they are worth summarising here. In determining procedural unfairness, the tribunal will inquire about (a) the general knowledge and understanding of the consumer; (b) the relative bargaining strength of the parties; (c) whether the agreement was negotiated or embodied in a standard form; (d) whether terms were in fine print or are difficult to read or understand; (e) the consumer's ability to appreciate the importance of a contract term of the contract or its implications by reason of age, sickness, or physical, mental, educational or linguistic disability, or emotional distress or ignorance of business affairs; (f) whether the consumer had access to legal advice; (g) the extent to which contract terms were explained to the consumer; and (h) whether the consumer relied on the skill, care or advice of the trader in entering into the contract.

For substantive unfairness, the Malaysia report stated that a tribunal will inquire whether the term (a) is in itself harsh or oppressive; (b) excludes or restricts liability for negligence; (c) excludes or restricts liability for breach of express or implied terms without justification; (d) imposes conditions that are difficult or impossible to comply with; (e) is contrary to reasonable standards of fair dealing; (f) will result in a substantially unequal exchange of value; and (g) will result in the benefits received by the consumer being manifestly disproportionate or inappropriate to his or her circumstances.[8] An additional factor might be whether the consumer was in a fiduciary relationship with the trader, in which case the consumer would justifiably have even higher expectations that the trader will observe standards of fair dealing.

While a list of factors such as these is helpful in defining the parameters of the unconscionability doctrine, one of the enduring strengths of the doctrine is its elasticity and ability to adapt to changing times and commercial practices. Although the unconscionability standard is not easy to satisfy, it is malleable enough to give consumers an opportunity to limit the effects of standard contract terms as consumer transactions evolve and new areas of commerce emerge.

B. Good Faith

Among legal doctrines that can limit the effect of standard terms in consumer contracts, the good faith doctrine has probably been the most controversial and has seen the most evolution over time.[9] Several of the reporters noted that some form of good faith

[8] This aspect of the Malaysian law (distinguishing between procedural and substantive unfairness) was influenced by the work of the Indian Law Commission in 2006. See Law Commission of India, '199th Report on Unfair (Procedural and Substantive) Terms in Contract' (August 2006); A Manaf and N Amiruddin, 'Comparative Study on Law of Unfair Contract Terms in Malaysia' in *Proceedings of ADVED 2018-4th International Conference on Advances in Education and Social Sciences, 15–17 October 2018*, Istanbul, Turkey, at n 17.

[9] Some of the discussion in this section is drawn from a previous paper by the author. See P Nehf, 'Bad Faith Breach of Contract in Consumer Transactions' in R Brownsword et al (eds), *Good Faith Contract: Concept and Context* (Aldershot: Dartmouth, 1999) 115.

doctrine exists as a limit on unfair terms in their countries. If a standard term addresses matters arising post-contract formation, that is, during contract performance, particularly if it gives the business discretion in performing its obligations, those obligations and responsibilities must be exercised in good faith.

Like the doctrine of unconscionability, the good faith concept is fluid, highly adaptable and not easily reduced to a concise formula. The official comment to the Restatement (Second) of Contracts acknowledges that 'its meaning varies somewhat with the context', but offers little in the way of guidance. It explains that good faith has something to do with the expectations of the parties and general principles of fairness and moral behaviour. Good faith 'emphasizes faithfulness to an agreed common purpose and consistency with the justified expectations of the other party', and in contrast, bad faith conduct 'violate[s] community standards of decency, fairness or reasonableness'. Similar characterisations of the good faith doctrine appear in some of the country reports. While there will always be some uncertainty when a party is charged with bad faith conduct, the problem is no different from the other disputes that require reasonable implications about the parties' legitimate expectations created in the bargain.[10]

III. Procedural Unfairness

Private law is legitimised by consent between individuals or groups. Contract law, in particular, has long been viewed as a legitimate creation of private law because it results from voluntary undertakings that direct the behaviour of two or more willing parties. Although the consent model of contract law is still taught in most law schools, it is widely viewed as an inadequate description of and normative justification for modern contractual relationships. Standard form consumer contracts are consent-based on only the most basic terms. In most transactions, at least one party (and sometimes both) has little awareness of contract terms, and it is difficult to defend term legitimacy on consent grounds alone.

One way of addressing this problem is to create an environment in which informed, subjective consent is more likely to occur. Laws calling for conspicuous disclosure of terms, notice of contract rights, plain language and mandatory rescission or cooling-off periods try to ensure that consumers make better informed and more voluntary decisions.

Several of the country reports discussed consumer protection laws that are designed to address procedural defects in consumer contracting. As a general matter, several country reports stated that ambiguous terms in a contract will be construed in the consumer's favour. That is sometimes the case in the United States as well, but only as a last resort. If other contract interpretation rules dictate a particular meaning, those rules will be followed.[11] Stating such a rule in a consumer protection statute seems like a

[10] Stephen Burton's Harvard Law Review article took Farnsworth's view in a different direction. See S Burton, 'Breach of Contract and the Common Law Duty to Perform in Good Faith' (1980) 94 *Harvard Law Review* 369.

[11] See, eg, *Klapp v United Insurance Group Agency, Inc*, 468 Mich 459, 471; 663 NW2d 447 (2003).

good idea. Other unfair procedural practices mentioned in the country reports include drafting a contract with important terms hidden or including important terms that are difficult to read (Indonesia), drafting contract terms that are difficult to understand (Indonesia), using aggressive sales tactics that undermine informed and deliberate consumer decision making (Macau), not making standard terms available to consumers for review prior to contract formation (Taiwan) and not providing copies of contracts to consumers to keep (Taiwan).

IV. Specific Prohibitions

Most of the country reports highlighted specific types of contract terms that are generally deemed to be unfair in consumer contracts, although some reports included more details than others. While the reports did not provide complete and exclusive lists of prohibited terms, when read together they give a general sense of the types of terms that are likely candidates for characterisation as unfair to consumers.

A. Exemption Clauses

Most prominent are clauses that seek to insulate the trader from liability: exempting liability for personal injury to the consumer (China, Hong Kong, Singapore), exempting liability for property damages to the consumer as a result of deliberate intent or gross negligence (China), waiver of a consumer's important legal rights (China, Japan, Taiwan) and excluding liability of the trader generally for nonconforming performance (Hong Kong, Indonesia, Japan, Taiwan, Thailand, Vietnam).

B. Trader Rights

Another common set of unfair terms concerns a trader's ability to make decisions unilaterally and arbitrarily without consumer consent: binding consumers to contracts by consumer inaction (Japan), arbitrary imposition of additional charges (Indonesia, Vietnam), permitting the trader to ignore contractual obligations, modify the contract, or terminate the contract unilaterally without cause (India, Thailand, Vietnam), refusing to accept return of defective goods (Indonesia) and failure to refund money for defective goods (Indonesia).

C. Dispute Resolution

Several of the reports addressed unfair terms regarding dispute resolution, including mandatory binding arbitration of consumer disputes (Hong Kong) and dispute resolution in a forum other than the consumer's domicile (Indonesia). This is one area where a stark contrast can be seen with the United States, where binding arbitration in consumer contracts is an increasingly common contract term. These clauses typically state that the trader can require that disputes between them be resolved by privately appointed arbitrators, sometimes with an exception for cases brought in small claims court (where the trader can go to collect an overdue payment). Where these clauses exist, the trader can block lawsuits from proceeding in a court of general jurisdiction. These clauses also typically bar consumers from bringing group claims (class actions) either in court or in the arbitration proceeding. As a result, no matter how many consumers are injured by the same conduct, consumers must resolve their claims individually against the company in binding arbitration. If the amount in controversy is relatively small, the costs of arbitration alone will deter most consumers (and lawyers) from bringing the case. Mandatory consumer arbitration has long been under attack by consumer advocates and others who have found fault with both the manner in which arbitration is agreed to, the process itself, and the results of arbitration proceedings. In a series of court decisions,[12] however, the US Supreme Court has generally enforced mandatory arbitration provisions in consumer contracts despite strong opposition from consumer groups and their lawyers, and despite the holdings of many lower courts that have been more sympathetic to consumers' concerns.[13]

D. Excessive Pricing and Profiteering

Excessive pricing and profiteering was another common theme: interest rate caps and exorbitant pricing (Thailand), unreasonably high security deposits (India), imposing unreasonable charges or obligations on a consumer (India) and disproportionate penalties for breach of contract (India, Japan).

E. Bad Faith

While the above lists can be viewed as enumerated examples of substantively unconscionable contract terms, a final group seen in the country reports might be characterised as instances of the traders not acting in good faith toward the consumer: exercising

[12] See *AT&T Mobility LLC v Concepcion*, 563 US 333 (2011), which declared the supremacy of the Federal Arbitration Act and its preemption of state laws banning class-arbitration waivers. Later in *DirecTV, Inc v Imburgia*, 136 S Ct 463 (US 2015), the Supreme Court affirmed an intermediate California state court's interpretation of idiosyncratic language in an arbitration clause, ensuring that a case would be sent to arbitration rather than proceeding as a class action in court. See also *CompuCredit Corp v Greenwood*, 132 S Ct 665 (2012); *American Express Co v Italian Colors Restaurant*, 133 S Ct 2304 (2013)(a contractual waiver of class arbitration is enforceable under the Federal Arbitration Act even though the plaintiff's cost of individually arbitrating a federal statutory claim exceeds the potential recovery).

[13] See, eg, *Carmona v Lincoln Millenium Car Wash, Inc*, 226 Cal App 4th 74, 88 (Cal Ct App 2014); *Samaniego v Empire Today LLC*, 205 Cal App 4th 1138, 1143 (Cal Ct App 2012); *Ajamian v CantorCO2e, LP*, 203 Cal App 4th 771, 799–800 (Cal Ct App 2012). Some courts continue to resist (or distinguish) Supreme Court precedent and refuse to enforce arbitration clauses with class action waivers. See, eg, *Meyer v Kalanick*, 2016 US Dist LEXIS 60816 (SDNY May 7, 2016).

undue influence over the consumer (India), failure to disclose a known defect (Japan), agreements that are immoral or contrary to public policy (India), refusing to accept early repayment of a consumer debt (India) and assignment of contracts to third parties causing detriment to the consumer without the consumer's consent (India, Vietnam).

V. Consequences of Including Unfair Terms

Consumer rights without effective remedies are almost worthless. In all of the country reports, if a contract term is deemed to be unfair it can be declared null and void by a court. In some countries (for example, Macau) certain unfair terms are void in all circumstances while other terms are voidable on a case-by-case basis. Along the same lines, Australia has a 'grey' list of fourteen contract terms that can be declared unfair depending on the circumstances.

The remedy of avoidance alone is not always effective, however, because there is no real penalty for including unfair terms if the only consequence is term avoidance. A trader has little to lose by including unfair terms if the only remedy is non-enforcement of the term. Several of the country reports discussed additional penalties for including unfair terms in contracts. In some countries there may be criminal liability (Indonesia, Macau, Malaysia, Myanmar). Others mentioned administrative fines and suspension of business activities as additional penalties (Indonesia, Vietnam), or require the trader to make restitution to consumers who are harmed by imposition of the unfair term (Vietnam).

The most common remedy in the United States is to render the unfair contract term null and void. Restatement (Second) of Contracts states:

> If a contract or term thereof is unconscionable at the time the contract is made a court may refuse to enforce the contract, or may enforce the remainder of the contract without the unconscionable term, or may so limit the application of any unconscionable term as to avoid any unconscionable result.[14]

It would be highly unusual for criminal penalties to result from a trader including unfair terms, although in extreme situations it might be possible to bring an action under the Racketeer Influenced and Corrupt Organizations (RICO) Act.[15] Occasionally a state or federal statute will provide for a monetary remedy when a trader includes particular prohibited term in a consumer contract. The federal Truth-In-Lending Act,[16] for example, has numerous disclosure rules which if violated can subject the creditor to monetary penalties that the consumer may recover.

[14] Uniform Commercial Code Section 2-302 has a similar provision for unconscionable terms in contracts for the sale of goods.

[15] 18 USC §§ 1961 et seq.

[16] 15 USC §§ 1601–1667f.

VI. Conclusion

Every country report addressed how standard form contracts are regulated. Some countries have adopted fairly rigid rules for traders who use standard terms in certain economic sectors, requiring them to use specified terms in their contracts or get state approval of their standard terms prior to their use. This pro-active approach is perhaps the starkest contrast to the regulation of unfair terms in the United States, where neither the federal nor state governments require that traders use a government sanctioned contract or require traders to submit their contracts for approval before using them in consumer transactions.[17] Consumer legislation certainly exists at federal, state and (sometimes) local/city levels. Often these enactments dictate that certain standard terms must be included in consumer contracts (most frequently disclosure requirements), and sometimes they dictate that certain terms may not be included in consumer contracts. But none go so far as to require that a trader must use an approved consumer contract in order to do business.

We still adhere to the pretence of consumer 'assent' to the non-negotiable terms that the traders foist upon us. We are constantly playing 'catch-up' as traders find new ways to take advantage of consumers. Legislation occasionally gets amended to address emerging trends. Litigation sometimes can challenge the use of unfair terms in court, but with the expansion of binding arbitration of consumer disputes the importance of court supervision of unfair terms is steadily diminishing. A more pro-active approach – standard terms agreed upon by industry, consumer representatives and state actors – seems to be a fairer and more efficient solution, but in legal system that frequently values trader autonomy over consumer welfare, it is not likely to happen anytime soon.

To the extent the national legislation discussed in this book has been influenced more by the European approach to regulating unfair contract terms than the American model, it is fair to say that consumer contracts in Asia are likely to be more protective of consumer interests than they are in the United States.

[17] One exception might be insurance contracts, where state insurance regulators provide some oversight of the insurers' contract provisions.

18

Product Liability

MICHEL CANNARSA

I. Introduction

Product liability refers to the liability of commercial suppliers of defective goods causing damage to persons and property. It is generally considered as an area of tort law even though, historically, contractual remedies have played a significant role in shaping producers' liability towards end-users of products. The rationale behind product liability is, through the possibility for victims of defective goods to claim compensation, to give producers incentives to ensure products' safety. Product liability is supposed to reach a fair allocation of risks among consumers and producers, who are in the best position to avoid defects in goods (that is, the cheapest cost avoiders).

In most jurisdictions, product liability developed as a part of contract law and/or tort law. Courts and legislators historically relied on warranty claims, before introducing more recently consumer regulations creating new legal grounds for direct producers' liability to the ultimate consumer, while introducing several binding product safety and product recall rules.[1] Though contractual and warranty claims never really left the scene, extracontractual producers' liability is supposed to be the most appropriate tool to deal with such cases, especially to prevent privity of contract from being an obstacle to compensation.[2] Extracontractual producers' liability has been first based on negligence or tortious misrepresentation, before switching to strict liability in tort, at least in some jurisdictions including the United States and the European Union.[3] As discussed

[1] For a general picture of product liability and consumer product safety law in the ASEAN region, see L Nottage and S Thanitcul, *Asean Product Liability and Consumer Product Safety Law* (Bangkok: Winyuchon Publication House, 2016).

[2] In China for example, liability for defective product is mainly considered as a specific category of liability in tort: see Chapter 5 of the 2009 Tort Law and Articles 1202–07 of the new Civil Code (Book VII Tort Liability, Chapter IV Product Liability, to enter into force on 1 January 2021). Several other provisions are more or less closely related to product liability: the Product Quality Law promulgated in 1993 and revised in 1999 (special law on product quality and liability, defining liabilities of producers and sellers and providing a framework for damage allocation), the Law on the Protection of Consumer Rights and Interests of 1993 (current version of 2013) and the Food Safety Law.

[3] US law has been a major source of influence in this legal area. In the 1980s, the European Economic Communities – now European Union (EU) – introduced the Council Directive 85/374/EEC of 25 July 1985 on the approximation of the laws, regulations and administrative provisions of the Member States

later,[4] the assumption that the liability regime is one of strict liability could be challenged though, not necessarily when we consider the ground of liability, but more when we look at defences available to the producers, especially the development risk defence.

The next few pages are dedicated to a comparative overview of product liability in Asia, mainly based on the national reports included in the present book. The various doctrines in the field of product liability and its central notions (producer, defect, damage, defences, etc) will constitute the reference points of the analysis, highlighting if and how they are included, interpreted and implemented in the various Asian jurisdictions under study. In addition, the recent development of digital technologies and digital goods will be considered in order to check whether the current product liability rules in the various jurisdictions covered are fit for the said digital age.[5] Indeed, though product liability generally takes a neutral standpoint vis-à-vis technology, many of the legal notions generally involved in product liability rules deserve to be analysed and possibly updated in the light of the digital evolution in order to preserve the said neutral standpoint and the fair allocation of risks among consumers and producers.

II. Strict Product Liability

Before strict product liability emerged, common law jurisdictions recognised that a duty of care was imposed on manufacturers in certain circumstances, relying on negligence-based tort liability. After US law,[6] English law moved in the same direction with the 1932 House of Lords decision in *Donoghue v Stevenson*,[7] introducing the general tort of negligence in a product liability case. Then, common law and civil law jurisdictions moved progressively from negligence-based liability in product liability cases to strict liability in tort, at least as far as manufacturing defects are concerned.[8] Strict product

concerning liability for defective products, OJ 1985 No L201, p 29 (Product Liability Directive), inspired to a large extent by US law. Due to the fast evolution of the digital economy, there is an ongoing assessment process of the Product Liability Directive. The conclusions of an expert group have been published in October 2019: Expert Group on Liability and New Technologies – New Technologies Formation, 'Liability for Artificial Intelligence and other emerging digital technologies'.

[4] See below, at s V, dedicated to burden of proof and defences.

[5] Though not within the scope of this Chapter dedicated to extracontractual rules on product liability, it is worth mentioning the recent adoption of Directive (EU) 2019/771 of 20 May 2019 on certain aspects concerning contracts for the sale of goods, OJ 2019 No L136, p 28. This new piece of legislation brings several updates, especially to consider the new technology-driven economy. It was introduced in parallel to Directive (EU) 2019/770 of 20 May 2019 on certain aspects concerning contracts for the supply of digital content and digital services, laying down rules on certain requirements concerning contracts for the said contracts, OJ 2019 No L136, p 1. Directive 2019/771 contains new rules regarding goods with digital content, introducing new aspects of conformity and seller's liability. These two new pieces of legislation might be of interest for the legislators in the various jurisdictions covered in this book in case of a need to update their own legislation.

[6] Court of Appeals of New York, *MacPherson v Buick Motor Co*, 111 NE 1050 (NY 1916).

[7] [1932] AC 562. The fact that *Donoghue v Stevenson* created a completely new category in the law of torts can be discussed: 'What Donoghue v Stevenson did may be described either as the widening of an old category or as the creation of a new and similar one. The general conception can be used to produce either categories in the same way', *Hedley Byrne v Heller* [1964] AC 465, 525, per Devlin LJ.

[8] There is a manufacturing defect when the product departs from its intended design even though all possible care was exercised in the preparation and marketing of the product (See US Restatement Third on Products Liability – US Restatement, § 2).

liability was formalised in the US Restatement (Second) of Torts, at § 402A, and later in 1985 in EU law when the Product Liability Directive was introduced. It is worth indicating that the vast majority of the jurisdictions covered by this book have specific laws, rather recent (consumer protection acts, most of the time) dealing, among others, with product liability. Depending on their history, the said jurisdictions have been influenced by civil law and/or common law models and have structured their legal systems accordingly, while developing domestic peculiarities. For all of them, the sources of product liability are, if not exclusively, mostly written sources.

Both in EU and US law, producers' liability is based on the defect of the product having caused damage.[9] A product is defective when 'it does not provide the safety which a person is entitled to expect'.[10] Safety is therefore a key notion and is not necessarily a unitary concept. Three different defects shall be considered, even if they are not formally distinguished in the various domestic product liability laws:[11] manufacturing defects, warning or instruction defects and design defects.[12] Strict liability applies fully only in case of manufacturing defects as it will highlighted later, while analysing the development risk defence. In India, a recent Consumer Protection Act 2019 contains provisions on strict product liability, where the liability is based on the defectiveness of the product causing harm. In Chinese law, the notion of defectiveness is also mainly based on the unreasonable lack of safety on one side, a concept very similar to the one in Article 6(1) of the Product Liability Directive, and on various national and industry safety standards on the other side. Product liability seems therefore to be a strict liability, according to Article 41 of the Chinese Tort Law. However, Article 42 of the Tort Law provides for a negligence-based liability in tort, in certain circumstances. In Australia, a strict product liability regime exists, when goods having a safety defect caused harm. In practice, the strict product liability regime seems however often argued in conjunction with an action based on the tort of negligence, where the negligence argument predominates. In Japan, the Product Liability Act 1994 is the main legal basis when defective goods caused damage.[13] In Taiwan, product liability derives from the Consumer Protection Act and corresponds to a strict liability. In Thailand, the Unsafe Product Liability Act of 2008 defines defectiveness by relying on the concept of safety and introduced a strict extracontractual liability regime.[14] In Indonesia, the

[9] According to Article 1 of the Product Liability Directive (EU): 'The producer shall be liable for damage caused by a defect in his product'. In US law, the statement is the same: 'one engaged in the business of selling or otherwise distributing products who sells or distributes a defective product is subject to liability for harm to persons or property caused by the defect' (US Restatement, § 1). See M Reimann, 'Liability for Defective Products and Services: Emergence of a Worldwide Standard?' (2003) 51(4) *American Journal of Comparative Law* 751.

[10] Product Liability Directive (EU), Art 6.

[11] Unlike the Product Liability Directive (EU), the US Restatement formally distinguishes the three categories of defects in its § 2: 'A product is defective when, at the time of sale or distribution, it contains a manufacturing defect, is defective in design or is defective because of inadequate instructions or warnings'.

[12] The distinction between the three different defects is for example included in the Vietnamese Law on Consumer Protection, Art 3(3), as well as in the Thai Unsafe Product Liability Act and in the Indian Consumer Protection Act. Japanese law seems to make the distinction as well in practice.

[13] Japanese product liability seems in reality based on an objective concept of fault, rather than on a true no-fault liability.

[14] A bill on defective goods was discussed in the parliament in 2020.

legal regime is described as a strict liability one, even though the producer is entitled to prove that he was not at fault. Malaysian law also has a strict product liability regime, based on the Consumer Protection Act 1999, followed by Vietnam with its 2010 Law on Consumer Protection. At the opposite, in Hong Kong, product liability claims still rely on traditional rules applicable to sale of goods contracts,[15] or on negligence-based tort actions and it seems to be the case in Singapore as well, where no specific strict product liability exists.[16]

As far as digital goods are concerned, many ongoing works and reflexions aim at making sure that artificial intelligence (AI) and embedded AI is humancentric and trustworthy. A recent study by Harvard's Berkman Klein Center for Internet and Society mapped out and analysed not less than 36 AI principles documents.[17] In the various national reports of this book, there does not seem to be an indication of specific legal provisions dedicated to digital goods and/or AI. In the field of product liability, and elaborating on the current reflexions, one could foresee evolutions coming rather soon.[18] For example, we could imagine that products have to be 'ethical by design': if a product's design does not comply with the ethical principles developed in a given jurisdiction, then it might be deemed to constitute a form of design defect: the product would be deemed not to present the level of safety that may be legitimately expected, as it does not achieve a sufficient level of compliance with ethical rules. The increasingly connected nature of products also raises problems of vulnerability to cyberattacks. This being the case, the idea is envisaged of integrating into the notion of defectiveness, the level of cybersecurity that may be legitimately expected.[19]

III. Products and Producers

The notion of producer is generally quite broadly intended, even if not necessarily clearly defined. Depending on the jurisdictions concerned, the scope of this category can therefore be more or less extended. In the Product Liability Directive, the person liable in case of damage caused by a defective product is the producer. According to its Article 3, the importer into the EU and/or each supplier of the product shall be treated as its producer if the manufacturer is not based in the EU in the first situation,

[15] Hong Kong Sale of Goods Ordinance.

[16] Whereas liability based on the Sale of Goods Act is strict and not fault-based.

[17] J Fjeld et al, 'Principled Artificial Intelligence: Mapping Consensus in Ethical and Rights-based Approaches to Principles for AI', Research Publication No. 2020-1, available at: https://cyber.harvard.edu/publication/2020/principled-ai. The authors note that '[i]n the past several years, seemingly every organization with a connection to technology policy has authored or endorsed a set of principles for AI. As guidelines for ethical, rights-respecting, and socially beneficial AI develop in tandem with – and as rapidly as – the underlying technology, there is an urgent need to understand them, individually and in context'.

[18] The European Commission is conducting a review of the Product Liability Directive in order to improve it and to address the challenges of the digital economy and AI. A possible adaptation of the Directive could be proposed by the end of 2022.

[19] See Expert Group on Liability and New Technologies – New Technologies Formation, 'Liability for Artificial Intelligence'.

and if the manufacturer (or the importer) cannot be identified in the second case.[20] In the US Restatement Third on Products Liability (US Restatement), the liability rules are applied to manufacturers and other commercial sellers and distributors engaged in the business of selling or otherwise distributing the type of product that harmed the plaintiff.[21] Most Asian product liability laws target the producer or importer as well,[22] even though they tend to go beyond the strictly defined notion of producer. In Thailand for example, claims can be directed against sellers as well, even when the seller is not aware of the defect, while the court can call the manufacturer or the importer into the case. In India too, it seems that not only producers but also sellers can be sued in case of harm caused by defective goods.

Concerning products, goods that traditionally fall into the scope of application of the relevant provisions are movables, tangible personal property distributed commercially for use or consumption, but also electricity,[23] having been put into circulation. Because many of the domestic rules in the various Asian countries under study are rather recent, it seems that intangible goods are more likely to be included into the concept of 'product'.[24] Even though the Product Liability Directive and other similar provisions take a neutral standpoint vis-à-vis technology, the notion of product contained within it has been conceived in terms of, and is aimed primarily at, tangible objects. The EU legislator seems to consider software programs as products, notably via the Machinery Directive,[25] Radio Equipment Directive[26] and the Medical

[20] Product Liability Directive (EU), Art 3: '(1) "Producer" means the manufacturer of a finished product, the producer of any raw material or the manufacturer of a component part and any person who, by putting his name, trade mark or other distinguishing feature on the product presents himself as its producer. (2) Without prejudice to the liability of the producer, any person who imports into the Community a product for sale, hire, leasing or any form of distribution in the course of his business shall be deemed to be a producer within the meaning of this Directive and shall be responsible as a producer. (3) Where the producer of the product cannot be identified, each supplier of the product shall be treated as its producer unless he informs the injured person, within a reasonable time, or the identity of the producer or of the person who supplied him with the product. The same shall apply, in the case of an imported product, if this product does not indicate the identity of the importer to in paragraph 2, even if the name of the producer is indicated'.

[21] Comment (c) to § 1 states: 'The rule stated in this Section applies only to manufacturers and other commercial sellers and distributors who are engaged in the business of selling or otherwise distributing the type of product that harmed the plaintiff ... Whether a defendant is a commercial seller or distributor within the meaning of this Section is usually a question of law to be determined by the court'. According to comment (e), 'The rule stated in this Section provides that all commercial sellers and distributors of products, including nonmanufacturing sellers and distributors such as wholesalers and retailers, are subject to liability for selling products that are defective. Liability attaches even when such nonmanufacturing sellers or distributors do not themselves render the product defective and regardless of whether they are in a position to prevent defects from occurring'. This rule is designed to offer the greatest protection to the injured person and to prevent the absence of compensation when the manufacturer is insolvent. A manufacturer of a defective product component will also be subject to the liability (US Restatement, § 5; Product Liability Directive (EU), Art 3(1)).

[22] See eg Consumer Protection Act 1999 (Malaysia), s 68(1), according to which the liable person is the producer of the product, or the person putting his name/mark on the product, or the importer.

[23] Product Liability Directive (EU), Art 2; US Restatement, § 19.

[24] This is the case, for example, in Indonesia.

[25] Directive 2006/42/EC of the European Parliament and of the Council of 17 May 2006 on machinery, OJ 2006 No L157, p 24.

[26] Directive 2014/53/EU of the European Parliament and of the Council of 16 April 2014 on the harmonisation of the laws of the Member States relating to the making available on the market of radio equipment, OJ 2014 No L153, p 62.

Devices Regulations,[27] which regards software programs as products. Another factor to be taken into consideration when studying the notion of a product in the context of emerging digital technologies is the evolutive, non-static and partly unpredictable nature of new 'smart devices'. The so-called 'autonomous' systems, which possess machine-learning capability, present the dual characteristic of being both autonomous (given that their 'behaviour' is not necessarily entirely predictable) and also evolutive (the producer of this type of system might then take the view that it cannot be held liable for any unpredictable and autonomous 'adverse behaviour' on the part of its products). These various features impact primarily on the liability regime binding the producer and more particularly on the latter's capacity to deny liability, in whole or in part, based on the notion either of development risk or of the victim's wrongdoing. At this stage, the phenomenon is still recent and quite evolutive in nature. Hence, it does not seem to be considered in the various Asian legislation.

IV. Recoverable Damages

Recoverable damages in product liability claims are generally harm to persons or property: personal injury and property damage.[28] Traditionally, damages caused to the defective product itself are not recoverable under strict products liability rules.[29] Indeed, both the US Restatement and the Product Liability Directive exclude pure economic losses from the list of recoverable damages, these damages being generally recoverable under warranty laws and general contractual law rules. Considering the fact that boundaries between contractual and extracontractual liabilities in Asian jurisdictions seem sometimes to be blurred, consumers' claims could also include compensation for damage caused to the product itself. On another note, punitive damages are a feature of product liability in the United States, in contrast to the EU. Some Asian jurisdictions, as China and Thailand for example, have provisions imposing punitive damages, especially when the liable person knew about the defect and the risk, and did not act to prevent the harm to occur.

Concerning non-material damages, they are not always recoverable on the basis of the specific product liability rules. In the EU for example, non-material damages are recoverable on the basis of domestic rules, and not on the basis of the Product Liability Directive. Since one of the main features of the ecosystem based on emerging digital

[27] Regulation (EU) 2017/745 of the European Parliament and of the Council of 5 April 2017 on medical devices, OJ 2017 No L117, p 1; Regulation (EU) 2017/746 of the European Parliament and of the Council of 5 April 2017 on in vitro diagnostic medical devices, OJ 2017 No L117, p 176.

[28] See eg US Restatement, § 21. According to Art 9 of the Product Liability Directive (EU), damage means damage caused by death or by personal injuries; damage to, or destruction of, any item of property other than the defective product itself (with a minimum threshold of 500 euro) provided that the item of property is of a type ordinarily intended for private use or consumption and was used by the injured person mainly for his own private use or consumption.

[29] The US Restatement § 21, Comment (d) states that 'when a product defect results in harm to the product itself, the law governing commercial transactions sets forth a comprehensive scheme governing the rights of the buyer and seller'. This kind of loss is therefore recoverable under contractual claims.

technologies is its increasingly immaterial and intangible dimension, the harm that may be caused within its context will in all likelihood be of the same nature. The fact that information lies at the heart of the ecosystem in question should encourage reflection on the nature of any harm caused by erroneous/defective information. The prejudice suffered as a result of the unauthorised disclosure of personal data comes to mind quite naturally in this context, in addition to questions of how product liability will work in conjunction with the EU General Data Protection Regulation.[30]

V. Burden of Proof and Defences

The injured person must usually prove the damage, the defect and the causal relationship between defect and damage.[31] In the US Restatement, there are presumptions of defectiveness in certain circumstances: 'when the incident that harmed the plaintiff was of a kind that ordinarily occurs as a result of a product defect and was not, in the particular case, solely the result of causes other than product defect existing at the time of sale or distribution'.[32] In several Asian jurisdictions, it seems that the reversal of the burden of proof is a tool to come closer to a strict liability regime, producers being called to prove that they were not at fault.[33] For example, in Chinese law, there seems to be a presumption that, in case of damage, the product was defective and that the damage was caused by the defective product. Indeed, it is up to the producer to prove that there was no causal relationship between the defect and the damage or that the product was not defective. In Indonesia, the producer can escape liability by proving that he was not at fault, which means therefore that the regime is fault-based and not a strict liability regime. Most product liability legislations provide for exonerating circumstances.[34] The Product Liability Directive grants to the EU Member States the option whether to adopt a development risk defence or not.[35] Most EU Member States have adopted it as did the majority of jurisdictions in the United States. The Chinese Product Quality Law includes a development risk defence exemption. Indeed, the producer is not liable if, when the product was put into circulation and taking into account the scientific and technical knowledge, the defect could not be discovered.[36] The development risk defence

[30] Regulation (EU) 2016/679 of the European Parliament and of the Council of 27 April 2016 on the protection of natural persons with regard to the processing of personal data and on the free movement of such data, and repealing Directive 95/46/EC (General Data Protection Regulation), OJ 2016 No L119, p 1.

[31] See eg Product Liability Directive (EU), Art 4.

[32] US Restatement, § 3.

[33] It is stated for example that, in Indonesia, defendants have to prove that they are innocent. In Taiwan, liable producers can escape liability by proving that the product was in conformity with security standards.

[34] Usual defences are, alternatively, that the product was not put into circulation by the producer; that the defect did not exist at the time when the product was put into circulation; that the product was neither manufactured for sale or any form of distribution for economic purpose nor manufactured or distributed professionally; that the defect is due to compliance of the product with mandatory regulations issued by public authorities (this latter defence is present in some of the Asian jurisdictions studied, as for example in China, possibly inspired by a similar rule in the US Restatement, at § 4(a)).

[35] A producer can avail himself of the said defence when the state of scientific and technical knowledge at the time when he put the product into circulation was not such as to enable the existence of the defect to be discovered (see Article 15(b) of the Product Liability Directive).

[36] Product Quality Law (China), Art 41(2) No 3.

exists in other jurisdictions as Australia, Malaysia[37] and Vietnam,[38] and is absent in others as in Thailand.

Development risks are a key issue in the various legal regimes and are the main indicator of a true strict liability regime. Indeed, if producers can escape liability by proving that the state of scientific and technical knowledge at the time when they put the product into circulation was not such as to enable the existence of the defect to be discovered, liability for design defects will be mainly based on negligence, that is, based on the fact that the producer could have discovered it by relying on the state of scientific and technical knowledge but he did not because of a lack of diligence.[39]

VI. Conclusion

The combined short analysis of US-American and EU product liability rules on one side, and the various Asian legislation on the other side, leads to some observations. At first glance, the various legal regimes seem to rely, at least to some extent, on the same concepts and the same liability rules. This probably highlights the initial influence of US law, and the subsequent influence of EU law. Taking these various product liability legislations as a whole, one could suggest some adjustments, especially considering the digital revolution. For example, a clarification of the various defect categories might be beneficial in the current thinking, notably as far as a lack of information or defective information are concerned. Given that information occupies a pivotal position in the new ecosystem, we should look closely at its potential defects. We might also consider a new category of defect, namely that of a 'behavioural' defect, for autonomous systems. It could also be interesting to reflect on the growing role of technical and safety regulations of technological goods and services on one side, and on the ethical rules for a trustworthy AI on the other side.

Also, the debate relating to the development risk defence is even more crucial in the context of AI, Internet of Things, etc. Indeed, in the field of machine learning and autonomous systems, producers could rely on the fact that the product was defect-free when put into circulation and that it later became defective, unpredictably, on the basis of its self-learning capacities/features. This would mean that more and more losses, caused by unforeseen consequences of emerging digital technologies and cybersecurity threats, would be supported by consumers. One of the issues here is therefore to determine whether the development risk clause should be maintained in the various legal regimes from an innovation perspective: a fair allocation of risks and losses between producers and consumers is a key concern in order to make digital goods and markets socially acceptable.

[37] Consumer Protection Act 1999 (Malaysia), Art 72(1)(d).
[38] Law on Consumer Protection 2010 (Vietnam), Art 24.
[39] See on this issue G Howells and M Mildred, 'Is European Products Liability More Protective than the Restatement (Third) of Torts: Products Liability?' (1998) 65 *Tennessee Law Review* 985.

More generally speaking, in the various Asian jurisdictions, something which is striking is the apparent lack of reported cases and, possibly, the lack of effectivity of the rules on product liability. Even though administrative bodies in charge of monitoring and, sometimes, introducing claims are quite frequent,[40] increasing therefore the level of effectivity of the rules concerned, it seems that one of the central points to be improved in the said jurisdictions are the means of enforcement and access to justice: legislative reforms could focus on it in the future.

[40] In Thailand for example, the Consumer Protection Board and, in Indonesia, the Consumer Dispute Settlement Agency.

19

Adaptation of Asian Consumer Law to the Digital Age

ALBERTO DE FRANCESCHI

I. Consumer Law Facing the Digital Age: The Global Challenge

Groundbreaking changes and challenges posed by the digital revolution require a legislative framework which proves to be fit for the digital age and takes into account current and emerging needs.[1] Such a framework has to provide businesses with the legal certainty they need to invest in this field and to support technological development, while adequately protecting buyers, users and data subjects.

Within the so-called Industry 4.0, digital technology significantly changes the balance in society and economic relationships, offering new opportunities for innovative business models. This raises challenging questions affecting several aspects of the law as for example the legal classification of data, data mining, trade in data,[2] the related intellectual property issues and the protection of personal data, Internet of Things, artificial intelligence[3] and algorithmic regulation,[4] online platforms,[5] etc.

[1] See eg G Howells, 'Protecting Consumer Protection Values in the Fourth Industrial Revolution' (2020) 46 *Journal of Consumer Policy* 145; H-W Micklitz et al (eds), *Verbraucherrecht 2.0. – Verbraucher in der digitalen Welt* (Baden-Baden: Nomos, 2017); R Brownsword, *Law 3.0: Rules, Regulation and Technology* (London: Routledge, 2020); A De Franceschi and R Schulze (eds), *Digital Revolution – New Challenges for Law. Data Protection, Artificial Intelligence, Smart Products, Blockchain Technology and Virtual Currencies* (Munich: CH Beck – Baden-Baden: Nomos 2019); C. Busch and A. De Franceschi, Algorithmic Regulation and Personalized Law (Munich: CH Beck – Oxford: Hart – Baden-Baden: Nomos, 2021).

[2] See S Lohsse, R Schulze and D Staudenmayer (eds), *Trading Data in the Digital Economy: Legal Concepts and Tools* (Baden-Baden: Nomos, 2017).

[3] See eg in the EU: European Commission, 'Report on the safety and liability implications of Artificial Intelligence, the Internet of Things and robotics' COM(2020) 64 final (2020); European Parliament, 'Resolution of 20 October 2020 with recommendations to the Commission on a civil liability regime for artificial intelligence' (2020/2014(INL)), P9 TA(2020)0276 (2020); Expert Group on Liability and New Technologies, 'Liability for Artificial Intelligence and other emerging Digital Technologies, Ethics guidelines for trustworthy AI' (2019).

[4] See eg S Lohsse, R Schulze and D Staudenmayer (eds), *Liability for Artificial Intelligence and the Internet of Things* (Baden-Baden: Nomos, 2019); C Busch and A De Franceschi (eds), *Algorithmic Regulation and Personalized Law*.

[5] See nn 10 and 11 below.

In the data-driven economy, data is handled both as a tradeable commodity and as a counter-performance:[6] transactions concerning data involve contract, property law and the protection of personality rights. This raises new issues, which impact on the very core of legal systems.

With the Digital Revolution expanding into increasingly more areas of life, new data-driven business models are being developed at a rapid pace which are based on the technological possibilities of Big Data analytics.[7] The spectrum ranges from personalised marketing on the Internet to telematics-based insurance and personalised medicine. In other areas, the new analytical tools are used for prognostic purposes, such as 'predictive maintenance' of machinery. Similarly, public agencies are using the technological possibilities of Big Data in the fight against crime through 'predictive policing'. The rise of Big Data analytics is fundamentally changing the legal system itself and the way legal rules are designed and applied.[8]

Contemporarily, the digitalisation of products, services and business processes has delivered a huge contribution to the spread and growth of online platform business models. The rise of the 'platform economy' is having a disruptive effect on both established business models and the associated legal rules.[9] Important problems and questions continue to arise not only concerning private law issues, but also regarding competition, administrative law and tax law.[10]

This is stimulating increased debate[11] and provoking legislative responses such as recently in the EU the proposals for a Data Governance Act and for a Data Act,[12] a Digital Services Act[13] and a Digital Markets Act.[14] The growing relevance of e-commerce exacerbates these problems, even more so after the outbreak of the Covid-19 pandemic. Furthermore, the digital revolution is now increasingly facing challenges concerning climate change and sustainability.

As Asia is one of the global leaders in the development of digital technologies, the case law and legislative activity concerning the emergence of digital technologies have taken off considerably in recent years. It is against this background that this contribution directs the attention towards the tasks and the problems arising from the Digital

[6] See S Lohsse, R Schulze and D Staudenmayer (eds), *Data as Counter-Performance – Contract Law 2.0?* (Baden-Baden: Nomos, 2020).

[7] See eg M Leistner, L Antoine and T Sagstetter, *Big Data* (Tübingen: Mohr Siebeck, 2021); P Hacker, *Datenprivatrecht* (Tübingen: Mohr Siebeck, 2020).

[8] H-W Micklitz, 'De- or Re-Typification through Big Data Analytics? The Case of Consumer Law', in Busch and De Franceschi, *Algorithmic Regulation*, 203–20.

[9] See C Busch et al, 'An Introduction to the ELI Model Rules on Online Platforms' (2020) 9 *Journal of European Consumer and Market Law* 61. Cf DS Evans and R Schmalensee, *Matchmakers: The New Economics of Multisided Platforms* (Boston: Harvard Business Review Press, 2016).

[10] NM Davidson, M Finck and JJ Infranca (eds), *The Cambridge Handbook of the Law of the Sharing Economy* (Cambridge: Cambridge University Press, 2018).

[11] See European Law Institute, 'Model Rules on Online Platforms' available from the ELI homepage under https://europeanlawinstitute.eu.

[12] See European Commission, 'Proposal for a Regulation of the European Parliament and of the Council on European Data Governance (Data Governance Act)' COM(2020) 767 final; European Commission, 'Proposal for a Regulation of the European Parliament and of the Council on harmonized rules on fair access to and use of data (Data Act)' COM(2022) 68 final.

[13] European Commission, 'Proposal for a Regulation of the European Parliament and of the Council on a Single Market for Digital Services (Digital Services Act)' COM(2020) 825 final.

[14] European Commission, 'Proposal for a Regulation of the European Parliament and of the Council on contestable and fair markets in the digital sector (Digital Markets Act)' COM(2020) 842 final.

Revolution in Asian countries, with the aim of assessing them from a global perspective, in order to stimulate solutions alongside national law at the 'junction' between national and international rules, so also and particularly within world regions and in regional supranational communities.

II. Origins, Jurisdiction, Borrowings

There is no underlying coherence in the consumer law regulation of digital technologies in Asia. Indeed, starting from diverse colonial influences, there are still relevant national differences.

When Singapore assumed the Chairmanship of the Association of Southeast Asian Nations (ASEAN) in 2018, it focused its efforts on realising an 'Asian Digital Single Market'. Agreements at member state level have therefore been reached regarding creating common rules or comparable standards for consumer protection and data protection insofar as these affect the intra-ASEAN digital trade in goods and services.[15] Meanwhile, ASEAN started a close cooperation with the European Commission and with the United States, in order to strengthen synergy in the regulation of the digital economy.[16]

Mainland China, Singapore and South Korea are leading in the process of adapting their legal system to the digital age. In particular, the e-commerce reform in China, which entered into force in 2019, signalled an important step for modernisation in continental Asia.[17] Meanwhile, the draft Chinese Internet Information Service Law is also in the preparatory stage.[18] These laws take a hybrid legal reception approach, and rely on the existing legislative experiences of the EU and the United States. The latest amendment to The Law on the Protection of Consumer Rights and Interests[19] introduced, inter alia, specific rules on online shopping.[20]

Other Asian legal systems are still at a very early stage of development as regards the regulation of the digital economy. Malaysia released in 1998 a now old-fashioned Communications and Multimedia Act and, in 2010, a Personal Data Protection Act. Hong Kong consumer law can still be considered 'analogue law' as it hardly deals with legal issues of the digital age.[21] Indeed, it does not have rules mandating consumer information in online sales and does not provide a mandatory cooling-off period for online consumers. Furthermore, Hong Kong has not adopted any specific rules related

[15] Eg 'ASEAN Framework on Digital Data Governance of 6 December 2018'; 'ASEAN Agreement on Electronic Commerce of 27 March 2019'.

[16] See eg: 'The EU and ASEAN: Building stronger digital economy & connectivity cooperation'; 'US-ASEAN Business Council, Digital Data Governance in ASEAN'.

[17] E-Commerce Law of the People's Republic of China, adopted at the Fifth Session of the Standing Committee of the 13th National People's Congress on 31 August 2018. See J Jing, 'China', in this volume.

[18] See Regulation on Internet Information Service of the People's Republic of China of 25 September 2000.

[19] The Law on the Protection of Consumer Rights and Interests came into force in 1993 and was amended twice in 2009 and 2013 respectively. In this regard, see Jing, 'China'.

[20] The Law on the Protection of Consumer Rights and Interests (China), Art 25.

[21] See M Durovic, G Howells and A Janssen, 'Hong Kong', in this volume.

to digital consumer contracts, for instance for digital downloads (for example apps) or streaming which are not covered by the existing consumer legislation.[22] Nevertheless, it has adopted modern data protection legislation.[23] It also has an Electronic Transactions Ordinance. The current focal point of Hong Kong's consumer policy (that is, from the past decade) is on sustainable consumption and personal privacy.[24] Vietnamese law is at a very early stage of development. There are almost no rules regarding digital products. In Indonesia, there is also little development of rules on consumer protection in the digital era. As a first attempt, in August 2018 several members of the Indonesian FinTech Association signed the Code of Conduct of Responsible Lending.[25]

Countries within the common law tradition (for example Australia, India, Singapore, Hong Kong) and countries with a civil law approach (for example Indonesia, Japan, Macau, Taiwan, Thailand and Vietnam) have been influenced by European and English law. The recent development in UK consumer law (in particular the Consumer Rights Act 2015) but also EU legislative instruments such as the new Digital Content Directive[26] and the Sale of Goods Directive[27] as well as the aforementioned EU Digital Services Act and EU Digital Markets Act might therefore represent good inspirations for related progress of national law in Asian countries. When it comes to digital means to be used for the resolution of consumer disputes, there are some recent developments in Asia of Online Dispute Resolution (ODR), for example India and Macau.[28] Here the EU and Brazilian ODR laws might serve as useful models, too.[29]

III. The Notions of Digital Goods and Digital Services

A big question regards the taxonomy of goods, digital products and digital services.[30] Some Asian jurisdictions already adapted their law in order to take into account the new entities in the realm of the digital economy. This will be an ongoing issue for transactions involving tangibles and software.

According to Hong Kong legislation, 'Goods' under the Sale of Goods Ordinance are defined to include all chattels personal other than things in action and money.[31]

[22] L Chen, 'Consumer Sales Law in Hong Kong' in L Chen et al (eds), *Comparative Consumer Sales* (London: Routledge, 2018) 74.

[23] Personal Data (Privacy) Ordinance (Cap 486); see S Wong and G Zhu, *Personal Data (Privacy) Law in Hong Kong: A Practical Guide on Compliance* (Hong Kong: City University of Hong Kong Press, 2016).

[24] Consumer Council, 'Landmark Events of the Council in 40 Years'.

[25] The code of conduct is put together by AFTECH's working group on financial inclusion and agreed upon voluntarily by its members providing online loans to consumers in Indonesia. See on this J Gunawan and BM Waluyo, 'Indonesia', in this volume.

[26] Directive (EU) 2019/770 of the European Parliament and of the Council of 20 May 2019 on certain aspects concerning contracts for the supply of digital content and digital services, OJ 2019 No L136, p 1.

[27] Directive (EU) 2019/771 of the European Parliament and of the Council of 20 May 2019 on certain aspects concerning contracts for the sale of goods, OJ 2019 No L136, p 28.

[28] See below, s VI.

[29] See Regulation (EU) No 524/2013 of the European Parliament and of the Council of 21 May 2013 on online dispute resolution for consumer disputes (Regulation on consumer ODR), OJ 2013 No L165, p 1. See below s VI. Cf Durovic, Howells and Janssen, 'Hong Kong'.

[30] See on this G Pearson, 'Sale of Goods: A Comparative Perspective', in this volume.

[31] Sale of Goods Ordinance (Hong Kong), s 2(1).

From this definition, it seems that digital content supplied in tangible form (for example as a CD or DVD) is subject to the rights and remedies provided for in the sale of goods legislation, but digital content supplied in intangible form (through downloads, streaming or other means) is not subject to similar statutory regulation. There is no other specific statutory regime for digital content yet in Hong Kong. However, the Consumer Council recommends to take action and to regulate this area of law.[32]

In Singapore, there is no specific consumer legislation regulating digital products:[33] this is perhaps an indication either that in the eyes of the policymaker, digital products are no different than real world products, or that the likely impact of digital products in the Singapore market is at present not significant enough to warrant legislative attention.[34] Vietnamese law regarding this issue is also at a very early stage of development. There are almost no special rules regulating digital products.[35] Under the current legal system in China, there is no clear normative system for digital content and digital services. China has neither introduced special rules on digital content within the current system of the Civil Code nor has it implemented separate legislation focused on digital content: such proposals for individual legislation have not been found at any legislative level. Under existing law, protection can only be based on copyright or trade secrets law, depending on the specific type of data. Litigation disputes related to digital content can only be resolved by returning to the existing general rules, that is, applying the general norms of the Civil Code.[36]

In passing it is interesting to note that the Australian Consumer Law definition of goods includes 'Computer software'; its definition of services specifically excludes 'rights or benefits being the supply of goods'.[37] A contract for services can include a supply of goods. In this respect, the Australian Federal Court held that downloads from an international online delivery platform for video games may be a supply of goods.[38] In order to work, the video games needed computer software and also included 'non-executable data such as music and html images'.[39] This given, the Australian Federal Court decided that the non-executable data was not goods. It accompanied and was incidental to the computer software, and it was 'hard to see how it could be decoupled from the computer software'[40] which was goods.[41] In this regard, the Court rejected the argument that because consumers required a licence to obtain and use the video games, there was no supply of goods.[42]

[32] Consumer Council, 'Online Retail: A Study on Hong Kong Consumer Attitudes, Business Practices and Legal Protection' (November 2016), 84 et seq. See Durovic, Howells and Janssen, 'Hong Kong'.

[33] There is no agenda tabled by the government on this issue, and, indeed, no discussion at present on the need to regulate digital products.

[34] G Low, 'Singapore', in this volume.

[35] N Van Cuong, 'Vietnam', in this volume.

[36] Jing, 'China'.

[37] Australian Consumer Law, s 2(1).

[38] *Australian Competition and Consumer Commission v Valve Corporation (No 3)* [2016] FCA 196 at [13]–[23].

[39] ibid at [138], [139].

[40] ibid, at [156].

[41] What was being supplied was games, computer software was at the heart of the provision of the games. Consumers believed they were purchasing computer software; ibid, at [157].

[42] See G Pearson, 'Australasia', in this volume.

IV. Data Protection

Regulation on data protection is experiencing an increasing development in Asian countries. In this regard, existing EU law is playing an important role. The EU General Data Protection Regulation[43] significantly influenced Thai legislation on data protection.[44] Taking inspiration from the EU Regulation, Singapore put in place rules governing the flow of information, which includes legislation aimed at protecting the collection and use of personal data.[45] As under the EU approach, the primary basis for consumer data protection in Singapore is consent: the Personal Data Protection Act requires consumers' consent to be obtained before personal data may be collected and used. Consumers may revoke consent at any time; if that happens, their personal data must be destroyed and proof of destruction must be provided. In particular, the Personal Data Protection Act established a nationwide Do-Not-Call Registry, which obliges telemarketers to check whether a consumer's telephone number is listed under the registry, before cold-calling. The protection of personal data is also regulated through sector-specific legislation such as the Statistics Act, the Banking Act and the Official Secrets Act. The Personal Data Protection Act specifically exempts[46] public institutions from complying with its obligations. This indicates that the statute is solely intended to regulate the flow of personal data between private persons. Taking inspiration from the EU General Data Protection Regulation again, Singapore is looking to establish standards for data portability, giving consumers greater control over personal data collected by businesses.

The Vietnamese legal system also provides for special rules regarding the flow of consumers' personal information.[47] Accordingly, where a trader authorises a third party to collect and store consumers' personal information, the contract between the two parties must clearly define the responsibility of each party to comply with data protection legislation and relevant regulations on the protection of personal information. Where this does not occur, the trader will be liable in case of unlawful collection, storage and use of personal information of consumers by third parties. In addition, traders who collect and use consumers' personal information shall formulate and communicate their personal information protection policy, which must be clearly displayed to consumers before or at the time of information collection. If the information collection is conducted through e-commerce websites of information collection units, the personal information protection policy must be publicly displayed at an easy-to-spot position on these websites. Pecuniary fines are provided for violations related to consumers' personal information such as illegal collection and storage of consumers' personal information.[48]

[43] Regulation (EU) 2016/679 of the European Parliament and of the Council of 27 April 2016 on the protection of natural persons with regard to the processing of personal data and on the free movement of such data, and repealing Directive 95/46/EC (General Data Protection Regulation), OJ 2016 No L119, p 1.

[44] Personal Data Protection Act BE 2562 (2019) (Thailand).

[45] The Personal Data Protection Act (Singapore) entered into force in 2012, and established the statutory Personal Data Protection Commission as the body charged with regulating all matters pertaining to personal data.

[46] While the Personal Data Protection Act (Singapore) does not apply to public agencies, these agencies are subject to similar data protection obligations under the Singapore Government Instruction Manual.

[47] Decree 52/2013/ND-CP (Vietnam).

[48] Fines up to 30,000,000 VND (approximately 1300 USD) per violation, as stipulated in Article 84 of Decree 15/2020/ND-CP.

Furthermore, Taiwan published a Computer-Processed Personal Data Protection Law[49] and Hong Kong has adopted modern data protection legislation.[50]

V. E-Commerce

E-commerce regulation is addressed in very different ways in the Asian countries. Some countries (such as China) take a hybrid legal reception approach, and rely on the existing legislative experiences from the EU and the United States. Other countries (for example Taiwan) take significant inspiration from EU law, and in particular from the rules contained in the Consumer Rights Directive.[51] Following this path, some Asian countries (as for example China, Taiwan and South Korea) provide a statutory right of withdrawal. Other countries (for example Hong Kong, Japan and Macau) do not provide such a right. Furthermore, the UNCITRAL Model Law on electronic commerce significantly influenced national regulation in Singapore and Thailand.

China plays a leading role in this regard as it adopted a modern and extensive e-commerce law, which entered into force in 2019. As noted above, not only is a draft Internet Information Service Law in the preparatory stage, but the Chinese Law on the Protection of Consumer Rights and Interests contains specific rules on online shopping, with information disclosure obligations covering specific areas such as online shopping, video shopping, mail order and financial services.[52] Under this Law, for some goods the consumer has a right to withdraw his consent without reason. This applies to distance sales and e-commerce and other 'non-traditional' sales. The right to withdraw without reason does not apply to perishable goods, digital products and the like, newspapers that have been delivered, or goods that have been custom made. Furthermore, if at the time of the conclusion of the sales contract the consumer acknowledges that the goods are not suitable for return without reason, the goods cannot be returned. This could give rise to abuses by the sellers who may use this way in order to introduce exclusion clauses.[53]

In revising its Consumer Protection Act in 2015, by extending information duties of the business operators and the consumers' withdrawal right to Internet-related sales, Taiwan took inspiration from the EU Consumer Rights Directive. In particular, the Taiwan Consumer Protection Act, resembling Article 10 of the Consumer Rights Directive, provides that when business operators fail to provide consumers with information on matters related to the consumer's right to rescind contracts upon receipt of goods or services, the seven-day period provided for exercising the withdrawal right shall not be counted until the information duty is fulfilled. The withdrawal right would be lost if the seven-day period has lapsed for four months.[54] Following the consumer's

[49] See JG Fong, 'Taiwan (Republic of China)', in this volume.

[50] Personal Data (Privacy) Ordinance (Cap 486); see Wong and Zhu, *Personal Data (Privacy) Law*.

[51] Directive 2011/83/EU of the European Parliament and of the Council of 25 October 2011 on consumer rights, OJ 2011 No L304, p 64.

[52] See Jing, 'China', in this volume.

[53] See also Pearson, 'Sale of Goods: A Comparative Perspective', in this volume.

[54] Taiwan Consumer Protection Act (Taiwan), Art 19(3).

notification of withdrawal to business operators in writing according to Article 19, the business operators must retrieve the goods within fifteen days and make a refund within fifteen days after retrieving the goods.[55] Following the path traced by Article 16 of the EU Consumer Rights Directive, the Taiwan legislator provided seven exceptions to the withdrawal right in distance and door-to-door sales.[56]

Taking inspiration from EU and German law, the South Korean 'E-Commerce Act'[57] came into force in 2002, addressing in particular information duties and the right of withdrawal.[58] In this regard, Article 13(2) of the E-Commerce Act regulates the duties to provide information on the identity of the seller and transaction conditions, including exercise and effects of withdrawal from the contract. The seller who provides false information regarding their identity can be punished with a fine up to 10 million Won (approximately 8,800 USD).[59] A consumer who has concluded a contract through email order distributor for the purchase of goods or services can withdraw the contract within a period of seven days from the date of receipt of a document regarding the content of the contract, except for the cases in which: (1) the goods have been destroyed or damaged due to a cause attributable to the consumer,[60] although this shall not apply where the package has been damaged for just checking the content of the goods;[61] (2) the value of the goods has substantially decreased due to consumer's use or partial consumption or where the value of the goods has substantially decreased due to the elapse of time, making resale difficult or impossible;[62] (3) the package of copyable goods is opened (this exception applies, for example, if digital content is supplied on a tangible medium, such as a CD or a DVD); (4) the provision of services or digital content has commenced. However, in cases of a contract comprising divisible services or divisible digital content, the effects of the withdrawal do not touch the portion for which the provision of such services or digital content has not commenced.[63] In contrast to the situation under EU law,[64] the right of withdrawal can be exercised in principle also in passenger transport service contracts and accommodation contracts.[65]

By contrast, Japanese e-commerce regulation does not provide a mandatory right of withdrawal. Indeed, traders are allowed to indicate if they are willing to allow consumers a right of withdrawal. In the absence of an indication that there is no right of withdrawal, consumers benefit from a cooling-off period of eight days.[66]

[55] ibid, Art 19-2. Moreover, after rescinding the contract, the restitution provision shall be null and void if it is more adverse to the consumers than the provision prescribed in Art 259 of the Civil Code.

[56] See on this JG Fong, 'Taiwan (Republic of China)', in this volume.

[57] Act on the Consumer Protection in Electronic Commerce, etc.

[58] See Jung, 'South Korea', in this volume.

[59] E-Commerce Act (South Korea), Art 43(1) and (2).

[60] ibid, Art 17(2) No 1.

[61] See also Consumer Rights Directive EU), Art 14(2) and recital 47.

[62] E-Commerce Act (South Korea), Art 17(2) Nos 2 and 3.

[63] ibid, Art 17(2) No. 5.

[64] See eg Consumer Rights Directive (EU), Art 3(3)(k) and recital 27.

[65] According to Art 3(4) of the E-Commerce Act (South Korea), only transactions of securities by investment traders and investment brokers under the Korean Financial Investment Services and Capital Markets Act and transactions of financial instruments by financial companies are excluded from the scope of this Act.

[66] See Act on Specified Commercial Transactions (Japan), Art 15-3. See also H Hirose, K-F Lenz and T Shiraishi, 'Japan', in this volume.

Although Hong Kong has an Electronic Transactions Ordinance, it does not have rules mandating consumer information in online sales or a mandatory cooling-off period for online sales. In Macau, there is also no legislation dealing specifically with substantive aspects of electronic transactions. This means that e-commerce consumer transactions and related disputes are regulated by the existing consumer law and subsidiarily by the general provisions of the Civil Code 1999 and of the Civil Procedural Code 1999, respectively. The increasing significance of e-commerce has been considered in the Draft Consumer Protection Law 2019, which aims to consolidate many of the legal solutions currently scattered or only indirectly regulated,[67] imposing strict information duties on business operators, a cooling-off period of seven days, extended to an additional 30-day period in case of violation of the duty of information on the right of withdrawal.

In Malaysia, there are several legislative acts under the jurisdiction of different ministries, which directly or indirectly regulate or have an impact on the conduct of online shopping. The primary legislation governing e-commerce transactions is the Electronic Commerce Act 2006, which provides for legal recognition of electronic messages in commercial transactions, the use of the electronic messages to fulfil legal requirements. Consumer protection in e-commerce has been recently further strengthened by the enactment of the Electronic Trade Transactions Regulations 2012. Furthermore, the Direct Sales and Anti-pyramid Scheme Act 1993 was amended in 2010 to include e-commerce in the definition of mail order sales.[68]

In India, the online sale of goods or services,[69] including online transactions through electronic means or by teleshopping or direct selling or multi-level marketing, has been regulated for the first time by the Indian Consumer Protection Act 2019, which defines e-commerce as buying or selling of goods or services including digital products over digital or electronic networks. The Ministry of Consumer Affairs, Food and Public Distribution has also released the Consumer Protection (E-Commerce) Rules, 2020,[70] which requires e-commerce entities, inter alia, to be registered under the Companies Act 2013 or under Foreign Exchange management Act 1999 and to provide a series of information to consumers and prohibits discrimination among them.[71]

The UNCITRAL Model Law on Electronic Commerce significantly influenced legislation governing e-commerce in Singapore,[72] in particular as regards the validity of electronic records in the formation of contracts and pre-contractual statements.[73] In Thailand, e-commerce regulation borrows several solutions from the UNCITRAL Model Law on Electronic Commerce. The Electronic Transactions Act provides the legal framework for validity of electronic signatures and electronic transactions.

[67] Draft Consumer Protection Law of 5 March 2019 (Macau), revised in September 2020. See D Wei and Â Patrício Rafael, 'Macau', in this volume.

[68] See N Amin and R Mohd Nor, 'Online Shopping In Malaysia: Legal Protection For E-Consumers' (2013) 5 *European Journal of Business and Management* 79.

[69] Consumer Protection Act 2019 (India), s 2(7)(b).

[70] Those rules came into force on 23 July 2020.

[71] See A Patil, 'India', in this volume.

[72] See Electronic Transactions Act (Singapore). For a general overview and background to the introduction of this Act, see J Chan, 'Legal Issues in E-Commerce and Electronic Contracting: The Singapore Position' (8th ASEAN Law Association General Assembly 2003).

[73] Electronic Transactions Act (Singapore), s 2.

A Commission on Electronic Transactions is established for supervising the application of this law.[74] A businessman who wishes to conducts business via electronic transactions is required to register his business with the Ministry of Commerce.[75] Furthermore, there are laws guaranteeing the security of consumers in the electronic transactions, especially in the case of electronic payments.[76]

VI. Online Dispute Resolution

The existence of simple, efficient, fast and low-cost ways of resolving disputes is key to making national legal systems more effective. Following this path, in 2016 the Government of India established the 'Online Consumer Mediation Centre' as a pilot project at the National Law School of India University to cater for e-consumers and e-commerce companies. The mission of the Centre is to provide innovative technology for e-consumers and e-commerce companies to manage and resolve conflicts and to enhance the use of online mediation as a first choice to resolving consumer disputes. The Centre runs with a vision to provide for an innovative online mediation tool that affords consumers better access to justice through quick and easy redress mechanism and at the same time provides opportunity for businesses to maintain good customer relations. The core values of the Centre include easy accessibility, security, confidentiality, cost-effectiveness, neutrality and integrity.[77]

The Council of Consumers of Macau has successfully installed an online dispute resolution system (Centre for Arbitration of Consumer Conflicts of Macau), whose purpose is to promote the resolution of consumer disputes of no more than 50,000 MOP (approximately 6250 USD) in the territory of Macau through mediation, conciliation and arbitration. Furthermore, the Council of Consumers established in March 2018 an online dispute resolution system, which is especially aimed at dealing with cross-border consumer disputes. In this regard, the Council of Consumers concluded cooperation agreements with its counterparts of the Greater Bay Area, which includes cities from the Guangdong province in mainland China and Hong Kong. The plan is to gradually extend the use of this online dispute resolution system to cross-border disputes involving parties not only from mainland China but also from other parts of the world.[78]

Although online dispute resolution systems play a role in many Western legal systems, in Asian countries there is still little development in this regard. Here the EU Regulation on Online Dispute Resolution might serve as a useful model to look at,[79]

[74] Electronic Transactions Act (Thailand), s 36.

[75] Decree of Ministry of Commerce on the registration of the e-commerce (Thailand), s 5.

[76] Those laws in Thailand are, for example, the Royal Decree on Regulating of Electronic Payment Services, the Royal Decree on Security Procedures in Electronic Transaction and the Royal Decree on Regulating of Electronic Payment Services of Certains Financial Institutes.

[77] See Patil, 'India', in this volume.

[78] See Wei and Patrício Rafael, 'Macau', in this volume.

[79] See eg J Morais Carvalho and J Campos Carvalho, 'Online Dispute Resolution Platform. Making European Contract Law More Effective' in A De Franceschi (ed), *European Contract Law and the Digital Single Market. The Implications of the Digital Revolution* (Cambridge: Intersentia, 2016) 245–66; P Cortés and AR Lodder, 'Consumer Dispute Resolution Goes Online: Reflections on the Evolution of European Law for Out-of-Court Redress' (2014) 21 *Maastricht Journal of European and Comparative Law* 14.

even if it is still not yet very well known among EU consumers and could be more effective if the incentives for both parties, traders and consumers, to use ODR were reinforced.[80] On this point, Brazil offers an Online Dispute Resolution Platform, which is proving to be particularly effective and becoming popular among Brazilian consumers.[81] One of the reasons for this popularity is the procedural design of that platform, which serves as a direct communication channel between the trader and the consumer. The Brazilian model delivers therefore useful input on how the potential of ODR can be better utilised.[82]

VII. Between Fragmentation and Cross-contamination: Asian Digital Consumer Law Facing the Global and the Environmental Challenges

There is no underlying coherence in the consumer law regulation of digital technologies in Asia. Mainland China and Singapore are leading in the process of adapting their legal system to the digital age. Moreover, countries have adopted a hybrid legal reception approach and rely on the existing legislative experiences of the EU and the United States, with also the UNCITRAL Model Law on Electronic Commerce significantly influencing legislation governing e-commerce in several Asian countries.

When Singapore assumed the Chairmanship of ASEAN in 2018, it focused its efforts on realising an 'Asian Digital Single Market'. Agreements at member state level have therefore been reached for creating common rules or comparable standards for consumer protection and data protection insofar as these affect intra-ASEAN digital trade in goods and services, in particular by adopting the 2018 ASEAN Framework on Digital Data Governance[83] and the 2019 ASEAN Agreement on Electronic Commerce.[84] Meanwhile, in order to strengthen global synergies in the regulation of

[80] The EU Commission announced in its Communication on A New Deal for Consumers that it is planning to make the framework for the European ODR platform more effective: see European Commission, 'A New Deal for Consumers' COM(2018) 183 final; European Commission, 'Report on the application of Directive 2013/11/EU of the European Parliament and of the Council on alternative dispute resolution for consumer disputes and Regulation (EU) No 524/2013 of the European Parliament and of the Council on online dispute resolution for consumer disputes' COM(2019) 425 final.

[81] See the dataset from Consumidor.gov.br, consisting of a sample of more than 800,000 consumer complaints. While 2,228,819 complaints were resolved (*finalizadas*) through Consumidor.gov.br since its creation in 2014 (609,000 only in 2018), the EU ODR platform has only received 36,000 complaints in its second year of functioning and a total of 60,000 since its launch in February 2016, European Commission, 'Report on the application of Directive 2013/11/EU of the European Parliament and of the Council on alternative dispute resolution for consumer disputes and Regulation (EU) No 524/2013 of the European Parliament and of the Council on online dispute resolution for consumer disputes, 25 September 2019' COM(2019) 425 final. See M-J Schmidt-Kessen, R Nogueira and M Cantero Camito, 'Success or Failure? – Effectiveness of Consumer ODR Platforms in Brazil and in the EU' (2020) 46 *Journal of Consumer Policy* 659; C Lima Marques and P Galindo da Fonseca, 'Consumer Protection in Brazil: The 2016 Report for the International Academy of Consumer Law' in H-W Micklitz and G Saumier (eds), *Enforcement and effectiveness of Consumer Law* (Cham: Springer, 2018) 99.

[82] See Schmidt-Kessen, Nogueira and Cantero Camito, 'Success or Failure?'.

[83] 'ASEAN Framework on Digital Data Governance' (6 December 2018).

[84] 'ASEAN Agreement on Electronic Commerce' (27 March 2019).

the digital economy, ASEAN started a close cooperation with the European Union as well as with the United States. In particular, the 10 Southeast Asian countries are closely cooperating with the EU Commission – in the framework of the 'Enhanced Regional EU-ASEAN Dialogue Instrument' – with regard to the elaboration of legal instruments for the digital economy, including policy, regulation and digital innovation ecosystem in general, as well as specific issues such as international roaming, data governance and disinformation.[85] On the same path, the US-ASEAN Business Council (US-ABC) offered a series of recommendations to foster a data-driven economy.[86]

A source for inspiration and an incentive towards an enhanced cooperation between Asian and European legislators may be delivered by some of the most recent developments in the European Union, such as the proposed Data Governance Act, the Digital Services Act and the Digital Markets Act – even though these proposals are rather disappointing from a consumer law perspective – and the Proposal for a Regulation on Markets in Crypto-assets.[87] Even if approved, the provisions would in practice be of limited reach, especially in the context of cross-border transactions. Therefore, the effectiveness of the proposed rules largely depends on the upgrading of other regional consumer protection laws. For the same reason, synergy between Asian and the EU legislators shall be strengthened also concerning the regulation of Artificial Intelligence (AI), in which regard the European Parliament[88] and the European Commission[89] recently published a set of proposals, resolutions, guidelines, communications and working papers, paving the way for creating a comprehensive European industrial policy on AI and robotics, with the aim to deal with technological, ethical, legal and socio-economic aspects to boost the EU's research and industrial capacity and to put AI and robots at the service of European citizens and the economy, in order to improve working conditions, reduce human exposure to harmful and hazardous conditions, and bring an added value in the general public interest, such as health, energy and transport.

Within the outlined scenario, legislators shall also address the synergy between the digital transformation and the climate disruption, by exploring measures to ensure that digital technologies such as artificial intelligence, 5G, cloud and edge computing and the Internet of Things can accelerate and maximise the impact of policies to deal with climate change and protect the environment.[90]

[85] See eg 'The EU and Asean: Building stronger digital economy & connectivity cooperation' (23 October 2019).

[86] US-ASEAN Business Council, 'Digital Data Governance in ASEAN', 23 August 2019, available at www.usasean.org/system/files/downloads/digital_data_governance_in_asean-key_elements_for_a_data-driven_economy.pdf.

[87] European Commission, 'Proposal for a Regulation of the European Parliament and of the Council on Markets in Crypto-assets, and amending Directive (EU) 2019/1937' COM(2020) 593 final.

[88] See eg European Parliament, Resolution on a comprehensive European industrial policy on artificial intelligence and robotics of 12 February 2019' (2018/2088(INI)).

[89] See eg European Commission, Proposal for a Regulation of the European Parliament and of the Council laying down harmonised Rules on Artificial Intelligence (Artificial Intelligence Act) and amending certain Union Legislative Acts, COM/2021/206 final; European Commission, 'Communication on Artificial Intelligence for Europe' COM(2018) 237 final; European Commission, 'Report on the safety and liability implications of Artificial Intelligence, the Internet of Things and robotics' COM(2020) 64 final; European Commission, 'White Paper on Artificial Intelligence – A European approach to excellence and trust' COM(2020) 65 final; European Parliament, 'Resolution of 20 October 2020 with recommendations to the Commission on a civil liability regime for artificial intelligence' (2020/2014(INL)), P9 TA(2020)0276 (2020).

[90] See H-W Micklitz, 'Squaring the Circle? Reconciling Consumer Law and the Circular Economy' in B Keirsbilck and E Terryn (eds), *Consumer Protection in a Circular Economy* (Antwerp: Intersentia, 2019) 329.

It is clear that many questions which arise for the law from this dramatic shift in our daily lives cannot be solved solely, or even for the most part, within the national legal framework. Isolated national solutions would hardly satisfy the cross-border (or practically borderless) nature of the communication, the activities and the risks in the digital world. Global answers to global changes would therefore be the best path to follow. However, it is apparent that the different political perceptions and economic interests at present would, despite the efforts, only have limited effect, if any, particularly when one considers the 'big players' in the production and use of digital content (such as China and the United States).

From a policy perspective, there is therefore much in favour of the approach to find solutions alongside national law at the 'junction' between national and international rules: so also and particularly within world regions and in regional supranational communities. This offers an excellent opportunity of cooperation and discussion between continents: in this regard, ASEAN is already playing an important role as a bridge for enhancing such cooperation.

20

Commercial Practices

HANS-W MICKLITZ*

I. Introduction

Seen through the consumer lens the law on commercial practices is deeply connected to the 'right to information' which plays a prominent role in consumer law from the 1962 declaration of President Kennedy onwards. I am using here the modern term 'commercial practices' which covers advertising and sales promotion and which has been introduced by the EU Unfair Commercial Practices Directive and I will not hide that I am looking at the ASEAN laws on Unfair Commercial Practices through European eyes, this means through the eyes of the most recent and most developed model of supranational legislation.[1] It seems that the EU Unfair Commercial Practices Directive could turn into a success story similar to the Product Liability Directive.[2]

Roughly speaking, the distinction between advertising and sales promotion is the following: advertising measures carry some sort of information which shall entice the consumer to buy a product or a service. The concern of the consumer is that the information is 'correct' and 'true' and does not mislead them. Sales promotion instead focuses on marketing strategies such as doorstep selling, rebates, promotional sales, gifts, sale at a loss, tied promotion, three for the price of two, etc. Whilst there might be an informational element, however, contrary to advertising, the emphasis is not on information but on promotional activities. The consumer concern however might not only result from misleading advertising and sales promotion techniques, but much more generally from being treated 'unfairly'. Until today and in particular in cross-cutting analyses which cover many different countries, cultures and traditions, 'fairness' or 'deception' remain relatively open legal concepts, which are more often than not tailored to the

* In writing this chapter I took inspiration from G Pearson, 'Sale of Goods: A Comparative Perspective', in this volume.

[1] Directive 2005/29/EC of the European Parliament and of the Council of 11 May 2005 concerning unfair business-to-consumer commercial practices in the internal market ('Unfair Commercial Practices Directive'), OJ 2005 No L149, p 22.

[2] Council Directive 85/374/EEC of 25 July 1985 on the approximation of the laws, regulations and administrative provisions of the Member States concerning liability for defective products, OJ 1985 No L210, p 29. On the success of this Directive see M Reimann, 'Product Liability in a Global Context: the Hollow Victory of the European Model' (2003) 11(2) *European Review of Private Law* 128.

national particularities. The law on unfair commercial practices plays a prominent role in legal research and has attracted attention far beyond Europe.[3]

II. Origins, Jurisdictions and Borrowing

The law on commercial practices is much older than consumer law. In Europe, the nation states began to use civil and common law or to adopt specific legislation in the beginning of the twentieth century to exercise some sort of control of the competitive behaviour of companies. There is an old saying that the law on commercial practices aims at preventing companies from being 'too aggressive' with each other, whereas the law on antitrust is meant to prevent companies from being 'too nice' to each other. The traditional means to fight 'aggressive practices' was via tort law, in continental Europe via the respective rules in the civil codes and in common law countries via the rules of the common law.[4] Tort law requires that the victim suffers damage or is at the very least endangered to suffer damage and that the incriminated behaviour is based on negligence.

There were also countries that adopted specific legislation to tackle aggressive practices, either explicitly limited to b2b relations or unlimited but with a clear focus on b2b transactions, though without excluding the applicability of the general rules of civil and commercial law. France adopted the Loi Sur Fraudes et Falsifications en Matière de Produits et Service in 1905, Germany adopted the Gesetz gegen unlauteren Wettbewerb in 1909.[5] The two countries demonstrate the coherence as well as the differences in legislative action. The common denominator is the fight against misleading advertising in business transactions, however, the remedies differ. France relied on administrative enforcement and criminal sanctions, Germany – together with Austria – favoured private enforcement through business organisations who have to go to court and seek an injunction. The basic structure survived the whole twentieth century and is still very much alive today. This means the starting point for the control of commercial practices remains tort law, coupled to particular legislation which is divided through the way in which the law is enforced and by whom. Many of the legal orders of the countries under review are shaped by their colonial legacy. Even in countries which were not colonised, such as Japan and Thailand, the Western influence remained strong. The divide between civil law (China, Indonesia, Japan, Macau, Taiwan and Vietnam) and common

[3] There are a number of publications which take a comparative perspective. However, the law on unfair commercial practices is fast moving. That is why the publications are not always up to date. P Schotthöfer and F Steiner (eds), *International Advertising Law* 3rd ed (Alphen aan den Rijn: Kluwer, 2017) with reports on China by R Kok and India by G Anand and R Anand; F Henning-Bodewig (ed), *International Handbook on Unfair Competition* (Munich: CH Beck, 2012) with reports inter alia from China by Y Bu, India by R Mittal and Japan by C Heath. On the Directive 2005/29/EU, G Howells, H-W Micklitz and T Wilhelmsson, *European Fair Trading Law. The Unfair Commercial Practices Directive* (Aldershot: Ashgate, 2006), on the national laws through a consumer lens prior to the adoption of the Directive 2005/29/EU, H-W Micklitz and J Keßler (eds), *Marketing Practices Regulation and Consumer Protection in the EC Member States and the US* (Baden-Baden: Nomos, 2002).

[4] N Reich and H-W Micklitz, *Consumer Legislation in the EC Countries, A Comparative Analysis* (New Yok: Van Nostrand Reynolds, 1980) 65 et seq.

[5] See the reports from K Boesche on Germany, S Nérisson on France in Henning-Bodewig, *International Handbook.*

law (Australia, India, Malaysia and Singapore) can still be observed. Where common law prevails the reference point is English law and English case law, where civil law sets the standards, the origins in the Dutch Code with respect to Indonesia, the German Civil Code with regard to Japan and the French Civil Code in Vietnam have to be taken into account. Language and familiarity oftentimes over more than a century explain the path dependency.

The second wave of legislation goes hand in hand with the rise of the consumer society. Contrary to the United States, the consumer society in Europe fully unfolded after the Second World War. Nation states intervened so as to integrate consumer protection into the special legislation and gradually established administrative enforcement agencies. In Europe, the United Kingdom took the lead with the Fair Trading Act 1973. The then newly established Director of Fair Trading was granted powers to ensure proper market conduct to protect the consumer. The Nordic Countries, with Denmark and Sweden as forerunners, adopted Market Practices Legislation which established the Consumer Ombud and a Market Court with special jurisdiction.[6] Today there is a nearly universal trend towards administrative enforcement where public agencies interfere in the collective interest as a consumer. This is clearly reflected in the Asian/Pacific countries here under review, where more recently also in Japan, consumer policy trusts much more in administrative enforcement than in private individual enforcement.

The rise of special legislation coupled with the establishment of administrative authorities does not mean that the civil law and the common law no longer have a role to play. Quite the contrary seems true. The general rules of civil law or common law or special rules on consumer contract law remain of crucial importance; for example, in Japan where a comprehensive law in its straight sense on unfair commercial practices is missing until today, although a comprehensive body on unfair commercial practices is gradually being formed since 2009[7] or in India where the common law remained the only effective remedy until the establishment of the Central Consumer Protection Agency in 2019.[8] However, with the shifting focus from b2b to b2c the remedy changed from tort law to contract law. To stay with the metaphor: the aggression in b2b relations is rejected through tort law. The competitive order needs to be protected so as to guarantee competition between the companies. The consumer society brought the consumer into the limelight not as a competitor but as the buyer of products and services. Now the companies fight between each other so as to make their products attractive to consumers. Advertising and sales promotion techniques are mobilised to seduce the consumer and pull them into a contract that they might not have wanted to conclude. Until today the question is when and under what conditions a consumer might be entitled to rescind a contract which is the result of problematic advertising and sales promotion strategies. India requires even consideration, which means the consumer must have concluded

[6] On Sweden A Bakardijeva-Engelbrekt in Henning-Bodewig, *International Handbook* and from the same author, 'Fair Trading Law in Flux?: National Legacies and Institutional Choice and the Process of Europeanisation', PhD thesis, Stockholm University (2003).

[7] See Heath, 'Japan', 345 et seq., but more particularly the Japanese national report in this volume.

[8] N Reich, 'Reflections on Hans Micklitz's Plea For a Movable System (of Consumer Law) – Anything to Learn from the Experience of Indian Consumer Law' in K Purnhagen and P Rott (eds), *Varieties of European Economic Law and Regulation, Liber Amicorum Hans Micklitz* (Vienna: Springer, 2014) 651 et seq.

a contract before a consumer can take action against advertising and sales promotion strategies. But even when the rules are less strict when neither consideration nor the existence of a contract is required, when the advertisement is treated like an offer, like in Taiwan, the comparison demonstrates that the reliance on individual consumers to fight for their rights in courts meets a number of barriers.[9] Occasionally, consumers might rely on the support of administrative agencies in getting their rights enforced before the courts.[10] Last but not least there is also Inter Asian/Pacific transfer, for instance from Indian common law to Myanmar.

III. Distribution of Sources in the Law on Commercial Practices[11]

Table 1 shows and summarises the different legal sources on which the law on unfair commercial practices is based. It demonstrates the variety of sources, the old common and civil law, particular legislation on commercial practices on b2b, later on consumer protection legislation and last but not least legislation dealing with particular goods and services, health and financial services as well as particular forms and methods of sales promotion in particular. It is striking to see though that none of the countries under review adopted particular legislative measures to deal with environmental advertising.

The different sources can be linked to different types of external influences. The establishment of the international economic order after the Second World War with GATT and IMF and after the Uruguay round with the introduction of the WTO and TRIPS put pressure on those states who intended to join to adopt legislation on unfair commercial practices. The required protection of intellectual property rights served as a trigger, such was the case in China and Japan. This explains the focus on b2b relations. It took until 1985 before the United Nations was ready to agree on the UN Guidelines on Consumer Protection.[12] These Guidelines were taken into consideration by countries such as Malaysia and Vietnam. Most of the countries under review, however, took inspiration in the shaping of their consumer laws from the former colonial power on which their legal order was based. As all of them are or have been – in the case of the United Kingdom – members of the EU, the countries implicitly integrated the nationally implemented version of the European law on unfair commercial practices into their legal systems. Only occasionally, EU law has been explicitly chosen as a benchmark. Hong Kong, Singapore and Macau (Draft) were inspired by the EU Unfair Commercial Practices Directive, Taiwan and Thailand by the Consumer Rights Directive,[13] which covers doorstep and distance selling.

[9] H-W Micklitz and G Saumier, 'Enforcement and Effectiveness of Consumer Law – General Report' in H-W Micklitz and G Saumier (eds), *Enforcement and Effectiveness of Consumer Law* (Cham: Springer, 2018) 3–45.

[10] In so far see M Cantero Gamito, 'Consumer Access to Justice in a Comparative Perspective', in this volume.

[11] Table taken from Pearson, 'Sale of Goods: A Comparative Perspective', in this volume and adjusted to commercial practices.

[12] UN Guidelines on Consumer Protection have been revised twice, see the contribution by M Durovic and J Pui, 'The Effect of the United Nations Guidelines on Consumer Protection on Consumer Law in Asia', in this volume.

[13] Directive 2011/83/EU of the European Parliament and of the Council of 25 October 2011 on consumer rights, OJ 2011 No L 304, p 64.

Table 1 Sources of unfair commercial practices regulation

Jurisdiction	Chief Commercial Practices Law	Major influence: civil law, common law, other	Is commercial practices in a general law, consumer law, or other?	Special laws for particular goods and services?	Special rules for different methods of commercial practices	Special rules for commercial practices on financial products?
Australia	Competition and Consumer Act 2010 (CCA) Sale of Goods Acts	Common law	Consumer law	Yes	Yes, in CCA: distance selling; no special e-commerce	Limited carve outs[1]
China	Anti-Unfair Competition Law	Sui generis		Interim Measures for Administration of Internet Advertising and specifies the regulation in the area of Internet advertising	Regulation on pyramid selling Rules on bundling and coercion Rules on sales promotion	
Hong Kong	Trade Descriptions (Unfair Trade Practices) (Amendment) Ordinance (Cap. 362)	Common law	Both			
India	Consumer Protection Act 2019	Common law	Both	Yes, eg Food Safety and Standards Act 2006	See Consumer Protection Act 2019	

(continued)

[1] For details see Table 2 in Section 6 of the Japanese report in this volume.

Table 1 *(Continued)*

Jurisdiction	Chief Commercial Practices Law	Major influence: civil law, common law, other	Is commercial practices in a general law, consumer law, or other?	Special laws for particular goods and services?	Special rules for different methods of commercial practices	Special rules for commercial practices on financial products?
Indonesia	Consumer Protection Act 1999	Civil law, Dutch law	Both			
Japan	Basic Act on Consumer Policies, Consumer Contract Act Act on Specified Commercial Transactions Act against Unjustifiable Premiums and Misleading Representations Civil Code	Civil law	Both	Premiums and Representation Act Food Labelling Act Household Goods Quality Labelling Act Pharmaceuticals and Medical Devices Act Consumer Product Safety Act	Act on Specified Commercial Transactions	Instalment Sales Act Money Lending Business Act Interest Rate Regulation Act
Macau	Civil Code 1999 Commercial Code 1999 Act on Advertising Activities 1989	Civil law, Portuguese civil law	Both	Special rules on health advertising	Consumer Protection Law 1988 Various special acts	
Malaysia	Consumer Protection Act 1999 Trade Description Act 2011	Common law		Special law on health advertising	Direct Sales and Anti-Pyramid Scheme Act 1993	

Myanmar	Consumer Protection Act, 2018 Penal Code 1860 (Art 415)	Common law	Consumer law rules on fraud	Consumer Protection Act on health Special rules for food 1997 and drug advertising 1992		
Singapore	Consumer Protection (Fair Trading) Act 2007	Common law, but increasing influence from non-UK countries		Yes, eg Sale of Food Act		Yes
South Korea	Consumer Protection Act 2008 Act on Fair Labelling and Advertising	Civil law			E-commerce Door-to door sales Telemarketing	
Taiwan	Fair Trading Act 1991 Consumer Protection Act 1994/2015 dual jurisdiction	Civil law from various European countries	Also Consumer Protection Act 1994/2015	Yes	Consumer Protection Act 2015: Mail order Door-to-door sales	Financial Consumer Protection Act 2011
Thailand	Consumer Protection Act 1979 Criminal Code	Both Civil law and Common Law	Both	Yes	Direct Sales and Direct Marketing Act	Yes
Vietnam	Civil Code 2015 Socialist tradition Consumer Protection 2010	Civil law, French Civil Code		Criminal law on counterfeited goods		

IV. The Scope and Reach of the Law on Commercial Practices

The EU Unfair Commercial Practices Directive provides for the most advanced regulatory design to deal with unfair commercial practices.[14] It is based on a threefold structure. The first layer consists of a general clause which prohibits unfair commercial practices and serves as a safety net. The second layer is composed of two particular general clauses – one dealing with the prohibition of misleading actions and misleading omissions, the other with aggressive practices. The third layer is the prohibition of blacklisted practices. The legislative process was full of conflicts. The United Kingdom resisted the introduction of a general prohibition of unfair commercial practices and most of the Member States did not agree with the Nordic approach to positively oblige advertisers to provide information which is true, transparent and comprehensive. Whilst the majority of the Member States agreed on a general clause on fairness, they rejected the introduction of a positive information obligation and instead advocated the prohibition of misleading omissions.

Table 2 indicates that the Asian/Pacific countries remain behind the sophisticated European law with its different layers of general clauses and blacklisted practices, perhaps with the exception of Hong Kong and Singapore. Overall, there is no agreement on the need and feasibility of a general clause that prohibits unfair commercial practices, independent of how unfairness is defended, as a reasonableness in the common law tradition or as a good faith test in the civil law tradition. The EU Unfair Commercial Practices Directive uses professional diligence as a benchmark, however, professional diligence did not turn into a common denominator. The focus lies on the prohibition of misleading advertising, often coupled with particular rules on sensitive products, such as pharmaceuticals. However, there is no general move to oblige information based advertising to be 'true'. Asian/Pacific law accepts that exaggeration and entertainment is a legitimate part of commercial practices. Restrictions on sales promotion constitute a second major field, be it in doorstep selling, online sales or particular forms of marketing strategies, such as rebates, gifts etc. Interestingly there are no rules in the laws under review that tie advertising to particular religious requirements.[15] In Thailand, the King and the Royal Family enjoy a particular status of protection.

[14] On the design, the history and the conflicts, see Howells, Micklitz and Wilhelmsson, 'European Fair Trading law'; the most comprehensive analysis of the Directive 2005/29/EU in form of a commentary is available in German only, H-W Micklitz and M Namyslowska, 'Kommentierung der Richtlinie über unlautere Geschäftspraktiken' in *Münchener Kommentar zum UWG* 3rd edn (Munich: CH Beck, 2020) 654–945.

[15] This might be different in Islamic countries, see H-W Micklitz and Y Atamer, 'The Implementation of EU Consumer Protection Directives in Turkey' (2009) 27 *Penn State Int Law Review* 551.

Table 2 Regulatory approaches

Jurisdiction	Rules on unfairness	Rules on misleading practices	Particular Rules (eg sales promotion)	Black listed practices
Australia	No embracing concept of unfair commercial practices, but unconscionability doctrine	Most powerful tool	Yes	
China	Principle of voluntariness, equality, fairness, honesty and good faith, adhere to generally recognised business morals	Deceptive advertising		
Hong Kong	Prohibition of misleading information and unfair trading practices	Omitting or concealing material information Providing material information in an unclear, unintelligible or untimely manner Failing to identify material information	Six types of unscrupulous trade practices will be prohibited: – Applying false trade descriptions of goods and services – Misleading omissions – Aggressive commercial practices – Bait advertising; – Baiting and switching – Wrongly accepting payment	
India	Prohibition of any unfair method or unfair or deceptive practice	Unfair method or unfair or deceptive practice	Particular rules on forms and conditions	

(continued)

Table 2 *(Continued)*

Jurisdiction	Rules on unfairness	Rules on misleading practices	Particular Rules (eg sales promotion)	Black listed practices
Indonesia	Offering, promoting advertising or providing incorrect or misleading statements regarding the price or rate of a certain good and/or service business actors are obliged to, amongst other things, act in good faith in conducting business			
Japan	Good faith Principle and public policy and good morals requirement in Civil Code	Consumer Contract Act Act on Specified Commercial Transactions. A general rule on misleading representations by Act against Unjustifiable Premiums and Misleading Representations, and special rules in various other laws	Door-to-door sales (and purchase) Telemarketing and multilevel marketing transactions, Business opportunity sales Mail order sales Specified continuous services providing contract.	Extended versions of fraud and duress in Consumer Contract Act, Seven types of prohibitions in Act on Specified Comm. Transactions Special Acts on pyramid selling, etc.
Macau	Principles of truthfulness; free and fair competition and consumer protection	Draft on misleading omissions	Draft on aggressive marketing practices	Draft on blacklisted practices
Malaysia		Prohibition of false trade descriptions and false or misleading statements, conduct, and practices		

Myanmar		Prohibition of incorrect and misleading advertising	mixing goods with the good products and lower quality products, using exaggeration in the information, increasing the price of the goods before sale promotion,	
Singapore	Reasonableness test	Do anything or to omit to do or say anything such as to reasonably deceive or mislead a consumer		Twenty blacklisted practices
South Korea		False or exaggerated advertising Deceptive advertising Unfairly comparative advertising Slanderous advertising		
Taiwan	Fair Trade Act Prohibition of false and misleading advertising as well as deceptive or unfair conduct	Consumer Protection Act: only false and misleading advertising		Pyramid selling; multilevel marketing
Thailand	Considered as unfair to consumers or which may harm society as a whole	Consumer Protection Act: Misleading advertising and fake labels	Pyramid selling, Distance selling Doorstep selling	
Vietnam	No	Deceiving or misleading advertisement	Special rules on coercion and harassment, sales promotion and unsolicited goods	

V. Private and Public, Individual and Collective Enforcement

Enforcement is the proof of the pudding. Theoretically, there are three actors who could set the control procedure into motion: the individual consumer, consumer organisations and public authorities entrusted with the enforcement.[16] Whereas consumers and consumer organisations (with standing) have to go to court to enforce their rights, public authorities enjoy powers to take regulatory action through civil law remedies or through administrative and even penal sanctions. Whilst regulatory action is subject to judicial review, whilst conflicts may end up in courts, this is not the rule. It is a common characteristic that public authorities which are granted regulatory power use all sorts of soft law means to influence the behaviour of the companies before they take hard regulatory action.

The civil law and common law rules on contract and tort serve as a kind of a safety net in individual litigation. However, overall these general rules require the existence of a contract which harmed the consumer due to the illegitimate commercial practices that had triggered them to conclude the contract. It is only under rather particular requirements that the consumer may enjoy rights and remedies resulting from infringements prior to the contract, *culpa in contrahendo*: negligence in the pre-contractual stage. There is doctrinal debate over how to classify such an infringement, as a tortious or contractual action.[17] Be that as it may, what matters is that individual enforcement is not preventive but compensatory. This is different from collective enforcement, be it through consumer organisations or public agencies. If a particular commercial practice is *likely* to mislead the consumer or is *likely* to treat them unfairly, both may intervene as far as they have standing. In theory collective enforcement is designed in order to prevent the consumer from being harmed from concluding a contract that they do not want. In practice, it might very well happen that even public agencies only interfere after it becomes clear that the commercial practice has harmed the consumer.

It is striking to see that the rules on individual enforcement remained rather stable, whereas the rules on collective enforcement are under constant change. On this there is no difference between the Asian/Pacific and the European countries.[18] The country reports document that revisions of consumer law usually go hand in hand

[16] H-W Micklitz and F Cafaggi, 'Introduction and Conclusion' in F Cafaggi and H-W Micklitz (eds), *New Frontiers of Consumer Protection – the Interplay between Private and Public Enforcement* (Cheltenham: Edward Elgar, 2009) 1–46 and 401–46.

[17] The ECJ considered pre-contractual liability as tortious liability in Case C-334/00 *Tacconi* EU:C:2002:499.

[18] P Rott, 'Behördliche Durchsetzung von Verbraucherschutz in Großbritannien, den Niederlanden und den USA' in H Schulte-Nölke and Bundesministerium der Justiz und für Verbraucherschutz (eds), *Neue Wege zur Durchsetzung des Verbraucherrechts* (Vienna: Springer, 2017) 31–84; A Ottow, *Market and Competition Authorities, Good Agency Principles* (Oxford: Oxford University Press, 2015).

with a revision of the institutional infrastructure that should guarantee the protection of the collective interests of consumers. There are countries, such as Australia, China and Singapore, in which the enforcement of consumer law is entrusted to already existing public authorities which are in charge of enforcing antitrust law or unfair commercial practices in b2b relations. There are also countries, and this seems to be the majority, which have set up specialised authorities in the field of consumer law. Sometimes the specialised agency originally formed part of the competition authority, like in Japan. The problem the latter countries have to face is that the consumer enforcement authorities need to co-ordinate their control activities with other public authorities that enjoy overlapping competences, not only at the state/federal level but also at the local/county level, for instance in China. The interinstitutional exchange is the more complicated the more authorities compete with each other. There seems to be a correlation between the variety of sources and the variety of enforcement authorities.

The remedies of public authorities range from civil law remedies, injunctions, corrections and compensation over the issuance of guidelines and recommendations to administrative and even criminal sanctions. Taking the whole picture together it seems that the establishment of a public agency implies advocating 'sanctions' so as to punish the perpetrator be it through fines or even through imprisonment. This is particularly true with regard to Macau, Malaysia, Myanmar, Thailand, Taiwan and Vietnam. The more stable the enforcement structure has become, the stronger there is a move towards civil law remedies, in particular injunctions, but also the promotion of guidelines and recommendations, such as in Australia, India (since 2019), Japan, Hong Kong and Singapore. Effective enforcement is the Achilles heel of all consumer protection laws. The contributions were not expected to undertake socio-legal research in order to measure the impact of the national laws on advertising on the economy and the society. This would have been a different project. Overall, however, Asian/Pacific consumer law confirms what is known from Africa and South America. There is a gap between the law in the books and the law in action.[19] A classical means to close that gap is public interest litigation.[20] However, public interest litigation depends on professional NGOs which prepare the case, on the existence of legal standing and of courts which are ready to engage in conflicts that are on the border between law and politics. Table 3 provides for an overview of the remedies for individual consumers and for the protection of the collective interests as well as the key actors in the law enforcement.

[19] H-W Micklitz and G Saumier, 'General Report', 3–45.

[20] Cantero Gamito, 'Consumer Access to Justice', in this volume and more generally on public interest litigation, J Handler, *Social Movements and the Legal System* (New York: Academic Press, 1978); D Kelemen, *Eurolegalism. The Transformation of Law and Regulation in the European Union* (Cambridge, MA: Harvard University Press, 2011).

Table 3 Enforcement systems

Jurisdiction	Individual	Consumer organisations	Consumer Agencies	Injunction, correction and compensation	Guidance and guidelines	Administrative + criminal sanctions
Australia			Australian Competition and Consumer Commission	Yes	Yes	Yes
China	Private party complaints before courts		Administration for Industry and Commerce, but competing competences with other national and county level	Injunction, correction, confiscation of illegal income		Administrative sanctions, Criminal sanctions only with respect to misappropriation of business and commercial bribery
Hong Kong			Intellectual Property Investigation Bureau (IPIB) Trade Descriptions Investigations Bureau (TDIB).	Yes (since 2012)	Consumer Council through naming and shaming	Criminal law as default
India	Provided the consumer concluded a contract (consideration doctrine)		Central Consumer Protection Agency	Injunction and corrective measures	Yes	Penalties

Indonesia			Consumer Dispute Settlement Agency			On business actors violating certain articles in the form of determining compensation up to a fixed maximum
Japan	Administrative and private ADRs (individual litigation before courts remains important)	Qualified Consumer Organisations (QCO) and Specific Qualified Consumer Organisations[2]	Consumer Affairs Agency[3]	Injunctions (by QCOs). Specific Qualified Consumer Organisations Collective consumer litigation for compensation.	Yes	Criminal sanctions by ordinary administrative authorities possible
Macau	Joint and several liability of the owners of advertising apparatus and the advertising agent with the advertiser for damages caused to third parties as a result of dissemination of illegal advertising messages					Administrative and criminal sanctions

(continued)

[2] For details see the report on Japan, in this volume.
[3] The description by Heath, 'Japan' is outdated.

Table 3 *(Continued)*

Jurisdiction	Individual	Consumer organisations	Consumer Agencies	Injunction, correction and compensation	Guidance and guidelines	Administrative + criminal sanctions
Malaysia	Individual complaints of consumers are dealt with by the tribunal of consumer claims					Criminal sanctions under the Trade Description Act
Myanmar			Since 2020: Consumer Protection Commission At the local level: inspector with considerable surveillance power		Notifications	Yes
Singapore	A false or misleading advertisement is not per se actionable unless brought by a consumer who has entered into a consumer contract involving that unfair practice		Competition and Consumer Commission of Singapore (CCCS) Self-regulatory body Advertising Standards Authority of Singapore (ASAS)	Injunction		

South Korea			Korea Fair Trade Commission Korea Consumer Agency	Suspension of the relevant violation, publication of the fact that a corrective order has been issued to the relevant trader or corrected advertising) to the relevant trader to correct the unfair advertising		
Taiwan			Taiwan Fair Trade Commission Consumer Protection Committee Department of Consumer Protection		FTA Regulations and guidelines	Fines in case of infringement under the FTA and the CPA
Thailand	When a consumer commits to the advertisement, a contract is validly entered into based on the advertisement		Office of the Consumer Protection Board (OCPB) Office of Prime Minister and the Committee of Advertisement Direct Sales and Direct Marketing Commission	No civil law remedies under the CPA	Three notifications on guidelines by the Committee of Advertising	
Vietnam			Vietnam Competition and Consumer Authority			Administrative fines and criminal sanctions

21

Access to Justice

MARTA CANTERO GAMITO*

I. Introduction

The effectiveness of consumer protection legislation is contingent on effective access to justice by aggrieved consumers. Without access to justice, consumers cannot enforce their rights and, therefore, the rights granted by consumer legislation would materialise if adequate mechanisms are not put in place. Yet, the nature of consumer claims and the variety of mechanisms for solving consumer disputes expose the ever growing gap between a literal (and liberal) understanding of access to justice, as equality before the law, and the actual possibilities for consumers to obtain redress.[1]

Consumer law is premised on the natural imbalance of the parties. This is also reflected on the behaviour of consumers following wrongdoings by traders. Typically, consumers will not go to court for low claims, accepting the loss that they have suffered. Effective consumer access to justice then requires the availability of suitable procedures for the particularities of consumer claims, generally of low value. Cappelletti and Barth identified three waves to overcome traditional barriers to access to justice. This included the development of legal aid, the representation of diffuse interests and the development of alternative methods for dispute resolution, including those aimed at preventing disputes.[2] Consequently, mapping consumer access to justice requires the examination of the existing mechanisms for redress at all three levels.

This chapter provides a comparative analysis of consumers' access to justice based on the different country reports featured in this volume. The analysis is grouped in three major mechanisms for redress somewhat related to Cappelletti's and Barth's identified waves. The chapter focuses, first, on judicial mechanisms for consumer redress (Section II). Secondly, the chapter maps different variations of alternative dispute resolution (ADR) available to consumer disputes (Section III). Thirdly, the growing

* University of Tartu. I would like to thank the editors of this volume for the great opportunity and experience offered by inviting me to exchange these ideas in Hong Kong (January 2017) with the rest of the contributors to this volume.

[1] See I Ramsay, 'Consumer Redress and Access to Justice' in CEF Rickett and TGW Telfer (eds), *International Perspectives on Consumers' Access to Justice* (Cambridge: Cambridge University Press, 2003) 17.

[2] M Cappelletti and B Garth (eds), *Access to Justice: A World Survey* (Milan: Giuffrè, 1978).

role of regulators and the administrative enforcement of consumer law require the examination of these mechanisms not only as to their capacity for consumer law enforcement but also as effective venues for obtaining consumer redress (Section IV). The Annex to this chapter contains the specific particularities of the examined mechanisms based on the rules of the different jurisdictions, for comparative purposes. Lastly, Section V provides a summarised overview of the main challenges and opportunities for consumers' access to justice identified within the national jurisdictions covered in this contribution.

II. Judicial Consumer Redress

When talking about access to justice, the main representation that comes to mind is that of a court where the judges deliver justice by adjudicating disputes. This representation involves the possibility for the aggrieved parties to submit their pleadings and to be heard in front of a neutral party, the judge, who will settle the dispute by assessing the facts and applying the pertaining rules. The effectiveness of the law is then materialised in the availability of suitable mechanisms and procedures for the exercise of the rights conferred by its rules and the availability of effective remedies where such rights have been violated. In the case of consumer law, this is translated in the capacity of the consumer to obtain redress based on the rights and remedies conferred upon consumer protection rules.

The application of consumer law, though, is faced with a significant challenge: consumer disputes rarely reach the courts.[3] The nature of consumer claims, generally of low value, disincentivise consumers to engage in often lengthy and costly court procedures to obtain redress. As a result, consumers often accept the loss they have suffered, especially where it only involves small pecuniary damages. Most of the national reports signal this situation. Physical accessibility to courts, often located in the city, also remains an issue for consumers located in rural areas. As noted in the Malaysian and Indian country reports, consumers in rural areas will most likely avoid travelling to the city to fill a claim in front of the court, face a long procedure, or go through the psychological trouble of attending a court hearing, especially in those areas lacking a litigation culture.

A second important challenge in the enforcement of consumer law is the lack of specialised consumer law jurisdictions to handle consumer-related disputes and to resolve them according to the rights and remedies provided by consumer law. Typically, consumer claims will be dealt with in front of civil courts, which in many instances will apply civil law rules to the case at stake, potentially undermining the application of consumer law provisions. For instance, as reported in China, courts are more likely to apply civil law or contract law, instead of consumer law, to consumer disputes.[4]

In order to make consumer redress (relatively) more accessible, specialised consumer courts such as the Malaysian Tribunal for Consumer Claims (TCC), established in 1999,

[3] Cf in Europe, European Commission, 'Consumer Conditions Scoreboard: Consumer at Home in the Single Market' (2015). Only 2 per cent of consumers facing a problem took the business concerned to court.

[4] See J Jin, 'China', in this volume.

or the Indian Consumer Redressal Forums, were created to deal with consumer-related disputes. These dedicated courts operate under more accessible procedures to consumers as they are designed to serve the particularities of consumer cases, usually low-value claims. The purpose of these specific procedures is to make it easier for the consumer to seek judicial redress. For instance, consumers can file a complaint electronically at the e-Tribunal system of the Malaysian Tribunal for Consumer Claims.[5] The counter-claim can also be submitted electronically. Consumers do not need the representation of a lawyer, reducing litigation costs.[6] The TCC functions under a speedy procedure: consumer-disputes submitted to the TCC are required to be heard and adjudicated within 60 days,[7] and the national report states that most cases are heard and settled within 40 days.[8] The cases can be adjudicated by the TCC or the parties can reach an agreement. As to the enforceability of the award, every award made by the TCC or the decision containing the agreement are final and binding on all parties to the proceedings.[9] However, the TCC's awards can be subject to judicial review by the High Court. Failures to comply with an award after 14 days from the date it was given by the TCC entails a criminal offence, involving economic fines or even imprisonment.[10]

The Indian Consumer Redressal Forums, set up under the 1986 Consumer Protection Act, is a three-level quasi-judicial mechanism for consumer cases depending on the value of the claim. By virtue of the new Indian Consumer Protection Act (2019) now the District Commission deals with claims up to approximately USD 117,000; claims above that amount are dealt with by the National Consumer Disputes Redressal Commission (NCDRC). The new system to determine the jurisdiction is made on the basis of the 'value of goods or service paid as consideration',[11] rather than the value of the claim, which leave outside the scope of the District Commission cases where, although the value of the good or service exceeds that amount, the aggrieved party seeks compensation below that sum. In some instances, this may hinder the possibility of litigation under this scheme as the consumer can decide to avoid submitting a claim in front of the NCDRC when it would rather do it locally. Similarly to the Malaysian TCC, the 2019 Consumer Act reform in India has made it possible for consumers to submit their complaints online.[12] Court fees are also low.[13] However, unlike the Malaysian TCC, the procedure in front of the Indian District Commission seems complex and lengthy. While the admissibility of the complaint shall ordinarily be decided within 21 days from the date on which the complaint was filed,[14] the rest of the procedure can prolong

[5] Consumer complaints can be filed at https://ttpm.kpdnhep.gov.my/login. The system requires users' registration.

[6] To submit a claim, consumers pay a flat-rate fee of approximately USD 1.20, and litigation costs are capped at approximately USD 48.

[7] See https://ttpm.kpdnhep.gov.my/portal/award/tribunal.

[8] See Z Zakaria, 'Malaysia', in this volume.

[9] Consumer Protection Act 1999 (Malaysia), s 116.

[10] See https://ttpm.kpdnhep.gov.my/portal/award/penalty.

[11] Consumer Protection Act 2019 (India), s 34.

[12] Available at https://edaakhil.nic.in/edaakhil/.

[13] For instance, for claims up to Rs 20 lakhs (approximately USD 27,000), fees are about USD 7 and about USD 7 in front of the NCDRC.

[14] Consumer Protection Act 2019 (India), s 36(2).

the resolution of the dispute, which may take from one to five years. Yet, although the procedure is still lengthy, redress in front of Consumer Redressal Forums is comparatively shorter than ordinary judicial routes in India.[15]

Similarly important to the creation of tailor-made procedures for consumer disputes, with shorter and cheaper venues for judicial redress, is the usability of such mechanisms. Do consumer use these mechanisms? How many disputes are resolved through these dedicated proceedings? The Malaysian TCC proved a successful case. Consumers referred more than 10,000 disputes in 2011. However, a sharp decline has been observed in recent years, with less than 5,000 cases submitted in 2017, casting doubts on its authority to solve consumer disputes.[16] By contrast, as shown in the Indian country report, Indian Consumer Redressal Forums have received more than five million cases since its creation in 1988 and, on average, more than 90 per cent of the cases have been cleared. Therefore, and despite the decline in the submission of cases to the Malaysian TCC – an issue that would require separate attention – consumer courts provide a relief to the load of general civil courts while establishing more responsive procedures to the consumer problems and litigation attitudes.

Other countries have opted for an intermediary route establishing simplified procedures for small claims, which are the majority of consumer disputes. Under such approach, consumer claims are conducted through a special or summary procedure inside civil courts, such as for instance in Thailand, Australia or Vietnam. Consumer legislation in Thailand has simplified the procedure for consumer claims by admitting oral proceedings and providing assistance to consumers through the different stages of the procedure. This system also reduces the burden of proof and allows the possibility of amending the calculation of already awarded damages where they produce last-long-ing effects on the subjects concerned. Another example of a hybrid model between the possibility or seeking redress in front of a specialised consumer court or to do it via a normal civil litigation rule is that of Australia. As part of the Queensland Civil and Administrative Tribunal (QCAT) a special consumer division has jurisdiction to hear matters under the Australian Consumer Law up to AUS 25,000 (approximately USD 18,500), excluding interest. The application form available in the QCAT website is fairly intuitive in guiding the consumer to define the claim appropriately.[17] The procedure also establishes an attempt at mediation for claims above AUS 1,500 (approximately USD 1,100). Where mediation fails, a hearing will take place and the judge will render a decision. The Civil Procedure Code in Vietnam has also put in place a simplified civil procedure for dealing with consumer law-value disputes (for transactions below VND

[15] For a recent analysis of the procedures in front of the Consumer Redressal Forums, see S Minhas, 'Consumer Disputes and Consumer Redressal Forums in India' (2019) 8 *International Journal of Engineering Science Invention* 1.

[16] S Sothi Rachagan and S Sothirachagan, 'Access to Justice – Addressing Consumer Redress in Malaysia' (2018), Intergovernmental Group of Experts on Consumer Law and Policy (IGE Consumer), available at https://unctad.org/system/files/non-official-document/cicplp3rd_c_nu_drr_en1.pdf.

[17] The form can be found at www.qcat.qld.gov.au/resources/forms under 'Consumer and trader disputes, and property damage disputes'.

100 million, approximately USD 4,500) where the length and the procedural steps are reduced.[18]

However, the effectiveness of these intermediary solutions seems limited. It has been reported that the advantages associated with the Thai summary procedure are shadowed in practice by a lack of resources to make the mechanism fully operational.[19] Likewise, to date, no cases have been brought in front of the court under the Vietnamese simplified civil procedure.[20] No data is publicly available regarding the performance of the consumer division inside the QCAT.

Notwithstanding the contribution of specialised consumer courts or summarised procedures to improve consumers' access to justice, the second challenge in the enforcement of consumer law, namely the effective application of consumer rules, is not entirely overcome. The creation of dedicated courts does not always guarantee the application of consumer protection rules. In principle, consumer courts have to adjudicate consumer disputes on the basis of the rules for which they were established, that is, consumer law. However, in Malaysia for instance, this has raised jurisdiction problems as to the interpretation of unfairness.[21] The Malaysian chapter reports a case that deserves attention. To what extent do specialised consumer courts have to apply consumer law? In 2015, pursuant to an appeal against a TCC's decision, the Malaysian High Court held that the TCC acted *ultra vires* by applying consumer law to a case falling outside the scope of the TCC.[22] Moreover, the TCC has freedom, therefore, to decide the appropriate remedy to be granted from a contract modification or replacement of the goods to monetary compensation for any loss or damage suffered by the claimant.[23] This leaves aside the application of specific consumer remedies if the adjudicator wishes to. At the same time, the Malaysian Consumer Protection Act leaves to the discretion of the TCC whether to refer questions of law to the High Court. As a result, it can be concluded that despite dedicated consumer courts, an effective application of consumer rules does not always take place.

A closer examination of the jurisdiction of specialised consumer courts reveals yet another problem, namely the competence of an adjudicator to resolve sector-specific consumer disputes such as those arising in connection to financial services or telecommunications, for example. In such cases, depending on the competent jurisdiction, the dispute will be decided on the basis of civil/contract law, general consumer law or sector-specific consumer law, where it exists. In many instances, sector-specific consumer provisions provide for specific sectorial remedies, such as the right of contract termination without penalty in telecommunications services. The situation with more general consumer remedies is similar. The variety of applicable regimes and remedies results

[18] See N Van Cuong, 'Vietnam', in this volume.

[19] See A Techaapikun, 'Thailand', in this volume.

[20] See Van Cuong, 'Vietnam'.

[21] For a further analysis, see Sothi Rachagan and Sothirachagan, 'Access to Justice'.

[22] *Fairview International School Subang Sdn Bhd v Tribunal Tuntutan Pengguna Malaysia & Anor* [2015] 9 MLJ 581.

[23] See at https://ttpm.kpdnhep.gov.my/portal/award/tribunal.

in a fragmented landscape, where an identical problem can be resolved in a completely different manner depending on the court handling the case. The level of expertise of the adjudicator also impacts the application of consumer legislation, most notably when it comes to the interpretation of consumer provisions.[24] In the case of Thailand, the lack of specialised consumer lawyers impacts the way the procedure is conducted. For instance, the national report shows that a consumer lawyer would normally conduct an accusatorial procedure rather than an inquisitorial one. Insufficient specialisation of consumer lawyers also have an effect on the determination of punitive damages.[25]

Remaining jurisdictions not included in the examples above have opted for dealing with consumer disputes under simplified or small claim procedures; for example, Hong Kong, Singapore or Vietnam. Small claims procedures are fitting to the nature of consumer disputes (low-value), while reducing the duration and costs of the procedure. However, the problem with small claims solutions is that, in some instances, these expeditious venues not only reduce time and cost of resolving consumer disputes but also decrease procedural guarantees. For example, in Macau there is no possibility of appealing decisions made by the court of first instance under the procedure for small claims.[26] Moreover, the costs of enforcing small claims decisions disincentivise consumers from seeking redress under this mechanism.[27]

An additional means to enhance access to justice is the collective representation of diffuse interests. As a matter of fact, collective claims are allowed in most of the countries covered in this volume.[28] The configuration of collective redress in these jurisdictions in the form of representative actions differs, however, from the US-style class action system. Seemingly, collective redress incentivises litigation by allowing aggregation.[29] In practice, consumers face significant hurdles to use this route for obtaining redress. In India, for example, the identification of what constitutes a consumer case is not clearly defined. Therefore, the difficulties in identifying what constitutes a consumer case and the affected parties in the case of opt-in systems, together with high litigation costs, also prevent consumers from using this mechanism. Besides, a worrying situation is observed in China, where the mechanism of class action has been gradually watered down by the courts' inadmissibility based on the 'social stability' argument.[30]

Lastly, the limited number of consumer cases reaching the courts results in little case law on consumer cases; for instance, rulings under small claims procedures are not usually published. The lack of accessibility of case law makes the identification of recurrent consumer problems considerably difficult.

[24] In this regard, see Jing, 'China' and Techaapikun, 'Thailand'.

[25] See Techaapikun, 'Thailand'.

[26] See D Wei and Â Patrício Rafael, 'Macau', in this volume.

[27] See G Low, 'Singapore', in this volume.

[28] Myanmar remains the exception. No reference is made in the national report or information found regarding collective redress in Myanmar.

[29] BT Fitzpatrick, 'Do Class Action Lawyers Make Too Little' (2010) 158(7) *University of Pennsylvania Law Review* 2043.

[30] T Daffer, 'I am Fighting for the Right to Eat, and I Will Keep Fighting – The Truth Is on Our Side: Class Action Litigation as a Means of Enacting Social Change in China' (2006) 75 *UMKC Law Review* 227; see also

III. Alternative Dispute Resolution (ADR)

A different understanding of justice involves allowing parties the possibility to resolve their disputes among themselves in a non-adversarial manner, even while requiring the intervention of a third party. Parties may reach a restorative solution while avoiding complex procedures in front of the court or where the outcome escapes their control. The option for one model or another largely depends on the legal culture. Jurisdictions with a strong litigation culture would establish redress structures where the role of the court in resolving private disputes is substantial. Conversely, in other jurisdictions less prone to litigation more prominence will be given to out-of-court procedures. By way of example, Confucian influences for instance in China,[31] Singapore,[32] Taiwan[33] and Vietnam[34] explain the preference for instances facilitating extrajudicial settlement rather than adversarial procedures, while in Australia a non-adversarial dispute resolution approach finds its origins in ancient indigenous communities despite the adoption of the English common law system.[35] Non-adversarial out-of-court procedures are a religious heritage, for instance in Malaysia where, pursuant to the influence of Islam, a third party, or *Suhl*, would be in charge of providing conciliation, mediation and even arbitration.[36]

Different modalities and configurations of procedures are found across the ADR spectrum. Some ADR mechanisms simply facilitate negotiation or conciliation (for example Hong Kong's privately run Consumer Council). Other models involve mediation and even adjudication through arbitration, typically under a two-tiered procedure by which adjudication takes place where mediation fails. The latter model is found in most jurisdictions covered in this volume such as, for example, the Dispute Resolution Committee within the National Consumer Affairs Center of Japan (NCAC) or the Consumer Arbitration Centre of the Macau Government Consumer Council. This two-stage model is also more frequent when it comes to ADR procedures provided by sectoral bodies (sector-specific ombudsman, regulators, etc) as reported in India, for instance.

Generally, the purpose of ADR is to provide a faster, cheaper, more efficient and more amicable venue for settling disputes than the court. These features make ADR

JH Shoo, 'Class Action Mechanisms in Chinese and Taiwanese Contexts – A Mixture of Private and Public Law' (2014) 28 *Emory International Law Review* 237.

[31] AHY Chen, 'Mediation, Litigation, and Justice: Confucius Reflections in a Modern Liberal Society' in DA Bell and H Chaibong (eds), *Confucianism for the Modern World* (Cambridge: Cambridge University Press 2003) 259.

[32] See Low, 'Singapore'.

[33] T Thanh, 'Consumer Dispute Settlement in Vietnam and Taiwan: A Comparative Perspective' (2018), available at www.researchgate.net/publication/328999908_Consumer_dispute_settlement_in_Vietnam_and_Taiwan_A_comparative_perspective.

[34] ibid.

[35] MA Noone and LA Ojelabi, 'Alternative Dispute Resolution and Access to Justice in Australia' (2020) 16(2) *International Journal of Law in Context* 108.

[36] R Hassan et al, 'Setting Up a Sulh-based, Community Mediation-Type of Online Dispute Resolution (ODR) in Malaysia' in *5th International Conference on Information and Communication Technology for the Muslim World (ICT4M)* (2013), 1.

appealing to consumers seeking redress. ADR is also a practical solution to the increasing workload of civil courts, optimising existing resources. The time for processing and resolving complaints is shortened compared to judicial proceedings. Consumer disputes in front of ADR bodies or following ADR procedures are said to be processed and resolved within weeks, although no specific data was found concerning the actual duration of representative ADR procedures featured in the different country reports. In terms of costs, consumer ADR mechanisms are generally free (for example Macau, Vietnam or mediation in front of the Insurance Ombudsman in India) or they involve a small fee (Singapore).

Another major advantage of ADR mechanisms is their accessibility. Generally, ADR is more fitting to the nature of consumer disputes, not only because of simplified procedures vis-à-vis the courts, but also because of their geographic proximity; it is common that local consumer centres provide ADR (for example Japan). ADR also offers a high potential owing to the possibilities of technology. Consumers not only can submit their complaints electronically, but also the procedure can be entirely conducted online, through Online Dispute Resolution (ODR) methods.

Although not completely taking off over the last two decades, ODR is gaining momentum nowadays due to the Covid-19 pandemic. By way of example, the Department of Justice of Hong Kong has set up a Covid-19 Online Dispute Resolution Scheme, launched in June 2020.[37] This scheme covers Covid-19 related-claims under 500,000 HKD (approximately 65,000 USD). It consists of a multi-tiered dispute resolution mechanism comprising e-negotiation, e-mediation and e-arbitration. The service is provided by the International Online Dispute Resolution Centre Limited (eBRAM), a private company.[38] The use of this service requires an online registration fee of 200 HKD (approximately 25 USD) to be paid by both parties, claimant and respondent. Timeframes are reduced; for instance, in case of reaching the arbitration stage, the award shall be rendered within seven calendar days from the filing of the last submission.[39] The arbitration award is final and binding. However, the design of the procedure, especially the appointment of neutrals and the requirement for both parties to pay the registration fee, although open to the general public, does not seem intended for consumer disputes. Rather, the procedure stands as a fast-track mechanism for micro, small and medium-sized enterprises.[40]

The scalability of ODR makes it very effective for resolving mass consumer claims, while reducing legal expenses. As noted, ODR offers substantial capacity for resolving disputes in an accessible, cheap and fast manner.[41] The Online Consumer Mediation Centre of the National Law School of India University aims at providing an accessible

[37] For further information see Department of Justice, 'Press Release: COVID-19 Online Dispute Resolution Scheme launched today' (29 June 2020), available under www.doj.gov.hk/en/community_engagement/press/20200629_pr1.html.

[38] www.ebram.org/covid_19_odr.html.

[39] eBRAM Rules for the Covid-19 ODR Scheme, Art 8(8).

[40] Department of Justice, 'Press Release: COVID-19'.

[41] EE Katsh, ME Katsh and J Rifkin, *Online Dispute Resolution: Resolving Conflicts in Cyberspace* (Hoboken: John Wiley & Sons, 2001).

venue to manage and resolve consumer disputes through online mediation based on a set of procedural guarantees: easy accessibility, security, confidentiality, cost-effectiveness, neutrality and integrity.[42] In Indonesia, the new amendment of consumer legislation envisages the use of ODR.[43] Regrettably, the potential of ODR is not yet fully explored.[44]

Despite the benefits associated with the use of ADR, including ODR, for solving consumer disputes, it is important that the fairness of the procedure is preserved. For example, the Vietnamese Law on Consumer Protection establishes certain procedural guarantees for mediation and arbitration procedures.[45] Ensuring procedural fairness is also particularly important in cases where the decision arising from an ADR procedure is not only binding but also produces *res judicata* effects. For example, in Indonesia, the decision of the Consumer Dispute Settlement Agency (CDSA) is binding and final. Secondly, it is important that, while enhancing access to redress, ADR also preserves the rule of law. Consumers should not be deprived of their right to obtain redress in court. As a result, arbitration clauses are generally prohibited.[46] Thirdly, ADR procedures should be transparent and open. However, one of the main appeals of ADR procedures, in particular for arbitration, is their secrecy and confidentiality. Generally, there is no obligation to publish arbitration awards. As a result, the accessibility of the data on disputes resolved via ADR is limited and, therefore, it prevents the early identification of recurrent consumer problems, where they exist.

Court-based ADR is growing and increasingly becoming part of civil justice systems. ADR can be embedded in the judiciary by establishing attempts at conciliation before trial (for example in China). It can be argued that this is also a reminiscence of the Confucian influence over the legal culture. Moreover, in some instances, these attempts at conciliation become even a mandatory condition of admissibility; for example, the new Indian Consumer Protection Act (2019) fosters mediation, while the Commercial Court Act makes it mandatory for commercial disputes over INR 300,000 (approximately USD 4,000) to undergo mediation before filing proceedings in court.[47] In Australia, for issues falling under the jurisdiction of the Federal Court, the Civil Dispute Resolution Act requires parties to take genuine actions to settle their disputes before initiating proceedings.[48]

Softer forms of ADR involve the requirement to handle consumer complaints in-house. For example, the Indian Telecoms Regulatory Authority requires the compulsory establishment of in-house complaints centre to handle consumer complaints, with a possibility to appeal in front of an in-house body established under the requirements

[42] http://onlinemediationcenter.ac.in.

[43] See Chapter IV of Law on Consumer Protection. For a further analysis see J Gunawan and BM Waluyo 'Indonesia', in this volume.

[44] For an analysis of the effectiveness of ODR in the EU and Brazil, see MJ Schmidt-Kessen, R Nogueira and M Cantero Gamito, 'Success or Failure? – Effectiveness of Consumer ODR Platforms in Brazil and in the EU' (2020) 43 *Journal of Consumer Policy* 659.

[45] See Van Cuong, 'Vietnam'.

[46] Consumer Protection Law in Vietnam establishes that arbitration clauses in standard form contracts are not binding on consumers (Art 38), see also ibid.

[47] Commercial Court Act (India), s 21A(2).

[48] Noone and Ojelabi, 'Alternative Dispute Resolution'.

established by the regulator.[49] In some instances, however, this requirement may delay obtaining redress where the trader is not obliged to respond to consumer claims, since the consumer cannot take any action before contacting the trader.

The ADR landscape in the analysed jurisdictions is complex and fragmented; for example in Australia.[50] Some forms of ADR are provided by public bodies (Indian Consumer Forums, Indonesian CDSA or the NCAC in Japan, while there is an increasing offer of commercial ADR solutions, such as the Hong Kong Consumer Council or the China International Economic and Trade Arbitration Commission (CIETAC).[51] In other instances, the availability of ADR mechanisms is limited. For instance, in Hong Kong, civil action remains virtually the only redress option for consumers, with the exception of insurance-related disputes, which can be settled in front of the Insurance Complaints Bureau (ICM).[52] In Japan, the NCAC may initiate mediation and arbitration to resolve 'important consumer disputes'. However, what would constitute an 'important consumer dispute' is not clearly defined in the legislation.[53]

IV. Administrative Enforcement and the Role of Regulators

A third approach to the materialisation of consumer protection rules is the granting of enforcement powers to public authorities. For example, the lack of judicial precedent may explain administrative enforcement as one additional tool for ensuring compliance of consumer protection rules. In some instances, public enforcement and regulatory authorities may investigate misconduct and consumer law violations by traders. A significant example is the Indian 2019 Consumer Protection Act, which entitles the Consumer Protection Authority to investigate consumer complaints, issue safety notices for goods and services and even injunctions. However, it is noted that in most jurisdictions the enforcement powers of regulatory authorities are generally limited for the following reasons.

First, as shown above, public regulators do not typically resolve disputes. For instance, in Hong Kong, the Consumer Council is not a law enforcement agency and

[49] Telecom Consumers Complaint Redressal Regulations, 2012; available at https://trai.gov.in/consumer-info/telecom/grievance-redressal-mechanism.

[50] Noone and Ojelabi, 'Alternative Dispute Resolution'. For consumer ADR, see L Nottage, 'The New Australian Consumer Law: What About Consumer ADR' (2009) 9 *Queensland University of Technology Law & Justice Journal* 176.

[51] Not typically designed for consumer disputes but consumers can use it.

[52] Adjudication for claim-related complaints (for claims that do not exceed HKD 1 million, approximately USD 128,500) and mediation for non-claim related complaints. See also M Durovic, G Howells and A Janssen, 'Hong Kong', in this volume.

[53] Section 2 of the Act on National Consumer Affairs Center of Japan (Act No 123 of 2002; Amendment of Act No 43 of 2017), which establishes and regulates the 'Important Consumer Dispute Resolution procedure', does not explicitly define the criteria for identifying these disputes. The literature understands that an 'important consumer dispute' involves transactions that affect larger groups of consumers (eg mass claims) or transactions that have caused or will cause material damages to individuals; see H Habuka and C Rule, 'The Promise and Potential of Online Dispute Resolution in Japan' (2017) 4 *International Journal of Online Dispute Resolution* 74.

is not vested with the power of investigation or adjudication.[54] In Australia, consumers can obtain information and even draft a complaint with the tools offered by the Australian Competition and Consumer Commission (ACCC).[55] Yet, the ACCC can only advise to go to the court or other third party, such as the Industry Ombudsman, if the problem persists after contacting the business.

Secondly, public regulators are usually not competent to grant remedies to affected consumers; for example, as a rule, they do not establish compensation to consumers. In Japan, qualified consumer organisations, that is, those certified by the Government, may issue injunctions in case of unfair clauses and unfair practices, but a claim for damages is not allowed.[56]

Thirdly, it has also been argued that even in the event regulatory bodies are competent to prosecute consumer law breaches, they may lack the resources to investigate every violation.[57] Some administrative bodies are not endowed with proper powers or even resources for providing dispute resolution. For example, in Hong Kong, the Consumer Council proposed to put in place a Consumer Dispute Resolution Centre (CDRC). However, as noted in the national report, it still remains unclear the extent of the powers and operation of the CDRC. As a result, ineffective enforcement led to more and more problems such as unfair sales tactics in the gym and beauty industries.[58]

Despite these limitations, the role of regulators and administrative enforcement is still critical to improve consumers' access to justice. First and foremost, it is important to not disregard the fact that consumer disputes are, generally, private disputes. As a result, a *caveat emptor* approach is the prevailing rule. Such approach has an impact in the configuration of mechanisms for seeking redress, usually consisting of venues for private enforcement. However, some consumer law violations may have implications for citizens at large, not only for contracting parties; for example misleading advertising or defective products. Increasingly, consumer law frameworks are granting public authorities the tools not only to investigate breaches but also to restrain certain practices by acting as a deterrent or even as an incentive to be compliant with consumer law. For instance, the Hong Kong Consumer Council elaborates public lists naming traders for non-compliance with consumer rules.[59] Naming and shaming is also used in Singapore and Vietnam.

Some jurisdictions, however, go beyond merely deterrent mechanisms and open the door to public interest litigation. For instance, in Indonesia, consumer protection NGOs

[54] See Durovic, Howells and Janssen, 'Hong Kong'.

[55] The ACCC is the regulator as per the Competition and Consumer Act 2010 (Schedule 2, s 2).

[56] See H Hirose, K-F Lenz and T Shiraishi, 'Japan', in this volume.

[57] Cf for an EU-centric perspective, P Cortés, *The Law of Consumer Redress in an Evolving Digital Market: Upgrading from Alternative to Online Dispute Resolution* (Cambridge: Cambridge University Press, 2017) 19–20.

[58] See Durovic, Howells and Janssen, 'Hong Kong'.

[59] A list of traders being named by the Hong Kong Consumer Council can be accessed here: www.consumer.org.hk/ws_en/named-list. However, traders report lack of transparency in the methodology used for product testing; in the case of sunscreen, see K Magramo, 'Industry backlash against Hong Kong Consumer Council study which finds 83 per cent of sunscreen products do not meet protective claims', scmp.com, 15 October 2020.

have the legal standing to sue business actors before the general court. Another initiative in this direction is the 2019 Consumer Protection Act in India, which enables the public authority to investigate cases which are harmful to the public interest.[60] However, consumer public interest litigation in India has been traditionally considered limited[61] and the plurality of authorities in India makes it difficult to navigate available venues for consumer redress. Other bodies, while not necessarily representing consumers in front of the court, can increase access to justice by providing funding for litigations costs, such as the Bar Free Legal Service Scheme in Hong Kong.[62] Despite the noted limitations, public interest litigation is still an important tool for consumer law enforcement, especially where consumers do not have the resources to seek redress. Yet, it is important to note that, generally, public enforcement is not an adequate venue for recovering damages due to the private law nature of consumers disputes. This contrasts with the EU, where there is a growing role for public regulators to establish mechanisms to compensate consumers.[63]

To conclude, a possible way to enhance consumers' access to justice by using administrative structures while preserving the private law nature of consumer disputes is to reinforce cooperation between ADR bodies and administrative authorities. A positive example could be the Malaysia Aviation Commission Act 2015 which established an in-house mechanism for mediation and adjudication of consumer disputes related to passenger rights.[64] Consumers are increasingly relying on this mechanism; for instance, complaints submitted to this body increased by 89 per cent in 2017 as compared to 2016.[65] However, the main limitation of this body is that for disputes related to aviation services not covered in the 2016 Malaysian Aviation Consumer Protection Code 2016, consumers would have to initiate proceedings in front of the Malaysian TCC.[66] This makes it difficult for consumers to effectively identify the competent venues for obtaining consumer redress.

[60] Pursuant to s 19(1) of the 2019 Consumer Protection Act, '[T]he Central Authority may, after receiving any information or complaint or directions from the Central Government or of its own motion, conduct or cause to be conducted a preliminary inquiry as to whether there exists a prima facie case of violation of consumer rights or any unfair trade practice or any false or misleading advertisement, by any person, which is prejudicial to the public interest or to the interests of consumers and if it is satisfied that there exists a prima facie case, it shall cause investigation to be made by the Director General or by the District Collector'.

[61] SH Shah, 'Consumer Interest Litigation under the Consumer Protection Act, 1986 in India: A Critical Analysis' (2013) *Nirma University Law Journal* 3.

[62] See Durovic, Howells and Janssen, 'Hong Kong'.

[63] See P Cortés, 'Enforcing EU Consumer Policy More Effectively: A Three-Pronged Approach' in S Drake and M Smith (eds), *Effective Enforcement of EU Law and Policy* (Cheltenham: Edward Elgar, 2016).

[64] Malaysia Aviation Commission Act 2015, ss 69 et seq.

[65] Sothi Rachagan and Sothirachagan, 'Access to Justice'.

[66] ibid.

V. Conclusions

This chapter has examined different venues for consumers to obtain redress in the different countries covered in this volume. It has noted that despite the assorted possibilities for resolving consumer disputes, the actual mechanisms for obtaining consumer redress remain complex and fragmented.

Existing judicial consumer redress mechanisms are deficient as shown by their limited appeal to consumers. Specialised consumer courts and summary small claims procedures appear more suitable to the nature of consumer disputes. However, while data on the use of these mechanisms shows an initial enthusiasm for these procedures, the steady decline in the use of these mechanisms signals the lack of effectiveness of these venues for obtaining redress. The analysis also suggests that judicial consumer redress is detached from consumer markets. In large countries such as China or India, going to the court can be geographically distant for consumers located in rural areas. The introduction of electronic systems for initiating judicial proceedings or even the possibility of wholly or partially conducting the procedure online would bridge that gap; provided that the economic and digital divide are appropriately solved. Online mechanisms in which procedural guarantees are preserved (fairness, hearing, appeal, etc), would also have the capacity of rendering judicial redress more accessible, so that consumers would not feel as intimidated as going through a formal procedure in front of the court.

The current consumer ADR scenario does not look much better. Consumer ADR is scattered among a mixture of private and public bodies, governed by public and private rules, with different procedures from negotiation to arbitration and covering different sectors. This creates confusion as to the better venues for obtaining adequate redress. Moreover, a piecemeal approach to consumer disputes means that for areas left aside of specific consumer redress such as healthcare or professional services consumers need to resort to litigation. Opportunities are found in the introduction of ODR as an effective mechanism for consumer redress in all sort of disputes, not only for those arising from e-commerce transactions. However, it is important that ODR procedures preserve minimum procedural guarantees.

To conclude, it is important to highlight the lack of availability of consumer case law and data on the use and effectiveness of existing procedures as well as their outcomes. Such information would be highly useful as a tool to better design dispute resolution procedures. Finally, it is suggested that a closer cooperation between public authorities and ADR bodies could provide credible and practicable possibilities for consumer access to justice and effective consumer law enforcement. On the one hand, ADR bodies could exchange data with administrative authorities on recurrent consumer disputes, which would contribute to the early identification of problems. On the other, administrative authorities could host ADR mechanisms. Their de-centralised structure and official character can increase consumers' confidence in these bodies as venues in which to effectively obtain redress.

Annex*

1. Judicial Consumer Redress

	Competent court	Small claims procedure	Possibility of appeal	Length and costs of the procedure	Class actions
Australia	Special Consumer division within the Civil and Administrative Tribunal that has jurisdiction to hear matters under the Australian Consumer Law up to AUS 25,000 (excluding interest).	Yes. For domestic disputes under AUS 20,000.	Matters can go to an Appeal Panel on limited grounds including cases where the decision of the Tribunal was not fair and equitable.	/	Yes
China	No special courts but special procedural rules for consumer issues and public interest litigation (limited to food safety cases).	Yes. Judgments are final.	No	/	Yes. Formally called representative lawsuits, *daibiaoren susong*.
Hong Kong	No specialised courts for consumer disputes.	Yes. Informal, quick and inexpensive for claims up to HKD 50,000. Main claims: debts, services charges, damage to property, goods sold and consumer claims.	Yes (but very limited grounds)	Possibility of legal aid for going to the court under fulfilment of certain conditions related to the merits of the case and the financial resources of the consumer.	No specifically class action but representative action. Opt-in system.

India	Specialised courts for consumer disputes, *Consumer Redressal Forums*, with a high rate of resolved cases (on average 90 percent of the initiated procedures).	No specific procedure for small claims.	Yes	Low court fees (max equivalent to approx USD 70).	Representative actions. Opt-out system. However, with the new Consumer Protection Law (2019) consumers shall now go first to the Central Consumer Protection Authority to request the enforcement of consumer provisions.
Indonesia	No specialised courts for consumer disputes, which are solved in general courts.	Small claim procedure in ordinary courts.	Uncertain in practice[1]	Civil proceedings based on simple, fast and low-cost principle although high costs and lengthy procedures in case of appeals, which usually take place. Execution, esp. where collateral is asked to be seized, is not considered cheap.	Yes. Opt-out system. For instance, consumer protection NGOs have the legal standing to sue business actors before the general court.
Japan	No specialised courts for consumer disputes. However, consumer-related cases can be handled in summary courts, where it is possible to litigate without the representation of a lawyer.	Small claims before a summary court for cases below JPY 600,000 (approx 5500 USD).	No	Costly procedures and the absence of a 'loser pays' approach act as a deterrent to initiate judicial proceedings. The Japan Legal Support Center may offer some legal counselling for free and even to anticipate attorney's fees.	Yes. Out-in system. It consists of a two-stage litigation procedure where a qualified consumer organisation brings an action seeking a declaratory judgment that, if successful, serves as a basis for claiming damages (exception: human injuries).

(continued)

(Continued)

	Competent court	Small claims procedure	Possibility of appeal	Length and costs of the procedure	Class actions
Macau	No specialised courts. Consumer cases will be handled by courts of first instance under a small claims' procedure for cases below MOP 100,000 (approx USD 12,400), an expeditious procedure for claims under MOP 250,000, and general procedure above that sum.	Yes, for cases below MOP 100,000.	No	Lengthy procedures	Yes. Class action can be initiated by the consumer organisation.
Malaysia	Specialised jurisdiction for consumer-related disputes: Tribunal for Consumer Claims for claims below R 50,000 (approx USD 12,000). Two-stage phase: court-assisted negotiation + trial if negotiation fails.	Yes	Decisions by the TCC can be reviewed.	Low fees (filling fee only RM 5, approx USD 1.20). Cases are heard and solved within 60 days.	Representative actions. Opt-in system.
Myanmar	No specialised courts for consumer disputes. However, criminal proceedings can be initiated where the consumer has been deceived.	Procedure for small claims.	/	/	No

Singapore	No specialised courts for consumer complaints. State Courts for disputes below SGD 250,000 (approx. USD 180,000). For disputes above that sum, it is competence of the Supreme Court.	Small Claims Tribunal for disputes below SGD 10,000 (approx USD 7,300). Originally devised for consumers disputes. Enforceable decisions.		Filing fee of SKD 10 (USD 7.5), and SGD 20 (USD 15) for claims between SGD 5,000 and 10,000.	Representative actions. Opt-in.
South Korea	No specialised courts for consumer disputes. Instead, the out-of-court procedure in front of the Korea Consumer Agency (KCA) stands as a mechanism for redress and a procedural step before going to the court. In fact, the Consumer Dispute Settlement Commission (CDSC) within the KCA is considered a quasi-judicial authority. See below, ADR.	Small-sum civil suit for disputes that have not been solved by the CDSC or for cases that fulfil certain requirements such as cases under KRW 30 million (approx USD 26,500) or cases involving vulnerable consumers.	Yes		Only for securities-related damages and in certain product liability matters under the Consumer Act of Korea. Current proposed rules in late 2020 to expand the scope for class actions.
Taiwan	No specialised court for consumer disputes but specific procedure for consumer disputes, and even the possibility to claim punitive damages up to five times the amount of the damages.	Yes	Yes	Reduced court fees and the possibility of being waived.	Yes, Group litigation. Opt-in system. Qualified consumer protection organisations may institute a lawsuit in its name after at least twenty consumers who have suffered from the same factual grounds assign their rights to claim to such consumer protection organisation.

(continued)

(Continued)

	Competent court	Small claims procedure	Possibility of appeal	Length and costs of the procedure	Class actions
Thailand	No specialised court but specific simplified procedure for consumer disputes. This special procedure also allows for specific remedies and damages such as punitive damages or the right to repair and to replace the defective goods. It is also possible to initiate civil and criminal proceedings against consumer protection infringements.	/	Yes	/	Yes. Opt-out system.
Vietnam	No specialised courts for consumer disputes but simplified civil procedure, for consumer-related and simple dispute below VND 100 million (approx USD 5,000).	Yes	Yes	Consumers are exempted from paying court fees in advance.	Not provided under civil procedural law, but a civil case against Apple Inc. to the People's Court of Ho Chi Minh City.

* The information contained in this Annex is based on the country reports contained in this volume and independent research conducted in preparation for the analysis contained in this chapter. The content of this comparative analysis should not be considered or used as legal advice.

[1] For an analysis on the topic, see M Syamsudin, 'The Failure of the Court to Protect Consumers: A Review of Consumer Dispute Resolution in Indonesia' (2020) 44 *Journal of Consumer Policy* 117.

2. Alternative Dispute Resolution

	Entities	Procedure	ODR	Costs & Time
Australia	Public			
	Community Justice Centres (CJC)	Mediation	/	/
	Judicial ADR and referral to CJC from courts of first instance	Mediation		
	Private			
	Industry ombudsmen (depending on the sector concerned)	Two-stage procedure (Mediation + arbitration)		
China	Public			
	Judicial conciliation	Before trial, judges usually attempt conciliation	Internet Courts in Hangzhou, Beijing and Guangzhou	/
			Shenzhen E-business Better Service Centre (EBS)[1]	/
	Private			
	China International Economic and Trade Arbitration Commission (CIETAC)[2]	Arbitration (although conciliation is generally attempted first)	CIETAC Online Dispute Resolution Center for electronic commerce disputes and domain name disputes (arbitration)	/

(continued)

(Continued)

	Entities	Procedure	ODR	Costs & Time
Hong Kong	Consumer Council	It is possible to lodge a complaint at the website of the HK Consumer Council. The Consumer Council provides only a venue for conciliation. It does not resolve disputes.	COVID-19 Online Dispute Resolution Scheme[3] for COVID-19 related-claims under HKD 500,000. Multi-tiered dispute resolution mechanism comprising negotiation, mediation and arbitration. Electronic Business-related Arbitration and Mediation Platform (currently under proposal).	COVID-19 Online Dispute Resolution Scheme: HKD 200 fee
	Sectoral schemes			
	Financial Dispute Resolution Centre (FDRC)	Mediation and arbitration		HKD 200 application fee, plus HKD 1,000–2,000 depending on the claim for mediation or HKD 5,000 (documents only) or HKD 12,500 (in-person hearing) for arbitration.[4]
	Insurance Complaints Bureau (ICM)	Mediation for non-claim related Adjudication for claim-related complaints (for claims that do not exceed HK$1,000,000) and mediation for non-claim related complaints.		No fees for claim-related complaints. Average time for processing a complaint is 4–6 months.[5]

India	Public			
	National Consumer Dispute Redressal Commission (NCDRC), State Consumer Dispute Redressal Commission (SCDRC), and District Consumer Dispute Redressal Commission (DCDRC)	New Consumer Protection Act (2019) to foster mediation	Consumer Commission Online-Application Portal[6]	/
	Sectoral Ombudsmen			
	(Banking, Insurance, Income Tax and Electricity)	Banking: arbitration if the complaint is not resolved by the provider.	Banking: Consumer complaints can be submitted online.[7]	Banking: Consumer complaints shall be solved within 30 days.
		Insurance: mediation and arbitration. The Ombudsman will issue a recommendation, if not followed it will issue an arbitral award.[8]		Insurance: no fees. There is a time-limit (30 days) for the insurer to comply with the award but no info about the duration of the procedure.
	Sectoral regulators			
	(Telecoms Regulatory Authority, Food Safety and Standard Authority of India, Security and Exchange Board of India, Central Electricity Regulatory Commission)	Telecoms: Compulsory establishment of in-house complaints centre to handle consumer complaints, with a possibility to appeal (in-house as well) in front of a body established under the requirements established by the regulator.[9]		Telecoms: telecoms providers should respond to consumer complaints within 3 days.[10]
	Other entities: National Law School of India University (NLSIU)		Online Consumer Mediation Centre (OCMC)	

(continued)

(Continued)

	Entities	Procedure	ODR	Costs & Time
Indonesia	Consumer Dispute Settlement Agency (CDSA)	Mediation, conciliation or arbitration based on the agreement of the parties.	The new amendment of consumer law envisages the use of ODR.	No later than 21 working days from the time the request is received by the CDSA Secretariat.
	Sectoral regulators	The Financial Services Authority requires financial services providers to establish procedures for the investigation and handling of consumer complaints.		
Japan	National Consumer Affairs Center (NCAC) – ADR Committee	The NCAC may initiate mediation and arbitration to resolve 'important consumer disputes'.[11]		
	Local Consumer Affairs Centers			
Macau	Macau Consumer Council (Consumer Arbitration Center)	Conciliation, mediation and arbitration mechanisms for small claims (below MOP 100,000, approx USD 12,600).	Complaints can be submitted online.[12]	Free of charge. Any case applied for arbitration will be scheduled for arbitration within 12 working days from the date of filing.
Malaysia	Tribunal for Consumer Claims	Assisted negotiation[13]	/	
	The National Consumer Council	Mediation		
	Penang Consumer Association	Mediation		

Myanmar	Public			
	Department of Consumer Affairs	Mediation and adjudication	Complaints can be submitted online.[14]	
	Other entities:			
	Myanmar Consumer Union (MCU)	Mediation	Complaints can be submitted online.[15]	
Singapore	Public			
	Small Claims Tribunal	No	No ADR, but consumers can access e-Court services at the Community Justice and Tribunals System (CJTS) for claims not exceeding SGD 10,000 (approx USD 7,500). There are also some online options for e-negotiation.	
	Other bodies			
	Consumers Association of Singapore (CASE)	Mediation and arbitration	Complaints can be submitted online.[16]	Depending on the claim amount (between USD 12 approx and USD 260).
South Korea	Public			
	Korea Consumer Agency (KCA)	First stage: free counselling to the consumers encountering problems. Second stage: Mediation. Binding agreement between the parties. Third stage: Conciliation by the Consumer Dispute Settlement Commission (CDSC). Binding decision.	The application for mediation can be submitted online.	Free of charge

(continued)

(Continued)

	Entities	Procedure	ODR	Costs & Time
Taiwan	Public			
	Consumer Protection Committee (CPC)	Mediation	Yes. Complaints can be submitted electronically.[17]	/
	Sector-specific			
	Financial Ombudsman Institution (FOI) for financial disputes	Two-tiered procedure: mediation (agreements are binding) and adjudication where mediation fails.[18]		
Thailand	Public			
	Office of the Consumer Protection Board (OCPB)	Negotiation and mediation	/	/
	Entities	**Procedure**	**ODR**	**Costs & Time**
Vietnam	Public			
	Vietnam Competition and Consumer Authority	Mediation (resulting agreement not binding) and adjudication.	Consumer complaints can be submitted online.[19]	Free of charge. Disputes are resolve within 15 days since the submission of the complaint.
	Private			
	Commercial ADR is allowed under consumer protection rules.	Mediation (resulting agreement not binding). Arbitration (consumers can decide on the application of arbitration clauses).	Hanoi International Arbitration Center[20]	Depends on scheme

[1] www.ebs.org.cn.
[2] Not typically designed for consumer disputes but consumers may use it.
[3] Launched in June 2020.
[4] See FDRC Fees – For cases of Standard Eligible Dispute under Terms of Reference, available at www.fdrc.org.hk/en under 'Resolving Disputes': 'fees'.
[5] HK Insurance Complaints Bureau, 'Terms of Reference', available at www.icb.org.hk.
[6] https://edaakhil.nic.in/edaakhil/.
[7] Complaints to Banking Ombudsman can be submitted online, however link is not operative (June 2021) and consumers have been reporting the non-functioning of the link to submit a complaint since May 2020.
[8] FAQs on Insurance Ombudsman Rules 2017; available under www.irdai.gov.
[9] Telecom Consumers Complaint Redressal Regulations, 2012; available at https://trai.gov.in/consumer-info/telecom/grievance-redressal-mechanism.
[10] ibid.
[11] What would constitute an 'important consumer dispute' is not defined within s 2 of the Act on National Consumer Affairs Center of Japan (Act No 123 of 2002; Amendment of Act No 43 of 2017) that establishes and regulates the 'Important Consumer Dispute Resolution procedure'. The literature understands that an 'important consumer dispute' involves transactions that affect larger groups of consumers (eg mass claims) or transactions that have caused or will cause material damages to individuals; see H Habuka and C Rule, 'The Promise and Potential of Online Dispute Resolution in Japan' (2017) *International Journal of Online Dispute Resolution* 4, 74.
[12] https://app.consumer.gov.mo/.
[13] However, scholars argue that the TCC could be more effective in providing mediation, see R Ismail and Z Osman, 'Alternative Dispute Resolution Process in the Tribunal for Consumer Claims of Malaysia: A Way Forward' (2019) 9(5) *International Journal of Asian Social Science* 342.
[14] www.doca.gov.mm/complaint/ (only in Burmese).
[15] www.myanmarconsumersunion.org/en/home/. However, the link to submit the actual complaint does not work (at least on the English version of the site).
[16] www.statecourts.gov.sg/CJTS/#!/index1.
[17] https://appeal.cpc.ey.gov.tw/EN/step_three_2_en.aspx.
[18] In the event of adjudication, the decision will enjoy *res iudicata* effects.
[19] http://en.vcca.gov.vn under 'consumer protection': 'Handling consumer requests'.
[20] http://en.hiac.vn/.

3. Administrative Enforcement and the Role of Regulators

	Entities	Enforcement action(s)	Public interest litigation	Dispute resolution
Australia	Australian Competition and Consumer Commission (ACCC)[21]	Injunction Sanctions Damages	Yes	No. Consumer can obtain information and even draft a complaint with the tools offered by the ACCC. However, the ACCC advice to go to court or other third party, such as Industry Ombudsman, if the problem persists after contacting the business. The ACCC registers the issue.
	State and Territorial consumer organisations			
China	China Consumer Association (CCA) and other consumer bodies under the Government.		Yes	
Hong Kong	Consumer Council	No. The Consumer Council is not a law enforcement agency and is not vested with the power of investigation or adjudication. However, naming and shaming techniques are used and proven to have a deterrent effect to unfair practices. Enforcement action is taken by the Customs and Excise Department (civil and criminal actions).	No. However, there is the Consumer Legal Action Fund (CLAF) for providing legal assistance to consumers in cases where there is a public interest (under a non-refundable application fee and with a strong emphasis on mediation).	

India	*NEW* Consumer Protection Authority (CPA)	Yes. Under the 2019 Consumer Protection Act, the CPA can investigate into consumer complaints, issue safety notices for goods and services and injunctions.	Yes[22]	
Indonesia	National Consumer Protection Agency (NCPA)	No	No. However, Consumer Protection NGOs have the legal standing to sue business actors before the general court.	
Japan	Qualified consumer organisations, certified by the Government	Yes. Injunctions (in case of unfair clauses and unfair practices, but it does not allow to claim damages).		
	National Consumer Affairs Center of Japan (NCAC)	No	Yes. The NCAC may initiate mediation and arbitration to resolve 'important consumer disputes.'[23]	No. NCAC only provides consultation and negotiation support.
Macau	Macau Consumer Council	Monitoring and soft-law.	Based on consumer complaints, matters are brought to the Consumer Mediation and Arbitration Center of the Council of Consumers.	Yes. Conciliation, mediation and arbitration of consumer disputes.

(continued)

(Continued)

	Entities	Enforcement action(s)	Public interest litigation	Dispute resolution
Malaysia	Consumer Advisory Council	Yes	/	Handling of consumer complaints.
	Ministry of domestic trade and consumer affairs			
	Sector-specific			
	Communications and Multimedia Consumer Forum of Malaysia (CFM)			Yes. The CFM deals with disputes related to a communication and multimedia.
Myanmar	Department of Commerce and Consumer Affairs	Monitoring through inspectors	It can initiate criminal proceedings against businesses infringing consumer protection rules.	Dispute resolution
	Myanmar Consumer Protection Commission (MCPC)	MCPC decides on fines for consumer protection rules violations presented by the Department of Commerce and Consumer Affairs.	Not specifically, but under new consumer protection rules (2019) they can hold emergency meetings where consumers are facing serious harms or loss.	MCPC can resolve consumer disputes.
	Consumer Affairs Committees	Administrative fines		Dispute resolution (adjudication). Not only damages but also administrative fines and injunctions.
Singapore	Competition and Consumer Commission of Singapore (CCSS)	Yes. Imposition of administrative fines. Naming and shaming.	Yes. Injunctions applications against persistent violations of consumer protection rules.	No. The CCS does not resolve consumer complaints.

South Korea	Korea Consumer Agency (KCA)	Yes. Product test and inspection. Monitoring of unfair business practices.	/	Yes. Mediation by the KCA and conciliation by the CDSC. Binding decisions (see above).
Taiwan	Consumer Protection Committee (CPC)	Yes. Monitoring powers and imposition of administrative fines.	/	The CPC registers consumer complaints.
	Local consumer organisations: eg Consumers' Foundation Chinese Taipei (CFCT)			Yes
Thailand	Office of the Consumer Protection Board (OCPB)	No. Only monitoring powers.[24]	Yes. Civil and criminal proceedings against violations of consumer protection rules.	Yes
Vietnam	Vietnam Competition Authority (VCA)	Yes. Imposition of administrative fines. Naming and shaming.	Yes	Yes. Complaints handling and resolution (within 15 working days since submission).

[21] The ACCC is the regulator as per the Competition and Consumer Act 2010 (Schedule 2 Chapter 1, s 2).

[22] Pursuant to s 19(1) of the 2019 Consumer Protection Act, '[T]he Central Authority may, after receiving any information or complaint or directions from the Central Government or of its own motion, conduct or cause to be conducted a preliminary inquiry as to whether there exists a prima facie case of violation of consumer rights or any unfair trade practice or any false or misleading advertisement, by any person, which is prejudicial to the public interest or to the interests of consumers and if it is satisfied that there exists a prima facie case, it shall cause investigation to be made by the Director General or by the District Collector]'.

[23] See n 53.

[24] The national report signals lack of resources.

22

Consumer Product Liability and Safety Regulation: ASEAN in Asia

LUKE NOTTAGE AND SAKDA THANITCUL*

I. Introduction

The Association of Southeast Asian Nations (ASEAN) brings together 10 diverse and dynamic states with a collectively large population, growing middle class and extensive economic impact within the wider Asian region.[1] It is worth taking a closer look at its consumer law harmonisation initiatives in the key field of consumer product safety law, beginning with regulation from public authorities and more recently product liability within private law developments.[2] The analysis includes some comparison with other parts of Asia, but also leaves lessons that may resonate beyond Southeast Asia when considering the current and likely trajectory for consumer law in other parts of the Asian region.

ASEAN has been accelerating trade and investment liberalisation among its 10 Member States under the ASEAN Economic Community (AEC) project since 2007, while trying to avoid a regulatory race to the bottom. The ASEAN Economic Community Blueprint 2025, agreed in November 2015, set outs out a further 10-year plan to advance the AEC, involving some renewed emphasis on developing harmonised consumer law and policy, including for product safety:

> 28. Consumer protection is an integral part of a modern, efficient, effective and fair market place. Consumers will demand the right of access to: adequate information to enable them to make informed choices, effective redress, and products and services that meet standard and safety requirements. …
>
> 29. Strategic measures include the following: …
>
> iii. Build higher consumer confidence and cross-border commercial transactions by strengthening product safety enforcement, stronger participation of consumer representatives, and promotion of sustainable consumption.

* We thank James Tanna, student intern at the Centre for Asian and Pacific Law at the University of Sydney (2020), for superlative research and editorial assistance.

[1] For details, see L Nottage and S Thanitcul, 'ASEAN Economic Integration and Consumer Protection in Southeast Asia', in this volume.

[2] See M Cannarsa, 'Product Liability', in this volume.

This initiative is also consistent with the 2017 ASEAN High-Level Principles on Consumer Protection, including recommendations for national law and policy initiatives consistent with Principle 3: protecting consumers from harmful goods (and services). Product safety is an area of consumer law that is usually more high-profile, and so a field that develops relatively early and more easily, especially for product safety regulation but also more recently through private law mechanisms. However, challenges remain across Southeast Asia due to fragmented or omitted regulatory powers as well as credible access to courts or other avenues of consumer redress.[3] These parts draw upon earlier research conducted by the authors.[4] Such challenges are also evident in other parts of Asia, as indicated in many national reports and comparative reports for other topic areas in this volume.

II. Fragmented Product Safety Regulation

A. Pre-market Controls

In terms of pre-market controls over product safety by public authorities,[5] after the AEC project was agreed in 2007 Singapore introduced the Consumer Protection (Consumer Goods Safety Requirements) Regulations 2011. General consumer goods (ordinarily supplied for private use or consumption) must now meet safety standards from four specified overseas bodies, subject to any Singaporean government amendments, or otherwise 'regional' or national standards. Exceptions include products regulated by specific laws (such as healthcare products, foods, drugs, pesticides and vehicles), as well as second-hand or used products (when the supplier has clearly declared them as such). The regulator can also decide that a safety standard provision is 'inappropriate for application' because it fails to take into account the tropical climate of Singapore, for example, 'or any other reason'.[6] This regime complements an older regime that imposes minimum safety standards for dozens of specific (higher-risk) general consumer goods.[7] Some early evidence (for example for toys) suggested significant safety improvements since the Regulations were introduced in 2011.[8] However, there are various problems with the Singaporean Regulations, including product coverage, costs of and disparities among the approved foreign standards and lack of direct sanctions.

By contrast, Malaysia's Consumer Protection Act 1999 imposes a full-scale general safety provision enforced by the consumer affairs regulator, demanding that all 'goods'

[3] For more details, see L Nottage, 'Product Safety Law' in L Nottage et al, *ASEAN Consumer Law Harmonisation and Cooperation: Achievements and Challenges* (Cambridge: Cambridge University Press, 2019) 122.

[4] L Nottage and S Thanitcul (eds), *ASEAN Product Liability and Consumer Product Safety Law* (Bangkok: Winyuchon, 2016).

[5] For a brief comparison of pre- and post-market public regulation of consumer product safety, see generally, Australian Competition & Consumer Commission, 'The state of product safety: Jurisdiction comparisons' (2013), available under www.productsafety.gov.au/about-us/publications.

[6] Consumer Protection (Consumer Goods Safety Requirements) Regulations 2011 (Singapore), reg 2(2).

[7] Consumer Protection (Safety Requirements) Regulations 2002 (Singapore).

[8] See the report submitted by S Tab of the Singapore Consumer Product Safety Department, 'Consumer Product Safety – Balancing Regulation and the Enterprise' (May 2021).

be reasonably safe (if 'primarily purchased, used or consumed for personal, domestic or household purposes').[9] Paralleling the Consumer Protection Act 1987 in the United Kingdom before the latter's general safety provision was superseded by Article 3(1) of the EU General Product Safety Directive[10] for goods 'intended for consumers or likely, under reasonably foreseeable conditions, to be used by consumers' (including used products), or Singapore's partial approximation in its 2011 Regulation, Malaysia's Consumer Protection Act does not directly reference standards set by international bodies. It does not even include any analogue to Article 3(3) of the EU General Product Safety Directive, which provides for the safety requirement to be assessed in light of national standards, European Commission recommendations, sectoral product safety codes of good practices, 'the state of the art and technology' and 'reasonable consumer expectations concerning safety'. A lack of further detail in the Malaysian Act may explain why there is little evidence of its section 21 being applied by the general consumer regulator. The regulator has also only set a few specific mandatory performance standards, mostly quite recently, even though section 19 is comparatively broad. It allows the general consumer regulator to set safety standards for all consumer goods (and indeed services), except foods and healthcare products, even if regulated also by other laws and regulators.

Thailand, which like Malaysia has comparatively influential consumer NGOs, enacted in 2019 further amendments to its Consumer Protection Act 1979. Section 29(2) introduces a general safety provision with some parallels to EU law (emphasis added):

> Section 29(2). The goods that the entrepreneur intends to sell, presents for sale, enters into an agreement for sale, presents by advertisement or any other methods or put on the market **have to be safe goods.**
>
> The practice concerning the safety of goods shall be considered using the following:
>
> (1) The **characteristic and type of goods**, as well as their components, designs, packaging and packages, instructions concerning their assembly, installations, maintenance, and expectations that the general consumers should have concerning the goods;
> (2) **How the goods are presented** and labeled, and their warnings and instructions concerning usage, disposal and destruction as well as indications and any information concerning the goods, including the advertisement of the goods;
> (3) The effects on the safety of the goods if the goods are being used with other goods;
> (4) The **consumers who are especially at risk** from the consumption of goods, such as children, pregnant women, the elderly, patient, and the disabled;
> (5) The **safety standard generally accepted for that type** of goods;
> (6) **Best practic**e of the business sector.

A new section 29(3) adds that the supplier 'must not produce, order, or import into the Kingdom to sell for sale goods that are dangerous, and must not recommend or advertise said goods'. Section 29(1) clarifies that: '"Dangerous goods" means goods that cause or may cause danger to life, body, health, mental state, or property. This does not include goods with other laws already legislated specifically on their concerns.' It remains to be seen how these new provisions will be implemented in practice.

[9] Consumer Protection Act 1999 (Malaysia), s 21.

[10] Directive 2001/95/EC of the European Parliament and of the Council of 3 December 2001 on general product safety, OJ 2001 No L11, p 4.

This new general safety provision is accompanied by longstanding powers for the regulators to declare goods to be 'label controlled' if they may cause physical or mental harm (section 30). Suppliers must then ensure true and non-misleading information is provided to consumers (section 31), otherwise the regulator can ban their supply. The 2019 amendments add extra requirements for entrepreneurs dealing with such label-controlled goods, or for any gazetted services declared to create risks for consumers, 'to prevent or eliminate' the associated risks (section 29(4)). Entrepreneurs have the following specific obligations:

> (1) Constantly inspect the safety of their goods or services during the warranty period of said goods or services, and keep the statistics or related reports.
> (2) Appropriate measures for the goods or the services allowing to detect the risk which may occur according to the condition of goods and services for the sake of said risk prevention.
> (3) Contact channel where consumer can receive and communicate information, verification and processing of information notified by consumer and reporting of result without delay. Records and reports concerning the notification and the result must be made and kept.
> (4) Measures to keep track of the goods which have been sold including names and details of the producer, the importer, or the distributor, and the reference number on the goods or its package.
> (5) Measures to keep track of the services provided, including name and address of the consumer receiving the service and the details of the service.

Those who sell such products or services must disclose their risks to consumers, as well as keep documentation for tracking them – to provide to regulators on request (section 29(5)).

In other ASEAN countries, there is still no general safety requirement as in Malaysia, Singapore's approximation introduced in 2011, and Thailand since 2019. Indeed, the general consumer affairs regulators typically have very limited jurisdiction to set minimum safety standards even for specific goods (such as foods or toys).[11] Instead, those powers are reserved for other, usually longer-established and better-resourced government departments. The latter may also be more concerned to promote the regulated industries' immediate economic interests than the more diffuse interests associated with consumer protection.

B. Post-market Controls

Such limited powers for most general consumer regulators in Southeast Asia also sit awkwardly with their typically more wide-ranging powers to implement post-market controls to ensure the safety of consumer products, for example by banning goods found to be unsafe or forcing a recall. General consumer regulators can usually intervene at this stage either with or without cooperation from any relevant national sectoral

[11] See L Nottage, 'Policy Digest 20: Food Safety Regulation Under National and International Law: Integrating Consumer Regulators in Proliferating Standardisation Projects' in ASEAN Secretariat (ed), *Consumer Protection Digests and Case Studies* (Jakarta: ASEAN Secretariat, 2015) Vol 2, 75.

regulators. However, there were exceptions even under new Consumer Protection statutes enacted in Vietnam in 2010, and Myanmar in 2014, where general bans on 'hazardous goods or services' remain the exclusive responsibility of specialist regulators. (By contrast, sections 30 and 31 of Myanmar's 2019 law gave banning powers to the Department of Consumer Affairs of the Ministry of Commerce.) In addition, Brunei still lacks a framework for consumer product safety legislation altogether.

In Thailand, the Consumer Protection Act has allowed the consumer regulator to ban unsafe products and conduct testing, but there was uncertainty about the scope of its powers. Under 2019 amendments, it can order a temporary ban and require suppliers to have risky products tested, and then consider such results in deciding whether or not to remove the ban or instead make it permanent and require a recall (section 29(9)).

A further challenge across ASEAN countries is that there have been few requirements for suppliers to notify their national consumer regulators even if conducting a voluntary product recall (as required, for example, in Australia since 1986), let alone if they become aware of a serious product-related accident (as in Australia since 2010, following EU General Product Safety Directive in 2001 but with narrower scope for such reporting requirements).[12] The closest provision had been under Vietnamese legislation since 2010, requiring specific public notices of recalls if suppliers learn of a product 'defect'.[13]

Under section 29(6) introduced by Thailand's 2019 amendments, but only if the regulator has gazetted a product as label-controlled or a service as risky for consumers, where the entrepreneur under sections 29(4) and 29(5):

> has a reasonable cause to suspect that the goods or services could be dangerous, said entrepreneur may alert the producer, the importer, the seller, the reseller, or the service provider as well as advertiser, consumers, and the general public. In the case where it has become known that the goods or the services are dangerous, or that dangerous goods or services has caused a person death, grave injury, or harm a physical or mental well-being, or pose danger to other properties, the entrepreneur … must inform the producer, the importer, the seller, the reseller, or the service provider as well as advertiser, consumers, and the general public and promptly notify the Office of the Consumer Protection Board of the danger of the goods or services.

The last sentence creates a mandatory reporting requirement for suppliers concerning goods or services known to be 'dangerous' (extending under section 29(1) to potential harm to health or property, not just actual harm), but only for this subset of gazetted goods and services. Suppliers informed about such goods and services must eliminate their risks eg by suspending supplies and conducting recalls, and promptly report such measures to the consumer regulator (section 29(7)).

Across ASEAN, the persistent lack of a general obligation to notify national regulators about serious product safety accidents or risks – or even voluntary recalls by

[12] L Nottage, 'ASEAN Product Liability and Consumer Product Safety Regulation: Comparing National Laws and Free Trade Agreements' (2015) 15/07 *Sydney Law School Research Paper*. The Appendix to this paper summarises the key legislative features and provisions in ASEAN Member States' general consumer product safety regulations and product liability statutes, at that time. Full-text translations in English of many of these laws can also now be found via https://aseanconsumer.org/.

[13] PTP Anh, 'Vietnamese Law on Consumer Protection: Some Points for Traders' (2013) *Vietnam Law & Legal Forum* 16–20.

suppliers – limits the capacity of regulators to accurately analyse injury risk data and then actually use what powers are legislated for them. It also restricts the usefulness of the ASEAN Committee's 'Product Alerts' webpage,[14] compared to the EU's extensive 'Safety Gate' database.[15] The gap further makes it harder to develop regional Recall Guidelines.[16]

III. Private Law Redress for Unsafe Products

The AEC has also provided further encouragement for ASEAN to reform private law mechanisms that indirectly encourage suppliers to improve product safety, by promising fuller compensation to injured consumers. Sometimes following EU consumer contract law, for example voiding unfair terms, most now have legislation limiting the scope for direct sellers to avoid contractual liability to consumers.[17] Upstream suppliers or manufacturers may still be permitted to seek to limit their own liability for compensation claims from such sellers, but the latter are then incentivised to source safer products from other suppliers.

Singapore's Consumer Protection (Fair Trading) Act 2003 also facilitates consumer contract claims by imposing a presumption of non-conformity at the time of delivery if goods fail within six months of delivery.[18] This too follows earlier EU law, namely Article 5(3) of the Consumer Sales Directive;[19] but the latter goes further, for example by mandating at least a minimum two-year statutory guarantee.[20] The Philippines also enacted a more bright-line 'Lemon Law' in 2013, but only for automobiles.[21]

In addition, many ASEAN countries now allow consumers to bring statutory tort claims directly against manufacturers, importers and certain others in the supply chain providing unsafe products, even in the absence of a contractual relationship. Indonesia's Consumer Protection Law 1999 reversed the usual burden of proof, so that the

[14] See https://aseanconsumer.org/alerts/. For a recent consultancy project to improve such reporting mechanisms, but without mandatory requirements, see https://c-tif.ca/portfolio/projects/strengthening-consumer-protection-in-asean/.

[15] Formerly known as 'Rapex' (Rapid Exchange of Information Sytem), see https://ec.europa.eu/safety-gate-alerts.

[16] See L Nottage, 'Policy Digest 23: Developing ASEAN Recall Guidelines for Consumer Products' in ASEAN Secretariat, *Consumer Protection Digests*, 109.

[17] L Nottage and J Paterson, 'Consumer Contracts and Product Safety Law in Southeast Asia: Partly Trading Up?' in P Hsieh and B Mercurio (eds), *ASEAN Law in the New Regional Economic Order* (Cambridge: Cambridge University Press, 2019) 329.

[18] Consumer Protection (Fair Trading) Act 2003 (Singapore), s 12B(3). See generally A Loke, 'The Lemon Law and the Integrated Enhancement of Consumer Rights in Singapore' (2014) 2 *Singapore Journal of Legal Studies* 285.

[19] Directive 1999/44/EC of the European Parliament and of the Council of 25 May 1999 on certain aspects of the sale of consumer goods and associated guarantees, OJ 1999 No L171, p 12. Note that this Directive has since been repealed by Directive (EU) 2019/771 of the European Parliament and of the Council of 20 May 2019 on certain aspects concerning contracts for the sale of goods, OJ 2019 No L136, p 28 (Sale of Goods Directive).

[20] Consumer Sales Directive (EU), Art 5(1); see Sale of Goods Directive (EU), Art 10.

[21] The Act Strengthening Consumer Protection in the Purchase of Brand New Motor Vehicles 2013 includes rights of repair or replacement for consumers within the first 12 months from delivery in the case of established non-conformity amounting to a defect or fault, which the supplier or manufacturer has not been able to repair after four attempts.

manufacturer (and even the services provider) has to prove that it was *not* negligent in supplying a product that harms a consumer.[22] Five other countries have taken the next step of imposing EU-like strict product liability.[23] Indeed, their statutes often go further than the EU law in terms of the substantive rights given to consumers, sometimes even compared to other countries in the broader Asia-Pacific region that have also enacted strict liability regimes.[24] Table 1 below summarises some of these differences in ASEAN Member States compared to several other countries in the Asian region that have also introduced strict liability regimes.[25]

Table 1 Product Liability Legislation in ASEAN Member States (*) and other Selected Regions

Year of enactment (enforcement, if different)	Country or Jurisdiction	Statute	Significant differences from the 1985 European Product Liability Directive
1992	Philippines*	Consumer Act	Only for unsafe 'consumer' (purpose) goods; some intermediate suppliers liable as well; no 'development risks' defence; manufacturer must prove goods were safe.
1992	Australia	Trade Practices Act (renamed Australian Consumer Law in 2010)	Regime added similar to EU for product liability; another from 1987 (amended in 2010 in light of New Zealand's 1993 Act) extended consequential loss claims for non-consumer property (as in Malaysia – below); representative actions permitted by regulator.
1993	New Zealand	Consumer Guarantees Act	Only for certain consequential property loss (personal injury claims are covered instead by a state no-fault compensation scheme).
1993	China	Product Quality Act	Consumer must prove causal link between abnormal performance and harm; double damages.
1994	Taiwan	Consumer Protection Act	Treble damages for wilful misconduct; consequential loss to non-consumer goods; manufacturers must prove goods were safe.

(continued)

[22] Consumer Protection Law 1999 (Indonesia), Art 19(5).

[23] See Nottage, 'Case Study 4: ASEAN consumer product safety law' in ASEAN Secretariat, *Consumer Protection Digests*, 149. Generally: Nottage and Thanitcul, 'ASEAN Product Liability'.

[24] See also J Kellam (ed), *Product Liability in the Asia-Pacific* (Sydney: Federation Press, 2009), with several chapters updated as well as completely new chapters in Nottage and Thanitcul, 'ASEAN Product Liability'.

[25] For detail, see Cannarsa, 'Product Liability'.

Table 1 ***(Continued)***

Year of enactment (enforcement, if different)	Country or Jurisdiction	Statute	Significant differences from the 1985 European Product Liability Directive
1995	Japan	Product Liability Act	Consequential loss to non-consumer goods; extended limitation period for toxic torts.
1999	Indonesia*	Consumer Protection Act	Reversed burden of proof of negligence (not clearly strict liability); but covering defective services as well as goods; representative actions by regulators (for large-scale harm) or certified consumer NGOs.
1999	Malaysia*	Consumer Protection Act	Part X similar to the EU (limiting consequential damages to goods ordinarily and actually used for personal use); but Part VII (influenced by New Zealand's Consumer Guarantees Act 1993) extends strict liability also to consequential loss to non-consumer goods if the unsafe goods themselves (lacking 'acceptable quality') were ordinarily and actually for personal use.
2002	South Korea	Product Liability Act	Consequential loss also to non-consumer property; treble non-compensatory damages (since 2018).
2007 (2011)	Cambodia*	Civil Code (Art 751)	Consequential loss also to non-consumer property (influenced by Japan's Product Liability Act 1994).
2008 (2009)	Thailand*	Product Liability Act	Consumer need only prove harm from product used normally (then manufacturer must prove goods were safe); up to double damages; consequential losses also for non-consumer property; defence if consumer knew the goods were unsafe; no (express) 'development risks' defence; extended limitation period for toxic torts; representative actions by regulator and certified NGOs.
2010 (2011)	Vietnam*	Law on Protection of Consumer Rights	Consumer may only need to prove harm from product used normally; representative actions by certified NGOs.

Elaborating on Table 1 above, under Malaysia's Consumer Protection Act 1999, section 50 allows the consumer to claim damages directly against the manufacturer for violating the guarantee of 'acceptable quality' set out in section 32(2)(a) (specifically including safety), but not for violating the fitness for purpose guarantee (owed therefore only by the retailer or direct seller). Section 51 also allows anyone to claim against the manufacturer for all types of consequential damages caused by the lack of acceptable quality in a consumer good.[26] By contrast, section 69(1)(c) follows the law in the 1985 European Product Liability Directive:[27] plaintiffs can only be awarded damages for personal injury and to property (other than the defective product itself) that is ordinarily and actually intended for personal or household use.

In addition, inspired by what became the European Unfair Commercial Practices Directive,[28] statutory reforms in Singapore (2003) and then Brunei (2011) introduced strict liability for misleading conduct.[29] Section 4(a) of Singapore's Consumer Protection (Fair Trading) Act 2003 defines an 'unfair practice' to include conduct of a 'supplier' that could result in a consumer being reasonably misled. Section 2 defines 'supplier' to include a person who manufactures goods as a business. Section 7(4) allows claims for damages suffered from unfair practices, including in small claims tribunals. This may allow consumers to bring claims at least regarding alleged warning or information defects, but there is little awareness of this possibility and no case law. Anyway, claims for design or one-off manufacturing defects remain subject to proving negligence on the part of the manufacturer.

Myanmar's Consumer Protection Law, as enacted in 2014, might have allowed the new statutory consumer settlement bodies to order compensation only for warning defects.[30] But there were no known cases brought by regulators and the 2019 statute does not help on this point. Nor have there been reports of any claims by alleging negligence against manufacturers. Myanmar's court system was anyway severely weakened by decades of military government.[31]

Cambodia's Law on Consumer Protection 2019 prohibits businesses engaging in 'unfair acts', including misleading or deceptive conduct whether intentionally or not, and in such acts regarding goods (including concerning their characteristics,

[26] Consumer Protection Act 1999 (Malaysia), s 3 defines 'consumer good' as a product ordinarily for personal use, and not for resupply or using up in a manufacturing process.

[27] Council Directive 85/374/EEC of 25 July 1985 on the approximation of the laws, regulations and administrative provisions of the Member States concerning liability for defective products, OJ 1985 No L210, p 29.

[28] Directive 2005/29/EC of the European Parliament and of the Council of 11 May 2005 concerning unfair business-to-consumer commercial practices in the internal market OJ 2005 No L149, p 22.

[29] See generally J Paterson and V Wong, 'Consumer Protection in Singapore: Statute and the Ongoing Influence of the General Law' (2016) 28 *Singapore Academy of Law Journal* 1079. Similar provisions can be found in Brunei's Consumer Protection (Fair Trading) Order 2011. By contrast, from both statutory interpretation and access to justice perspectives, it is unlikely that requirements to provide 'accurate information on production' of goods under s 35(3) of the Consumer Protection Act 2010 in Laos, or for 'entrepreneurs' to give 'simple and correct information' regarding goods and services under s 21(a) of Myanmar's Consumer Protection Law 2019, would generate effective private law remedies against manufacturers omitting adequate product warnings or safety instructions.

[30] Consumer Protection Law 2014 (Myanmar), ss 7(b) and 19(c).

[31] See generally: N Cheesman, *Opposing the Rule of Law: How Myanmar's Courts Make Law and Order* (Cambridge: Cambridge University Press, 2015); M Crouch and T Lindsey (eds), *Law, Society and Transition in Myanmar* (Oxford: Hart, 2014).

standards or quality).[32] Yet the National Consumer Protection Committee (assisted by an Investigating Officer) has no statutory powers to order compensation to harmed consumers, and nor do consumer organisations regulated under this recent legislation.[33] Instead, as indicated above, since Cambodia's Civil Code came into force from 2011 (after significant legal technical assistance from Japanese experts), individual consumers (and even potentially businesses, for business-use consequential property loss) could bring strict product liability claims against manufacturers.[34] Nonetheless, despite longer-standing efforts to create a more functional court system compared to Myanmar, civil litigation remains difficult in Cambodia and there are no reports of product liability claims.

More generally in Southeast Asia, problems of access to justice and a lack of consumer awareness – often linked to weak consumer NGOs – limit the practical effectiveness even of EU-style product liability statutes. Even in Malaysia, for example, small claims tribunals typically only give oral decisions, leaving no reported judgments to guide future consumer claims or supplier behaviour. In the Philippines and Indonesia, and more recently Cambodia and Vietnam, there seem to be no significant reported decisions either.

Thailand is the regional exception. Thanks in part to a unique statute facilitating consumer claims generally through regular courts, also enacted in 2008, large numbers of claims have been filed since the Product Liability Act was passed. Consumer NGOs are also active, and have a long history.[35] However, almost all lawsuits still settle, leaving only a few court judgments.[36] It remains to be seen what will result from the enactment of a US-style (opt-out) class action procedure in early 2015, which had an even longer gestation period.[37] It was applied for the first time in a mass claim by Ford automobile users filed on 3 April 2017, after not making progress by involving the Office of the Consumer Protection Board.[38] That claim resulted in the Southern Bangkok Civil Court ordering Ford to pay 291 automobile owners compensation ranging from THB 20,000

[32] Law on Consumer Protection 2019 (Cambodia), Arts 9–10.

[33] A translation of this 2019 Law has recently become available at https://aseanconsumer.org/file/pdf_file/Law-on-Consumer-Protection.pdf, along with the other main consumer protection laws enacted in ASEAN Member States, and an earlier translation is at https://ibccambodia.com/laws-and-reforms/. Product safety regulation remains separately covered in the Law on the Management of Quality and Safety of Products, enacted in 2000 to allow the consumer regulator to ban unsafe products (but only enforce ex ante any minimum safety standards set by other regulators).

[34] Cambodian Civil Code, Art 751.

[35] F Munger, 'Revolution Imagined: Cause Advocacy, Consumer Rights, and the Evolving Role of NGOs in Thailand' (2014) 9(1) *Asian Journal of Comparative Law* 29.

[36] S Thanitcul, 'Law and Legal Process of the Product Liability Act in Thailand' (2012) 20(2–3) *Journal of International Cooperation Studies* 27; updated and expanded in Nottage and Thanitcul, 'ASEAN Product Liability' 273–304.

[37] For early legislative history of the class action reform proposal, see C Ratanachaichan, 'A Primer on the Thai Draft Law on Class Actions' (2006), Paper presented at the 9th General Assembly of the ASEAN Law Association. Regarding its eventual enactment, see C Thongpakdee et al, 'New Class Action Law in Thailand', *Lexology* (19 May 2015).

[38] On the pioneering lawsuit against Ford, see S Mokkhasan, 'Thai Ford Owners File Class-action Lawsuit Over Faulty Cars', khaosodenglish.com, 4 April 2017.

to 200,000 each (approximately USD 640–6,400).[39] A class action regime introduced years earlier in Indonesia has not proved to be very functional, by contrast, especially for product liability claims.[40]

Collective redress mechanisms for consumers are nonetheless attracting more attention from legislators and policy-makers in the Asia-Pacific region, as in Europe.[41] Until these become more functional in ASEAN, perhaps with some push from the 2017 ASEAN High-Level Principles on Consumer Protection and related projects especially through the ASEAN Committee on Consumer Protection established in 2007, it is likely that the introduction of strict product liability regimes will continue to have only little (although sometimes still significant) direct influence on supplier and insurer behaviour. After all, a similar result for the wider Asian region was found almost a decade ago by broader survey research.[42] It is still only in the United States that strict liability litigation became and remains extensive, due to that country's unique combination of factors associated primarily with its civil justice system and underlying socio-economic structures.[43]

IV. Conclusions

Product safety is often an issue that arises early on as countries modernise and industrialise, and which becomes politically quite salient – even for authoritarian governments. Accordingly, product safety law reform has attracted relatively widespread attention among legislators, regulators, consumers and businesses across Southeast Asia, including more recently in the developing country Member States of ASEAN. This chapter has focused mainly on the diverse and dynamic states within Southeast Asia, one of our areas of particular expertise in consumer law. The sub-region has attracted less commentary than several other parts of Asia, even though there have been some intriguing reforms even in some of the developing country Member States of ASEAN, and the themes

[39] See P Maikaew, 'Ford to pay B23m to car owners in class-action ruling', bangkokpost.com, 22 September 2018.

[40] See E Sundari, 'The Cost Barrier of Consumers Class Action in Indonesia' (2013) 9(31) *European Scientific Journal* 97–120, and generally: J Kellam, 'The Asia-Pacific Region' in P Karlsgott (ed), *World Class Actions: A Guide to Group and Representative Actions* (Oxford: Oxford University Press, 2012) 438–52. Thus, in a case of drugs mixed up by Kalbe Farma (the largest publicly listed pharmaceutical company in Southeast Asia), the Indonesian Consumers Foundation pointed out that families of the two patients consequently suffering fatal injuries could sue the hospital, which would have to disprove negligence and bring Kalbe Farma into the lawsuit. The Foundation also urged prosecutors to claim under the Criminal Code for negligence causing death. See H Jong, 'Govt Freezes Kalbe Drug Licenses Following Deaths', jakartapost.com, 18 February 2015.

[41] See L Nottage, 'Policy Digest 16: Enforcing Product Liability' in ASEAN Secretariat, *Consumer Protection Digests*.

[42] J Kellam and L Nottage, 'Europeanisation of Product Liability in the Asia-Pacific Region: A Preliminary Empirical Benchmark' (2008) 31(2) *Journal of Consumer Policy* 217.

[43] Cf generally M Reimann, 'Liability for Defective Products at the Beginning of the Twenty-First Century: Emergence of a Worldwide Standard?' (2003) 51 *American Journal of Comparative Law* 751; L. Nottage, *Product Liability and Safety Law in Japan: From Minamata to Mad Cows* (London: Routledge Curzon, 2004); G Howells and D Owen, 'Products Liability Law in America and Europe' in G Howells et al (eds), *Handbook of Research on International Consumer Law* 2nd edn (Cheltenham: Edward Elgar, 2018) 202–30.

emerging from analysing Southeast Asia have some parallels or implications for the wider Asian region.

Despite evidence of 'trading up' to higher consumer safety law standards, amidst ASEAN trade and investment liberalisation,[44] the original and probably still major focus has been on regulation by public authorities, with various gaps persisting. As indicated above, consumer regulators (often quite newly established and under-resourced) often have limited pre-market powers to set minimum safety standards for particular types of products; instead, they enforce standards set by other sectoral regulators, which may have different aims than consumer protection. Most ASEAN states' laws lack an overarching general safety requirement, enforceable with sanctions against suppliers. The consumer regulators sometimes even have limited jurisdiction to engage in post-market activities, such as banning goods found to be unsafe, and rarely have a requirement for suppliers to notify regulators about serious product-related accidents. These gaps are quite often found even in the larger economies in the Asian region.[45]

As for private law impacting on consumer product safety, the AEC project since 2007 has also led to more enactments of strict product liability law in ASEAN Member States. Quite often these include substantive rights that are more pro-plaintiff than the underlying EU law model. A notable example, found also for instance in Japan and South Korea, is legislation allowing businesses to claim against others for consequential losses to business-use property caused by a manufacturer's unsafe product. Yet these enactments in Southeast Asia have been patchy and are missing in five ASEAN states, although there may be scope for consumers to bring strict product liability claims at least for warning or information defects in Singapore and Brunei. Even in the other five ASEAN states that have enacted strict product liability legislation, the impact has been quite small. The exception seems to be when this law reform is combined with measures facilitating access to justice generally, as in Thailand, although such measures are more politically controversial and therefore less common. This clear finding resonates with other national and comparative reports in this volume, highlighting the divergence between consumer law 'in books' and 'in action'.

Going forward, we can expect ASEAN through the ACCP, sometimes with financial or in-kind support from other Asian states or regional partners like Australia, to keep encouraging Member States to improve both the public regulation and private law on consumer product safety. This will likely be done mainly through guidelines and networking, drawing on the consensus-based 'ASEAN Way' and wider patterns of contemporary 'international regulatory cooperation'.[46] The 10-yearly review of the 2009 ASEAN–Australia–New Zealand Free Trade Agreement (AANZFTA) may add consumer protection topics to the short original Chapter 14 on Competition,[47] going beyond those found in Chapter 16 of the Comprehensive and Progressive Agreement

[44] See Nottage and Thanitcul, 'ASEAN Economic Integration'.

[45] L Nottage, 'Improving the Effectiveness of the Consumer Product Safety System: Australian Law Reform in Asia-Pacific Context' (2020) 43 *Journal of Consumer Policy* 829.

[46] See Nottage and Thanitcul, 'ASEAN Economic Integration'; D Gill (ed), *Interconnected Government: International Regulatory Cooperation in ASEAN* (Central Jakarta: Economic Research Institute for ASEAN and East Asia, 2020).

[47] See AANZFTA, 'General Review: Recommendations for the 23rd AEM-CER Consultations'.

for Trans-Pacific Partnership involving many of the 12 AANZFTA Member States. Such FTA provisions are likely to remain 'best efforts' obligations (not subject anyway to binding inter-state dispute settlement procedures) for each state to introduce some national law addressing broad topics in consumer law, including around product safety. Nonetheless, they might be useful to promote further collaboration not just among ASEAN (and Australian or New Zealand) consumer regulators, but also with other government departments (namely trade and foreign affairs ministries) within each ASEAN state, and even the business sector.[48]

A more specific useful addition to the relevant Free Trade Agreements would be an obligation, or at least power, for consumer regulators in each ASEAN state to share product accident reports.[49] The data provided through the websites for ACCP 'product alerts', and even more recently the OECD Global Recalls Portal,[50] is provided only voluntarily and partially. Formalising information-sharing through a Free Trade Agreement, or even a binding cross-border Memorandum of Understanding among regulators, could in turn prompt enactment of accident reporting requirements for local suppliers.

[48] See also J Malbon and J Paterson, 'Key Reflections and Future Directions' in Nottage et al, *ASEAN Consumer Law Harmonisation*, 415.

[49] See generally L Nottage, 'Asia-Pacific Regional Architecture and Consumer Product Safety Regulation Beyond Free Trade' in S Frankel and M Lewis (eds), *Trade Agreements at the Crossroads* (London: Routledge, 2014) 114–38.

[50] See https://globalrecalls.oecd.org/.

PART 4

Asian Law in Comparative Perspective

23

European Union Consumer Law

MATEJA DUROVIC, GERAINT HOWELLS, ANDRÉ JANSSEN AND HANS-W MICKLITZ

I. Introduction

The European Union has gradually taken over the regulatory powers in the field of consumer protection in the aftermath of the Single European Act (1986) in Europe. Initially the European Union aimed at adopting minimum standards built on the then existing national consumer laws. These minimum standards provided for a common platform from which, however, Member States could deviate so as to set higher standards of protection. At the 2000 Lisbon Summit the European Commission gained political support from the head of states to shift European consumer law-making from minimum to full harmonisation. Since then the European Commission has gradually realised its objective. With the so-called 'New Deal for Consumers' (2019), the new Modernisation Directive[1] on modernisation and better enforcement of EU consumer law, the development has come to a preliminary end.[2] The Unfair Contract Terms Directive[3] still remains as the last bulwark of minimum harmonisation. The dense net of European consumer law covers nearly all substantive areas of consumer relevant economic transactions. Today, EU consumer law is the most advanced regional system of consumer law globally and the European consumer law defines the benchmark of protection not only within the EU, but far beyond the EU around the globe. Currently the EU is working on proposals in order to 'green' European consumer law.

[1] Directive (EU) 2019/2161 of the European Parliament and of the Council of 27 November 2019 on the better enforcement and modernisation of Union consumer protection rules, OJ 2019 No L328, p 7.

[2] See M Durovic, 'Adaptation of Consumer Law to the Digital Age: The Case of the New European Directive 2019/2161 on Modernisation and Better Enforcement of Consumer Law' (2020) 68(2) *Belgrade Law Review* 120.

[3] Council Directive 93/13/EEC of 5 April 1993 on unfair terms in consumer contracts, OJ 1993 No L95, p 29.

II. Information and Right of Withdrawal

A. Information

The European Union has placed the information paradigm at the centre of its consumer protection agenda.[4] This is useful from an internal market perspective as it allows technical specification barriers to be removed if information provision is seen as a viable alternative.[5] It also promotes the model of an active autonomous consumer able to look after their own interests. However, this concept may be more theoretical than real given the behavioural economics insights into the effectiveness of information as a consumer protection strategy.[6] Nevertheless, the rhetoric of consumer protection as an information asymmetry problem has been compelling. It has been promoted through several sectoral directives on topics such as timeshare, package holidays, consumer credit and financial services. Information was also a key element of the regulation of distance selling and e-commerce. The duty to provide information took a significant step forward in the Unfair Commercial Practices Directive[7] by rendering omitting material information a breach of the duty not to mislead the consumer.[8] However, the depth of the obligation to inform the consumers is fully exposed by the Consumer Rights Directive.[9] This not only strengthened the information rules for distance and off-premises contracts, but also created a general information obligation for all other contracts. In distance and off-premises contracts this information is given legal effect by becoming part of the terms of the contract.[10]

In several Asian countries there is recognition of the right of consumers to be informed. However, the practical implementation varies.[11] In some countries, like Malaysia, there have been few steps to develop an information policy. Some like Singapore and Taiwan have developed rules in specific sectors such as doorstep sales. Japan has a fairly extensive patchwork of rules. The most extensive rules seem to be in China, Macau and Vietnam. Macau seems to resonate with the European language by talking about the need to inform consumers of the goods' essential characteristics. In Hong Kong something similar may be achieved by copying the EU rules on misleading

[4] For example, the 'Consumer Policy Strategy 2002–2006' COM(2002) 208 final talked about measures giving 'consumers the means to protect their own interests by making autonomous, informed choices'. Empowering consumers was in the title of the 'Consumer Policy Strategy 2007–2013' COM(2007) 99 final. In general, see G Howells, C Twigg-Flesner and T Wilhelmsson, *Rethinking EU Consumer Law*, (London: Routledge, 2018) 31–36 and 94–112.

[5] Case 261/81 *Rau* EU:C:1982:382: see S Weatherill, 'The Role of the Informed Consumer in EC Law and Policy' (1994) *Consumer Law Journal* 49.

[6] G Howells, 'The Potential and Limits of Consumer Empowerment by Information' (2005) 32 *Journal of Law and Society* 349.

[7] Directive 2005/29/EC of the European Parliament and of the Council of 11 May 2005 concerning unfair business-to-consumer commercial practices in the internal market, OJ 2005 No L149, p 22.

[8] Unfair Commercial Practices Directive (EU), Art 7.

[9] Directive 2011/83/EU of the European Parliament and of the Council of 25 October 2011 on consumer rights, OJ 2011 No L304, p 64.

[10] Consumer Rights Directive (EU), Art 6(5).

[11] For a full account see M Etkins and E Webb, 'Information and Right of Withdrawal', in this volume.

omissions. There are certainly rules about information scattered across Asia. However, one does not get the sense that the rhetoric of information as empowerment is as firmly embedded in Asia as it is in Europe. In particular, one might have expected the growth of the Internet selling age to have spawned more rules about mandatory disclosure on the Internet.

B. Right of Withdrawal

The European Union has been a strong promoter of the right of withdrawal.[12] This breaches the principle of *pacta sunt servanda* by giving the consumer the right to terminate the contract and return any goods without having to give any reasons – even where the goods or services are in full conformity with the contract. There are various motivations for granting such a right. It may be because the consumer is concluding the contract under circumstances where there is a risk they will be pressured, for example in their home or when being sold a timeshare at a promotional event. Being sold a timeshare when on holiday may ironically be risky as the consumer may be too relaxed.[13] In some instances it is an extension of the information policy, as a consumer buying over the Internet may only be able fully to appreciate the qualities of the goods when they receive them. The importance of the transaction may also justify a right to cancel, for instance for life insurance.[14] Some feel the rights are too extensive and open to abuse and even potentially environmentally unfriendly as goods returned increase demands for transportation. Others see them as being well intentioned, but potentially ineffective as consumers may not be motivated to use them.[15] They are certainly cloaked in complex regulation to manage the exercise of the right and its consequences. There has been an attempt to simplify the rules in the Consumer Rights Directive that also sees a move towards fixing 14 days as the normal withdrawal period.[16]

Asia has several examples of rights of withdrawal being granted. Often this is in relation to doorstep selling and sometimes it has been extended to forms of distance selling. However, as with information there has not been a clear trend to ensure Internet sales are included. Indeed, in Hong Kong it has been argued that Internet sales should not be included in order to help promote this selling medium which often involves low value goods. Singapore provides rights to withdraw for timeshare, life insurance and investment products. Hong Kong does not yet have any rights of withdrawal, but they have been proposed for fitness and beauty services following local scandals. Macau does not yet have

[12] See Howells, Twigg-Flesner and Wilhelmsson, *Rethinking EU Consumer Law*, 36 and 113–26.

[13] Arts 6–8 of Directive 2008/122/EC of the European Parliament and of the Council of 14 January 2009 on the protection of consumers in respect of certain aspects of timeshare, long-term holiday product, resale and exchange contracts, OJ 2008 No L33, p 10.

[14] Art 186 of Directive 2009/138/EC of the European Parliament and of the Council of 25 November 2009 on the taking-up and pursuit of the business of Insurance and Reinsurance (Solvency II), OJ 2009 No L335, p 1.

[15] J Luzak, 'To Withdraw or Not to Withdraw? Evaluation of the Mandatory Right of Withdrawal in Consumer Distance Selling Contracts Taking into Account its Behavioural Effects on Consumers' (2013) 37 *Journal of Consumer Policy* 91.

[16] Consumer Rights Directive (EU), Arts 9–16.

a right of withdrawal, but a general right is proposed which in the case of distance and off-premises contracts would be extended to 30 days where information about the right of withdrawal had not been provided. Hong Kong had also flirted with a very broad right to withdraw before pulling back. There may indeed be some concerns if the right of withdrawal were extended to regular contracts. Where there are rights of withdrawal they tend to be generally for less than the 14-day period that is becoming conventional within the EU, outside the field of life insurance.

III. Sale of Goods

The centrepiece of EU consumer law with regard to sale of goods was beyond doubt for more than 20 years the Consumer Sales Directive.[17] This piece of legislation regulated some of the most important aspects of business to consumer sales in the EU, namely non-conformity, remedies (but not damages), presumption of lack of conformity with the first six months after delivery and limitation. This minimum harmonisation directive was partly modelled after the UN Convention on Contracts for the International Sale of Goods (especially non-conformity and remedies), but also showed several consumer-related unique new features (for example the presumption of non-conformity). The Directive did not only have a harmonising EU-wide effect in the field of consumer sales law, but the obligation to implement the Directive was also the reason for some important national reforms. One example for that is the German Reform of the Law of Obligations of 2002 (the so-called *Schuldrechtsreform*), which is considered to be the most important revision of the German Civil Code (BGB) since its enactment in 1900. The Consumer Sales Directive was repealed in 2019 by the Sale of Goods Directive.[18] The new Directive contains many elements of the old Directive but it also shows some important changes. The two most important conceptual changes are that the new Directive is a full harmonisation directive and as the EU wanted to have a 'digital age ready consumer sales law', the new Directive also applies to digital content or digital services which are incorporated in or inter-connected with goods, and are provided with the goods under the sales contract.[19]

Most Asian jurisdictions seem to agree that consumers in a business to consumer sales scenario need extra protection.[20] Here the subsequent question is whether those consumer protection rules are incorporated into the general private law or whether they can be found in a separate consumer law act. However, some jurisdictions still have no or very little additional protection for a consumer-buyer, as for example the Hong Kong legal system shows. An open borrowing from the Consumer Sales Directive is seldom

[17] Directive 1999/44/EC of the European Parliament and of the Council of 25 May 1999 on certain aspects of the sale of consumer goods and associated guarantees, OJ 1999 No L171, p 12.

[18] Directive (EU) 2019/771 of the European Parliament and of the Council of 20 May 2019 on certain aspects concerning contracts for the sale of goods, OJ 2019 No L136, p 28. The corresponding national provisions are to apply from 1 January 2022.

[19] Sale of Goods Directive (EU), Art 3(3).

[20] For a full account G Pearson, 'Sale of Goods: A Comparative Perspective', in this volume.

(see for an exception the proposed consumer law of Macau). Sometimes though it seems that some Asian legal systems have 'silently' transplanted elements of the Consumer Sales Directive into their consumer protection law, as one might suspect with the Singaporean Consumer Projection (Fair Trading) Act. However, even without an open or silent borrowing some Asian (consumer) sales laws show commonalities with the Consumer Sales Directive as they both were influenced by the UN Convention on the International Sale of Goods – especially with regard to non-conformity and remedies. The 'digital age problem' dealt with by the new Sale of Goods Directive (where digital content or digital service are incorporated or inter-connected with the goods) is not yet tackled by most Asian legal systems.

IV. Unfair Terms

EU law submits the standard contract terms to a transparency and a fairness test. The judiciary is empowered to declare intransparent and unfair terms as 'non-binding' which comes close to them being 'void'. The Unfair Contract Terms Directive is nearly 30 years old now. Over time it has turned into one of the most powerful means of European consumer law, not least in the aftermath of Lehman Brothers and the Euro Crisis.[21] The Directive has introduced a general fairness test of contract terms in consumer contracts, complemented by an indicative list of potentially unfair terms.[22] The Directive has established a twofold enforcement mechanism, not only individual consumers are granted the right to challenge the fairness of unfair terms, but also so-called collective entities – such as consumer agencies and consumer associations – are given the power to initiate an action for injunction. The European Court of Justice has developed a fruitful judicial practice which is often described as manifesting a very pro-consumer oriented approach.[23]

When it comes to unfair contract terms, the examined Asian jurisdictions demonstrate much less similarity than in the case of the unfair commercial practices. Common law jurisdictions, such as Hong Kong or Singapore, tend to rely on the legislative instruments developed under UK law in the pre-EU consumer law era, primarily on the Unfair Contract Terms Act 1977 which provides much less protection than the EU consumer law and the Unfair Terms Directive as well as rather outdated English law doctrines on unconscionability and inequality of bargaining powers.[24] However, there are some exceptions to this as is the case with Malaysia which has adopted legislation with more protective rules on unfair contracts terms than is the case in other common law jurisdictions. The Asian civil law jurisdictions, logically, seem to be more receptive to the

[21] H-W Micklitz and N Reich, 'The Court and the Sleeping Beauty, The Revival of the Unfair Contract Terms Directive (UCTD)' (2014) 51 *Common Market Law Review* 771.

[22] Unfair Terms Directive (EU), Art 3(1).

[23] See, inter alia, Case C-472/10 *Invitel* EU:C:2012:242; Case C-26/13 *Kásler* EU:C:2014:282; Case C-484/08 *Caja de Ahorros* EU:C:2010:309; Case C-186/16 *Andriciuc* EU:C:2017:703; Case C-143/13 *Matei* EU:C:2015:127; Case C-415/11 *Aziz* EU:C:2013:164.

[24] *Lloyds Bank Ltd v Bundy* [1974] EWCA 8.

European rules as is the case, for example, with South Korea's rules on unfair contract terms. Similarly, Taiwan also has very powerful rules on unfair contract terms, but they are different than the EU ones.

V. Product Liability

The primary and most general piece of EU legislation governing product liability is the Product Liability Directive,[25] which is at the same time one of the earliest consumer law directives that is still in place (1985). The Directive is clearly inspired to a large extent by US Law and introduces a uniform no-fault liability system for defective products. This idea of a strict tort liability of producers (and importers) without the need to establish any fault or negligence on their side can be considered as the most important improvement of the Directive in comparison with general national tort law. As the Directive is meant to operate alongside national product safety and liability laws, claimants may have various other contract and/or tort avenues to establish liability – depending on the law of the relevant Member State. The practical relevance of the Directive is quite disappointing or to agree with *Reimann*: 'While the European model has more or less conquered the world of product liability law on the books … it has had amazingly little impact on the law in action'.[26] As the core of the Directive is from 1985, it could not foresee the technological changes to come like the importance of software nowadays, or the rise of artificial intelligence or autonomous systems. Therefore, there is no wonder that there is an intense debate in the EU right now as to whether the Directive is still fit for purpose or whether it needs to be revised to make it fit for the twenty-first century.[27]

The sources of product liability in Asia are mainly, but not exclusively, written ones.[28] To the vast majority they have been influenced by US Law and by the Product Liability Directive even though direct references to both legal systems by Asian legislators are hard to find. Due to the US and European models it is not surprising that most Asian jurisdictions follow (with some differences) the no-fault/strict liability approach in the field of product liability. Examples here are Indonesia, Malaysia, Taiwan, Thailand and Vietnam. However, some Asian jurisdictions follow a different path: in Hong-Kong the product liability claims are (still) based on traditional rules applicable to sales contracts or on negligence-based tort actions. The same seems to apply to Singapore where no specific strict liability for product liability exists. In addition, it is noteworthy that in the Asian legal systems the number of reported product liability cases is also low. Hence, one might in general question the effectiveness of the rules on product liability as such.

[25] Council Directive 85/374/EEC of 25 July 1985 on the approximation of the laws, regulations and administrative provisions of the Member States concerning liability for defective products, OJ 1985 No L210, p 29.

[26] M Reimann, 'Product Liability in a Global Context: The Hollow Victory of the European Model' (2003) 11 *European Review of Private Law* 128–54.

[27] The conclusions of an expert group have been published in October 2019: 'Liability for Artificial Intelligence and other emerging digital technologies', Report from the Expert Group on Liability and New Technologies – New Technologies Formation.

[28] For a full account M Cannarsa, 'Product Liability', in this volume.

VI. Product Safety

Ensuring products are safe and yet not allowing technical differences to be barriers to trade has been a central aspect of building the internal market.[29] There was a major push to harmonise standards as part of the project to build the internal market in 1992 in which the new approach to technical harmonisation was central.[30] This favoured directives for broad categories of products that avoided detailed technical regulation and instead set out essential safety requirements that could be met by complying with standards drafted by the European body CEN and adopted by national bodies. The need for detailed rules on market surveillance, requirements for conformity assessment and the application of remaining national technical rules has also been addressed and is found in a suite of pieces of legislation from 2008.[31]

Undoubtedly the most important development in EU consumer safety regulation was the adoption in 1992 of the General Product Safety Directive[32] and the establishment of a general safety requirement that captured all aspects of consumer safety not covered by specific rules. It also made it a requirement to have a government agency with powers to protect consumers. These powers were strengthened in the current General Product Safety Directive 2001[33] by for example granting the right to recall products in the hands of consumers and placing an obligation on traders to notify the authorities when they had safety concerns. The general safety regime has been subject to intense review throughout its history. There was a proposal for further reform in 2013, which has stalled over the inclusion of rules on disclosing the country of origin.[34]

Hong Kong and Malaysia have a general requirement of product safety modelled on the EU approach, although not fully updated to take account of reforms after the first directive.[35] Singapore also has an elaborate system that both prescribes certain categories of consumer goods that have to be registered before being supplied and also a general safety regulation which divides goods into those products for which there is an international standard from the four standards bodies listed and other products for which local standards might be adopted. Indeed, in many Asian countries standardisation is important and is often closely related to government. India is said not to have a consumer safety regime, but for most other countries there are some forms of safety rules which often include powers to recall dangerous products. They might consider whether having a general safety requirement would be a useful addition; as is indeed currently being discussed in Australia.[36]

[29] Howells, Twigg-Flesner and Wilhelmsson, *Rethinking EU Consumer Law*, 258 et seq.

[30] Council resolution on a new approach to technical harmonisation and standards, OJ 1985 No C136, p 1.

[31] Regulation (EC) 764/2008, OJ 2008 No L218, p 21; Regulation 765/2008 OJ 2008 No L218, p 30; Decision 768/2008/EC, OJ 2008 No L218, p 82.

[32] Council Directive 92/59/EEC of 29 June 1992 on general product safety, OJ 1992 No L228, p 24.

[33] Directive 2001/95/EC of the European Parliament and of the Council of 3 December 2001 on general product safety, OJ 2001 No L11, p 4.

[34] COM(2013) 75 final. See however the new proposal COM(2021) 346 final.

[35] For a full account, L Nottage and S Thanitcul, 'Consumer Product Liability and Safety Regulation: ASEAN in Asia', in this volume.

[36] L Nottage, 'Improving the Effectiveness of the Consumer Product Safety System: Australian Law Reform in Asia-Pacific Context' (2020) 43 *Journal of Consumer Policy* 829.

VII. Adaptations to the Digital Age

The European Union entered the arena in 1997 with the adoption of the Directive on Distance Selling[37] (today Consumer Rights Directive 2011) followed by the E-Commerce Directive[38] in 2000. The Consumer Rights Directive regulates online trade. It obliges the supplier to provide the consumer with information prior to the conclusion of the contract and to grant a right to withdraw from the contract within 14 days. The E-Commerce Directive, which is currently under review,[39] provides until today the ground rules for the digital economy and/or the platform economy. Two major principles are still relevant today: first the so-called country of origin principle which prevents the recipient state of digital services from double checking the control standards of the host state, secondly the recognition of platforms as mere intermediaries which by and large have no liability for the content they make available to the customer. Twenty years later and in line with the revision of the Consumer Sales Directive the EU adopted the Digital Content Directive,[40] which enters into force on the 1 January 2022. The Directive defines digital content and makes the supplier liable in case of non-conformity. In December 2021 the European Commission presented a proposal for a Digital Markets Act and a Digital Services Act.[41] These proposals are supposed to revise the full exemption of liability of the platform providers maybe to introduce some sort of a subsidiary liability and take account of the risks which result from platforms as gatekeepers. It seems that the EU is ready to take the lead in the regulation of the digital economy, hopefully taking the consumer interests into account.

Mainland China, Singapore and South Korea are leading in the process of adapting their legal system to the digital age.[42] In particular, the e-commerce reform in China, which entered into force in 2019, signalled an important step for modernisation in the Asian continent. Other Asian legal systems are still at a very early stage of development as regards the regulation of the digital economy. Malaysia released in 1998 a by now old-fashioned Communications and Multimedia Act and, in 2010, a Personal Data Protection Act. Hong Kong consumer law hardly deals with legal issues of the digital age, but has introduced modern data protection legislation and an Electronic Transactions Ordinance. Vietnamese Law is at a very early stage of development as is Indonesian law. Overall the development is very much in flux and it seems as if there is room for some sort of loose co-ordination between European and US approaches.

[37] Directive 97/7/EC of the European Parliament and of the Council of 20 May 1997 on the protection of consumers in respect of distance contracts, OJ 1997 No L144, p 19.

[38] Directive 2000/31/EC of the European Parliament and of the Council of 8 June 2000 on certain legal aspects of information society services, in particular electronic commerce, in the Internal Market, OJ 2000 No L178, p 1.

[39] COM(2020) 825 final.

[40] Directive (EU) 2019/770 of the European Parliament and of the Council of 20 May 2019 on certain aspects concerning contracts for the supply of digital content and digital services, OJ 2019 No L136, p 1.

[41] Digital Services Act, COM(2020) 825 final; Digital Markets Act, COM(2020) 842 final.

[42] For a full account A De Franceschi, 'Adaptation of Asian Consumer Law to the Digital Age', in this volume.

VIII. Unfair Commercial Practices

For the regulation of unfair commercial practices under the European law, the most important and powerful piece of legislation has been the Unfair Commercial Practices Directive. This Directive provides a complete and advanced legal framework for consumer protection in case of business-to-consumer commercial practices.[43] The Unfair Commercial Practices Directive is a very promising instrument which applies to all commercial practices of a trader that in any manner may affect or affect, directly or indirectly, consumer's economic behaviour.[44] The Modernisation Directive provides, first, new rules related to the enforcement and introduces individual remedies to consumers as victims of unfair commercial practices, and second, adapts the rules on unfair commercial practices to the challenges brought by the pending digitalisation of the marketplace.

The comparative examination of the selected jurisdictions in Asia has demonstrated that most of the jurisdictions have some rules on unfair commercial practices that are similar or inspired by the EU rules (China, Hong Kong, Macau draft, Vietnam).[45] Also most of the jurisdictions have very detailed rules on information requirements, some tightly connected with the rules on unfair commercial practices (for example Taiwan). However, similarly like in the case of the European Union, in most of the jurisdictions in Asia, individual consumers are not given any kind of individual remedies in situations when they have become victims of unfair commercial practices.[46] Although most of the examined Asian jurisdictions have developed rules on unfair commercial practices, their modernisation and adaptation to challenges of the increasingly digitalised market is necessary and a potentially good model to follow is the one provided by the recently adopted Modernisation Directive on better enforcement and modernisation of Union consumer protection rules which has addressed some of the most important consumer law challenges brought by the digitalisation of commerce.

IX. Access to Justice

The European Treaties limit the competence of the EU to adopt rules on the substantive level of protection, whereas the Member States remain in charge to guarantee effective law enforcement. However, with the backing of the European Court of Justice, the EU succeeded in using its legislative competences to adopt minimum standards for the enforcement of EU consumer law. The result of nearly 20 years of piecemeal regulation is

[43] For more info, see M Durovic, *European Law on Unfair Commercial Practices and Contract Law* (Oxford: Hart, 2016).

[44] As confirmed already in the first case law on the Directive 2005/29/EC Joined Cases C-261/07 and C-299/07 *VTB-VAB* EU:C:2009:244; Case C-304/08 *Plus Warenhandelsgesellschaft mbH* EU:C:2010:12; Case C-522/08 *Telekomunikacja Polska* EU:C:2010:135; Case C-540/08 *Mediaprint Zeitungs- und Zeitschriftenverlag* EU:C:2010:660.

[45] For a full account H-W Micklitz, 'Commercial Practices: A Comparative Perspective', in this volume.

[46] M Durovic, 'Contract Law Remedies for Breach of the Unfair Commercial Practices Directive – What Can Be Improved' in M Cantero et al (eds), *Transformation of Economic Law* (Oxford: Hart, 2019) 29–42.

a rather messy scenario. Overall, it seems appropriate to distinguish between individual and collective as well as between private and public enforcement.[47]

With regard to private individual enforcement, the European Union put emphasis on establishing a new layer outside and beyond access to courts through alternative dispute resolution (ADR)[48] and online dispute resolution (ODR) procedures.[49] ADR mechanisms reach from non-binding decisions to consumer arbitration, often preceded by mediation procedures.[50] With regard to collective enforcement, in 1998[51] the EU introduced the action for injunction as a minimum standard in the field of commercial practices and unfair terms. The respective directives leave it for the Member States to decide whether legal standing should be granted to public authorities and/or to consumer organisations. In 2020 and after a decade-long discussion the EU adopted the Representative Action Directive[52] which grants public and/or private entities the power to initiate collective compensation claims based on an opt in procedure. Member States remain free to go further and follow the American class action model where consumers have to opt out. Particular rules exist on the transborder co-operation of public authorities and/or consumer organisations as regards consumer law enforcement.[53]

Whilst the EU legal body on enforcement is gradually taking shape, mastering the broad varieties of national enforcement cultures, the ASEAN countries demonstrate overall large differences.[54] When it comes to consumer redress in the courts, the practical problems resulting from access to justice look relatively similar. Only India and Malaysia have introduced specialised consumer tribunals, others have opted for an intermediary route establishing simplified procedures for small claims. Consumer claims are conducted through a summarised procedure inside civil courts, such as for instance in Thailand or Vietnam. Contrary to EU law, collective redress be it through consumer organisations, aggregate claims or consumer agencies is comparatively underdeveloped, except in Japan.

The availability of out of court dispute resolution mechanism is widespread. Legal culture matters. Confucian influences in China, Singapore, Taiwan and Vietnam explain the preference for extrajudicial settlement rather than adversarial procedures. Similarly, in Australia a non-adversarial dispute resolution approach finds its origins in ancient

[47] P Rott, 'The EU Legal Framework for the Enforcement of Consumer Law' in H-W Micklitz and G Saumier (eds), *Enforcement and Effectiveness of Consumer Law* (Cham: Springer, 2018) 249.

[48] Directive 2013/11/EU of the European Parliament and of the Council of 21 May 2013 on alternative dispute resolution for consumer disputes, OJ 2013 No L165, p 63.

[49] Regulation (EU) No 524/2013 of the European Parliament and of the Council of 21 May 2013 on online dispute resolution for consumer disputes, OJ 2013 L165, p 1.

[50] Directive 2008/52/EC of the European Parliament and of the Council of 21 May 2008 on certain aspects of mediation in civil and commercial matters, OJ 2008 No L136, p 3.

[51] Directive 2009/22/EC of the European Parliament and of the Council of 23 April 2009 on injunctions for the protection of consumers' interests, OJ 2009 No L110, p 30.

[52] Directive (EU) 2020/1828 of the European Parliament and of the Council of 25 November 2020 on representative actions for the protection of the collective interests of consumers, OJ 2020 No L409, p 1.

[53] Regulation (EU) 2017/2394 of the European Parliament and of the Council of 12 December 2017 on cooperation between national authorities responsible for the enforcement of consumer protection laws and repealing Regulation (EC) No 2006/2004, OJ 2017 No L345, p 1.

[54] See for a full account M Cantero Gamito, 'Consumer Access to Justice in a Comparative Perspective', in this volume.

indigenous communities, despite the adoption of the English common law system. Last but not least, just as in the EU, there is a certain tendency to strengthen administrative enforcement mechanisms, although their institutional setting, the procedure and the available remedies differ considerably. Overall, it seems as if consumer organisations do not play a prominent role in the enforcement of consumer law, again with the exception of Japan.

X. Conclusion

Seen through the lens of the existing body of EU consumer law, it is fair to conclude that EU law is ahead of the curve. This is not only true in the first generation of consumer law – the regulation of unfair terms, commercial practices, consumer sales, tourism, but also in the second generation of consumer law – the consumer law 2.0 on the digital age.[55] It seems as if the EU is ready to take the lead, although the concrete impact of the envisaged directives and regulations on consumer protection cannot be determined. It might take another two to three years before the consumer law 2.0 that started with the Digital Content Directive will take shape. The EU has managed to achieve a certain level of homogeneity even in the field of consumer law enforcement, where there are perhaps the most important differences.

[55] H-W Micklitz, 'Consumer Law in the Digital Economy' in T Kono et al (eds), *Transnational Commercial and Consumer Law* (Vienna: Springer, 2018) 111–52.

24

Regulation of Unfair Terms in Consumer Contracts: An American Perspective

JAMES P NEHF

I. Introduction

In the typical merchant-consumer transaction, standard terms are of course the norm. Consumer transactions are documented by contracts of adhesion where most, if not all, of the terms are drafted by the merchant and are not negotiable. Even if they were negotiable, the vast majority of consumers will either not be aware of this possibility or, quite reasonably, will conclude that they cannot bargain effectively over terms either because they do not understand their legal import or they cannot envision alternatives that would better serve their interests.

Sometimes those standard terms are so one-sided in favour of the merchant that they inflict unfair hardship on the unknowing consumer. In the United States, there is no omnibus law on unfair contract terms that applies uniformly throughout the country. Regulation of unfair terms is addressed piecemeal, with limited protection in certain sectors at the federal level and most of the regulatory norms imposed by the individual states. Those norms can take statutory or common law form, and while they can vary widely from state to state, there are some parallel themes.

II. Regulation of Unfair Terms by Statutes

Consumer legislation exists at federal, state and (sometimes) local/city levels. Consumer protection at the federal level is extensive, particularly in the area of consumer credit. Over the years, states and municipalities have adopted laws addressing a wide variety of consumer contracting situations including consumer credit, distance selling, payday loans and numerous others. Often these enactments, whether state or federal, dictate that certain terms must be included in consumer contracts (particularly disclosure requirements), and often they dictate that certain unfair terms not be included in consumer contracts. These statutes may prohibit certain merchant conduct (for example pyramid schemes, door-to-door selling, 'bait and switch' advertising), while others provide a regulatory framework for a particular type of commercial activity or industry (for example rent-to-own contracts or the timeshare industry). Although there are common themes present in the array of state laws, and some areas in which federal law controls, for the most part each state adopts its own approach to protecting its residents from deceptive and unfair practices in consumer contracts. Similarly, agency regulations such as Regulation Z (truth in lending) and Regulation E (electronic funds transfers) impose mandatory disclosure requirements and some limitations on contract terms in consumer contracts under their scope.

A. Background

Statutes regulating unfair terms in consumer contracts became popular in the 1950s and 1960s during the rise of post-war consumerism in the United States. Prior to that time, the Federal Trade Commission (FTC) was the principal government agency charged with protecting consumer rights. The FTC promulgated consumer protection regulations under the Federal Trade Commission Act[1] (FTC Act) and brought enforcement actions to combat widespread merchant misconduct in areas such as deceptive advertising, fraudulent business opportunity schemes, abuses arising from home solicitation sales and unfair debt collection tactics. Protection at the state level was comparatively weak. Much of the objectionable merchant conduct did not rise to the level of common law fraud. Even when it did, the difficulties of proving the elements of fraud, especially the scienter requirement, and the high cost of litigation as compared to the injury suffered, often discouraged enforcement actions. Existing state statutes governing business conduct, such as the Uniform Commercial Code (UCC), included few consumer protection provisions. The FTC therefore began encouraging the states to create statutory enforcement mechanisms designed specifically to promote consumer rights, and by the end of the 1970s most states had enacted at least one general consumer protection law to curb unfair or deceptive acts and practices, and a variety of industry-specific laws.

The various state laws enacted in this period shared certain common characteristics because many of them originated from one of two sources. The National Conference of Commissioners on Uniform State Laws (NCCUSL), as well as the FTC, drafted model statutes and strongly encouraged states to adopt one of the forms. The NCCUSL proposed two model laws. The Uniform Deceptive Trade Practices Act prohibited 11 specific deceptive trade practices along with a general prohibition of 'any other conduct which similarly creates a likelihood of confusion or misunderstanding'. The Uniform Consumer Sales Practices Act prohibited deceptive acts and practices generally and also enumerated specific types of deceptive conduct and unconscionable acts. The FTC proposed three alternative versions of an Unfair Trade Practices and Consumer Protection Law. The first alternative mimicked the FTC Act and prohibited 'unfair methods of competition and unfair or deceptive acts or practices in the conduct of any

[1] 15 USC §§ 41–58.

trade or commerce'. The second alternative enjoined 'false, misleading, or deceptive acts or practices in the conduct of any trade or commerce'. The third alternative was similar to the Uniform Deceptive Trade Practices Act and included a list of specific prohibited practices.

B. Fragmentation to Convergence

Today, state consumer statutes vary among the states to an even greater extent because states have frequently amended their statutes in non-uniform ways, either to resolve ambiguities in statutory language, to clarify or supplement consumer rights or to address new consumer problems. Nevertheless, despite the largely uncoordinated and ad-hoc enactment and amendment process, there has been some convergence of laws regulating unfair terms over time.[2] As a few states begin to address a new problem (for example telemarketing fraud in the 1980s), other states have usually followed suit, and over time most states now address the same basic set of consumer issues, although the laws may differ somewhat in scope and content.

State consumer protection statutes list a large number of specific unfair practices. For example, Pennsylvania's statute lists 21 specific unfair practices, California's lists 27 and Texas's lists 31. Many of these statutes follow a uniform law that was proposed in the 1960s and therefore list the same types of practices. For example, there are several common unfair practices in the Pennsylvania, California, and Texas statutes:

- Passing off goods or services as those of another.
- Misrepresenting the source, sponsorship, approval or certification of goods or services.
- Misrepresenting the affiliation, connection or association with, or certification by, another.
- Using deceptive representations or designations of geographic origin in connection with goods or services.
- Representing that:
  - goods or services have sponsorship, approval, characteristics, ingredients, uses, benefits or quantities which they do not have.
  - a person has a sponsorship, approval, status, affiliation or connection which they do not have.
  - that goods are original or new if they have deteriorated unreasonably or are altered, reconditioned, reclaimed, used or second-hand.

[2] As a result of differing statutory language in enacted laws and evolving court interpretations of those laws, consumer protection norms under the array of state statutes continue to vary among the 50 states. And while there are occasional calls for uniformity or a more national and harmonised approach, the calls generally have not gained widespread support. Indeed, in the last decade or so, calls for harmonisation typically originate in the business community, seeking adoption of a national law that will insulate members from liability under state laws that are perceived to be less business-friendly than they would prefer.

- Representing that goods or services are of a particular standard, quality or grade, or that goods are of a particular style or model, if they are of another.
- Disparaging the goods, services or business of another by false or misleading representation of fact.
- Advertising goods or services with intent not to sell them as advertised.
- Advertising goods or services with intent not to supply reasonably expectable demand, unless the advertisement discloses a limitation of quantity.
- Making false or misleading statements of fact concerning reasons for, existence of, or amounts of price reductions.

The consensus among consumer representatives is that a state-by-state approach is preferred unless there is a strong need for uniformity in a particular area of commerce. The approach has worked fairly well over time and carries several advantages. First, it allows for a healthy degree of experimentation and an evolutionary approach to consumer protection nationwide. As states adopt different laws and models to address similar problems, there is opportunity to evaluate which laws and models work best. Over time, the good ideas take hold in other states, and the weak approaches get strengthened or jettisoned.

Second, a particular consumer problem (for example fraud in the home mortgage market) may be more prevalent in one state or region before it takes hold in others. A state where the problem is most serious may enact protective legislation that can serve as a guide to other states where the problem is only in its early stages.

Third, state legislatures have been able to react more quickly to emerging consumer problems than the US Congress. Proposed national legislation, or a proposed amendment to existing national legislation, is perceived as a high stakes political event, and competing interest groups are inclined to expend tremendous resources to get their views heard. This often results in legislation either stalling in Congress or being enacted in a diluted form that is the least objectionable to major stakeholders but does little to solve the problem.

Regarding warranty disclaimers, there is large uniformity in contracts to sell goods, which are governed by the UCC in every state. Although a few states have modified these uniform rules, the uniform provisions prevail in the vast majority of states. A seller, even a merchant selling goods to a consumer, may disclaim all warranties so long as it complies with the mandates of UCC § 2-316.[3] The seller may choose to give no express warranties and may, in writing, conspicuously disclaim the implied warranty of merchantability (by using that term), or can state that it is selling the goods 'as is' or 'with all fault' or similar language. While a disclaimer of all warranties is not common for common new goods sold by merchants in stores, it is often used when a merchant is selling used products, particularly used motor vehicles.

[3] Under the federal Magnuson-Moss Warranty Act (PL 93-637), 15 USC §§ 2301 et seq, a merchant does not have to give any express or implied warranties when selling goods to consumers. If it chooses to give an express warranty, however, the implied warranty of merchantability cannot be disclaimed entirely and can only be limited to the duration of the express warranty.

III. Regulation of Unfair Terms by Common Law Decision-Making

A. Role of the Common Law

In addition to statutes, regulation of unfair terms in consumer contracts is addressed through the common law, that is, judges deciding cases in published opinions.[4] At the centre of common law regulation are the two most important common law doctrines of unconscionability and good faith. Those two doctrines have played a central role in regulating standard terms in consumer contracts over the years.

In a common law judicial system, courts decide cases and, in the process of doing so, create law. While a legislature creates law through the enactment of statutes, and administrative agencies through rulemaking (and enforcement proceedings), courts create law by deciding cases, writing opinions and publishing them for the world to see.[5] Courts are generally bound by precedent and must follow decisions of higher courts, and all courts are supposed to give serious consideration to the rationale of others deciding similar cases.[6]

Through the process of judicial decision-making, courts create, define and refine legal rights, supplementing those created by statutes or agency rules.[7] Courts serve a 'gap-filling' role, deciding cases involving transactions that are not directly addressed

[4] The term 'common law' can have more than one meaning. Early definitions saw common law as 'customary law, the law of "long use" and "custom"'. JF Stinneford, 'The Original Meaning of "Unusual": The Eighth Amendment as a Bar to Cruel Innovation' (2008) 102 *Northwestern University Law Review* 1739, 1768 (quoting E Coke, *The Compleat Copyholder* (1630)). As used in this chapter, however, the definition of common law is judge-made law, through published decisions, that exists as vehicle for law creation, development and change over time.

[5] The importance of common law as a supplement to statutory law has been described as follows: 'Our society has an enormous demand for legal rules that actors can live, plan, and settle by. The legislature cannot adequately satisfy this demand. The capacity of a legislature to generate legal rules is limited, and much of that capacity must be allocated to the production of rules concerning governmental matters, such as spending, taxes, and administration; rules that are regarded as beyond the courts' competence, such as the definition of crimes; and rules that are best administered by a bureaucratic machinery, such as the principles for setting the rates charged by regulated industries. Furthermore, our legislatures are normally not staffed in a manner that would enable them to perform comprehensively the function of establishing law to govern action in the private sector. Finally, in many areas the flexible form of a judicial rule is preferable to the canonical form of a legislative rule. Accordingly, it is socially desirable that the courts should act to enrich that supply of legal rules that govern [business] conduct-not by taking on lawmaking as a free-standing function, but by attaching much greater emphasis to the establishment of legal rules than would be necessary if the courts' sole function was the resolution of disputes'. CA Carr and MR Jenks, 'The Privatization of Business and Commercial Dispute Resolution: A Misguided Policy Decision' (1999) 88 *Kentucky Law Journal* 183, 193. See generally JM Feinman, 'Un-Making Law: The Classical Revival in the Common Law' (2004) 28 *Seattle Law Review* 1 (discussing changes and trends in the development of the common law).

[6] Among the distinguishing characteristics of common law are: '[I]ts development of law by a system of judicial precedent, its use of the jury to decide issues of fact, and its all-pervading doctrine of supremacy of the law – that the agencies of government are no more free than the private individual to act according to their own arbitrary will or whim, but must conform to legal rules developed and applied by courts'. HF Stone, 'The Common Law in the United States' (1936) 50 *Harvard Law Review* 4, 5.

[7] R Alderman, 'The Future of Consumer Law in the United States – Hello Arbitration, Bye-Bye Courts, So-Long Consumer Protection', University of Houston Law Center, 19 September 2007.

by legislation or were only partially or ambiguously addressed.[8] Courts also help maintain consistency between similar rights in the absence of legislative action.[9] Sometimes courts create law in areas where the legislature has done little or nothing, making law in the classic common law tradition. In the field of consumer law, courts provide remedies and define rights for individuals who feel that they have been wronged by businesses, supplementing legislative and regulatory dictates through the development of common law rules and principles. Courts play a pivotal role in policing market failure as they protect consumers from what they perceive as the unjustified exercise of market power, and courts provide a means by which consumers can seek redress from perceived abuses in the marketplace. While critics of this process sometimes argue that in so doing judges usurp the authority of the elected legislature to create the rules governing market participants, any usurpation is at most temporary because legislatures are free to enact laws that reverse judicial decisions if they so choose. The fact that they frequently allow those decisions to stand can be seen, at a minimum, as legislative acquiescence in the role that courts play in policing market behaviour in consumer transactions. Without common law regulation of consumer contracts, all public sector limitations on standard terms would have to come from the other branches of government. While there certainly are advantages to legislative and agency deliberation and subsequent enactment of consumer contract norms, the role of courts in policing consumer transactions is longstanding and is generally accepted as a legitimate and important exercise of judicial power.

B. Unconscionability and Good Faith

At common law, the regulation of unfair terms in consumer contracts can take many forms but the most often used and well-developed common law doctrines are the doctrines of unconscionability and good faith. Each plays a different role. Unconscionability is generally used to limit the legal effect of unfair terms as evaluated at the time the contract was made. It prevents overreaching by the contract drafter in the contract formation process. The good faith doctrine generally is used to evaluate the legal effect of contract terms throughout the post-contract period of contract performance. It prevents overreaching and abuse of discretion by the contract drafter during contract performance.

i. The Unconscionability Doctrine

At common law, the unconscionability doctrine is one of the few doctrines that allows a consumer to avoid harsh contract terms to which it has technically agreed either by signing, clicking or manifesting some other form of assent to those terms. In the absence

[8] See RA Posner, *Divergent Paths: The Academy and the Judiciary* (Cambridge, MA: Harvard University Press, 2016) 112 (describing 'judges not as interpreters of legislation but as partners of the legislators' when they 'interpret' statutes).

[9] Alderman, 'The Future of Consumer Law'.

of statutory or regulatory mandates, the unconscionability doctrine stands as one of the few defences to harsh terms imposed by the business in the contract formation process.

As the unconscionability doctrine developed at common law in the United States, courts have generally asked whether two elements are present: procedural infirmities and substantive unfairness.[10] As stated in *Williams v Walker Thomas Furniture Co*, the consumer must show that they had an absence of meaningful choice (the procedural infirmity) in manifesting assent to the term, and a term that is unreasonably favourable to the party imposing that term (substantive unfairness).[11] In consumer contracts, the procedural element is seldom an issue. Almost by definition, a typical consumer 'adhesion' contract will not give the consumer any meaningful choice regarding standard contract terms.

The substantive element, however, is often contested. Drawing on judicial decisions, the draft Restatement elaborates on what is meant by 'substantive' unconscionability. A contract term is substantively unconscionable if it (1) excludes or limits the consumer's remedies for death or personal injury caused by a wrongful act of the business, or for loss caused by an intentional or negligent act of the business, (2) unreasonably expands the business's remedies or its enforcement powers or (3) unreasonably limits the consumer's ability to seek reasonable redress for a violation of a legal right.[12] This leaves to the courts much discretion to determine what constitutes an 'unreasonable' term.[13] Courts have, generally speaking, found terms unconscionable if they have an unreasonably adverse effect on a consumer's justifiable expectations in the context of the transaction. Examples of terms held to be unconscionable include a term whereby a consumer receives a product that does not work but is barred from a refund by a warranty disclaimer,[14] clauses that require arbitration in a foreign jurisdiction or where the filing fee greatly exceeds the amount of the claim[15] and a term that gives the merchant the unfettered power to act unilaterally, such as where the agreement includes open terms and the seller has the right to fill in any term it chooses.[16] In *Williams v*

[10] See generally, M Frey, 'A Consumer's Guide to Unconscionable Sales Contracts' (1974) 2 *Loyola Consumer Law Review* 5.

[11] 350 F2d 445 (DC Cir 1965). As phrased in the draft Restatement, a term will be voidable as unconscionable only if it is: '(1) Substantively unconscionable, namely unfair or unreasonably one-sided, and (2) Procedurally unconscionable, amounting to unfair surprise or depriving the consumer of meaningful choice'. Draft Restatement of the Law, Consumer Contracts, § 5(b).

[12] ibid, § 5(c).

[13] Note that the draft specifically references, as potentially unconscionable, contract terms that restrict a consumer's ability to obtain redress of their rights. This could become important as consumers continue to challenge mandatory arbitration provisions as unconscionable. The Supreme Court has made it difficult for consumers to challenge arbitration provisions on unconscionability grounds, but it is still possible to do so, as several courts have held. See, eg, *Armendariz v Foundation Health Psyche Services, Inc*, 24 Cal 4th 83 (2000); *Sanchez v Valencia Holding Company*, 61 Cal 4th 899 (2015).

[14] See *Universal Leasing Servs, Inc v Flushing Hae Kwan Restaurant*, 169 AD2d 829, 565 NYS2d 199 (2d Dep't 1991); *Industralease Automated & Scientific Equipment Corp v RME Enterprises, Inc*, 58 AD2d 482, 396 NYS2d 427 (2d Dep't 1977).

[15] *Brower v Gateway 2000, Inc*, 246 AD2d 246, 676 NYS2d 569 (1st Dep't 1998); *Teleserve Sys, Inc v MCI Telecomm. Corp*, 230 AD2d 585, 659 NYS2d 659 (4th Dep't 1997).

[16] *Sunbeam Farms, Inc v Troche*, 110 Misc 2d 501, 442 NYS2d 842 (Civ Ct, Bronx Co 1981); cf *Nalezenec v Blue Cross of WNY*, 172 AD2d 1004, 569 NYS2d 264 (4th Dep't 1991); *Zuckerberg v Blue Cross & Blue Shield*, 119 Misc 2d 834, 888, 464 NYS2d 678 (Sup Ct, Nassau Co 1983), rev'd on other grounds, 108 AD2d 56, 487 NYS2d 595 (2d Dep't 1985), aff'd, 67 NY2d 688, 499 NYS2d 920 (1986).

Walker Thomas Furniture Co.,[17] the DC Circuit held that a term in a consumer credit contract requiring cross-collateralisation with a pro-rata pay-out could well be deemed unconscionable because the goods that Mrs Williams bought on credit might remain as collateral far longer than a consumer would reasonably expect.[18]

One of the enduring strengths (and some might say the central weakness) of the unconscionability doctrine is its elasticity and ability to adapt to changing times and commercial practices. If cross-collateralisation with a pro-rata pay-out is held to be unenforceable, credit sellers may react by including other terms that seek to achieve similar goals, such as a term granting the seller a security interest in all of the consumer's household items with each new purchase. When that clause is held unconscionable,[19] they may inflate the stated 'cash price' of the goods in an effort to ensure profitability on a credit sale to a high risk consumer. When extremely high prices are challenged as unconscionable, the transaction might be restructured as a rent-to-own lease instead of a credit sale, and on it goes. While the unconscionability standard is not easy to satisfy, and like all common law development moves in fits and starts, it is malleable enough to give consumers an opportunity to limit the effects of standard contract terms as consumer transactions evolve and new areas of commerce emerge.

ii. The Good Faith Doctrine

Among common law doctrines that can limit the effect of standard terms in consumer contracts, the good faith doctrine has probably been the most controversial and has seen the most evolution over time.[20] If a standard term addresses matters arising post-contract formation, that is, during contract performance, particularly if it gives the business discretion in performing its obligations, those obligations and responsibilities must be exercised in good faith.[21] According to most courts, the meaning of good faith at common law is now the same as in the UCC: honesty in fact and observance of reasonable standards of fair dealing.[22]

a. Development

The good faith doctrine in consumer transactions has gone through periods of revision and re-evaluation over the years. Courts (and legislatures) have taken up the task of delineating the boundaries of the doctrine, identifying specific types of behaviour that constitute bad faith in contract settings. Most courts in the United States did not

[17] 350 F2d 445 (DC Cir 1965).

[18] Under the agreement, every purchase that Mrs Williams made at the store was deemed to be collateral for all other debts she had incurred in the past and might incur in the future, and because of the pro-rata payout provision she would own none of the collateral (household items) free and clear until all of the purchased items had been paid off in full.

[19] Or rendered unenforceable by statute or regulation, as in the Uniform Consumer Credit Code, or the FTC's Credit Practices Rule.

[20] Some of this discussion is drawn from a previous paper by the author. See JP Nehf, 'Bad Faith Breach of Contract in Consumer Transactions' in R Brownsword et al (eds), *Good Faith Contract: Concept and Context* (Aldershot: Dartmouth, 1999) 115.

[21] Draft Restatement of the Law, Consumer Contracts, § 4.

[22] ibid, § 1(7).

recognise good faith as an independent duty, with the same legal significance as other express or implied contractual duties, until the latter half of the twentieth century. Prior to this point, good faith was frequently referenced, but only as an interpretive tool to give meaning to some other contractual duty. It is the relatively recent acceptance of good faith as an independent duty which has generated much activity in the courts (and law journals) over the years.

American judges initially embraced the doctrine of *caveat emptor* with even more enthusiasm than their English brethren,[23] but even in early reported cases the notion that contracting parties owe a duty of good faith to each other can be found. At the end of the nineteenth century, during the pinnacle of liberal economic thought, Bishop's treatise on contract law observed that

> the law presumes each [party] to be acting in good faith toward the other; and it binds each to the other, to whatever good faith requires. The implication may be derived from the words employed, from the acts of the parties viewed in connection with the thing contracted for, or from the nature of the transaction.[24]

By the beginning of the twentieth century, judges routinely referred to the implied obligation of good faith performance.[25]

Despite considerable support for an implied duty of good faith in the case law, the American Law Institute (ALI) in 1920 did not give explicit recognition to the doctrine when it drafted the Restatement (First) of Contracts. Nevertheless, courts continued to impose good faith duties, and by the 1970s, when the ALI prepared the revised Restatement (Second) of Contracts, the doctrine was more firmly rooted in American law. Section 205 of the Restatement (Second) proclaims: 'Every contract imposes upon each party a duty of good faith and fair dealing in its performance and its enforcement'. The Restatement has been highly influential in American jurisprudence, and has frequently been cited by courts when recognising the duty of good faith in a variety of commercial and consumer contexts. The doctrine's inclusion solidified it as a central tenet of the common law of contracts, though the absolute rule was probably overstated at the time, and it has not been applied rigorously in every contract since its publication. It is applied consistently enough, though, to be fairly regarded as one of the defining characteristics of American contract law, particularly in consumer transactions.[26]

b. Defining Good Faith?

Like the doctrine of unconscionability, the good faith concept is fluid, highly adaptive and not easily reduced to a concise formula. The official comment to the restatement (second) acknowledges that 'its meaning varies somewhat with the context', but offers little in the way of guidance. It explains that good faith has something to do with the

[23] See M Horwitz, *The Transformation of American Law, 1780–1860* (Cambridge, MA: Harvard University Press, 1977) 180.

[24] JP Bishop, *Bishop on Contracts* (Chicago: TT Flood, 1878) s 106, 37–38.

[25] In one of the early precedents to modern good faith litigation of insurer liability, a New York court required the insurer to act with 'entire good faith and fair dealing' in its transactions with the insured when demanding that the insured provide proof of loss. *Armstrong v Agricultural Ins Co*, 29 NE 991, 992 (NY 1892).

[26] The draft Restatement of Consumer Contracts continues this treatment by including good faith as one of the central tenets of interpreting and enforcing consumer contract terms.

expectations of the parties and general principles of fairness and moral behaviour. Good faith 'emphasizes faithfulness to an agreed common purpose and consistency with the justified expectations of the other party', and in contrast, bad faith conduct 'violate[s] community standards of decency, fairness or reasonableness'. Through case decisions over time, however, the doctrine gains meaning. Precedent leads to more precedent, and while cases are seldom consistent, over time a body of law emerges.

Various commentators have attempted to provide a definitional foundation to assist judges in developing the good faith doctrine, but none has gained general acceptance in the courts. Robert Summers, whose writings on the subject were influential in the drafting of the Restatement, advocated an 'excluder' analysis of good faith. He argued that good faith has no general meaning of its own, and that attempting to construct a positive meaning is both unnecessary and futile.[27] Good faith can best be described by excluding activities that constitute bad faith in particular situations. He called for the compilation of a list of what courts would find to be bad faith conduct under certain circumstances or in particular types of transactions; good faith conduct then becomes all behaviour not on the list. Good faith, then, is not really an affirmative obligation imposed upon the parties, but more resembles a default position attained when a party avoids bad faith conduct. This framework has some appeal because, if we view good faith conduct as the generally accepted behaviour of contracting parties, compiling a list or attempting to describe all such instances will surely be a hopeless task. On the other hand, it should be less burdensome to identify those fewer instances which deviate from the norm as examples of unacceptable behaviour. Moreover, as a practical matter, courts are seldom asked to identify good faith conduct, but are frequently asked to address specific conduct one party says constitutes bad faith by the other. We are therefore more likely to find an ample supply of bad faith conduct in published cases to inform the inquiry.

The other dominant definitional framework is an extension of the bargain model, to attempt a reconstruction of the legitimate expectations of the parties at the time of contracting and then ask whether the conduct is consistent with those expectations. Early in the debate, Alan Farnsworth took the view that good faith is simply one application of basic principles of contract law.[28] The task is to imply terms that are consistent with the parties' reasonable expectations, an exercise judges do all the time in similar contexts. Over the years, certain tools have become accepted as legitimate inquiries to assist courts in divining these expectations (custom, trade usage, past dealings, etc), which helps quiet criticism that the good faith standard has no normative base and gives judges too much discretion, leading to unpredictable results. While there will always be some uncertainty when a party is charged with bad faith conduct, the problem is no different from the other disputes that require reasonable implications about the parties' legitimate expectations created in the bargain (for example mistake, consequential damages, liquidated penalties, contract formation).[29]

[27] RS Summers, 'Good Faith in General Contract Law and the Sales Provisions of the Uniform Commercial Code' (1968) 54 *Virginia Law Review* 195, 198.

[28] A Farnsworth, 'Good Faith in Contract Performance' in J Beatson and D Friedmann (eds), *Good Faith and Fault in Contract Law* (Oxford: Clarendon Press, 1995) 153, 161 (reprising earlier observations and endorsing the comments of Justice Antonin Scalia in *Tymshare, Inc v Covell*, 727 F2d 1145 (DC Cir 1984).

[29] Stephen Burton's *Harvard Law Review* article took Farnsworth's view in a different direction. S Burton, 'Breach of Contract and the Common Law Duty to Perform in Good Faith' (1980) 94 *Harvard Law Review* 369.

Each of these (and other) discussions of the definitional problem with the good faith doctrine has found some measure of acceptance in legal commentary and support in the case law. Law reform advocates have been content to see the definition develop piecemeal in the common law tradition. While definitional uncertainties and normative inquiries remain, there currently seems to be less dissatisfaction with the present state of the law compared with previous eras. After a few decades living with uncertainties and seeing neither calamitous consequences result nor better solutions proposed, the tendency is to accept the good faith doctrine, at least in consumer transactions, more readily. Besides insurance law, one of the most important of these areas is the consumer banking industry, where an ongoing relationship between the financial institution and its customers is the norm, and opportunities to perform discretionary duties abound. American courts have not hesitated to imply a good faith obligation in consumer contracting relationships, and on occasion have imposed heavy penalties, including punitive damages, for a breach of the duty.[30]

IV. The Draft Restatement of Law: Consumer Contracts

Commenting on both of these common law doctrines, in April 2016 a team of contract and consumer law experts at the American Law Institute released a draft Restatement of the Law, Consumer Contracts.[31] This Restatement draft, focusing solely on consumer contracts, is an attempt to supplement the more general Restatement (Second) of Contract principles, recognising that consumer contracts present unique challenges and situations that justify special treatment. The Restatement drafters approached the project by recognising two important trends in consumer law that have emerged over the past several decades.

A. Contract Formation

First is the emphasis courts place on contract formation principles: a requirement that there be mutual assent to contract terms. The draft recognises that this trend has generally favoured businesses because they have found little difficulty getting consumers to 'agree' to standard contract terms without understanding the details or import of what they are agreeing to. Technological developments have facilitated this trend, as 'clickwrap' agreements proliferate and consumers find themselves agreeing to something but not taking the time (or having the ability) to understand the standard terms to which they are expressing their consent. The contract formation process is thus not a process of true

[30] See Note, 'Implied Covenants of Good Faith and Fair Dealing: Loose Cannons of Liability for Financial Institutions' (1987) 40 *Vanderbilt Law Review* 1197.

[31] The Restatement has no force of law in the United States. But like the Restatement (Second) of Contracts (and Restatements of the law in numerous other fields), an ALI-approved Restatement addressing consumer contracts could prove influential in the development of consumer contract law across the United States. Courts often use Restatement provisions when deciding cases, and when they do so the Restatement provisions become part of the common law of the United States.

'mutual assent', yet courts usually hold consumers to the standard contract terms unless they are prohibited by statute or regulation, are deemed to be unconscionable or breach a duty of good faith and fair dealing that the business is deemed to owe the consumer.

B. Prohibited Terms

The second trend recognised by the drafters is the tendency of government regulators (for example the FTC, state agency enforcers or legislatures) to prohibit the use of certain terms in consumer contracts that are deemed to be particularly unfair, surprising or oppressive. The draft recognises the interplay between this trend and the 'mutual assent' trend. Businesses get consumers technically to 'assent' to terms that favour the business more and more, and regulators react by putting limits on how far they can go in imposing onerous terms on unwitting consumers. The draft thus provides that standard contract terms become part of a consumer contract only if the consumer has been given 'reasonable notice of the standard contract terms' and a 'meaningful opportunity to review them'.[32] The draft also permits businesses to impose standard contract terms after the consumer has first signified assent to the transaction, but only if the consumer has a reasonable opportunity to terminate the contractual relationship after the standard terms are available for review. Modifications of standard contract terms are covered by these same rules (reasonable opportunity for review and right to terminate).[33] Moreover, if a standard term gives the business discretion in performing its obligations, that discretion must be exercised in good faith.[34] The meaning of good faith is the same as in the UCC: honesty in fact and observance of reasonable standards of fair dealing.[35]

V. Conclusion

While there are a wide variety of statutes and common law decisions that prohibit the use of unfair contract terms in consumer contracts in the United States, there are numerous areas of commerce that go unaddressed. Particularly as new forms of contracting and new types of consumer transactions emerge, it becomes difficult for state and federal regulators to monitor unfair terms in their various and evolving forms. Even more difficult is the ability of courts to monitor unfair terms at common law. Cases must first be brought to court for a decision. Given the small amount in controversy in many consumer cases, the vast majority of disputes do not get litigated. Moreover, fewer

[32] Draft Restatement of the Law, Consumer Contracts, § 2. The draft does not specify what constitutes 'reasonable notice' and 'meaningful opportunity to review', although draft Comment 7 states that 'the test for adequacy of notice depends on whether it is conspicuous enough to reasonably alert the consumer to the existence of terms'. Presumably, courts would give meaning to these terms as they decide individual cases or class actions.

[33] Adopting the rule of Art 2 of the Uniform Commercial Code, modifications of standard terms do not need new consideration to be binding, so long as they comply with the doctrine of good faith. Draft Restatement of the Law, Consumer Contracts, § 3.

[34] Draft Restatement of the Law, Consumer Contracts, § 4.

[35] ibid, § 1(7).

consumer cases are being litigated in court due to the increased presence of mandatory arbitration in consumer contracts. Even cases that make it to court often take years to complete, which makes for painstakingly slow going in the regulation of unfair terms by case decisions.

At present, there is little political impetus to address unfair terms at the federal level, and this is not likely to change for the foreseeable future. That leaves the regulation of unfair terms largely to the states and their elected legislative bodies, which leads to a wide variety of approaches depending on the political climate in each state. Given these circumstances, the American experiment with incremental, piecemeal regulation of unfair contract terms can be expected to continue for many years to come.

25

Australasia

GAIL PEARSON

I. Structure of Law

Australia does not have a consumer Code. It is a Federation with Commonwealth (national) and State law. The Competition and Consumer Act 2010 (Cth) which includes the Australian Consumer Law as Schedule 2, is both Commonwealth and State law.[1] For financial services, the Australian Securities and Investments Commission Act 2001 (Cth) partly echoes the Australian Consumer Law.[2] The Corporations Act 2001 (Cth) and the National Consumer Credit Protection Act 2009 (Cth) also provide financial consumer protection. A major driver for the Competition and Consumer Act, which replaced the Trade Practices Act 1974 (Cth), was harmonisation between Australian and New Zealand consumer laws, namely the Consumer Guarantees Act 1993 and the Fair Trading Act 1986.[3] There is ongoing cooperation through Consumer Affairs Australia New Zealand (CAANZ). The Australian Consumer Law may apply to cross-border transactions.[4] Other influences include the laws of the United Kingdom,[5] European Union[6] and United States.[7]

[1] Australian Consumer Law and Fair Trading Act 2012 (Vic), s 8. Fair Trading Act 1987 (NSW), s 28. The reason for this dual State, Federal law is the Commonwealth Constitution which sets out Commonwealth heads of power. Residual powers to make law lie with the States. On jurisdiction see *Walker v Sell* [2016] FCA 1259 [77]–[88]. See also S Corones et al (eds), 'Comparative Analysis Overseas Consumer Policy Frameworks' (April 2016), paras 1.2, 1.3.

[2] Competition and Consumer Act 2010 (Cth), s 131A(1). The bifurcation in consumer protection between financial services and the rest, occurred in 1989. Previously the then Trade Practices Act 1974 (Cth) applied economy-wide. This has persisted despite recommendations by the Productivity Commission for one national consumer law, including financial services. See Productivity Commission, 'Review of Australia's Consumer Policy Framework' 2 vols (2008).

[3] This is particularly evident in consumer guarantees. J Paterson, 'The New Consumer Guarantee Law and the Reasons for Replacing the Regime of Statutory Implied Terms in Consumer Transactions' (2011) 35(1) *Melbourne University Law Review* 252.

[4] In *ACCC v Valve Corporation (No 3)* [2016] FCA 196 a choice of law and a choice of jurisdiction clause were ineffective in respect of an e-commerce transaction.

[5] For a useful account see J Goldring, 'The Contracts Review Act (NSW)' (1981) 4 *University of New South Wales Law Journal* 1.

[6] See D Harland, 'Influence of European Law on Product Liability' (1995) 17 *Sydney Law Review* 336; M Tsui, 'The State of the Art Defence: Defining the Australian Experience in the Context of Pharmaceuticals' (2013) 13 (1) *Queensland University of Technology Law Review* 132; M Guihot, 'Putting the "Personal" back into injury: An interpretation of Pt 3-5 of the ACL' (2014) 21(3) *Competition and Consumer Law Journal* 232.

The strong culture of voluntary business self-regulation and industry codes of conduct is partly associated with the notion of responsive regulation.[8] There is private and public enforcement of consumer laws. Individuals are likely to commence in state tribunals or complain to an ombudsman body. Regulatory litigation is likely to commence in the Federal Court or if by a State, the Supreme Court or a tribunal. The 2017 review of the Australian Consumer Law recommended easier enforcement and increased penalties, which were then raised.[9]

II. Information and Right of Withdrawal

There is no general right to pre-contractual information, though some products and transactions require pre-contractual disclosure, which includes information about the person the consumer may deal with and the product or service. The Australian Consumer Law regulates information for unsolicited consumer agreements, including the right to terminate within 10 days, which persists even if the contract is executed.[10] If the requisite information is not supplied, the cooling-off period is extended to six months and the dealer may be liable to a pecuniary penalty.[11] Advocates discuss opt-in as an alternative to ineffective cooling-off.[12] There are no comparable provisions under the Australian Securities and Investments Commission Act. There is a generic precontractual information disclosure regime for financial services in the Corporations Act,[13] which does have cooling-off provisions.[14]

The Australian Consumer Law includes mandatory information standards for some goods,[15] including product information standards about care of clothes.[16] An information standard can be made by digital publication.[17] There are also State product information standards,[18] including for second-hand cars.[19]

[7] RM Dietrich, 'Federal Trade Commission and Consumer Protection' (1973) 1 *Australian Business Law Review* 204. For s 52 (now s 18 of the Australian Consumer Law) and the Australian Securities and Investments Commission Act, s 12DA see Corones et al, 'Comparative Analysis Overseas', para 2.2.

[8] Some Codes, particularly those regulating business to business conduct are mandatory, eg the Franchising Code see www.accc.gov.au/business/industry-codes.

[9] 'Australian Consumer Law Review: Final Report' (March 2017), pp 80, 87.

[10] Australian Consumer Law, ss 69, 74, 76, 82(2), 86.

[11] ibid, s 82(3)(d), ss 74–77.

[12] See http://consumeraction.org.au/cooling-off-periods-consumers-dont-work-study/; *Australian Competition & Consumer Commission v Origin Energy Electricity Limited* [2015] FCA 278.

[13] Corporations Act (Australia), ss 941D, 941A, 941B, 1012A, 1012B, 1012C, 1014A, 946C, 942DA, 947E.

[14] ibid, s 1019B.

[15] Australian Consumer Law, ss 134, 135. Supplying goods or services that do not conform with the information standards is prohibited: Australian Consumer Law, ss 136, 137. It is an offence to supply goods or services that do not comply with the information standards: Australian Consumer Law, ss 203, 204. Standards under the Trade Practices Act became standards under the Australian Consumer Law: Trade Practices Amendment (Australian Consumer Law) Act (No 2) 2010, Schedule 7 item 5.

[16] See Australian Competition & Consumer Commission, 'Care labelling for clothing and textile products: Supplier guide' (2011).

[17] Australian Consumer Law, s 134.

[18] Fair Trading Regulation 2012 (NSW).

[19] See *Burton v Chad One Pty Limited* [2013] NSWDC 301.

There is a distinction in the Australian Consumer Law between consumer guarantees and express warranties against defects such as a representation by the supplier that he will repair or replace the goods. Any express warranty against defects must include a statement that goods already come with non-excludable guarantees that could provide a refund, compensation, repair or replacement.[20]

The regulator may issue a notice requiring a supplier to substantiate claims made about a product.[21] This is an important aid in ensuring consumers obtain accurate information.

III. Sale of Goods

There are two regimes for the sale of goods. The Australian Consumer Law national regime stipulates mandatory consumer guarantees if goods are supplied to a consumer in the course of trade and commerce. Most are familiar. They provide that the seller has the right to dispose of the goods; the consumer will have undisturbed possession; that the goods are free from undisclosed securities; of acceptable quality; fit for a disclosed purpose; correspond with description; and if sold by sample or demonstration model, will correspond; that spare parts and repair will be available for a reasonable period; and compliance with an express warranty given by the manufacturer or supplier.[22] The second regime is the implied terms in the State sale of goods legislation.[23] For services, there is a consumer guarantee the service will be rendered with due skill and care, fit for a communicated purpose, and supplied within reasonable time.[24]

Both an implied term and a consumer guarantee may be relevant. One is a contractual term and the other a statutory right. The preservation of both is important for the case of sales that are not in trade or commerce.[25] It was not uncommon for matters to be run using both State law and the now repealed Trade Practices Act.[26]

As State tribunals have considered consumer guarantees more than courts, there has been limited development of the distinction between a major failure and a non-major one for the purpose of remedies.[27] There is a statutory remedial regime for the guarantees. If the failure of the guarantee is non-major, the supplier can choose a refund, replacement or repair.[28] If it is a major failure, or if the supplier fails to remedy, the consumer may reject the goods or claim compensation.[29] Rejection allows the consumer

[20] Competition and Consumer Regulations 2010 (Cth), reg 90(2).

[21] Australian Consumer Law, s 219; Australian Securities and Investments Commission Act, s 12GY.

[22] Australian Consumer Law, ss 51–59.

[23] For example, Sale of Goods Act 1923 (NSW). This retains the consumer sale provisions.

[24] Australian Consumer Law, ss 60–62; Australian Securities and Investments Commission Act, s 12ED.

[25] See *Walker v Sell* [2016] FCA 1259 [69], [72] which involved 'an informal online sales platform used by private individuals'.

[26] *Sovereign Grange Pty Ltd v Bridgestone Australia Ltd* [2014] WADC 147.

[27] See *ACCC v Jayco Corporation Pty Ltd* [2020] FCA 1672.

[28] Australian Consumer Law, s 261. See Productivity Commission, 'Issues Paper, Right to Repair' (December 2020), which also addresses software.

[29] Australian Consumer Law, s 263, s 259. See *ACCC v Ford Motor Company of Australia Limited* [2018] FCA 703.

to claim a refund or replacement goods.[30] The consumer can take action against the supplier or the manufacturer.[31] The regulator can bring an action against the supplier or manufacturer for failure to comply with the consumer guarantees.[32]

Court action brought by the Australian Competition and Consumer Commission (ACCC) and state agencies on the consumer guarantees has focused on misleading conduct regarding the effect of the guarantees more than failure to comply with a consumer guarantee.[33] Representations about extended or 'voluntary' warranties (a form of warranty against defects) which are sold to consumers, risk being misleading.[34]

IV. Unfair Contract Terms

Prior to the Australian Consumer Law, there was no national regime for unfair contract terms in consumer contracts.[35] Under both State and national laws the entirety of the contract or part of the contract could be set aside for unjustness[36] or for unconscionability.[37] The provisions of the Australian Consumer Law on unfair terms address substantive unfairness. They apply to standard form contracts with consumers and small business, terms of which are void if unfair.[38] The Australian Competition and Consumer Commission recommends unfair terms should be prohibited, not just void.[39]

The legislation does not apply to terms that define the main subject matter of the contract or set the upfront price under the contract.[40] It contains a grey list of 14 types of terms that may, or may not, be unfair.[41] In comparison with the earlier Victorian unfair terms legislation, lack of good faith is not an explicit requirement to find a term is unfair.[42] Good faith comes in as a statutory norm through the list of factors that a court may consider to decide if conduct is unconscionable, not if a term is unfair. This is formulated as 'the extent to which the acquirer and the supplier acted in good faith'.[43]

The unfair contract terms regime in the Australian Consumer Law is echoed in the Australian Securities and Investment Commission Act and both agencies, the Competition and Consumer Commission and the Securities and Investments Commission, have enforcement obligations. Neither regulator pre-approves terms.

[30] Australian Consumer Law, s 263.

[31] ibid, s 271. Actions against the manufacturer are limited to acceptable quality, description, express warranties and repairs or spare parts.

[32] ibid, s 227.

[33] *ACCC v Jetstar Airways Pty Ltd* [2019] FCA 797.

[34] *ACCC v Fisher & Paykel Customer Services Pty Ltd* [2014] FCA 1393.

[35] There were provisions in the Fair Trading Act 1999 (Victoria) (repealed).

[36] Contracts Review Act 1980 (NSW).

[37] Trade Practices Act 1974 (Cth) (repealed).

[38] Australian Consumer Law, s 23; Australian Securities and Investments Commission Act, s 12BF. See *ACCC v Get Qualified Australia Pty Ltd (in liquidation) (No 2)* [2017] FCA 709.

[39] ACCC, 'Customer Loyalty Schemes, Final Report' (December 2019), Recommendation 2 at p vii; ACCC, 'Digital Platforms Inquiry' (July 2019), Recommendation 20 at p 27.

[40] Australian Consumer Law, s 26(1).

[41] ibid, s 25.

[42] Commenting on this see A, Sims, 'Unfair Contract Terms: A New Dawn in Australia and New Zealand' (2013) 39(3) *Monash University Law Review* 739 at 754.

[43] Australian Consumer Law, s 22.

Both regulators may enforce the law and a person may bring a private action. Regulatory action and private action take the form of seeking a declaration from the court that a term is unfair. For the person, this means that the term is void and if the contract cannot survive without the term, the contract is void. If a party seeks to rely on an unfair term, the court may make a variation order.

A court may also grant an injunction.[44] An injunction may be ordered for a past contravention whether or not it appears the person will engage in the conduct again or there is damage to another person.[45]

V. Product Liability

Australia has a strict product liability regime. Directed to overcoming problems with proving negligence, it is often argued in conjunction with an action for negligence. Product liability actions were also brought alongside breach of the contractual term of merchantable quality.

Product liability in the Australian Consumer Law rests on the goods having a safety defect. The standard is that goods should be as safe as 'persons generally are entitled to expect' having regard to matters including marketing, packaging, instructions and warnings, what might reasonably be expected to be done with them and the time the manufacturer supplied them.[46] This is an objective standard not linked to any particular person; it does not mean that goods are risk free.[47]

Liability rests on the manufacturer or manufacturers. The manufacturer may include the importer or a person who puts their mark on the goods.[48] There are four liability actions: a defective good injuries and causes loss to an individual; the above occurs and some other person suffers loss; defective goods damage other domestic goods and cause loss; and defective goods damage land used for a domestic purpose and cause loss.[49] Liability arises at the time of supply, that is when goods are supplied by their actual manufacturer.[50] There is no action if the matter is governed by a workers' compensation claim or if the loss could be recovered under a law giving effect to an international agreement.[51]

Australia has a state-of-the-art defence. This was successful in *Merck Sharp & Dohme*.[52]

[44] ibid, s 232.

[45] ibid, s 29(1)(m). In *ACCC v Chrisco Hampers Australia Limited No 2* [2016] FCA 144 the court considered but did not order an injunction as there was little chance Chrisco would continue to use a written and website term that had been declared unfair. This was about false representation of rights to terminate the agreement, in this case a lay-by agreement.

[46] Australian Consumer Law, s 9.

[47] *ACCC v Glendale Chemical Products Pty Ltd* (1998) 40 1PR 619, per Emmett J at 629; *Carey-Hazell v Getz Bros & Co (Aust) Pty Ltd* (2004) ATPR 42-014 at [186]; *Merck Sharp & Dohme (Australia) Pty Ltd v Peterson* [2011] FCAFC 128 at [191].

[48] Australian Consumer Law, s 7.

[49] ibid, ss 138–41.

[50] ibid, s 143(2).

[51] ibid, s 146.

[52] This was successful in *Merck Sharp & Dohme (Australia) Pty Ltd v Peterson* [2011] FCAFC 128.

The consumer guarantees can be enforced against a manufacturer and safety comes in via acceptable quality.[53] There are restrictions on recovering from the manufacturer including a time limit.[54] Damages include consequential loss that is loss reasonably foreseeable as a result of the failure of the guarantee.[55]

VI. Product Safety

A general product safety obligation is being considered. The architecture for safety regulation is complex as it is divided between the multiple regulator model through which the Australian Consumer Law is administered and a series of specialist regulators. Different regulators are responsible for different products.[56]

Unsafe products that may injure any person may be subject to an interim ban[57] or banned outright.[58] The Australian Consumer Law prohibits and imposes pecuniary penalties for supplying products or product related services that do not comply with product safety standards,[59] or are banned permanently or in the interim.[60] There is a prohibition on exporting goods that do not comply with a safety standard;[61] compulsory and voluntary product recalls;[62] and warning notices if goods are under investigation for causing injury.[63] There is a further safeguard. Suppliers must report if goods or related services are associated with death, serious injury or illness.[64] The supplier's knowledge may come from a range of sources including consumers, resuppliers, repairers and insurers.[65]

There are around 40 mandatory safety standards on the Product Safety Australia website run by the Australian Competition and Consumer Commission.[66] They are predominantly about products used for or by children and now include button battery products.[67] Product safety standards may involve markings or warnings on a product. Failure to provide the correct warning may result in a product recall.[68]

[53] Australian Consumer Law, s 271.
[54] ibid, s 273.
[55] ibid, s 272(1)(b).
[56] www.productsafety.gov.au/about-us/who-regulates-what; Productivity Commission, 'Consumer Law Enforcement and Administration Report' (March 2017).
[57] Australian Consumer Law, s 109.
[58] ibid, s 114.
[59] ibid, ss 106, 107.
[60] ibid, ss 119, 118.
[61] ibid, s 106(5). It is possible to obtain permission to do so.
[62] ibid, ss 122, 128.
[63] ibid, s 129.
[64] ibid, ss 131, 132. See ibid, s 2 for a definition of serious injury or illness. This is something that requires medical or surgical treatment under the supervision of a medical practitioner or nurse. It is an offence if the supplier fails to give the required notice: s 202.
[65] ibid, s 131(4).
[66] www.productsafety.gov.au/product-safety-laws/safety-standards-bans/mandatory-standards. The Federal Register of legislation shows twenty made under the Competition and Consumer Act. www.legislation.gov.au/Browse/Results/ByTitle/LegislativeInstruments/InForce/C/73/0/principal.
[67] Consumer Goods (Products Containing Button/Coin Batteries) Safety Standard 2020; ACCC, 'Button battery safety Assessment of regulatory options Consultation paper' (March 2020).
[68] *BMW Australia Limited v Australian Competition & Consumer Commission* [2004] FCAFC 167.

VII. Adaption to the Digital Age

The 'Digital Platforms Inquiry' is an international landmark embracing data protection, competition and consumer protection.[69] There are consumer data rights in the Competition and Consumer Act.[70] Digital products and services fall under the generic consumer law. The Australian Competition and Consumer Commission was successful against Apple, which contravened the Australian Consumer Law by misleading the public about the characteristics of goods.[71] It was unsuccessful against Google when it argued that Google was liable for misleading 'sponsored link' advertisements generated via a Google service.[72] Other decisions include misleading price comparison claims on an international platform,[73] advertisements for subscriptions to mobile phone ringtones and video games[74] and for so called 'free bets' on gambling websites.[75]

The decision in *Valve Corporation (No 3)* held that downloads from an international online delivery platform for video games may be a supply of goods.[76] The definition of goods includes 'Computer software'.[77] The definition of services in the Australian Consumer Law specifically excludes 'rights or benefits being the supply of goods'.[78] A contract for services can include a supply of goods. In order to work, the video games needed computer software and also 'non-executable data such as music and html images'.[79] The Court said that the non-executable data was not a good. It accompanied and was incidental to the computer software, and it was 'hard to see how it could be decoupled from the computer software'[80] which was a good. What was being supplied was games; computer software was at the heart of the provision of the games. Consumers believed they were purchasing computer software.[81] The Court rejected Valve's argument that since consumers required a licence to obtain and use the video games, there was no supply of goods.

VIII. Unfair Commercial Practices

There is no embracing concept of unfair commercial practices to prohibit conduct that in all the circumstances is unfair.[82] Lack of fairness is considered obliquely in concert

[69] ACCC, 'Digital Platforms Inquiry' (July 2019).
[70] Competition and Consumer Act, Part 1VD.
[71] Australian Consumer Laws 33; *ACCC v Apple Pty Limited* [2012] FCA 646.
[72] *Google Inc v ACCC* [2013] HCA 1 [20].
[73] *ACCC v Trivago NV* [2020] FCA 16.
[74] *Global One Mobile Entertainment Pty Ltd v ACCC* [2012] FCAFC 134.
[75] *ACCC v Hillside (Australia New Media) Pty Ltd trading as Bet365* [2015] FCA 1007.
[76] *ACCC v Valve Corporation (No 3)* [2016] FCA 196 at [13]–[23].
[77] Australian Consumer Law, s 2(1). This circumvented the issue of whether the characterisation of digital data was different depending on whether it was supplied on a physical medium or not. See [2016] FCA 196 [137].
[78] Australian Consumer Laws, s 2 (1).
[79] [2016] FCA 196 [138], [139].
[80] ibid, [156].
[81] ibid, [157].
[82] However, see ACCC, 'Digital Platforms Inquiry', Recommendation 21 at p 37.

with other doctrines, in particular misleading or deceptive conduct, unconscionable conduct and the prohibition on unfair terms in standard form contracts. The first applies to all consumer and commercial dealings, with limited carve-outs for designated financial services documents;[83] the second applies to consumer and business contracts other than those with a listed public company;[84] the third also applies to consumer and small business contracts.[85] These doctrines sometimes fall short.[86]

It is fair to say that the prohibition against misleading or deceptive conduct or conduct that is likely to mislead or deceive is the one of the most powerful provisions in Australian law. It cuts across traditional boundaries of legal categories and is as influential in property and intellectual property law as in contract and consumer law. It can be enforced by anyone with an interest (the public in general), and there is a range of statutory remedies from injunction to damages. Provisions that explicitly prohibit certain types of false representations about goods or services complement the general prohibition.[87]

The first unconscionable conduct provision imports Australia's highly developed equity jurisprudence into the statute.[88] The second looks specifically to the supply of goods and services and provides a list of factors a court may take into account.[89] Mere disparity of bargaining power and the exercise of that power will, not of itself, make a bargain unconscionable.[90] Unconscionable conduct is conduct against conscience by reference to the norms of society.[91]

The unfair terms provisions apply to consumer and small business contracts.[92] There is a grey list of potentially unfair terms.[93] Two deal with industry codes of practice.

IX. Access to Justice

The framework for consumer claims changed with consolidation of civil and administrative tribunals. The Civil and Administrative Tribunal (NSW) has a commercial and consumer division,[94] and jurisdiction to hear matters under the Australian Consumer Law.[95] Matters can go to an Appeal Panel on limited grounds including if the decision of the Tribunal was not fair and equitable.[96] Matters can be transferred from the tribunal

[83] Australian Consumer Law, s 18; Australian Securities and Investments Commission Act, s 12DA.
[84] Australian Consumer Law, ss 20–22; Australian Securities and Investments Commission Act, ss 12CA, 12CB, 12CC.
[85] Australian Consumer Law, s 23; Australian Securities and Investments Commission Act, s 12BF.
[86] *ACCC v Kobelt* [2019] HCA 18.
[87] Australian Consumer Law, ss 29, 34, 48. *ACCC v viagogo AG* [2019] FCA 544.
[88] Australian Consumer Law, s 20.
[89] ibid, ss 21, 22.
[90] *Paciocco v Australia and New Zealand Banking Group Limited* [2016] HCA 28 [293] per Keane J. See also *ACCC v Woolworths Limited* [2016] FCA 1472.
[91] *ACCC v Lux Distributors Pty Ltd* [2013] FCAFC 90 at [41].
[92] Australian Consumer Law, s 23(3), (4).
[93] ibid, ss 27, 25.
[94] Civil and Administrative Tribunal Act 2013 (NSW), s 16. Until October 2015, the relevant legislation in New South Wales was the Consumer Claims Act 1998 (NSW).
[95] *Lam v Steve Jarvin Motors* [2016] NSWCATAP 186.
[96] Civil and Administrative Tribunal Act 2013 (NSW), Schedule 4, s 12(1).

to a court if the parties agree or if the Tribunal so directs.[97] The Tribunal can make orders if the proceedings are conducted in a way that disadvantages a party.[98] There are ombudsmen services for financial services, energy and telecommunications but no retail ombudsman.

It is possible to bring class actions against suppliers. A class may be defined by individuals or criteria and involve a litigation funder. The bank fees case was a class action. This was unsuccessful, but did alter the law on penalties in Australia.[99]

The regulators can and do take enforcement action. This includes taking an undertaking, which if breached can be subject to a court order.[100] Other actions include substantiation notices, public warning notices, and other non-punitive orders,[101] instituting proceedings for pecuniary penalties, seeking an injunction and compensation orders.[102] The regulator can take a defective goods representative action on behalf of persons who have suffered loss or damage.[103]

[97] ibid, Schedule 4, s 6.
[98] ibid, Schedule 4, s 10.
[99] [2016] HCA 28; *Andrews v Australia and New Zealand Banking Group Ltd* [2012] HCA 30.
[100] Australian Consumer Law, s 218.
[101] ibid, ss 219, 223, 246.
[102] ibid, ss 228, 232, 237.
[103] ibid, s 149(1).

26

Latin America

MARTA CANTERO GAMITO

I. Introduction

This chapter provides a short comparative analysis of the main issues and trends in Asian consumer law as identified in the different national reports of this volume. The exploration is made from the different experiences in the development and application of consumer protection legislation in selected Latin American countries. A key basis for this chapter is a project analysing consumer law in Latin America.[1] Similarly to the chapters in this volume on consumer protection in Asia, national experts in Latin American countries produced national reports providing an overview of the most salient issues regarding specific substantive aspects and identified the main consumer problems as well as the institutional and procedural design for the application of consumer rules in each jurisdiction.

The origin, evolution and influences of consumer law in Latin American countries offer certain similarities to the general observations made in relation to the Asian consumer law perspectives: relatively 'young' regimes, similar consumer-related problems, limited judicial application of consumer rights and remedies and notable influences (more indirectly than directly) from European consumer law and from other countries at the forefront regarding consumer law within the respective regions.

The chapter offers, first, a brief overview of consumer protection law in Latin America. Secondly, it provides some observations regarding identified influences in the development of Latin American consumer law. Before the examination of substantive aspects, this contribution highlights the focus of consumer protection legislation on consumers' vulnerability as a central feature of consumer law in the American region, and contrasting with the understanding of consumer protection in Asia. Then the chapter succinctly highlights parallel issues in both regional areas under examination, and concludes with perceived similarities in the enforcement of consumer rules and their implications for consumers' access to justice.

[1] 'An Introduction to the Issue of Consumer Law in South America' *Journal of Consumer Policy* 45(3):1–6 (March 2022).

II. Consumer Protection in Latin America: An Overview

The adoption of consumer protection legislation in Latin America came about in the late 1980s to early 1990s, comparatively later than other consumer regimes such as those in the United States or European Union.[2] The deeper reason is the belated democratisation process in countries such as Argentina, Brazil and Chile which, after the Second World War, had suffered from difficult years of dictatorship, and economic and political turmoil. That is why, contrary to the United States and the earlier EU Member States, the rise of consumer protection is deeply connected to the democratisation process, a phenomenon which is known also in Portugal and Spain. These particular circumstances have left deep traces in the understanding and the role of consumer protection. Consumer law in Latin American countries is more often than not anchored in the national Constitution and consumer rights are connected to fundamental rights.[3] Key questions about the direction the law has to take, like the societal and social dimension of consumer policy, are turned into constitutional conflicts, where the highest courts in these countries have to decide. More down to earth there is another reason, the late privatisation of former public utilities which boosted consumer protection in the EU after democratisation processes and led to consumer protection rules even in countries like Cuba, which has a mixed economy, a dual currency, dual ownership and dual markets. However, the late incorporation of consumer rules to national regulatory frameworks did not prevent Latin American countries from rapidly 'catching up' with their international counterparts so that throughout the 1990s most Latin American countries had already enacted consumer-related rules.

Despite existing divergences between the different countries and legal cultures, the development of consumer protection legislations in Latin America, as well as their problems, run in parallel across jurisdictions. Generally, problems reside in the enforcement of consumer rules, with only few cases reaching the court, and resulting in an excessive reliance on administrative authorities which, although not always institutionally efficient, have become the main venue for obtaining consumer redress.

To date, consumer protection in Latin American countries is largely harmonised as a result of international initiatives, such as the UN Guidelines for Consumer Protection or the UNCTAD COMPAL Programme,[4] and the mediated incorporation of EU consumer law through the inspiration in consumer rules from countries such as France, Spain or Portugal in the design of the different national regimes, resulting in a certain Europeanisation of Latin American consumer law. Brazil, though, has taken the lead in

[2] For a very comprehensive overview of the reasons leading to a late flourishing of consumer law in Latin America see C Carranza Álvarez and OA Alcántara Francia, 'Consumer Protection in Peru: Origins, Evolution and Main Regulatory Influences' *Journal of Consumer Policy* forthcoming. For an English reference, see RG Vaughn, 'Consumer Protection Laws in South America' (1993) 17 *Hastings International & Comparative Law Review* 275.

[3] E Arcelia Quintana Adriano, 'Fundamental Rights and Consumer Protection in Mexico' *Journal of Consumer Policy* forthcoming.

[4] COMPAL is an UNCTAD programme providing capacity building and institutional strengthening on competition and consumer protection matters to 17 beneficiary countries in Latin America (https://unctadcompal.org/). See also A Izaguerri, 'UNCTAD's Technical Cooperation Programme on Consumer Protection for Latin America: COMPAL' *Journal of Consumer Law* forthcoming.

South America. The Brazilian Consumer Protection Code has set a benchmark for the whole region. More often than not other South American countries refer either directly or indirectly to Brazilian legal rules and to their interpretation.

III. Influences in the Development of Consumer Law in Latin America

When Latin American countries started to develop consumer law, the United States and western European countries, and to some extent the European Economic Community (EEC), had already prepared the ground. In the United States consumer law started in the 1960s, in the old continental Member States and the United Kingdom in the 1970s, in the EEC (later the EU) by and large only after the adoption of the Single European Act in 1986, which paved the way for majority decision in the Council of Ministers. Projects that had been under discussion for more than a decade quickly passed the legislative process in the 1990s, for instance the Unfair Terms Directive.[5] Before 1986 the adoption of secondary EU legislation required unanimity. This was only achieved with regard to four directives: the Misleading Advertising Directive,[6] Product Liability Directive,[7] Doorstep Selling Directive[8] and the (first) Consumer Credit Directive.[9] This means when Latin American countries developed their consumer laws, the EU had also laid down a set of rules, but overall EU consumer law started to blossom under the majority principle in the 1990s. The influence of EU law varies between the countries, but overall it can be easily traced. The search for the EU influence, however, should not divert attention from the much more important fact that Brazil played a much stronger role than the EU in the making and the understanding of consumer law in the region.[10] At the same time, the 1990 Brazilian Consumer Code received influence from Europe (France, Germany, Spain and EU consumer law).[11] The EU's influence in the local consumer legislation can be summarised in the following.

The European Directive 93/13/EEC on unfair terms in consumer contracts and, later, the Unfair Commercial Practices Directive,[12] significantly influenced consumer

[5] Council Directive 93/13/EEC of 5 April 1993 on unfair terms in consumer contracts, OJ 1993 No L95, p 29.

[6] Council Directive 84/450/EEC of 10 September 1984 relating to the approximation of the laws, regulations and administrative provisions of the Member States concerning misleading advertising, OJ 1984 No L250, p 17.

[7] Council Directive 85/374/EEC of 25 July 1985 on the approximation of the laws, regulations and administrative provisions of the Member States concerning liability for defective products, OJ 1985 No L210, p 29.

[8] Council Directive 85/577/EEC of 20 December 1985 to protect the consumer in respect of contracts negotiated away from business premises, OJ 1985 No L372, p 31.

[9] Council Directive 87/102/EEC of 22 December 1986 for the approximation of the laws, regulations and administrative provisions of the Member States concerning consumer credit, OJ 1987 No L42, p 48.

[10] See Carranza Álvarez and Alcántara Francia, 'Consumer Protection in Peru'.

[11] See C Lima Marques and P Galindo da Fonseca, 'Consumer Protection in Brazil: The 2016 Report for the International Academy of Consumer Law' in H-W Micklitz and G Saumier (eds), *Enforcement and Effectiveness of Consumer Law* (Cham: Springer, 2018) 99.

[12] Directive 2005/29/EC of the European Parliament and of the Council of 11 May 2005 concerning unfair business-to-consumer commercial practices, OJ 2005 No L149, p 22.

protection in Latin America. The EU concept of unfairness was transplanted into national law, for example, in Chile and Cuba.[13] In Peru, the EU Product Liability Directive influenced the local regime for liability for defective products and the EU Unfair Terms Directive was received via the influence of Spanish consumer protection legislation, and incorporated the system of 'black' and 'grey' lists as well as the respective absolute and relative ineffectiveness of the clauses included in those lists.[14] The 1992 EU General Product Safety Directive[15] served as a model for product safety regulation in Uruguay,[16] while the Misleading Advertising Directive influenced advertising regulation in Brazil.[17]

Some Latin American countries have also adopted EU regulatory standards in certain sectors. Chilean legislation adopted the European approach regarding transparency requirements and essential contractual aspects included in the latest Consumer Credit Directive.[18] More recently, the EU General Data Protection Regulation (GDPR),[19] notoriously known for having set a benchmark for data protection legislations around the world, has been largely replicated as a data protection framework in Brazil.[20] Other examples include the incorporation of a similar mechanism to the European RAPEX[21] system (Rapid Exchange of Information System for dangerous products) in Chile.[22]

The regulatory influence of the European consumer *acquis* is also the result of commercial commitments. For instance, EU trade agreements required contracting parties to put in place mechanisms of consumer protection in e-commerce transactions.[23] Another example is the 2002 EU-Chile association agreement, currently under revision, which calls for more compatible consumer legislation with a view to reduce barriers to trade.[24] Past attempts at the harmonisation of European private law, such as the Principles of European Contract Law (PECL), also had an impact on these jurisdictions (for example in Argentina's consumer protection or the Cuban Civil

[13] R Momberg, ME Morales and A Pino-Emhart, 'Enforcement and Effectiveness of Consumer Law in Chile: A General Overview', in Micklitz and Saumier (eds), *Enforcement and Effectiveness of Consumer Law* 151.

[14] See Carranza Álvarez and Alcántara Francia, 'Consumer Protection in Peru', *Journal of Consumer Law* forthcoming.

[15] Council Directive 92/59/EEC of 29 June 1992 on general product safety, OJ 1992, No L228, p 24.

[16] D Szafir and H Marks, 'Influences of Comparative Law in Uruguayan Consumer Protection Law' *Journal of Consumer Policy* forthcoming.

[17] For a detailed overview of the EU rules that impacted Brazilian consumer protection legislation, see C Lima Marques and R Castellanos Pfeiffer, 'Dissemination of Consumer Law and Policy in Brazil: The Impact of European Law' *Journal of Consumer Policy* forthcoming.

[18] 2008/48/EC on credit agreements for consumers V Andrade, 'Chilean Consumer Law & Policy: A Brief Outlook' 16th Conference of the International Association of Consumer Law: Workshop 'Dissemination of Consumer Law and Policy in Africa, Asia, The Americas, and Australia'.

[19] Regulation (EU) 2016/679 of the European Parliament and of the Council of 27 April 2016 on the protection of natural persons with regard to the processing of personal data and on the free movement of such data, OJ 2016 No L119, p 1.

[20] Lei Geral de Proteção de Dados Pessoais (LGPD), Lei no 13.709, de 14 de agosto de 2018.

[21] Now 'Safety Gate'.

[22] Andrade, 'Chilean Consumer Law & Policy: A Brief Outlook', *Journal of Consumer Policy* forthcoming.

[23] For example, Article 166 of 'Trade Agreement between The European Union and its Member States, of the one part, and Colombia and Peru, of the other part' OJ 2012 No L354, p 3.

[24] Agreement establishing an association between the European Community and its Member States, of the one part, and the Republic of Chile, of the other part, OJ 2002 No L352, p 3; see Art 29.

Code). Some other sources of influence or inspiration are national laws, such as Italian or Spanish civil law in Argentina.[25] Also the incorporation of the UN and OECD guidelines on consumer protection have also influenced domestic regimes and contributed to the harmonisation of consumer law in the region. This does not mean though that Latin American countries are replicating consumer rules from each other or from the EU. Despite said influences, the current configuration of consumer law in some countries is the result of an idiosyncratic development of this field of law in their territories (for example Mexico, Chile or Argentina) or due to influences from within the region. One of the major characteristics is that each and every country defends its own particularities quite often in a sense of belongingness to the South American continent as a whole.

IV. The South American Particularity: Focus on the Vulnerable Consumer

Brazilian consumer protection is built around the vulnerability of consumers resulting in the imbalance of the contractual parties.[26] Due to the influence of the Brazilian Consumer Code on other jurisdictions, consumer vulnerability is also central in the development of consumer rules in Mexico, Bolivia, Colombia, El Salvador and Ecuador.[27] The recent recognition of consumer vulnerability in Argentina is seen as a necessary step towards a better consumer protection legislation.[28] Consumer protection legislation was also designed around the idea of consumer vulnerability in Venezuela until the socialist government replaced consumer legislation with a model entirely based on State control over private companies, resulting in the eventual repeal of consumer protection legislation in the country. This means that 'consumers' are no longer a special legal category which can use freedom of choice to decide which goods or services to acquire, but 'persons' with guaranteed access to the goods and services regulated by the administration.[29]

Lastly, despite the developments in consumer law over the last decades in Latin America, there are issues that remain unattended such as hypervulnerability and over-indebtedness of consumers, now especially critical due to Covid-19.[30] The pandemic has triggered an increase in prices and the escalation of consumer problems in the region, such as the increase of the electricity bill in Peru during lockdowns[31] or the lack

[25] P Aberastury and EB Sacristán, 'Argentina: Enforcement and Effectiveness of Consumer Law' in Micklitz and Saumier (eds), *Enforcement and Effectiveness of Consumer Law* 49.

[26] C Lima Marques, *Contratos No Código de Defesa Do Consumidor. O novo régime das relações contratuais* 6th ed (São Paulo: Editora Revista Dos Tribunais 2011).

[27] See Carranza Álvarez and Alcántara Francia, 'Consumer Protection in Peru'.

[28] Aberastury and Sacristán, 'Argentina: Enforcement and Effectiveness of Consumer Law', in Micklitz and Saumier (eds), *Enforcement and Effectiveness of Consumer Law* 49.

[29] JI Hernández, 'Compliance and Effectiveness of Consumer Law in Venezuela' in Micklitz and Saumer (eds), *Enforcement and Effectiveness of Consumer Law* 697.

[30] For a comprehensive analysis of consumers' vulnerability as a result of the pandemic, see L Pérez Bustamante, 'El consumidor latinoamericano como hipervulnerable: aspectos culturales, estructurales y geopolíticos de la desigualdad' *Deconomi*, Año III, n 4, p 1.

[31] 'Recibos de luz: ¿Por qué se facturó más durante la cuarentena?', rpp.pe, 17 July 2020.

of reimbursement due to flight cancellations in Chile, resulting in a collective claim, which was temporarily suspended by the court.[32]

V. The Substance of Consumer Law

A. Approach

Depending on the degree of sophistication, drawn with a rather broad brush, the consumer laws in South America are looking very much like those of the EU Member States. They are all enshrined in a consumer code, keeping the consumer law distinct from other bodies of law, in particular the respective civil codes. This might be due to their rather political character and the intention to set a sign with the adoption of a new law that is different from the old traditions and that heralds a new era, economically of a market society focused on the protection of the vulnerable, politically anchored in the new Constitution which reflects the achieved democracy. In the EU, consumer law is neither generally enshrined in a separate piece of law nor is it necessarily attached to the national Constitution. One of the key conflicts is whether EU consumer law is governed by the market rationale and whether and to what extent Member States can maintain and defend a more social outlook.[33]

The starting point in Latin American consumer codes is the 'consumer relationship': what in the western language is enshrined as business-to-consumer in Latin American countries is subject to political and even constitutional debates, cherished and condensed in the call for the protection of the vulnerable. By contrast, the constitutional dimension of consumer law is not that visible in Asia. Rather, there is a tendency to regard consumer protection as a market regulation tool than a individual right. As a result, the focus is not the consumer or the consumer rights, but the prevention of practices that may impair commercial transactions.[34]

Like in the United States and in the EU, consumer law focuses on consumer sales, on economic transactions that deal with the transfer of property of goods, potential defects and the call for appropriate remedies. Here potential tensions between the civil codes and the consumer codes are easily foreseeable and reflected in the reluctance of civil courts to apply the new consumer law in sales contracts, like for instance in Uruguay. There is not much new under the sun, neither in the distinction between hidden and apparent defects, nor in the available remedies, repair, price reduction, replacement or termination of the contract. Perhaps with one crucial exception: in Argentina, Brazil and Uruguay, the different actors in the supply chain are jointly liable. Another common element is the introduction of product liability. When it comes to consumer services, similar deficiencies as those identified in EU and Asian consumer law can be observed. Rules and services remain incremental and are mainly related to telecommunications, energy or financial services.

[32] 'Justicia chilena suspende demanda colectiva interpuesta contra Latam por cancelación de vuelos', larepublica.co, 21 July 2020.

[33] H-W Micklitz et al, *European Consumer Law* 2nd edn (Cambridge: Intersentia, 2014).

[34] F Trentmann, *Empire of Things* (London: Penguin, 2016) 355.

B. Information

Similarly to the Asian experience, the circumspect consumer does not appear to be a paradigm in the Latin American approach to consumer protection. While in the EU the information paradigm relies on the trader who has a duty to provide information by virtue of consumer law, in Latin America information is generally more of a right conferred by the civil or the commercial codes than a requirement to the trader.[35] As a result, information rights are actionable as a remedial solution, as it is found also in Macau.[36] This is significant in light of the shift in the burden of the proof; an issue contested in the different updates of EU consumer law and replicated in the renewal of the Brazilian Consumer Code.[37] The situation is different, however, when it comes to specific sectors such as consumer credit or off-premises consumer transactions.

C. Right of Withdrawal

Regarding the right of withdrawal, this is not generally granted under Latin American consumer legislation unless the transaction took place online[38] or concerns defective products, although as identified in Uruguay the application of withdrawal rights in case of defective products is often problematic.[39] This situation contrasts with that of Asian consumer protection, where cooling-off periods are more frequent even in transactions not necessarily conducted off-premises.[40] Such observation is remarkable in light of the foundation of consumer protection in Latin America. Despite the elevation of consumer protection as a fundamental right constitutionally protected, its operationalisation is more limited in these countries than in Asia.

D. Sale of Goods

Unlike other EU consumer law Directives, the Consumer Sales Directive[41] has not significantly influenced Latin American regimes. This is also the situation with regard to the incorporation of EU consumer law in Asia which, with exceptions, has not openly adopted the European approach to non-conformity remedies in consumer sales. By way of example, in Argentina, in case of non-conformity, the consumer should request the repair of the good and can only in case of unsatisfactory repair request the replacement

[35] For example, see G Sozzo and LV Bianchi, 'Influence of European Law on the Argentinian Consumer Law', *Journal of Consumer Policy*, forthcoming.

[36] See Wei and Patrício Rafael, 'Macau', in this volume.

[37] Lima Marques and Castellanos Pfeiffer, 'Dissemination of Consumer Law and Policy in Brazil', Journal of Consumer Policy (2022). https://doi.org/10.1007/s10603-022-09503-w.

[38] Sozzo and Bianchi, 'Influence of European Law on the Argentinian Consumer Law', Journal of Consumer Policy, 45, pp 7–26 (2022).

[39] D Szafir and H Marks, 'Influences of Comparative Law in Uruguayan Consumer Protection Law', Journal of Consumer Policy, 45, pp 103–119 (2022).

[40] See T Naude, 'Asian Consumer Law: An African Perspective', in this volume.

[41] Directive 1999/44/EC of the European Parliament and of the Council of 25 May 1999 on certain aspects of the sale of consumer goods and associated guarantees, OJ 1999 No L171, p 12.

of the good, the reduction of the price or the resolution of the contract.[42] Similarly, in Chile, the consumer must first exhaust the statutory guarantee before requesting the replacement of the good or the termination of the contract.[43]

E. Unfair Contract Terms

The development with regard to unfair contract terms is different from the substantive issues analysed so far. Thus, while the influence of the EU Unfair Terms Directive has been limited in Asian countries, it has been widely incorporated in Latin America under the influence of Spanish consumer protection legislation. Generally, consumer protection legislation in these jurisdictions has incorporated the EU system of 'black' and 'grey' lists as well as the respective absolute and relative ineffectiveness of the clauses included in those lists.[44] However, the lack of adoption of the European approach in Asia does not mean that legislation against unfair contract terms is not developed in these countries. For example, Taiwan has very sophisticated rules on unfair contract terms.[45]

F. Product Liability

The European Product Liability Directive widely influenced Latin American regimes of liability for defective products. As a result, and similarly to what has been observed in the majority of Asian jurisdictions, strict liability regimes are found in Argentina, Brazil, Chile or Uruguay as a result of the influence of the United States and the European models of product liability, and 'state of the art' defence is allowed. However, in Peru for instance, its application depends on whether liability is assessed by the court (compensation) or by the administrative entity in charge of consumer protection (remedies) and depending on whether the defect refers to a product or a service.[46]

G. Product Safety

Due to the constitutional nature of consumer protection in Latin America, product safety is of paramount importance, including the consideration of consumer safety as a constitutional right in Argentina and Uruguay. Generally, product safety rules provide not only specific consumer remedies but also detailed safety and information requirements on traders before placing the product or service in the market, similarly to the model established in the European General Product Safety Directive. In this regard, public authorities play an important role in controlling access to market and monitoring

[42] Sozzo and Bianchi, 'Influence of European Law on the Argentinian Consumer Law'.
[43] Andrade, 'Chilean Consumer Law & Policy'.
[44] See Carranza Álvarez and Alcántara Francia, 'Consumer Protection in Peru'.
[45] For details, see JG Fong, 'Taiwan (Republic of China)', in this volume. See also the reports for Hong Kong and Singapore.
[46] Carranza Álvarez and Alcántara Francia, 'Consumer Protection in Peru'.

safety requirements. However, product safety rules are scattered across different sectors. Although no specific reference to compliance with international standards is made in the national reports, MERCOSUR has created a Resolution establishing a system for harmful defective products,[47] but to date few countries have adopted this system.[48] Instead, international cooperation takes place only under bilateral trade agreements. The Chilean consumer authority, on the other hand, has opted for adopting the European RAPEX system (Rapid Exchange of Information System for dangerous products) for safety warnings regarding consumer goods, such as cars, electronic devices and toys.[49]

H. Adaptation to the Digital Age

Regarding the adaption of consumer rules to the digital age, Latin American countries are adopting specific regimes for online transactions. Brazil adopted in 2013 a consumer protection code for e-commerce, which took inspiration from the EU E-Commerce Directive,[50] the Distance Selling Directive[51] and the E-Privacy Directive.[52] More recently, the EU General Data Protection Regulation has been fundamentally replicated as a data protection framework in the country. The EU E-Commerce Directive has also influenced Argentinian consumer online protection. The situation in both Asia and Latin America is very similar in this regard, with a leading country incorporating changes and other slowly following. Thus, in the case of Latin America, while Brazil is at the forefront in the incorporation of the EU model of consumer protection online, other countries such as Cuba or Peru are still falling behind in the adaptation of the consumer legal framework to the digital age. In Chile, for instance, provisions concerning e-commerce transactions are argued to be insufficient.[53] Latin American jurisdictions are, nonetheless, currently adapting their legislations to the digital age, with such adaptation taking place under the consideration of consumer vulnerability in online environments.

I. Unfair Commercial Practices

The European rules have also influenced the regulation of unfair commercial practices in Latin America. Information obligations and the prohibition of misleading advertising are central in this regard. Similar to the Asian experiences, it is not surprising that no individual consumer remedies are provided, but rather administrative regimes

[47] Available at www.loa.org.ar/legNormaDetalle.aspx?id=29693.

[48] Szafir and Marks, 'Influences of Comparative Law in Uruguayan Consumer Protection Law'.

[49] Andrade, 'Chilean Consumer Law & Policy'.

[50] Directive 2000/31/EC of the European Parliament and of the Council of 8 June 2000 on certain legal aspects of information society services, in particular electronic commerce, in the Internal Market, OJ 2000 No L178, p 1.

[51] Directive 97/7/EC of the European Parliament and of the Council of 20 May 1997 on the protection of consumers in respect of distance contracts, OJ 1997 No L144, p 19.

[52] Directive 2002/58/EC of the European Parliament and of the Council of 12 July 2002 concerning the processing of personal data and the protection of privacy in the electronic communications sector, OJ 2002 No L201, p 37.

[53] Andrade, 'Chilean Consumer Law & Policy'.

consisting of prohibitions and fines in the event of unfair practices. The concept of unfairness remains largely homogeneous throughout the region. However, it is important to note that while the rationale of the EU regime of unfair commercial practices is mainly the proper functioning of the internal market, in Latin American countries the justification of prohibiting certain abusive practices is not purely instrumental but rather the materialisation of the consumer's dignity.[54]

VI. Enforcement of Consumer Law and Access to Justice

The enforcement of consumer law in Latin American countries largely relies on administrative enforcement. Consumer authorities play a very significant role in enforcing consumer protection in Argentina, Brazil, Mexico, Chile, Venezuela or Uruguay. However, the nature of these bodies is not as enforcement agencies. There have been legal and political discussions about the constitutionality of consumer authorities' powers. By way of example, in 2018, the Chilean Constitutional Court overruled the *ex officio* quasi regulatory powers of the Chilean Consumer authority (SERNAC: *Servicio Nacional del Consumidor*) granted by the national consumer protection legislation. The Constitutional Court held that adjudication powers would constitute the performance of activities typically of a judiciary nature, such as 'compulsory' mediation and conciliation, since it would involve the existence of conditions that would guarantee independence and impartiality and due process requirements which would be expected of any judicial procedure.[55] Notwithstanding this, the new legislation still reinforced SERNAC's powers and allowed the power of the authority to initiate collective procedures.

In terms of access to justice, the number of consumer disputes reaching the courts is small. In Cuba, for example, this is mainly due not only to high judicial fees and lengthy procedures but mainly to lack of consumer awareness about their rights.[56] Access to data on consumer-related cases is limited and it results in difficulty tracking the volume of consumer disputes reaching the judiciary given that these are classified as civil liability cases and not as consumer claims. Moreover, the design of small claims procedures does not generally take into account consumer needs and the characteristics of consumer disputes, which results in depriving consumers of effective judicial protection. The Brazilian Consumer Code established the creation of consumer law-specialised chambers in the courts, although special civil courts (*Juizado Cível Especial*) also play a role in the resolution of consumer-related disputes. However, the lengthy procedures (about one year to attend a hearing) offset the advantages associated with an institutional design that prioritises consumer enforcement.[57]

[54] Sozzo and Bianchi, 'Influence of European Law on the Argentinian Consumer Law'.

[55] Tribunal Constitucional, 18 de enero de 2018, Rol No 4012-17, available at www.tribunalconstitucional.cl/wp/ver.php?id=3621. Interestingly, this contrasts with the interpretation of the ECJ in joined cases C-317/08, C-318/08, C-319/08 and C-320/0, *Alassini and others* EU:C:2010:146, which concluded that a mandatory attempt at settlement does not involve, with regard to the objectives pursued, a disproportionate and intolerable interference which infringes upon the very substance of the rights guaranteed.

[56] N de la C Ojeda Rodríguez and T Peña Lorenzo, 'Consumer Protection Law in Cuba' *Journal of Consumer Policy*.

[57] Lima Marques and Galindo da Fonseca, 'Consumer Protection in Brazil'.

Collective redress is also a mechanism widely used for consumer-related problems. Despite not being regulated in an specific manner, Argentina has an opt-out system of collective action due to developments in the case law, which followed with specific rules in the consumer protection framework and amendments to the civil and commercial codes. Collective action for consumer problems is also growing in Chile, but although class action procedures have been in place in the country since 2004, few cases have been successful.[58]

Furthermore, despite the *lex specialis* character of consumer protection legislation, its application remains limited. There is an evident conflict between consumer law and the civil and commercial codes, where they exist. This is especially so in situations where a consumer case is decided in front of civil courts, where civil law provisions are usually applied. Moreover, consumer protection provisions have been gradually incorporated to specific sectors, such as public utilities or financial services. In those cases, although less common these days, civil judges have been traditionally prone to apply civil and contract law rules rather than what once was considered purely administrative provisions. In this regard, it is particularly interesting that the gradual incorporation of public law instruments in more recent revisions of consumer rules, such as the 2019 Chilean consumer protection legislation, has improved the application of consumer rules.

In sum, in Latin American jurisdictions, administrative enforcement systems based on monitoring, public prosecution and collective action remains a more efficient mechanism than private enforcement in the application of consumer law provisions.[59] However, in some instances, the number of layers of administrative enforcement makes it difficult for consumers to identify the competent body to which refer their complaints.[60] In this light, we find similarities in the enforcement of consumer rules between the two regions, namely an important role of administrative enforcement, a deficient system for judicial enforcement and a timid emergence of ODR mechanisms which is helping consumers to obtain (some) redress.

VII. Conclusions

From the perspective of consumer protection in Latin America, it can be said that the development of consumer law in Asia follows a similar path. Globalisation partially explains the perceived growing harmonisation of consumer protection rules across the globe. The global benchmark is set by those regimes that provide the most sophisticated rules as well as by those which rapidly respond to new scenarios. This explains why, despite the gradual displacement of economic power from Western economies, neither Asian nor Latin American countries are the ones setting the tone in establishing the rules for commerce in the twenty-first century. The rulemaker role is still performed by

[58] E. Muñoz Lamartine, 'The Politics of Consumer Rights in Latin America', available at https://clas.berkeley.edu/publications/politics-consumer-rights-latin-america.

[59] Lima Marques and R Castellanos Pfeiffer, 'Dissemination of Consumer Law and Policy in Brazil: The Impact of European Law' (2022) *Journal of Consumer Policy*, https://doi.org/10.1007/s10603-022-09503-w.

[60] Aberastury and Sacristán, 'Argentina: Enforcement and Effectiveness of Consumer Law', 49.

the United States and the EU legislator, and to some extent by private regulators establishing international technical standards.

Inside each of the regions compared in this chapter, there are leading countries which imprint their character into the consumer law within the region. In this regard, in particular Brazil, but also Macau and Singapore, stand as the countries where consumer law is most developed. Despite notable borrowings from susbtantive EU consumer law, each region is developing its own enforcement system, with significant variations across countries. Yet, it can be concluded that the enforcement of consumer rules seems limited across the globe. This appears to be the main challenge when it comes to consumer protection. In this light, it is important to note that while in the EU online dispute resolution has not fully taken off, countries such as Brazil or China are rapidly developing seemingly effective online venues for consumer redress.[61] The challenge is to replicate procedural guarantees and to materialise the rights conferred upon consumer law through new venues of enforcement.

[61] MJ Schmidt-Kessen, R Nogueira and M Cantero Gamito, 'Success or Failure? – Effectiveness of Consumer ODR Platforms in Brazil and in the EU' (2020) 43 *Journal of Consumer Policy* 659.

27

African Perspective

TJAKIE NAUDE

I. Introduction

This chapter aims to give an African perspective on the Asian reports in this book. South African law will be referred to most, but also a few other African laws. Space constraints prevent a more thorough study.

There is little conformity in Anglophone African consumer laws in respect of the various topics studied in this contribution. Although parts of the South African Consumer Protection Act[1] have influenced other laws in Africa,[2] wholescale transplanting has not taken place, and there remain differences in the details. It could be that attempts to create a single continental market via the African Continental Free Trade Agreement may at some point lead to some harmonisation of consumer law, in which case it may be justified to start speaking of an 'African consumer law' in the singular.

In places, this chapter refers to articles on consumer law in Anglophone Africa published in a special issue of the *Journal of Consumer Policy.*[3] For that project, contributors were asked to comment particularly on product safety and product liability, remedies for defective products, telecommunication services as well as interaction between their consumer law and foreign or supranational laws and agencies.[4] Although the parameters of that project are therefore not exactly the same as this one on Asian law, there is overlap and the projects were conceived of as linked from the start, inter alia with the goal of making scholarship on consumer law from Africa, Asia and South America more accessible.[5]

Before commenting on the particular aspects of consumer law covered by the Asian reports, the chapter will briefly comment on the scope of application of consumer protection law.

[1] Act No 68 of 2008.

[2] Including the Kenyan Consumer Protection Act No 46 of 2012, the Seychelles Consumer Protection Act No 30 of 2010, the Nigerian Federal Competition and Consumer Protection Act 2018, and the Zimbabwean Consumer Protection Act No 5 of 2019 (Cap 14:44).

[3] (2018) 41 *Journal of Consumer Policy*: 'Special Issue on Consumer Law and Policy in Africa'.

[4] See H-W Micklitz et al, 'Dissemination of Consumer Law and Policy in Africa, Asia, the Americas and Australia' (2018) 41 *Journal of Consumer Policy* 303.

[5] ibid.

II. Scope of Application of Consumer Protection Laws

South Africa has a more radical approach than the Asian countries regarding the scope of consumer protection laws. The South African Consumer Protection Act and the National Credit Act[6] protect not only traditional consumers but all sole traders and small juristic persons acting for the purpose of their businesses, regardless of the type of goods or services.[7] The juristic persons protected are defined with reference to asset value and annual turnover. Some of the provisions apply to franchising contracts, regardless of the franchisee's asset value or annual turnover. An example is the right to fair contract terms. The Kenyan Consumer Protection Act seems to have a similarly wide definition of consumers,[8] but does not even limit that definition to natural persons or otherwise to small juristic persons, as is done in South Africa.[9] By contrast, in Asian countries, protection is more limited. For example, in China the consumer must be a natural person who is purchasing goods or services 'for daily consumption'.[10] Similarly, in India if the customer obtains goods or services for resale or commercial purpose, they are not a consumer.[11] In Indonesia the consumer must be an end consumer, therefore not selling on the goods or services.[12]

III. Information Duties and Right of Withdrawal

A. Pre-contractual Information Duties

Some of the Asian countries impose greater duties to give pre-contractual information than South African law. For example, in Vietnam there is a general obligation to give information and fines are imposed if the supplier does not provide information on risks, availability of spare parts and warranties.[13] China requires information on quality, performance, use, validity period of goods and services.[14]

In South Africa, the National Credit Act does provide for a mandatory pre-contractual quotation document regarding, for example, the total cost of credit, which enables consumers to shop around.[15] The Kenyan Consumer Protection Act requires that such a disclosure document be given either before or at the time of contracting.[16]

[6] Act No 34 of 2005.
[7] Consumer Protection Act (South Africa), s 1 ('consumer') read with s 5(2)(b).
[8] Consumer Protection Act (Kenya), s 2(1) ('consumer'). This includes 'a person to whom particular goods or services are marketed in the ordinary course of the supplier's business' and franchisees in their dealings with franchisors.
[9] Consumer Protection Act (South Africa), s 2(1) ('consumer').
[10] The Law on the Protection of Consumer Rights and Interests (China), Art 2.
[11] Consumer Protection Act 2019 (India), s 2(7).
[12] Law No 8/1999 concerning Consumer Protection (Indonesia), Art 2(2).
[13] Decree 185/2013/ND-CP (Vietnam), Art 66.
[14] The Law on the Protection of Consumer Rights and Interests (China), Art 20.
[15] National Credit Act (South Africa), s 92.
[16] Consumer Protection Act (Kenya), s 65.

The South African Consumer Protection Act does not have a general obligation to give pre-contractual information. However, four types of clauses must be drawn to the consumer's attention before the earlier of the time at which the consumer concludes the agreement or enters the facility or pays consideration.[17] This must be done in a conspicuous manner and form likely to attract the attention of an ordinarily alert consumer.[18] These are exemption clauses, indemnity clauses, assumption of risk clauses and acknowledgements of facts. The Consumer Protection Act also requires pre-contractual warnings concerning activities or facilities that are subject to certain risks, for example, that could result in serious injury or death or of which an ordinarily alert consumer could not reasonably be expected to contemplate.[19] In addition, there are requirements for product labelling and trade descriptions.[20] The Consumer Protection Act regulations also require intermediaries such as booking agents and estate agents to provide certain information, including commission payable to them.[21]

There are also special rules on pre-contractual disclosure in legislation dealing with financial services. For example, the South African policy holder protection rules issued under the Long-Term and Short-Term Insurance Acts,[22] provide a list of aspects that must be disclosed to the potential insured.[23] The Code of Conduct applicable to financial advisors and intermediaries regulated by the Financial Advisory and Intermediary Services Act[24] also requires precontractual information regarding inter alia all fees or monetary obligations payable to the supplier of the financial product.[25] South African law should also consider mandatory information requirements in respect of certain goods such as second-hand cars.

The South African Electronic Communications and Transactions Act[26] and the Kenyan Consumer Protection Act provide for information that must be supplied on a website offering goods or services to consumers.[27] This legislation also requires that consumers must be able to review an online agreement and withdraw from it before finally placing an order.[28]

In line with some Asian countries' legislation, a South African consumer has a right to a copy of the written contract. If the agreement was not in writing, the supplier must keep a record of transactions entered into over the phone or any other recordable form.[29]

[17] Consumer Protection Act (South Africa), s 49(1); see also the Federal Competition and Consumer Protection Act 2018 (Nigeria), s 128.

[18] Consumer Protection Act (South Africa), s 49(4)(a).

[19] ibid, s 49(2).

[20] ibid, s 24.

[21] Consumer Protection Act Regulations (South Africa) of 1 April 2011, reg 9.

[22] Acts No 52 of 1998 and No 53 of 1998, respectively.

[23] Long-Term and Short-Term Insurance Acts (South Africa), rule 4.3.

[24] Policyholder Protection Rules (Short-Term Insurance), 2017 and Policyholder Protection Rules (Long-Term Insurance) 2017, rule 11.

[25] Section 3 of the General Code of Conduct for Authorised Financial Services Providers and Representatives.

[26] Act No 25 of 2002.

[27] Consumer Protection Act (Kenya), s 31; South African Electronic Communications and Transactions Act (South Africa), s 43.

[28] ibid.

[29] Consumer Protection Act (South Africa), s 50.

B. Right of Withdrawal

Asian countries sometimes provide for cooling-off rights in respect of doorstep selling and other forms of distance selling (for example China, Japan, Macau (draft legislation), Vietnam, Thailand and Malaysia). In some Asian countries, cooling-off rights also apply to other types of contracts, for example, timeshare contracts, insurance contracts and investment schemes (Singapore) and to contracts resulting from direct marketing (Thailand). The Kenyan Consumer Protection Act also recognises a cooling-off right for various types of contracts, including timeshare contracts and personal development contracts (such as gym contracts), and loan brokering and credit repair contracts of 10 days after receipt of the written agreement.[30] In respect of remote agreements, that is any agreement not concluded in the presence of both parties, a Kenyan consumer has a cooling-off period of seven days after receipt of a copy of the agreement if the supplier did not provide the consumer with the prescribed information before concluding the contract.[31] If the consumer does not receive a written copy of any of these agreements, the cooling-off period is for one year after conclusion of the agreement. The Kenyan Consumer Protection Act provides for an unlimited right to withdraw from a direct agreement, defined as an agreement concluded in person away from the supplier's place of business, or at a trade fair, etc.[32]

The South African Consumer Protection Act provides for a cooling-off right where the contract resulted from direct marketing, similar to the position in Thailand and Zimbabwe.[33] Although the South African Act obliges the supplier to inform the consumer of the cooling-off right,[34] unfortunately no provision is made for a sanction for non-compliance such as extension of the cooling-off period. In respect of electronic transactions, the South African Electronic Communications and Transactions Act creates a seven-day cooling-off period after delivery of goods and after conclusion of a contract for services. As is the case in some Asian countries, the e-commerce cooling-off right does not apply to all types of goods and services. Some are excluded, such as foodstuffs, books and accommodation (for example also in China). There are also cooling-off rights in respect of some South African financial services agreements, such as a 30-day cooling-off period in relation to insurance contracts.[35]

Therefore in both Asian and African countries, cooling-off rights are widely recognised. To give these teeth, there should be a sanction if the supplier does not inform the consumer of the right. For example, the EU Consumer Rights Directive provides for an extension of the withdrawal period for up to 12 months if the consumer was not informed of the withdrawal right as required.[36]

[30] Consumer Protection Act (Kenya), ss 23, 29, 41.

[31] ibid, s 38.

[32] ibid, s 35.

[33] Consumer Protection Act (South Africa), s 16; Consumer Protection Act (Zimbabwe), s 25; Direct Sales and Direct Marketing Act (Thailand), s 27.

[34] Consumer Protection Act (South Africa), s 32.

[35] Policyholder Protection Rules (Long-Term Insurance) 2007 (South Africa), rule 4.

[36] Art 10 of Directive 2011/83/EU of the European Parliament and of the Council of 25 October 2011 on consumer rights, OJ 2011 No L 304, p 64.

IV. Consumer Sales: Remedies

Some of the Asian countries have legislation based on the English Sale of Goods Act, which provides for implied terms as to quality of the goods etc (for example Singapore). In Hong Kong as well, remedies depend on whether an implied term is a condition or a warranty as these concepts are also understood in English law. In some African countries which used to be English colonies, such as Kenya, Ghana and Nigeria, protection against defective goods is also along the lines of the English Sale of Goods Act.[37] Some other Asian countries are influenced by the EU Consumer Sales Directive.[38] Macau in its draft legislation and Singapore both have the Directive's six months' presumption that a defect was already present at delivery.[39]

In some Asian countries, the consumer quite sensibly does not have a free choice between the remedies of repair, refund or replacement. For example, in Singapore the supplier has a right to offer a repair or replacement in the first instance, but in certain cases a consumer may insist on price reduction or refund (for example if a repair or replacement would be significantly inconvenient).[40] In China, the consumer may ask for rescission within seven days if statutory requirements are met.[41] If these are not met, the consumer may require a replacement or repair. Parties need to make a reasonable choice between remedies.

By contrast, the South African Consumer Protection Act is quite radical as it gives the consumer a right that the goods shall remain useable and durable for a reasonable amount of time plus the choice of repair, replacement or refund in the case of a defect arising within six months after the sale, regardless of the seriousness of the defect.[42] It is also not a requirement that the defect must have existed at delivery – as long as it arose within six months, the consumer has the choice of remedies. However, in practice the National Consumer Tribunal has effectively ignored the consumer's free choice at times and sometimes awarded a different remedy from what was sought.[43] The Zimbabwean Consumer Protection Act contains similar provisions to the South African ones.[44]

South African and Zimbabwean consumers may ask for a refund, repair or replacement not only against the eventual supplier, the retailer, but also against the manufacturer, importer and distributor who did not deal with the consumer.[45]

[37] Consumer Protection Act (Kenya), s 5, read with the Kenyan Sale of Goods Act, Cap 31; Ghanaian Sale of Goods Act 1962; Nigerian Sale of Goods Act 1893; see also C Dowuona-Hammond, 'Consumer Law and Policy in Ghana' (2018) 41 *Journal of Consumer Policy* 333, 344; F Monye, 'An Overview of Consumer Law in Nigeria and Relationship with Laws of Other Countries and Organisations' (2018) 41 *Journal of Consumer Policy* 373, 376.

[38] Directive 1999/44/EC of the European Parliament and of the Council of 25 May 1999 on certain aspects of the sale of consumer goods and associated guarantees, OJ 1999 No L171, p 12.

[39] Draft Consumer Protection Law 2019 (Macau), Art 33(2); Consumer Protection (Fair Trading) Act (Singapore), s 12B(3).

[40] See Consumer Protection (Fair Trading) Act (Singapore), s 12C.

[41] The Law on the Protection of Consumer Rights and Interests (China), Art 24.

[42] Consumer Protection Act (South Africa), ss 55(2), 56(2).

[43] *Lazarus and Another v RDB Project Management CC t/a Solid and Another* (NCT/36112/2016/75(1)(b)) [2016] ZANCT 15 (9 June 2016).

[44] Consumer Protection Act (Zimbabwe), ss 10 and 11.

[45] ibid, s 11(2); Consumer Protection Act (South Africa), s 56(1).

Although the Nigerian legislation copied out section 55 of the South African Consumer Protection Act dealing with the standards which goods must comply with,[46] its remedies to the consumer are much less drastic: the consumer may return the defective goods to the supplier who must either repair or replace them or give a refund.[47] Ethiopian consumers have a choice between a refund or replacement for a limited period of 15 days from the date of sale.[48]

V. Unfair Contract Terms

To some extent, South African law on unfair terms control is more radical than a number of Asian countries' legislation. The court's power to set aside unfair contract terms under the Consumer Protection Act not only applies to standard form contracts, or only to exemption clauses, but even to the negotiated terms in the business-to-small business contracts covered by the Consumer Protection Act. Core terms are not excluded from review, and an unfair price is specifically prohibited.[49] Regulations on price gouging were made during the Covid-19 pandemic, by the Competition Commission and National Consumer Commission acting jointly.[50] The consumer's right to a fair price in the Consumer Protection Act were relied upon as justification for the promulgation of these regulations. In Ethiopia there is price regulation for basic goods and services anyway.[51]

As in China and Zimbabwe, the unfair term may be amended by a court,[52] which is probably not a good thing as then businesses may continue to insert unfair terms hoping that they will simply be amended and not completely struck out.

Unfortunately, the South African Consumer Protection Act has a very short red list of prohibited terms (traditionally referred to in Europe and elsewhere as a black list).[53] Apart from prohibiting terms that purport to waive the consumer's rights under other provisions under the Act, section 51 only prohibits the following types of terms: exemption clauses in respect of gross negligence; cessions of claims against the Guardian's Fund; false acknowledgements that no representations or warranties were made or that goods or services or required documents were received; certain forfeiture clauses, as well as five types of clauses which can be grouped together as 'unfair enforcement clauses',

[46] Federal Competition and Consumer Protection Act 2018 (Nigeria), s 131.

[47] ibid, s 132.

[48] Trade Competition and Consumers Protection Proclamation No 813/2013 (Ethiopia), Art 20; see EN Stebek 'Consumer Protection Law in Ethiopia: The Normative Regime and the Way Forward' (2018) 41 *Journal of Consumer Policy* 309, 315.

[49] Consumer Protection Act (South Africa), s 48.

[50] Consumer and Customer Protection and National Disaster Management Regulations and Directions (N R 350 in Government Gazette 43116 of 19 March 2020).

[51] Trade Competition and Consumers Protection Proclamation No 813/2013 (Ethiopia), Art 25; Stebek, 'Consumer Protection Law in Ethiopia', 317.

[52] Consumer Protection Act (South Africa), s 52; Consumer Protection Act (Zimbabwe), s 36.

[53] The pejorative use of 'black' may be perceived as insensitive by some. For an argument that South Africa's short red list must be extended, see T Naude, 'Towards Augmenting the List of Prohibited Contract Terms in the Consumer Protection Act 68 of 2008' (2017) *Journal of South African Law* 138.

for example an undertaking to sign in advance documentation relating to enforcement of the agreement. The South African orange list (or grey list), promulgated as regulations under the Act, contains all the terms of the list of the EU Unfair Contract Terms Directive,[54] plus some additional items.[55]

Amongst African legal systems, the rules on unfair terms in the Seychelles Consumer Protection Act[56] appear to be closest to the Unfair Contract Terms Directive. It only relates to non-negotiated terms and not to core terms for example. It contains a similar list of terms that are considered potentially unfair under the Directive, although the Seychelles list is formulated as a list of prohibited terms. Macau has a list of outright prohibited clauses (red list) and a list of relatively prohibited clauses (presumably an orange list) in its legislation.[57] Japan, for example, has only a short red list.[58] In several countries, certain exemption clauses are prohibited (for example China, Hong Kong, Singapore and Japan), whereas some types of exemption clauses are not prohibited in the South African Consumer Protection Act, but may be challenged under the general prohibition on unfair terms.

Some Asian countries have legislation that draws on the English Unfair Contract Terms Act (for example Thailand).

Red and orange lists of unfair contract terms are critical for the effective protection of consumers. Certainly, the South African red list is insufficient and South Africa should look to other countries which have longer red lists, or, alternatively, more non-derogable rights for consumers.

VI. Product Liability

South Africa's product liability regime is more radical than some of the Asian and other African regimes in certain respects. Section 61 of the South African Consumer Protection Act gives a claim against the producer, importer, distributor and/or retailer when defective or unsafe goods are sold or inadequate warnings are given regarding hazards and cause injury, death or harm to property and resultant economic loss. Liability against the producer and importer is strict. However, distributors and retailers are not liable if they can show that they could not have been aware of the defect, having regard to their role in marketing the goods. So effectively retailers and distributors bear the burden of proving the absence of negligence. The Zimbabwean sections on product liability largely mirrors the South African provision.[59] This reverse burden of proof is to be found in Indonesia too.[60]

[54] Council Directive 93/13/EEC of 5 April 1993 on unfair terms in consumer contracts, OJ 1993 No L95, p 29.

[55] Consumer Protection Act: Regulations (GN No R 293 of 2011) (South Africa), reg 44.

[56] Act No 30 of 2010.

[57] Standard Form Contract Clauses Law 1992 (Macau), Arts 12 and 13.

[58] Consumer Contract Act (Japan), Arts 8 and 8-2.

[59] Consumer Protection Act (Zimbabwe), ss 16 and 17.

[60] Law No 8/1999 concerning Consumer Protection (Indonesia), Art 28.

In Vietnam and Thailand there is strict liability for producers, importers and parties who affixed their trade mark or name to the goods.[61] The same is true of Seychelles.[62] In Nigeria, this is true of a supplier who supplied the goods, regardless of whether the consumer concluded an agreement with that supplier.[63] Kenyan provisions make the manufacturer strictly liable as well as any supplier who cannot indicate who manufactured the goods.[64]

There is no 'state of the art' or 'development risks' defence in South Africa or Nigeria, contrary to the position in some Asian countries, including Malaysia and Japan, and in Africa, the Seychelles,[65] Kenya[66] and Ethiopia.[67] In this regard, South African law mirrors that of Thailand which also does not specifically recognise a state of the art/development risks defence. The definition of defect in the South African Consumer Protection Act, one of the possible bases for product liability, does however, contain a consumer expectations test.[68] So it depends on what consumers were reasonably entitled to expect. This could arguably imply a state of the art defence – consumers could be entitled only to expect that the goods would comply with what could reasonably be expected given the state of scientific and technical knowledge at the time. However, the alternative ground for liability, namely where the goods are unsafe, does not depend on a consumer expectation test.[69]

Thai product liability law is also more protective of consumers than the laws of other Asian countries as a claim for emotional distress is allowed. The South African Consumer Goods and Services Ombud has written an explanatory note on the basis on which consumers can claim damages for emotional distress under the common law of delict (tort).[70]

In other respects, the South African provision is more conservative than its Asian counterparts. The consumer must prove the bases of liability, for example a hazard or that goods had a defect or were unsafe, and must also prove causation, although leading writers argue that the courts should apply the *res ipsa loquitur* doctrine here. In Taiwan by contrast, the manufacturer must prove the goods were safe.[71] Similarly, in Thailand the consumer must prove harm from the product used normally, after which the manufacturer must prove that the goods were safe.[72] In some systems punitive damages are

[61] Product Liability Act B.E. 2551 (2008) (Thailand), ss 4 ('entrepreneur), 5; Law on Consumer Protection of 2010 (Vietnam), Art 23.

[62] Consumer Protection Act (Seychelles), s 45.

[63] Federal Competition and Consumer Protection Act 2018 (Nigeria), s 136.

[64] Competition Act No 12 of 2010 (Kenya), ss 64–65.

[65] Consumer Protection Act (Seychelles), s 45.

[66] Competition Act (Kenya), s 66.

[67] Trade Competition and Consumers Protection Proclamation No 813/2013 (Ethiopia), Art 20; see Stebek, 'Consumer Protection Law in Ethiopia', 315–16.

[68] Consumer Protection Act (South Africa), s 53.

[69] Unsafe is defined in s 53 as 'due to a characteristic, failure, defect or hazard, particular goods present an extreme risk of personal injury or property damage to the consumer or other persons'. Hazard in turn includes 'a significant risk of injury to any person or damage to property' and 'failure' means 'the inability of the goods to perform in the intended manner or to the intended effect'.

[70] Consumer Goods and Services Ombud, 'Advisory Note 8: Emotional distress suffered from contaminated food' (29 January 2014).

[71] Consumer Protection Act (Taiwan), Art 7-1.

[72] Product Liability Act (Thailand), ss 6–7.

awarded, for example double or triple damages are payable (China and Taiwan, depending on whether the misconduct was wilful).[73]

VII. Product Safety

Various safety standards exist in Asian countries, some of them compulsory, but voluntary certification is also provided for (for example by the Bureau of Indian Standards). Sector-specific legislation also deal with product safety standards, for example in relation to food and drugs. Legislation provides for enforcement of safety standards in various ways, including through product recalls.

The same is true of South Africa. The National Regulator for Compulsory Specifications recommends to the Minister which standards should be compulsory, including labelling requirements. Certain legislation deals with standards as well, such as for agricultural products.[74] This approach of some standards being set by a national authority acting in terms of general legislation and some standards being set by sectoral legislation and bodies is found in other African countries as well, including Ethiopia.[75] South Africa does not have sufficient safety standards, for instance there is no compulsory specification in respect of furniture, such as to guard against flammability of upholstery.[76]

There is also a general requirement in the South African Consumer Protection Act that goods supplied must be safe (as in Malaysia and Ethiopia).[77] But the South African National Consumer Commission does not itself set safety standards, although it does have a product recall programme.[78] The Consumer Product Safety Recall Guidelines interprets section 60 of the Act to require that suppliers inform the Commission if they are conducting a voluntary product recall or if they are aware of a safety hazard that may cause injury (as in Vietnam).

It is interesting that some Asian legislation obliges suppliers to comply with the standards set by well-known supra-national or overseas standard-setting authorities (for example the ISO and IEC) subject to local government amendments, or otherwise regional or national standards (for example Singapore). This may be an example to follow for South Africa. However, to some extent international standards do play a role in the standards set by South African and some other African authorities. For example, the compulsory standards for foodstuffs are typically based on those set by Codex Alimentarius.[79]

[73] ibid, s 11(2).

[74] Agricultural Product Standards Act No 119 of 1990.

[75] Stebek, 'Consumer Protection Law in Ethiopia', 317–18 and legislation there cited.

[76] T Naude 'Dissemination of Consumer Law and Policy in South Africa' (2018) 41 *Journal of Consumer Policy* 411, 416.

[77] Consumer Protection Act (South Africa), s 55; Trade Competition and Consumers Protection Proclamation No 813/2013 (Ethiopia), Art 22; see Stebek, 'Consumer Protection Law in Ethiopia', 316.

[78] In terms of the Consumer Product Safety Recall Guidelines, Notice 490 of 13 June 2020.

[79] See also eg Monye, 'An Overview of Consumer Law in Nigeria', 391 on the role played by ISO and Codex Alimentarius standards in Nigeria.

A proactive approach to prevent the influx of sub-standard goods is necessary to deal with the high volume of unsafe, imported goods in some African countries.[80]

VIII. Adaptation to the Digital Age

The Thai Electronic Transactions Act is primarily based upon the UNCITRAL Model Law on Electronic Commerce, which also heavily influenced the South African Electronic Commerce and Transactions Act.[81] As noted above,[82] this South African Act requires pre-contractual information disclosure, provides for a cooling-off right and gives the consumer a right to withdraw if they were not able to review the details of the transaction before finally paying for it.[83] The Consumer Protection Act and common law also apply to electronic transactions, and software are regarded as goods in the Act.[84] However, some sections in the Consumer Protection Act are not applicable, for example the cooling-off right in respect of direct marketing and section 19 on consumer's rights with respect to the time within which delivery of goods or supply of services must take place, as the Electronic Commerce and Transactions Act requires performance within 30 days.[85]

It appears that a number of Asian countries' legislation on digital issues could be improved. Examples of countries where more detailed legislation may be needed are Macau, China, Malaysia and India. It appears that there are modern data protection regimes in some Asian countries (for example Hong Kong, Singapore and Vietnam). South Africa has modern data protection regulation in the form of the Protection of Personal Information Act.[86] It draws on the EU Data Protection Directive.[87] Many companies in South Africa make sure that they also comply with the EU General Data Protection Regulation,[88] which is not vastly different from the Protection of Personal Information Act.

[80] Dowuona-Hammond, 'Consumer Law and Policy in Ghana', 343; M Rizzi, 'Reflections on Consumer Law and Policy in Seychelles' (2018) 41 *Journal of Consumer Policy* 395, 405 (who decries the lack of human resources to prevent importation of sub-standard goods). On a successful programme in this regard in Nigeria, see ibid, 379. Tanzania has a 'Pre-shipment Verification of Conformity' to prevent unsafe goods from being imported, but in practice unsafe counterfeit goods still enter the country, T Mwenegoha, 'Dissemination of Consumer Law and Policy in Tanzania' (2018) 41 *Journal of Consumer Policy* 435, 442–43. The same is true of Uganda, F Zeija, 'Consumer Protection in Uganda – the Law in Theory and Practice' (2018) 41 *Journal of Consumer Policy* 455, 465–66.

[81] Act No 25 of 2002.

[82] At Section III.B.

[83] Electronic Commerce and Transactions Act (South Africa), s 20.

[84] Consumer Protection Act (South Africa), s 1 ('goods').

[85] Section 46 of the Electronic Commerce and Transactions Act (South Africa) provides that the supplier must execute the order within thirty days after the day on which the supplier received the order, unless the parties have agreed otherwise. Also not applicable is catalogue marketing provisions.

[86] Act No 4 of 2013.

[87] Directive 95/46/EC of the European Parliament and of the Council of 24 October 1995 on the protection of individuals with regard to the processing of personal data and on the free movement of such data, OJ 1995 No L281, p 31.

[88] Regulation (EU) 2016/679 of the European Parliament and of the Council of 27 April 2016 on the protection of natural persons with regard to the processing of personal data and on the free movement of such data, and repealing Directive 95/46/EC (General Data Protection Regulation), OJ 2016 No L119, p 1.

IX. Unfair Commercial Practices

Some Asian countries have been influenced by the EU Unfair Commercial Practices Directive,[89] for example Macau and to some extent Singapore, which recognises this concept and lists 20 specific practices deemed unfair.[90] Hong Kong also lists some unfair commercial practices in its 'Trade Description Ordinance'. Several other Asian countries deal with unfair prices like misleading advertising, pyramid selling and deception (Taiwan), and on misleading and false labelling (Thailand).

The concept of 'unfair commercial practice' is not used as such in South Africa. However, as is the case in Asian countries, there are rules in African consumer laws on misleading and deceptive conduct in the form of false, misleading or deceptive representations and failure to disclose material facts in a deceptive manner and failure to correct an apparent misapprehension on the part of the consumer.[91] In addition, the South African Consumer Protection Act prohibits the use of duress, undue influence, unfair tactics or similar conduct during the whole life of the contract.[92] The same section also prohibits the supplier knowingly to take advantage of the consumer's inability to protect their own interests due to factors such as illiteracy, ignorance, and inability to understand the language of an agreement. Section 13 of the Kenyan Consumer Protection Act borrows from this South African section, but purports to rather prohibit unconscionable representations as opposed to unconscionable conduct more generally. In addition, various types of marketing are dealt with in the South African Act such as negative option marketing, bait marketing, referral selling and pyramid schemes,[93] as is the case with some Asian legislation (for example provisions on bait marketing in the Hong Kong Trade Ordinance and on pyramid selling in Taiwan and Thailand).

Therefore there are similarities in the various regimes.

X. Access to Justice

It seems that small claims tribunals are important in some Asian countries to create access to justice, although not necessarily the most important avenue of redress (for example in Singapore and Hong Kong – although mediation is more important than small claims tribunals in these countries). Other Asian countries have a simplified procedure for small claims (Vietnam, Thailand and Macau). The South African small claims courts are very accessible to consumers as there are many small claims courts even in remote rural areas and legal representation is not allowed. However, unfortunately the Consumer Protection Act provides that the consumer must first exhaust all other remedies before approaching a court.[94] These other avenues include ombuds and

[89] Directive 2005/29/EC of the European Parliament and of the Council of 11 May 2005 concerning unfair business-to-consumer commercial practices in the internal market, OJ 2005 No L149, p 22.

[90] Consumer Protection (Fair Trading) Act (Singapore), Schedule 2.

[91] Section 12 of the Kenyan Consumer Protection Act is based partially on s 41 of the South African Consumer Protection Act which deals with false representations.

[92] Consumer Protection Act (South Africa), s 40.

[93] ibid, Parts E and F of Chapter 2.

[94] ibid, s 69. The small claims courts are regarded as courts.

regulators that have offices in only the major cities and which are not therefore very accessible to low-income consumers in rural areas. This requires legislative amendment to enable consumers to approach a small claims court directly.[95] Nigeria has not made the same mistake as South Africa in this regard, and Nigerian consumers may approach a sectoral regulator or the Federal Competition and Consumer Protection Commission, but may also directly approach a court for relief.[96]

Mediation and other forms of ADR are important avenues of redress in various Asian countries (see for example Hong Kong, Taiwan, Singapore, Vietnam and Thailand).

Currently enforcement of consumer law in South Africa relies heavily on ombud schemes. Ombuds for financial services have already been in place years before the Consumer Protection Act took effect in 2011. These schemes are effective in resolving disputes and funded by industry levies. Typically the supplier but not the consumer is bound by a determination of the dispute by a financial ombud. As far as disputes outside of financial services are concerned, there are two ombuds accredited under the Act. First, the Consumer Goods and Services Ombud deals with all goods and services not covered by another industry code of conduct. The other accredited ombud is the Motor Industry Ombudsman. Moves are afoot to accredit more industry codes with ombud schemes.[97] These two ombuds typically first attempt to resolve disputes by mediation. Their rulings are currently not binding.[98] The Community Schemes Ombud Service was created by statute to resolve and adjudicate disputes within community schemes (sectional title schemes and homeowners associations).[99] This ombud may apply the Consumer Protection Act against managing agents as the latter are suppliers of services under the Act, although the Consumer Goods and Services Ombud has been lobbying for a change in the current rules so that her decisions would become binding on suppliers (subject to an appeal to the National Consumer Tribunal).

The National Consumer Commission is one of the bodies that may be approached by consumers, but it has not been very active in resolving individual consumer complaints lately and habitually refers these to the ombuds.[100] It rather focuses on 'systemic complaints'. There are also provincial enforcement agencies and consumer tribunals. The National Consumer Tribunal may also hear cases relating to the Consumer Protection Act.

What is lacking in South Africa which is present in some Asian countries are strong consumer organisations which are prepared to take legal action on behalf of consumers, educate consumers and advocate for better laws and enforcement. There appears to be only one dedicated functioning South African consumer organisation, but its website does not clearly indicate that it takes legal action on behalf of consumers. It appears that

[95] As often pointed out, eg by T Naude and J Barnard, 'Enforcement and Effectiveness of Consumer Law in South Africa' in H-W Micklitz and G Saumier (eds), *Enforcement and Effectiveness of Consumer Law* (Cham: Springer, 2018) 581.

[96] Federal Competition and Consumer Protection Act 2018 (Nigeria), s 146.

[97] The National Consumer Commission is considering a possible Franchising Industry Code of Conduct (franchisees are also protected under many but not all of the sections of the Consumer Protection Act).

[98] See the Ombud's website, which confirms this at www.cgso.org.za/cgso/the-process/.

[99] Community Schemes Ombud Service Act 9 of 2011.

[100] See 'Complaints to the NCC' available from the regulator's website www.thencc.gov.za.

strong consumer organisations contribute significantly to effective consumer redress in some Asian countries. This includes Malaysia and Singapore. Whereas in Kenya consumer organisations have also played an important role in strengthening consumer protection,[101] other African scholars have pointed out the need for active consumer organisations in their countries.[102] This is particularly important in countries where government agencies are not sufficiently resourced.

XI. Conclusion

There is not conformity amongst Asian countries in respect of the various topics studied in this book. The same can also be said of Anglophone African Consumer Law: there is significant divergence. Although parts of the South African Consumer Protection Act has influenced other corresponding laws in Anglophone Africa, including in Kenya, the Seychelles, Zimbabwe and Nigeria, this has not been wholescale transplanting and there remains much difference in the details. It could be that attempts at integration in Africa via the African Continental Free Trade Agreement may at some point aim to harmonise consumer law more, in order to facilitate the objective of a single continental market.

African countries can learn much from Asian countries. One important lesson is that strengthening consumer organisations is vital if there is to be real consumer protection in developing countries, as such organisations often make a vital contribution to consumer education, law reform and litigation on behalf of consumers. The South African National Consumer Commissioner has informally expressed the opinion some years ago that the National Consumer Commission does not have enough funding to fund consumer organisations.

Another lesson is to be stricter about prohibiting exemption clauses as Asian countries appear to be. In South Africa, by contrast (but with some qualifications), a supplier is not prohibited outright from exempting itself from liability for services performed negligently, as long as the conspicuousness requirements for the exemption clause are met.[103]

African countries can also learn from those Asian countries who have lists of prohibited contract terms in their unfair contract terms legislation, although the Seychelles should be commended for also taking a strict stance in favour of consumers by including a long list of prohibited terms.

Although consumer law should be tailored to local conditions and needs, it is valuable to benchmark proposed legislation against international best practice. Some Asian and African countries have done some comparative research before drafting their legislation. For example, Macau has drawn greatly on European Directives and some African countries have drawn on consumer protection legislation in South Africa.

[101] J Malala, 'Consumer Law and Policy in Kenya' (2018) 41 *Journal of Consumer Policy* 355, 360.
[102] Stebek, 'Consumer Protection Law in Ethiopia', 330; Zeija, 'Consumer Protection in Uganda', 468.
[103] Consumer Protection Act (South Africa), s 49.

However, all of these laws are not perfect and it is recommended that countries in these regions request a peer review of their consumer law by the UNCTAD (United Nations Conference on Trade and Development) Intergovernmental Group of Experts, who have wide-ranging expertise in consumer law.[104] It would be best if that could be done as a regional bloc, given that there are some benefits to greater convergence of consumer law within a region.[105]

[104] T Naude, 'Fragmentation versus Convergence of Consumer Law within One Legal System and across Legal Systems: An African Perspective' (2020) 43 *Journal of Consumer Policy* 11, 27.
[105] ibid.

28

ASEAN Economic Integration and Consumer Protection in Southeast Asia

LUKE NOTTAGE AND SAKDA THANITCUL*

I. Introduction

The Association of Southeast Asian Nations (ASEAN) originated in the Bangkok Declaration of 8 August 1967, signed by the foreign ministers of Indonesia, Malaysia, the Philippines, Singapore and Thailand. Brunei Darussalam joined in 1984, soon after gaining independence from the United Kingdom, followed by Vietnam (1995), Laos and Myanmar (1997) and Cambodia (1999).[1] ASEAN began with a strong emphasis on security cooperation, but since the end of the Cold War it has increasingly focused on economic integration.[2]

The ASEAN Free Trade Area was established in 1992 to reduce tariffs and other impediments to goods exports among the Member States. The ASEAN Framework Agreement on Trade in Services generated rounds of liberalisation commitments from 1995, and the ASEAN Comprehensive Investment Agreement (signed in 2009 and in effect from 2012) developed two earlier treaties to both liberalise and protect cross-border investments.[3]

* We thank James Tanna, student intern at the Centre for Asian and Pacific Law at the University of Sydney (2020), for superlative research and editorial assistance.

[1] For more details surrounding the history of ASEAN, see http://asean.org/asean/about-asean/history; H Hill and J Mennon, 'ASEAN Economic Integration: Driven by Markets, Bureaucrats or Both?' in M Kreinin and M Plummer (eds), *Oxford Handbook of International Economic Policy* (New York: Oxford University Press, 2012) 357–86 (outlining four phases: from 1967; the Bali Summit of 1976, followed by four ineffective economic cooperation programmes; from 1992, announcing the ASEAN Free Trade Area; and the current phase, following the Asian Financial Crisis of 1997).

[2] For various comparisons with other regional integration initiatives, including within Europe, see eg L Brennan and P Murray, *Drivers of Integration and Regionalism in Europe and Asia: Comparative Perspectives* (Abingdon: Routledge, 2015).

[3] See J Chaisse and S Jusoh, *The ASEAN Comprehensive Agreement* (Cheltenham: Edward Elgar, 2016).

In addition, since 2004, ASEAN has signed five 'ASEAN+' Free Trade Agreements (FTAs) to promote trade in goods, services and/or investment with respectively China, Japan, Korea, India, Australia and New Zealand.[4] The 16 countries also began negotiations in late 2012 towards an (ASEAN+6) FTA known as the Regional Comprehensive Economic Partnership, mostly in force from 2022. In addition, individual ASEAN Member States have concluded many bilateral FTAs and investment treaties with partners outside the region. Singapore, Malaysia, Vietnam and Brunei also negotiated from 2010 for an expanded Trans-Pacific Partnership FTA, including notably the United States, which was signed in 2016. However, it only came into force from 2019, with minor revisions involving six Member States without the United States, as the 'Comprehensive and Progressive Agreement for Trans-Pacific Partnership'.[5]

In 2003, ASEAN leaders further committed to creating a single ASEAN community, comprising an ASEAN Economic Community (AEC), a Security Community and a Socio-Cultural Community. Originally aiming for 2020, in 2007 they agreed to establish this community by the end of 2015. The 10 states also agreed on an AEC Blueprint or action plan to accelerate the creation of an internal free market, which was extended in November 2015 for the ensuing decade as the AEC Blueprint 2025.[6] In addition, the 10 ASEAN Member States signed a Charter in 2007 that formalised various aspects of ASEAN, including giving it the status of an international organisation.[7] Such normative instruments underpin an 'evolving legal architecture' throughout Southeast Asia, and new patterns of 'international regulatory cooperation' within and for ASEAN.[8]

Already, in 2011, ASEAN brought together over 600 million people (nine per cent of the world's population), and three per cent of the world's GDP (calculated in US dollars), extending to 24 per cent in combination with its closely linked Northeast Asian dialogue partners, China, Japan and Korea.[9] Next to China, ASEAN enjoyed strong GDP growth over 2001–13.[10] Growth is increasingly bolstered by the services

[4] V Bath and L Nottage, 'The ASEAN Comprehensive Investment Agreement and "ASEAN Plus" – The Australia-New Zealand Free Trade Area (AANZFTA) and the PRC–ASEAN Investment Agreement' in M Bungenberg et al (eds), *International Investment Law* (Oxford: Oxford University Press, 2015) 283–303.

[5] V Bath and L Nottage, 'Asian Investment and the Growth of Regional Investment Agreements' in C. Antons (ed), *Routledge Handbook of Asian Law* (Abingdon: Routledge, 2017) 182; L Nottage, 'The Investment Chapter and ISDS in TPP: Lessons From and For Southeast Asia' in C Lee and P Bhattacharya (eds), *The Comprehensive and Progressive Agreement for Trans-Pacific Partnership: Implications for Southeast Asia* (Singapore: ISEAS, 2021); J Chaisse, H Gao and C Lo (eds.), *Paradigm Shift in International Economic Law Rule-Making TPP as a New Model for Trade Agreements?* (Singapore: Springer, 2017). See also generally V Bath and L Nottage, 'International Investment Agreements and Investor-State Arbitration in Asia' in J Chaisse, L Choukroune and S Jusoh (eds), *Handbook of International Investment Law and Policy* (Singapore: Springer, 2020) 1.

[6] See http://asean.org/communities/asean-economic-community; PL Hsieh and B Mercurio, 'ASEAN Law in the New Regional Economic Order: an Introductory Roadmap to the ASEAN Economic Community' in PL Hsieh and B Mercurio (eds), *ASEAN Law in the New Regional Economic Order: Global Trends and Shifting Paradigms* (Cambridge: Cambridge University Press, 2019) 3.

[7] Charter of the Association of Southeast Asian Nations; generally L Leviter, 'The ASEAN Charter: ASEAN Failure or Member Failure?' (2010) 43 *New York University Journal of International Law and Politics* 159.

[8] B Bitas, 'Legal Convergence, Transnational Rule-Making and Regional Integration in ASEAN – From "Open Regionalism" to "Open Legal Architecture"' (2014) *Lawasia Journal* 1; D Gill (ed), *Interconnected Government: International Regulatory Cooperation in ASEAN* (Central Jakarta: Economic Research Institute for ASEAN and East Asia, 2020).

[9] See http://investasean.asean.org/index.php/page/view/about-the-asean-region/view/707/newsid/932/integrated-asean.html.

[10] See http://asiamattersforamerica.org/asean/data/.

sector, and overall GDP is significantly higher when calculated on a Purchasing Power Parity basis.[11] ASEAN also constitutes a major destination for inbound foreign direct investment (FDI), and has been recently expanding intra-ASEAN FDI and investment outside the region.[12] A report by McKinsey & Company has highlighted how ASEAN is a growing hub of consumer demand, yet is not a monolithic market.[13]

On the last point, other studies confirm considerable socio-economic disparity among the 10 Member States, as indicated for example by human development indices.[14] A top priority on the ASEAN Socio-Cultural Community agenda is to improve human development – including education, health, work, poverty, the environment and community participation.[15] Another challenge for Southeast Asia, but also a potential strength, is the extensive variation among Member States in terms of cultures and legal traditions.[16]

Particularly since the global financial crisis in 2008, some concerns have also emerged among citizens and policymakers within ASEAN about the goal of working towards a common internal market, promoting free movement in goods, services, capital and labour. Trade and investment protectionism was rising in Indonesia, for example, alongside some 'resource nationalism'.[17] More generally, there is some awareness that enhanced liberalisation might lead to a 'regulatory race to the bottom', lowering standards for the protection of consumers and the environment within ASEAN Member States.

II. Free Trade (Agreements) Promoting ASEAN Consumer Protection

As David Vogel documented in the mid-1990s in the context of closer regional integration through the EU, the North American FTA and the establishment of the multilateral World Trade Organization, closer economic integration can often lead instead to 'trading up' to higher safety standards.[18] Partly this is because exporters may need to improve safety features to comply with requirements set by public or private law in the

[11] See http://asean.org/news/asean-secretariat-news/item/asean-gdp-remains-robust-backed-by-services.

[12] See http://asean.org/resources/item/asean-unctad-launches-asean-investment-report-2013-2014-2.

[13] See http://mckinsey.com/insights/public_sector/understanding_asean_seven_things_you_need_to_know. On consumer demand, see eg The Economist Corporate Network, *Riding the ASEAN Elephant* (February 2013).

[14] See generally http://undp.org/content/undp/en/home/librarypage/hdr/2014-human-development-report/.

[15] See eg United Nations Development Programme, 'Thailand Human Development Report 2014' (2014).

[16] A Black and G Bell (eds), *Law and Legal Institutions of Asia: Traditions, Adaptations and Innovations* (Cambridge: Cambridge University Press, 2011; C Antons (ed), *Routledge Handbook of Asian Law* (London: Routledge, 2017). For a very helpful summary Table and discussion of divergences within ASEAN regarding institutional and commercial policy environments, welfare indicators and population, economic size and structure, see Hill and Mennon, 'ASEAN Economic Integration'. See also (primarily written by) L Nottage, 'Introduction' in L Nottage, J Malbon, J Paterson and C Beaton-Wells, *ASEAN Consumer Law Harmonisation and Cooperation: Achievements and Challenges* (Cambridge: Cambridge University Press, 2019) 1.

[17] See eg Lowy Institute for International Policy (A Patunru and S Rahardja), 'Trade Protectionism in Indonesia: Bad Times and Bad Policy' (July 2015).

[18] D Vogel, *Trading Up: Consumer and Environmental Regulation in a Global Economy* (Cambridge, MA: Harvard University Press, 1997).

destination country. It is then often inefficient to remove such features for products also sold into local markets, where requirements may initially be lower, or if features are removed consumers and regulators in local markets will more readily press for local safety standards to be raised. Instead, exporters can band together in coalition with local consumer groups seeking to raise standards to the levels found overseas, creating competitive pressure on local firms less oriented towards foreign markets.

Free Trade Agreements and other international agreements can also facilitate enactment of better consumer product safety laws. The European Economic Community (EEC), now the European Union (EU), was an early example. In 1979, the Treaty of Rome was interpreted to require 'mutual recognition': goods produced to safety standards required in one EU Member State would be deemed to satisfy standards in an importing country. However, in order to avoid a regulatory race to the bottom, the EU also developed a new and more effective approach to setting joint minimum safety standards.

In 1985, the EEC Product Liability Directive[19] required national legislatures to introduce a harmonised regime providing compensation for consumers suffering injuries or consequential property loss caused by goods containing a safety 'defect'. Such a regime premised on strict liability, rather than consumers having the more difficult burden of proving fault or negligence by manufacturers, indirectly encourages those manufacturers to achieve a minimum level of consumer safety as well as providing more scope for compensation if harm nonetheless arises.[20]

Intriguingly, Southeast Asia appears to be experiencing similar developments, at least in some fields – especially product safety law.[21] Indeed, four years after all the 10 current Member States had committed to the ASEAN Free Trade Area in 1999, they also agreed on an ASEAN Cosmetics Directive.[22] This provided initially for mutual recognition, but then a fully harmonised regime, completed in 2012. The regime establishes common technical standards (for example, for prohibited ingredients) as well as powers for national regulators, which are based on an earlier EEC Directive[23] rather than the less stringent US model.[24] Partly this is because ASEAN cosmetics

[19] Council Directive 85/374/EEC of 25 July 1985 on the approximation of the laws, regulations and administrative provisions of the Member States concerning liability for defective products, OJ 1985 No 210, p 29. For theoretical rationales and recent developments, see G Howells, 'Product Liability Along the Belt and Road' in L Nottage and S Thanitcul (eds), *ASEAN Product Liability and Consumer Product Safety Law* (Bangkok: Winyuchon, 2016) 55–66.

[20] See G Howells, *Comparative Product Liability* (Aldershot: Dartmouth, 1993); and more generally G Howells, *Consumer Product Safety* (Aldershot: Dartmouth, 1998) and L Nottage, 'Product Safety' in G Howells et al (eds), *Handbook of Research on International Consumer Law* 2nd edn (Cheltenham: Edward Elgar, 2018) 231–66.

[21] See L Nottage and S Thanitcul 'Consumer Product Liability and Safety Regulation: ASEAN in Asia', in this volume.

[22] L Nottage, 'Policy Digest 22: Cosmetics Regulation Under National and ASEAN Law' in ASEAN Secretariat (ed), *Consumer Protection Digests and Case Studies* (December 2015), vol 2, p 99.

[23] Council Directive of 27 July 1976 on the approximation of the laws of the Member States relating to cosmetic products, OJ 1976, No L262, p 169; repealed by Regulation (EC) No 1223/2009 of the European Parliament and of the Council of 30 November 2009 on cosmetic products, OJ 2009 No 342, p 59, in force from 2013.

[24] Z Zakaria, 'Cosmetic Safety Regulations: A Comparative Study of Europe, the USA and Malaysia', PhD thesis, University of Manchester (2012); Z Zakaria, 'Regulation of Cosmetics: What has Malaysia Learnt from the European System?' (2014) 38 *Journal of Consumer Policy* 38.

manufacturers are already major exporters to the EU and other markets worldwide.[25] Developing countries such as Myanmar may still face problems in enforcing these standards, but at least they now have a regulatory scheme, thanks to an international agreement.

III. Developing Consumer Protection: Mostly Still in the 'ASEAN Way'

More generally, despite the gradual emergence of 'hard law' elements within ASEAN, improvements in consumer protection law have come about mostly in the more traditional 'ASEAN Way'. This involves building consensus over core principles, suggesting (but not requiring) the enactment and enforcement of key elements.[26] Since 2008, pursuant to the (first) AEC Blueprint, a new ASEAN Committee on Consumer Protection (ACCP) has worked to ratchet up consumer protection law and policy.[27] The ACCP has encouraged capacity-building, regulatory cooperation and significant improvements in Member States. This Committee is supported by the ASEAN Secretariat based in Jakarta and the latter's partners such as the Australian government[28] and the United Nations Conference on Trade and Development.[29]

With such support, a new wave of general consumer protection laws have been enacted, particularly in the developing Member States of ASEAN.[30] But some counted as such are in name only. For example, Brunei's Consumer Protection (Fair Trading) Order 2011 only contains EU-like prohibitions on unfair commercial practices, largely copied from Singapore's Consumer Protection (Fair Trading) Act 2003. Other consumer protection laws are very general (for example Laos') and/or hard to interpret (for example Myanmar, even after revisions in 2019).[31] Cambodia experienced lengthy delays in enacting a comprehensive statute: the Law on Consumer Protection 2019.[32]

[25] See also eg D Gill, *International Regulatory Cooperation: Case Studies and Lessons Learnt* (Wellington: New Zealand Institute of Economic Research, 2018).

[26] See (primarily written by) J Malbon and L Nottage, 'Theoretical Perspectives on ASEAN and Consumer Law Developments' in L. Nottage et al, 'ASEAN Consumer Law Harmonisation', 53; T Yukawa, 'The ASEAN Way as a Symbol: An Analysis of Discourses on the ASEAN Norms' (2018) 31(3) *The Pacific Review* 298.

[27] See http://aseanconsumer.org.

[28] Recently incorporated into Australia's Department of Foreign Affairs and Trade, <http://aadcp2.org/supporting-research-dialogue-on-consumer-protection/>. See, especially, *ASEAN Consumer Protection Digests and Case Studies: A Policy Guide* (Volumes 1 and 2, 2014 and 2015, with contributions by L Nottage et al).

[29] See 'Six Modules on Strengthening Technical Competency on Consumer Protection in ASEAN' (2015), especially on 'Product Safety and Labelling' (lead-authored by L Nottage).

[30] The main consumer laws of each ASEAN Member States can be downloaded via https://aseanconsumer.org/accp, except for a translation of the 2019 Cambodian statute. See also generally L Nottage, 'Introduction'; *Handbook on ASEAN Consumer Protection Laws and Regulations* (Jakarta: ASEAN Secretariat, 2018).

[31] See N Oo and S Park, 'New Consumer Protection Law Enacted in Myanmar' (5 April 2019) www.tilleke.com/insights/new-consumer-protection-law-enacted-myanmar/.

[32] See J Cohen and P Bunthan, 'Cambodia Enacts a New E-commerce Law and a Consumer Protection Law' (14 November 2019) www.tilleke.com/insights/cambodia-enacts-new-e-commerce-law-and-consumer-protection-law/.

Pursuant to the (second) AEC Blueprint 2025, the ASEAN Strategic Action Plan for Consumer Protection 2016–2025 aims to:[33]

(1) Establish a Common ASEAN Consumer Protection Framework through higher levels of consumer protection legislation, improve enforcement and monitoring of consumer protection legislations through peer reviews and make available redress mechanisms, including alternative dispute resolution mechanisms;
(2) Promote a higher level of consumer empowerment and knowledge by addressing consumer concerns and strengthening consumer associations as well as enhancing consumer knowledge and advocacy;
(3) Build higher consumer confidence and cross-border commercial transactions by strengthening product safety enforcement, addressing cross-border complaints through online dispute resolution and promoting sustainable consumption;
(4) Encourage consumer-related matters in ASEAN policies through impact assessment of consumer protection policies and development of knowledge-based policies; and
(5) Promote consumer protection measures in products and services sectors such as finance, e-commerce, air transport, energy and telecommunications.

Elaborating the first Strategic Goal above, the 2017 ASEAN High-Level Principles on Consumer Protection were developed with input from a former senior UNCTAD official, containing significant parallels with the UN Consumer Protection Guidelines (as revised in 2015). These Principles provide

> a broad framework on consumer protection for ASEAN … a consistent context for ASEAN laws and arrangements and, in so doing, promote a common base level of cooperation and exchange of experiences and best practices … [also with] the purposes of:
>
> – setting benchmarks on key aspects of consumer protection;
> – addressing legislative and information gaps as a basis for the modernisation of consumer protection legislation;
> – providing an agreed set of criteria for peer reviews and peer learning that enhances regional cooperation and convergence in policy.[34]

Recommendations are developed around the following eight Principles:

(1) Enforcement of consumer protection laws is to be fair, consistent, effective and proportionate.
(2) Consumers are equipped with the skills, knowledge, information and confidence to exercise their rights.
(3) Consumers are protected from harmful goods and services.
(4) Consumers have access to appropriate and convenient sources of advice and redress including alternative dispute resolution (ADR).
(5) Consumers understand the impact of consumption decisions on the shared environment.

[33] See 'ASEAN Strategic Action Plan on Consumer Protection (ASAPCP) 2016–2025'.
[34] See 'ASEAN High-Level Principles on Consumer Protection'.

(6) Strong consumer advocacy is promoted.
(7) High levels of cooperation between different levels of government and with business and other stakeholders.
(8) Consumers in e-commerce are protected.

Particular challenges arise regarding Principle 1 on Enforcement, as consumer protection regulators are still folded into other government departments with potentially conflicting mandates (like a Commerce Ministry, as in Vietnam) and/or are very new (as in Myanmar and Laos). Relatedly, Principle 7 is problematic, as consumer agencies have fewer financial and personnel resources compared to more well-established and politically connected 'line ministries', and may not even have legal jurisdiction over some issues covered by those other ministries. Consumer regulators are often still distinct from competition law regulators, which themselves can be quite new and under-resourced.[35] Consumer regulator interests have been seen as marginal, or indeed antithetical, to those of foreign or trade ministries negotiating and managing FTAs, especially as FTAs begin to go beyond the WTO in addressing non-tariff barriers to trade and other 'beyond the border' issues that can emerge for protectionist rather than genuine public health reasons. Where consumer regulators are stronger, they can be seen as rights-driven and antagonistic to business, rather than sharing common interests in building trust in the marketplace to promote economic growth – the messaging long preferred by the EU, the OECD and many developed countries.

Consumer advocacy and NGOs remain weak (Principle 6), in the shadow of often authoritarian governments, although with some exceptions (notably in Thailand and Malaysia). Consumer education (Principle 2) is being promoted through the spread of the Internet, which is also underpinning growth in e-commerce and a corresponding push for harmonised standards (Principle 8).[36] Consumer education is also being given more emphasis through the ACCP and linked projects, for example, but developing country Member States face wider challenges in their education systems.[37] These factors also constrain the development and usage of consumer redress mechanisms, both through courts (sometimes influenced by corruption within Member States) and ADR procedures.[38] Limits on consumer redress hinder the credibility and impact of measures introduced to protect consumers from harmful products (Principle 3).[39]

[35] See further (primarily written by) C Beaton-Wells, 'Integration with Competition Policies, Laws and Institutions' in Nottage et al, 'ASEAN Consumer Law Harmonisation', 365. See also generally B Ong, *The Regionalisation of Competition Law and Policy within the ASEAN Economic Community* (Cambridge: Cambridge University Press, 2018); ASEAN, *ASEAN Regional Guidelines on Competition Policy* (Jakarta: ASEAN Secretariat, 2010).

[36] Note the existence of the 'ASEAN Work Programme on Electronic Commerce 2017–2025', the 'ASEAN Coordinating Committee on E-Commerce' and the 'Telecommunications and Information Technology Senior Officials Meeting'. One specific output, recently in March 2020, is the 'ASEAN Online Business Code of Conduct'.

[37] L Guan, *Education and Globalization In Southeast Asia: Issues and Challenges* (Singapore: ISEAS, 2017).

[38] See the summary Table 1 and related discussion in Nottage, 'Introduction'.

[39] See Nottage and Thanitcul, 'Consumer Product Liability'.

IV. Conclusions

The AEC Blueprint 2025, published in November 2015, recognises 'consumer protection [as] an integral part of a modern, efficient, effective and fair market place'. Accordingly, it aims to 'establish a common ASEAN consumer protection framework through higher levels of consumer protection legislation, improve enforcement and monitoring of consumer protection legislation, and make available redress mechanisms, including [ADR]' as well as to 'build higher consumer confidence and cross-border commercial transactions by strengthening product safety enforcement, stronger participation of consumer representatives, and promotion of sustainable consumption'.[40]

As such, further momentum can be expected at least towards implementing general consumer protection laws, as seen recently in Cambodia. There may also be moves to introduce a framework for consumer product safety regulation in Brunei, as well as strict product liability laws in the five ASEAN Member States that currently lack such protections.[41] Improving and harmonising access to justice remains a bigger challenge, even in developed countries (such as Australia),[42] as this impinges on court systems (with their own organisational dynamics) and risks more backlash from business and other vested interests.

However, an examination of ASEAN confirms that 'trading up' to higher levels of consumer protection has occurred more in the case of end-product standards, such as requirements that final goods achieve minimum environmental or safety features, as found by Vogel in the United States in the 1990s.[43] Coalitions between export-oriented firms and local consumer groups are arguably less likely to form regarding 'process standards' that focus on how goods or services are generated, such as regulations on factory emissions, which is why less trading up seems to occur in that field.[44] Such process standards may arguably include rules regulating not only the criteria for entry into consumer contracts but also the substantive content of those contracts.[45] Consumer contract law reforms may also have been more sporadic as cross-border liberalisation has been less extensive in ASEAN regarding services compared to tangible products.[46]

[40] At 13. This Blueprint goes on (at 14) to highlight several services sectors (finance, air transport and telecommunications), but also areas implicating products (e-commerce and energy), for future consumer protection measures.

[41] See Nottage and Thanitcul, 'Consumer Product Liability'.

[42] Cf eg L Nottage, 'The New Australian Consumer Law: What About Consumer ADR?' (2009) 9(2) *QUT Law and Justice Journal* 176, and the renewed recommendations for better internal harmonisation made by the Productivity Commission, 'Review of Australia's Consumer Policy Framework- Productivity Commission Inquiry Report' (2008), chapter 5 recommendation 5.1.

[43] Vogel, 'Trading Up'.

[44] D Vogel and R Kagan, 'Introduction: National Regulations in a Global Economy' in D Vogel and R Kagan (eds), *The Dynamics of Regulatory Change: How Globalization Affects National Regulatory Policies* (Berkeley: University of California Press, 2004) 1, especially at 10.

[45] L Nottage and J Paterson, 'Consumer Contracts and Product Safety Law in ASEAN: Partly Trading Up?' in Hsieh and Mercurio, *ASEAN Law in the New Regional Economic Order*, 392.

[46] See further (mainly written by J Paterson) 'Regulating Consumer Contracts in ASEAN', in L Nottage et al, *ASEAN Consumer Law Harmonisation*, 205.

More broadly, the ASEAN experience reveals partial but potentially significant 'transgovernmentalism', first theorised by Anne-Marie Slaughter.[47] So far, such cross-border networks serving to strengthen consumer law have been primarily among *national regulators* in Southeast Asia, with only incipient institutional networks among *legislators* and virtually none among *judges* in ASEAN Member States. Nonetheless, facilitated by growing interest from various international organisations (such as the OECD and UNCTAD), this emergent regional transgovernmentalism has developed not only an *information-sharing* function, but also a role in *harmonisation* and (to a limited extent) the actual *enforcement* of consumer law.[48] Although this legal harmonisation process is a much softer process than that found in the EU, the latter's more ambitious approach can risk backlashes – as seen dramatically with the 'Brexit' referendum vote in the United Kingdom in 2016.[49]

Anyway, there are examples of harder, treaty-based harmonisation initiatives even within Southeast Asia. The most prominent is the ASEAN Cosmetics Directive, modelled closely on the EU regime. But there are also now opportunities through intra-ASEAN and 'ASEAN+' FTAs.[50] Nonetheless, the latter still tend to focus on removing discriminatory non-tariff barriers to trade rather than actively 'trading up' to harmonised baseline levels of consumer product safety standards.

The EU's influence is already clearly discernible in national law reforms throughout the region. However, sometimes this is bolstered or filtered through variants of the EU approach adopted by neighbouring economies such as Australia, New Zealand,[51] Korea or Japan.[52] In general, the EU has responded since 2012 to greater American attention towards Asia by implementing its own 'pivot', including more high-level visits to, and funding in, Southeast Asia. The EU's closest links have been mostly with the ASEAN Secretariat, which still struggles to attract sustainable resourcing and policymaking leadership within ASEAN. However, the EU is becoming more aware of the need to help implement initiatives more effectively at the level of individual ASEAN Member States, with greater attention therefore being paid to 'domestification'. This recent programme is also boosted by the ongoing reformulation of consumer rights as economic (or instrumentalist), evident from the ASEAN Economic Community blueprints, rather than

[47] See generally AM Slaughter, *A New World Order* (New Jersey: Princeton University Press, 2004); AM Slaughter and T Hale, 'Transgovernmental Networks' in M Bevir (ed), *SAGE Handbook of Governance* (London: SAGE, 2011) 342.

[48] For more details on theories of transgovernmentalism – as well as comparative regionalism, 'trading up' and legal transplants – applied to consumer law harmonisation generally in Southeast Asia, see in general Nottage et al, 'ASEAN Consumer Law Harmonisation', esp chs 1, 2 and 8. Comparing international regulatory cooperation more generally in ASEAN and New Zealand, see also Gill, 'Interconnected Government'.

[49] For background (and possible implications of Brexit for the development of private law), see eg H Eidenmüller, 'Collateral Damage: Brexit's Negative Effects on Regulatory Competition and Legal Innovation in Private Law' (2018) 26(4) *Zeitschrift für Europäisches Privatrecht* 868.

[50] See eg the review underway since 2019 for the ASEAN-Australia-New Zealand FTA, potentially expanding the Competition law chapter to promote consumer protection: Nottage, 'Introduction'.

[51] For example, Malaysia's Consumer Protection Act 1999 includes Part VII on mandatory consumer guarantees modelled on New Zealand's legislation enacted in 1993, which was also adopted in the Australian Consumer Law reform of 2010 in lieu of (quite similar) mandatory statutory implied warranties.

[52] For example, Australia, Korea and Japan all adopted strict product liability laws based on the 1985 EU Product Liability Directive, with Japan's extension of its scope to consequential loss even to non-consumer-use property being found also in the enactments in Cambodia, Thailand and Malaysia.

linked predominantly to human rights, which have traditionally been a feature of the EU's self-identity but more controversial within ASEAN.[53]

Nonetheless, on the one hand, the impact of the more rights-based UN Guidelines on Consumer Protection[54] has been and is likely to remain significant in Southeast Asia. On the other hand, as the United Kingdom has now left the EU and may begin to tread its own path again in consumer law reform, this may complicate matters in Southeast Asia. This seems especially likely in countries traditionally influenced by the English common law, such as Singapore, Malaysia and Brunei.[55] After all, even when working within the EU system, the United Kingdom has tended to press for lighter or more market-based forms of consumer protection law.[56]

Whatever happens in Southeast Asia, developments will probably increasingly 'boomerang' back especially to neighbouring countries in the wider region, such as Australia. Already, for example, a governmental inquiry over 2016–17 reviewing the Australian Consumer Law considered Singapore's 2011 Regulations as an option for introducing a general safety provision, alongside the broader approach adopted in the EU (and followed in Malaysia, as well as more recently in Canada).[57] Australian ministers agreed to a recommendation in the regulators' 2017 Final Report to examine such a provision and other options for improving consumer product safety law, and a Treasury-led public consultation is still underway with some commentators bringing in ASEAN and Asia-Pacific perspectives.[58] As part of the review, moreover, an Australian government-commissioned study into other areas of consumer law also paid close attention to developments in Singapore.[59] Consequent reforms in Australia (and possibly then New Zealand) may in turn feed back into developments in Southeast Asia and further afield, including the EU.

[53] Cf generally P Murray, 'Europe and the World: The Problem of the Fourth Wall in EU-ASEAN Norms Promotion' (2015) 23 *Journal of Contemporary European Studies* 238.

[54] See generally L Nottage, 'Policy Digest 21: Best Practices for Developing Consumer Protection Policy', in ASEAN Secretariat, *Consumer Protection Digests*, 85.

[55] On influences on case law from England and other common law systems in Southeast Asia, see generally KH Ng and B Jacobson, 'How Global is the Common Law? A Comparative Study of Asian Common Law Systems – Hong Kong, Malaysia, and Singapore' (2017) 12(2) *Asian Journal of Comparative Law* 209.

[56] For example, the Thatcher government resisted the EU's introduction of strict product liability; and the UK was more sceptical about responsible lending obligations (not to mention price regulation of consumer loans, which still devolves to national law). See generally G Howells, I Ramsey and T Wilhelmsson, 'Consumer Law in its International Dimension' in Howells et al, *Handbook*, 1; N Reich et al, *European Consumer Law* 2nd edn (Amsterdam: Intersentia, 2014).

[57] Consumer Affairs Australia and New Zealand, 'Australian Consumer Law Review – Interim Report' (October 2015), especially at 83.

[58] L Nottage, 'Improving the Effectiveness of the Consumer Product Safety System: Australian Law Reform in Asia-Pacific Context' (2020) 43 *Journal of Consumer Policy* 829.

[59] S Corones et al., 'Comparative Analysis of Overseas Consumer Policy Frameworks' (April 2016) https://eprints.qut.edu.au/95636/.

29

The Effect of the United Nations Guidelines on Consumer Protection on Consumer Law in Asia

MATEJA DUROVIC AND JEREMY PUI

I. The United Nations Guidelines for Consumer Protection

The United Nations Guidelines for Consumer Protection (hereinafter: 'the UN Guidelines') were first adopted in April 1985 by a consensus resolution of the General Assembly, and have been acknowledged as the most important source of international consumer law.[1] At its core, the UN Guidelines are 'a valuable set of principles for setting out the main characteristics of effective consumer protection legislation',[2] and they aim to establish a minimum standard of protection in the field of consumer law for the 193 UN Member States. These principles have been particularly important in emerging economies with an inadequate framework or a lack of rules pertaining to consumer law, as they are able to build a system of consumer law using the UN Guidelines as inspiration. In most cases, it is observed that countries taking into account the UN Guidelines go beyond the suggested minimum standard in implementing national laws. At a regional level, the idea of a minimum standard of protection has fostered cooperation, with the ASEAN Committee on Consumer Protection on Consumer Protection referring to the Guidelines as a basis for developing a common approach among its Member States.[3]

Driven by a long campaign by consumer associations such as Consumers International, the Economic and Social Council (ECOSOC) initially began working with the Secretary General in 1977 to examine the status of consumer protection legislation and the role of national consumer agencies around the world. Taking this research

[1] United Nations General Assembly, Consumer protection: resolution / adopted by the General Assembly, 16 April 1985, A/RES/39/248. For details see M Durovic, 'International Consumer Law: What Is It All About?' (2020) 43 *Journal of Consumer Policy* 125.

[2] United Nations, 'United Nations Guidelines for Consumer Protection' (2016).

[3] ASEAN, *Handbook on ASEAN Consumer Protection Laws and Regulations: One Vision One Identity One Community* (Jakarta: ASEAN Secretariat, 2018).

into account, in addition to advice from the OECD and various consumer groups, the guidelines would be drafted in the following years, culminating in their adoption in 1985.

The UN Guidelines focus on seven fundamental principles of consumer law: the protection of health and safety of consumers; the protection of economic interests of consumers; the provision of consumers with adequate information; consumer education; accessibility of consumer to an effective means of redress; the establishment of consumer associations and consumer participation in the decision-making process; and sustainable consumption.[4]

Since their inception, the UN Guidelines have been amended twice, resulting in a broader scope of the principles. The first modifications were made in 1999.[5] The main addition was a section on sustainable consumption, reflecting a recognition of the important interplay between modern consumerism patterns and environmental protection.

The UN Guidelines were most recently amended in December 2015, led by the United Nations Conference for Trade and Development (UNCTAD) and revised by the General Assembly.[6] These revisions focused on adapting the UN Guidelines to changes created by technological developments and a modernisation of the global economy, for example, new advertising techniques. New fundamental principles of consumer law were introduced, including: e-commerce, financial services, data protection, misleading energy advertising, cross-border trade, transport, access to universal services, access to knowledge, tourism and consumer redress. Additionally, the Guidelines were amended to be more inclusive to a diverse range of consumers, with a recognition of the need to protect vulnerable and disadvantaged consumers. These revisions also introduced a new Intergovernmental Group of Experts (IGE) on consumer protection law and policy, acting as a forum for Member States to discuss the implementation of the Guidelines.[7] Following these amendments, UNCTAD produced a Manual on Consumer Protection in 2017 to support policymakers in emerging economies in the implementation and practicalities of the UN Guidelines.[8]

A common criticism of the potential effectiveness of the UN Guidelines is the fact that they are merely guidelines and a form of 'soft law', and are therefore not legally binding.[9] Although Member States are encouraged to adopt the principles of these guidelines into national legislation for consumer protection, there is no legal obligation to do so. This is reflected in the text of the guidelines, stating that 'Member States should take appropriate steps at the national or regional levels to implement these guidelines'.[10] However, the fact that the UN Guidelines are soft law and do not impose legal obligations on Member States can be beneficial towards its widespread adoption. It is more likely for there to be consensus between countries to implement the principles without

[4] United Nations, 'Guidelines for Consumer Protection', 7–9.
[5] United Nations Economic and Social Council resolution, 26 July 1999, E/1999/INF/2/Add.2.
[6] United Nations General Assembly, Consumer protection: resolution / adopted by the General Assembly, 22 December 2015, A/RES/70/186.
[7] ibid.
[8] UNCTAD, *Manual on Consumer Protection* (Geneva: United Nations, 2017).
[9] Durovic, 'International Consumer Law', 129.
[10] United Nations, 'Guidelines for Consumer Protection', 28.

the burden of repercussions from non-compliance. Furthermore, the UN Guidelines offer significant discretion to governments in how the fundamental principles are transposed into national consumer law. According to the wording of the Guidelines, the principles should be considered 'in accordance with the economic, social and environmental circumstances of the country',[11] allowing legislators to build frameworks around the particularities of domestic priorities. Even after two revisions to the Guidelines, the requirements are still broad enough to be accommodated by various legal systems around the world. The non-binding nature of the UN Guidelines also allows for dynamic growth. When changes are made or new principles are introduced, they are more likely to be accepted, making it easier for updates to be made as the needs of the global economy evolve and new problems arise. Ultimately, in practice, it can be argued that the UN Guidelines impose a moral obligation. This can be attributed to the fact that the principles were adopted by consensus, as well as the reputation and prominence of the United Nations as a leading, global institution. A 2013 report by UNCTAD aligns with this view, noting that '[s]ince 1985, the United Nations Guidelines on Consumer Protection have been widely implemented by Member States of the United Nations [and that] all areas of the current Guidelines remain valid and useful'.[12]

II. The Impact of the UN Guidelines on Consumer Protection in Asia

This section will analyse the consumer law frameworks in various Asian jurisdictions and evaluate the influence of the UN Guidelines in light of their main principles. An assessment will be made regarding compliance of these principles, and instances will be noted in which countries have gone beyond the minimum threshold of protection.

A. Product Safety and Product Liability

Product safety and product liability are covered by Sections V(B) and V(D) of the UN Guidelines. Under the Guidelines, there are three notable aspects to these principles. There should be standards to ensure that products are 'safe for either intended or normally foreseeable use', consumers should be 'instructed in the proper use of goods' and informed of associated risks of using the goods and there should be appropriate policies in place to deal with products that are found to be defective.

Wide compliance with these principles is observable when looking at the legal frameworks of Asian jurisdictions, rooting these areas in tort law and going beyond the minimum standard. Often, the definition of which actors would be liable as a 'producer' was left quite broad, to the benefit of consumers. It was commonly observed that there were strict requirements with a heavy burden of proof falling on potentially liable

[11] ibid, 7.

[12] UNCTAD, 'Implementation report on the United Nations Guidelines on Consumer Protection (1985–2013)' (2013), para 43.

entrepreneurs. In countries such as Indonesia and Taiwan, there is a standard of strict liability when dealing with defective products, and the business actor is presumed to be at fault immediately upon the infliction of harm.[13] Moreover, in Taiwan, consumer protection laws force joint tortfeasors, distributors and marketers to be jointly and severally liable with the business operators.[14] In Japan, liability for defective products can fall on the State, for example, in cases where the government may have negligently approved medical products with dangerous side-effects.[15]

The importance of this area of consumer law is highlighted by several national laws stipulating punitive damages in certain scenarios. For example, in Thailand, where an entrepreneur knows that a product is unsafe but fails to take proper action to prevent the damage, the court has the power to award punitive damages.[16] It is also possible for affected consumers to claim damages for mental distress caused by unsafe products in Thailand.[17] In China, not only are punitive damages available where defective products cause death or disability,[18] but consumers can claim damages of up to 10 times the price of the goods in the case of food-related products under the Food Safety Law.[19] Similarly, in South Korea, producers who, despite having knowledge of the defect, cause serious damage to the life or body of a person as a result of not taking necessary measures against a defective product may be liable for up to three times the damage sustained by the victim.[20]

B. Unfair Contract Terms

Section V(C) of the UN Guidelines concerns the principles relating to unfair contract terms. Paragraph 26 states that '[c]onsumers should be protected from such contractual abuses as one-sided standard contracts, exclusion of essential rights in contracts and unconscionable conditions of credit by sellers'.[21] It appears that this suggestion has been duly transposed into the legislative frameworks across Asia, with all jurisdictions having specific provisions for this area of consumer law.

Most commonly, in jurisdictions such as Indonesia and Japan, if any terms in consumer contracts are found to be unfair, they will be void and unenforceable against the consumer.[22] For example, in China, sellers are prohibited from '[imposing] unfair or unreasonable rules on consumers to exclude or restrict consumer rights, reduce or waive the responsibilities of sellers, or aggravate the responsibilities of consumers'.[23]

There is some variation in how the 'unfairness' of a term is defined across different countries. In Thailand, the courts are granted powers by statute to consider if a contract

[13] Indonesian Civil Code, Art 1365; Consumer Protection Act (Taiwan), Art 7(1).
[14] Consumer Protection Act (Taiwan), Arts 7–8.
[15] State Redress Act (Japan).
[16] Unsafe Product Liability Act (Thailand), s 11(2).
[17] ibid, s 11(1).
[18] The Law on the Protection of Consumer Rights and Interests (China), Art 49.
[19] Food Safety Law (China), Art 148.
[20] Product Liability Act (South Korea), Art 3(2).
[21] United Nations, 'Guidelines for Consumer Protection', 13.
[22] Consumer Protection Law (Indonesia), Art 18 (IDN); Consumer Contract Act (Japan), Art 10.
[23] The Law on the Protection of Consumer Rights and Interests (China), Art 26.

is unfair on a case-by-case basis, taking the facts and context into consideration and applying their discretion.[24] Other jurisdictions such as Hong Kong and Taiwan use a general fairness test to assess the validity of contractual terms. In Hong Kong, a 'reasonableness' test is employed, assessing 'whether the term was a fair and reasonable one to be included having regard to the circumstances which were, or ought reasonably to have been, known to or in the contemplation of the parties when the contract was made'.[25] The courts are guided by considerations such as the relative bargaining positions of the parties or any inducement of the consumer to agree to the term.[26] Taking a different approach, in Vietnam, there is no general standard of what constitutes an 'unfair term', and instead, statutory provisions specify a list of terms that will always be unfair.[27] Macau's consumer protection laws are similar, stipulating a list of 'absolutely prohibited' and 'relatively prohibited' clauses as opposed to a general fairness test.[28]

In Thailand, there is increased protection for consumer contracts in certain industries, with statutory requirement for these agreements to be overseen by the Committee on Contract.[29] The affected industries are those that typically create contracts that consumers need assistance with, such as apartment rental, used car purchase and consumer credit.

C. Unfair Commercial Practices

Paragraphs 21–23 of the UN Guidelines contain recommendations regarding unfair commercial practices. Specifically, there are guidelines to prevent 'adverse practices', 'restrictive and other abusive business practices' and 'false or misleading claims in marketing'.[30] While many consumer protection frameworks across Asia have provisions against misleading and aggressive practices, they are manifested in different ways.

In Singapore, an approach is taken similar to that of the UK's Consumer Protection from Unfair Trading Regulations. The law outlines a blacklist of 20 specific practices deemed to always be unfair, for example, the concealment of onerous or material terms in small print.[31] Businesses are prohibited from committing any of these listed practices. It is also important to note that the rules in Singapore acknowledge the standard of a vulnerable consumer, in line with the UN Guidelines of fair and equitable treatment.[32] Supplementing this, there are soft law provisions to regulate advertising, and while not legally binding, sellers are threatened with having their advertising space withheld.[33] Vietnam also details a blacklist of commercial practices considered to be unfair or coercive.[34]

[24] Unfair Contract Terms Act (Thailand), s 4(1).
[25] Control of Exemption Clauses Ordinance (Hong Kong), s 3(1).
[26] ibid, Schedule 2.
[27] Law on Consumer Protection 2010 (Vietnam), Art 16.
[28] Standard Form Contract Clauses Law 1992 (Macau), Arts 12–13.
[29] Consumer Protection Act (Thailand), s 35.
[30] United Nations, 'Guidelines for Consumer Protection', 12–13.
[31] Consumer Protection (Fair Trading) Act (Singapore), Schedule 2.
[32] United Nations, 'Guidelines for Consumer Protection', 9.
[33] Advertising Code of Practice (Singapore), 6.1.
[34] Law on Consumer Protection (Vietnam), Art 10.

In Hong Kong, the Trade Descriptions Ordinance outlines six types of prohibited trade practices: applying false trade descriptions of goods and services; misleading omissions; aggressive commercial practices; bait advertising; baiting and switching; and wrongly accepting payment.[35] The fairness of commercial practices follows a similar assessment to that of the EU's average consumer standard, where the average consumer is understood as a reasonably well informed and circumspect and observant consumer.[36] The law aims to deter this type of behaviour by imposing punishments of up to five years' imprisonment.[37]

Although Thailand does not have specific laws for unfair commercial practices, there are a variety of laws that regulate business practices. For example, doorstop selling and pyramid selling matters are overseen by the Direct Sales and Direct Marketing Act. The law also aims to make it easier for consumers to access justice in this regard, as consumers facing problems of misleading advertising can notify the Office of the Consumer Protection Board who will assist the consumer in mediation.

D. Dispute Resolution and Redress

Dispute resolution and redress are covered by Section V(F) of the UN Guidelines. This principle aims to ensure that consumer protection agencies have the capacity to promote compliance amongst businesses and to facilitate effective redress for affected consumers. In Asia, this guideline has been duly respected across consumer law systems with a straightforward process for consumers to seek redress. It is notable that in China, it is possible to bring public interest litigation in regard to consumer protection issues.[38] The China Consumers' Association and consumer associations of individual provinces can file lawsuits in the people's courts against the infringement of lawful rights and interests of vast numbers of consumers. Public prosecutors can also initiate litigation, although this is limited to claims pertaining to food safety.[39]

In Thailand, the Consumer Case Procedure Act 2008 established several provisions favouring the plaintiff in consumer law proceedings. These rules include simplified rules of evidence for the plaintiff, the introduction of punitive damages and the ability to seek assistance from a case official for the drafting of claims. Since 2015, it has also been possible for a group of consumers to bring a claim as a class action lawsuit.[40] This was observed in 2018, when 291 car owners succeeded in receiving compensation for their claim for defective products.[41] Since 2016, a class action lawsuit can also be raised in Japan.[42]

[35] Trade Descriptions Ordinance (Hong Kong), ss 13E–13I.
[36] ibid, s 13D.
[37] ibid, s 18(1).
[38] The Law on the Protection of Consumer Rights and Interests (China), Art 47.
[39] ibid, Art 55.
[40] Act Amending the Civil Procedure Code of Thailand.
[41] Judgment of the Civil Court Black No 492/2560, 21 September 2018 (Thailand).
[42] Act on Special Measures Concerning Civil Court Proceedings for the Collective Redress for Property Damage Incurred by Consumers (Japan).

In Singapore, where it is more common for consumers to seek redress directly with traders at the Small Claims Tribunal, measures have been taken to minimise barriers for the access of justice. The financial threshold to bring a claim is low.[43] A similar approach has been taken in Malaysia, with the aim of avoiding a burdensome experience for consumers who wish to file a claim, both in terms of time and money. Redress can be sought through a consumer tribunal for a low fee, with most cases heard and settled within 40 days.[44]

South Korea also offers a simple method for the resolution of consumer disputes. Led by the Korea Consumer Agency and Korea Consumer Dispute Settlement Commission, consumers and trades are able to settle issues in a free out-of-court method. The process involves free counselling for the consumer managed by a nationwide call centre, consumer mediation with the Korea Consumer Agency, and finally, conciliation with the Consumer Dispute Settlement Commission. The Commission makes a conciliation proposal to the parties as a solution to the dispute, which can become binding if the terms are mutually accepted by the parties.[45] Embracing innovation, the Council of Consumers in Macau established an online dispute resolution system in 2018 for disputes between Macau and China, with aims to expand the platform to cross-border disputes around the world.

Consumer protection agencies have commonly been empowered to oversee litigation and evaluate the state of consumer law in their respective countries. In Myanmar, the Myanmar Consumer Protection Commission has a duty to submit annual reports of consumer protection to the Union government. The group also advises on further protection based on these regular findings.[46] A similar role is undertaken by the Office of the Consumer Protection Board in Thailand, who are responsible for overseeing and receiving complaints from consumers, in addition to conducting research on relevant consumer protection issues.[47]

Hong Kong's Consumer Council, established in 1974, plays a role in resolving consumer complaints through conciliation. The body is also involved in policy, working with the OECD and participating in the 2015 revisions of the UN Guidelines.[48]

E. E-Commerce and the Digital Age

A section on electronic commerce was added to the aforementioned 2015 revisions of the UN Guidelines. The provisions suggest for Member States to '[ensure] a level of protection that is not less than that afforded in other forms of commerce' and

[43] Small Claims Tribunal Act (Singapore), s 54.

[44] Consumer Protection Act 1999 (Malaysia), s 85.

[45] Korea Consumer Agency, 'Criteria for the Settlement of Consumer Disputes' (KFTC Notification No 2019-3).

[46] Union Cabinet's Executive Order No 38/2014. No 112/2016 and No 15/2017 (Myanmar),

[47] Consumer Protection Act (Thailand), ss 19–20.

[48] Consumer Council, 'Hong Kong Consumer Council's Comments on the OECD's Draft G20 High-level Principles on Financial Consumer Protection Public Consultation' (26 August 2011).

'where appropriate, review existing consumer protection policies to accommodate the special features of electronic commerce and ensure that consumers and businesses are informed and aware of their rights and obligations in the digital marketplace'.[49]

Overall, while many legal frameworks in Asia have laws regulating the collection and use of personal data, it is rare to find rules specifically pertaining to digital content and consumer protection.

There is more emphasis on this matter in South Korea, where there have been laws in place covering information duties and right of withdrawal for e-commerce transactions since 2002.[50] The law imposes information duties on businesses, requiring disclosure of the seller's address, telephone number and email address among other details. If false information is provided, the seller may be dealt a fine of up to 10 million won (approximately USD 8,900).[51] There is also significant protection in Japan, with safeguards in place for the use and navigation of online shopping websites.[52] The law provides that in certain circumstances, if induced by mistake, consumers may be able to rescind a contract if they clicked and accidentally purchased an item or ordered a different quantity than intended.

It is possible that the lack of specific consumer protection laws in this area suggests that the existing rules are technology-neutral and are capable of sufficiently protecting the consumer. If this is the case, the countries would still be complying with the UN Guidelines, as revisions would only need to be made 'where appropriate'. If this is the case, it would be most important that there is equal recognition between the processes of electronic and physical transactions. For example, in Macau and Thailand, electronic documents and signatures have the same legal value as written documents.[53]

[49] United Nations, 'Guidelines for Consumer Protection', 20.
[50] Act on the Consumer Protection in Electronic Commerce (South Korea).
[51] ibid, Art 13.
[52] Act on Special Provisions to the Civil Code Concerning Electronic Consumer Contracts of 2001 (Japan).
[53] Law No 5/2005 (Macau), Art 3; Electronic Transaction Act (Thailand).

PART 5

Conclusion

30

Some Concluding Remarks

Future Prospects for Consumer Law in Asia

MATEJA DUROVIC AND ANDRÉ JANSSEN

I. General Observations

This edited collection has provided an in-depth examination of consumer law regimes in selected jurisdictions of the Asian continent, in particular the legal systems of East, South East and Southern Asia. As a major general observation, it can be concluded that, during the last years and decades, all of the jurisdictions analysed here have developed their own consumer law regimes, regulating broad numbers and types of business-to-consumer relations, each with some similarities and some national particularities, while the level of consumer protection and its success in practice differ largely in the Asian legal world.

Besides the national reports on the Asian jurisdictions, the book has also provided a comparative general examination of the most important fields of consumer law (such as consumers' access to justice, adaption of the consumer law to the digital age, consumer sales law, unfair contract terms, product liability, product safety and unfair commercial practices) from a regional perspective as well as from comparative observations of the Asian consumer laws from the viewpoint of consumer legislation of the other continents (Africa, Australasia, Europe, etc).

Through this triple approach (national reports, comparative reports and ultimately reports which put the Asian consumer law in a global perspective), the book has secured a proper critical overview over national consumer laws in Asia. Moreover, it also drew some comparative conclusions about the development of major areas of consumer law and positioned Asian consumer law in global regulatory and political perspectives.

II. Challenges and Opportunities for Asian Consumer Laws and Policies

When it comes to future prospects for consumer laws and policies in Asia, the principal question is whether consumer laws in Asia are ready to properly address the challenges brought by the ongoing processes of globalisation and digitalisation as well as challenges related to securing proper enforcement of consumer law in practice. Both phenomena, the globalisation and the digitalisation of the markets, economies, societies, products and services represent an omnipresent and ongoing development which require not only adequate national solutions for consumer law but also efficient *supranational* responses.[1] Likewise, the enforcement of consumer law traditionally represents a continuously challenging aspect of consumer law. Therefore, one of main goals of this book is the attempt to address the discrepancy between consumer law in books and consumer law in practice.

III. Globalisation and Cross-Border Consumer Transactions

Globalisation is substantially affecting not only consumer laws and policies in general but also the behaviour of consumers on a large scale. The Covid-19 pandemic has contributed to an even faster rise of the Internet as *the* dominant marketplace which facilitates also cross-border transactions: consumers no longer need to travel to other countries in order to make transactions with a cross-border dimension. Through the Internet, consumers get access to goods or services which are not available domestically or at least only at a higher price. The increasing importance of the Internet for consumer transactions is not only observable in Europe or the United States but is clearly a worldwide trend which is even fuelled by the pandemic. From the perspective of economy, the increase of cross-border consumer transactions is great, but it causes serious consumer law consequences, which demand a greater supranational response to avoid that consumers are in a disadvantageous legal position when making cross-border transactions.

However, unlike the consumer law in the European Union (EU), where there exists some unified or at least harmonised EU consumer law aiming at protecting consumers as fundamentally important players of the European internal market, in the case of Asia, we are still talking about *consumer laws in Asia*, and not of one *Asian consumer law*. Different Asian legal traditions have been influenced by diverse legal systems, ideologies and other factors, and overall show a higher degree of diversity than the EU Member States. Moreover, the process of globalisation also enables a never-before-seen process of development of global traders whose business practices affect consumers in all or a majority of the examined jurisdictions as it is the case with, for example, Amazon, Alibaba, WhatsApp or WeChat. In such a manner, individual consumers are exposed to extremely powerful global traders with an enormous market power.

Some attempts to develop a supranational consumer law response in Asia are noticeable. In case of the examined jurisdictions, a regional organisation has been developed – the Association of Southeast Asian Nations (ASEAN) – where one of the goals is also to harmonise the consumer laws of its Member States, as an example of regionalisation of

[1] One might for example also think about legal aspects which are put in the spotlight by the increasing globalisation, eg the idea of sustainability and social responsibility within consumer law.

consumer law.[2] ASEAN is a regional union of 10 countries that geographically belong to South East Asia. It includes Indonesia, Singapore, Myanmar, Brunei, Malaysia, the Philippines, Vietnam, Cambodia, Laos and Thailand.[3] ASEAN was founded already in 1967, but only recently rising efforts towards the development of a common consumer law policy can be noted. In that context, three areas of mutual cooperation amongst the ASEAN Member States have been identified: information exchange, cross-border redress and capacity-building. The recently established ASEAN Committee on Consumer Protection plays an essentially important role, being in charge of the cross-border system of complaints. Its main objective is to provide a channel or facility for ASEAN consumers to complain or claim for any loss incurred (in respect of any goods or services purchased or acquired) in a less cumbersome, speedier manner and at a minimal cost.[4] The EU as the most advanced regional system of consumer protection has influenced this development of a regionalisation of consumer law in Asia.

Likewise, some of the examined Asian jurisdictions, such as South Korea or Japan, belong to the Organisation for Economic Cooperation and Development (OECD), hence it is an international organisation that among others also aims to contribute to the development of consumer policy. In the last year, the OECD has been very active in developing some global minimum requirements of consumer protection. Similarly, all of the examined Asian jurisdictions seem to comply, to a large extent, with the minimum standards of consumer protection set up by the United Nations Guidelines for Consumer Protection from 1985 (with revisions in 1999 and 2015; hereinafter: UN Guidelines).

Again, the UN Guidelines represent only the absolute minimum standards that the (Asian) jurisdictions are expected to follow. Within the UN framework, Asian countries can profit from the voluntary peer review of the consumer protection law and policy to be performed by the so-called Intergovernmental Group of Experts on Consumer Protection Law and Policy. After the substantial reform of the UN Guidelines in 2015, this Group is mandated, inter alia, to conduct voluntary peer reviews of national consumer protection laws and policies of the Member States, as implemented by the consumer protection authorities. This was something that some Asian countries have indeed profited from, as is the case with Indonesia.[5]

IV. Digitalisation and New Technologies

Like everywhere in the world, the increasing process of digitalisation of (electronic) commerce represents a particular challenge for consumer protection regimes in Asia. In the ongoing era of the so-called Fourth Industrial Revolution, the consumer law framework, on the one side, in general needs to ensure that the level of consumer protection remains the same irrespective of the type of technology used (for example the Internet

[2] See M Durovic and HW Micklitz, *Internationalization of Consumer Law* (Basel: Springer, 2017) 21.
[3] https://asean.org/asean/asean-member-states/.
[4] www.aseanconsumer.org.
[5] https://unctad.org/system/files/official-document/cicplpd18_en.pdf.

becoming the main marketplace for consumer transactions), but, on the other side, that consumer law does not represent a disproportionate obstacle to the development and application of new technologies. Striking the balance between these two values might be easy in theory, but to achieve it in practice is something that needs to be addressed by the Asian consumer laws. The national reports have demonstrated that the Asian consumer law frameworks have actually developed (though at different levels), some digital consumer market specific rules, but their continuous adaptation is a must.

Some developments in consumer law and policy can be observed here. For example, again on the regional level of ASEAN, Singapore's initiative while chairing ASEAN in 2018 was to develop an 'Asian Digital Single Market' to develop common rules on consumer protection and data protection in the context of the intra-ASEAN digital trade in goods and services. Likewise, the e-commerce law reform in China entered into force in 2019. These all show some clear signs of the development taking place in the Asian jurisdictions connected with the digital age. However, in general the Asian jurisdictions seem to have to some extent a 'digital backlog' in comparison with the EU as innovative legal acts as the new Sale of Goods Directive,[6] the Digital Content Directive[7] or proposals for a Digital Services Act[8] or Digital Markets Act[9] are regularly still lacking in Asia. Here the development at EU level might serve as an important impetus for Asian jurisdiction, but further developments are awaited.

It is important to note that the development of new technologies certainly creates a number of benefits for consumers, as it is the case, for example, with making markets more competitive through enabling collaborative economy to develop. However, the new technology also poses new risks for consumers and regulators. For example, Big Data allows online price discrimination of consumers. In that sense, a response from the Asian jurisdiction is expected. Consumer laws in Asia have to be modified and broadened in order to address innovations brought by new technologies, as well as by modern economics.

In case of challenges posed by digitalisation, Big Data has proven a high relevance among different legal areas, primarily among competition law, consumer law and data protection law which is of essential importance for a proper regulation of the market. Accordingly, a proper regulatory response requires a close coordination in the development of rules related to Big Data as it is the case, for instance, with a number of proceedings against Facebook throughout the world where this inter-connection can be noticed. Importantly, in the case of Asia, competition law and, in particular, data protection law are still at an early stage of development in most of the examined jurisdictions, so, for instance, consumer law can also be used as a remedy to protect consumers from negative consequences of commercialisation of consumer data.

[6] Directive (EU) 2019/771 of the European Parliament and of the Council of 20 May 2019 on certain aspects concerning contracts for the sale of goods, OJ 2019 No L136, p 28.

[7] Directive (EU) 2019/770 of the European Parliament and of the Council of 20 May 2019 on certain aspects concerning contracts for the supply of digital content and digital services, OJ 2019 No L136, p 1.

[8] 'Proposal for a Regulation of the European Parliament and of the Council on a Single Market for Digital Services (Digital Services Act)' COM(2020) 825 final.

[9] 'Proposal for a Regulation of the European Parliament and of the Council on contestable and fair markets in the digital sector (Digital Markets Act)' COM(2020) 842 final.

V. Enforcement of Consumer Law

Consumer rights need effective and efficient enforcement and redress mechanisms as otherwise they tend to be without any practical impact. However, on a global and comparative level, the enforcement of consumer law represents one of the most difficult issues of consumer protection. Designing a truly working system of consumer law enforcement is a real challenge for legal systems in general and unsurprisingly also for most Asian jurisdictions in particular. The main aims of consumer law enforcement are, in a nutshell, to prevent businesses from further infringements and to provide consumers with an efficient redress mechanism.

Some, but not all, of the examined Asian jurisdictions are part of the International Consumer Protection and Enforcement Network (ICPEN).[10] The ICPEN is the most important global framework for the cooperation in the area of consumer protection. It is an excellent model of how a less formal manner can be established as a pathway for cooperation among the different national consumer protection authorities as well as a forum for a multi-stakeholder dialogue. It seems that it would be beneficial for the examined part of the world if the currently non-participating countries decides to join the ICPEN as this existing framework could help strengthening the enforcement of consumer law.

In Asia, as demonstrated in the book chapters, consumer law is primarily enforced by diverse forms of national public authorities: private enforcement of consumer law plays only a secondary role. Collective redress mechanisms have not yet developed properly, or in the jurisdictions where a such a legal framework was put in place, the operationality of collective redress mechanisms does not function on a satisfactory level in practice.

Consumer organisations traditionally represent one of the main pillars of the enforcement mechanism in Europe and in the United States. However, in Asia this movement is still under underdeveloped. Much more effort needs to be invested to secure an appropriate regulatory, but also a financial mechanism which strengthens and empowers consumer organisations in Asia. In this respect, it appears that there is still a long way to go.

VI. Final Concluding Observations

It can be observed that all of the examined Asian jurisdictions have developed their own systems of consumer protection and that there seems to be continuous work on modernisation of consumer law in this part of the world. However, some of the analysed consumer laws in Asia represent more advanced models of regulatory regimes of consumer protection, which is certainly the case with Japan, China or South Korea. This also demonstrates that the level of economic development of a country has a notable influence on the level of development of consumer law as the more economically developed countries also tend to have a more developed consumer protection regime.

[10] https://icpen.org.

INDEX

Abbreviations used in the index

AANZFTA (ASEAN–Australia–New Zealand Free Trade Agreement (2009))
ACCC (Australian Competition and Consumer Commission)
ACCP (ASEAN Committee on Consumer Protection)
ACL (Australian Consumer Law)
ADR (alternative dispute resolution) 64
AEC (ASEAN Economic Community)
AI (artificial intelligence)
ALI (American Law Institute) 475
APSA (Agricultural Products Standard Act 2008)
ASAS (Advertising Standards Authority of Singapore)
ASCT (Act on Specified Commercial Transactions 1975/2016 (Japan))
ASEAN (Association of Southeast Asian Nations)
ASIC (Australian Securities and Investments Commission)
ASICA (Australian Securities and Investment Commission Act)
B2B (business-to-business)
B2C (business-to-consumer)
BACP (Basic Act on Consumer Policies)
CA (Contract Act)
CAA (Consumer Affairs Agency) 106
CAANZ (Consumer Affairs Australia New Zealand)
CAC (Myanmar Consumer Affairs Committee)
CASE (Consumers Association of Singapore)
CC (Civil Code)
CC (Consumer Commission/Consumer Council)
CCA (Consumer Contract Act)
CCA (Establishment of the Consumer Council Act 2019 (Thailand))
CCC (Civil and Commercial Code)
CCCS (Competition and Consumer Commission of Singapore)
CCJ (Cross-border Consumer Center Japan)
CCPA (Central Consumer Protection Authority)
CCPA (Competition and Consumer Protection Act)
CCPA (Consumer Cases Procedure Act)
CCSPECC 2001 (Civil Code Concerning Electronic Consumer Contracts 2001)
CDMC (Consumer Dispute Mediation Commission)
CDRC (Consumer Dispute Resolution Centre)
CDSA (Consumer Dispute settlement Agency)
CDSB (Consumer Dispute Settlement Bodies)
CECO (Control of Exemption Clauses Ordinance)
CFCT (Consumers' Foundation Chinese Taipei)
CGSO (Consumer Goods Safety Ordinance)
CISG (UN Convention on Contracts for the International Sale of Goods)
CL (Contract Law)

CLAF (Consumer Legal Action Fund)
CMAC (Consumer Mediation and Arbitration Centre)
ComC (Commercial Code)
ComL (Commercial Law)
CompA (Competition Act)
CompL (Competition Law)
CorpL (Corporation Law)
CP (consumer protection)
CP (ETT) (Consumer Protection (Electronic Trade Transactions))
CPA (Consumer Protection Act)
CPB (Consumer Protection Bill)
CPB (Consumer Protection Board)
CPC (Civil Procedure Code)
CPC (Consumer Protection Commission/Committee)
CPC (Consumer Protection Council)
CPCC (Consumer Protection Central Committee)
CPFA (Consumer Protection Fundamental Act)
CP(FT)A (Consumer Protection (Fair Trading) Act)
CPL (Civil Procedure Law)
CPR (Consumer Protection (E-Commerce) Rules)
CPSA (Consumer Product Safety Act)
CPSS (Committee on Products and Services Safety)
CrimC (Criminal Code)
CSA (Consumer Safety Act)
DA (Drug Act)
DCCA (Department of Commerce and Consumer Affairs)
DCP (Department of Consumer Protection)
DSA (Direct Sales and Anti-Pyramid Scheme Act (Malaysia))
DSA (Direct Sales and Direct Marketing Act)
DSDMA (Direct Sales and Direct Marketing Act)
DSE (Directorate of Economic Services)
DTDSA (Door-To-Door Sales Act)
ECA (Electronic Commerce Act/E-Commerce Act)
ECJ (European Court of Justice)
ETA (Electronic Transactions Act)
FA (Food Act)
FAA (Act on Fair Labelling and Advertising 1999 (South Korea))
FDA (Food and Drug Administration)
FDI (inbound foreign direct investment)
FIDReC (Financial Industries Dispute Resolution Centre (Singapore))
FLA (Food Labeling Act)
FSA (Financial Services Agency)
FSL (Food Safety Law)
FSSA (Food Safety and Standards Act 2006 (Myanmar))
FTA (Fair Trade Act)
FTA (Free Trade Agreement)
FTA (Monopoly Regulation and Fair Trade Act 2015 (South Korea))
FTC (Federal Trade Commission)
HGQLA (Household Goods Quality Labeling Act (Japan))
HKBL (Hong Kong Basic Law)
IL (Investment Law)
IMDA (Infocommunications and Media Development Authority)
IPIB (Intellectual Property Investigation Bureau)
JFTC (Japan Fair Trade Commission)

KCA (Korea Consumer Agency)
KCDSC (Korean Consumer Dispute Settlement Commission)
KCPA (Korea Consumer Protection Agency)
KEDTA (Korean Electronic Documents and Transactions Act 2002)
KFAC (Korea Framework Act on Consumers)
KFTC (Korea Fair Trade Commission)
LCA (Vietnam Law on Commercial Arbitration)
LCP (Law on Consumer Protection)
LQPG (Law on Quality of Goods and Products)
LRC (Law Reform Commission)
MCPC (Myanmar Consumer Protection Commission)
MO (Misrepresentation Ordinance)
MOC (Ministry of Commerce)
MPA (Act Against Unjustifiable Premiums and Misleading Representations 1962 (Japan))
MTI (Ministry of Trade and Industry)
MyCC (Malaysia Competition Commission)
NCA (National Credit Act)
NCAC (National Consumer Affairs Center)
NCCC (National Consumer Complaints Centre)
NCCUSE (National Conference of Commissioners on Uniform State Laws)
NCCUSL (National Conference of Commissioners on Uniform State Laws)
NCDRC (National Consumer Disputes Redressal Commission)
NCPA (National Consumer Protection Agency)
NDL (National Drug Law)
OCPB (Office of the Consumer Protection Board)
ODR (online dispute resolution)
OECD (Organisation for Economic Co-operation and Development)
(OPCB (Office of the Consumer Protection Board))
PDPA (Personal Data Protection Act)
PDPC (Personal Data Protection Commission)
PICC (UNIDROIT Principles of International Commercial Contracts)
PIL (public interest litigation)
PLA (Product Liability Act)
PLL (Product Liability Law)
PMDA (Pharmaceuticals and Medical Devices Act 2014)
PQL (Product Quality Law)
QCAT (Queensland Civil and Administrative Tribunal)
QCO (Qualified Consumer Organisation)
QUAT (Queensland Civil and Administrative Tribunal)
RAPEX (rapid exchange of information system for dangerous products) 492
SBTA (Standard Business Terms Act)
SFCCL (Standard Form Contract Clauses Law)
SGA/SGO (Sale of Goods Act/Ordinance)
SPRING (Standards Productivity and Innovations Board)
SQCO (Specified Qualified Consumer Organisation)
SRA (Specific Relief Act)
TCC (Malaysian Tribunal for Consumer Claims)
TDA/TDO (Trade Descriptions Act/Ordinance)
TDIB (Trade Descriptions Investigations Bureau)
TFTC (Taiwan Fair trade Commission)
TIPSA (Thailand Industrial Products Standards Act 1968)
TL (Tort Law)
UCC (Uniform Commercial Code)
UCO (Unconscionable Contracts Ordinance)
UCTA (Unfair Contract Terms Act)

UNCTAD (UN Conference on Trade and Development)
UNGA (UN General Assembly) 526
UNGCP (UN Guidelines on Consumer Protection)
UPICC Uniform Principles of International Commercial Contracts
VCA (voluntary compliance agreement)
VCCA (Vietnam Competition and Consumer Authority)
VICOPRO (Vietnam Consumers Protection Association)
WTO (World Trade Organization)
YLKI (Yayasan Lembaga Konsumen Indonesia) (Indonesian Consumers Foundation)

www.ingramcontent.com/pod-product-compliance
Ingram Content Group UK Ltd.
Pitfield, Milton Keynes, MK11 3LW, UK
UKHW020224290926
15470UKWH00001B/367

9 781509 957538